## Conditional Proof (CP)

Premises

Assume

$$p \rightarrow q \quad \text{CP}$$

Reduct...

To prove a negat...

Premises

$$
\begin{array}{ll}
p & \text{Assume} \\
\vdots & \\
(q \cdot \sim q) & \\
\sim p & \text{RAA}
\end{array}
\qquad
\begin{array}{ll}
\sim p & \text{Assume} \\
\vdots & \\
(q \cdot \sim q) & \\
p & \text{RAA}
\end{array}
$$

---

## INFERENCE RULES FOR PREDICATE LOGIC

### Universal Instantiation (UI), in two forms

$$(\mathbf{x})\mathcal{P}$$
$$\therefore \mathcal{P}\mathbf{c}$$

Where **c** stands for any constant, and $\mathcal{P}\mathbf{c}$ is an instance of $(\mathbf{x})\mathcal{P}$.

$$(\mathbf{x})\mathcal{P}$$
$$\therefore \mathcal{P}\mathbf{y}$$

Where **y** stands for any variable, and $\mathcal{P}\mathbf{y}$ is an instance of $(\mathbf{x})\mathcal{P}$.

---

### Existential Instantiation (EI)

$$(\exists\mathbf{x})\mathcal{P}$$
$$\therefore \mathcal{P}\mathbf{y}$$

Where $\mathcal{P}\mathbf{y}$ is an instance of $(\exists\mathbf{x})\mathcal{P}$, and **y** is any variable not occurring free previously in the proof.

---

### Universal Generalization (UG)

$$\mathcal{P}\mathbf{y}$$
$$\therefore (\mathbf{x})\mathcal{P}$$

Where **y** stands for any variable, $\mathcal{P}\mathbf{y}$ is an instance of $(\mathbf{x})\mathcal{P}$, **y** is not free in any line derived by an application of EI, **y** does not occur free in $(\mathbf{x})\mathcal{P}$, and **y** does not occur free in an assumption for CP or RAA.

---

### Existential Generalization (EG), in two forms

$$\mathcal{P}\mathbf{c}$$
$$\therefore (\exists\mathbf{x})\mathcal{P}$$

Where **c** is any constant and $\mathcal{P}\mathbf{c}$ is an instance of $(\exists\mathbf{x})\mathcal{P}$.

$$\mathcal{P}\mathbf{y}$$
$$\therefore (\exists\mathbf{x})\mathcal{P}$$

Where **y** is any variable and $\mathcal{P}\mathbf{y}$ is an instance of $(\exists\mathbf{x})\mathcal{P}$.

---

### Quantifier Negation (QN), in two forms

$$\sim(\exists\mathbf{x})\mathcal{P} \ :: \ (\mathbf{x})\sim\mathcal{P}$$
$$\sim(\mathbf{x})\mathcal{P} \ :: \ (\exists\mathbf{x})\sim\mathcal{P}$$

# The Power of Logic
## Third Edition

## C. Stephen Layman
*Seattle Pacific University*

Boston   Burr Ridge, IL   Dubuque, IA   Madison, WI   New York
San Francisco   St. Louis   Bangkok   Bogotá   Caracas   Kuala Lumpur
Lisbon   London   Madrid   Mexico City   Milan   Montreal   New Delhi
Santiago   Seoul   Singapore   Sydney   Taipei   Toronto

The McGraw-Hill Companies

**Mc Graw Hill** **Higher Education**

THE POWER OF LOGIC, Third Edition

Published by McGraw-Hill, a business unit of The McGraw-Hill Companies, Inc., 1221 Avenue of the Americas, New York, NY 10020. Copyright © 2005 by The McGraw-Hill Companies, Inc. All rights reserved. Previous editions © 2002, 1999 by Mayfield Publishing Company. No part of this publication may be reproduced or distributed in any form or by any means, or stored in a database or retrieval system, without the prior written consent of The McGraw-Hill Companies, Inc., including, but not limited to, any network or other electronic storage or transmission, or broadcast for distance learning.

Some ancillaries, including electronic and print components, may not be available to customers outside the United States.

ISBN-13: 978-0-07-287587-4
ISBN-10: 0-07-287587-9

5 6 7 8 9 0 FGR/FGR 0 9 8 7 6

| | |
|---|---|
| Vice president and editor-in-chief: *Thalia Dorwick* | Art director: *Jeanne M. Schreiber* |
| Publisher: *Chris Freitag* | Design manager and cover designer: *Preston Thomas* |
| Sponsoring editor: *Jon-David Hague* | Art manager: *Robin Mouat* |
| Marketing manager: *Zina Craft* | Art editor: *Emma Ghiselli* |
| Production editor: *Jennifer Mills* | Production supervisor: *Randy Hurst* |

The text was set in 10.5/12.5 Goudy by TBH Typecast, Inc., and printed on acid-free 45# New Era Matte by Quebecor World, Fairfield.

*Chapter Opening Photos:* Ch. 1 Copyright © 1996 PhotoDisc, Inc.; Ch. 2 Copyright © 1993 PhotoDisc, Inc.; Ch. 3 Copyright © 1997 PhotoDisc, Inc.; Ch. 4 Copyright © 1992 PhotoDisc, Inc.; Ch. 5 Copyright © 1996 PhotoDisc, Inc.; Ch. 6 Copyright © 1996 PhotoDisc, Inc.; Ch. 7 Copyright © 1993 PhotoDisc, Inc.; Ch. 8 Copyright © 1992 PhotoDisc, Inc.; Ch. 9 Copyright © 1992 PhotoDisc, Inc.; Ch. 10 Copyright © 1995 PhotoDisc, Inc.; Ch. 11 Copyright © 1994 PhotoDisc, Inc.

*Credits:* Cover image © William Whitehurst/Corbis; p. 134 Steven Fellows/Letter to *The Seattle Times*, July 19, 2000. Copyright © 2003 Seattle Times Company. Used with permission; p. 137 Jim Spellman/Letter to *The Seattle Times*, July 5, 2000. Copyright © 2003 Seattle Times Company. Used with permission.

**Library of Congress Cataloging-in-Publication Data**
Layman, Charles S.
    The power of logic / C. Stephen Layman.—3rd ed.
        p. cm.
    Includes index.
    ISBN 0-07-287587-9
    1. Logic.    I. Title.
    BC61.L28 2004
    160—dc22

2003067466

www.mhhe.com

# Contents

# *Preface*

**W**e live in a time when many cultural forces and academic trends are unfavorable to the study of logic. Accordingly, my goal in writing this book has been to provide a text that removes as many obstacles to the learning of logic as possible. These obstacles include dull or wordy writing, a shortage of interesting exercises, and an imbalance of content.

It is difficult to overemphasize the importance of writing style in a logic textbook. While logic is undeniably technical at many points, *The Power of Logic* is written with the conviction that a cut-to-the-chase style is a great asset. The response to previous editions indicates that many readers agree, and I've made every effort to stay loyal to this conviction.

*The Power of Logic* is also written with the conviction that the tools of logic are indeed powerful and that the study of logic is one of the best ways to increase students' skills in critical thinking. Rather than requiring the student to acquire powerful logical tools *only* to apply them to uninteresting arguments, this book illustrates, chapter by chapter, that the tools of logic can be put to work in analyzing and evaluating significant arguments on important subjects.

*The Power of Logic* is written in the belief that the best introductory courses in logic include a mix of traditional logic (including informal logic) and modern symbolic logic. Too much emphasis on traditional and informal methods leaves students unacquainted with the most powerful tools logic has to offer. Too much emphasis on symbolic methods tends to produce students who can manipulate symbols but cannot apply logic to English arguments.

The study of logic increases one's ability to understand, analyze, evaluate, and construct arguments. For this reason, logic makes a vital contribution to the curriculum of the modern university. Accordingly, if this book does something to make logic a bit easier both to learn and to teach, it will have achieved its purpose.

## What's New in the Third Edition?

- This edition contains a new formulation of the rule of addition (Chapter 8). By allowing two forms of addition, the rule becomes more flexible and many proofs can be shortened by one step. Also, since a similar rule, simplification, was given in two forms in previous editions, this change increases stylistic consistency, thereby making both rules a bit easier to remember.

■ This edition contains new and different formulations of the inference rules of predicate logic (Chapter 9). These formulations (courtesy of Chris Menzel) are clearer and more rigorous and yet are more simply expressed. While nothing can make predicate logic easy, these formulations are, due to their relative simplicity, significantly easier to remember than those used in the previous editions.

■ There are a number of improvements in Chapter 4 (Informal Fallacies). The definitions of some of the informal fallacies have been sharpened, and the material on equivocation and amphiboly has been significantly revised and simplified. Also, throughout Chapter 4, the information in the boxes is presented with greater stylistic consistency, increasing clarity and aiding memory.

■ Throughout the entire text, exercises that have been judged less-than-optimal for one reason or another have been replaced or modified, and new exercises have been added in a number of places. While these changes are not highly visible, they make the text significantly easier to use.

## Enduring Features

■ Each chapter includes numerous exercises designed to show the power of logic as a tool for (a) formulating issues in a revealing way and (b) evaluating significant arguments on interesting topics.

■ Regarding the order of presentation, early chapters focus on relatively informal methods. More technical material is introduced gradually, with symbolic logic receiving thorough treatment in Chapters 7, 8, and 9.

■ The writing is concise and lively throughout the text. You'll be the judge of this, of course, but if *The Power of Logic* is more readable than most texts that cover similar topics, then it has at least one important pedagogical advantage.

■ The chapter on truth tables includes a discussion of the material conditional and its relation to the English "if-then" and emphasizes abbreviated truth tables.

■ The system of natural deduction for statement logic is entirely standard, consisting of eight implicational rules, ten equivalence rules, conditional proof, and *reductio ad absurdum*.

■ The chapter on induction includes standard material on statistical syllogisms, induction by enumeration, arguments from authority, Mill's methods, scientific reasoning, and arguments from analogy.

■ The exercises on arguments from analogy require students to evaluate a stated criticism of each argument, which makes the exercises relatively easy to grade.

■ The chapter on probability keeps the focus on argument evaluation. The exercises on Bayes' theorem involve a wide variety of applications, including applications to philosophical issues.

Various paths through this book are possible, depending on the time available, the needs of the students, and the interests of the instructor. Here are three possibilities:

*Path A:* A course emphasizing traditional and informal logic, covering Chapters 1–6 and 10: Basic Concepts, Identifying Arguments, Logic and Language, Informal Fallacies, Categorical Logic: Statements, Categorical Logic: Syllogisms, and Induction

*Path B:* A course giving roughly equal emphasis to informal and symbolic logic, covering Chapters 1–4, 7, and 8: Basic Concepts, Identifying Arguments, Logic and Language, Informal Fallacies, Statement Logic: Truth Tables, and Statement Logic: Proofs

*Path C:* A course emphasizing symbolic methods, covering Chapters 1, 2, 7–9, and 11: Basic Concepts, Identifying Arguments, Statement Logic: Truth Tables, Statement Logic: Proofs, Predicate Logic, and Probability

*Note:* Instructors who wish to treat more advanced topics may find the online treatment of modal (statement) logic useful. It is available at www.mhhe .com/layman3e.

Perhaps I should add here that this text is not designed for self-mastery. It is for courses taught by instructors. Thus, I have not tried to answer every question that might come to a student's mind as he or she works on assignments. The dangers of a highly detailed approach are that students will miss the forest for the trees or feel that coming to class is unnecessary. Thus, I have tried to write a text that explains the crucial points but avoids excessive detail. I will have achieved my purpose if instructors find that the text makes it easier to keep students interested and willing to take on the next topic.

## Ancillary Package

A comprehensive ancillary package has been developed to accompany *The Power of Logic:*

■ The online *Logic Tutor*, accessible through the book's website at www .mhhe.com/layman3e, allows students to do a vast majority of the book's exercises online with feedback. This includes creating Venn diagrams, truth tables, and proofs.

- The book's website, www.mhhe.com/layman3e, has a *Student Resource Center* that includes access to chapter overviews, learning objectives, flash cards, and the online *Logic Tutor*.

- The enhanced *Solutions Manual and Test Bank* includes both the complete answer key and the following features:

  - "Tips on Teaching Logic" (including a detailed lesson plan for the first day of class)

  - Three illustrative syllabi

  - "Basic Concepts: Alternative Schemes" (a short essay comparing and contrasting the definitions of "valid," "invalid," "sound," etc., in *The Power of Logic* with the definitions used in other popular texts)

  - Many new items in the *Test Bank* for Chapters 1, 8, and 9.

- Teachers also have free access to McGraw-Hill's *PageOut* course management system at www.pageout.net. *PageOut* brings all the elements of *The Power of Logic* package together: *Logic Tutor* homework can be automatically graded and compiled, and tests can be created and administered online using all the items from the *Test Bank*. Additionally, teachers can build proof, truth table, and symbolization questions of their own that are also graded by the *Logic Tutor* and compiled into the *PageOut* grade book.

## Acknowledgments

Many individuals have helped me with this book. I should start with the logic teachers who got me hooked on the subject (in temporal order): Carl Ginet, Alvin Plantinga, Donald Kalish, and David Kaplan. I have also been helped by colleagues and former colleagues, who read and commented on parts of the book and sometimes used drafts of the early chapters in the classroom: Terence Cuneo, Phillip Goggans, Daniel Howard-Snyder, and Richard McClelland. My students have also provided many helpful criticisms over the years; I have learned much from them.

I am indebted to a number of textbooks that I have used in the classroom over the years. These include Irving M. Copi and Carl Cohen, *Introduction to Logic*; Wilfred Hodges, *Logic*; Howard Kahane, *Logic and Philosophy: A Modern Introduction*; Donald Kalish, Richard Montague, and Gary Mar, *Logic: Techniques of Formal Reasoning*; Richard L. Purtill, *A Logical Introduction to Philosophy*; and Wesley C. Salmon, *Logic*. Other texts from which I have drawn inspiration and insight include Patrick Hurley, *A Concise Introduction to Logic*, and Brian Skyrms, *Choice and Chance*.

Thanks are due to the editors at McGraw-Hill for their support and advice throughout the project. Special thanks go to Ken King, who not only coached me through the first edition but also provided wise counsel for the second edition. For the third edition, I am grateful to Jon-David Hague, my current editor. And I must add a word of thanks to the specialists at McGraw-Hill who gave invaluable technical assistance: Allison Rona, Editorial Assistant, and Jen Mills, Production Editor.

I am greatly indebted to the reviewers, who provided me with a tremendous amount of constructive criticism. For the third edition, I am grateful to:

Ken Akiba, University of Wisconsin, Eau Claire

Anne L. Bezuidenhout, University of South Carolina

Darian C. De Bolt, University of Central Oklahoma

Peter Dlugos, Bergen Community College

Rachel Hollenberg, Long Beach City College

Ron Jackson, Clayton College & State University

Bernard F. Keating, West Virginia Wesleyan College

Eric Saidel, The George Washington University

Benjamin Shaeffer, Humboldt State University

For previous editions, I thank James K. Derden, Jr., Humboldt State University; William J. Doulan, Salem State College; Nancy Slonneger Hancock, Northern Kentucky University; Paul M. Jurczak, Lansing Community College; Eric Kraemer, University of Wisconsin, La Crosse; Joseph Le Fevre, Xavier University of Louisiana; Sander Lee, Keene State College; Charles Seymour, Valparaiso University; Mark Storey, Bellevue Community College; Patricia A. Ross, University of Minnesota, Twin Cities; and Michael F. Wagner, University of San Diego.

Special thanks are due to Colin Allen and Chris Menzel, who in their role as designers of the web-tutorial, have offered many helpful suggestions for improving the text. I am especially indebted to Chris for the new formulations of the inference rules for predicate logic in Chapter 9.

I also wish to thank Paul Draper for a number of thoughtful suggestions for improving the text, based on his experience in the classroom.

My friend and former colleague Greg Oakes took on the exacting job of checking the entire text and the *Solutions Manual and Test Bank* for errors in logic. I greatly appreciate his efforts, although, of course, I must take responsibility for any errors or infelicities that remain.

I dedicate this book to my mother, Velma P. Layman, whose love of books has shaped my life in more ways than I can tell.

## Chapter 1

# Basic Concepts

Everyone thinks. Everyone reasons. Everyone argues. And everyone is subjected to the reasoning and arguing of others. We are bombarded daily with reasoning from many sources: books, speeches, radio, TV, newspapers, employers, friends, and family.

Some people think well, reason well, and argue well. Some do not. The ability to think, reason, and argue well is partly a matter of natural gifts. But whatever our natural gifts, they can be refined and sharpened. And the study of logic is one of the best ways to refine one's natural ability to reason and argue. Through the study of logic, one learns strategies for thinking well, common errors in reasoning to avoid, and effective techniques for evaluating arguments.

But what is logic? Roughly speaking, **logic** is the study of methods for evaluating arguments. More precisely, logic is the study of methods for evaluating whether the premises of an argument adequately support (or provide good evidence for) its conclusion. To get a better grasp of what logic is, then, we need to understand the key concepts involved in this definition: *argument*, *premise*, *conclusion*, and *support*. This chapter will give you an initial understanding of these basic concepts.

An **argument** is a set of statements, one of which, called the *conclusion*, is affirmed *on the basis* of the others, which are called the *premises*. The premises of an argument are offered as support (or evidence) for the conclusion, and that support (or evidence) may be adequate or inadequate in a given case. But the set of statements counts as an argument as long as one statement is affirmed on the basis of others. Here is an example of an argument:

1. All Quakers are pacifists. Jane is a Quaker. So, Jane is a pacifist.

The word "so" indicates that the conclusion of this argument is "Jane is a pacifist." And the argument has two premises—"All Quakers are pacifists" and "Jane is a Quaker."

> An **argument** is a set of statements, one of which, called the *conclusion,*
> is affirmed *on the basis* of the others, which are called the *premises.*

What is a statement? A **statement** is a sentence that is either true or false.
For example:

2. Some dogs are collies.

3. No dogs are collies.

4. Some dogs weigh exactly 124.379 pounds.

Statement (2) is true—that is, it describes things as they are. And (3) is false
because it describes things as other than they are. Truth and falsehood are the
two possible **truth values**. So, we can say that a statement is a sentence that has
truth value. The truth value of (2) is *true* while the truth value of (3) is *false*, but
(2) and (3) are both statements. Is (4) a statement? Yes. You may not know its
truth value, and perhaps no one does, but (4) is either true or false, and hence it
is a statement.

Are any of the following items statements?

5. Get your dog off my lawn!

6. How many dogs do you own?

7. Let's get a dog.

Item (5) is a *command*, and one may obey or disobey a command, but it makes
no sense to pronounce it true or false. So, although (5) is a sentence, it is not a
statement. Item (6) is a *question*, and as such it is neither true nor false; hence, it
is not a statement. Finally, item (7) is a *proposal*, and proposals are neither true
nor false, so (7) is not a statement.[1]

The **premises** of an argument are the statements on the basis of which the
conclusion is affirmed. To put it the other way around, the **conclusion** is the
statement that is affirmed on the basis of the premises. In a well-constructed
argument, the premises *give good reasons for believing that the conclusion is true*. But
a poorly constructed argument is still an argument. For example, compare the
following arguments:

8. All uncles are male. Chris is an uncle. Hence, Chris is male.

9. Some uncles are skinny. Chris is an uncle. So, Chris is skinny.

The premises of argument (8) support (or provide a basis for) the conclusion in
this sense: If they are true, then the conclusion must be true. But the premises of
(9) fail to support the conclusion adequately: Even if true, they do not provide

good reason to believe that the conclusion is true. So, (9) is a bad argument, but it is still an argument.

Arguments are used frequently in our verbal and written interactions with others. And we may use arguments either to *persuade* others or to *discover truth*. For example, we often use arguments to persuade others to believe our political or ethical views. But we also use arguments as tools for *discovering truth*. Suppose a detective is investigating a crime: Who shot Alvin Smith? There are only two suspects, Griggs and Brooks. The detective establishes that Brooks was out of town at the time of the shooting and argues as follows:

> 10. Either Brooks or Griggs shot Smith. Brooks did not shoot Smith. Therefore, Griggs shot Smith.

In this case, the argument is used to discover truth. Of course, a given argument can be used *both* to discover truth *and* to persuade others to believe the conclusion. Persuasion and truth seeking are often compatible goals. Sometimes, however, one of these goals interferes with the other. For example, in a political campaign, one candidate might try to persuade the voters that his opponent is dishonest even though he knows his opponent is honest.

We now have a preliminary understanding of what logic is. We can gain a deeper understanding by taking a closer look at what it means for the conclusion of an argument to be adequately *based on* or *supported by* the premises. And we can best do this by exploring the basic concepts introduced in the remaining sections of this chapter—concepts such as validity, soundness, argument form, strength, and cogency.

---

> **Logic** is the study of methods for evaluating whether the premises of an argument adequately support (or provide good evidence for) its conclusion.

---

## 1.1 Validity and Soundness

A valid argument is one in which the premises support the conclusion *completely*. More formally, a **valid argument** has this essential feature: It is necessary that if the premises are true, then the conclusion is true. Two key aspects of this definition should be noted immediately. First, note the important word "necessary." In a valid argument, there is a *necessary connection* between the premises and the conclusion. The conclusion doesn't just happen to be true given the premises; rather, the truth of the conclusion is *absolutely guaranteed* given the truth of the premises. We could put this negatively by saying that a valid argument has this characteristic: It is *impossible* for the conclusion to be false assuming that the premises are true. Second, note the conditional (if–then) aspect of the definition. It does *not* say that the premises and conclusion of a valid argument are in fact true. Rather, the definition says that, necessarily, *if* the premises are true, *then* the conclusion is true. In other words, if an argument is valid, then *on the assumption that* its premises are true, its conclusion must be true also. Each of the following arguments is valid:

11. All biologists are scientists. John is not a scientist. So, John is not a biologist.

12. If Alice stole the diamonds, then she is a thief. And Alice did steal the diamonds. Hence, Alice is a thief.

13. Either Bill has a poor memory or he is lying. Bill does not have a poor memory. Therefore, Bill is lying.

In each case, it is necessary that if the premises are true, then the conclusion is true. Notice that one doesn't have to know whether the premises of an argument actually *are* true in order to determine its validity. One simply has to ascertain that the conclusion must be true *assuming* the premises are true.

In everyday English, the word "valid" is often used simply to indicate one's overall approval of an argument. But logicians focus their attention on the link-age between the premises and the conclusion rather than on the actual truth or falsity of the statements composing the argument. Thus, "valid" has a less precise meaning in ordinary English than it does for logicians.

The following observations about validity may help prevent some common misunderstandings. First, notice that an argument can have one or more *false* premises and still be valid. For instance:

14. All birds have beaks. Some cats are birds. So, some cats have beaks.

Here, the second premise is plainly false, and yet the argument is valid, for *on the assumption* that the premises are true, the conclusion must be true also. And in the following argument, both premises are false, but the argument is still valid:

15. All sharks are birds. All birds are politicians. So, all sharks are politicians.

Although the premises of argument (15) are in fact false, if they *were* true, the conclusion would *have* to be true as well. It is *impossible* for the conclusion to be false *assuming that* the premises are true. So, the argument is valid.

Second, we cannot rightly conclude that an argument is valid simply on the grounds that its premises are all true. For example:

16. Some Americans are women. Tom Hanks is an American. Therefore, Tom Hanks is a woman.

The premises here are true, but the conclusion is in fact false. So, obviously, it is *possible* that the conclusion of argument (16) is false while its premises are true; hence, (16) is not valid. Is the following argument valid?

17. Some Americans work in the movie industry. Meryl Streep is an American. Hence, Meryl Streep works in the movie industry.

Here, we have true premises and a true conclusion. But it is not *necessary* that if the premises are true, then the conclusion is true. (Streep could switch to another line of work while remaining an American.) So, even if an argument has true premises and a true conclusion, it isn't necessarily valid, for the premises may not support the conclusion in the right way. (Of course, in many cases, we simply do not know whether the premises of an argument are true or false, and yet we may know that the argument is valid.) Thus, the question "Are the premises actually true?" is distinct from the question "Is the argument valid?"

Third, suppose an argument is valid and has a false conclusion. Does it necessarily have at least one false premise? Yes. If it had true premises, then it would have to have a true conclusion, since it is valid. *Validity preserves truth;* that is, if we start with truth and reason in a valid fashion, we will always wind up with truth.

Fourth, does validity also preserve falsehood? In other words, if we start with false premises and reason validly, are we bound to wind up with a false conclusion? It is tempting to answer yes because "error in its own right breeds error—if the first step in an argument is wrong, everything that follows will be wrong."[2] But the correct answer is no. Consider the following argument:

18. All dogs are ants. All ants are mammals. So, all dogs are mammals.

Is argument (18) valid? Yes. It is impossible for the conclusion of (18) to be false *assuming that* its premises are true. However, the premises here are false while the conclusion is true. So, *validity does not preserve falsehood.* In fact, false premises plus valid reasoning may lead to either truth or falsity, depending on the case. Here is a valid argument with false premises and a false conclusion:

19. All birds are cats. Some dogs are birds. So, some dogs are cats.

*The lesson here is that although valid reasoning guarantees that we will end up with truth if we start with it, we may wind up with either truth or falsehood if we reason validly from false premises.*

---

A **valid argument** has this essential feature: It is necessary that if the premises are true, then the conclusion is true.

---

An **invalid argument** has this essential feature: It is *not necessary* that if the premises are true, then the conclusion is true. In other words, even on the assumption that the premises are true, the conclusion could still be false. Each of the following arguments is invalid:

20. All dogs are animals. All cats are animals. Hence, all dogs are cats.

21. If Pat is a wife, then Pat is a woman. But Pat is not a wife. So, Pat is not a woman.

22. Bill likes Sue. Therefore, Sue likes Bill.

The premises of argument (20) are in fact true, but its conclusion is false; so, (20) is obviously invalid. Argument (21) is invalid because its premises leave open the possibility that Pat is an unmarried woman. And (22) is invalid because even if Bill does like Sue, that is no guarantee that she likes him. In each of these cases, then, the conclusion could be false while (i.e., assuming that) the premises are true.

---

An **invalid argument** has this essential feature: It is *not necessary* that if the premises are true, then the conclusion is true.

---

Validity matters because true premises by themselves do not make good arguments. But we obviously want our arguments to have true premises. A **sound argument** has two essential features: *It is valid, and all its premises are true.* Notice that a sound argument cannot have a false conclusion. Because a sound argument is valid and has only true premises, it must have a true conclusion. Here are two sound arguments:

23. All collies are dogs. All dogs are animals. So, all collies are animals.

24. If Akron is in Ohio, then Akron is in the United States. Akron is in Ohio. Hence, Akron is in the United States.

---

Valid + All Premises True = Sound

---

An **unsound argument** falls into one of the following three categories:

It is valid but has at least one false premise.
It is invalid, but all its premises are true.
It is invalid *and* has at least one false premise.

In other words, an unsound argument is one that either is invalid or has at least one false premise. For example, both of the following arguments are unsound:

25. All birds are animals. Some grizzly bears are not animals. Therefore, some grizzly bears are not birds. *true* *false* *F* *Valid argument* *unsound*

26. All birds are animals. All grizzly bears are animals. So, all grizzly bears are birds. *False*

Argument (25) is unsound, because although it is valid, it has a false (second) premise. And (26) is unsound, because although it has true premises, it is invalid. We can easily construct an unsound argument of the third type—that is, one that both is invalid *and* has at least one false premise—by replacing "birds" in (26) with "trees":

27. All trees are animals. All bears are animals. So, all bears are trees.

---

An **unsound argument** is one that either is invalid or has at least one false premise.

---

Here is a map of the main concepts we've discussed so far:

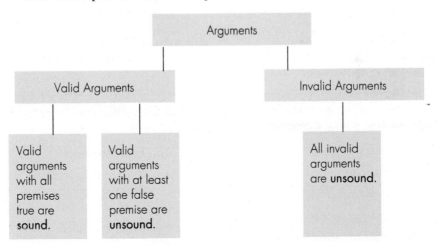

**Deductive logic** is the part of logic that is concerned with tests for validity and invalidity.[3] And much of this book is devoted to an exploration of deductive logic. In fact, the next two sections will provide us with some initial tests for establishing the validity and invalidity of arguments.

A note on terminology is in order at the close of this section. Given our definitions, *arguments* are neither true nor false, but each *statement* is either true or false. On the other hand, *arguments* can be valid, invalid, sound, or unsound; but *statements* cannot be valid, invalid, sound, or unsound. Therefore, a given premise (or conclusion) is either true or false, but it cannot be valid, invalid, sound, or unsound.

---

### Summary of Definitions

An **argument** is a set of statements, one of which, called the *conclusion*, is affirmed *on the basis* of the others, which are called the *premises*.

**Logic** is the study of methods for evaluating whether the premises of an argument adequately support (or provide good evidence for) its conclusion.

A **valid argument** has this essential feature: It is necessary that if the premises are true, then the conclusion is true.

An **invalid argument** has this essential feature: It is *not* necessary that if the premises are true, then the conclusion is true.

A **sound argument** has two essential features: *It is valid, and all its premises are true.*

An **unsound argument** is one that either is invalid or has at least one false premise.

**Deductive logic** is the part of logic that concerns tests for validity and invalidity.

---

The following exercises provide you with an opportunity to explore the concepts introduced in this section.

## ◆ Exercise 1.1

*Note:* For each exercise item preceded by an asterisk, the answer appears in the Answer Key at the end of the book.

**Part A:** Recognizing Statements   Write "statement" if the item is a statement. Write "sentence only" if the item is a sentence but not a statement. Write "neither" if the item is neither a sentence nor a statement.

* **1.** The sky is blue.

  **2.** Let's paint the table red.

  **3.** Please close the window!

* **4.** Murder is wrong.

  **5.** Abraham Lincoln was born in 1983.

  **6.** If San Francisco is in California, then San Francisco is in the U.S.A.

* **7.** It is not the case that Ben Franklin.

  **8.** "Why?" asked Socrates.

  **9.** Table not yes if.

* **10.** Either humans evolved from apes or apes evolved from humans.

  **11.** Davy Crockett died at the Alamo.

  **12.** How are you?

* **13.** If seven is greater than six, then six is greater than seven.

  **14.** Let's have lunch.

  **15.** Go!

* **16.** Shall we dance?

  **17.** Patrick Henry said, "Give me liberty or give me death."

  **18.** If punishment deters crime.

* **19.** "Stand at attention!" ordered General Bradley.

  **20.** Despite the weather.

**Part B: True or False?** Which of the following statements are true? Which are false?

F * 1. All valid arguments have at least one false premise.

T 2. An argument is a set of statements, one of which, called the *conclusion*, is affirmed *on the basis* of the others, which are called the *premises*.

F 3. Every valid argument has true premises and *only* true premises.

T* 4. Logic is the study of methods for evaluating whether the premises of an argument adequately support its conclusion.

F 5. Some statements are invalid.

F 6. Every valid argument has true premises *and* a true conclusion.

F 7. A sound argument can have a false conclusion.

T 8. Deductive logic is the part of logic that is concerned with tests for validity and invalidity.

T 9. If a valid argument has only true premises, then it must have a true conclusion.

F* 10. Some arguments are true.

T 11. If a valid argument has only false premises, then it must have a false conclusion.

T 12. Some invalid arguments have false conclusions but (all) true premises.

T* 13. Every sound argument is valid.

T 14. Every valid argument with a true conclusion is sound.

T 15. Every valid argument with a false conclusion has at least one false premise.

F* 16. Every unsound argument is invalid.

F 17. Some premises are valid.

F 18. If all of the premises of an argument are true, then it is sound.

T* 19. If an argument has (all) true premises and a false conclusion, then it is invalid.

T 20. If an argument has one false premise, then it is unsound.

T 21. Every unsound argument has at least one false premise.

F* 22. Some statements are sound.

F 23. Every valid argument has a true conclusion.

T 24. Every invalid argument is unsound.

F* 25. Some arguments are false.

F 26. If an argument is invalid, then it must have true premises and a false conclusion.

27. Every valid argument has this feature: Necessarily, if its premises are true, then its conclusion is true.

* 28. Every invalid argument has this feature: It is possibly false that if its premises are true, then its conclusion is true.

29. Every sound argument has a true conclusion.

30. Every valid argument has this feature: Necessarily, if its premises are false, then its conclusion is false.

**Part C:** Valid or Invalid?   Much of this text concerns methods of testing arguments for validity. While we have not yet discussed any particular methods of testing arguments for validity, we do have definitions of "valid argument" and "invalid argument." Based on your current understanding, which of the following arguments are valid? Which are invalid?

* 1. If Lincoln was killed in an automobile accident, then Lincoln is dead. Lincoln was killed in an automobile accident. Hence, Lincoln is dead.

2. If Lincoln was killed in an automobile accident, then Lincoln is dead. Lincoln was not killed in an automobile accident. Therefore, Lincoln is not dead.

3. If Lincoln was killed in an automobile accident, then Lincoln is dead. Lincoln is dead. So, Lincoln was killed in an automobile accident.

* 4. If Lincoln was killed in an automobile accident, then Lincoln is dead. Lincoln is not dead. Hence, Lincoln was not killed in an automobile accident.

5. Either 2 plus 2 equals 22 or Santa Claus is real. But 2 plus 2 does not equal 22. Therefore, Santa Claus is real.

6. Either we use nuclear power or we reduce our consumption of energy. If we use nuclear power, then we place our lives at great risk. If we reduce our consumption of energy, then we place ourselves under extensive governmental control. So, either we place our lives at great risk or we place ourselves under extensive governmental control.

* 7. All birds are animals. No tree is a bird. Therefore, no tree is an animal.

8. Some humans are comatose. But no comatose being is rational. So, not every human is rational.

9. All animals are living things. At least one cabbage is a living thing. So, at least one cabbage is an animal.

* 10. Alvin likes Jane. Jane likes Chris. So, Alvin likes Chris.

11. All murderers are criminals. Therefore, all nonmurderers are noncriminals.

12. David is shorter than Saul. Saul is shorter than Goliath. It follows that David is shorter than Goliath.

* **13.** It is possible that McGraw will win the next presidential election. It is possible that Lambert will win the next presidential election. Thus, it is possible that both McGraw and Lambert will win the next presidential election.

  **14.** All physicians are singers. Madonna is a physician. Therefore, Madonna is a singer.

  **15.** Samuel Morse invented the telegraph. Alexander Graham Bell did not invent the telegraph. Consequently, Morse is not identical with Bell.

**Part D:** Soundness   Which of the following arguments are sound? Which are unsound? If an argument is unsound, explain why.

* **1.** All cats are mammals. All mammals are animals. So, all cats are animals.

  **2.** All collies are dogs. Some animals are not dogs. So, some animals are not collies.

  **3.** All citizens of Nebraska are Americans. All citizens of Montana are Americans. So, all citizens of Nebraska are citizens of Montana.

* **4.** "Let's party!" is either a sentence or a statement (or both). "Let's party!" is a sentence. So, "Let's party!" is not a statement.

  **5.** No diamonds are emeralds. The Hope Diamond is a diamond. So, the Hope Diamond is not an emerald.

  **6.** All planets are round. The earth is round. So, the earth is a planet.

* **7.** If the Taj Mahal is in Kentucky, then the Taj Mahal is in the U.S.A. But the Taj Mahal is not in the U.S.A. So, the Taj Mahal is not in Kentucky.

  **8.** All women are married. Some executives are not married. So, some executives are not women.

  **9.** All mammals are animals. No reptiles are mammals. So, no reptiles are animals.

* **10.** All mammals are cats. All cats are animals. So, all mammals are animals.

  **11.** Wilber Wright invented the airplane. Therefore, Orville Wright did not invent the airplane.

  **12.** All collies are dogs. Hence, all dogs are collies.

* **13.** William Shakespeare wrote *Hamlet*. Leo Tolstoy is identical with William Shakespeare. It follows that Leo Tolstoy wrote *Hamlet*.

  **14.** If San Francisco is in Saskatchewan, then San Francisco is in Canada. But it is not true that San Francisco is in Saskatchewan. Hence, it is not true that San Francisco is in Canada.

  **15.** Either Thomas Jefferson was the first president of the U.S.A. or George Washington was the first president of the U.S.A., but not both. George Washington was the first president of the U.S.A. So, Thomas Jefferson was not the first president of the U.S.A.

## 1.2 Forms and Counterexamples

We have seen that deductive logic is the part of logic that concerns tests for validity and invalidity. This section introduces the concept of an argument form and explains how an understanding of argument forms can be used to establish that an argument is valid or invalid.

Consider the following two arguments:

28.  1. All oaks are trees.          29.  1. All emotivists are prescriptivists.
     2. All trees are plants.             2. All prescriptivists are metaethicists.
So, 3. All oaks are plants.          So, 3. All emotivists are metaethicists.

These two arguments have the same *form*—that is, they exemplify the same pattern of reasoning. We can represent the form as follows:

Form 1

1. All *A* are *B*.
2. All *B* are *C*.
So, 3. All *A* are *C*.

Here, the letters A, B, and C stand for *terms*. For the purposes of this chapter, let us say that a **term** is a word or phrase that stands for a class (i.e., collection or set) of things, such as the class of oaks or the class of trees. Thus, the words "oaks," "trees," and "plants" are terms in argument (28) above. (Certain descriptive phrases such as "oak trees less than 2 years old" also count as terms in the sense defined.) Form 1 provides a representation of the pattern of reasoning common to arguments (28) and (29). With regard to (28), A stands for the term "oaks," B for the term "trees," and C for the term "plants." With regard to (29), A stands for the term "emotivists," B stands for the term "prescriptivists," and C stands for the term "metaethicists."

Argument (28) is clearly valid: If all members of class A (oaks) are members of class B (trees), and all members of class B (trees) are members of class C (plants), then all members of A (oaks) are members of C (plants). We can diagram the logic as follows:

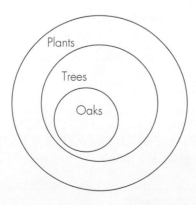

And as regards argument (29), even if its technical terms are unfamiliar, one can still see that if its premises are true, its conclusion must be true as well; hence, it is valid. In fact, any argument having Form 1 will have the following feature: On the assumption that its premises are true, its conclusion must be true. Thus, *the validity of the argument is guaranteed by its form and does not depend on its content* (i.e., its specific subject matter).

Using Form 1, we can generate valid arguments at will by substituting terms for the letters A, B, and C. An argument that results from uniformly replacing letters with terms (or statements) in an argument form is called a **substitution instance** of that form. Note that the replacement must be uniform. For example, if "oaks" replaces A in one instance, "oaks" must replace A in all instances. (In this section, we will focus primarily on argument forms in which the letters stand for terms; in the next section, we will focus on argument forms in which the letters stand for statements.)

Here is another valid form of argument, along with two substitution instances:

Form 2

    1. All *A* are *B*.
    2. Some *C* are not *B*.
So, 3. Some *C* are not *A*.

Substitution Instances

30. 1. All emeralds are gems.
    2. Some rocks are not gems.
So, 3. Some rocks are not emeralds.

31. 1. All collies are dogs.
    2. Some animals are not dogs.
So, 3. Some animals are not collies.

In argument (30), "emeralds" replaces A, "gems" replaces B, and "rocks" replaces C. In (31), "collies" replaces A, "dogs" replaces B, and "animals" replaces C. Every argument having this form is valid. We can diagram the logic as follows:

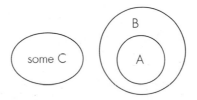

Clearly, if all members of class A are members of class B, and some members of class C are not members of B, then some members of C are not members of A. Thus, necessarily, if an argument of this form has true premises, then it has a true conclusion.

---

An **argument form** is a pattern of reasoning.
An argument that results from uniformly replacing letters in an argument form with terms (or statements) is called a **substitution instance** of that form.

Let us now consider the relationship between form and invalidity. The following argument has true premises and a false conclusion, so it is plainly invalid.

32.  1. All birds are animals.
     2. All dogs are animals.
So, 3. All birds are dogs.

If we let A stand for "birds," B for "animals," and C for "dogs," we can represent the form of the argument as follows:

Form 3
    1. All *A* are *B*.
    2. All *C* are *B*.
So, 3. All *A* are *C*.

This argument form is invalid because it allows us to move from true premises to a false conclusion. Argument (32) proves this, for it is a substitution instance of Form 3.

The relationship between argument (32) and Form 3 suggests a procedure for showing that an argument is invalid. First, identify the form of the argument. Second, if the validity of the argument is suspect, produce a substitution instance of the argument form in which the premises are true and the conclusion is false. This will show that the argument form is invalid. Third, given that the validity of the argument depends on the form identified, we may conclude that the argument itself is invalid. Let us now make this procedure a bit more explicit and note some complications that may arise.

Consider the following argument:

33.  1. All determinists are fatalists.
     2. Some fatalists are not Calvinists.
So, 3. Some Calvinists are not determinists.

Argument (33) has this form:

Form 4
    1. All *A* are *B*.
    2. Some *B* are not *C*.
So, 3. Some *C* are not *A*.

We can prove that this form is invalid by producing a substitution instance that has premises known to be true and a conclusion known to be false. For example:

34.  1. All dogs are animals. [true]
    2. Some animals are not collies. [true]
So, 3. Some collies are not dogs. [false]

A substitution instance with premises known to be true and a conclusion known to be false is a **counterexample** to the form in question. A counterexample demonstrates the invalidity of an argument form by showing that the form does not preserve truth—that is, that the form can lead from true premises to a false conclusion. A good counterexample must have the following features:

It must have the correct form.

Its premises must be *well-known* truths.

Its conclusion must be a *well-known* falsehood.

> A **counterexample** to an argument form is a substitution instance whose premises are *well-known* truths and whose conclusion is a *well-known* falsehood.

Counterexample (34) shows that Form 4 is invalid: "All A are B; some B are not C; so, some C are not A." And argument (33)—"All determinists are fatalists; some fatalists are not Calvinists; so, some Calvinists are not determinists"—has Form 4. Therefore, we may provisionally conclude that (33) is invalid. (The *provisional* nature of the conclusion will be explained shortly.)

    Now, let's break the process of finding a counterexample down into steps. We begin with an argument:

35.  1. No capitalists are philanthropists.
    2. All philanthropists are altruists.
So, 3. No capitalists are altruists.

If we let A stand for "capitalists," B for "philanthropists," and C for "altruists," we can represent the form as follows:

Form 5

    1. No A are B.
    2. All B are C.
So, 3. No A are C.

Next, we construct a substitution instance whose premises are well-known truths and whose conclusion is a well-known falsehood. It is best to employ terms whose interrelations are well understood—for example, simple biological terms such as "dog," "collie," "mammal," "cat," and "animal," or simple geometrical terms such as "square," "figure," "rectangle," and "circle." It often helps to begin by writing a blatantly false conclusion and then work backward. For instance:

36. 1. No dogs are B.
    2. All B are animals.
  So, 3. No dogs are animals.

Notice that since "dogs" replaces A in the conclusion, it must also replace A in the first premise; and because "animals" replaces C in the conclusion, it must replace C in the second premise. Now we merely need to find a term to replace B with—a term that will make the premises well-known truths. "Cats" is an obvious choice. So, our completed counterexample looks like this:

37. 1. No dogs are cats.
    2. All cats are animals.
  So, 3. No dogs are animals.

Because the premises are well-known truths but the conclusion is a well-known falsehood, Form 5 is invalid ("No A are B; all B are C; so, no A are C"). And we may provisionally conclude that argument (35) is invalid.

The counterexample method has some limitations and complications that should be noted at this time. First, although the counterexample method can be used to prove that an invalid argument form is invalid, it cannot show that a valid form is valid. For example, suppose we show that a given argument form has a substitution instance that has true premises and a true conclusion. Does that show that the argument form is valid? No. Invalid forms often have such substitution instances. Here is one for Form 5 ("No A are B; all B are C; so, no A are C):

38. 1. No cats are collies. [true]
    2. All collies are dogs. [true]
  So, 3. No cats are dogs. [true]

Nevertheless, the argument form remains invalid because it *can* lead from true premises to a false conclusion, as counterexample (37) illustrates. Again, the point is that the counterexample method cannot establish validity, but only invalidity.

Of course, it is impossible to construct a counterexample to a valid form. If an argument form is valid, then any substitution instance with true premises is bound to have a true conclusion. This indicates a second limitation of the counterexample method. What if we suspect that an argument form is invalid but have difficulty constructing a counterexample? Perhaps the form is valid after all, or perhaps we simply need to be more creative in thinking of substitution instances. How do we tell which? The counterexample method does not answer this question.

A minor complication that arises when constructing counterexamples concerns the word "some." In logic, the word "some" means "at least one." Hence, the statement "Some dogs are animals" is true: At *least one dog* is an animal. And "Some dogs are animals" does *not* imply that some dogs are not animals. Both of the following are true statements: "Some dogs are animals" and "All dogs are animals."

A more interesting complication regarding counterexamples stems from the fact that an argument can have more than one form. This complication explains why the counterexample method allows us to draw only *provisional* conclusions regarding the invalidity of *arguments* (as opposed to argument *forms*). Let's consider an argument having Form 1:

39. 1. All cats are mammals.

    2. All mammals are animals.

So, 3. All cats are animals.

Like all arguments having Form 1, argument (39) is valid. But suppose we let the letters A, B, and C stand for *statements* (instead of terms, as we have been doing). Such a use of letters is entirely legitimate; indeed, we will focus on forms in which letters stand for statements in the next section. And if we let A stand for the first premise, B for the second premise, and C for the conclusion, we can rightly say that argument (39) has the following form:

40. 1. A.

    2. B.

So, 3. C.

This form, however, is invalid—here is a counterexample:

41. 1. Trees exist.

    2. Frogs exist.

So, 3. Unicorns exist.

(To obtain the counterexample, simply substitute "Trees exist" for A, "Frogs exist" for B, and "Unicorns exist" for C.) Have we shown that argument (39) is invalid? No. We have merely shown that it has *one* form that is invalid. As a matter of fact, we might add that every argument has at least one invalid form because we can represent *any* argument as a series of statements, followed by a conclusion, along these lines: "A; B; C; D; so, E" (where the letters stand for *statements*). And it is easy to construct a counterexample similar to (41) to prove that any such form is invalid.

Very well, then. A single argument can have both valid and invalid forms. But here is a key point to remember: *An argument is valid if any of its forms is valid.* In other words, if an argument has a valid form, then it is impossible for its conclusion to be false while its premises are true. To illustrate, argument (39) is valid because it has a valid form, namely, Form 1.

We can now see why the counterexample method yields only provisional results. Suppose we have correctly identified one of the argument's forms and shown *that* form to be invalid by means of a counterexample. It remains possible—at least in theory—that the argument has an additional form that is valid. And, as we have just seen, it is not the possession of an invalid form that makes an argument invalid; rather, it is the lack of a valid form that makes an argument invalid.[4]

What good is it, then, to show that an argument has a form that is invalid? Generally speaking, if we identify the form of an argument *with due sensitivity to its key logical words and phrases*, and if the form thus identified is invalid, then the argument has no further valid form, and so it is invalid. And this is why the counterexample method is a powerful tool for evaluating arguments even though it cannot rigorously prove that a given *argument* is invalid. In addition, bear in mind that the counterexample method *can* be used to prove *rigorously* that invalid *forms* are invalid, and it is of great value for this reason also.

The following exercise gives you some practice in identifying argument forms and constructing counterexamples. In this exercise, the capital letters in the argument forms stand for terms. In the next section, we will focus on argument forms in which the capital letters stand for statements.

---

### Process for Constructing a Counterexample

1. Identify the form of the argument, using capital letters to stand for terms (or for statements).

2. Find English terms (or statements) that, if substituted for the capital letters in the conclusion of the argument form, produce a *well-known* falsehood. Substitute these English terms (or statements) for the relevant capital letters uniformly throughout the argument form.

3. Find additional English terms (or statements) that, if substituted uniformly for the remaining capital letters in the argument form, produce premises that are *well-known* truths.

4. Check to make sure that your counterexample is a substitution instance of the argument form and that its conclusion is a *well-known* falsehood while each premise is a *well-known* truth. In checking your counterexample, here's a good question to ask yourself: "Will my classmates readily agree that the premises of my counterexample are well-known truths and that its conclusion is a well-known falsehood?"

# ◆ *Exercise 1.2*

**Counterexamples** Use counterexamples to show that the following arguments are invalid. Remember, it is usually best to employ terms whose interrelations are well known, such as "dog," "cat," "collie," "animal," and "mammal."

* **1.** No genuine Americans are communist spies. Some Oregonians are not communist spies. Therefore, some Oregonians are genuine Americans.

  **2.** All dogmatists are hypocrites. All dogmatists are bigots. So, all bigots are hypocrites.

  **3.** All who seek public office are noble. Some who seek public office are not wise persons. So, some wise persons are not noble.

* **4.** No rock is sentient. Some mammals are sentient. Hence, no mammal is a rock.

  **5.** All fatalists are determinists. Some predestinarians are not fatalists. So, some predestinarians are not determinists.

  **6.** All vegetarians who refuse to eat animal products are vegans. No vegetarians who refuse to eat animal products are cattle ranchers. Hence, no vegans are cattle ranchers.

* **7.** Some intelligent people are highly immoral. All highly immoral people are unhappy. Therefore, some unhappy people are not intelligent.

  **8.** No perfect geometrical figures are physical entities. No physical entities are circles. Therefore, no circles are perfect geometrical figures.

  **9.** All Fabians are socialists. Some socialists are not communists. So, some Fabians are not communists.

* **10.** All trespassers are persons who will be prosecuted. Some trespassers are not criminals. So, some criminals are not persons who will be prosecuted.

  **11.** All observable entities are physical entities. Some quarks are not observable entities. Therefore, some quarks are not physical entities.

  **12.** No wines are distilled liquors. Some beers are not distilled liquors. So, some beers are not wines.

* **13.** All statements that can be falsified are scientific. All empirical data are scientific. Hence, all statements that can be falsified are empirical data.

  **14.** All diligent persons are individuals who deserve praise. Some students are individuals who deserve praise. So, some students are diligent persons.

  **15.** All black holes are stars that have collapsed in on themselves. All black holes are entities that produce a tremendous amount of gravity. So, every entity that produces a tremendous amount of gravity is a star that has collapsed in on itself.

* **16.** Every rock musician is cool. No nerd is a rock musician. Hence, no nerd is cool.

**17.** All miracles are highly improbable events. Some highly improbable events are cases of winning a lottery. So, some cases of winning a lottery are miracles.

**18.** No positrons are particles with a negative charge. No neutrons are particles with a negative charge. Therefore, some positrons are neutrons.

* **19.** All people who despise animals are neurotic. No veterinarian is a person who despises animals. Hence, no veterinarian is a neurotic.

**20.** All destructive acts are evil. Some wars are evil. So, some wars are destructive acts.

## 1.3 Some "Famous" Forms

We have seen how the concept of an argument form can be used to establish that an argument is invalid. And we have seen that if an argument has a valid form, then it is valid. In this section, we will identify some forms that occur so often that they have been given names by logicians. Five of these forms are valid, and two are invalid. Because these forms appear very frequently, let us call them "famous" forms. Prior to identifying these forms, however, we need to understand conditional ("if-then") statements because some of the most important argument forms centrally involve conditional statements.

### Understanding Conditional Statements

Each of the following are conditional statements (often called simply "conditionals" by logicians):

**42.** If it is snowing, then the mail will be late.

**43.** If Abraham Lincoln was born in 1709, then he was born before the American Civil War.

**44.** If Abraham Lincoln was born in 1809, then he was born after the American Civil War.

Conditionals have several important characteristics. First, note the components of conditionals. The if-clause of a conditional is called its **antecedent**; the then-clause is called the **consequent**. But the antecedent does not include the word "if." Hence, the antecedent of statement (42) is "it is snowing," not "*If* it is snowing." Similarly, the consequent is the statement following the word "then," but it does not include that word. So, the consequent of (42) is "the mail will be late," not "*then* the mail will be late."

Second, conditionals are hypothetical in nature. Thus, in asserting a conditional, one does not assert that its antecedent is true. Nor does one assert that its consequent is true. Rather, one asserts that *if* the antecedent is true, *then* the consequent is true. Thus, statement (43) is a true conditional even though its antecedent is false (Lincoln was born in 1809, not 1709). If Lincoln was born in 1709, then, of course, his birth preceded the American Civil War, which began in 1861. And (44) is a false conditional even though its antecedent is true. If Lincoln was born in 1809, then he certainly was not born *after* the American Civil War.

Third, there are many ways to express a conditional in ordinary English. Consider the following conditional statement:

> **45.** If it is raining, then the ground is wet.

Statements (a) through (f) following are all **stylistic variants** of (45), that is, alternate ways of saying the same thing:[5]

   a. *Given that* it is raining, the ground is wet.

   b. *Assuming that* it is raining, the ground is wet.

   c. The ground is wet *if* it is raining.

   d. The ground is wet *given that* it is raining.

   e. The ground is wet *assuming that* it is raining.

   f. It is raining *only if* the ground is wet.

Each of the above statements is logically equivalent to (45). Two statements are **logically equivalent** if each validly implies the other. Since each of (a) through (f) is logically equivalent to (45), (45) can be substituted for each of them in an argument. And as we will see, making such substitutions is an aid to identifying argument forms. Accordingly, a close look at these stylistic variants is warranted. Consider (c). Note that "if" comes not at the beginning but in the middle of the statement. Yet, (c) has the same underlying logical meaning as (45). And the phrase "given that" in (d) plays a role exactly analogous to the "if" in (c). We might generalize from these examples by saying that "if" and its stylistic variants (e.g., "given that" and "assuming that") *introduce an antecedent*. But we must hasten to add that this generalization applies only when "if" or its stylistic variants appear by themselves. When combined with "only," as in (f), the situation alters dramatically. Statement (f) has the same logical force as (45), but the phrase "only if" is confusing to many people and bears close examination.

To clarify the logical force of "only if," it is helpful to consider very simple conditionals, such as the following:

> **46.** Rex is a dog *only if* Rex is an animal.

> **47.** Rex is an animal *only if* Rex is a dog.

Obviously, (46) and (47) say different things. Statement (47) is false. Rex may well be an animal even if Rex isn't a dog. Thus, (47) says, in effect, that "If Rex is an animal, Rex is a dog." But (46) says something entirely different, and something true—namely, that if Rex is a dog, then Rex is an animal. In general, statements of the form "A only if B" are logically equivalent to statements of the form "If A, then B." They are *not* logically equivalent to statements of the form "If B, then A." Another way to generalize the point is to say that "only if" (unlike "if") *introduces a consequent*, that is, a then-clause.

## The Argument Forms

We are now ready to examine some "famous" argument forms.

### Modus Ponens

Let us begin with **modus ponens**. Consider the following argument:

> 48.  1. If it is raining, then the ground is wet.
>      2. It is raining.
> So, 3. The ground is wet.

This argument is obviously valid: On the assumption that its premises are true, its conclusion must be true also. Using letters to stand for statements, the form of the argument is as follows:

> Modus Ponens
>      1. If A, then B.
>      2. A.
> So, 3. B.

(A stands for "it is raining"; B stands for "the ground is wet.") This form of argument is always valid. It is called *modus ponens* (which means "the mode of positing") because the second premise posits (i.e., sets down as fact) the antecedent of the conditional (first) premise.

Two points about *modus ponens* are worth noting. First, the order of the premises does not matter. For example, both of the following count as *modus ponens*:

> 49. If Einstein was a physicist, then he was a scientist. Einstein was a physicist. So, Einstein was a scientist.

> 50. Einstein was a physicist. If Einstein was a physicist, then he was a scientist. So, Einstein was a scientist.

In other words, arguments of the form "A; if A, then B; so, B" count as examples of *modus ponens*.

Second, the conditionals involved in *modus ponens* can be rather long and complex. For example:

> 51. If every right can be waived and each person has a right to life, then eutha-
> nasia is permitted in those cases in which the person to be "euthanized"
> waives his or her right to life. Moreover, every right can be waived and each
> person has a right to life. Hence, euthanasia is permitted in those cases in
> which the person to be "euthanized" waives his or her right to life.

The conditional premise in argument (51) is relatively long and complex, but the form is still *modus ponens*. ("Every right can be waived and each person has a right to life" replaces A; "euthanasia is permitted in those cases in which the person to be euthanized waives his or her right to life" replaces B.)

### Modus Tollens

A second basic argument form is called **modus tollens**. Like *modus ponens*, one of its key premises is a conditional:

> 52. 1. If it is raining, then the ground is wet.
> 2. The ground is not wet.
> So, 3. It is not raining.

*Modus tollens* means "the mode or way of removing." The argument form gets its name from the second premise, which denies (removes the truth of) the conse-quent of the first premise. The form is as follows:

> *Modus Tollens*
> 1. If A, then B.
> 2. Not B.
> So, 3. Not A.

"Not A" and "not B" stand for negations. A **negation** of a statement is its denial. For example, in argument (52), "the ground is not wet" plays the role of "not B." The negation of a statement can be formed in various ways. Take the statement "the ground is wet." Each of the following is a negation of it:

> a. *It is not the case that* the ground is wet.
> b. *It's false that* the ground is wet.
> c. *It is not true that* the ground is wet.
> d. The ground is *not* wet.

As with *modus ponens*, the order of the premises does not matter. In other words, arguments of the form "Not B; if A, then B; so, not A" count as *modus tollens*.

Consider a more complicated example of *modus tollens*. According to some physicists who endorse the Big Bang theory, the universe cannot be infinitely old. The second law of thermodynamics tells us that in a closed physical system entropy always tends to increase; that is, energy gets diffused over time. (For instance, the radiant energy of a star will gradually become spread out evenly into the space surrounding it.) According to these physicists, if the physical universe has existed for an infinite period, there are now no concentrations of energy (e.g., no stars or planets). But obviously, there are stars and planets, so the physical universe has not existed for an infinite period. We can put this reasoning explicitly into the *modus tollens* form as follows:

53. 1. If the physical universe has existed for an infinite period, then all the energy in the universe is spread out evenly (as opposed to being concentrated in such bodies as planets and stars).

    2. It is not true that all the energy in the universe is spread out evenly (as opposed to being concentrated in such bodies as planets and stars).

    So, 3. It is not true that the physical universe has existed for an infinite period.

Notice how putting the argument into explicit form helps to focus attention on the key issues. There is no debate whatsoever about the second premise of this argument. Stars and planets exist, so energy is not in fact spread out evenly throughout the physical universe. Nor is there any debate about the validity of the argument. Every argument having the form *modus tollens* is valid. The focus of the debate, therefore, must be on the first premise, and that is just where physicists have placed it. For example, some physicists think that the universe oscillates, that is, goes through a cycle of "Big Bangs" and "Big Crunches." And if the universe can oscillate, then its diffuse energy can be reconcentrated into usable forms, in which case the first premise is doubtful.[6]

## Denying the Antecedent

Having examined two valid forms of argument, let us now take note of two invalid forms with which they are often confused. These invalid forms are called *fallacies*. (A fallacy is an error in reasoning.) Let us begin with the **fallacy of denying the antecedent**, which is often confused with *modus tollens*. Consider:

54. 1. If it is raining, then the ground is wet.

    2. It is not raining.

    So, 3. The ground is not wet.

The first premise here is a conditional, as in the case of *modus tollens*. However, whereas the second premise of *modus tollens* denies the consequent of the conditional, the second premise of this argument denies the antecedent. This difference in form is crucial because even if the premises of this argument were true, the conclusion could still be false. For example, let us suppose that the ground is soaking wet due to a sprinkler having been left on all night. Then, even if it is not raining, the ground is wet. (And remember, the first premise, being hypothetical, does not assert or imply that it is raining.) Denying the antecedent is an invalid form of argument. We can represent its form as follows:

Fallacy of Denying the Antecedent
1. If A, then B.
2. Not A.
So, 3. Not B.

(The order of the premises does not matter; hence, arguments of the form "Not A; if A, then B; so, not B" count as examples of denying the antecedent.) Here is a counterexample that shows that denying the antecedent is invalid:

55. 1. If lemons are red, then lemons have a color. [true]
2. Lemons are not red. [true]
So, 3. Lemons do not have a color. [false]

In thinking about this counterexample, it is important to recall that conditionals are hypothetical statements. Thus, premise (1) does not say that lemons *are* red; it merely says that *if* lemons are red, *then* they have a color.

## Affirming the Consequent

A second fallacy, often confused with *modus ponens*, is the **fallacy of affirming the consequent**. Here is an example:

56. 1. If it is raining, then the ground is wet.
2. The ground is wet.
So, 3. It is raining.

The form is as follows:

Fallacy of Affirming the Consequent
1. If A, then B.
2. B.
So, 3. A.

(The order of the premises does not matter; hence, arguments of the form "B; if A, then B; so, A" are examples of affirming the consequent.) Again, the example of a sprinkler left on overnight reveals the invalidity of the argument. One cannot assume that rain is the only thing that will make the ground wet. The fallacy of affirming the consequent gets its name from its second premise, which affirms the consequent of the conditional premise. Here is a counterexample that shows that the form is invalid:

57. 1. If lemons are red, then lemons have a color. [true]
   2. Lemons have a color. [true]
So, 3. Lemons are red. [false]

Again, in thinking about this counterexample, bear in mind that the conditional premise is hypothetical in nature.

Two issues should be considered here before going on. First, it is sometimes alleged that we can imagine circumstances in which *modus ponens* or *modus tollens* fails—that is, in which the premises are true and the conclusion is false. For example, let's go back to *modus ponens*: "If it's raining, then the ground is wet. It's raining. So, the ground is wet." What if the ground is covered, you might ask? What if the whole earth were enclosed in a plastic bag? Then, even if it was raining, the ground wouldn't be wet. Wouldn't *modus ponens* fail in such (admittedly farfetched) circumstances? No. These are not circumstances in which the premises are true and the conclusion is false. Rather, they are circumstances in which the conditional premise ("If it's raining, the ground is wet") is false. And remember: When we are testing for validity, we must assume that the premises are true and consider whether this assumption forces us to assume that the conclusion is true as well.

Second, although the invalidity of denying the antecedent and affirming the consequent is readily apparent in the examples used thus far, the error isn't always quite so obvious. Consider the following example of affirming the consequent:

58. If lying causes ill feelings, then it is wrong. And lying is wrong. Therefore, it causes ill feelings.

Argument (58) is invalid because it overlooks the possibility that an act might be wrong for some reason other than its causing ill feelings. For instance, some say lying is wrong simply because society disapproves of it or because the liar violates a moral rule. The following example of the fallacy of denying the antecedent involves a similar error:

59. If using placebos causes harm, then doing so is wrong. But using placebos does not cause harm. Hence, using placebos is not wrong.

Argument (59) overlooks the possibility that an act might be wrong even if it doesn't harm anyone. For example, some say that acts are wrong simply because God disapproves of them (and regardless of the effects the actions have on other people).

## Hypothetical Syllogism

Let us now return to valid forms. Consider the following argument:

> 60. 1. If tuition continues to increase, then only the wealthy will be able to afford a college education.
>
> 2. If only the wealthy will be able to afford a college education, then class divisions will be strengthened.
>
> So, 3. If tuition continues to increase, then class divisions will be strengthened.

We can represent the form as follows; it is called **hypothetical syllogism**:

### Hypothetical Syllogism

> 1. If $A$, then $B$.
> 2. If $B$, then $C$.
> So, 3. If $A$, then $C$.

(The order of the premises does not matter; hence, arguments of the form "If $B$, then $C$; if $A$, then $B$; so, if $A$, then $C$" are examples of hypothetical syllogism.) The argument is called *hypothetical syllogism* because it involves only hypothetical (i.e., conditional) statements. *Syllogism* comes from Greek roots meaning "to reason together" or to put statements together into a pattern of reasoning. Every argument that exemplifies the form hypothetical syllogism is valid. Here is another example of this form:

> 61. If I am morally responsible, then I can choose between good and evil. If I can choose between good and evil, then some of my actions are free. Therefore, if I am morally responsible, then some of my actions are free.

Note that the conclusion of a hypothetical syllogism is a conditional statement.

## Disjunctive Syllogism

Thus far in this section, we have focused on argument forms that involve conditional statements. Not all argument forms are like this. Some make central use of **disjunctions**, that is, statements of the form "Either $A$ or $B$." For example:

> 62. 1. Either Michelangelo painted *Guernica* or Picasso painted it.
>
> 2. Michelangelo did not paint *Guernica*.
>
> So, 3. Picasso painted *Guernica*.

The argument has the following form, which is called **disjunctive syllogism** because of its "either-or" premise:

Disjunctive Syllogism

    1. Either *A* or *B*.

    2. Not *A*.

So, 3. *B*.

Arguments having this form are *always* valid. (The order of the premises does not matter; hence, arguments of the form "Not *A*; either *A* or *B*; so, *B*" are examples of disjunctive syllogism.)

Some brief remarks about disjunctions are in order here. First, some terminology: The statements comprising a disjunction are called its **disjuncts**. For instance, the disjuncts of premise (1) in argument (62) are "Michelangelo painted *Guernica*" and "Picasso painted *Guernica*."

Second, we will take "Either *A* or *B*" to mean "Either *A* or *B* (or both)." This is called the **inclusive** sense of "or." For instance, suppose a job announcement reads: "Applicants must have either work experience or a bachelor's degree in the field." Obviously, an applicant with *both* work experience *and* a bachelor's degree is not excluded from applying.

Third, some authors speak of an **exclusive** sense of "or," claiming that "Either *A* or *B*" sometimes means "Either *A* or *B* (but not both)." For example, in commenting on a presidential election, one might say, "Either Smith or Jones will win the election," the assumption being that both will not (indeed cannot) win. However, it is a matter of controversy whether there really are two different meanings of the word "or" *as opposed to* there simply being cases in which the context indicates that *A* and *B* are not (or cannot) both be true. Rather than let this controversy sidetrack us, let us simply assume that the locution "Either *A* or *B*" means "Either *A* or *B* (or both)."

Having made this assumption, however, we must immediately add that arguers are free to use the locution "Either *A* or *B* (but not both)." This locution is equivalent to two statements: "Either *A* or *B*. Not both *A* and *B*." Consider the following argument:

    63. Either Millard Fillmore was the 13th president of the United States, or Zachary Taylor was the 13th president of the United States (but not both). Millard Fillmore was the 13th president. So, Zachary Taylor was not the 13th president.

We can represent the form of argument (63) as "Either *A* or *B*; not both *A* and *B*; *A*; so, not *B*." This form is valid, but notice that it differs from disjunctive syllogism.

Also note that disjunctive syllogism differs from the following form of argument:

    64. Either Hitler was a Nazi, or Himmler was a Nazi (or both were). Hitler was a Nazi. Therefore, it is not the case that Himmler was a Nazi.

The form of argument (64) can best be represented as "Either A or B (or both); A; therefore, not B." As a matter of historical fact, the premises of (64) are true, but its conclusion is false, so this argument form is definitely invalid.

Now, what is the form of the following argument?

> 65. Either Bloggs is guilty or Brennan is guilty. It is false that Bloggs is guilty. Hence, Brennan is guilty.

Yes, the form is disjunctive syllogism, and the argument is valid.

### Constructive Dilemma

Let's look at one more "famous" argument form. This form is called the **constructive dilemma**, and it combines both conditional and disjunctive statements. Here is an example:

> 66. 1. Either Donna knew the information on her tax returns was inaccurate, or she did not know it.
> 2. If Donna knew the information was inaccurate, she was lying.
> 3. If Donna did not know the information was inaccurate, then she was negligent.
> So, 4. Either Donna was lying, or she was negligent.

The form of this argument is as follows:

### Constructive Dilemma

> 1. Either A or B.
> 2. If A, then C.
> 3. If B, then D.
> So, 4. Either C or D.

Arguments of this form are always valid. (The order of the premises in a constructive dilemma does not matter. For example, sometimes the conditional premises are given first, followed by the disjunctive premise.) The age-old problem of evil can be put in the form of a constructive dilemma:

> 67. If God cannot prevent suffering, then God is not omnipotent. If God does not want to prevent suffering, then God is not perfectly good. But either God cannot prevent suffering or God does not want to prevent suffering. So, either God is not omnipotent or God is not perfectly good.

This dilemma nicely illustrates how logic can be used to formulate a problem in a revealing way. Because argument (67) is valid, the conclusion must be true if the premises are true. And the first premise seems undeniable. Moreover, theists, against whom the argument is directed, can hardly deny the third (disjunctive) premise. (If God *can* prevent suffering, then God must not want to prevent it for some reason.) Historically, the second premise has been the focus of debate, with theologians suggesting that God does not want to eliminate all suffering because suffering is the necessary means to certain good ends (e.g., the spiritual maturation of free creatures).

## The Process

The "famous" forms we now have in hand are quite useful for determining the validity of arguments. Many arguments either possess one of these forms or, when briefly summarized, are naturally put into one of these forms. In order to make use of these new tools, we employ the following process. First, we identify the component statements in the argument, labeling them with capital letters as we have throughout this section. To avoid errors, write the capital letter by each instance of the statement it stands for, taking negations into account, like this:

      *A*            *B*            *not B*

68. Ken is old *only if* he is over seventy. But Ken is not over seventy, and hence he is not old.
    *not A*

Second, rewrite the argument using capital letters instead of English statements and eliminating the stylistic variants. Rewriting argument (68) in this fashion, we get:

69. 1. If *A,* then *B.*
    2. Not *B.*
    So, 3. Not *A.*

Third, identify any "famous" forms that appear and evaluate for validity. Here the form is *modus tollens,* so the argument is valid. If none of our "famous" forms is employed and the argument seems invalid, try to construct a counterexample. Of course, if the argument is valid, it won't be possible to construct a counter-example. And in order to assess a wider range of valid arguments, we will need additional tools such as those introduced in subsequent chapters of this book.

It may be useful to highlight some complications that can arise when employing our three-step process. Consider the following argument:

     *A*           *B*

70. Alice is a fast runner *if* she can run the mile in under four minutes. But Alice cannot run the mile in under four minutes. Therefore, Alice in not a fast runner.
         *not B*                    *not A*

When we rewrite the argument using capital letters and eliminating stylistic variants, we get:

71. 1. If *B*, then *A*.
2. Not *B*.
So, 3. Not *A*.

Our labeling results in the conditional "If *B*, then *A*" rather than "If *A*, then *B*." But this is not a problem—there is no need to try to make the letters appear in alphabetical order. The important thing to note is that the second premise *denies the antecedent* of the conditional premise, while the conclusion denies the consequent of the conditional premise. Thus, we have an instance of the fallacy of denying the antecedent, and the argument is invalid.

Here's another argument that illustrates a slight complication that can arise when applying our three-step process:

          *A*                    *B*                   *A*
72. The sun is shining; but the room is hot *given that* the sun is shining; hence, the room is hot.
     *B*

We may rewrite the argument as follows:

73. 1. *A*.
2. If *A*, then *B*.
So, 3. *B*.

The conditional premise appears second, but that's not a problem—the order of the premises does not matter. What matters is this: We have a conditional and its antecedent as premises, with the consequent of the conditional as the conclusion. Thus, the argument form is *modus ponens*, and the argument is valid.

Another complication arises when you need to construct a counterexample for an argument that involves conditional statements. For example:

             *A*                           *B*
74. If computer hacking causes harm, it should be penalized. So, if computer hacking should be penalized, then it causes harm.
     *B*                                *A*

The form of the argument is as follows:

75. 1. If *A*, then *B*.
So, 2. If *B*, then *A*.

Now, we follow our usual procedure in constructing a counterexample, beginning with a conclusion that is a *well-known* falsehood. For instance, "If Tom Hanks is over 2 years old, then he is over 100 years old." Notice that this conditional has a true antecedent and a false consequent. *Conditionals with a true*

---

### *Using Forms to Test for Validity*

Step 1. Identify the component statements in the argument, labeling each with a capital letter.

Step 2. Rewrite the argument using capital letters instead of English statements. Eliminate any stylistic variants.

Step 3. Identify any "famous" forms that appear, and evaluate for validity. If none of the "famous" forms is employed and the argument seems invalid, try to construct a counterexample.

---

*antecedent and a false consequent are always false*. The counterexample looks like this:

> 76. 1. If Tom Hanks is over 100 years old, then he is over 2 years old. [true]
>
> So, 2. If Tom Hanks is over 2 years old, then he is over 100 years old. [false]

Remember, the premise does not say that Hanks is over 100 years old; it just says that *if* he is over 100, then he's over 2, which is obviously true. The following additional counterexamples to form (75) will give you some ideas for constructing your own counterexamples to arguments involving conditional statements:

> 77. 1. If Abe Lincoln was over 10 feet tall, then he was over 4 feet tall. [true]
>
> So, 2. If Abe Lincoln was over 4 feet tall, then he was over 10 feet tall. [false]

---

### *Summary of Forms*

**Valid Forms**

*Modus ponens:* If A, then B. A. So, B.

*Modus tollens:* If A, then B. Not B. So, not A.

*Hypothetical syllogism:* If A, then B. If B, then C. So, if A, then C.

*Disjunctive syllogism:* Either A or B. Not A. So, B.

*Constructive dilemma:* Either A or B. If A, then C. If B, then D. So, either C or D.

**Invalid Forms**

*Denying the antecedent:* If A, then B. Not A. So, not B.

*Affirming the consequent:* If A, then B. B. So, A.

**78.** 1. If lemons are red, then lemons have a color. [true]

So, 2. If lemons have a color, then lemons are red. [false]

(Note that the false conditionals here have a true antecedent and a false consequent.) As always, when constructing counterexamples, it is important that the premises be well-known truths and the conclusion a well-known falsehood.

The following exercise gives you an opportunity to use your knowledge of the "famous" forms in order to assess the validity of arguments.

## ◆ Exercise 1.3

**Part A:** Arguments to Evaluate    Identify the forms of the following arguments, using capital letters to stand for statements and eliminating any stylistic variants. If the argument form is one of the "famous" forms, give the name of the form and indicate whether it is valid. If the argument form is not one of the "famous" forms, construct a counterexample to show that the form is invalid.

* **1.** If the solution turns blue litmus paper red, then the solution contains acid. The solution turns blue litmus paper red. So, the solution contains acid.

  **2.** If the solution turns blue litmus paper red, then the solution contains acid. The solution does not contain acid. So, the solution does not turn blue litmus paper red.

  **3.** Lewis is a famous author only if he knows how to write. But Lewis is not a famous author. Hence, Lewis does not know how to write.

* **4.** If Susan is a famous author, then she knows how to write. Moreover, Susan knows how to write. So, she is a famous author.

  **5.** Souls transmigrate. But it is wrong to eat animals if souls transmigrate. Hence, it is wrong to eat animals.

  **6.** Either Jones is an innocent bystander, or Jones fired a shot at the mayor. Jones is not an innocent bystander. Therefore, Jones fired a shot at the mayor.

* **7.** Rilke is a dreamer if he is a poet. Therefore, Rilke is a poet.

  **8.** Either you marry young, or you wait. If you marry young, you incur a high risk of divorce. If you wait, the field of available partners grows ever smaller. So, either you incur a high risk of divorce, or the field of available partners grows ever smaller.

  **9.** It is not wrong to kill spiders. But if spiders have eternal souls, then it is wrong to kill them. Thus, it is false that spiders have eternal souls.

* **10.** If you study hard, you refine your communication skills. If you refine your communication skills, then your job opportunities increase. Hence, if you study hard, your job opportunities increase.

  **11.** If Mubarak is from Egypt, then he is from Africa. Therefore, if Mubarak is not from Egypt, then he is not from Africa.

12. Ben is a rat. Ben is a rat only if Ben is a mammal. So, Ben is a mammal.

* **13.** Sam is wealthy if he has more than a billion dollars. But Sam does not have more than a billion dollars. Therefore, Sam is not wealthy.

**14.** There is life on Mars given that there is life on Earth. Hence, there is life on Mars.

**15.** It is true that corrupt institutions are hard to reform. It is false that individuals are totally depraved. Therefore, if corrupt institutions are hard to reform, then individuals are totally depraved.

**Part B:** More Arguments to Evaluate   Identify the forms of the following arguments, using capital letters to stand for statements and eliminating any stylistic variants. If the argument form is one of the "famous" forms, give the name of the form and indicate whether it is valid. If the argument form is not one of the "famous" forms, construct a counterexample to show that the form is invalid.

* **1.** The sky is blue. The sky is cobalt blue only if it is blue. Hence, the sky is cobalt blue.

**2.** Abortion in the case of ectopic pregnancy is not wrong. But if it is always wrong to kill an innocent human being, then abortion in the case of ectopic pregnancy is wrong. So, it is not always wrong to kill an innocent human.

**3.** Kidnapping is wrong if society disapproves of it. Kidnapping is wrong. So, society disapproves of kidnapping.

* **4.** Eating meat is unhealthy if meat contains a lot of cholesterol. Meat does contain a lot of cholesterol. Therefore, eating meat is unhealthy.

**5.** Either the "eye for an eye" principle is interpreted literally, or it is interpreted figuratively. If it is interpreted literally, then the state should torture torturers, maim maimers, and rape rapists. If the "eye for an eye" principle is interpreted figuratively, then it does not necessarily demand death for murderers. So, either the state should torture torturers, maim maimers, and rape rapists, or the "eye for an eye" principle does not necessarily demand death for murderers.

**6.** Affirmative action is preferential treatment of disadvantaged groups, and preferential treatment of disadvantaged groups is reverse discrimination. If affirmative action is preferential treatment of disadvantaged groups and preferential treatment of disadvantaged groups is reverse discrimination, then affirmative action is wrong. Hence, affirmative action is wrong.

* **7.** If the zygote lacks a brain, then the zygote lacks a soul. If the zygote lacks a soul, then killing the zygote is permissible. So, if the zygote lacks a brain, then killing the zygote is permissible.

**8.** If Mary is a psychiatrist, then she is a physician. Mary is not a physician. Therefore, Mary is a psychiatrist.

9. If you want to ruin your life, you should take hard drugs. But you don't want to ruin your life. So, you should not take hard drugs.

* 10. Lying causes social discord. Hence, lying is wrong.

11. It is not true that acts are right because God approves them. But either acts are right because God approves them, or God approves of acts because they are right. Therefore, God approves of acts because they are right.

12. If Dracula is a vampire, then he is dangerous. But Dracula is not a vampire. Hence, he is dangerous.

* 13. Either the animals used in research are a lot like humans, or they are not a lot like humans. If the animals are a lot like humans, then experimenting on them is morally questionable. If the animals are not a lot like humans, then experimenting on them is pointless. So, either experimenting on animals is morally questionable, or it is pointless.

14. The state cannot uphold the value of life by taking it. And if the state cannot uphold the value of life by taking it, then the death penalty should be abolished. Therefore, the death penalty should be abolished.

15. If my society approves of genetic engineering, then genetic engineering is right. But my society does not approve of genetic engineering. Hence, genetic engineering is not right.

**Part C:** Still More Arguments to Evaluate   Identify the forms of the following arguments, using capital letters to stand for statements and eliminating any stylistic variants. If the argument form is one of the "famous" forms, give the name of the form and indicate whether it is valid. If the argument form is not one of the "famous" forms, construct a counterexample to show that the form is invalid.

*  1. Overeating is foolish only if it causes disease. Overeating does not cause disease. So, overeating is not foolish.

2. Either films depicting graphic violence have caused the increase in violent crime or bad parenting has caused it (or both). Movies depicting graphic violence have caused the increase in violent crime. Therefore, bad parenting has not caused the rise in violent crime.

3. Corporations contribute huge sums of money to political campaigns. If that is so, then corporations exert undue influence on elections. So, corporations exert undue influence on elections.

*  4. You will win the chess tournament if you are very good at chess. Unfortunately, you are not very good at chess. Hence, you will not win the chess tournament.

5. Either virtue is good for its own sake, or it is good as a means to an end. It is not the case that virtue is good for its own sake. So, virtue is good as a means to an end.

6. You should be *B* an optimist if pessimists are less likely *A* to succeed than optimists. And it is a fact that pessimists are less likely to succeed than optimists.
   Therefore, you should be an optimist.

* 7. If God can arbitrarily decide what is morally right, then God can make cruelty right. And if God cannot arbitrarily decide what is morally right, then
   morality is not entirely in God's control. But either God can arbitrarily
   decide what is morally right, or God cannot arbitrarily decide what is
   morally right. Therefore, either God can make cruelty right, or morality is
   not entirely in God's control.

8. The dinosaurs vanished due to a sudden, extreme drop in temperature. The
   earth must have suffered some sort of cataclysm millions of years ago, assuming that the dinosaurs vanished due to a sudden, extreme drop in temperature. So, the earth must have suffered some sort of cataclysm millions of
   years ago.

9. Assuming that you treat like cases alike, you are fair. Hence, you are fair only
   if you treat like cases alike.

* 10. The death penalty is inequitably applied to the poor and to minorities. And
   given that the death penalty is inequitably applied to the poor and to
   minorities, it is unjust. Therefore, the death penalty is unjust.

11. Philosophy is important if ideas are important. And assuming that ideas
   change lives, ideas are important. Hence, if philosophy is important, then
   ideas change lives.

12. If you join the military, you give up a lot of freedom. If you go to college, you
   incur enormous debts. However, you either join the military, or you go to
   college. Therefore, you either give up a lot of freedom, or you incur enormous debts.

* 13. Mercy killing is morally permissible only if it promotes a greater amount of
   happiness for everyone affected than the alternatives do. And mercy killing
   does promote a greater amount of happiness for everyone affected than the
   alternatives do. Therefore, mercy killing is morally permissible.

14. You must either love or hate. If you love, then you suffer when your loved
   ones suffer. If you hate, then you suffer when your enemies flourish. Hence,
   either you suffer when your loved ones suffer, or you suffer when your enemies flourish.

15. A severe depression will occur given that the economy collapses. The economy collapses if inflation soars. So, inflation soars only if a severe depression
   will occur.

**Part D: Constructing Arguments**   Construct your own substitution instances for
each of the following argument forms: *modus ponens, modus tollens*, hypothetical
syllogism, disjunctive syllogism, constructive dilemma, denying the antecedent, and
affirming the consequent. Make your substitution instances for the two fallacies
counterexamples.

## 1.4  Strength and Cogency

Our discussion to this point may leave the impression that, from a logical point of view, each argument is either valid or not, and if an argument is not valid, then it is entirely without logical merit. But matters are not quite this simple. Even if an argument is not valid, its premises may still provide significant support for its conclusion. A strong argument is one in which the premises provide *partial* support for the conclusion. More precisely, a **strong argument** has this essential feature: It is probable (but not necessary) that if its premises are true, then its conclusion is true. In other words, it is improbable (but possible) that the conclusion is false *on the assumption that* the premises are true. For example:

> 79.  Ninety percent of American males over 50 years of age cannot run a mile in less than 6 minutes. Thomas is an American male over 50 years of age. So, Thomas cannot run a mile in less than 6 minutes.

The premises of argument (79) do not absolutely guarantee the truth of the conclusion. Possibly Thomas belongs to that small percentage of American men over 50 who can run a mile in less than 6 minutes. Nevertheless, it is probable that if the premises of (79) are true, then its conclusion is true also.

Now, let's alter argument (79) systematically to clarify the concept of strength. Suppose we replace "ninety" with "ninety-nine." Does the argument remain strong? Yes, of course. In fact, it is even stronger. This indicates that *strength*, unlike validity, is very much a matter of degree. Suppose we replace "ninety" with "fifty-one." Is the argument then strong? Strictly speaking, yes, because the conclusion remains *slightly* more probable than not. Of course, once we replace "ninety" with "fifty-one," the argument is of little value: The amount of support given to the conclusion is scarcely worth mentioning. But the important point to keep in mind is that because strength comes in degrees, we can legitimately speak of arguments that are *slightly* strong, *moderately* strong, or *very* strong. By contrast, it would make no sense to speak of "slightly valid" or "moderately valid" arguments. Validity is an all-or-nothing affair.

What if we replace "ninety" with "fifty" in argument (79)? Then the argument is not strong, but weak. A **weak argument** has this essential feature: *It is not probable that if its premises are true, then its conclusion is true.* If we replace "ninety" with "fifty," then it is as probable, given the premises, that Thomas *can* run the mile in less than 6 minutes as that he *cannot*. So, the argument is weak. And, of course, the argument becomes progressively weaker as we replace "ninety" with "forty," "thirty," and so on.

At the other end of the scale, what if we replace "Ninety percent of" with "All" in argument (79)? Does the argument remain strong? No. At that point, the argument becomes *valid*—necessarily, if its premises are true, its conclusion is true also. But, by definition, in a strong argument, it is *possible* that the conclusion is false while the premises are true. Thus, no valid argument is strong, and no strong argument is valid.

---

A **strong argument** has this essential feature: It is probable (but not necessary) that if the premises are true, then the conclusion is true.

A **weak argument** has this essential feature: It is not probable that if its premises are true, then its conclusion is true.

---

We will explore the concept of strength more fully in subsequent chapters, but it will be helpful at this point to consider some additional examples of strong arguments in order to underscore the fact that they come in very different types. For instance, **arguments from authority** can be strong. They have the following structure:

> 80.  1. *R* is a reliable authority regarding *S*.
>      2. *R* sincerely asserts that *S*.
>      So, 3. *S*.

(Here, *R* stands for a person or reference work, while *S* stands for any statement.) For example:

> 81. According to historian Howard Zinn, by 1933, the worst year of America's Great Depression, one-fourth to one-third of America's labor force was out of work. Therefore, one-fourth to one-third of American workers were unemployed in 1933.[7]

This appeal to authority is legitimate, but authorities can make mistakes, so it is possible that the conclusion of (81) is false while its premises are true—possible, but unlikely. Hence, the argument is strong. Yet it would be impossible to state the degree of strength with numerical precision.

Like arguments from authority, **arguments from analogy** are very common, and they, too, can be strong. The structure of an argument from analogy is as follows:

> 82.  1. Object (event or situation) *A* is similar to object (event or situation) *B* in certain relevant respects.
>      2. *B* has property *P*.
>      So, 3. *A* has property *P* also.

Here is an example. Suppose Jack and Jill are riding horseback. Jill's horse jumps a fence, but Jack is unsure whether his horse can jump the fence. Jill points out that his horse is very similar to hers in size, speed, strength, and training. She adds that because Jack is an experienced rider and weighs no more than she does, Jack's horse is not operating with a handicap. She concludes that Jack's horse can jump the fence, too. We could outline Jill's reasoning as follows:

> 83. Jack's horse is similar in relevant respects to Jill's horse (and is similarly situated). Jill's horse is able to jump the fence. Hence, Jack's horse is able to jump the fence also.

This argument is not valid because its conclusion can be false while its premises are true. For example, unknown to Jill, Jack's horse may have been given a drug that renders it unable to jump well today. Still, it is more probable than not that if the premises of (83) are true, then the conclusion is true, and hence the argument is at least slightly strong.

To say that an argument is strong is *not* to say that its premises are in fact true (just as to say that an argument is valid is *not* to say that its premises are in fact true). Let us use the phrase **cogent argument** to refer to any argument that is both strong and has only true premises (just as we use the phrase *sound argument* to refer to any argument that is both valid and has only true premises). Here is an example of a cogent argument:

> 84. All or nearly all lemons that have been tasted were sour. So, all or nearly all lemons are sour.

This argument is not valid because the conclusion concerns not merely the lemons that have been tasted but lemons in general, *including those that have not been tasted*. And the premise does not rule out the *possibility* that a large percentage of untasted lemons are not sour. Nevertheless, it is unlikely that the conclusion is false given that the premise is true. And the premise is true. So, the argument is cogent.

A cogent argument can have a false conclusion, for its premises do not absolutely guarantee the truth of its conclusion. In this respect, cogent arguments differ markedly from sound arguments. A sound argument cannot have a false conclusion because it is valid and all its premises are true. (And if a valid argument has only true premises, its conclusion must be true also.)

---

Strong + All Premises True = Cogent

---

An **uncogent argument** is one that is either (a) weak or (b) strong with at least one false premise. (Note that by this definition a weak argument with a false premise counts as uncogent.) Here is an example of an argument that is uncogent because it is weak:

> 85. Slightly less than 50 percent of Americans are men. Julia Roberts is an American. Therefore, Julia Roberts is a man.

Although argument (85) has true premises, the premises do not provide even partial support (in our technical sense) for the conclusion: It is *not* probable that if the premises are true, then the conclusion is true. (*Note:* This is not because Julia Roberts is a woman. If we replace "Julia Roberts" with "Woody Allen," the argument is still weak even though its conclusion is true.)

Here is an example of an argument that is uncogent because it is strong but has a false premise:

> 86. There is intelligent life on all of the following planets: Mercury, Venus, Earth, Jupiter, Uranus, Neptune, and Pluto. So, there is intelligent life on Mars.[8]

As far as we know, the premise of argument (86) is false, and so is the conclusion. But it is improbable that the conclusion is false *on the assumption that* the premise is true. So, the argument is strong but uncogent.

---

An **cogent argument** has two essential features:
It is strong, and all its premises are true.

An **uncogent argument** is one that is either
(a) weak or (b) strong with at least one false premise.

---

Note that according to our definitions, no sound argument is cogent, for no valid argument is strong. Similarly, no cogent argument is sound, since no strong argument is valid. Note also that a valid argument with a false premise is unsound, but it is not uncogent because a valid argument is neither strong nor weak.

We have defined deductive logic as the part of logic that is concerned with methods of evaluating arguments for validity and invalidity. Let us now add that **inductive logic** is the part of logic that is concerned with methods of evaluating arguments for strength and weakness. Thus, we have defined deductive and inductive logic not in terms of the kinds of arguments they treat but in terms of the standards and methods employed. And indeed, we might use methods from both branches of logic on the same argument. For example, we might use a method from deductive logic to determine that an argument is invalid and then use a method from inductive logic to determine that the same argument is strong (or that it is weak). Since, by definition, any argument that is either strong or weak is invalid, we can draw a map of the main concepts discussed in this section as follows:

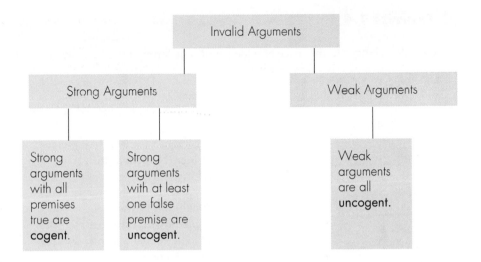

Note that strong arguments with at least one false premise are unsound (as well as uncogent). They are unsound for two reasons: (a) They are invalid, and (b) they have a false premise. Of course, weak arguments are also unsound, for every weak argument is invalid. And if a weak argument has at least one false premise, then it is unsound both because it is invalid and because it has a false premise.

---

A **strong argument** has this essential feature: It is probable (but not necessary) that if the premises are true, then the conclusion is true.

A **weak argument** has this essential feature: It is not probable that if its premises are true, then its conclusion is true.

A **cogent argument** has two essential features: It is strong, and all its premises are true.

An **uncogent argument** is one that is either (a) weak or (b) strong with at least one false premise.

**Inductive logic** is the part of logic that concerns tests for strength and weakness.

---

Some general remarks on terminology are in order. Notice that given our definitions, *arguments* can be strong, weak, cogent, or uncogent. But *arguments* are never true, and they are never false. Both *premises* and *conclusions* are either true or false. But neither *premises* nor *conclusions* are ever strong, weak, cogent, or uncogent.

The following exercises give you an opportunity to apply the concepts introduced in this section.

## ◆ **Exercise 1.4**

**Part A:** Matching    In the space provided, write the letter of the item on the right that best characterizes the item on the left.

_____ **1.** Valid

_____ **2.** Invalid

_____ **3.** Strong

_____ **4.** Weak

_____ **5.** Sound

_____ **6.** Cogent

_____ **7.** Statement

_____ **8.** Unsound

_____ **9.** Uncogent

_____ **10.** Deductive logic

_____ **11.** Inductive logic

_____ **12.** Logic

_____ **13.** Argument

_____ **14.** Arguments from analogy

_____ **15.** Arguments from authority

**A.** A sentence that is either true or false.

**B.** An argument that is either invalid or has a false premise.

**C.** A strong argument with (all) true premises.

**D.** The part of logic concerned with tests for validity and invalidity.

**E.** It is not probable that if the premises are true, then the conclusion is true.

**F.** A valid argument with (all) true premises.

**G.** The part of logic concerned with tests for strength and weakness.

**H.** The study of methods for testing whether the premises of an argument adequately support its conclusion.

**I.** It is necessary that if the premises are true, then the conclusion is true.

**J.** A set of statements, one of which, called the *conclusion,* is affirmed *on the basis* of the others, which are called the *premises.*

**K.** *R* is a reliable authority regarding *S. R* sincerely asserts that *S.* So, *S.*

**L.** An argument with the following essential feature: It is possible that the conclusion is false while the premises are true.

**M.** Object *A* is similar to object *B* in certain relevant respects. *B* has property *P.* So, *A* has property *P* also.

**N.** It is probable (but not necessary) that if the premises are true, then the conclusion is true.

**O.** An argument that is either (a) weak or (b) strong but has a false premise.

**Part B:** True or False?

* **1.** All arguments having only true premises are cogent.
  **2.** All strong arguments are cogent.
  **3.** All weak arguments are uncogent.
* **4.** All arguments with a false premise are uncogent.
  **5.** Some cogent arguments have a false conclusion.
  **6.** Some sound arguments have a false conclusion.
* **7.** The following argument is true: "Over 90 percent of Americans speak English. Hank Williams is an American. So, Hank Williams speaks English."

8. The following argument is an argument from analogy: "According to Flew's *Dictionary of Philosophy*, the British philosopher Bertrand Russell died in 1970. So, Bertrand Russell died in 1970."

9. A strong argument has this essential feature: It is impossible for its conclusion to be false while its premises are true.

* 10. Every uncogent argument has at least one false premise.

11. Every uncogent argument is weak.

12. Some arguments have valid premises, and some do not.

* 13. The following argument is an argument from authority: "Scholars are like the Roman emperor Nero. Nero, you'll recall, played his violin while Rome burned. Similarly, scholars play with ideas while civilization is threatened by the 'flames' of greed, poverty, racism, and violence. Now, plainly, Nero was morally irresponsible. Hence, scholars are morally irresponsible also."

14. A strong argument has these two features: (a) It is possible that if its premises are true, then its conclusion is false, and (b) it is probable that if its premises are true, then its conclusion is true.

15. A weak argument has this essential feature: It is not likely that if its premises are true, then its conclusion is true.

**Part C:** Valid or Invalid? Strong or Weak?    As best as you can determine, which of the following arguments are valid? Invalid? Which are strong? Weak?

* 1. Fifty percent of serial killers were abused as children. Ted Bundy was a serial killer. Therefore, Bundy was abused as a child.

2. This lovely china plate is similar in size, weight, and composition to the one I just dropped. The one I just dropped broke. So, if I drop this lovely china plate, it will break.

3. According to Lillian Roxon's *Rock Encyclopedia*, Buddy Holly, who wrote "Peggy Sue," "That'll Be the Day," and other early rock hits, died in an airplane crash on February 3, 1959. So, Buddy Holly died in an airplane crash in 1959.

* 4. One hundred percent of all the frogs that have ever been dissected had hearts. Therefore, 100 percent of the entire frog population have hearts.

5. It is always wrong to kill an innocent human intentionally. A fetus is an innocent human. So, it is always wrong to kill a fetus intentionally.

6. Research based on Gallup polls indicates that a random sample of 4000 is sufficient to support highly accurate conclusions about large populations—conclusions having a margin of error of only 2 percentage points. And according to a recent poll, 83 percent of a random sample of 4000 American voters favor Jones for president. Thus, approximately 83 percent of American voters favor Jones for president.

* 7. A porpoise is similar to a human being. It has lungs rather than gills. It is warm-blooded rather than cold-blooded. And porpoises nurse their young with milk. Therefore, porpoises, like humans, are capable of speaking languages.

8. Every serial killer is a psychopath. Some criminals are not psychopaths. So, some criminals are not serial killers.

9. Ninety percent of the cars in the parking lot were vandalized, and your car was in the parking lot. Therefore, your car was vandalized.
* 10. No spiders are humans. Dawn is a human. Thus, Dawn is not a spider.
11. All observed emeralds have been green. Therefore, the next emerald to be observed will be green.
12. Linda is younger than Maria. Hence, Maria is older than Linda.
* 13. According to H. W. Janson, professor of fine arts at New York University, the Norwegian artist Edvard Munch painted *The Scream* in 1893. So, Munch painted *The Scream* prior to 1900. (See Janson's *History of Art* [New York: Abrams, 1971], p. 513.)
14. Sixty-five percent of the students at St. Ambrose College are Democrats. Joan is a student at St. Ambrose College. Therefore, Joan is a Democrat.
15. Mark Twain is identical with Samuel Clemens. Mark Twain wrote *Huckleberry Finn*. It follows that Samuel Clemens wrote *Huckleberry Finn*.
* 16. No circles are squares. All circles are figures. So, no figures are squares.
17. According to Lewis Hopfe, a noted authority on world religions, the religion called Jainism originated in India in the sixth century B.C.E. It is the goal of Jainism to liberate the soul from matter. All life, but especially animal life, is sacred to the Jains. And the Jains hold that the gods cannot help humans attain salvation. Therefore, at least one religion holds that the gods cannot help humans attain salvation. (See Hopfe's *Religions of the World*, 4th ed. [New York: Macmillan, 1987], pp. 134–138.)
18. In a certain factory, there is a machine that produces tin cans. Quality-control inspectors examine (in a random fashion) one-tenth of all the tin cans produced by the machine. Of the tin cans examined by the inspectors, 5 percent are malformed. So, approximately 5 percent of all the tin cans produced by the machine are malformed.
* 19. Computers are similar to humans in that both are capable of complex calculations. Humans generally feel ashamed if they make a mistake. Hence, computers generally feel ashamed if they make a mistake.
20. According to the *Encyclopedia Britannica*, the first use of poison gas as a weapon in modern warfare occurred on April 22, 1915, when the Germans launched a highly successful chlorine gas attack against the Allied positions at Ypres, Belgium. So, the first use of poison gas as a weapon in modern warfare occurred on April 22, 1915.

**Part D:** Cogency   Which of the following are cogent? Which are uncogent? (If the argument is uncogent, explain why.) Which of the arguments are neither cogent nor uncogent?
*  1. Most humans fear death. Woody Allen (the famous comedian and filmmaker) is a human. Therefore, Woody Allen fears death.
2. Fifty percent of the students at Seattle Pacific University are Republicans. Kathy is a student at Seattle Pacific University. So, Kathy is a Republican.
3. All humans are mortal. Socrates is a human. Hence, Socrates is mortal.
*  4. All of the birds that have been observed (in the entire history of the world) can fly. Therefore, all birds can fly.

5. War is similar to playing a game of chess. For instance, in both war and chess, strategy is important. And in both war and chess, there is a struggle for victory. Now, when one is losing a game of chess, one should not attack one's opponent with lethal weapons. So, when a nation is losing a war, it should not attack its opponent with lethal weapons.
6. Ninety percent of Americans speak Chinese. Harrison Ford (the famous actor) is an American. Thus, Harrison Ford speaks Chinese.
* 7. Sue is taller than Tom. Tom is taller than Fred. It follows that Sue is taller than Fred.
8. The vast majority of Americans are fluent speakers of English. The Queen of England is an American. So, the Queen of England is a fluent speaker of English.
9. Most Americans live in Nevada. Aretha Franklin (the famous singer) is an American. Hence, Aretha Franklin lives in Nevada.
* 10. Forty percent of students at Reed College are from the Northwest. Sally is a student at Reed College. So, Sally is from the Northwest.

## Notes

1. I have said that arguments are composed of statements. Some logicians would prefer to say that arguments are composed of *propositions*. For more about this issue, see section 3.1.
2. C. S. Lewis, *The Problem of Pain* (New York: Macmillan, 1962), p. 116.
3. My characterizations of deductive and inductive logic are borrowed from Brian Skyrms, *Choice and Chance*, 3rd ed. (Belmont, CA: Wadsworth, 1986), p. 12.
4. Some logicians would qualify this statement. These logicians are not convinced that validity is always due to form. Their views are based on such examples as the following: "Some things are green. So, some things have a color." This argument is clearly valid, but it is difficult to specify any valid form for which it is a substitution instance. Of course, one might reply that the argument has an unstated premise: "All green things have a color." But some logicians would counter that the argument already seems to be valid without *adding* a premise, so why insist that validity is always determined by form? From this perspective, validity is sometimes due to specific content, even if it is typically determined by form.
5. A more complete list of stylistic variants for "if-then" is provided in Chapter 7. The intent here is to provide a short list of the more common stylistic variants.
6. For a useful discussion of these issues, see P. C. W. Davies, *The Physics of Time Asymmetry* (Berkeley and Los Angeles: University of California Press, 1977), chap. 7, pp. 185–200.
7. Howard Zinn, *A People's History of the United States* (New York: HarperCollins, 1995), p. 378.
8. This example is borrowed from Skyrms, *Choice and Chance*, p. 9.

Chapter 2

# Identifying Arguments

The arguments we examined in the previous chapter were short and simple. Moreover, it was obvious which statements were premises and which conclusions. But, as you probably already realize, authors don't commonly state their arguments quite so simply and straightforwardly. The conclusion may be given first or sandwiched between various premises. And a long argument may actually be a chain of shorter arguments, in which case it becomes vital to distinguish between the final (or overall) conclusion of the argument and the various subconclusions that lead up to it.

This chapter tells you how to identify arguments as they appear in ordinary language, how to distinguish extraneous verbiage from premises and conclusions, and how to identify the structure of the argument (i.e., which statements support which).

## 2.1 Arguments and Nonarguments

We must first learn to distinguish arguments from nonarguments. Recall that an argument is a set of statements, one of which, called the *conclusion*, is affirmed on the basis of the others, which are called *premises*. Obviously, one can do many things with language besides argue: extend greetings, tell a story, make a request, express one's feelings, provide information, tell a joke, pray, and so on. In this section, we will examine some nonargumentative uses of statements that are sometimes confused with arguments.

In general, it is important to distinguish between arguments and **unsupported assertions**. For example:

1. From 1964 to 1972, the wealthiest and most powerful nation in the history of the world made a maximum military effort, with everything short of atomic bombs, to defeat a nationalist revolutionary movement in a tiny, peasant country [Vietnam]—and failed.[1]

As it stands, this passage is not an argument but simply a statement about the war in Vietnam. No supporting statements (i.e., premises) are provided here, and no inferences are drawn. Of course, supporting statements could be supplied, but because they do not appear in the quoted passage, it is not an argument in and of itself.

Unsupported assertions come in a variety of types, some of which may be confused with arguments. For example, a **report** is a set of statements intended to provide information about a situation, topic, or event. A report may contain many informational statements without containing any arguments. For instance:

> 2. Total global advertising expenditures multiplied nearly sevenfold from 1950 to 1990. They grew one-third faster than the world economy and three times faster than world population. In real terms, spending rose from $39 billion in 1950 to $256 billion in 1990—more than the gross national product of India or than all Third World governments spent on health and education.[2]

Again, these statements could be backed up with further statements, but the passage, as it stands, is a report and not an argument. No inferences are drawn—the passage merely contains a series of informational statements.

An **illustration** is a statement together with an explanatory or clarifying example:

> 3. Mammals are vertebrate animals that nourish their young with milk. For example, cats, horses, goats, monkeys, and humans are mammals.

Because the word "thus" is often used to indicate the conclusion of an argument, illustrations are easily confused with arguments when the word "thus" is used to introduce the examples:

> 4. Whole numbers can be represented as fractions. Thus, 2 can be represented as 8/4, and 5 can be represented as 15/3.

In statement (4), the examples seem merely illustrative. Sometimes, however, examples are given not merely to explain or clarify but to support (provide evidence for) a thesis, in which case the passage in question is an argument rather than an illustration:

> 5. You just said that no mammal can fly, but that is inaccurate. At least one mammal has wings and can fly. For example, bats are mammals.

And sometimes a passage can reasonably be interpreted either as an illustration or as an argument. It all depends on the answer to this question: Do the examples merely clarify (or explain) a statement, or are they used to *provide evidence* for it? If the examples are used to provide evidence, then the passage is an argument.

An **explanatory statement** provides a reason for the occurrence of some phenomenon. For example:

6. Judy got sick because she ate too much.

7. The dinosaurs are extinct because a "large comet or asteroid struck the earth some 65 million years ago, lofting a cloud of dust into the sky and blocking sunlight, thereby suppressing photosynthesis and . . . drastically lowering world temperatures. . . ."[3]

Such passages are easily confused with arguments since the word "because" is often used to indicate a premise. For example, "Not all mammals are land animals *because* whales are mammals." Here the word "because" indicates the premise "whales are mammals." (More on this use of "because" in the next section.) But consider cases (6) and (7) carefully. Statement (6) does not seem to be an argument for the conclusion that Judy got sick, with "she ate too much" as a premise. Rather, (6) is simply the *assertion* that Judy's sickness was caused by her overeating. And of course there are other possible explanations for Judy's sickness, such as an encounter with viruses or food poisoning. But (6) provides no reason to think the "overeating explanation" is true; that is, (6) includes no premises. Hence, (6) is not an argument. Similarly, (7) doesn't seem to be an argument for the conclusion that dinosaurs are extinct. It is merely the assertion that one possible explanation of the extinction of the dinosaurs is correct.

However, if an explanatory hypothesis is supported by further statements, then we have an argument. For example, many arguments are arguments to the effect that a certain statement or hypothesis is the *best explanation* of some phenomenon (or that some statement is probably true *because* it is the best explanation of some phenomenon). These are arguments rather than mere assertions because premises are provided. For instance:

8. Three explanations have been offered for the extinction of the dinosaurs. First, a global rise in temperature caused the testes of male dinosaurs to stop functioning. Second, certain flowering plants (namely, angiosperms) evolved *after* the dinosaurs evolved; these plants were toxic for the dinosaurs, which ate them and died. Third, a large comet struck the earth, causing a cloud of dust that blocked out the sunlight, which in turn created a frigid climate for which the dinosaurs were ill suited. Now, there is no way to get any evidence either for or against the first hypothesis. And the second hypothesis is unlikely because it is probable that angiosperms were in existence 10 million years before the dinosaurs became extinct. There is, however, some evidence in favor of the third hypothesis. If the earth was struck by a large comet at the time the dinosaurs became extinct (some 65 million years ago), then there should be unusually large amounts of iridium (a rare metal) in the sediments of that period, for most of the iridium on Earth comes from comets and other objects from outer space. And, as a matter of fact, unusually large amounts of iridium have been found in the sediments of that period. So, the third explanation seems best.[4]

Passage (8) is an argument because evidence is given to support the claim that one of the three explanations is best.

**Conditional statements**, taken by themselves, are typically not arguments. For instance,

> 9. If Lucy works hard, then she will get a promotion.

There is some temptation to think that the antecedent (if-clause) of a conditional is a premise and that the consequent (then-clause) is a conclusion. But this is typically not the case. Remember that a conditional statement is hypothetical in nature. Thus, statement (9) merely asserts that if Lucy works hard, then she will get a promotion. It does not assert that Lucy works hard. Nor does it assert that she will get a promotion. By contrast, consider the following argument:

> 10. Lucy works hard. Therefore, Lucy will get a promotion.

Here, we clearly have a premise–conclusion structure. And the conclusion is asserted on the basis of the premise (which is also asserted).

Although conditionals, taken by themselves, are not arguments, in context they may serve to express an argument. For example, during a tournament, a tennis coach might give this advice to one of the players: "If you want to win, you should hit to your opponent's backhand." In this context, "you want to win" need not be explicitly stated; it can be assumed. So, by expressing a conditional, the coach may in effect be offering a *modus ponens*–type argument: "If you want to win, then you should hit to your opponent's backhand. You want to win. So, you should hit to your opponent's backhand." Note, however, that adding unstated premises (and conclusions) to arguments can get tricky; we will return to this issue in a later chapter. The main point here is that outside of special contexts, conditionals by themselves are not arguments.

The following exercise will test your understanding of the difference between arguments and nonarguments.

---

**Unsupported assertions** are not arguments. But some types of unsupported assertions may be confused with arguments—for example, reports, illustrations, explanations, and conditionals.

---

## ◆ Exercise 2.1

**Part A:** Arguments and Nonarguments   Which of the following passages are arguments? Which are not arguments? If a passage is an argument, identify its conclusion. If a passage is not an argument, classify it as a report, illustration, explanation, or conditional statement.

* **1.** Americans are materialistic because they are exposed to more advertising than any other people on Earth.

**2.** A person is dead if his or her brain has stopped functioning.

**3.** The world fish catch dropped from its 1989 high of 100 million tons to 97 million tons in 1990 and has remained at about that figure ever since. Harvests have increased in some oceans but have fallen in others. And rising catches of some species are offset by falling catches of others. Breaking with a historical trend of constantly growing catches, stagnation in the global catch now appears likely to continue . . . —Hal Kane, "Fish Catch No Longer Growing," in Lester Brown, Hal Kane, and Ed Ayres, eds., *Vital Signs 1993: The Trends That Are Shaping Our Future* (New York: Norton, 1993), p. 32.

* **4.** Waging war is always wrong because it involves killing human beings. And killing humans is wrong.

**5.** When we calculate what the surface temperature of the planet should be, based on the heat it radiates to space, we find the whole globe should be a frozen wasteland, colder than today by about 33 degrees Celsius (60 degrees Fahrenheit) on average. The force saving us from this frigid fate is the atmosphere. The layer of air surrounding our globe contains important gases such as water vapor and carbon dioxide, which absorb the heat radiated by Earth's surface and reemit their own heat at much lower temperatures. We say they "trap" Earth's radiation and call this planetary warming mechanism the "greenhouse effect." —National Oceanic and Atmospheric Administration, *The Climate System* (Winter 1991), p. 7

**6.** Never has the nation been safer from foreign menaces, and never before has the nation been graduating students less well educated than those of the immediately preceding generation. These facts warrant this conclusion: Today the principal threat to America is America's public-education establishment. —George F. Will, *The Leveling Wind* (New York: Viking Press, 1994), p. 199

* **7.** Since particle-like behavior and wave-like behavior are the only properties that we ascribe to light, and since these properties now are recognized to belong not to light itself, but to our interaction with light, . . . it appears that light has no properties independent of us! To say that something has no properties is the same as saying that it does not exist. The next step in this logic is inescapable. Without us, light does not exist. —Gary Zukav, *The Dancing Wu Li Masters* (New York: Bantam Books, 1979), p. 95

**8.** If humans are created beings, then the Creator wills the ultimate fulfillment of each human.

**9.** U.S. food producers feed livestock 20 million tons of plant protein per year that could be consumed by humans, and the livestock yields only 2 million tons of protein.

* **10.** Wars occur because humans desire to control other humans.

 **11.** The earth is getting warmer. Why? There are many reasons, but here are two important ones. First, the burning of coal, oil, and natural gas has greatly increased the carbon dioxide in the atmosphere. And carbon dioxide retains heat. Second, chlorofluorocarbons, which are used in air conditioners and refrigerators, have attacked the ozone layer, thus leaving the earth exposed to ultraviolet rays from the sun.

 **12.** In 1950, the population of the world was about 2.5 billion. In 1967, the population of the world was almost 3.5 billion. In 1980, the population of the world was almost 4.5 billion. And in 1992, the population of the world was almost 5.5 billion. So, the population of the world has grown both steadily and rapidly since 1950.

* **13.** Global oil demand still lies well below the peak level of 1979. Improved energy efficiency and the expanding role of natural gas in many countries is cutting into petroleum's market. But oil is still the world's leading source of energy, supplying 40 percent of the total . . . —Christopher Flavin and Hal Kane, "Oil Production Steady," in Lester Brown, Hal Kane, and Ed Ayres, eds., *Vital Signs 1993: The Trends That Are Shaping Our Future* (New York: Norton, 1993), p. 46

 **14.** Either James died because he was shot, or James died because he was hanged. It's false that James died because he was shot. Hence, James died because he was hanged.

 **15.** Not all mob bosses avoid prison because John Gotti was a mob boss and Gotti was sent to prison.

* **16.** Prime numbers are divisible only by themselves and one. For example, 3, 5, 7, and 11 are prime numbers.

 **17.** If Oswald did not kill Kennedy, then someone else did.

 **18.** Roman numerals as well as Arabic numerals can be used to stand for numbers. Thus, the Roman numeral IX stands for the number 9.

* **19.** If one sets one's heart on humaneness, one will be without evil. —Confucius, *The Analects* (New York: Oxford University Press, 1993), p. 13

 **20.** During the Cold War, the United States pursued a policy of nuclear deterrence. Missiles with nuclear warheads were aimed at many locations in the former Soviet Union. The threat of destruction was real. Had the missiles been launched, millions of innocent people would have been killed. But in my opinion, the U.S. policy of nuclear deterrence was immoral. Let me give you an analogy. Suppose two angry men face each other with machine guns. Behind each one stands many innocent bystanders. Each man holds the other in check by threatening to pull the trigger and thus kill many innocent people. I submit that it is obvious that such men would be acting immorally. Hence, the U.S. policy of nuclear deterrence was immoral also.

21. If it is permissible for humans to eat animals, then it is permissible for super-intelligent extraterrestrials to eat humans.

* 22. The good don't always die young because Mother Teresa was a good person.

23. America is a powerful nation primarily because it has one of the strongest economies in the world.

24. Some metals are liquids at room temperature because mercury is a metal.

25. If driving on the left side of the road is wrong simply because society disapproves of it, then stealing is wrong simply because society disapproves of it. And driving on the left side of the road is wrong simply because society disapproves of it. Therefore, stealing is wrong simply because society disapproves of it.

**Part B:** Constructing Arguments   Each of the following statements can be made the conclusion of an argument. For each statement, write down at least one premise that provides some degree of support for it.

* 1. It is morally permissible to experiment on nonhuman animals.

2. It is wrong to eat animals.

3. Marijuana should be legalized.

* 4. Only violent criminals should be imprisoned.

5. Handguns should be outlawed.

6. Society has an obligation to provide housing for the homeless.

* 7. Americans are too individualistic.

8. The world is overpopulated with humans.

9. It is foolish to live in a modern city.

* 10. Beauty is in the eye of the beholder.

11. Large corporations have too much political power.

12. Nuclear deterrence is irrational.

* 13. It is wrong to misrepresent one's income on a tax form.

14. It is not always wrong for a nation to wage war.

15. Lying is morally permissible in some cases.

## 2.2 Well-Crafted Arguments

Arguments in ordinary English are often stated in ways that obscure their important logical features. For instance, excess verbiage may make it difficult to determine what the premises actually are. The conclusion may be "camouflaged" in a tangle of premises. Repetition may give the appearance of many premises where there are in fact few. An unhelpful variation in the vocabulary employed may obscure the linkage between the premises (and/or between the premises and the conclusion). And so on.

Obviously, arguments are easier to evaluate when stated in such a way that their important logical features are explicit. When an argument is so stated, we will refer to it as a **well-crafted argument**. Because well-crafted arguments are, from a logical point of view, easier to evaluate than their less-well-crafted cousins, one of the most important logical skills is the ability to take an argument in ordinary English and rewrite it as a well-crafted one. In this section, we will discuss the principles involved in producing **well-crafted versions** of arguments found in ordinary English.

Principle 1:  Identify the premises and the conclusion.

Recall that the **premises** of an argument are the statements on the basis of which the conclusion is affirmed, and the **statements** are sentences that are either true or false. Each step of an argument, whether premise or conclusion, must be a statement. Consider the following simple example:

11.  We should abolish the death penalty because it does not deter crime.

This is an argument. The word "because" often indicates a premise, and it does so in this case. A well-crafted version of argument (11) looks like this:

12.  1. The death penalty does not deter crime.
So, 2. We should abolish the death penalty.

From now on, when constructing well-crafted versions of arguments, let us adopt the convention of making the conclusion of the argument the final step. Let us also write "so" to mark a conclusion, as I have done here. Further, let us place a number before each step of the argument (whether premise or conclusion). A step of an argument without the word "so" in front of it will be understood to be a premise. In this case, statement (1) is the only premise. We can drop the word "because" since our convention tells us that (1) is a premise.

Short as it is, argument (11) illustrates at least two things worth noting. First, the conclusion of an argument often comes first in English prose. For example, the thesis sentence in a paragraph is often a conclusion that is supported by the statements appearing later in the paragraph. Thus, one cannot assume that an author will first state his or her premises and then draw a conclusion later on. In ordinary prose, the order is often reversed.

Second, argument (11) illustrates a typical use of premise indicators—in this case, the word "because." **Premise indicators** are frequently followed by a premise, that is, a supporting reason. Common premise-indicator words or phrases include these:

| | |
|---|---|
| because | after all |
| since | the reason is that |
| for | in light of the fact that |
| as | based on the fact that |

Now, one cannot assume that these words and phrases indicate premises on every occasion of their use. As we have already seen, the word "because" is often used in explanations. But the point here is that these words are frequently used as premise indicators, and knowing this is a great aid when rewriting an argument as a well-crafted one.

Just as premise indicators typically signal premises, **conclusion indicators** typically signal conclusions. Common conclusion indicators include:

| | |
|---|---|
| so | thus |
| therefore | accordingly |
| hence | consequently |
| implies that | we may infer that |
| it follows that | which proves that |

Consider the following argument:

13. I was bitten by several dogs when I was a child. Therefore, dogs are dangerous.

A well-crafted version of argument (13) looks like this:

14. 1. I was bitten by several dogs when I was a child.
So, 2. Dogs are dangerous.

Of course, this argument is weak, but a weak argument is still an argument.

At this point, you know what premise and conclusion indicators are. The good news is that authors frequently use such words and phrases to clarify their intentions. The bad news is that authors often rely on more subtle methods (e.g., context, order, emphasis) to identify the structure of their reasoning. There is no substitute in such cases for logical and linguistic insight. But *a good rule of thumb is to identify the conclusion first.* Once you figure out what the author is trying to prove, the rest of the argument often falls into place.

Let's now consider a slightly more complicated argument:

15. Since the average American consumes 30 times the amount of the earth's resources as does the average Asian, Americans (taken as a group) are selfish. After all, excessive consumption is a form of greed. And greed is selfish desire.

What is the conclusion of the argument? That Americans (taken as a group) are selfish. "Since" is a premise indicator, and so is "after all." Thus, a well-crafted version of the argument looks like this:

16. 1. The average American consumes 30 times the amount of the earth's resources as does the average Asian.
    2. Excessive consumption is a form of greed.
    3. Greed is selfish desire.
    So, 4. Americans (taken as a group) are selfish.

You may be wondering whether the order of the premises matters. From the standpoint of logic, the order makes no difference, so we simply list the premises in the order in which they appear in the original. Note, however, that if an argument is well crafted, the premises must precede the conclusion. For our conventions tell us that in a well-crafted version of an argument, the last statement *is* the conclusion.

As we saw in Chapter 1, conditional statements have a number of stylistic variants. When writing a well-crafted version of an argument, you should put any conditional premises or conclusions into **standard form**—that is, "If A, then B"—for two reasons. First, most people find it easier to grasp the logical meaning of conditionals when they are in standard form. Second, putting conditionals into standard form facilitates the recognition of argument forms. Consider the following example:

17. It is not permissible to eat cows and pigs, for it is permissible to eat cows and pigs only if it is permissible to eat dogs and cats. But it is not permissible to eat dogs and cats.

Rewriting this argument as a well-crafted one, we get:

18. 1. If it is permissible to eat cows and pigs, then it is permissible to eat dogs and cats.
    2. It is not permissible to eat dogs and cats.
    So, 3. It is not permissible to eat cows and pigs.

The argument form is *modus tollens*. Recall that common stylistic variants of "If A, then B" include "B if A," "B assuming that A," "B given that A," "A only if B," "Given that A, B," and "Assuming that A, B."

Before leaving the topic of identifying premises and conclusions, we need to address two slight complications involving rhetorical questions and commands. As noted in Chapter 1, not all sentences are statements. For example, questions are sentences, but questions are not statements. There is, however, one kind of question that serves as a disguised statement, namely, the so-called rhetorical question. A *rhetorical question* is used to emphasize a point. No answer is expected because the answer is considered apparent in the context. For example:

19. The common assumption that welfare recipients like being on welfare is false. Does anyone like to be poor and unemployed? Does anyone like to be regarded as a parasite?

In this context, the arguer clearly expects a "no" answer to both questions. So, these questions are in effect statements. And when producing a well-crafted version of the argument, we change them into statements, like this:

**20.** 1. No one likes to be poor and unemployed.

   2. No one likes to be regarded as a parasite.

So, 3. The common assumption that welfare recipients like being on welfare is false.

*Commands* (or imperatives) are also sentences but not statements. If someone issues the command "Shut the door!" it makes no sense to reply, "That's true" (or "That's false") because no truth claim has been made. However, imperatives sometimes turn up as premises or conclusions in arguments. Such imperatives are disguised "ought" statements. For example, consider the following argument:

**21.** Be a doctor! You've got the talent. You would enjoy the work. You could help many people. And you could make a lot of money!

In this case, the imperative "Be a doctor!" is naturally interpreted as "You ought to be a doctor," and this latter sentence expresses something either true or false.[5] When an imperative is a disguised "ought" statement, you should make this explicit when constructing a well-crafted version of the argument:

**22.** 1. You've got the talent.

   2. You would enjoy the work.

   3. You could help many people.

   4. You could make a lot of money.

So, 5. You ought to be a doctor.

It would be equally correct to write the conclusion this way: "You should be a doctor."

**Principle 2:** Eliminate excess verbiage.

Four types of excess verbiage are extremely common in arguments. One is discounts. A **discount** is an acknowledgment of a fact or possibility that might be thought to render the argument invalid, weak, unsound, or uncogent. For example:

**23.** Although certain events in the subatomic realm occur at random, I still say that the universe as a whole displays a marvelous order. Perhaps the best evidence for this is the fact that scientists continue to discover regularities that can be formulated as laws.

The conclusion of this argument is "the universe as a whole displays a marvelous order." The premise is "scientists continue to discover regularities that can be formulated as laws." But what are we to do with "Although certain events in the subatomic realm occur at random"? It does not seem to be a premise, for events that occur at random are not evidence of order. In fact, the statement "certain events in the subatomic realm occur at random" seems to be evidence *against* the conclusion of the argument. And that is why it is best regarded not as a premise but as a discount.

Discounts are very important rhetorically. Roughly speaking, **rhetorical elements** in an argument are ones that increase its psychological persuasiveness without affecting its validity, strength, soundness, or cogency. And discounts often increase the psychological persuasiveness of an argument by anticipating potential objections. An audience is often disarmed to some degree by the realization that the arguer has already considered a potential objection and rejected it. But discounts aren't premises, since they don't support the conclusion. Therefore, we shall omit them when producing a well-crafted version of an argument. To illustrate, here is a well-crafted version of argument (23):

> **24.** 1. Scientists continue to discover regularities that can be formulated as laws.
> So, 2. The universe as a whole displays a marvelous order.

Words or phrases often used as **discount indicators** include these:

| | |
|---|---|
| although | while it may be true that |
| even though | while I admit that |
| in spite of the fact that | I realize that . . . , but |
| despite the fact that | I know that . . . , but |

A second type of excess verbiage is repetition. Authors and speakers who use **repetition** restate a premise or conclusion, perhaps altering the wording slightly. When this occurs, select the formulation that seems to put the argument in its best light and drop the others. Here's an example:

> **25.** The study of logic will increase both your attention span and your patience with difficult concepts. In other words, if you apply yourself to the subject of logic, you'll find yourself able to concentrate for longer periods of time. You will also find yourself increasingly able to approach complex material without feeling restless or frustrated. Therefore, a course in logic is well worth the effort.

A well-crafted version of argument (25) might look like this:

> **26.** 1. The study of logic will increase both your attention span and your patience with difficult concepts.
> So, 2. A course in logic is well worth the effort.

Now, you may feel that something is lost in dropping the repetition in a case like this, and indeed, something of rhetorical importance *is* lost. Repetition itself aids memorization. And a slight alteration of terminology can correct possible misunderstandings and/or make an idea more vivid. But our well-crafted version has advantages of its own; in particular, it enables us to focus on the argument's essential logical features.

A third type of excess verbiage is the assurance. An **assurance** is a statement, word, or phrase that indicates that the author is confident of a premise or inference. For example:

> 27. Ben will do well in the marathon, for he is obviously in excellent condition.

Here is a well-crafted version of the argument:

> 28. 1. Ben is in excellent condition.
> So, 2. Ben will do well in the marathon.

The word "obviously" indicates the author's confidence in the premise, but it does not contribute to the validity, strength, soundness, or cogency of the argument. Common assurances include these:

| | |
|---|---|
| obviously | everyone knows that |
| no doubt | it is well known that |
| certainly | no one will deny that |
| plainly | this is undeniable |
| clearly | this is a fact |

Assurances are rhetorically important because confidence often helps win over an audience. But they seldom affect the validity, strength, soundness, or cogency of an argument, so they should seldom appear in the well-crafted version of an argument.

A fourth type of excess verbiage is the hedge, which is the opposite of an assurance. That is, a **hedge** is a statement, word, or phrase that indicates that the arguer is tentative about a premise or inference. For instance:

> 29. In my opinion, we have lost the war on drugs. Accordingly, drugs should be legalized.

"In my opinion" is a hedge, so the well-crafted version of the argument would be as follows:

> 30. 1. We have lost the war on drugs.
> So, 2. Drugs should be legalized.

Common hedges include these:

| | |
|---|---|
| I think that | I believe that |
| it seems that | I guess that |
| perhaps | it is reasonable to suppose that |
| maybe | this seems reasonable |
| in my opinion | this is plausible |

Hedges are rhetorically important because without them one sounds dogmatic and close-minded. But hedges usually do not contribute to the validity, strength, soundness, or cogency of an argument. So, hedges usually should not appear in the well-crafted version of an argument.

Assurances and hedges *usually* can be dropped when we are producing a well-crafted version of an argument. But they cannot always be dropped, for they sometimes contribute to the validity, strength, soundness, or cogency of the argument. For example:

31. I am in pain if it seems to me that I am in pain. And it seems to me that I am in pain. Therefore, I am in pain.

Here's a well-crafted version of the argument:

32. 1. If it seems to me that I am in pain, then I am in pain.
    2. It seems to me that I am in pain.
    So, 3. I am in pain.

The main point of this argument is that in the case of pain, there is a special connection between what *seems* to be so and what *is* so. Hence, while we can usually drop "it seems to me that" as a hedge, in this case we cannot. This example underscores the fact that we must remain vigilant when rewriting an argument as a well-crafted one. The role of every word or phrase must be carefully evaluated in context.

Principle 3: Employ uniform language.

Compare the following two arguments:

33. If God is omniscient, then God knows whether or not you will steal a car tomorrow. And, in fact, God is all-knowing. So, God is cognizant of whether or not you will commit car theft tomorrow.

34. If God is omniscient, then God knows whether you will steal a car tomorrow. And, in fact, God is omniscient. So, God knows whether you will steal a car tomorrow.

The logical links between premises and conclusions in these arguments are strongly dependent on the terms involved: "omniscient," "steal," "all-knowing," and so on. Argument (33) appears to have been written by someone using a thesaurus, substituting "omniscient" for "all-knowing," "commit car theft" for "steal a car," "is cognizant of" for "knows," and so on. In short, the language in (33) is not uniform but varied. The result is that the linkage between premises and conclusion is obscured. By contrast, the premise–conclusion linkage is crystal clear in (34). And yet the underlying form of argument is the same in both cases, namely, *modus ponens*.

Here is one well-crafted version of argument (33):

**35.**  1. If God is all-knowing, then God knows whether you will steal a car tomorrow.

2. God is all-knowing.

So, 3. God knows whether you will steal a car tomorrow.

Of course, you might just as well have used "omniscient" in place of "all-knowing." The important thing is to stick with one term throughout the argument so as to highlight the logical form or pattern of reasoning.

Before leaving the topic of uniform language, let's consider one more example:

**36.** If you study other cultures, then you realize what a variety of human customs there is. If you understand the diversity of social practices, then you question your own customs. If you acquire doubts about the way you do things, then you become more tolerant. Therefore, if you expand your knowledge of anthropology, then you become more likely to accept other people and practices without criticism.[6]

Once again, the lack of uniform language makes it difficult to see whether (and how) the premises logically connect with the conclusion. Here is one well-crafted version of the argument:

**37.**  1. If you study other cultures, then you realize what a variety of human customs there is.

2. If you realize what a variety of human customs there is, then you question your own customs.

3. If you question your own customs, then you become more tolerant.

So, 4. If you study other cultures, then you become more tolerant.

Now, we can see that the argument actually is a tightly linked chain of reasoning. The use of uniform language is enormously beneficial in exhibiting the logical structure of an argument. By clarifying the linkages between premises and conclusions, uniform language helps us avoid fuzzy thinking, which frequently stems from the careless use of words with *similar but slightly different* meanings.

Principle 4: Be fair and charitable in interpreting an argument.

*Fairness* involves being loyal to the original, not distorting the clear meaning. *Charity* is needed when the original is ambiguous in some respect; it involves selecting an interpretation that puts the argument in its best possible light. Both of these concepts need to be explained in some detail.

With regard to fairness, many people tend to read more into an argument than they should. Instead of letting the author speak for him- or herself, they re-create the argument in their own image. Key statements may be loosely reworded or couched in emotionally loaded phrasing. Important premises may be omitted. New premises not provided in the original may be added. And so on. Now, there is indeed a place for identifying assumed but unstated premises in evaluating an argument. (We'll get to this in Chapter 6.) But before one can usefully identify unstated assumptions, one must first accurately represent the *stated* or *explicit* version of the argument without distorting the meaning.

Fairness demands that we not let our biases interfere with the process of providing a well-crafted version that is true to an author's original intent. For example, if an author argues in favor of euthanasia for permanently comatose patients, it almost certainly distorts his intent to describe himself as in favor of our "playing God." Similarly, a person who argues against promiscuity does not necessarily believe that all sex is evil, and she should not be so represented in the absence of solid evidence to the contrary. Or, again, someone who supports affirmative action isn't necessarily advocating the use of strict quotas to achieve greater equality. It is unfair to interpret this person as advocating strict quotas unless he or she has *clearly* stated or implied this.

At the same time, we must not conceive of fairness in too narrow or wooden a fashion. To interpret well, we must take into account various rhetorical devices, such as irony and deliberate exaggeration. Suppose an American newspaper reporter argues as follows:

38. Oh, yes, we are all deeply appreciative of the full and accurate information we received from our government during the Vietnam War. So, how can anyone doubt that we received full and accurate information during the war in the Persian Gulf?

Since it is well known that Americans were sometimes not told the truth by their own government during the Vietnam War, the reporter's real meaning is probably the exact opposite of the surface meaning of her words. A well-crafted version of the argument would therefore involve some changes, perhaps along these lines:

39. 1. Americans did not receive full and accurate information from their government during the Vietnam War.

So, 2. Americans possibly (or probably) did not receive full and accurate
   information from their government during the war in the Persian Gulf.

Incidentally, notice that in the well-crafted version, the rhetorical question is
phrased as a statement.

Charity enters the picture when an argument has been presented unclearly.
Perhaps a premise can be understood in either of two ways. Or perhaps the structure of the argument is unclear—which statement is supposed to support which?
Where such ambiguities occur, charity demands that we put the argument in its
best possible light. In other words, when we are confronted with an interpretive
choice, we should try to select an interpretation that makes the argument valid,
strong, sound, or cogent (as the case may be) rather than invalid, weak, unsound,
or uncogent. For instance:

40. Flag burning should be outlawed. I realize that there are worse things than flag
   burning, such as murder or kidnapping, but it ought to be illegal. Many people
   are disturbed by it. And it is unpatriotic. How important is freedom of
   expression, anyway?

Consider the following attempt at a well-crafted version:

41. 1. Many people are disturbed by flag burning.
   2. Flag burning is unpatriotic.
   3. Freedom of expression is not important.
   So, 4. Flag burning should be outlawed.

Premise (3) is stated in an uncharitable fashion. Admittedly, the meaning of the
question "How important is freedom of expression, anyway?" is unclear. But as
stated, premise (3) is an easy target. Charity demands that we rephrase premise
(3), perhaps along these lines: "Freedom of expression is not the most important
thing" or "Freedom of expression is not the highest value."

   Principle 5: Do not confuse subconclusions with (final) conclusions.

Some arguments proceed by establishing subconclusions, which, in turn, become
premises supporting the (final) conclusion of the argument. A **subconclusion**,
then, has a dual role: It is supported by a premise (or premises), but it also
supports at least one further statement (which may be either the conclusion or
another subconclusion). Consider this example:

42. It is not always moral to save five lives at the cost of one life. For if it is always
   moral to save five lives at the cost of one life, then it is moral to remove the
   organs of a healthy person *against his wishes* and transplant them in five
   people who need organ transplants. But it is not moral to perform such transplants because doing so violates the rights of the healthy person. Therefore,
   it is not always morally right to save five lives at the cost of one life.

Here is a well-crafted version of the argument:

**43.** 1. If it is always moral to save five lives at the cost of one life, then it is moral to remove the organs of a healthy person against his wishes and transplant them in five people who need organ transplants.

2. Removing the organs of a healthy person *against his wishes* and transplanting them in five people who need organ transplants violates the rights of the healthy person.

So, 3. It is not moral to remove the organs of a healthy person *against his wishes* and transplant them in five people who need organ transplants.

So, 4. It is not always moral to save five lives at the cost of one life.

Note that premise (2) supports subconclusion (3). This structure is required by the premise indicator "because" in argument (42). And final conclusion (4) follows from (3) and (1), which work together as a logical unit (the form is *modus tollens*). To make the structure of the argument clear, shorthand expressions in the original, such as "doing so," are here expanded and made explicit. (The extent to which this is helpful in a given case is a matter of judgment.)

Let us adopt the convention of always listing the (final) conclusion of the argument as the last step in the well-crafted version, marked by the word "So." Subconclusions are also marked by the word "So" and are distinguished from (final) conclusions because they have a dual role—that is, they are supposed to follow from earlier steps in the argument and to support later steps. Of course, a subconclusion in fact may not be adequately supported by earlier steps, and it may not adequately support any later steps. But the well-crafted version is supposed to represent the arguer's intentions, even if those intentions are logically flawed.

Let us consider another argument that contains subconclusions:

**44.** Murder victims X, Y, and Z were apparently killed by the same person, whom police call "the Golden Gunner," for victims X, Y, and Z were all shot with a gold-plated bullet from the same .38-caliber pistol. Now, we know that most serial killers select members of their own ethnic group as victims. And X, Y, and Z are white. Finally, nearly all serial killers are men. We may infer that the Golden Gunner is a white male.

Here is a well-crafted version of the argument:

**45.** 1. Murder victims X, Y, and Z were all shot with a gold-plated bullet from the same .38-caliber pistol.

So, 2. Victims X, Y, and Z were killed by the same person, whom police call "the Golden Gunner."

3. Most serial killers select members of their own ethnic group as victims.

4. Victims X, Y, and Z are white.

5. Nearly all serial killers are men.

So, 6. The Golden Gunner is a white male.

Here, subconclusion (2) is supported by statement (1). And steps (2), (3), (4), and (5) combine to support final conclusion (6).

When evaluating an argument with subconclusions, one must evaluate the support for each subconclusion as well as the support for the final conclusion of the argument. For example, if the argument for a given subconclusion is weak or invalid, then the overall argument is logically flawed. However, even if a given subconclusion is poorly supported by a premise that is supposed to support it, the overall argument may still retain merit under two conditions: (a) The subconclusion is adequately supported by other premises in the argument, and/or (b) the subconclusion is plausible taken all by itself.

---

### Principles for Rewriting Arguments as Well-Crafted Ones

1. Identify the premises and the conclusion.
2. Eliminate excess verbiage (e.g., discounts, repetition, assurances, hedges).
3. Employ uniform language.
4. Be fair and charitable in interpreting an argument.
5. Do not confuse subconclusions with (final) conclusions.

---

You now have in hand five principles to employ when constructing a well-crafted version of an argument. The following exercises give you some practice in producing well-crafted versions of arguments.

### ◆ *Exercise 2.2*

**Part A:** Identifying Arguments    If a given passage is an argument, write a well-crafted version of it. (Be sure to apply the five principles developed in this section. Pay especially close attention to premise and conclusion indicators. Do NOT add unstated premises. Do NOT delete premises unless they are repetitious.) If a passage is not an argument, simply write "not an argument."

* **1.** The defendant is not guilty of murder since she is insane.

   **2.** One does not worry about the fact that other people do not appreciate one. One worries about not appreciating other people. —Confucius, *The Analects*, trans. Raymond Dawson (New York: Oxford University Press, 1993), p. 5

   **3.** Folly is a more dangerous enemy to the good than malice. You can protest against malice, you can unmask it or prevent it by force. Malice always contains the seeds of its own destruction, for it always makes men uncomfortable,

> ### Writing Well-Crafted Versions of Arguments: A Series of Questions to Ask
>
> 1. What is the main conclusion? (Look for conclusion indicators.)
> 2. Are there any subconclusions? (Again, look for conclusion indicators).
> 3. What are the premises? (Look for premise indicators.)
> 4. Have you put conditional statements into standard form? Have you rewritten commands and rhetorical questions as statements?
> 5. Have you removed excess verbiage? (Look for discounts, repetition, assurances, and hedges.)
> 6. Is the language uniform? (Look for variations in word use that may obscure the logical linkages within the argument.)
> 7. Have you been fair and charitable? Have you changed the meaning of the original? Have you added any statements not in the original? If the original is ambiguous, have you chosen an interpretation that makes the argument *harder* to refute?

if nothing worse. There is no defense against folly. Neither protests nor force are of any avail against it, and it is never amenable to reason. —Dietrich Bonhoeffer, *Prisoner for God: Letters and Papers from Prison*, ed. Eberhard Bethge (New York: Macmillan, 1959), p. 18

\* **4.** Will power, the kind that, if need be, makes us set our teeth and endure suffering, is the principal weapon of the apprentice engaged in manual work. But, contrary to the usual belief, it has practically no place in study. The intelligence can only be led by desire. [And] for there to be desire, there must be pleasure and joy in the work. —Simone Weil, *Waiting for God* (New York: Harper & Row, 1951), p. 110

**5.** It can hardly be denied that people fear death more than they fear life imprisonment. Are we not then forced to conclude that the death penalty is a greater deterrent than life imprisonment?

**6.** Science does not deal with the whole of life. For there are many kinds of human experiences, and science can deal with only a portion of them. Specifically, the task of science is to describe the behavior of the material (or physical) world. —A. R. Patton, *Science for the Non-Scientist* (Minneapolis: Burgess, 1962), p. 3 (*Note:* This passage has been slightly altered for use as an exercise.)

\* **7.** Since affirmative action involves giving a less qualified person the job, affirmative action is unjust. After all, the most qualified person deserves the job.

**8.** Abraham Lincoln died because John Wilkes Booth shot him with a pistol.

**9.** If alcoholism is a disease, then it is treated medically. But alcoholism is not treated medically, for the primary mode of treatment is the 12-step program of Alcoholics Anonymous. And AA's 12-step program is religious in nature. Therefore, alcoholism is not a disease.

* **10.** Since the Vietnam War, America has been reluctant to get militarily involved except in situations where success was virtually certain.

**11.** A galaxy is a complex system of many stars. The galaxy in which we live is called the Milky Way. It is shaped like a hamburger bun 10,000 light years thick and 100,000 light years in diameter. It contains most of the stars we are able to see at night. But there is one of these stars which we can never see at night; we call this star the Sun. It is about 93 million miles away. Orbiting the Sun at 66,600 miles per hour is our own personal space vehicle, the planet Earth. . . . The Milky Way is also spinning around. We are in orbit around the center of the Milky Way at the fantastic speed of 600,000 miles an hour. —A. R. Patton, *Science for the Non-Scientist* (Minneapolis: Burgess, 1962), p. 27

**12.** While it is true that people in general fear death more than they fear life in prison, most murders are crimes of passion. That is to say, most murderers, at the time when they commit the act, are so full of hate or anger that they are completely unconcerned with the long-term consequences of their actions. How, then, can anyone assert with confidence that the death penalty deters murder?

* **13.** The familiar statement that God cannot be proved is fundamentally ambiguous. On one hand it may mean that the existence of the One whom Christ called Father cannot be proved beyond a shadow of a doubt, but on the other hand it may mean, and often does mean, that there is no valid evidence for the being of God. One does not need to be a professional philosopher to see that these two meanings differ. . . . —Elton Trueblood, *A Place to Stand* (New York: Harper & Row, 1969), p. 21

**14.** Pacifists are either deeply insightful or greatly mistaken. But if pacifists are deeply insightful, then it is immoral for a police officer to kill a sniper who is firing at schoolchildren. Frankly, I don't think it takes a moral genius to see that it isn't wrong for a police officer to kill a sniper who is firing at schoolchildren. So, in my opinion, pacifists are not deeply insightful. And hence, in my estimation, they are greatly mistaken.

**15.** All wrong translations, all absurdities in geometry problems, all clumsiness of style, and all faulty connection of ideas in compositions and essays, all such things are due to the fact that thought has seized upon some idea too hastily, and being thus prematurely blocked, is not open to the truth. The cause is always that we have wanted to be too active; we have wanted to carry out a search. —Simone Weil, *Waiting for God* (New York: Harper & Row, 1951), p. 112

* **16.** Obviously, empirical data are scientific. But only what can be falsified (i.e., what can in principle be shown false) is scientific. Therefore, although many people regard empirical data as fixed and unchangeable, empirical data can be falsified.

17. Joan and Carl had been living together for a year and had maintained their separate friendships with both sexes. They were in agreement that they were committed to monogamy, but did not want to sacrifice the opportunity to have close friends. This informal contract proved to be workable, until Carl began spending time with his young research assistant who was in the process of going through a divorce. In response, Joan found herself feeling jealous, threatened, and angry. —Harriet Goldhor Lerner, *The Dance of Anger* (New York: Harper & Row, 1985), p. 104

18. In spite of the fact that the vast majority of contemporary scientists and intellectuals accept the theory of evolution, it is highly questionable for at least two reasons. First, the probability of life evolving from nonlife is so low as to be in the category of the miraculous. Second, if evolution is true, then there are "missing links" (e.g., animals midway between reptiles and birds). But apparently there are no "missing links" since the fossil record contains none. Therefore, the theory of evolution is very much open to question.

* 19. In Stanley Milgram's obedience experiments, first performed at Yale in 1963, subjects were ostensibly recruited to take part in a study of memory. They were then duped into believing they were to be "teachers" in an experiment in which they would administer painful electric shocks of increasing strength to "learners" whenever the latter made mistakes. The so-called learners were actually actors who grunted, screamed, begged to be released from the experiment. As the subject-teachers administered what they thought was ever stronger punishment, they were observed to see whether they continued or protested, and what their reactions were. A large fraction of them were induced to give the highest range of electric shock, even when the pseudo-learners cried out that they feared a heart attack. —Sissela Bok, *Lying: Moral Choice in Public and Private Life* (New York: Random House, 1978), p. 193

20. While many endorse the principle of *equal pay for equal work*, the principle is untrue, for it would have disastrous results if it were applied to college employees. Why? Because faculty salaries differ markedly by discipline (e.g., professors of engineering receive much higher salaries than professors of English literature). So, if colleges gave equal pay for equal work, they would either (a) go broke paying all faculty high salaries or (b) demoralize the more highly-paid faculty with severe pay cuts. Obviously (a) would be disastrous, and so would (b).

**Part B:** More Identifying Arguments   If a given passage is an argument, write a well-crafted version of it. (Do NOT add unstated premises. Do NOT delete premises unless they are repetitious.) If a passage is not an argument, simply write "not an argument."

* 1. The ozone layer has a hole in it primarily because of the large amounts of chlorofluorocarbons that have been released into the atmosphere. These

chemicals are manufactured by human beings for use in refrigerators and air conditioners.

2. The most essential and fundamental aspect of culture is the study of literature, since this is an education in how to picture and understand human situations. —Iris Murdoch, *The Sovereignty of the Good* (London: Ark, 1970), p. 34

3. Language is the incarnation of the mentality of the race which fashioned it. Every phrase and word embodies some habitual idea of men and women as they ploughed their fields, tended their homes, and built their cities. For this reason there are no true synonyms as between words and phrases in different languages. —Alfred North Whitehead, *The Aims of Education and Other Essays* (New York: Macmillan, 1929), p. 66

\* 4. That our minds contain elements which are normally inaccessible to us is made clear by the phenomenon of hypnotism. For by plunging a man into a state of profound hypnosis, he can be made to remember events that have long vanished from his normal mind, and that he is quite unable to recover by ordinary voluntary effort—events belonging, for example, to his very early childhood. —J. W. N. Sullivan, *The Limitations of Science* (New York: Viking Press, 1957), pp. 116–117 (*Note:* This passage is slightly altered for use as an exercise.)

5. If someone believes something, we needn't always be able to answer the question "Why does he believe it?"; but if he knows something, then the question "How does he know?" must be capable of being answered. —Ludwig Wittgenstein, *On Certainty*, eds. G. E. M. Anscombe and G. H. von Wright (New York: Harper and Row, 1972), p. 72

6. We live in the best of all possible worlds. For there is a God. And if God exists, a perfect being exists. Moreover, if God exists, God created the world. So, a perfect being created the world. But if a perfect being created the world, then we live in the best of all possible worlds.

\* 7. I emphatically deny that each culture should be judged only by its own moral standards, for if each culture should be judged only by its own moral code, then no culture's moral standards should be criticized. But the ethical standards of some cultures ought to be criticized because some cultures permit slavery, cannibalism, and/or the oppression of women. Hence, it is not the case that each culture should be judged only by its own ethical standards.

8. Failure to study literature in a technical way is generally blamed, I believe, on the immaturity of the student, rather than on the unpreparedness of the teacher. I couldn't pronounce on that, of course, but as a writer with certain grim memories of days and months of just "hanging out" in school, I can at least venture the opinion that the blame may be shared. At any rate, I don't think the nation's teachers of English have any right to be complacent about their service to literature as long as the appearance of a really fine work of fiction is so rare on the best-seller lists, for good fiction is written more often

than it is read. —Flannery O'Connor, *Mystery and Manners* (New York: Noonday Press, 1957), p. 127

9. Americans of this generation read less than those of the previous generation. What explains this fact? In a word, television.

*10. We [Americans] had roughly 10,000 handgun deaths last year. The British had 40. In 1978, there were 18,714 Americans murdered. Sixty four percent were killed with handguns. In that same year, *we had more killings with handguns by children 10 years old and younger than the British had by killers of all ages.* The Canadians had 579 homicides last year; we had more than 20,000. —Adam Smith, "Fifty Million Handguns," *Esquire*, April 1981, p. 24

11. Either murderers are rational enough to be deterred by the death penalty, or they are not. If they are not rational enough to be deterred by the death penalty, then the death penalty is not necessary. On the other hand, if murderers are rational enough to be deterred by the death penalty, then they are rational enough to be deterred by life imprisonment. And if murderers are rational enough to be deterred by life imprisonment, then capital punishment isn't necessary. So, the death penalty is not necessary. Now, if the death penalty isn't necessary, it should be abolished. Therefore, we should get rid of capital punishment.

12. It may fairly be said that a just man becomes just by doing what is just, and a temperate man becomes temperate by doing what is temperate, and if a man did not so act, he would not have much chance of becoming good. But most people, instead of acting, take refuge in theorizing; they imagine that they are philosophers and that philosophy will make them virtuous; in fact, they behave like people who listen attentively to their doctors but never do anything that their doctors tell them. But a healthy state of the soul will no more be produced by this kind of philosophizing than a healthy state of the body by this kind of medical treatment. —*Aristotle's Nicomachean Ethics*, trans. James Weldon (New York: Macmillan, 1897), Bk. II, chap. 3

*13. It is now widely recognized that absolute proof is something which the human being does not and cannot have. This follows necessarily from the twin facts that deductive reasoning cannot have certainty about its premises and that inductive reasoning cannot have certainty about its conclusions. —Elton Trueblood, *A Place to Stand* (New York: Harper & Row, 1969), p. 22

14. Although advocates of the "prochoice" view sometimes claim that a woman has an unlimited right over what happens in and to her own body, this claim is plainly false. For if a woman has an unlimited right over what happens in and to her own body, then she has the right to drink heavily during pregnancy. But if drinking lots of alcohol during pregnancy causes birth defects, then a woman does not have the right to drink heavily during pregnancy. And it is a well-known fact that heavy drinking during

pregnancy does cause birth defects. So, a woman does not have the right to drink heavily during pregnancy. And therefore, a woman does not have an unlimited right over what happens in and to her own body.

15. Although rewards and punishments do indeed play a role in its formation, they do not by themselves *yield* the moral life. The tendency to avoid acting in a racist manner may first be developed in children by rewards and punishments, but they are not yet moral agents until they act in nonracist fashion even when discipline is not in view, and do so by acting *on the principle* of love and respect. —Nicholas P. Wolterstorff, *Educating for Responsible Action* (Grand Rapids, MI: Eerdmans, 1980), pp. 48–49

\* 16. The conscientious law breaking of Socrates, Gandhi, and Thoreau is to be distinguished from the conscientious law testing of Martin Luther King, Jr., who was not a civil disobedient. The civil disobedient withholds taxes or violates state laws knowing he is legally wrong but believing he is morally right. While he wrapped himself in the mantle of Gandhi and Thoreau, Dr. King led his followers in violation of state laws he believed were contrary to the federal Constitution. But since Supreme Court decisions in the end generally upheld his many actions, he should not be considered a true civil disobedient. —Lewis H. Van Dusen, Jr., "Civil Disobedience: Destroyer of Democracy," in Lynn Z. Bloom, ed., *The Essay Connection*, 4th ed. (Lexington, MA: Heath, 1995), pp. 564–565

17. Youth is imaginative, and if the imagination be strengthened by discipline this energy of imagination can in great measure be preserved through life. The tragedy of the world is that those who are imaginative have but slight experience, and those who are experienced have feeble imaginations. Fools act on imagination without knowledge; pedants act on knowledge without imagination. Therefore, the task of a university is to weld together imagination and experience. —Alfred North Whitehead, *The Aims of Education* (New York: Macmillan, 1929), p. 93 (*Note:* This passage is slightly altered for use as an exercise.)

18. Terrorism is the threat or use of violence against noncombatants for political purposes. In ordinary war, the deaths of civilians are side effects of military operations directed against military targets. In terrorist operations, the civilian is the direct and intentional target of attack. Therefore, George Washington was not a terrorist; but neither were the truck-bombers who attacked the Marine compound in Beirut in 1983, though they are commonly described as such; on the other hand, when states use murder and torture to crush political dissent (a common occurrence throughout the twentieth century), they engage in terrorism. —Douglas P. Lackey, *The Ethics of War and Peace* (Englewood Cliffs, NJ: Prentice-Hall, 1989), p. 85 (*Note:* Parts of the conclusion are paraphrased.)

\* 19. I find every [religious] sect, as far as reason will help them, make use of it gladly: And where it fails them, they cry out. It is a matter of faith, and above reason. —John Locke, *An Essay Concerning Human Understanding*, Bk. IV, chap. XVIII, p. 2

20. All segregation statutes are unjust because segregation distorts the soul and damages the personality. It gives the segregator a false sense of superiority, and the segregated a false sense of inferiority. To use the words of Martin Buber, the great Jewish philosopher, segregation substitutes an "I-it" relationship for the "I-thou" relationship, and ends up relegating persons to the status of things. So segregation is not only politically, economically and sociologically unsound, but it is morally wrong and sinful. Paul Tillich has said that sin is separation. Isn't segregation an existential expression of man's tragic separation, an expression of his awful estrangement, his terrible sinfulness? So I can urge men to disobey segregation ordinances because they are morally wrong. —Martin Luther King, Jr., "Letter from the Birmingham City Jail," in James Rachels, ed., *The Right Thing to Do* (New York: Random House, 1989), pp. 242–243

**Part C:** Argument Forms and Well-Crafted Arguments   Write a well-crafted version of each of the following arguments. Indicate which steps support each sub-conclusion. Also, identify the following forms wherever they appear: *modus ponens*, *modus tollens*, hypothetical syllogism, disjunctive syllogism, and constructive dilemma. To save laborious writing, use capital letters (as indicated) to stand for the statements composing the arguments. (See the Answer Key for an illustration.)

* 1. Large corporations have done much to weaken family ties given that the corporations require a high degree of mobility on the part of their employees, for a high degree of mobility ensures that families will be separated geographically. And the corporations do require a high degree of mobility on the part of their employees. Hence, large corporations have done much to weaken family ties. (L: Large corporations have done much to weaken family ties; M: The corporations require a high degree of mobility on the part of their employees; H: A high degree of mobility ensures that families will be separated geographically.)

  2. It is wrong to risk one's life unnecessarily. But given that it is wrong to risk one's life unnecessarily, it is wrong to race autos. Hence, it is wrong to race autos. And if it is wrong to race autos, then the Indy 500 should be banned, even though most Americans enjoy watching it. Therefore, the Indy 500 should be banned. (W: It is wrong to risk one's life unnecessarily; A: It is wrong to race autos; I: The Indy 500 should be banned.)

  3. If God exists, his existence is necessary. If God does not exist, his existence is impossible. Either God exists or he does not exist. It follows that God's existence is either necessary or impossible. (G: God exists; N: God's existence is necessary; I: God's existence is impossible.) —C. Stephen Evans, *Philosophy of Religion* (Downers Grove, Ill: InterVarsity Press, 1985), p. 48 (*Note:* The passage is slightly altered for use as an exercise.)

* 4. God predestines human acts only if God fully causes human acts. God fully causes humans acts only if humans lack free will. So, God predestines human

acts only if humans lack free will. But humans do not lack free will. Hence, God does not predestine human acts. (P: God predestines human acts; C: God fully causes human acts; F: Humans lack free will.)

5. Nowadays many people are moral relativists; that is, they hold that one should act in the way one's society says one should act. But consider the following argument: "If moral relativism is true, then everyone who advocates reform (i.e., changing the societal code) is mistaken. Not everyone who advocates reform is mistaken. Therefore, moral relativism is not true." (M: Moral relativism is true; E: Everyone who advocates reform is mistaken.) —Fred Feldman, *Introductory Ethics* (Englewood Cliffs, NJ: Prentice-Hall, 1978), p. 166 (*Note:* The passage is slightly altered for use as an exercise.)

6. Either the order in the world is due merely to chance, or the order in the world is due to intelligent design. The order in the world is not due merely to chance. So, the order in the world is due to intelligent design. Now, there is a God, assuming that the order in the world is brought about by intelligent design. Hence, God exists. (O: The order in the world is due merely to chance; D: The order in the world is due to intelligent design; G: God exists.)

\* 7. By a *dependent being* we mean *a being whose existence is accounted for by the causal activity of other things*. By a *self-existent* being we mean *a being whose existence is accounted for by its own nature*. Armed with these two concepts, we can now state the first part of the Cosmological Argument: Either every being (that exists or ever did exist) is a dependent being or at least one being is a self-existent being. Not every being is a dependent being. Therefore, there exists a self-existent being. (D: Every being is a dependent being; S: At least one being is a self-existent being.) —William L. Rowe, *Philosophy of Religion*, 2nd ed. (Belmont, CA: Wadsworth, 1993), p. 18 (*Note:* The passage is slightly altered for use as an exercise.)

8. Either the defendant should be put to death, or he should be permanently hospitalized. For either the defendant is guilty, or he is insane. And assuming that he is guilty, he should be put to death. But assuming that he is insane, he should be permanently hospitalized. Obviously, the defendant should not be put to death if the evidence is less than compelling. And the evidence is less than compelling. So, the defendant should not be put to death. And hence, the defendant should be permanently hospitalized. (D: The defendant should be put to death; H: The defendant should be permanently hospitalized; G: The defendant is guilty; I: The defendant is insane; E: The evidence is less than compelling.)

9. Humans have souls. For, assuming that humans are identical with their bodies, human acts are determined by prior states of the physical universe. And if human acts are determined by prior states of the physical universe, then humans lack free will. So, humans lack free will if humans are identical with their bodies. But obviously, humans do not lack free will. Therefore, humans are not identical with their bodies. And if humans are not identical with

their bodies, then they must have souls. (S: Humans have souls; B: Humans are identical with their bodies; D: Human acts are determined by prior states of the physical universe; F: Humans lack free will.)

* **10.** If Syria attacks Israel, Israel will counterattack. If Israel counterattacks, then the other Arab states will join in. So, if Syria attacks Israel, then the other Arab states will join in. If the other Arab states join in, then the United States will defend Israel. So, if Syria attacks Israel, the United States will defend Israel. And if the United States defends Israel, there will be a world war. Therefore, if Syria attacks Israel, there will be a world war. (S: Syria attacks Israel; C: Israel will counterattack; A: The other Arab states will join in; U: The United States will defend Israel; W: There will be a world war.)

## Notes

1. Howard Zinn, A *People's History of the United States: 1492–Present* (New York: HarperCollins, 1995), p. 460.
2. Alan Thein Durning, "World Spending on Ads Skyrockets," in Lester Brown, Hal Kane, and Ed Ayres, eds., *Vital Signs 1993: The Trends That Are Shaping Our Future* (New York: Norton, 1993), p. 80.
3. Stephen Jay Gould, "Sex, Drugs, Disasters, and the Dinosaurs," in Stephen R. C. Hicks and David Kelley, eds., *The Art of Reasoning: Readings for Logical Analysis* (New York: Norton, 1994), p. 145.
4. This argument is a summary of some of the main ideas in Gould, "Sex, Drugs, Disasters, and Dinosaurs," pp. 144–152.
5. Some philosophers, such as the emotivists, have denied that "ought" judgments are either true or false. But I am here speaking from the standpoint of common sense. For a classic statement of the emotivist position, see Alfred Jules Ayer, *Language, Truth and Logic* (New York: Dover, 1952), pp. 102–120. This work was first published in 1935.
6. This example is borrowed from Anthony Weston, *A Rulebook for Arguments* (Indianapolis, IN: Hackett, 1987), p. 8. My well-crafted version of this argument also is borrowed from Weston.

## Appendix to Chapter 2: Argument Diagrams

As we have seen, by producing a well-crafted version of an argument, one gains insight into the logical structure of the argument (i.e., which statements support which). Argument diagrams are another tool for exploring the logical structure of arguments. Argument diagrams are of interest for at least two reasons: (a) They provide a shorthand method of representing logical relationships and (b) they highlight certain important differences in the types of logical structure.

To diagram an argument, one first places brackets around each statement in the argument, taking note of any premise or conclusion indicators and numbering each statement. To illustrate:

46. ¹[Campaign reform is needed] because ²[many contributions to political campaigns are morally equivalent to bribes.]

We will use an arrow to indicate the relationship of support between premise and conclusion. The arrow is drawn downward from the number that stands for the premise to the number that stands for the conclusion. Thus, the diagram for argument (46) looks like this:

The arrow means that (1), the conclusion, is affirmed on the basis of (2), the premise. In other words, (2) is given as a support for (1).

Subconclusions can readily be accommodated using this procedure. Here is an example:

47. ¹[Charles is unpleasant to work with] since ²[he interrupts people constantly.] Therefore, ³ [I do not want to serve on a committee with Charles.]

This diagram says that premise (2) is given as a support for (1), the subconclusion, and that (1) is given as a support for (3), the conclusion.

Sometimes two or more premises provide *independent* support for a single conclusion. In such a case, if one of the premises were removed, the support provided by the other(s) would not decrease. For instance:

48. Although [1][Americans like to think they have interfered with other countries only to defend the downtrodden and helpless], [2][there are undeniably aggressive episodes in American history.] For example, [3][the United States took Texas from Mexico by force.] [4][The United States seized Hawaii, Puerto Rico, and Guam.] And [5][in the first third of the 20th century, the United States intervened militarily in all of the following countries without being invited to do so: Cuba, Nicaragua, Guatemala, the Dominican Republic, Haiti, and Honduras.]

The diagram is as follows:

Note that statement (1) is omitted from the diagram because it is a discount. The diagram says that the three premises support the conclusion *independently*.

Sometimes two or more premises are *interdependent*. In such a case, the premises work together as a logical unit, so that if one is removed, the support of the others is decreased. Here's an example:

49. [1][No physical object can travel faster than light.] [2][A hydrogen atom is a physical object.] Hence, [3][no hydrogen atom can travel faster than light.]

If two or more premises provide *interdependent* support for a single conclusion (or subconclusion), write their numbers in a horizontal row, joined by plus signs, and underline the row. The plus signs serve as an abbreviation for "in conjunction with." To illustrate, the diagram for argument (49) looks like this:

This diagram tells us that premises (1) and (2) provide *interdependent* support for conclusion (3).

Because English grammar is subtle and flexible, there are no hard-and-fast rules for bracket placement. But the main goal is to bracket the argument in a way that fully reveals the patterns of reasoning within it. The following rules of thumb will help you do this.

First, always take note of any premise and conclusion indicators. For instance, two statements joined by the premise indicator "because" need to be bracketed separately, since one is a premise and one is a conclusion (or subconclusion).

Second, recognize that statements joined by the words "and" or "but" often need to be separated into distinct units for the purpose of diagramming. For example, whenever the word "and" joins two premises, the diagram must indicate whether the premises operate independently or interdependently. Again, the overriding principle is to bracket the statements in such a way as to make an accurate picture of the logical structure of the argument. For instance:

50. ¹[The defendant is guilty.] After all, ²[he confessed to stealing the jewels] and ³[he was undoubtedly present at the scene of the crime] since ⁴[his fingerprints are on the safe.]

The argument can be diagrammed as follows:

The diagram indicates that premises (2) and (3) support conclusion (1) *independently*. In addition, (4) supports (3) but not (2).

Third, note that conditionals (if-then statements) and disjunctions (either-or statements) should *never* be broken down into parts and joined with the plus sign. As noted previously, the plus sign is a special form of "and," linking statements that operate in a logically *interdependent* fashion. Of course, "and" is very different from "if-then" or "either-or." For example, take the statement "If I will fall, then I will hurt myself." This conditional statement obviously does *not* have the same meaning as, "I will fall, *and* I will hurt myself." So, we must treat conditional statements as units for the purposes of diagramming. The same goes for disjunctions. The following words form compounds that should be treated as a single unit in diagramming arguments:

| | |
|---|---|
| if . . . then | assuming that |
| only if | either . . . or |
| given that | neither . . . nor |

Consider the following example:

51. ¹[If China attacks Taiwan, Taiwan will fight,] for ²[the Taiwanese are ready to defend themselves.] ³[Their air force is formidable.] ⁴[And their navy is well trained and well equipped.]

Argument (51) can be diagrammed as follows:

Note that conclusion (1) stands for an entire conditional statement.

When bracketing and numbering an argument, simply take the statements in the order in which they appear in the original, marking the first statement (1), the second (2), and so on. This will help ensure that your numbering system is similar to that of your classmates. All statements should be numbered even though some statements, such as discounts and repeated statements, may not appear in your diagram. This convention helps in two ways: It makes the process of bracketing and numbering relatively mechanical, and it ensures that your numbering system is like that of your classmates. (This, in turn, is a great aid to communication.) Finally, where rhetorical questions and commands serve as premises or conclusions, they, too, should be bracketed and numbered.

The complexity of an argument diagram mirrors the complexity of the original. Accordingly, argument diagrams can become rather complex. Here's an example:

52. Although ¹[some have argued that nuclear weapons introduce nothing genuinely new into the disputes about the morality of war,] I believe that ²[nuclear weapons raise novel moral issues.] First, ³[nuclear weapons have new and undreamed-of long-term effects] since ⁴[the radioactive fallout pollutes the environment and alters human genes.] Second, ⁵[a nuclear war could destroy human civilization in its entirety.] Third, ⁶[in case of nuclear war, the dust caused by the explosions would prevent the sun's rays from reaching the earth's surface.] So, ⁷[a nuclear war would result in a drastic lowering of the earth's temperature.] In other words, ⁸[a nuclear war would result in a "nuclear winter."] And ⁹[no human or human group has a right to gamble with the very climate upon which life itself is based.]

The argument can be diagrammed as follows:

A number of things are worthy of note in this diagram. First, statement (1) is omitted from the diagram because it is a discount. Second, statement (8) is omitted because it is a repetition of (7). One could put (8) in the diagram, but in that case, one would omit (7). Third, the conclusion is supported by three *independent* lines of reasoning:

- ■ (4) supports (3), which, in turn, supports (2).
- ■ (5) supports (2).
- ■ (6) supports (7), and (7) operates in conjunction with (9) to support (2).

Each of these lines of reasoning is independent of the others because if we eliminate any one of them, the support of the others remains unaltered. Finally, statements (7) and (9) operate as an *interdependent* logical unit.

The following exercises will test your understanding of the principles of argument diagramming.

## ◆ Exercise: Appendix to Chapter 2

**Part A:** Argument Diagrams    Make a photocopy of the arguments below. Then, on your photocopy, bracket and number the statements in the arguments, using the techniques outlined in the previous section. Finally, construct a diagram for each argument, placing it beside the argument on the photocopy.

\*  **1.** Photography makes representational art obsolete because no one, not even the best artist, can be more accurate than a camera.

**2.** In spite of the fact that electrons are physical entities, they cannot be seen for electrons are too small to deflect photons (i.e., light particles). Hence, electrons are invisible.

**3.** There is a healthy kind of individualism—the kind that is resistant to group tyranny. . . . But capitalist individualism is not concerned about promoting the growth of the person into emotional, intellectual, ethical and cultural fullness; rather, it fosters the development of individual traits only so far as these are useful for maximizing profits. Thus, ironically, capitalist individualism turns into a group despotism under which personal becoming is sacrificed to the external tyrannies of material gain. —Eugene C. Bianchi, "Capitalism and Christianity Are Contradictory," in David L. Bender, ed., *American Values: Opposing Viewpoints* (San Diego: Greenhaven Press, 1989), p. 147

\*  **4.** While there is much wickedness in the world, there is also much good. For if there is evil, then there must be good, since good and evil are relative, like big and small. And no one will deny that evil exists.

**5.** Since major historical events cannot be repeated, historians aren't scientists. After all, the scientific method necessarily involves events (called "experiments") that can be repeated.

**6.** The scientific method doesn't necessarily involve experimentation. For if anything is a science, astronomy is. But the great cosmic events observed by astronomers cannot be repeated. And, of course, an experiment is by definition a repeatable event.

\* **7.** There is no better way to arouse the American citizen than to order him around or to tell him what to think. Although there are many people in this country who would like to organize us more thoroughly and tidy up the freedom we have by a little more control, we still reserve the personal right to plunge our own way into our own mistakes and discoveries, in art, philosophy, education, or politics. . . . —Harold Taylor, *Art and the Intellect* (New York: The Museum of Modern Art, 1960), p. 43

**8.** Although people often say that beauty is in the eye of the beholder, there are various reasons for thinking that beauty is objective. First, there is wide agreement about natural beauty. After all, virtually everyone finds the Grand Canyon, Niagara Falls, and the Rocky Mountains beautiful. Second, even though art critics frequently disagree with one another, they do defend their views with principled reasoning. Third, art critics tend to agree among themselves about which historical works of art are truly great. And this agreement is no mere coincidence since the critics are not, in general, reluctant to disagree with one another.

**9.** In the new order, when voters are concerned about what benefits the elected officer will provide them, promises, hypocrisy, deceit, log-rolling and clout are fast becoming the characteristics of electability. As Harold Blake Walker noted, of 21 Congressmen linked in one way or another with political wrongdoing or personal scandal prior to the 1976 election, 19 were re-elected. —John A. Howard, "Democratic Values Are Being Lost to Self-Interest," in David L. Bender, ed., *American Values: Opposing Viewpoints* (San Diego: Greenhaven Press, 1989), p. 57

\***10.** Despite the fact that contraception is regarded as a blessing by most Americans, using contraceptives is immoral. For whatever is unnatural is immoral since God created and controls nature. And contraception is unnatural because it interferes with nature.

**11.** Of course, of all the various kinds of artists, the fiction writer is most deviled by the public. Painters and musicians are protected somewhat since they don't deal with what everyone knows about, but the fiction writer writes about life, and so anyone living considers himself an authority on it. —Flannery O'Connor, *Mystery and Manners* (New York: Noonday Press, 1957), pp. 121–122

**12.** While some people seem to be under the impression that humans are making moral progress, I submit that the 20th century is a movement backwards into violence and cruelty. For in spite of the fact that science and technology have developed rapidly, the greatest mass murders in history have all occurred in this century. Millions died on the battlefields of World Wars I and II. Six million Jews died in Nazi prison camps. And from 1917 until the end of Stalin's reign, 20 million people died in Soviet work camps. More recently, we have Pol Pot's slaughter of the Cambodians as well as the atrocities in the former Yugoslavia.

* 13. There is no life after death. For what's real is what you can see, hear, or touch. And you cannot see, hear, or touch life after death. Furthermore, life after death is possible only if humans have souls. But the notion of a soul belongs to a prescientific and outmoded view of the world. And hence, the belief in souls belongs to the realm of superstition.

14. Politicians are forever attributing crime rates to *policies*—if the crime rates are decreasing, to their own "wise" policies; if the crime rates are increasing, to the "failed" policies of their opponents. But the fact is that crime rates are best explained in terms of demographics. For crime is primarily a young man's game. Whenever there is a relatively large number of young men between the ages of 15 and 30, the crime rates are high. And whenever this part of the population is relatively small, the crime rates are relatively low.

15. A liberal arts education is vital to any great nation. Why? For one thing, a liberal arts education provides the best possible skills in communication. And without good communication at all levels, a nation cannot move forward. For another, work is not the whole of life. And it is well known that a liberal arts education increases one's capacity to enjoy life by substantially broadening the range of one's interests.

* 16. For beginners, portrait painting is perhaps the most difficult branch of art to understand and enjoy *as painting*. If we happen to know, either from personal acquaintance or from photographs, what the subject of a portrait is actually like in physical appearance, we are inclined to think more about whether it is a good likeness than whether it is a good painting. And if it is a portrait of someone who lived long ago but is not in the history books, we may think that because the subject is of no interest to us the painting must also be without interest. —A. C. Ward, *Enjoying Paintings* (New York: Penguin Books, 1949), p. 90

17. Psychotherapy is a religion for many Americans. After all, fewer and fewer Americans regularly attend church, synagogue, or temple, but more and more see their psychotherapists regularly. And what do they talk about with their psychotherapists? They talk about their inner lives, or, in other words, about the state of their souls. For they speak of strange impulses, confess dark thoughts, and put their deepest fears into words. And because only 50 years ago these same outpourings would have occurred only in the presence of a priest or pastor, it seems fair to say that psychotherapy is indeed a religion for many Americans.

18. The human sciences have . . . made a major contribution to cynicism about human greatness, especially as they treat the subjects of motivation and freedom. We are told that human choice is not what it appears to be. If we accept the sophistications of some views of psychology, we know that what appears to be heroic—for example, a man or woman's act of courage in saving another's life—is, in fact, a desperate attempt to win the approval of a long-dead parent who had withheld love in the childhood years. What, then,

has become of the hero? He or she is transformed in our minds into a neurotic, and with a slight turn of the mind, admiration is changed to pity and condescension. —Dick Keyes, "America Must Rediscover Heroism," in David L. Bender, ed., *American Values: Opposing Viewpoints* (San Diego: Greenhaven Press, 1989), p. 84

* **19.** Violence as a way of achieving racial justice is both impractical and immoral. It is impractical because it is a descending spiral ending in destruction for all. The old law of an eye for an eye leaves everybody blind. It is immoral because it seeks to humiliate the opponent rather than win his understanding; it seeks to annihilate rather than to convert. Violence is immoral because it thrives on hatred rather than love. It destroys community and makes brotherhood impossible. —Martin Luther King, Jr., *The Words of Martin Luther King, Jr.*, selected and introduced by Coretta Scott King (New York: Newmarket Press, 1983), p. 73

  **20.** Although God created all *dependent* beings, God did not create everything. For numbers have existed from all eternity since God has existed from all eternity, and there has always been exactly *one* God. Moreover, nothing that has existed from all eternity is created because each cause must precede its effect.

**Part B:** More Argument Diagrams  Make a photocopy of the paragraphs below. Then determine which of the paragraphs are arguments and which are not. If a paragraph is not an argument, write "not an argument" beside the paragraph. If a paragraph is an argument, bracket and number the statements involved on your photocopy; then, beside the argument, construct a diagram.

*  **1.** John and Robert Kennedy and Martin Luther King were, like them or not, this country's last true national leaders. None of John Kennedy's successors in the White House has enjoyed the consensus he built, and every one of them ran into trouble, of his own making, while in office. In the same way, none of this country's national spokespeople since Robert Kennedy and Dr. King has had the attention and respect they enjoyed. —Warren Bennis, *Why Leaders Can't Lead* (San Francisco: Jossey-Bass, 1989), p. 61

  **2.** If . . . our government is to function, it must have dissent. Only totalitarian governments insist upon conformity, and they—as we know—do so at their peril. Without criticism abuses will go unrebuked; without dissent our dynamic system will become static. —Henry Steele Commager, "True Patriotism Demands Dissent," in David L. Bender, ed., *American Values: Opposing Viewpoints* (San Diego: Greenhaven Press, 1989), p. 248

  **3.** It is because of the ideal of freedom that we have organized our particular form of democracy, since the political structure of any society is . . . formed to support the demands which the people make for the attainment of certain values. Because of . . . the variety and richness of the social and natural resources with which the country has abounded, in order to realize the full potential which has always existed here, we have needed the idea of freedom as a social instrument to be used for our full development. —Harold Taylor, *Art and the Intellect* (New York: The Museum of Modern Art, 1960), p. 53

\* **4.** For a variety of reasons, private colleges are in trouble. First, private colleges have repeatedly increased tuition well beyond the rate of inflation. And any business that increases prices in such a fashion is likely to run into trouble. Second, many people are beginning to question the value of higher education since a college degree no longer guarantees an attractive salary. Third, rightly or wrongly, the American public believes that colleges have not practiced good financial management, and hence the public thinks that tuition dollars often subsidize inefficiency.

**5.** From 1979 through 1994, attacks by dogs resulted in 279 deaths of humans in the United States. Such attacks have prompted widespread review of existing local and state dangerous-dog laws, including proposals for adoption of breed-specific restrictions to prevent such episodes. —*The Journal of the American Medical Association*, 278(4) (1997): 278

**6.** The legalization of drugs is neither unwise nor immoral. It is not unwise because by legalizing drugs we would eliminate the illegal drug trade. Hence, by legalizing drugs, we would rid our nation of all the violence that goes along with the illegal drug trade. Furthermore, the legalization of drugs is not immoral because it can be combined with a massive program of moral education.

\* **7.** The Peloponnesian War deeply altered the future course of Greek history. By changing the movement of men, the geographical distribution of genes, values, and ideas, it affected later events in Rome, and through Rome, all Europe. . . . In turn, in the tightly wired world of today, . . . Europeans influence Mexicans and Japanese alike. Whatever trace of impact the Peloponnesian War left on the genetic structure, the ideas, and the values of today's Europeans is now exported by them to all parts of the world. Thus today's Mexicans and Japanese feel the distant, twice-removed impact of that war even though their ancestors, alive during its occurrence, did not. In this way, the events of the past, skipping as it were over generations and centuries, rise up to haunt and change us today. —Alvin Toffler, *Future Shock* (New York: Bantam Books, 1970), p. 16

**8.** During the 1930s, there were 1667 executions in the United States. During the 1940s, there were 1284. During the 1950s, there were 717. And during the rehabilitation-mad 1960s, the numbers plummeted to 191. Then came the *Furman v. Georgia* decision in 1972, which resulted in a grand total of 3 executions during the 1970s. While the numbers began to creep back up in the 1980s, with a total of 117 executions in that decade, we are forced to conclude that America has not had a serious practice of capital punishment since about 1960. Therefore, it is not true that America's currently high murder rate proves the ineffectiveness of the death penalty.

9. It is difficult, and you may be sure that we know it, for us to oppose your power and fortune, unless the terms be equal. Nevertheless we trust that the gods will give us fortune as good as yours, because we are standing for what is right against what is wrong; and as for what we lack in power, we trust that it will be made up for by our alliance with the Spartans. . . . Our confidence, therefore, is not so entirely irrational as you think. —The Melians to the Athenians, in Thucydides, *The Peloponnesian War*, trans. Rex Warner (New York: Penguin Books, 1954), p. 404 (The Athenians had demanded that the Melians surrender, but the Melians refused.)

\* 10. All Gaul is divided into three parts, one of which is inhabited by the Belgae, another by the Aquitani, a third by . . . [the] Celtae. . . . Of all these peoples the bravest are the Belgae, because they are farthest removed from the civilization and refinement of the Roman Province and are very rarely visited by traders who bring in those wares which tend to make people effeminate; and also because they are nearest to the Germans, who live across the Rhine, with whom they are constantly at war. —Julius Caesar, *Caesar's Gallic War*, trans. Joseph Pearl (New York: Barron's Educational Series, 1962), p. 1

11. Two distinct lines of reasoning support the thesis that the physical universe is temporally finite. First, the galaxies are speeding away from each other *and* from a central point. Moreover, there isn't enough matter in the universe to reverse this process. And if we trace this process back, it appears that the universe began with a "bang" roughly 15 billion years ago. Second, if the universe is temporally infinite, it must have gone through an infinite number of cycles (each Big Bang followed by a Big Crunch). But according to physicists, each Big Bang/Big Crunch cycle would cause a decrease in the overall amount of available energy. Thus, if the universe were temporally infinite, there would now be no energy available at all. But obviously, lots of energy is still available.

12. Besides the natural and the human law it was necessary for the directing of human conduct to have a divine law. And this for four reasons. First, because it is by law that man is directed how to perform his proper acts in view of his last end. . . . [And] since man is ordained to an end of eternal happiness which exceeds man's natural ability, . . . therefore it was necessary that, in addition to the natural and the human law, man should be directed to his end by a law given by God. Secondly, because, by reason of the uncertainty of human judgment . . . different people form different judgments on human acts. . . . Thirdly, because man . . . is not competent to judge of interior movements, that are hidden, but only of exterior acts which are observable; and yet for the perfection of virtue it is necessary for man to conduct himself rightly in both kinds of acts. . . . Fourthly, because . . . human law cannot punish or forbid all evil deeds, since, while aiming at doing away with all evils, it would do away with many good things. . . . —Anton C. Pegis, ed., *Introduction to St. Thomas Aquinas* (New York: Random House, 1948), pp. 621–622

* 13. While colleges and universities have come under heavy criticism in the last decade, they will undoubtedly remain a vital force in American social life for generations to come. For one thing, although both the public and the media seem to have a thirst for stories about people who've gotten rich or famous with only a high-school degree, the fact remains that a college or university degree is the surest way to increase one's social and occupational status. For another, college grads as a group indicate higher levels of satisfaction with their lives than do those with lesser educational attainments. Finally, you show me a nation with a weak system of higher education, and I'll show you a nation with little power. And Americans will never willingly accept a position of relative powerlessness among the nations of the world.

14. As I crisscross the United States lecturing on college campuses, I am dismayed to find that professors and administrators, when pressed for a candid opinion, estimate that no more than 25 percent of their students are turned on by classwork. For the rest, college is at best a social center or aging vat, and at worst a young folks' home or a prison that keeps them out of the mainstream of economic life for a few more years. —Caroline Bird, "College Is a Waste of Time and Money," in Stephen R. C. Hicks and David Kelley, eds., *The Art of Reasoning* (New York: Norton, 1994), p. 200

15. The war in Vietnam was immoral, for a variety of reasons. First, although America's leaders insisted that the war was needed to stop the expansion of communism, there was no good reason to suppose that communism would have spread from Vietnam to any place else significant. Second, the war in Vietnam was a civil war. Hence, North Vietnam was no more wrong to fight for union with South Vietnam than the northern states were wrong to fight for union with the southern states during the American Civil War. Third, in Vietnam, the Americans did a lot of indiscriminate killing through bombing and massive artillery strikes. Finally, during the war, the Americans (and their allies) killed some 600,000 Vietnamese. Only the achievement of a great good could justify so many deaths, but no great good was achieved.

* 16. There are no easy answers, no quick fixes, no formulas. It's time to face facts, lest we all follow Boesky, North, Hart, and the Bakkers into the abyss. We are not supermen. We cannot remake the world to suit us. It's not some mere trick of fate that the high and the mighty are tumbling off their pedestals in record numbers. It is rather the inevitable result of ambition outstripping competence and conscience. Whatever the question, competence and conscience are part of the answer. . . . —Warren Bennis, *Why Leaders Can't Lead* (San Francisco: Jossey-Bass, 1989), p. 154

17. Since God is love, he must always have had an object for his love. Since the world did not exist from everlasting, but was created at a certain moment in time, God must have had another object for his love in the countless aeons before this world was made. If there is an eternal Lover, there must be an eternal Beloved, since love without an object is an abstraction. The Son,

therefore, must have existed eternally as the object of the Father's love.
—Alan Richardson, *Creeds in the Making: A Short Introduction to the History of Christian Doctrine* (London: SCM Press, 1935), pp. 58–59

18. Although the great majority of homicides in the United States involve assailants of the same race or ethnic group, current evidence suggests that socioeconomic status plays a much greater role in explaining racial and ethnic differences in the rate of homicide than any intrinsic tendency toward violence. For example, Centerwall has shown that when household crowding is taken into account, the rate of domestic homicide among blacks in Atlanta, Georgia, is no higher than that of whites living in similar conditions. Likewise, a recent study of childhood homicide in Ohio found that once cases were stratified by socioeconomic status, there was little difference in race-specific rates of homicide involving children 5 to 14 years of age. —John Henry Sloan et al., "Handgun Regulations, Crime, Assaults, and Homicide: A Tale of Two Cities," in Stephen R. C. Hicks and David Kelley, eds., *The Art of Reasoning* (New York: Norton, 1994), p. 305

* 19. The only proof capable of being given that an object is visible is that people actually see it. The only proof that a sound is audible is that people hear it; and so of the other sources of our experience. In like manner, I apprehend, the sole evidence it is possible to produce that anything is desirable is that people do actually desire it. [Thus,] no reason can be given why the general happiness is desirable, except that each person . . . desires his own happiness. —J. S. Mill, *Utilitarianism* (New York: Bobbs-Merrill, 1957), pp. 44–45

20. There is an undoubted psychological easing of standards of truthfulness toward those believed to be liars. It is simply a fact, for instance, that one behaves differently toward a trusted associate and toward a devious, aggressive salesman. But this easing of standards merely explains the difference in behavior; it does not by itself justify lies to those one takes to be less than honest. Some of the harm the liar may have done by lying may be repaid by the harm a lie can do to him in return. But the risks to others, to general trust, and to those who lie to liars in retaliation merely accumulate and spread thereby. Only if there are separate, and more compelling, excuses, can lying to liars be justified. —Sissela Bok, *Lying: Moral Choice in Public and Private Life* (New York: Random House, 1978), p. 134

## Chapter 3
# Logic and Language

In order to construct, analyze, and evaluate arguments *well*, one must pay close attention to language. Many errors of logic stem from a careless or imprecise use of language, and many misunderstandings about logic stem from misunderstandings about the nature of language. This chapter provides a series of clarifications about the relationships between logic and language.

## 3.1 Logic, Meaning, and Emotive Force

Let us begin by noting that the meaning of words can change over time. For example, in the King James Version of the Bible, first published in 1611, we read, "Let no man despise thy youth, but be thou an example of the believers, in word, in conversation, in charity, in spirit, in faith, in purity" (1 Tim. 4:12). But the word "conversation" did not then mean, as it now does, "talking together." Rather, it meant what we should call "conduct," and this shift in meaning has been taken into account in more recent translations.

The fact that the meaning of words can change over time raises some important questions about the nature of logic. For example, do logical relationships change as linguistic meaning changes? Let us examine this question briefly.

In Chapter 1, we said that a statement is a sentence that has truth value (i.e., a sentence that is either true or false). And we said that arguments are composed of statements. Some logicians would prefer to say that arguments are composed of *propositions*—an interesting point that needs to be considered at this time. In order to grasp the concept of a proposition, consider the following sentences:

1. Grass is green.
2. *Das Gras ist grün.*

Sentence (2) translates sentence (1) into German. So, it is natural to suppose that (1) and (2) can be used to express the same truth (or falsehood). In other words, (1) and (2) can be used to express the same **proposition**—a proposition being a truth or a falsehood that may or may not be expressed in a sentence. Whereas a sentence (and hence a statement) belongs to a particular language, such as English or German, a proposition does not.

We can get at the distinction between statements and propositions in another way. Consider the following:

3. All squares are rectangles.

What if the meaning of the word "rectangle" were to change over time so that in, say, the year 2096, "rectangle" were to mean what we now mean by the word "circle"? Such reversals of meaning do sometimes occur in the history of a language. Would (3) become false? Not if by (3) we mean the *proposition* (i.e., truth) currently expressed by the *sentence* "All squares are rectangles" (assuming the words are used in the standard way). Given the current, conventional meaning of the terms, no square can fail to be a rectangle. But it could indeed happen that the meaning of the word "rectangle" would change, in which case we would have to use a different sentence to express the proposition that we now express via the sentence "All squares are rectangles." So, once again, there seems to be a distinction between a sentence and the truth (or falsehood) it expresses, and hence a distinction between statements and propositions.

As noted previously, some logicians regard arguments as *sets of propositions* rather than as sets of statements. We will not here enter into the highly theoretical debate about whether arguments are best regarded as sets of statements or sets of propositions. We do not need to do this in order to grasp an important point about the nature of logic that arises from that debate. Logic is sometimes characterized as a "word game," as if logical reasoning were simply a matter of manipulating words, with *any* conclusion being possible provided that the players are sufficiently clever. However, once we see that logic is fundamentally about the connections between truths and falsehoods, it becomes apparent that logic is not merely a word game. Of course, we must use words to communicate truths and falsehoods (and hence arguments). But logical connections are fundamentally connections between those truths and falsehoods, and this is so whether we regard arguments as composed of statements or propositions.

Thus far, we have considered the fact that the meanings of words can change over time. But we also need to take note of the fact that statements often have *emotive force* as well as *cognitive meaning*. Failure to distinguish these two factors can easily lead to errors in logic. Consider the following statements:

4. There are approximately 20,000 homicides in the United States each year, with handguns being the most frequently used instrument of death.

5. The number of murders per year in America is now so high that you've got to have a death wish to walk the streets, day or night. Every lunatic and every thug carries a "heater," just waiting to blow you away.

Statement (4) is designed primarily to provide information, whereas statement (5) is designed, at least in part, to express feelings or elicit an emotional response. To the extent that a sentence conveys information, it is said to have **cognitive meaning**. Words such as "approximately," "20,000," and "homicides" help give (4) its cognitive meaning. To the extent that a sentence expresses or elicits emotions, it is said to have **emotive force**. Words and phrases such as "death wish," "lunatic," "thug," and "blow away" contribute heavily to the emotive force of (5). Of course, a single sentence can have both cognitive meaning and emotive force. Take (4), for instance. It conveys information, and so it has cognitive meaning, but the information conveyed is itself apt to provoke emotions such as fear or outrage; hence, (4) also has emotive force.

Logic mainly has to do with cognitive meaning—that is, with the logical connections between the informational content of statements. But one often needs to distinguish between the cognitive meaning and the emotive force of a sentence in order to understand its logical relationships, for emotionally loaded language is apt to interfere with logical insight. This can happen in at least two ways. First, loaded language can interfere with our attempt to understand the cognitive meaning of a sentence. We may be so carried away with or blinded by the feelings a sentence evokes that we fail to grasp its informational content precisely. Second, emotionally loaded language can blind us to the need for evidence. When our positive emotions are aroused, we may be inclined to accept a statement without argument even though an argument is definitely called for.

Let's consider some examples:

6. Should capital punishment be abolished? No way! The inmates on death row are nothing but human vermin.

7. You should ignore the company's arguments against the strike. Those arguments are nothing but capitalist propaganda aimed at workers.

The phrase "human vermin" in argument (6) is apt to have considerable emotive force. Vermin are small, troublesome animals (such as mice or rats), and we routinely kill vermin without qualms. So, if we accept the label "vermin" for the inmates on death row, we may readily accept the claim that they should be killed. But what exactly is the *cognitive meaning* of the premise "The inmates on death row are nothing but human vermin"? Perhaps this: "The inmates on death row are very bad people, morally speaking." Putting the premise into emotionally neutral terms helps us not to be swayed too easily by the emotive force of the original verbiage. It also helps us to think of relevant critical questions to ask about the argument. For example, do we really believe that *all* "very bad people" should be put to death? Can't a person be very bad, morally speaking, without committing murder? If so, does argument (6) in effect extend the death penalty to many persons who have never killed anyone? It would seem so.

Argument (7) illustrates the way in which the emotive force of language may blind us to the need for evidence. Once we've labeled someone's reasoning as propaganda, we are apt to dismiss it out of hand. After all, propaganda is a systematic form of indoctrination, often involving deliberate deception or distortion of the facts. But if arguments have been offered, then we need to explain *why* they are rightly labeled as propaganda. For example, wherein lies the deception or distortion of facts? Perhaps some of the company's arguments against the strike are sound, even if it *is* in the company's interest to avoid a strike.

To underscore the distinction between cognitive meaning and emotive force, let's consider two further arguments:

8. If we harvest the organs (hearts, liver, kidneys, etc.) of certain animals, such as baboons, and transplant the organs into humans who need them, many human lives will be saved. Therefore, we ought to harvest the organs of baboons and use the organs to save human lives.

9. Most of the people at the party were bureaucrats. Therefore, not surprisingly, the party was quite boring.

Argument (8) illustrates how a word with positive emotive force can be used to downplay certain negative facts or aspects of an issue. Literally speaking, "to harvest" means "to gather in a crop," an agricultural activity that has everyone's approval. But, of course, "harvesting" the vital organs of animals involves killing the animals, and this unsavory or questionable aspect of obtaining the organs is to some degree obscured by the emotive force of the word "harvest." Again, there is less likelihood of downplaying negative aspects of the case if we express the argument in more neutral language—for instance: "If we remove the vital organs of certain kinds of animals, such as baboons, and transplant their organs into humans who need them, the animals will die, but many human lives will be saved. So, we ought to remove the vital organs of baboons and use the organs to save human lives."

As for argument (9), the word "bureaucrat" has a strong negative connotation. And the emotive force of the word may lead us to suppose that the premise of (9) supports its conclusion. But in less emotionally loaded language, the argument would look like this: "Most of the people at the party were government officials. So, the party was quite boring." Again, the more neutral language immediately suggests relevant critical questions: Are government officials on average less interesting than other people? If so, how is this known? What is the evidence? If not, then the premise seems to provide little support for the conclusion.

Thus far, we have emphasized that emotionally loaded language can interfere with logical insight. But this does not mean that arguments should always be expressed in emotionally neutral language. In fact, it is neither possible nor desirable to rid argumentative speech and writing of emotive force. For example, the information conveyed in the premises of almost any argument about a controversial moral issue is apt to have emotive force. Furthermore, it is often appropriate to engage the emotions of one's audience when defending an important belief or course of action. For example, it is entirely proper for a person to be stirred by a profound insight or by the revelation of serious injustice. "If you have a logical argument to back up a conclusion, there is nothing wrong with stating it in such a way that your audience will endorse it with their feelings as well as with their intellects."[1] The key point to remember, however, is that emotional verbiage should not be used as a substitute for sound arguments. If, upon "translating" an argument into emotionally neutral language, it becomes clear that the premises do not support the conclusion, then emotional language has replaced logic.

Let us here consider an argument that involves a skillful use of emotive language, taken from the famous "I Have a Dream" speech of Dr. Martin Luther King, Jr.:

> 10. I have a dream that one day this nation will rise up and live out the true meaning of its creed: "We hold these truths to be self-evident—that all men are created equal." I have a dream that one day, on the red hills of Georgia, the sons of former slaves and the sons of former slaveowners will be able to sit down together at the table of brotherhood. I have a dream that one day even the state of Mississippi, a state sweltering with the heat of injustice and oppression, will be transformed into an oasis of freedom and justice. I have a dream that my four little children will one day live in a nation where they will not be judged by the color of their skin but by the content of their character.[2]

While this passage has considerable emotive force, it does not substitute an appeal to the emotions for substantive argument. This can readily be seen if we restate its central argument in more neutral language: "All persons are created equal. So, people should not be judged by the color of their skin but by the content of their character."

The following exercise gives you some practice in distinguishing between cognitive meaning and emotive force.

## ◆ Exercise 3.1

Cognitive Meaning and Emotive Force   Each of the following arguments involves the use of emotionally loaded language. Write well-crafted versions of the arguments, replacing the emotionally loaded verbiage with more neutral language. You may find it helpful to use a dictionary.

* 1. Sir, terrorism in the Middle East is one of the greatest threats to world peace today. Therefore, I strongly recommend that we neutralize the leaders of each of the main terrorist groups.

2. Since the Chinese have a lousy record on human rights, to give China "Most Favored Nation" status is simply to give in to injustice.

3. It's pretty ridiculous to tell people to drive their cars less often in order to reduce air pollution. After all, we can't go back to the caves.

* 4. What's wrong with playing the lottery? Nothing. Playing the lottery simply involves making a modest investment with the possibility of a substantial return.

5. As Senator Smith is a demagogue, she should be removed from office. No free country should indulge a demagogue.

6. Ever since Franklin D. Roosevelt introduced welfare programs into American life, this country has become increasingly socialistic. But Americans reject socialism. So, the sooner we eliminate welfare, the better.

* 7. Your reluctance to take this job is beyond comprehension. The pay is good and the hours are reasonable. Furthermore, the work of a sanitary removal engineer is of great importance.

8. I admit that American foreign policy suffered a temporary setback in Vietnam during the late 1960s and early 1970s. But it's the essence of a great country to turn temporary setbacks into stunning success stories. Hence, all the moaning and groaning about the American "defeat" in Vietnam is just blather.

9. The CIA has engaged in electoral sabotage in some countries. For example, the CIA dropped a bomb on the elections in Brazil one year by giving a total of $20 million to conservative candidates.

* 10. If you're against genetic engineering, you're against progress. So, why don't you just accept the fact that genetic engineering is here to stay?

11. Plato lured us into a mystical realm of ideas separated from physical reality. Aristotle taught us how to be logic choppers. Descartes tried to frighten us with the possibility that we might be dreaming all the time. Kant did nothing but take ordinary moral rules and put them into his own pompous and obscure technical language. Haven't philosophers done a lot for the world?

12. I utterly repudiate the notion that God will punish the immoral, for it is nothing but a deception used to frighten children and weak-minded adults.

* 13. Gun control is utterly misguided! Do not be deceived: There is a war on. And politicians who promote gun control are collaborating with the enemy. But the enemy will remain fully armed—you can bet on that!

14. The lyrics of many rock music hits are obscene. We must cleanse our society of this moral filth. That's why I think rock music should be banned.

15. While the right wing of the Republican party masquerades as the bastion of moral values, it has in fact done little but provide rationalizations for the selfishness of the yuppies. As for the Democrats, they are a loose-knit coalition of left-wing ideologues and social outcasts. So, cast your lot with the moderate Republicans.

* **16.** The world is full of horror, shocking cruelty, grinding poverty, starvation, and debilitating illness. In short, we humans inhabit one gigantic disaster area. And yet, some people believe that a loving God controls the universe. It just goes to show: People believe what they want to believe regardless of the facts.

**17.** If a gang of criminals were systematically executing 1.6 million citizens per year in our society, decent folks would take a stand, using force of arms if necessary. But this is precisely the situation America is in given the current rate of abortion. Hence, I think that those who have bombed abortion clinics are fully justified.

**18.** The insanity plea is a joke. Here's how the process works: (a) Vicious murderers go out and kill innocent people in cold blood; (b) the police haul the sadistic killers into court, where the killers claim to have been temporarily insane at the time they performed their cruel deeds; and (c) the psychotic killers spend a few months being treated in a mental hospital, are miraculously "cured," and then are released so they can go out and massacre more law-abiding citizens.

* **19.** Son, you must not marry her! She's nothing but a selfish little Barbie Doll.

**20.** Would it be wrong to fight a nuclear war? Yes, of course. Just imagine it: Millions of people vaporized in a few moments. Millions more, including children and the aged, literally melting from the intense heat. Of those who aren't killed immediately, many freeze to death as great clouds of dust block out the sun's rays. The rest perish in agony from the nasty effects of radioactive fallout.

## 3.2 Definitions

Ambiguous or vague language often interferes with clear thinking. A word is **ambiguous** if it has more than one meaning. For example, in the statement "I walked to the bank," the word "bank" might mean either a kind of financial institution or the edge of a river. A word is **vague** to the extent that it is imprecise, and a word is imprecise if there are "borderline cases" in which there is no way to determine whether the word applies. For example, how much does a person have to have in the way of material possessions in order to count as *rich*? We would all agree that billionaires are rich. But as we mention successively lesser sums, there would come a point at which we would not be sure whether a person who has such-and-such a net worth is rich.

Definitions play an important role in argument because definitions can be used to clear up ambiguity and to make vague terminology more precise. In this section, we will examine various types of definitions, focusing on those types that are most helpful in clarifying and sharpening arguments.

## Types of Definitions

As we discuss the various types of definitions, we will focus mostly on *terms* rather than on words in general. For present purposes, a **term** *is a word or phrase that can serve as the subject of a statement.* For example, proper names, such as "Teddy Roosevelt," "New York City," and "Mount Rainier," are terms. Common nouns, such as "tree," "mammal," "human," "event," and "chair," are also terms. Finally, certain descriptive phrases, such as "the 16th president of the United States" and "the furniture in my office," serve as terms. Words or phrases that are not terms include verbs, adverbs, prepositions, and conjunctions—for example, "to waltz," "slowly," "of," and "but." (Note that this definition of *term* is broader than the one used in Chapter 1, in which *term* was defined as a word that stands for a class or collection of things.)

### Intensional and Extensional Definitions

We can attain greater clarity about linguistic meaning if we distinguish between the extension and the intension of a term. The **extension** of a term consists of the set of things to which the term applies. Thus, the extension of the term "collie" consists of Lassie, Rex, Shep, and so on. The **intension** of a term consists of the properties a thing must have in order to be included in the term's extension. In the case of "collie," the intension includes such properties as being a Scottish sheep dog, being long-haired, and having a narrow head and pointed nose.

---

The **extension** of a term consists of the set of things to which the term applies.

The **intension** of a term consists of the properties a thing must have in order to be included in the term's extension.

---

As Wesley Salmon observes, we "may specify the meaning of a word through its extension, or we may specify its meaning through its intension. There is thus a basic distinction between extensional definitions and intensional definitions."[3] Extensional definitions themselves come in two basic types: non-verbal (or ostensive) and verbal. To give an **ostensive definition**, one specifies the meaning of a term by pointing to objects in its extension. Usually, we can't point to them all, but only to a representative sample. Thus, if you are trying to teach a child the meaning of the word "rock," you might point to a rock, utter the word "rock," then point to another rock, utter the word "rock" again, and so on. Of course, this type of definition is not without its problems. For instance, if the rocks you point to are all small, the child may fail to realize that large rocks are rocks as well.

Many times, however, we use *verbal* extensional definitions to specify the meaning of a term. We can do this by naming the members of the extension *individually* or *in groups*. An **enumerative definition** names the members of the extension *individually*. For example:

11. "Philosopher" means someone such as Socrates, Plato, Aristotle, Descartes, Kant, or Hegel.

Such a definition may be either partial or complete. Definition (11) is partial since we have not listed every philosopher. An enumerative definition is complete if all members of the extension are listed. For instance:

12. "Scandinavia" means Denmark, Norway, Sweden, Finland, Iceland, and the Faroe Islands.

Generally speaking, however, it is either impossible or impractical to list all the members of a term's extension. For example, it is impossible to list all the whole numbers because there are infinitely many of them. And it would be impractical for most purposes to define "Ohioan" by listing all the inhabitants of that state.

Another kind of verbal extensional definition names the members of the extension *in groups* (rather than individually). This is called a **definition by subclass**. For instance:

13. "Feline" means tigers, panthers, lions, leopards, cougars, cheetahs, bobcats, house cats, and the like.

Definitions by subclass can also be partial or complete. Definition (13) is partial since some classes (kinds or types) of felines have been omitted, such as jaguars and lynxes. Here is an example of a complete definition by subclass:

14. "North American marsupial" means an opossum.[4]

While extensional definitions are sometimes very useful, they also have their drawbacks. One drawback is this: Some terms cannot be defined extensionally because their extensions are empty. To illustrate:

15. "Unicorn" means a horselike creature having one long, straight horn growing from the center of its forehead.

Because unicorns are mythical creatures, the extension of the term "unicorn" is empty. Nevertheless, "unicorn" has a meaning that can be specified via an intensional definition, as above. A second drawback of extensional definitions is that they are often inadequate for the purposes of argument and rational dialogue. For example, suppose Smith and Jones are debating whether affirmative action is just. Jones requests a definition of "justice." Smith mentions a few examples of just social practices—for example, punishment only for the guilty, the progressive income tax, and the prohibition against poll taxes for voters. Even if Jones agrees that these practices are just, such an extensional definition is unlikely to facilitate an enlightening discussion of the justice of affirmative action. Careful and insightful thinking about controversial issues demands more precise terminology—hence the need for intensional definitions, which specify the meaning of a term by indicating the properties a thing must have in order to be included in the term's extension.

### Lexical Definitions

A **lexical definition** *reports the conventional or established intension of a term.* Dictionary definitions are standard examples of lexical definitions. For example:

16. "Immanent" means existing or remaining within, that is, inherent.

17. "Imminent" means about to occur.[5]

Note that lexical definitions have truth value—that is, they are either true or false. They are true if they correctly report the established intension of the term and false if they fail to do this.

For the purposes of critical thinking, it is important to know when conventional meanings are at issue. To illustrate, in the middle of a philosophical conversation, someone may assert that no one knows what "truth" means. Well, thinking about the nature of truth may give rise to some puzzling questions, but since "truth" is a word in the English language, it has a conventional meaning. Surely no one would suggest that witnesses in court have *no idea* what a judge means when she admonishes them to "tell the truth, the whole truth, and nothing but the truth"!

### Stipulative Definitions

A **stipulative definition** *specifies the intension of a term independently of convention or established use.* For various reasons, a writer or speaker may wish to introduce a new word into the language or give an old word a new meaning. For example, the word "double-dodge" currently has no generally accepted meaning. But we could make a proposal:

18. "Double-dodge" means the anticipatory movements people commonly make when they nearly collide (as when walking toward each other in a confined space) and are trying to avoid such collision.[6]

To illustrate: "Marsha and Fred nearly ran into each other in the hallway; but at the last moment they double-dodged and then came to a full stop, whereupon

Fred burst into laughter." Thus, by introducing a stipulative definition, we can gain a shorthand means of expressing a complex idea.

Stipulative definitions are often useful in science. For example, in 1967, the physicist John Wheeler introduced the term "black hole" as shorthand for a star that has completely collapsed in on itself due to gravitational forces.[7] When first introduced, this definition was stipulative, for there was then no conventional use of "black hole" to refer to astronomical entities. (Of course, since 1967, "black hole" has come into common use so that it now has a conventional meaning that can be reported in a *lexical* definition.)

Note that a stipulative definition is a *recommendation* or *proposal* to use a term in a certain manner. In other words, a stipulative definition has the form "Let's use term X to mean . . ." And since a recommendation or proposal is neither true nor false, a stipulative definition is neither true nor false. However, if the recommendation to use a term in a certain manner takes hold and becomes part of established use, then the stipulative definition turns into a lexical one, as is the case with "black hole." And as we have seen, lexical definitions are true (or false) because they report conventional meanings.

### Precising Definitions

A **precising definition** *reduces the vagueness of a term by imposing limits on the conventional meaning.* It differs from a stipulative definition because it is not independent of the conventional meaning but rather simply sharpens the conventional meaning, making it more exact. For example, suppose we define a "very strong argument" as one such that there is at least a .95 probability that if the premises are true, then the conclusion is true. Obviously, this definition is more precise than the ordinary English phrase "very strong argument," but the definition is not stipulative because the conventional meaning is not ignored but simply rendered more exact.

Precising definitions are common in both science and law. For example, the term "velocity" simply means "speed" in ordinary English, but physicists have given it a more precise meaning for their own purposes, namely:

19. "Velocity" means rate of motion in a particular direction.

Precising definitions are also essential in constructing workable laws. For instance, suppose Congress wishes to write legislation that provides a tax break for the poor. Since the word "poor" is quite vague, a precising definition will be needed if the law is to be applicable—for example, a family of four will count as poor if it has an annual income of $15,000 or less. Or again, suppose a law is being written to determine when caregivers may remove a patient from life-support systems (such as a respirator). A precising definition of "dead" will be helpful for this purpose because presumably there are no objections to removing life-support systems if the patient is dead. But is a person "dead" when her heart has ceased to function? When she stops breathing? When she is permanently unconcious? When her brain has stopped functioning? For legal purposes, we obviously want to be rather precise about this. In most states, a person is now considered legally dead if he or she is "brain-dead." That is, a precising definition along these lines is used:

20. A "dead" person is one whose brain functions have permanently ceased.

And an electroencephalograph can be used to determine whether this definition applies in a given case.

## Theoretical Definitions

A theoretical definition is an intensional definition that attempts to provide an adequate understanding of the thing(s) to which the term applies. For example, when philosophers or scientists disagree about the definition of important terms, such as "knowledge," "virtue," "mass," "temperature," "space," or "time," they are not disagreeing about the lexical definitions. Nor are they simply trying to stipulate meanings or make conventional meanings more precise. They are trying to reach a deeper and more accurate understanding of the nature of things. For example, in one of Plato's dialogues (entitled "Euthyphro"), the following definition is discussed:

21. "Right" means approved of by the gods.[8]

This definition is not lexical, not stipulative, and not precising. Rather, it attempts to provide deeper insight into the nature of moral rightness. Interestingly, however, within the dialogue, Plato has his hero, Socrates, object to this definition, pointing out that the same act may be approved by one god but disapproved by another god. Would such an act be both right and not right, according to definition (21)? Apparently so. Thus, within the dialogue, the definition is rejected as inadequate. (Because the ancient Greek religious context was polytheistic, the possibility of conflict between the gods was acknowledged as relevant by all parties in the dispute.)

The scientific definition of "temperature" as "the motion of molecules" also provides an example of a theoretical definition (the more rapid the motion of the molecules, the higher the temperature). Obviously, this definition of "temperature" could not be given prior to the development of molecular theory. Note that in offering this definition of "temperature," scientists are not reporting the conventional meaning. Nor are they offering a stipulative definition or making a conventional definition more precise. They are offering a theoretical definition intended to provide a deeper and more adequate understanding of the nature of temperature.

## Definition by Genus and Difference

One technique for constructing definitions is worth special attention because it can be applied in a wide variety of cases and because it is one of the best ways to eliminate ambiguity and vagueness. This is the method of definition by *genus* and *difference*. This method is often useful in constructing stipulative, precising, and theoretical definitions, but we will here focus primarily on lexical definitions.

To explain this method, we need some technical terms. First, as is customary among logicians, let us call *the word being defined* the **definiendum**, and let us call *the word or words that do the defining* the **definiens**. To illustrate:

22. "Puppy" means young dog.

Here, "puppy" is the *definiendum*, while "young dog" is the *definiens*.

---

The **definiendum** is the word being defined.

The **definiens** is the word or words that do the defining.

---

Second, we need to define *proper subclass*. A class X is a **subclass** of another class Y given that every member of X is a member of Y. For example, the class of collies is a subclass of the class of dogs. Note, however, that the class of collies is also a subclass of itself. By contrast, class X is a **proper subclass** of class Y given that X is a subclass of Y but Y has members X lacks. Thus, the class of collies is a *proper* subclass of the class of dogs, but the class of collies is not a *proper* subclass of the class of collies.

Now we can say that the **species** is simply a *proper subclass* of the **genus**. This use of the terms differs from the use they are given in biology. For example, in logic (unlike biology), we may speak of the genus dog and the species puppy, of the genus animal and the species dog, or of the genus animal and the species mammal. The **difference** (or specific difference) is the attribute that distinguishes the members of a given species from the members of other species in the same genus. For example, suppose sibling is the genus and sister is the species. Then the difference is the attribute of being female, which distinguishes sisters from the species brother, which also belongs to the genus sibling. Or suppose dog is the genus and puppy is the species. Then the difference is the attribute of being young, which distinguishes puppies from other species in the same genus—for example, adult dogs.

The relationship among genus, species, and difference is shown in the accompanying diagram, with the rectangles standing for classes. Again, a species is a proper subclass of the genus. The difference is the attribute that distinguishes the members of a given species from the members of other species belonging to the same genus.

GENUS (Example: horse)

| SPECIES: Filly | SPECIES: Colt |
|---|---|
| DIFFERENCE: Young female | DIFFERENCE: Young male |

One constructs a definition by genus and difference as follows. First, choose a term that is more general than the term to be defined. This term names the genus. Second, find a word or phrase that identifies the attribute that distinguishes the species in question from other species in the same genus. Here are some examples:

| Species | | Difference | Genus |
|---|---|---|---|
| "Stallion" | means | male | horse |
| "Kitten" | means | young | cat |
| "Banquet" | means | elaborate | meal |
| "Lake" | means | large | inland body of standing water |

In many cases, of course, the difference is a rather complicated attribute that takes many words to describe. For example:

> 23. "Dinosaur" means any of a group of extinct reptiles of the Mesozoic Era, with four limbs and a long, tapering tail.[9]

The genus here is reptile, and the rest of the definition specifies the difference.

A definition by genus and difference is inadequate if it fails to meet certain criteria. Let us now examine the six standard criteria for evaluating definitions by genus and difference.

> **Criterion 1:** A definition should not be obscure, ambiguous, or figurative.

To illustrate:

> 24. "Desire" is the actual essence of man, insofar as it is conceived, as determined to a particular activity by some given modification of itself.[10]

This definition employs obscure technical jargon. And since the point of defining a term is to clarify its meaning, one should use the simplest words possible in the definiens.

Sometimes, a definiens contains a word that, in the context, has two possible meanings. Then the definition is ambiguous:

25. "Faith" means true belief.

Does "true belief" here mean "sincere or genuine belief," or does it mean "belief that is true as opposed to false"? Either meaning seems possible in the context of a definition of "faith," so the definition is ambiguous. Note, however, that many words have multiple meanings listed in the dictionary, and this mere fact does not render the words ambiguous in a given case. For instance, the word "store" may mean "a place where merchandise is sold," as in, "I bought a shirt at the store"; or it may mean "to provide for a future need," as in, "Squirrels store nuts for the winter." But the context usually indicates which of the meanings is relevant. It is only when the context does not make clear which meaning is relevant that ambiguity occurs.

Figurative (or metaphorical) definitions are generally either obscure or ambiguous. For example:

26. "Art" is the stored honey of the human soul, gathered on wings of misery and travail.[11]

Definition (26) may be suggestive and interesting, but as is common with figurative language, it invites multiple interpretations and so is ambiguous.

**Criterion 2**: A definition should not be circular.

A definition is circular if the definiendum (or some grammatical form thereof) appears in the definiens. To illustrate:

27. "Metaphysics" means the systematic study of metaphysical issues.

Of course, if one doesn't know the meaning of the term "metaphysics," one isn't likely to find a definition employing the word "metaphysical" informative. Note, however, that depending on the context, some kinds of circularity in definitions are not problematic. For instance, suppose my audience knows what a triangle is but does not know what an acute triangle is. In such a context, I might define "acute triangle" as follows:

28. "Acute triangle" means any triangle in which each of the three angles is less than 90 degrees.

This type of circularity is harmless because (in the context) the part of the definiendum that appears in the definiens (namely, "triangle") is not what needs to be defined.

**Criterion 3**: A definition should not be negative if it can be affirmative.

For example:

29. A "mineral" is a substance that is not an animal and not a vegetable.

30. "Mammal" means an animal that is not a reptile, not an amphibian, and not a bird.

A relatively affirmative definition is more informative than a relatively negative one and is therefore to be preferred. However, it is impossible to give affirmative definitions in every case. For instance, a typical dictionary definition of "geometrical point" is "something that has position in space but no size or shape." And the word "spinster" is defined as "an elderly woman who has never married." These definitions would be hard to improve on, though they are largely negative.

**Criterion 4**: Definitions should not be too wide (or too broad).

A definition is too wide (or too broad) if the definiens applies to objects outside the extension of the definiendum. For instance:

31. "Bird" means animal having wings.

Taken as a lexical definition, (31) is too wide, since bats and some types of insects have wings, and yet neither bats nor insects are birds.

In order to determine whether a definition is too wide, we need to know the context and/or type of definition. For example, in the context of the formal study of logic, the following definition is too wide:

32. A "valid" argument is one such that the premises support the conclusion.

In the context of the study of logic, definition (32) is too wide because the definiens also applies to strong arguments. But (32) may not be too wide if it is taken as a lexical definition, designed to report the conventional meaning of "valid."

**Criterion 5**: Definitions should not be too narrow.

A definition is too narrow if the definiens fails to apply to some objects in the extension of the definiendum. To illustrate:

33. "Bird" means feathered animal that can fly.

Taken as a lexical definition, (33) is too narrow because some birds cannot fly—for example, penguins, kiwis, ostriches, and cassowaries.

To determine whether a definition is too narrow, we need to know the context and/or type of definition. For example, in the context of the formal study of logic, the following definition is too narrow:

**34.** A "valid" argument is one that (a) has only true premises and (b) is such that its conclusion cannot be false while its premises are true.

This definition is too narrow because the definiens does not apply to valid arguments with false premises. Taken as a lexical definition, (34) is incorrect because it is far more precise than the established meaning of "valid." But (34) would probably be too narrow from this perspective as well because in ordinary English, "valid" is applied to strong arguments as well as to arguments that are valid in the logicians' technical sense.

As you may have realized, the same definition can be both too wide and too narrow. For example:

**35.** "Bird" means animal that can fly.

On the one hand, this definition is too wide because bats and certain insects are not birds, but they are animals that can fly. On the other hand, this definition is too narrow since the definiens does not apply to penguins, kiwis, ostriches, and so on, and yet these animals are birds.

Criterion 6: A definition is flawed if the definiens picks out the right extension via attributes that are unsuitable relative to the context or purpose.

For example, suppose we are trying to construct a lexical definition of the word "triangle." The following definition would violate Criterion 6:

**36.** "Triangle" means my favorite geometrical figure.

Since triangles are my favorite geometrical figure, the definiens applies to the correct extension, namely, the members of the class of triangles. But the attribute of "being my favorite geometrical figure" is unsuitable to the context of forming a lexical definition. What would be suitable is the attribute English speakers implicitly agree to mean by the term "triangle," namely, "being a closed-plane figure with three angles (or three sides)."

Because Criterion 6 is not always easy to apply, let us consider some further examples. For instance:

**37.** "Seven" means the number of days in a week.

Since there are indeed seven days in a week, the definiens picks out the right extension. But taken as a lexical definition, this definition is flawed because it does not make reference to the attribute associated with established usage, namely, "being one more than six." (In principle, one could know the ordinary meaning of "seven" without knowing how many days there are in a week.) Furthermore, taken as a theoretical definition, (37) is flawed because it fails to pick out attributes relevant for mathematical purposes—for example, that of "being a whole number between six and eight."

If we translate the proposal of certain ancient Greek philosophers into English, we get the following definition of "human":

38. "Human" means featherless biped.

Now, let's assume that this definition is neither too narrow nor too wide—that is, that all and only humans lack feathers *and* normally walk upright on two legs. Still, if (38) is taken as a lexical definition, it violates Criterion 6. As evidence, we can cite the fact that the attribute of "being a featherless biped" is not alluded to in dictionary definitions of the term "human." We might add that the attribute seems unsuitable if the definition is taken to be theoretical in nature, for (38) surely fails to provide any noteworthy insight into the nature of human beings.

To sum up, definitions can be used to eliminate ambiguity and vagueness. Both extensional and intensional definitions can be used for these purposes, but certain kinds of intensional definitions (e.g., stipulative, lexical, precising, and theoretical definitions) are especially useful in argumentation. The method of definition by genus and difference can often be used to construct stipulative, lexical, precising, and theoretical definitions; hence, this method is very useful for the purposes of constructing and evaluating arguments. Finally, definitions by genus and difference must conform to the six criteria set down in this section.

The following exercises give you an opportunity to apply the concepts introduced in this section.

## ◆ Exercise 3.2

**Part A:** Types of Definitions    Match the definition on the left to the letter of the item on the right that best characterizes it.

| | |
|---|---|
| \_\_\_\_ * **1.** Let us use the word "grellow" to mean the color of things that are either green or yellow. | **A.** Enumerative definition |
| \_\_\_\_ **2.** "Vixen" means female fox. | **B.** Definition by subclass |
| \_\_\_\_ **3.** "Southern state" means Alabama, Arkansas, Georgia, Louisiana, Mississippi, North Carolina, South Carolina, Tennessee, Texas, and Virginia. | **C.** Lexical definition |
| \_\_\_\_ * **4.** "Tall man" means male human over 6 feet in height. | **D.** Stipulative definition |
| \_\_\_\_ **5.** "Living things" means plants and animals. | **E.** Precising definition |
| \_\_\_\_ **6.** "Motorized vehicle" means cars, motorcycles, trucks, and the like. | **F.** Theoretical definition |
| \_\_\_\_ * **7.** "Tome" means large book. | |

*(list of definitions continues on the next page)*

_____   8. A "wrong act" is one that fails
to promote the general happiness.

_____   9. "Aunt" means sister of one's father
or mother.

_____   *10. A "sound argument" is one that (a) has only
true premises and (b) is valid (i.e., its conclusion cannot be false while its premises are
true).

_____   11. "Religion" means Hinduism, Christianity,
Judaism, Buddhism, Islam, Sikhism, and the
like.

_____   12. Let us use the term "zangster" to mean a person who steals zirconium.

_____   *13. "Human" means rational animal.

_____   14. "Subatomic particles" means electrons, protons, neutrons, quarks, and the like.

_____   15. "Miracle" means an event that (a) is an
exception to a law of nature and (b) is
brought about by the decision of a divine
being.

**Part B:** Lexical Definitions   Identify one defect in each of the following definitions, using the six criteria for definition by genus and difference.

1. Obscure, ambiguous, or figurative     4. Too wide
2. Circular                              5. Too narrow
3. Unnecessarily negative               6. Unsuitable attribute

Explain your answer briefly. For example, if you say a definition is too narrow, give
an example that illustrates your point. Assume that the definitions are meant to be
lexical definitions. You may find it helpful to use a dictionary.

* 1. "Penguin" means bird that can't fly, but not an ostrich, cassowary, or emu.

2. "Quadrilateral" means a closed-plane figure having four sides of equal length
and four right (i.e., 90-degree) angles.

3. "Marsupial" means an Australian mammal.

* 4. An "octagon" is a figure shaped like a stop sign.

5. "Square" means a closed-plane figure having four right (i.e., 90-degree)
angles.

6. "Right" means not wrong.

* 7. A "triangle" is a closed-plane figure having three sides of equal length.

8. "Jellyfish" means an animal without a spine.

9. "Wine" means a beverage made from grapes.

* **10.** An "ellipse" is a cross between a circle and a rectangle.

   **11.** "Coward" means a spineless person.

   **12.** "Wolf" is defined as a flesh-eating mammal having four legs.

* **13.** "Homosexual" means a man who is erotically attracted exclusively (or at least primarily) to other men.

   **14.** "Dog" means a flesh-eating domestic mammal similar to a wolf but having specifically doglike characteristics.

   **15.** A "murderer" is a human who has killed another human.

* **16.** A "wealthy person" is one who has as much money as Bill Gates or Donald Trump.

   **17.** "Camel" means ship of the desert.

   **18.** "Snake" means a widely feared animal that symbolizes evil or deception in many cultures.

* **19.** "Evil" is defined as the darkness that lies within the human soul.

   **20.** "Wife" means spouse who is not a husband.

**Part C:** More Lexical Definitions   Evaluate the following definitions, using the six criteria for definition by genus and difference.

   **1.** Obscure, ambiguous, or figurative       **4.** Too wide

   **2.** Circular                                 **5.** Too narrow

   **3.** Unnecessarily negative                   **6.** Unsuitable attribute

Explain your answer briefly. For example, if you say a definition is too narrow, give an example that illustrates your point. Assume that the definitions are meant to be lexical definitions. If a definition meets all six criteria, simply write "OK."

*  **1.** "Blue" means having a bluish color.

   **2.** "Fifty" means the number of states in the U.S.A.

   **3.** "Rectangle" means a plane figure having four equal sides and four right (i.e., 90-degree) angles.

*  **4.** Time is the great container into which we pour our lives.

   **5.** "Wise person" means one who displays wisdom.

   **6.** A "trapezoid" is a closed-plane figure that is not a triangle or a rectangle or a circle or an ellipse.

*  **7.** "Oligarchy" means a form of government in which the ruling power belongs to a few persons.

8. A "circle" is a closed-plane figure bound by a single curved line, every point of which is equally distant from the point at the center of the figure.

9. "Atheist" means person who believes that there is no God.

* 10. "Spherical" means shaped like the earth.

11. A "trumpet" is a brass wind instrument with three valves.

12. A "painting" is a picture made with water colors.

* 13. "Reptile" means snake.

14. A "scrupulous person" is one who has scruples.

15. "God" means a being Billy Graham often speaks about.

**Part D:** Precising Definitions   Evaluate the following as precising definitions *in the context of making law*. Since these are precising definitions, they may, without fault, depart from ordinary usage in some degree, but if they depart in a high degree, they may appropriately be judged too wide or too narrow (or otherwise flawed).

* 1. The elderly shall receive subsidized health care; "the elderly" means citizens over 92 years of age.

2. Euthanasia is permissible when a patient is permanently comatose. A patient shall be deemed permanently comatose when he or she has been in a coma for at least one week.

3. All serial killers shall receive the death penalty, a "serial killer" being anyone who has killed more than one person.

* 4. Pacifists shall be exempt from the draft, a "pacifist" being anyone who is willing to swear under oath that he or she is opposed to the use of violence against human beings under any circumstances.

5. Religion shall not be taught in public schools; "religion" means any belief system involving supernatural beings.

6. The penalty for terrorism shall be life imprisonment; "terrorism" means any use of violence against persons or property for political purposes.

* 7. Evolution shall be taught in the public high schools; "evolution" means the view that all life, including human life, came into existence through entirely natural causes, there being no supernatural Creator.

8. Killing in self-defense is justifiable homicide; one kills in self-defense when one kills a person who is immediately threatening one's life. A person's life shall be deemed under immediate threat provided that he or she passes a lie detector test indicating that he or she believed (at the time of the event) that he or she was about to be attacked with a lethal weapon.

9. Torture, defined as *inflicting physical pain on another person*, is a grave offense and merits incarceration.

* 10. The penalty for telling a lie shall be a fine of $1000; "one tells a lie" means one asserts a falsehood without being coerced.

**Part E:** Theoretical Definitions    Match the definiendum on the left with the *best* definiens available on the right. These definitions are theoretical in type.

*B* 1. Courage

*H* 2. Justice

*G* 3. Faith

*E* 4. Evidence

*C* 5. Wisdom

*I* 6. Virtues

*A* 7. Belief

*J* 8. Suspending judgment

*D* 9. Vices

*F* 10. Disbelief

A. Confidence that a proposition is true

B. A tendency to perform acts the agent considers dangerous but worth the risk

C. Knowledge of which ends are worth achieving and of how to achieve them

D. Traits that hinder one from living well

E. Considerations relevant to the truth of the proposition in question

F. Confidence that a proposition is false

G. Believing in spite of factors that may tend to cause doubt

H. Giving each individual his or her due

I. Traits enabling one to live well

J. A lack of confidence in the truth of a proposition combined with a lack of confidence in its falsehood

## 3.3 Using Definitions to Evaluate Arguments

In the absence of good intensional definitions, two negative results are likely to occur: equivocation and merely verbal disputes. **Equivocation** occurs when a word (or phrase) is used with more than one meaning in an argument but the validity of the argument depends on the word's being used with the same meaning throughout. For example:

39. John has a lot of pride in his work. He is already a superb craftsman, and he is constantly improving. But, unfortunately, pride is one of the seven deadly sins. So, John is guilty of one of the seven deadly sins.

Here, of course, the word "pride" is used with two different meanings. In the first occurrence, it means "appropriate self-respect." In the second occurrence, it means "arrogance" or "excessive self-regard." Clearly, these two meanings differ, and it is plainly invalid to argue that John has a serious moral flaw (namely, arrogance) simply on the grounds that he has appropriate self-respect with regard to his work.

The use of the single word "pride" in argument (39) gives it a superficial appearance of validity. But if we rewrite the gist of the argument, plugging in words that capture the two different meanings of "pride," any appearance of validity vanishes completely:

> 40. John has appropriate self-respect with regard to his work. Arrogance is one of the seven deadly sins. So, John is guilty of one of the seven deadly sins.

Etymologically, "equivocate" comes from two Latin words, one meaning "equal" or "same" and one meaning "voice" or "word." When one equivocates, one makes it sound as if the same word (or phrase) is being used with the same meaning throughout the argument, when, in fact, more than one meaning is present. Let's consider another example of equivocation:

> 41. Given the scientific evidence, the claim "Smoking is healthy" is nonsense. But if the claim is nonsense, it is without meaning. Hence, although "Smoking is healthy" may seem to be a meaningful sentence, in fact it is not. It's on a par with "Blug vie nok willinac."

Here the word "nonsense" is used with two different meanings. In its first occurrence, "nonsense" means "plainly false." In its second occurrence, "nonsense" means "meaningless." But we cannot reasonably pronounce a statement false unless we understand it, and we cannot understand it if it is meaningless. Accordingly, it is invalid to argue that *"Smoking is healthy" is meaningless* on the grounds that *"Smoking is healthy" is plainly false*.

A **merely verbal dispute** occurs when two (or more) disputants appear to disagree (i.e., appear to make logically conflicting assertions) but an ambiguous word (or phrase) hides the fact that the disagreement is unreal. Here is an example:

> 42. Mr. X: Bob is a good man. I can always count on him to do his job. And he doesn't make excuses. I wish I had more employees like him.
>
> Ms. Y: I disagree. Bob is not a good man. He has been divorced four times, he drinks too much, and he is addicted to gambling.

For Mr. X, "good man" means "good man on the job"—that is, a person who does quality work efficiently. But for Ms. Y, "good man" means "a morally virtuous person." Accordingly, there is no real disagreement here between Mr. X and Ms. Y, for there is no logical conflict between the statement that *Bob does quality work efficiently* and the statement that *Bob is not morally virtuous*. Even if Bob does have some moral vices, it may still be true that he is a good employee.

A merely verbal dispute is similar to equivocation in that a double meaning is involved. But a merely verbal dispute necessarily involves *two or more people* who misunderstand each other due to the ambiguity of a key word or phrase, whereas equivocation occurs when an ambiguity destroys the validity of an argument (and no dialogue partner need be involved). The American philosopher and psychologist William James provides a striking and humorous example of a merely verbal dispute:

> Some years ago, being with a camping party in the mountains, I returned from a solitary ramble to find everyone engaged in a ferocious . . . dispute. The *corpus* of the dispute was a squirrel—a live squirrel supposed to be clinging to one side of a tree-trunk; while over against the tree's opposite side a human being was imagined to stand. This human witness tries to get sight of the squirrel by moving rapidly round the tree, but no matter how fast he goes, the squirrel moves as fast in the opposite direction, and always keeps the tree between himself and the man, so that never a glimpse of him is caught. The resultant . . . problem now is this: *Does the man go round the squirrel or not?* He goes round the tree, sure enough, and the squirrel is on the tree; but does he go round the squirrel? In the unlimited leisure of the wilderness, discussion had been worn threadbare. Everyone had taken sides, and was obstinate. . . .[12]

At this point, the dispute can be summed up as follows:

43. Side 1: The man goes around the squirrel.

   Side 2: No. The man does not go around the squirrel.

James goes on to explain how he resolved the dispute:

> Mindful of the scholastic adage that whenever you meet a contradiction you must make a distinction, I immediately sought and found one, as follows: "Which party is right," I said, "depends on what you practically mean by 'going round' the squirrel. If you mean passing from the north of him to the east, then to the south, then to the west, and then to the north of him again, obviously the man does go round him, for he occupies these successive positions. But if on the contrary you mean being first in front of him, then on the right of him, then behind him, then on his left, and finally in front again, it is quite as obvious that the man fails to go round him, for by the compensating movements the squirrel makes, he keeps his belly turned toward the man all the time, and his back turned away."[13]

Here, the dispute is merely verbal, due to the ambiguity in the phrase "going round." The disputants fail to communicate because they do not realize that their assertions are logically compatible. There is an appearance of contradiction, but no real logical conflict is present.

Consider one last example of a merely verbal dispute:

**44.** Mr. X: Modern physics has shown that medium-sized physical objects, such as bricks, walls, and desks, are not solid.

Ms. Y: How absurd! If you think this wall isn't solid, just try putting your fist through it, buster.[14]

Mr. X presumably has in mind the fact that according to modern physics, medium-sized physical objects are composed of tiny particles—atoms, protons, electrons, quarks, and the like. And, according to modern physics, these particles are not packed tightly together. Rather, the spaces between the particles are vast relative to the size of the particles (just as the spaces between the sun and the planets in the solar system are vast relative to the size of these bodies). In a nutshell, the two parties talk past each other because Mr. X uses "solid" to mean "dense or tightly packed," while Ms. Y uses "solid" to mean "hard to penetrate."

At this point, we need to consider another error in reasoning that is sometimes confused with the merely verbal dispute. This is the improper use of persuasive definitions. A **persuasive definition** is one *slanted (or biased) in favor of a particular conclusion or point of view.* In practice, persuasive definitions often amount to an attempt to settle an argument by verbal fiat. Here's an example:

**45.** "Affirmative action" means reverse discrimination. But discrimination is always wrong. So, affirmative action is wrong.

Obviously, by defining "affirmative action" as "reverse discrimination," one puts a particular slant on matters. But this definition hardly characterizes a useful concept for the purposes of rational discussion. Notice that a person who did not know the conventional meaning of "affirmative action" would not get a clear grasp of the concept from this definition. A better definition of "affirmative action" would be "preferential treatment of disadvantaged groups." This definition enables us to focus on the heart of the issue: Should disadvantaged groups receive special treatment?

Persuasive definitions sometimes have considerable rhetorical power, and this power is often exploited in politics. Here's a typical example:

**46.** I will speak frankly and without the verbal fuzziness so typical of my opponent. "National health care" means socialized medicine. That's why I oppose it and why you should, too.

This argument may well succeed in associating national health care with something an audience fears or disapproves of, namely, socialism. But it is hardly a fair and neutral definition that will enable both sides to confront the issues squarely.

Persuasive definitions generally violate one or more of the six criteria for definition by genus and difference. Thus, they may be obscure, too wide, or too narrow, or they may involve attributes that are unsuitable relative to the context or purpose. The most common failing is this: When the context calls for a neutral (unbiased) definition of a key term for the purposes of rational discussion, then a persuasive definition makes reference to an attribute that is not suited to the purpose. A definition that slants things in favor of one side in the dispute is obviously not a definition acceptable to all parties in the dispute.

The use of persuasive definitions is sometimes confused with the phenomenon of the merely verbal dispute. This is the case especially when disputants trade persuasive definitions slanted in favor of opposing points of view. For example, a political conservative may define "conservative" as "a liberal who has wised up." In retaliation, the liberal may define "conservative" as "a person bent on protecting his own privileges." But the use of persuasive definitions differs from the merely verbal dispute precisely because definitions are provided. By contrast, in a merely verbal dispute, different meanings are employed but no definitions are provided.

It should be noted that it is not necessarily an error in reasoning to employ persuasive definitions. The error comes only when persuasive definitions are substituted for substantive argument. This error can be exposed by restating the argument without using any persuasive definitions. If such a restatement is an argument whose premises do not support its conclusion, then an error in reasoning has occurred. But such a summary may reveal a valid or strong argument, with plausible premises, that does not depend on persuasive definitions. In that case, persuasive definitions may well have been used appropriately as a rhetorical device. Persuasive definitions can be both humorous and insightful, and thus legitimate rhetorical tools, provided they are not substituted for arguments where arguments are needed.

The following exercises provide you with some practice in identifying equivocation, merely verbal disputes, and the misuse of persuasive definitions.

## ◆ **Exercise 3.3**

**Part A:** Equivocation    Each of the following arguments is invalid because it uses a word or phrase that has a double meaning. Identify the ambiguous word or phrase in each argument, and succinctly describe the double meaning involved. (It is a common tendency to ramble on in an attempt to identify such double meanings. Avoid this. Instead, provide two brief definitions of the relevant word or phrase.) You may find it helpful to use a dictionary. (See the Answer Key for an illustration.)

* 1. A boring job at the minimum wage is better than nothing. But nothing is better than going to heaven. So, a boring job at the minimum wage is better than going to heaven.

   2. If a tree falls in the forest and no one is there to hear it fall, does it make a sound? Modern science says, "Yes, for there are vibrations in the air even if no humans are nearby." But this is easily refuted. Sound is something heard.

That's really quite obvious when you think about it. So, if no one was there to hear the sound, there was no sound.

3. We are in the dark because the light bulb burned out. But if we are in the dark, then we are ignorant. Therefore, we are ignorant.

\* 4. The Bible says you need faith, but lots of people disagree with the Bible on this point. Unfortunately, these folks just aren't thinking straight. The fact that you go out to your car in the morning shows you have faith it's going to start. And the fact that you pull out of the driveway shows you have faith the car won't fall apart on the way to work. Everybody needs faith.

5. I phoned the museum, and the curator said that picture taking is permitted. So, when I visit the museum today, I should be allowed to take some of Rembrandt's pictures home with me.

6. When the recession hit us, I lowered your salary by 20 percent. You moved from $30,000 to $24,000. I know that was tough, and I'm sorry about it. But I have some good news. Things are looking up again. We're showing a profit. So, I'm going to raise your salary by 20 percent. I hope you appreciate this. I lowered your salary by 20 percent; now I'm raising it by 20 percent. So, you see, this policy will bring you back up to where you were before the recession hit.

\* 7. People nowadays say they can't believe in the Christian religion. They say they can't believe in miracles. Is it that they can't or that they won't? They believe in the miracles of modern science, don't they? You bet they do. They believe in vaccines, space-walks, and heart transplants. They believe in fiber optics, laser surgery, and genetic engineering. They can believe in miracles, all right. They just don't want to believe in the Christian miracles.

8. One milliliter of Nuclear Bug-Bomb Aerosol Spray will kill any pest. And Dennis McKenna is a pest. Hence, one-milliliter of Nuclear Bug-Bomb Aerosol Spray will kill Dennis.

9. You are a free creature. So, you are free to do good or evil. But if you are free to do evil, then you should not be punished for doing evil. Hence, you should not be punished for doing evil.

\* 10. See how foolish and inconsistent it is to say, "I would prefer not to be, than to be unhappy." The man who says, "I prefer this to that," chooses something; but "not to be" is not something, but nothing. Therefore, you cannot in any way choose rightly when you choose something that does not exist. You say that you wish to exist although you are unhappy, but that you ought not to wish this. What, then, ought you to have willed? You answer, "Not to exist." But if you ought to have willed not to exist, then "not to exist" is better. However, what does not exist cannot be better; therefore, you should not have willed this. —St. Augustine, *On Free Choice of the Will*, trans. Anna S. Benjamin and L. H. Hackstaff (Indianapolis, IN: Bobbs-Merrill, 1964), p. 104

11. I have a duty to do what is right. And I have a right to run for office. Hence, I have a duty to run for office.

12. We can all agree that sick people should not be punished for displaying the symptoms of their sickness. For instance, you shouldn't punish a flu victim for having a high fever. But, you know, a person has to be sick to commit murder. Murder is a symptom of a sick mind. Thus, contrary to popular belief, murderers should not be punished.

13. Alice is crazy. She'll do anything to get a laugh! Of course, if she is crazy, then she should be put in a mental hospital. So, Alice should be put in a mental hospital.

14. Something is better than material well-being. And a speck of dust is something. It follows that a speck of dust is better than material well-being.

15. It is good to act natural. And it is natural for boys to fight. Therefore, it is good for boys to fight.

**Part B:** Merely Verbal Disputes and Persuasive Definitions    The following brief dialogues provide examples of either merely verbal disputes or the improper use of persuasive definitions. If a persuasive definition is employed, explain its weakness in terms of the six criteria for definitions. Remember, a persuasive definition occurs *only when* an explicit definition of the relevant word or phrase appears. (And, of course, not every explicit definition is persuasive.) In the case of a merely verbal dispute, identify the word or phrase that has a double meaning, and provide a definition for both meanings. (*Note:* A merely verbal dispute is similar to equivocation in that a double meaning is involved, but a merely verbal dispute necessarily involves *two or more people* who misunderstand each other due to the ambiguity of a key word or phrase. Equivocation occurs when an ambiguity destroys the validity of an argument, and no dialogue partner need be involved.)

* 1. **Ms. Y:** Homework is sheer agony!

    **Mr. X:** Oh, come on. You love to do your logic homework.

    **Ms. Y:** Well, yes, but logic is fun. I can't really count logic assignments as homework.

2. **Ms. Y:** Pacifists are the only hope for the future of the human species.

    **Mr. X:** I disagree. "Pacifist" means a wimp who's afraid to stand up for his own rights. I see nothing hopeful about that.

3. **Ms. Y:** Secular humanism is a religion, for it is just as much a worldview or way of life as Judaism or Christianity. And yet, secular humanists claim to be free of religious bias.

    **Mr. X:** No. Secular humanism is not a religion. After all, secular humanists deny the supernatural altogether.

* 4. **Mr. X:** The Republican party will be the salvation of this country.

**Ms. Y:** Give me a break! The "Republican party" is best defined as the party whose primary concern is to protect the wealth of its own members. The only "country" Republicans will ever save is the country club.

5. **Mr. X:** I don't care for Reverend Boggs myself. Judging from his sermons, I don't even think he is a Christian. He denies the doctrine of the Trinity and the deity of Christ. Once he even preached a sermon claiming that heaven and hell are entirely mythical.

   **Ms. Y:** How can you say that! Reverend Boggs is a fine Christian man. He is genuinely loving, tolerant of others, and helps people in every way he can.

6. **Ms. Y:** This canyon is really beautiful. Look at these sweeping lines of natural geometry! And the background is the brightest blue sky imaginable.

   **Mr. X:** On the contrary, this canyon is nothing but a big, ugly hole in the ground.

   **Ms. Y:** You are mistaken. The word "beautiful" simply means enjoyable for the speaker to see or hear, and therefore the canyon is beautiful since I *do* enjoy looking at it.

\* 7. **Ms. Y:** Most atheists are inconsistent. On the one hand, they say there is no God, but then they turn around and say that certain things are right and certain things are wrong.

   **Mr. X:** Well, I'm an atheist and I don't get your point. Stealing and murder can be wrong whether or not there is a God.

   **Ms. Y:** No way. "Wrong" simply means disapproved of by God. So, the minute you say something is wrong, you imply that God exists. I rest my case.

8. **Mr. X:** Our society is losing its reverence for life. For example, euthanasia is widely practiced in American hospitals.

   **Ms. Y:** You are misinformed. Euthanasia is illegal, and in our litigious society, doctors have a tremendous motivation to avoid illegal procedures.

   **Mr. X:** But many patients are taken off respirators when their hearts are still pumping. Then they stop breathing and die. *That* is euthanasia.

   **Ms. Y:** No, it's not euthanasia because the electroencephalograms of the patients indicate that they were dead before the respirators were removed.

9. **Ms. Y:** We are not free because our behavior is determined by our genes in conjunction with environmental influences.

   **Mr. X:** I disagree. This is a free country. Americans are a free people!

\* 10. **Ms. Y:** Moral codes vary from society to society. For example, polygamy is "right" in some societies but "wrong" in others.

   **Mr. X:** No. Polygamy is never right. It is degrading to women.

11. **Mr. X:** I know that I am reincarnated.

   **Ms. Y:** Nobody can know that.

**Mr. X:** I disagree. "To know" means to believe with all your heart. And I believe with all my heart that I am reincarnated. Therefore, I know that I am reincarnated.

12. **Ms. Y:** Although many people claim to be atheists, there really are no atheists.

**Mr. X:** I beg to differ.

**Ms. Y:** Beg all you want, but "God" means the greatest being. And everyone thinks that something or other is the greatest being. For example, if you don't believe in supernatural entities, you will probably think that the entire physical universe is the greatest being. So, while not everyone accepts the traditional view of God, everyone does believe that God exists, and hence there are no atheists.

* 13. **Mr. X:** Did you have a nice weekend?

**Ms. Y:** Yes, we went to the Jackson Pollock exhibit at the art museum. He is truly one of the greatest artists of the century.

**Mr. X:** On the contrary, Pollock's abstract paintings aren't even art. You can't even tell what the paintings are supposed to be *of*.

14. **Ms. Y:** I'll never be a political conservative. Never!

**Mr. X:** Oh, but you are mistaken. After all, the word "conservative" means a liberal who has been mugged. So, given the rate of violent crime, I think you will likely one day find yourself a conservative.

15. **Mr. X:** Nietzsche was one of the most intelligent people in the history of the world. His books caused a revolution in philosophy.

**Ms. Y:** Intelligent? I don't think so. If Nietzsche was so smart, then why was his personal life such a total disaster? He couldn't keep a job, he alienated all his friends, and the older he got, the weirder he got. Personally, I think Nietzsche was stupid.

**Part C:** Equivocation and Persuasive Definition    Identify any equivocations or persuasive definitions that appear in the following arguments. In the case of equivocation, provide definitions to clarify the double meaning. Where persuasive definitions occur, explain why they are biased or slanted.

* 1. Every free action is prompted by a motive that belongs to the agent (i.e., the person who performs the action). So, every free act is pursued in an attempt to satisfy one of the agent's own motives. But, by definition, a "self-serving act" is one pursued in an attempt to satisfy one's own motives. Hence, every free act is self-serving.

2. Many people say there is poverty in America today. They cite the number of homeless men and women living on the streets. But there is no real poverty in America today. The people living on the streets of Calcutta are poor.

They are literally starving. Now that's poverty. Therefore, poverty doesn't really exist in America today.

3. Whenever 2 gallons of water are poured into a barrel and 2 gallons of alcohol are added, the barrel will contain slightly less than 4 gallons of liquid (due to the way water and alcohol combine chemically). Thus, when you add 2 and 2, you do not always get 4. Of course, this is entirely contrary to what any mathematician will tell you—namely, when 2 and 2 are added, you always get 4. Therefore, mathematics is sometimes contrary to empirical fact.

\* 4. There ought to be a law against psychiatry, for "psychiatrist" means person who makes a living by charging money for talking with deeply troubled people. And it is wrong to exploit deeply troubled people.

5. Many atheists complain about the harshness of nature "red in tooth and claw." They say that a loving Creator would not set up a system in which some animals must kill and eat other animals in order to live. Hogwash! "The law of the survival of the fittest" is best defined as God's way of achieving population control among the animals. Thus, although the struggle for survival *appears* harsh to us, the law of the survival of the fittest is in fact a very good thing. For without it the environment would be destroyed by an overabundance of animals.

6. Wherever there is a law, there is a person or group who established it. So, since the law of gravity is a law, there is a person or group who established the law of gravity. Now, no human or group of humans could establish the law of gravity. Therefore, some superhuman person or group of superhumans established the law of gravity.

\* 7. Any fetus of human parents is itself human. And if any fetus of human parents is itself human, then abortion is wrong if human life is sacred. Furthermore, since being human consists in having faculties higher than those of other animals (such as the capacity to choose between good and evil), human life is sacred. It follows that abortion is wrong.

8. Frankly, it amazes me that there are people who oppose capitalism. "Capitalism" means an economic system characterized by a free market, fair competition for the goods available, minimal interference from the state, and the sacred right to keep what you've earned. Accordingly, capitalism is a good thing, indeed, a marvelous thing. I can only conclude that those who oppose capitalism are either seriously confused or perverse.

9. If you become a socialist, you will be making a very big mistake. For "socialist" means someone who thinks the government should own everything and that the individual person has no moral value and no rights. So, the very foundations of socialism are evil.

10. It is reasonable to appeal to legitimate authority to settle disputes. If it is reasonable to appeal to legitimate authority to settle disputes and legitimate authority in a democracy resides in the people, then in America, it is

reasonable to appeal to the people to determine whether nuclear weapons are needed. And you will undoubtedly agree that legitimate authority in a democracy resides in the people. So, in America, it is reasonable to appeal to the people to determine whether nuclear weapons are needed. Now, if in America it is reasonable to appeal to the people to determine whether nuclear weapons are needed, then if the majority of Americans regard them as needed, they are needed. The majority of Americans regard nuclear weapons as needed. Hence, nuclear weapons are needed.

## Notes

1. David Kelley, *The Art of Reasoning,* exp. ed. (New York: Norton, 1990), p. 114.
2. *The Words of Martin Luther King, Jr.*, selected and introduced by Coretta Scott King (New York: Newmarket Press, 1983), p. 95.
3. Wesley Salmon, *Logic*, 3rd ed. (Englewood Cliffs, NJ: Prentice-Hall, 1984), p. 145.
4. This example is borrowed from Frank R. Harrison, III, *Logic and Rational Thought* (New York: West, 1992), p. 463.
5. Definitions (16) and (17) are taken from *The American Heritage Concise dic-tion-ar-y,* 3rd ed. (New York: Houghton Mifflin, 1994), p. 417.
6. I owe the interesting observation that the English language has no conventional term for this phenomenon to my friend Dr. Gary Gleb, in conversation.
7. This example is borrowed from Irving M. Copi and Carl Cohen, *Introduction to Logic*, 9th ed. (Englewood Cliffs, NJ: Prentice-Hall, 1994), p. 170.
8. See Plato, *Five Dialogues*, trans. G. M. A. Grube (Indianapolis, IN: Hackett, 1981), p. 12. My example is admittedly a loose paraphrase of the original for the sake of illustration.
9. *Webster's New World Dictionary of the American Language* (New York: World, 1966), p. 412.
10. Benedict de Spinoza, *The Ethics*, trans. R. H. M. Elwes (New York: Dover, 1955), p. 173. Quote marks added.
11. Definition (26) is borrowed from H. L. Mencken, ed., *A New Dictionary of Quotations on Historical Principles from Ancient and Modern Sources* (New York: Knopf, 1978), p. 62. Quote marks added. Mencken attributes (26) to Theodore Dreiser.
12. William James, *Pragmatism and Four Essays from* The Meaning of Truth (New York: New American Library, 1974), p. 41. This quotation is from chap. 2 of *Pragmatism*, "What Pragmatism Means." *Pragmatism* was originally published in 1907 by Longman, Green.
13. James, *Pragmatism*, pp. 41–42.
14. The gist of this example is borrowed from Salmon, *Logic*, p. 162.

## Chapter 4

# Informal Fallacies

**S**ome errors in reasoning are so obvious that no one is apt to be taken in by them. For example, probably no one would find the following argument persuasive:

1. Two plus 2 equals 4. Therefore, Santa Claus exists.

But other errors in reasoning tend to be psychologically persuasive; these are called **fallacies**. In this chapter, we will describe some of the more common informal fallacies and classify them by type. Our first question, then, is, What is an *informal* fallacy?

Let's begin with the contrasting concept of a formal fallacy. A **formal fallacy** involves the *explicit* use of an invalid form. We encountered a number of formal fallacies in Chapter 1. For example, the fallacy of affirming the consequent is a formal fallacy:

2. If nepotism is wrong, then it is destructive. And it is destructive. Hence, nepotism is wrong.

The form here is invalid: "If A, then B; B; so, A." The fallacy of denying the antecedent is another formal fallacy:

3. If good intentions make good sermons, then Reverend McGuire is a good preacher. Unfortunately, they don't; so he's not.

The form here is invalid as well: "If A, then B; not A; so, not B."

We have also seen how to use counterexamples to expose formal fallacies. For instance:

4. All cantaloupes are melons. All watermelons are melons. So, all watermelons are cantaloupes.

The form of argument (4) is "All A are B; all C are B; so all C are A." And here is a counterexample that shows that the form is invalid: "All dogs are animals; all cats are animals; so all cats are dogs."

Not all fallacies are formal fallacies. **Informal fallacies** are errors in reasoning that do not involve the *explicit* use of an invalid form. Furthermore, exposing an informal fallacy requires an examination of the argument's *content*. We took note of one kind of informal fallacy in Chapter 3, namely, equivocation. Here is a blatant example:

> **5.** My wife's brother is a real pig. You should see him eat! And if he is a pig, then he is not human. So, he is not human.

If we ignore the content, argument (5) appears to be an example of *modus ponens*. But if we examine the content, we notice that the word "pig" is used with two different meanings. In the first premise, "pig" means "person who habitually overeats." In the second premise, "pig" means "hog" (i.e., a domesticated animal with a long snout and fat body). Once we spot the double meaning, we see that it destroys the logical linkage between the two premises. While the form initially appears to be *modus ponens*, an analysis of the content indicates that the form would be more accurately identified as follows: "A; if B, then C; so, C." This form is obviously invalid, but it is not *explicitly* employed in argument (5)— it remains hidden due to the double meaning of the word "pig." Thus, equivocation is an *informal* fallacy.

There are many types of informal fallacies, and logicians do not agree on the best way to classify them. However, the attempt to classify them has benefits, for it enables us to see some commonalities among them. In this text, informal fallacies are divided into three groups: (a) fallacies involving irrelevant premises, (b) fallacies involving ambiguity, and (c) fallacies involving unwarranted assumptions. The reason for studying informal fallacies is simply this: By describing and labeling the more tempting ones, we increase our ability to resist their allure. (*Note:* Throughout this chapter, we will provide a contemporary name for each fallacy as well as the traditional Latin name when it is still used with some frequency.)

## 4.1 Fallacies Involving Irrelevant Premises

Some fallacies involve the use of premises that are logically irrelevant to their conclusions, but for psychological reasons, the premises may *seem* relevant. These fallacies are classified as *fallacies involving irrelevant premises*. Six varieties of this general class of fallacy are discussed in this section.

### 1. Argument Against the Person (Ad Hominem *Fallacy*)

The *argument against the person* (or *ad hominem* fallacy) involves attacking the person who advances an argument (or asserts a statement) as opposed to providing a rational critique of the argument (or statement) itself. (*Ad hominem* is a Latin phrase meaning "against the man.") In its most blatant form, the *abusive ad hominem*, this fallacy involves a direct personal attack, for example, an insult or allegation that the arguer has a moral flaw. For example:

> 6. Jones argues for vegetarianism. He says it is wrong to kill animals unless you really need to for food, and that, as a matter of fact, nearly everyone can get enough food without eating meat. But Jones is just a nerdy intellectual. So, we can safely conclude that vegetarianism remains what it has always been—nonsense.

Here, Jones's argument is not given a rational critique; rather, Jones himself is criticized. And even if Jones is a "nerdy intellectual," this does not show that Jones's argument is flawed, nor does it show that vegetarianism is nonsense. The personal attack on Jones is simply irrelevant to the soundness of Jones's argument and irrelevant to the issue of vegetarianism.

*Ad hominem* arguments need not employ outright verbal abuse. In more subtle forms, they involve the attempt to discredit an opponent by suggesting that the opponent's judgment is distorted by some factor in his or her circumstances—*even though the soundness of the opponent's argument (or truth of the opponent's view) is independent of the factor cited*. This form of *ad hominem* argument is sometimes called the *circumstantial ad hominem* because it involves an attempt to discredit an argument (or view) by calling attention to the circumstances or situation of those who advance it. For example:

> 7. Ms. Fitch argues in favor of equal pay for equal work. She says it doesn't make sense to pay a person more for doing the same job just because he is male or Caucasian. But since Ms. Fitch is a woman, it's to her personal advantage to favor equal pay for equal work. After all, she would get an immediate raise if her boss accepted her argument! Therefore, her argument is worthless.

Here, an attempt is made to discredit the argument by showing that the arguer has something to gain if her conclusion is accepted. Of course, the activity of arguing can be, in a given case, simply a way of getting something the arguer wants. But this fact, by itself, does not prove that the arguer's reasoning is flawed. What is needed is a rational critique of the premises or inferences in question.

Another form of the argument against the person involves an attempt to suggest that the opponent is hypocritical—that is, that his views or arguments conflict with his own practice or with what he has said previously. This form of *ad hominem* argument is sometimes called the *tu quoque* (pronounced "too kwo-kway"), meaning "you too." For instance, suppose a 12-year-old argues as follows:

> 8. Dad tells me I shouldn't lie. He says lying is wrong because it makes people stop trusting one another. But I've heard my Dad lie. Sometimes he calls in "sick"

> ### *Argument Against the Person*
> ### *(or Ad Hominem Fallacy)*
>
> Premises: Instead of providing a rational critique of a statement (or argument), attack the person who advances it.
>
> Conclusion: The statement is false or dubious. (Or the argument is unsound or uncogent.)
>
> The attack can take three forms:
>
> *Abusive ad hominem:* direct personal attack on the opponent
>
> *Circumstantial ad hominem:* attempts to discredit by calling attention to the circumstances or situation of the opponent
>
> *Tu quoque:* charges the opponent with hypocrisy or inconsistency

to work when he isn't really sick. So, lying isn't actually wrong—Dad just doesn't like it when I lie.

The *tu quoque* fallacy may succeed in embarrassing or discrediting the opponent, but the logical error should be clear upon reflection. For example, with regard to argument (8), that some people (including one's parents) lie in no way shows that lying is morally permissible. In general, the fact that some people violate a given moral rule does not show that the rule is incorrect. So, the premise of (8), that "Dad lies," is irrelevant to the conclusion.

Before we move on, let us consider one last example of the argument against the person:

9. During the 1980s, many American journalists passed harsh judgments on South African apartheid. They wrote that it was unjust, cruel, and immoral. But given the disgraceful history of race relations in America, these American journalists were in no position to pass judgment on South Africa. So, their judgments were without insight.

Here again, the premises are irrelevant to the conclusion. The journalists are accused of hypocrisy on the grounds that their own country has a disgraceful history of race relations, but what is needed is evidence contrary to the moral judgments of the journalists, and that has not been offered. Thus, (9) is an *ad hominem* of the *tu quoque* type.

## 2. Straw Man Fallacy

A *straw man* fallacy occurs when the arguer attacks a misrepresentation of the opponent's view. The idea is to describe something that *sounds like* the opponent's view but is easier to knock down and then to refute. This fallacy can be very effective from a rhetorical point of view if one's audience is not aware that the misrepresentation has taken place. However, when put bluntly, it is obvious that the premise is irrelevant to the conclusion:

> Premise: A misrepresentation of the view is false.
> Conclusion: The view is false.

Notice that the straw man fallacy results from a failure to honor Principle 4 of Chapter 2: *Be fair and charitable in interpreting an argument.* Fairness demands that we represent the original accurately; charity demands that we put an argument in its best light when we are confronted with interpretive choices.

In order to demonstrate that a straw man fallacy has occurred, one obviously must provide a more accurate statement of the view that has been misrepresented. Equally obviously, one does not always have in hand the information needed to do this. But one can often "smoke out" a straw man fallacy by asking such appropriate questions as these: What were the exact words used in the original? Have any key words or phrases been changed or omitted? Does the context suggest that the author was deliberately exaggerating or leaving obvious exception clauses unstated?

Straw man fallacies often appear in political contexts. Some years ago, when the Equal Rights Amendment was being hotly debated, arguments of the following sort were sometimes offered against it:

> 10. Backers of the ERA believe in the total equality of the sexes. "Equal pay for equal work" is just the tip of the iceberg. Few realize that to ratify the ERA is to insist that 50 percent of the players in the National Football League should be women. Few realize that to ratify the ERA is to insist that there should no longer be separate public bathrooms for men and women. Believe me, it would be a great mistake to ratify the ERA.

The entire text of the proposed Equal Rights Amendment runs as follows: "Equality of rights under the law shall not be denied or abridged by the United States or by any state on account of sex."[1] Now, like many statements in the U.S. Constitution itself, this proposed amendment leaves room for interpretation. But it certainly seems unfair to describe it as requiring that half the players on professional football teams be women or as requiring that men and women use the same public bathrooms. Argument (10) attacks a straw man rather than the ERA itself.

The straw man fallacy is also committed when a view or argument is alleged to involve assumptions that it does not (or need not) involve. For example:

> 11. Susan advocates the legalization of cocaine. But I cannot agree with any position based on the assumption that cocaine is good for you and that a society of drug addicts can flourish. So, I disagree with Susan.

Of course, one can consistently advocate the legalization of cocaine and yet believe that cocaine is not good for people. For example, one may think that although drugs are harmful, legalizing them is the best way to eliminate the illegal drug traffic (and hence the violence associated with it). Moreover, one can advocate the legalization of drugs without assuming or presupposing that a society of drug addicts can flourish. One might believe that legalization will not lead to a significant increase in the number of drug-addicted persons, especially if legalization is accompanied by a strong educational campaign on the dangers of using hard drugs.

---

### The Straw Man Fallacy

Premises: A misrepresentation of the view is false.
Conclusion: The view itself is false.

---

Sometimes a persuasive (i.e., biased) definition is used to set up a straw man:

12. Empiricism is the view that nothing should be believed in unless it can be directly observed. Now, no one can see, hear, taste, smell, or touch protons, electrons, or quarks. So, while empiricists pretend to be advocates of science, their views in fact rule out the most advanced physical science of our times.

Professor Anthony Flew, author of A *Dictionary of Philosophy*, defines "empiricism" as "the thesis that all knowledge or at least all knowledge of matters of fact (as distinct from that of purely logical relations between concepts) is based on experience."[2] Now, since the phrase "is based on" is somewhat vague, the concept of empiricism has rather fuzzy borderlines. But Flew's definition does not have the empiricists insisting that we know only those things we have *directly* observed. We might know about the existence of some entities by extrapolation or because the best theories presuppose their existence. This knowledge would still be "based on" experience because it would be inferred using observation statements. Thus, Flew's definition is fair to the empiricist tradition in philosophy, while the definition contained in argument (12) is biased. By including the phrase "direct observation," the arguer makes empiricism a straw man. Incidentally, argument (12) illustrates how the straw man fallacy can become quite subtle when complex issues are involved. If a seemingly minor but actually important aspect of a view is distorted or omitted, the view itself may appear much easier to refute than it really is.

## 3. Appeal to Force (Ad Baculum *Fallacy*)

The *appeal to force* (or *ad baculum* fallacy) occurs when a conclusion is defended by a threat to the well-being of those who do not accept it. (*Baculum* is Latin for "staff," the staff being a symbol of power.) The threat may be either explicit or implicit. Let's start with a case involving the threat of physical harm, reminiscent of scenes in films about organized crime:

13. Mr. Jones, you helped us import the drugs. For this, the Boss is grateful. But now you say you're entitled to 50 percent of the profits. The Boss says you're entitled to 10 percent. Unless you see things the Boss's way, you're going to have a very nasty accident. So, you're entitled to 10 percent. Got it?

Of course, the threatened "nasty accident" has no logical bearing on the conclusion ("Jones is entitled to 10 percent"). The logical error can be generalized as follows: "You can avoid harm by accepting this statement. So, the statement is true."

An autocratic employer might argue as follows:

14. Lately there has been a lot of negative criticism of our policy on dental benefits. Let me tell you something, people. If you want to keep working here, you need to know that our policy is fair and reasonable. I won't have anybody working here who doesn't know this.

Here, the threat of job loss is obviously irrelevant to the truth of the conclusion (that the dental policy is fair and reasonable). Nevertheless, it may be tempting to suppose that if one can avoid harm by believing $X$, then $X$ is true.

---

### Appeal to Force (*Ad Baculum* Fallacy)

Premises: You can avoid harm by accepting this statement.
Conclusion: This statement is true.

---

The *ad baculum* fallacy may involve any sort of threat to one's well-being, including one's psychological well-being. For instance:

15. Listen, Valerie, I know you disagree with my view about the building project. You've made your disagreement clear to everyone. Well, it's time for you to see that you are mistaken. Let me get right to the point. I know you've been lying to your husband about where you go on Wednesday afternoons. Unless you want him to know where you really go, it's time for you to realize that I've been right about the building project all along. You follow me?

Of course, the threat to expose the lie in no way constitutes evidence for anyone's view on a building project. But again, it may be tempting to suppose that a statement is true if one can avoid harm by accepting it.

## 4. Appeal to the People (Ad Populum *Fallacy*)

The *appeal to the people* (or *ad populum* fallacy) is an attempt to persuade a person (or group) by appealing to the desire to be accepted or valued by others. (*Populum* is Latin for "people" or "nation.") For instance, a speaker at a political rally may elicit strong emotions from the crowd, making each individual want to believe his conclusion so as to feel a part of the group:

> 16. I look out at you all, and I tell you, I am proud to be here. Proud to belong to a party that stands for what is good for America. Proud to cast my lot with the kind of people who make this nation great. Proud to stand with men and women who can get our nation back on its feet. Yes, there are those who criticize us, who label our view of trade agreements as "protectionist." But when I look at you hard-working people, I know we're right and the critics are wrong.

Of course, the strong feelings of the crowd do not lend logical support to anyone's view about trade agreements. Premises to the effect that "I am proud to be associated with you" and "you are hard-working people" are irrelevant to the conclusion (that "our view of trade agreements is right").

---

### Appeal to the People (Ad Populum *Fallacy*)

Premises: You will be accepted or valued if you believe this statement.
Conclusion: This statement is true.

---

One doesn't have to be addressing a large group to commit the *ad populum* fallacy. Any attempt to convince by appealing to the need for acceptance (or approval) from others counts as an *ad populum* fallacy. For instance:

> 17. Ms. Riley, are you saying that President Bush made a moral error when he decided to go to war with Iraq? I can't believe my ears. That's not how Americans feel. Not true Americans, anyway. You *are* an American, aren't you, Ms. Riley?

The mere fact that Ms. Riley is an American provides her with no logical support for the conclusion that America's war with Iraq was just or moral. But like most Americans, Ms. Riley may wish to avoid being regarded as unpatriotic, and so an appeal to the people may influence her thinking.

The appeal to the people is common in advertising:

> 18. The new Electrojet 3000 cabriolet isn't for everyone. But then, you've always stood apart from the crowd, haven't you? So, the Electrojet 3000 is the car for you.

Here, the *ad populum* fallacy takes the form of "snob appeal," that is, an appeal to the desire to be regarded as superior to others.

## 5. Appeal to Pity (Ad Misericordiam *Fallacy*)

The *appeal to pity* (or *ad misericordiam* fallacy) is the attempt to support a conclusion merely by evoking pity in one's audience *when the statements that evoke the pity are logically unrelated to the conclusion.* (*Misericordiam* is Latin for "pity" or "mercy.") For example, the chair of a faculty committee made the following speech to her dean:

> 19. We realize that our proposal concerning the library is flawed. But the merits of the proposal outweigh its flaws. After all, we worked awfully hard on it, and for so many hours! I hate to think we wasted all that time. Also, if you reject it, I might be denied my next promotion.

The premises here are simply irrelevant to the conclusion (that "the merits of the proposal outweigh its flaws"). Even if much time was spent developing the proposal, this in no way guarantees that its merits outweigh its flaws. And even if the dean's rejection of the proposal would lessen the likelihood of the arguer's receiving a promotion, this fact in no way supports the conclusion.

The appeal to pity is not, generally speaking, very subtle. But if the arguer succeeds in evoking sufficiently strong feelings of pity, he or she may distract the audience from the logic of the situation and create a desire to accept the conclusion. For this reason, lawyers often use the appeal to pity in an effort to convince judges and juries that their clients are not guilty or not deserving of a harsh sentence.

---

**Appeal to Pity (*Ad Misericordiam* Fallacy)**

Premises: You have reason to pity this person (or group).
Conclusion: You should do X for the benefit of this person (or group),
although doing X is not called for logically by the reason given.

---

The *ad misericordiam* fallacy must be distinguished from arguments that support the need for a compassionate response to persons whose plights call for compassion. For example, the following sort of argument is *not* an example of the *ad misericordiam* fallacy:

> 20. As a result of war and famine, thousands of children in country X are malnourished. You can help by sending money to Relief Agency Y. So, please send whatever you can spare to Relief Agency Y.

While the information in the premises of this sort of argument is apt to evoke pity, the information is also logically relevant to the conclusion. Hence, there is no *ad misericordiam* fallacy here.

## 6. Appeal to Ignorance (Ad Ignorantiam *Fallacy*)

The *appeal to ignorance* (or *ad ignorantiam* fallacy) involves one of the following: either (a) the claim that a statement is true (or may be reasonably believed true) simply because it hasn't been proven false or (b) the claim that a statement is false (or may be reasonably believed false) simply because it hasn't been proven true. Here are two corresponding examples:

21. After centuries of trying, no one has been able to prove that reincarnation occurs. So, at this point, I think we can safely conclude that reincarnation does not occur.

22. After centuries of trying, no one has been able to show that reincarnation does not occur. Therefore, reincarnation occurs.

Put starkly, the claim that a statement is false because it hasn't been proven is manifestly erroneous. By such logic, scientists would have to conclude that their unproven hypotheses are false. And surely it is wiser for scientists to take a "wait-and-see" attitude. After all, we do not have to believe or disbelieve every statement we consider, for we often have the option of suspending judgment—that is, of not believing the statement is true and (simultaneously) not believing it is false. We can remain neutral. Similarly, the claim that a statement is true (or may reasonably be believed true) simply because it hasn't been disproven is illogical. By this principle, every new scientific hypothesis is true (or at least it can reasonably be believed to be true) unless it has been disproven—*no matter how flimsy the evidence for it is.*

The *ad ignorantiam* fallacy is often committed in organizations during periods of change. Those opposing change may argue along the following lines:

23. It has not been proven that the proposed changes will be beneficial. Therefore, they will not be beneficial.

And the counterargument may be this:

24. There is no solid evidence showing that the proposed changes will not be beneficial. Therefore, they will be beneficial.

Both arguments are flawed. As for (23), there may be no way of obtaining the evidence apart from organizational experimentation—that is, trying the proposal. So, demanding the evidence may be unrealistic and unreasonable. As for (24), problems with the proposal may become evident once it is tried, so the current lack of evidence against it is obviously no guarantee that it will work.

**Appeal to Ignorance (*Ad Ignorantiam* Fallacy)**

Premises: This statement has not been proven true.
Conclusion: This statement is false
(or may be reasonably believed false).

Premises: This statement has not been proven false.
Conclusion: This statement is true
(or may be reasonably believed true).

Some confusion regarding the *ad ignorantiam* fallacy may stem from the assumption used in courts of law that a defendant is *innocent until proven guilty*. This important legal principle is *not* a principle of logic. The legal principle is

## Summary of Fallacies Involving Irrelevant Premises

For psychological reasons, the premises in these arguments may *seem* relevant to the conclusion, but in fact they are not.

1. **Argument Against the Person** (or *ad hominem* fallacy)
   Premises: Instead of providing a rational critique of a statement (or argument), attack the person who advances it.
   Conclusion: The statement is false or dubious. (Or the argument is unsound or uncogent.)

2. **Straw Man Fallacy**
   Premises: A misrepresentation of the view is false.
   Conclusion: The view itself is false.

3. **Appeal to Force** (or *ad baculum* fallacy)
   Premises: You can avoid harm by accepting this statement.
   Conclusion: This statement is true.

4. **Appeal to the People** (or *ad populum* fallacy)
   Premises: You will be accepted or valued if you believe this statement.
   Conclusion: This statement is true.

5. **Appeal to Pity** (or *ad misericordiam* fallacy)
   Premises: You have reason to pity this person (or group).
   Conclusion: You should do *X* for the benefit of this person (or group), although doing *X* is not called for logically by the reason given.

6. **Appeal to Ignorance** (or *ad ignorantiam* fallacy)
   Premises: This statement has not been proven true.
   Conclusion: This statement is false (or may be reasonably believed false).

   Premises: This statement has not been proven false.
   Conclusion: This statement is true (or may be reasonably believed true).

designed primarily to prevent the unjust punishment of the innocent, *not* to increase the chances of correctly identifying *all* those who have committed crimes. Undoubtedly, many defendants have committed the crimes they are accused of even though the evidence is not sufficient to prove them guilty according to accepted legal standards. Our legal system is deliberately designed to prevent one kind of unwanted result (namely, the punishment of the innocent) at the risk of allowing another unwanted result (namely, letting persons who have committed crimes go free). But we can recognize the usefulness and wisdom of the legal principle that "one is innocent until proven guilty" *without* supposing that it is a correct principle of logic.

The following exercise gives you an opportunity to identify examples of the fallacies discussed in this section.

## ◆ *Exercise 4.1*

**Part A:** Formal and Informal Fallacies   Most of the following passages exemplify either a formal fallacy or an informal fallacy. If a formal fallacy is committed, identify the argument form, using capital letters to stand for terms or statements (e.g., "All A are B; all C are B; so all A are C"). If an informal fallacy is committed, name the type of fallacy and explain why the passage is an example of that type. (In the case of *ad hominem* fallacies, indicate whether they are abusive, circumstantial, or *tu quoque* in type.) If no fallacy is committed, simply write "not a fallacy."

* **1.** Social Darwinists such as Herbert Spencer hold that the development and structure of human societies can be explained in terms of evolutionary principles such as the survival of the fittest. But I reject Social Darwinism because Spencer was a real bonehead.

  **2.** Your Honor, it's true that I killed my parents. I fully admit that I murdered them in cold blood. But I should get a light sentence. After all, I *am* an orphan.

  **3.** As I travel around and talk to people, I find that many do not even know what genetic engineering is. Well, genetic engineering is best defined as the most recent in a long line of attempts on the part of human beings to play God. Of course, the proponents of genetic engineering overlook just one little fact: We humans are not God. And that's why genetic engineering is profoundly immoral.

* **4.** All the really hot new thinkers are using principles from sociobiology. It's the new wave in ethics. So, you should accept the principles of sociobiology.

  **5.** Any politician who has lied to the nation is a person who has betrayed the public trust. Some U.S. presidents are politicians who have lied to the nation. Accordingly, some U.S. presidents are persons who have betrayed the public trust.

6. Although they've certainly tried, scientists have not been able to demonstrate that ESP is a myth. So, ESP is probably real.

* 7. It is quite clear what the proponents of legalized euthanasia are seeking. Put simply, they are seeking the power to kill anyone who has a serious illness. And that is why I stand opposed to legalized euthanasia.

8. All beautiful paintings are colorful objects. No charcoal drawings are beautiful paintings. Therefore, no charcoal drawings are colorful objects.

9. So many people these days are against prayer in the public schools! Of course, the assumptions underlying this view include (a) that there is no God, (b) that only matter exists, and (c) that life is essentially meaningless. That is why we must fight against these people who seek to remove prayer from our public schools.

* 10. Professor Jackson, this paper merits at least a "B." I stayed up all night working on it. And if I don't get a "B," I'll be put on academic probation.

11. If consuming large quantities of alcohol damages one's liver, then consuming large quantities of alcohol is unhealthy. Consuming large quantities of alcohol damages one's liver. Hence, consuming large quantities of alcohol is unhealthy.

12. Of course it is reasonable to believe that we have been visited by extraterrestrial beings. After all, plenty of skeptics have tried, but none has been able to disprove that such visitations have occurred.

* 13. Since you became a member of this club, you've raised quite a ruckus about women's rights. And I know you sincerely believe in feminism. But if you go on holding these extreme views, I will see to it that you are never voted in as an officer of this club. And you know I can make good on that threat. I hope you follow me: Your feminist views are too radical and need to be toned down.

14. The future free actions of humans can be known in advance only if time travel is possible. But you're a fool if you think time travel is possible. So, it is not true that the future free actions of humans can be known in advance.

15. If Norway is the world leader in per-capita electrical power generation, then the U.S.A. is not the world leader. And indeed the U.S.A. is not the world leader in per-capita electrical power generation. Therefore, Norway is the world leader in per-capita electrical power generation.

* 16. Dr. Herzheimer has written essays criticizing self-help books from the standpoint of logic and science. I realize Dr. Herzheimer is a famous philosopher, but I think it's immature and cold-hearted to criticize people who are trying to help others get their lives together. Thus, I myself give no credence to Dr. Herzheimer's work whatsoever.

17. Republicans are people who believe that the rich should get richer and the poor poorer. They are against welfare and against taxes for people who can well afford to pay taxes. Republicans also hold that the only good immigrants

are either wealthy or well educated. Thus, I strongly urge you not to be a Republican.

18. Excuse me, Mr. Smith, did I hear you correctly? Did you say that boxing should be banned? Sure, boxing is a little dangerous, but real men love boxing. Therefore, boxing should not be banned.

* 19. Mr. Johnson argues that we should stop eating meat. But did you know that Mr. Johnson owns the Vegetables Forever Produce Company? Oh yes, he stands to gain a lot, financially speaking, if the rest of us become vegetarians. I think we can safely ignore his line of argument.

20. Nowadays, everybody that's anybody believes in reincarnation. So, you should, too.

21. Given that most commuters are willing to ride trains, light rail is a good solution to gridlock on the highways. But most commuters are not willing to ride trains. Hence, light rail is not a good solution to gridlock on the highways.

* 22. I do not have very much information about Mr. Reed, but there is nothing in his file to disprove that he's a communist. So, he probably is one.

23. I find it mildly amusing that Mr. and Mrs. Billings are advocating school reforms. But I certainly do not see any reason to take their proposal seriously. Both of them were poor students in high school.

24. Intelligent, refined people insist on the best wines. And our Old World Merlot is the best red wine available. Obviously, Old World Merlot is for you.

* 25. The school needs a football team. I hope you agree. One thing I can tell you for sure: If you want to fit in around here, you'll see this issue the way the rest of us do. And we all think the school needs a football team.

26. Robert, I've heard you're a communist. So, let me tell you something. Around here, we know communism is evil. And we have ways of making communists see the error of their ways. The last communist who passed through this town suddenly saw the light after some of the boys had a little "talk" with him one night. I hope these facts will clarify things for you. You do understand that communism is evil, don't you?

27. Yes, Jill argues for deconstruction. But her mind is so open, her brains are falling out. You can safely ignore whatever she has to say.

* 28. In 1742, Christian Goldbach conjectured that every even number greater than 2 is the sum of two primes. Mathematicians have been trying to prove Goldbach's conjecture ever since, but no one has succeeded in doing so. After two and a half centuries, I think we can safely conclude that Goldbach was wrong.

29. It's interesting how the family of David Walker, the African American shot by Seattle police, complains that none of the jurors at the fact-finding hearing are black but has no problem that their attorney suing the city for

$5 million is not black. [Assume that the implicit conclusion is: The complaint is groundless.] —Letter to *The Seattle Times*, July 19, 2000, B7

30. After centuries of trying, no one has been able to prove that God exists. The attempt seems to be futile. So, at this point, I think we can safely conclude that there is no God.

**Part B:** Formal and Informal Fallacies   Most of the following passages exemplify either a formal fallacy or an informal fallacy. If a formal fallacy is committed, identify the argument form, using capital letters to stand for terms or statements (e.g., "All A are B; all C are B; so all A are C"). If an informal fallacy is committed, name the type of fallacy and explain why the passage is an example of that type. (In the case of *ad hominem* fallacies, indicate whether they are abusive, circumstantial, or *tu quoque* in type.) If no fallacy is committed, simply write "not a fallacy." *Note: In some cases, more than one fallacy is exemplified in a single passage; where this occurs, identify all the fallacies.*

*  1. What is the prochoice view? This: It is permissible to kill innocent human beings at will as long as they are small and helpless. By implication, then, the prochoice view would permit the slaughter of children on a wide scale. And that is why we should all oppose the prochoice view.

   2. Your Honor, my client does not deserve a year in prison. He has small children that need a father and a wife that needs a husband.

   3. You really think that drugs should be legalized? Think again. Dad will cut you out of the inheritance if you go on thinking like that. That should make it clear to you just how far off base your views really are.

*  4. Clairvoyance is the alleged ability to "see" with the mind's eye what cannot literally be seen. For example, some clairvoyants have claimed to "see" the death of a loved one from whom they were separated by many miles. Of course, you can imagine the kind of attention clairvoyants receive from the media, not to mention the money they can squeeze out of weak-minded people who are curious about the paranormal. Thus, I think the alleged reports of clairvoyance are just hype.

   5. Joe, I know you think that the new electronics plant should be located in Seattle. Well, you're wrong. It should be located in Spokane. How do I know? Joe, I'm your boss, right? And you're up for a promotion next month, right? You want the promotion, right? Well, then, the conclusion is obvious: The new electronics plant should be located in Spokane.

   6. Smoking cigarettes can harm one's health. So, it's best to avoid smoking, assuming one wants to be healthy.

*  7. No one has ever shown that miracles do not happen. Therefore, miracles do happen.

   8. Yates is guilty of murder, assuming that he pleads guilty. But Yates does not plead guilty. Therefore, Yates is not guilty of murder.

9. You have argued that it is wrong for me to hunt deer. Well, you eat hamburger, and that involves the killing of cows. Moreover, it is obvious that there is no moral difference between killing cows and killing deer, so your argument is unsound.

* 10. The poor people in many Third World countries are malnourished and highly susceptible to disease. These people are in need of help, for their poverty is so great that many of them can do little to help themselves. But many Americans have discretionary income well beyond what they need personally, and these (relatively) wealthy Americans could help the poor in the Third World—at least to some extent. Moreover, from a moral point of view, it is good to help those who really need help. So, from a moral point of view, it would be a good thing for these (relatively) wealthy Americans to help the poor in the Third World.

11. No one has been able to demonstrate that astrology is nonsense. For this reason I have concluded that astrology is not nonsense—rather, it is an insightful way of viewing our lives and the world around us.

12. No nuclear power plants are pollution-free forms of generating electrical power. Some waterwheels are pollution-free forms of generating electrical power. It follows that no nuclear power plants are waterwheels.

* 13. Christians teach the doctrine of the Triune God, namely, that "One God plus one God plus one God equals one God." But this doctrine is false, for it is obviously a mathematical impossibility, and only fools believe mathematical impossibilities.

14. Suzanne won the race only if she beat Marilyn. And Suzanne won the race. Therefore, Suzanne beat Marilyn.

15. Ingres' *Odalisque* is not a sexist painting. Of course, I admit that *Odalisque* is sexist if it treats women as sex objects. But you'd have to be the worst sort of uptight prude to think that *Odalisque* treats women as sex objects. In addition, no one has ever proven that *Odalisque* treats women as sex objects. Therefore, *Odalisque* does not treat women as sex objects, and so it is not sexist.

* 16. No contracts that contain a deliberate lie are legal contracts. All legal contracts are binding contracts. So, no contracts that contain a deliberate lie are binding contracts.

17. I don't deserve a speeding ticket, officer. Yes, I admit I was doing 60 in a school zone. But I've had a really rough day. I was angry about some stuff that happened at work. Everybody has to let off some steam once in a while, don't they? Give me a break.

18. Your Honor, the witness has just lied to the court three times. This has been verified by the tape recordings and by the reports of all of the other witnesses. Therefore, I submit that the witness's testimony is untrustworthy.

* 19. Real men drink El Belcho beer. Wimps drink the inferior brands. I can see you're a real man. So, El Belcho is the beer for you.

20. My dear sir, there are two reasons why you should agree that the money in your wallet is rightfully mine. First, I've had a lot of bad luck in my life, but you obviously enjoy health, wealth, and prosperity. So, if you are a man of compassion, you'll see that I deserve the wallet. Second, since I'm pointing a gun at your head, you owe your very life to my generosity and patience.

21. According to mind–body dualism, human beings have both a body and a nonphysical soul. But if mind–body dualism is true, then new energy is introduced from the soul into the brain. But dualists have never been able to show that new energy is introduced from the soul into the brain. Thus, we can safely conclude that new energy is not introduced from the soul into the brain. Furthermore, it's just crazy to suppose that a nonphysical thing (i.e., the soul) can have causal interactions with a physical thing (i.e., the brain). This, too, supports the claim that new energy is not introduced from the soul into the brain. I must conclude that mind–body dualism is not true.

*22. My opponent, the evolutionist, denies that we have our origin in God. Rather, according to the evolutionist, we humans have our origin in lower forms of life. Instead of having the dignity of being made in the image of God, we have the ignominy of being "made" in the image of apes, snakes, and bacteria.

23. You bet I'm in favor of stiff punishments for violent crimes. After all, punishment deters crime—no doubt about that. Yes, I'm aware that many bleeding-heart liberals have tried to prove that punishment doesn't really deter crime, but their feeble efforts have all failed miserably. It's just plain common sense that punishment deters crime.

24. If you want to die young, be one of those animals rights advocates. I mean, it's your business, but around here, folks don't have much patience with stupidity. Now, I know you really don't want to die young. So, don't be an animal rights advocate. And don't say I didn't warn you.

25. Wow! Just when you thought every state agency that possibly could had overdosed on dumb pills, here comes yet another. Kudos to Washington State Fish and Wildlife for opening the Lake Washington sockeye season on July 4th. They must have trundled to the very depths of their department to find a mind so brilliant as to make this kind of decision. Why would someone mix 3,000 boatloads of fishermen who are chomping at the bit to finally have a viable fishery in their front yard with several thousand people trying to launch their boats to attend the fireworks display on Lake Union? —Letter to *The Seattle Times*, July 5, 2000, B7

## 4.2 Fallacies Involving Ambiguity

Arguments are sometimes flawed because they contain ambiguous words (phrases or statements) or because they involve a subtle confusion between two closely related concepts. These we will call *fallacies involving ambiguity*, and we will discuss four kinds of them.

## 7. Equivocation

We first discussed this fallacy in section 3.3. Recall that *equivocation* occurs when two (or more) meanings of a word (or phrase) are used in a context in which validity requires a single meaning of that word (or phrase). Here is an example:

> 25. Only man is rational. But no woman is a man. Hence, no woman is rational.

Here, of course, the word "man" is used with two different meanings. In the first premise it means "humans," while in the second premise it means "male humans." If we rewrite the argument making the two meanings explicit, the invalidity is apparent:

> 26. Only humans are rational. No woman is a male human. So, no woman is rational.

The use of the single word "man" in argument (25) gives it a superficial appearance of validity. But our rewrite, argument (26), indicates that in reality, the two meanings of the word "man" destroy the logical linkage between premises and conclusion. Etymologically, "equivocate" comes from two Latin words, one meaning "equal" or "same" and one meaning "voice" or "word." When one equivocates, one makes it sound as if the same word (or phrase) is being used with the same meaning throughout the argument, when, in fact, more than one meaning is present.

Is the following an example of equivocation?

> 27. One of your answers on the math exam is not right. And if it's not right, it's wrong. Furthermore, what's wrong is immoral. So, one of your answers on the math exam is immoral.

Yes. The word "wrong" is used in two different senses. In its first occurrence, "wrong" simply means "incorrect" or "inaccurate." In its second occurrence, "wrong" means "morally wrong" or "unethical." And mathematical errors are not, in general, moral errors (although deliberate errors in math can of course be used to deceive others, and careless mathematical errors in research or business are irresponsible).

Now, let's consider a somewhat more subtle example of equivocation:

> 28. I agree with Christians in their claim that God is love. But unlike Christians, I'm not afraid to draw the obvious logical consequence: Love is God.

The gist of the argument is this: "God is love; therefore, love is God." And it might be tempting to suppose that the argument has this form:

29. *X* is identical with *Y;* therefore, *Y* is identical with *X.*

Form (29) is valid—for example, "Samuel Clemens is identical with Mark Twain; therefore, Mark Twain is identical with Samuel Clemens." But argument (28) does not really have form (29), for when Christians say, "God is love," they don't mean that God is identical with love. Rather, they mean that God has the attribute of being loving. Thus, in the premise of (28), "is" means "has the attribute of," while in the conclusion, "is" means "is identical with." Accordingly, argument (28) has the following form:

30. *X* has attribute *Y.* So, *Y* is identical with *X* (that is, *Y* is *one and the same thing as X*).

It is not hard to produce a counterexample to show that this form is invalid: "Tom Cruise (the famous actor) is male; that is, he has the attribute of maleness. So, maleness is identical with Tom Cruise." Here the premise is of course true, but the conclusion is false. Maleness is an attribute shared by many individuals, none of whom are identical with it. In particular, maleness is not *one and the same thing as* Tom Cruise.

---

### Equivocation

Premises: Contain a key word (or phrase) that is ambiguous.
Conclusion: Is reached not by valid logical inference but by trading on the ambiguity of the key word (or phrase).

---

## 8. Amphiboly

The fallacy of *amphiboly* is similar to equivocation except that the double meaning is due to a syntactic deficiency, such as a grammatical error or a mistake in punctuation (rather than to an ambiguous word or phrase). In other words, an *amphiboly* is an inference that is invalid because of its dependence on an ambiguity *that is due to sentence structure*. Here is an example:

31. Author Myron Mobbins warns about the negative effects of subtle lies in his book *Liars Tell Lies.* So, given that Mobbins's book contains subtle lies, perhaps it is best not to read it.

Presumably, Mobbins is not warning people about subtle lies *that occur in his own book;* rather, in his book, he is warning people about the negative effects of subtle lies that originate from other sources. But the conclusion drawn in argument (31) results from a different interpretation of the syntactically flawed premise. Amphiboly often occurs when someone interprets a syntactically deficient statement in a way that was not intended by the original author (or speaker).

Here is another example of amphiboly:

> 32. Professor Warren gave a lecture on homicide in Tiffany Hall, room 208. I gather that a lot of people have been murdered in that room.

The premise may mean simply that room 208 in Tiffany Hall is the location of the lecture, but the arguer takes it to mean that the lecture is about homicides that have occurred in that room. In the absence of additional information, the arguer's interpretation is not justified, so (32) is an example of the fallacy of amphiboly.

Now, consider the following two arguments. Are both examples of amphiboly? How do you know?

> 33. We were disturbed to read in the *Times* that during the past five years many of the middle school students searched illegally carried firearms. Obviously, they should fire the school administrators for conducting these illegal searches.
>
> 34. I'm sure we can agree that mentally abnormal people, such as psychotics, should be hospitalized. They shouldn't be living on the streets, and they shouldn't be put in prison. However, we must be willing to apply this principle consistently. And consider this fact: Geniuses, such as Albert Einstein, are mentally abnormal, for fewer than one in a million people have IQs as high as Einstein's. The conclusion is inescapable: Geniuses should be hospitalized.

Argument (33) is an example of amphiboly. Was it the searches or the carrying of firearms that was illegal? The arguer unjustifiably takes it to be the searches. Argument (34), on the other hand, is not an example of amphiboly; rather, it's an example of equivocation. The key phrase is "mentally abnormal." In its first use, "mentally abnormal" means "mentally ill." In its second use, "mentally abnormal" means simply "departing from the norm (or statistically rare)." Argument (34) is not an amphiboly because the ambiguity involved is not due to a structural flaw but simply due to the double meaning of the phrase "mentally abnormal."

---

### Amphiboly

Premises: Contain a sentence that is ambiguous due to faulty structure (e.g., grammar or punctuation).
Conclusion: Is reached not by valid logical inference but by trading on the structural ambiguity.

## 9. Composition

The label "fallacy of composition" applies to two similar types of invalid inference. The first type is *an invalid inference from the nature of the parts to the nature of the whole*. For instance:

> 35. Each of the parts of this airplane is very light. Therefore, the airplane itself is very light.

Of course, if enough light parts are conjoined, the airplane itself may be quite heavy, and so the argument is invalid. Here is another example of the parts-to-whole type of fallacy of composition:

> 36. Each player on the football team is outstanding. Hence, the team itself is outstanding.

Even if each of the players on a team is outstanding, the team itself may not be outstanding if there is a lack of teamwork or insufficient opportunity to practice together.

It should be noted that not all inferences from part to whole are invalid. For example:

> 37. Each part of the machine weighs more than one pound, and the machine has five parts. Consequently, the machine itself weighs more than one pound.

Obviously, argument (37) is valid. But (35) and (36) make it clear that the following argument form is *not* in general valid: "Each part of X has attribute Y; therefore, X itself has attribute Y." However, since composition is an *informal* fallacy, it cannot be detected simply by identifying the argument form. One must also examine the content, especially the attribute in question, before passing judgment on the validity of part-to-whole inferences. And there is no simple formula for determining whether a given attribute will lead to fallacies of composition. One must evaluate part-to-whole inferences on a case-by-case basis.

The second type of fallacy of composition is *an invalid inference from attributes of members of a group to attributes of the group itself*. Here is an example:

> 38. Elephants eat more than humans. So, elephants taken as a group eat more than humans taken as a group.

This argument illustrates the traditional distinction between *distributive* and *collective* predication. In the premise, "Elephants eat more than humans," the attribute of "eating more than" is predicated distributively; that is, each *individual* elephant is said to eat more than any *individual* human eats. In the conclusion, however, the attribute of "eating more than" is predicated collectively; that is, elephants *taken as a group* are said to eat more than humans *taken as a group*.

Thus, while the premise of (38) is true, its conclusion is false simply because there are so many more humans than elephants.

The two forms of the fallacy of composition are related because the relationship of parts to a whole is analogous to the relationship of members to a group (or collective). However, these relationships are not identical. A whole must have its parts organized or arranged in a particular way. For instance, if we take an automobile apart and ship the parts to hundreds of different locations, the automobile no longer exists, but the collection of parts still exists.

The fallacy of composition is here classified as a fallacy of ambiguity because it often gains its persuasive force from a confusion of concepts. Consider again this example: "The team members are excellent; so the team is excellent." While on reflection there is a clear distinction between the team members and the team, the two concepts are easily confused, since the team is merely its members *organized in a certain way*. So, a less-than-clear grasp of the concepts involved may obscure the error in reasoning.

It should be noted that in some cases it is a matter of controversy whether an argument exemplifies the fallacy of composition. For instance, some philosophers think the following argument is an example of the fallacy of composition while others do not:

> 39. Each part of the universe is a dependent entity (i.e., depends for its existence on some other entity). So, the universe itself is a dependent entity.

The conclusion of argument (39) has been used by some philosophers to argue for the existence of God. But does the premise of (39) support the conclusion? Some philosophers doubt that the concept of dependence is understood well enough to legitimate a conclusion about the universe as a whole (even if each part of the universe *is* a dependent entity). This controversy has yet to be settled in a definitive way.

---

**Composition**

Premises: The parts (or members) have attribute *X*.
Conclusion: The whole (or group) has attribute *X*.

---

## 10. Division

The fallacy of *division* is the reverse of the fallacy of composition. That is, the fallacy of division involves *an invalid inference from the nature of the whole to the nature of the parts, or from the nature of a group to the nature of its members*. Here is an example of the whole-to-part type of fallacy:

40. The airplane is heavy. So, each of its parts is heavy.

Of course, some of the parts of a heavy airplane may be very light. Thus, the argument is invalid. Here is another example of the whole-to-part variety of the fallacy of division:

41. The soccer team is excellent. Hence, each member of the team is excellent.

A team may be excellent due to teamwork and a few outstanding players and yet have members who are not themselves excellent players.

The fallacy of division does not always involve an inference from a whole to its parts. It may involve an inference from a group (or collective) to its members. For instance:

42. Grizzly bears are rapidly disappearing. So, Freddy, the grizzly bear at the zoo, must be rapidly disappearing.

This argument moves invalidly from a statement about grizzly bears (taken as a group) to a statement about a member of that group. The fallacy of division (like the fallacy of composition) is classified as a fallacy of ambiguity because it gains its persuasive force from a confusion of meanings or concepts. For instance, "grizzly bears" may mean "grizzly bears taken as group" or "individual grizzly bears." If one fails to distinguish these two meanings, one is readily taken in by the fallacy.

---

**Division**

Premises: The whole (or group) has attribute *X*.
Conclusion: The parts (or members) have attribute *X*.

---

The following exercise gives you an opportunity to identify fallacies involving ambiguity.

## ◆ *Exercise 4.2*

**Part A:** Fallacies Involving Ambiguity   Most of the following passages exemplify a fallacy introduced in this section, but some of the passages do not exemplify fallacies, and some exemplify a fallacy introduced in section 4.1. Identify all of the fallacies. In the case of equivocation and amphiboly, briefly explain the double meaning involved. Finally, if no fallacy is committed, simply write "not a fallacy."

* 1. The leader of this new religious group preaches the following message: "We shall wear no clothes to distinguish ourselves from our Christian brethren." Therefore, this religious group should be opposed. For it advocates nudity.

## Summary of Fallacies Involving Ambiguity

These fallacies result from double meanings or from a confusion between two closely related concepts.

7. **Equivocation**
   Premises: Contain a key word (or phrase) that is ambiguous.
   Conclusion: Is reached not by valid logical inference but by trading on the ambiguity of the key word (or phrase).

8. **Amphiboly**
   Premises: Contain a sentence that is ambiguous due to faulty structure (e.g., grammar or punctuation).
   Conclusion: Is reached not by valid logical inference but by trading on the structural ambiguity.

9. **Composition**
   Premises: The parts (or members) have attribute X.
   Conclusion: The whole (or group) has attribute X.

10. **Division**
    Premises: The whole (or group) has attribute X.
    Conclusion: The parts (or members) have attribute X.

2. No member of the crew can lift over 100 pounds. Therefore, the entire crew cannot lift over 100 pounds.

3. Monty is so much fun at a party! He's a real ham! But if he's a ham, then he is high in cholesterol. So, he is high in cholesterol.

\* 4. Every sentence in my book is well written. Accordingly, my book is well written.

5. The Acme Corporation is very important. So, since Ms. Griggs works for the Acme Corporation, she must be very important.

6. Your Honor, the witness said he saw a photograph of the defendant lying on the coffee table. Therefore, the defendant must have lain on the coffee table at some point.

\* 7. The Germans are mostly Lutheran. Karl Schmidt is a German. Accordingly, Karl is mostly Lutheran.

8. Each brick in the building is larger than my logic textbook, and the building is composed of many bricks. It follows that the building itself is larger than my logic textbook.

9. Nuclear weapons are more destructive than conventional weapons. Therefore, over the course of human history, more destruction has resulted from nuclear weapons (taken as a group) than from conventional weapons (taken as a group).

* **10.** If I have a strong desire to believe in God, then I have a motive for believing in God. And if I have a motive for believing in God, then I have a reason for believing in God. However, if I have a reason for believing in God, then I have evidence for my belief in God. Therefore, if I have a strong desire to believe in God, then I have evidence for my belief in God.

**11.** You have asked Lolla Lodge to contribute to the Krazykids Preschool fundraiser. I am sorry to inform you that we are unable to honor your request. We realize that you are under the impression that our previous director promised you that we would make a contribution this year. But what the previous director actually said was, "We promise to give $1000 and our best wishes to St. Mary's Hospital and Krazykids Preschool." So, St. Mary's gets the $1000, and Krazykids gets our best wishes.

**12.** Each cell in the human body is invisible. Therefore, the human body itself is invisible.

* **13.** Each square inch of the car's surface is red. It follows that the whole car is red.

**14.** If Maffeo Barberini was Pope Urban VIII, then if Pope Urban VIII had Galileo placed under house arrest, Maffeo Barberini had Galileo placed under house arrest. Maffeo Barberini was Pope Urban VIII. It follows that if Pope Urban VIII had Galileo placed under house arrest, Maffeo Barberini had Galileo placed under house arrest.

**15.** America is still a free country, right? You bet it is. That being so, how can you doubt that we are free to choose between good and evil? Every real American is free and knows it. I'm starting to wonder what country you're from.

* **16.** Immigrants come from every country in the world. Ms. Bashir is an immigrant. Consequently, Ms. Bashir comes from every country in the world.

**17.** Dear Sir: It is the duty of the *Williamsburg Post* to print all the news that's in the public interest. And whether you like it or not, there is tremendous public interest in clairvoyance. Hence, the *Post* would be remiss were it not to print articles on clairvoyance. —The Editors

**18.** Sparrows are plentiful. Pete, my pet bird, is a sparrow. Therefore, Pete is plentiful.

* **19.** All men are not losers. Therefore, all losers are nonmen.

**20.** According to the Declaration of Independence, all men are created equal. Well, I disagree. It is obvious that human beings differ in important respects from birth, for example, in intelligence, athletic ability, and physical attractiveness. Therefore, contrary to the Declaration of Independence, it is not the case that human beings are created equal.

**21.** Gareth Peterson argues that the war in Vietnam was unjust. He claims that American military personnel were largely unable to distinguish friend from foe, and so they engaged in a lot of indiscriminate killing. But Peterson is an embittered veteran of the conflict in Vietnam. So, his argument has little value.

* **22.** Piet Mondrian's famous painting, *Composition with Red, Blue, and Yellow,* is made up of a number of distinct rectangles, each of which is brightly colored and beautiful. Hence, the painting itself is beautiful.

**23.** People do what they want to do. You said you wanted to go to the party, but in fact you stayed home to study for your logic exam. So, you didn't really want to go to the party—what you really wanted to do was to study for the logic exam.

**24.** We Americans have got to get rid of the Electoral College! Why? Well, this is supposed to be a democracy, but it's not a democracy and never has been. As long as we have an electoral college, a presidential candidate can win the popular vote and lose the election. And that's not democracy. Furthermore, in a democracy, each person's vote counts equally. But again, as long as we have an electoral college, the votes of some people count more than the votes of others. Is that democracy? No way. Now, you do believe in democracy, don't you? Of course you do; all good people do.

* **25.** According to the *Seattle Times,* this year the State of Washington will not issue parking permits to fish. So, I guess the salmon won't be allowed to park anywhere this year.

**26.** If Edwin Hubble is an astronomer, then he must necessarily be a scientist. Edwin Hubble is an astronomer. So, Hubble must necessarily be a scientist. But if Hubble must necessarily be a scientist, then he has no choice but to be a scientist. Consequently, Hubble has no choice but to be a scientist.

**27.** Dear Editor: I am writing to voice my opposition to the proposed light rail system, which is supposed to solve the traffic problems in Seattle. First, do the math. The project will cost $3.5 billion. If you divide by ridership predictions, the cost per ride over the first 10 years of operation will be $12.13. Apparently, backers of light rail are a bunch of fat cats with no conception of how the other half lives! Second, no one has proved that the proposed light rail system will solve the traffic problem. So, we have a proposal that is (a) outrageously expensive and (b) won't even solve the problem it's supposed to solve. The sooner we get a better plan for dealing with the traffic issue, the better.

* **28.** That which can not-be at some time is not. Therefore, if everything can not-be, then at one time there was nothing in existence. —St. Thomas Aquinas, *Summa Theologica* (I, Q. 2. Art. 3), in Anton C. Pegis, ed., *Introduction to St. Thomas Aquinas* (New York: Random House, 1948), p. 26

**29.** God is love. Love is a character trait. Therefore, God is a character trait.

**30.** Sixty percent of the students at Seattle Pacific University are female. Pat is a student at Seattle Pacific. So, Pat is 60 percent female.

* **31.** I read in the *Seattle Times* that most traffic accidents occur within 5 miles of your home. Now, given this fact, I'm forced to conclude that it would be a

good idea for you to relocate to someplace *more than 5 miles* distant from your home.

32. For Communication 101, I'm required to give a speech on drugs. But I am personally opposed to using drugs for any reason, so I think the professor is being unfair. I mean, sure, like most people, I've wondered what it would be like to be on drugs, but I shouldn't have to violate my personal ethical standards in order to meet the class requirements.

33. I'm sorry to hear that many of the bars tested illegally sell alcohol to people under 21. I infer that the governor should put a stop to such illegal testing.

*34. According to the letter we received, your previous employer recommends you with no qualifications. But I'm afraid we here at the Grove Company hire only people that do have qualifications. So, there's really no point in our talking further.

35. In a recent sermon, Pastor Bob said that a good marriage takes more than just two people in love. I found the sermon quite disturbing. Apparently Pastor Bob no longer believes in monogamy.

**Part B:** Equivocation   For more examples of equivocation, see exercise 3.3, part A.

## 4.3 Fallacies Involving Unwarranted Assumptions

Some errors in reasoning result when the arguer makes an *unwarranted* assumption. An unwarranted assumption is one that, in context, stands in need of support. And because the support has not been provided, the assumption is illegitimate or unjustified, thus undermining the force of the argument. However, the unwary audience may not notice that an unwarranted assumption has been made, in which case the argument may be persuasive, although it *should not* be persuasive, and would not be to an ideally alert and rational audience.

### 11. Begging the Question (Petitio Principii)

An argument *begs the question* when it *assumes the point to be proved*. Begging the question is also known as arguing in a circle. (The Latin expression *petitio principii* means roughly "begging the first principle." It is pronounced variously but may be pronounced as "peh-TIT-ee-o prin-KIP-ee-ee.") Here is an example:

43. The defendant is not guilty of the crime, for she is innocent of having committed it.

The conclusion of this argument is merely a slightly rephrased version of the premise. So, the conclusion cannot be false given that the premise is true. And hence, argument (43) is valid. Therefore, if the premise is, as a matter of fact, true, then the argument is sound (by definition). Still, even if (43) is sound, one can see that it is defective in that it *assumes the point to be proved*.

The phenomenon of begging the question is interesting from the standpoint of logical theory, for it shows us that ultimately we want something more than valid arguments *with true premises*. But what is that something more? Here, we must keep in mind the two basic purposes for arguing: (a) convincing others and (b) discovering truth. From the standpoint of convincing others, we need premises that are somehow more acceptable to them than the conclusion. Of course, it's one of the facts of life that we cannot always convince others. As the old saying goes, "Convince a man against his will, he's of the same opinion still." But insofar as we wish to use an argument to persuade a person or group on a given issue, we need to employ premises that are more plausible to that person or group than the conclusion. And obviously, what's "more plausible" is, at least to some extent, relative to the person or group. We can sum this up by saying that in many cases, we need not only sound arguments but also convincing or persuasive ones.

But we use arguments not only to convince others but also to discover truth. And arguments that beg the question are flawed from this perspective as well because obviously one cannot reasonably claim to discover a truth *by inference* when that truth is itself included in the premises of one's argument. To discover a given truth via argument, each premise must be a different statement from the conclusion. Moreover, we usually want premises that we (rightly) take to be more probable than the conclusion prior to considering the argument.*

In sum, both from the standpoint of convincing others and from the standpoint of discovering truth, an argument that begs the question is deeply flawed. This is not to deny, of course, that question-begging arguments *do* sometimes convince a person or group. But such arguments *should not* be convincing because they illegitimately assume the point to be proved.

Does the following argument beg the question?

> **44.** Everyone must be allowed to speak his or her mind because otherwise freedom of speech would be violated.[3]

The premise, written out more explicitly, says that if someone were not allowed to speak his or her mind, then freedom of speech would be violated. The word "violated" presumably signals something that *should not* happen, and this being so, the premise of the argument is similar in content to the conclusion. Is the premise better known than the conclusion? It's hard to see any good reason for thinking so. Thus, the argument seems to beg the question.

It is not always immediately obvious whether an argument involves a fallacy of begging the question. Consider the following case:

---

*I say "usually" because sometimes a conclusion is well known on grounds independent of the premises of the argument, and yet the argument may be helpful from the standpoint of discovering the truth because it shows that the conclusion is supported by *more than one* line of evidence.

**45.** God exists because the Bible says so. But how do I know that what the Bible says is true? Because it is God's Word.

In well-crafted form, argument (45) would look like this:

1. The Bible is God's Word.
So, 2. What the Bible says is true. [from 1]
3. The Bible says that God exists.
So, 4. God exists. [from 2 and 3]

None of the premises here simply *restates* the conclusion that God exists. But the first premise (all by itself) *presupposes* that God exists. Therefore, the argument seems to beg the question.[4]

---

**Begging the Question (*Petitio Principii*):**
Assuming the point to be proved

The premises are similar in content to the conclusion
*but not better known* than the conclusion.

---

Sometimes, there is reasonable disagreement about whether an argument assumes the point to be proved. For one thing, there can be borderline cases because the extent to which a premise contains the information in the conclusion is a matter of degree. Furthermore, this entire issue is complicated by the fact that the premises of a *valid* argument, taken together, *must contain* the information in the conclusion. Ultimately, to identify a fallacy of begging the question, we need to determine whether each premise, taken by itself, is better known or more reasonably believed than the conclusion of the argument. If a given premise is similar in content to the conclusion but is *not* better known (or more reasonably believed) than the conclusion, then the argument begs the question. But there will sometimes be reasonable disagreement about whether a given premise is better known (or more reasonably believed) than the conclusion of the argument.

## 12. False Dilemma

The fallacy of *false dilemma* occurs when one uses a premise that unjustifiably reduces the number of alternatives to be considered. For example, the arguer may assume, without justification, that there are only two possible alternatives, when in fact there are three or more. Consider the following argument:

**46.** I'm tired of all these young people criticizing their own country. What I say is this, "America—love it or leave it!" And since these people obviously don't want to leave the country, they should love it instead of criticizing it.[5]

The argument presupposes that there are only two options: We can love America (uncritically) or we can emigrate. But there seem to be other possibilities. For example, surely one can be critical of one's country insofar as it has fallen short of its own ideals and yet still be devoted to it. And perhaps it is morally permissible for one to respect one's country (i.e., respect its laws and traditions) without loving it (assuming that loving one's country involves being especially fond of it).

Notice that the fallacy of false dilemma does not involve an invalid inference. Given that I have just two options ("love it" or "leave it"), and given that one of these ("leave it") is ruled out, I must take the other. Thus, as in the case of begging the question, the fallacy of false dilemma consists in assuming something without appropriate warrant or justification. In the case of a false dilemma, the arguer assumes that a certain list of alternatives is complete when it isn't. Here is a second example:

**47.** I do not know whether God's existence can be proven, but I do know that each person must be either a theist or an atheist. And by your own admission, you're no theist. Therefore, you must be an atheist.

This argument ignores or overlooks the possibility of agnosticism. While the theist believes that God exists and the atheist believes that God does not exist, the agnostic suspends judgment or remains neutral as regards the proposition that God exists. That is, the agnostic is not confident that this proposition is true, but he or she is not confident that it is false, either. The agnostic's mental state is a philosophical shrug of the shoulders, generally based on the principle that *one's confidence in a proposition should be proportional to the evidence for it*, and, therefore, when the evidence doesn't settle a matter, belief is inappropriate. In any case, since people often suspend judgment on an issue when they feel they have inadequate evidence, the agnostic's attitude is at least a possible one.

---

### False Dilemma

Using a premise that unjustifiably reduces
the number of alternatives to be considered

---

We can't identify a false dilemma unless we can specify at least one alternative that has been ignored. This is not always easy. Consider the following example:

48. Either your reasoning in any given case is based on an assumption or you have no place to start in your reasoning. If your reasoning is based on an assumption, then your conclusions are no more certain than a mere assumption. And if your conclusions are no more certain than a mere assumption, you do not gain knowledge by reasoning. Of course, if you have no place to start in your reasoning, then you are unable to make any inferences, and hence (once again) you do not gain knowledge by reasoning. Therefore, you do not gain knowledge by reasoning.

A chain of inferences has to start somewhere. And it seems that one cannot always defend one's premises with further arguments. Apparently, then, some of one's premises will be unsupported by further statements. Let us call these "first premises." Do first premises have the status of mere assumptions? If so, it would appear that all our reasoning is based on mere assumptions, in which case our reasoning never yields knowledge.

Many philosophers think there is a class of statements that do not *need* to be supported by further statements in order to be known or well grounded. But how do such statements differ from mere assumptions? How can a statement be known, warranted, or well grounded without being based on further statements? Here, some philosophers have called attention to allegedly self-evident statements, such as "No circles are squares." These are not *mere assumptions*, they claim, because to understand the statements is to see that they are true. Other philosophers have called attention to observation statements, such as "I see a piece of paper now." These are not mere assumptions, it is claimed, because they are somehow grounded in our sensory experience. But other philosophers have expressed doubts about the attempt to identify a privileged class of first premises. These philosophers are skeptical about the categories of self-evident statements and observation statements. The point here is simply that it takes philosophical creativity to explain how a first premise can be more than a mere assumption. Thus, it sometimes takes both creativity and hard intellectual work to make the case that a false dilemma fallacy has been committed.

## 13. Appeal to Unreliable Authority (Ad Verecundiam *Fallacy*)

The *appeal to unreliable authority* (or *ad verecundiam* fallacy) is an appeal to an authority *when the reliability of the authority may be reasonably doubted.* (Ad *verecundiam* is Latin for "appeal to authority.") A reliable authority is one who can be counted on, for the most part, to provide correct information in a given area. When an appeal to unreliable authority is made, the arguer assumes—*without sufficient warrant*—that the authority in question is reliable.

It is important to keep in mind that an appeal to *reliable* authority is generally appropriate. For example, when we cite encyclopedias, dictionaries, textbooks, or maps, we make an appeal to the authority of experts. This makes perfectly good sense as long as we are appealing to authorities whose reliability is not in doubt. However, when there is legitimate doubt about whether an authority is reliable, then the appeal to authority is fallacious.

*Ad verecundiam* fallacies are common in advertising when celebrities who lack the relevant expertise endorse products. For example:

> 49. Mike "Monster" Malone, left tackle for the Seattle Sea Lions, says that Chocolate Zonkers are a nutritional breakfast cereal. So, Chocolate Zonkers are a nutritional breakfast cereal.

Malone may be a fine athlete, but we need to know whether he is an expert in nutrition, and the argument leaves us in doubt on that point. Thus, an *ad verecundiam* fallacy has occurred.

A more subtle appeal to unreliable authority occurs when a well-known expert in one field is cited as an expert in another field even though he or she lacks expertise in it. This form of the fallacy is especially subtle if the two fields are related (at least in the minds of the audience). For example:

> 50. Professor Bloggs, the well-known astronomer, has done extensive research on distant galaxies. He points out that human bodies are composed of atoms that were once part of distant stars. According to Bloggs, this gives human life a sense of drama and significance equal to that inherent in the world's great mythologies and theologies. Thus, Bloggs corrects the common error of supposing that materialism reduces the drama or significance of human life.

Even if it *is* an error to suppose that materialism reduces the drama or significance of human life, the reasoning in argument (50) is flawed. An astronomer is an expert in the science of the stars and other heavenly bodies. So, as an astronomer, Professor Bloggs is in a position to tell us that the atoms in our bodies once belonged to the stars. But his authority about these matters does not automatically transfer to such philosophical topics as the comparative merits of mythologies, theologies, or worldviews in general. Expertise in one area doesn't necessarily "rub off" on another.

Argument (50) also reminds us of another point to keep in mind when evaluating an appeal to authority—namely, that the appeal to authorities in matters of controversy is often problematic. After all, in such matters, the authorities themselves often disagree. And when this occurs, if we have no good reason to suppose that one authority is more likely to be correct than another, then the appeal to authority should be unconvincing.

---

### Appeal to Unreliable Authority (*Ad Verecundiam* Fallacy)

Appealing to an authority when the reliability of the authority may reasonably be doubted (The arguer assumes, without sufficient warrant, that the authority in question is reliable.)

## 14. False Cause Fallacy

The *false cause* fallacy occurs when one possible cause of a phenomenon is assumed to be a (or the) cause *although reasons are lacking for excluding other possible causes*. This fallacy comes in various forms. Perhaps the most common form is called in Latin *post hoc, ergo propter hoc*, which means "after this, therefore because of this." This form of the false cause fallacy occurs whenever an arguer illegitimately assumes that because event X preceded event Y, X caused Y. Here is an example:

> 51. Since I came into office 2 years ago, the rate of violent crime has decreased significantly. So, it is clear that the longer prison sentences we recommended are working.

The longer prison sentences may be a causal factor, of course, but the mere fact that the longer sentences preceded the decrease in violent crime does not prove this. Many other possible causal factors need to be considered. For example, have economic conditions improved? Are more jobs available? Have the demographics of the area changed so that the population of young men (statistically the group mostly likely to commit violent crimes) is smaller relative to the population as a whole? Has there been an increase in the number of police officers on patrol?

Consider another example of the false cause fallacy:

> 52. Since sex education has become common, we've had a marked increase in promiscuity. So, sex education causes promiscuity.

Here, the arguer fails in two ways: (a) by ignoring other possible causal factors and (b) by failing to explain the alleged linkage between sex education and promiscuity. Regarding (a), it may be that promiscuity actually results from a third factor, such as the breakdown of the broadly Protestant sexual code that historically typified American attitudes. (This breakdown seems to have occurred gradually during the first half of the 20th century and then to have accelerated rapidly during the 1960s and 1970s.) Regarding (b), the arguer ignores the possibility that the causation may go *from* the phenomenon of promiscuity *to* sex education rather than vice versa. But surely the reason many people advocate sex education is that they are concerned about the increase in sexual activity among young people and seek to mitigate its negative consequences. So, it may be that promiscuity gives rise to sex education rather than vice versa. Again, the main point is that we cannot rightly assume that sex education causes promiscuity merely on the grounds that it precedes an increase in promiscuity.

Not all false cause fallacies involve the unwarranted assumption that if X precedes Y, then X causes Y. For instance:

53. The best professional athletes receive big salaries. Therefore, in order to guarantee that Smith will become one of the best professional athletes, we should give him a big salary.

Here the arguer assumes—without sufficient warrant—that if big salaries and outstanding athletic performance are correlated, the former causes the latter. But surely the causal relation goes in the reverse direction: It is successful athletic performance (in conjunction with the popular demand for spectator sports) that leads to big salaries for some athletes. Obviously, one cannot turn a mediocre athlete into a star simply by paying him a big salary.

Another version of the false cause fallacy occurs when many causes are (or may well be) operative but one of them is illegitimately assumed to be the sole cause:

54. The scores on standardized tests have been dropping for several decades. What accounts for this? Well, during these same decades, the average time a child spends watching TV (per day) has increased. So, the cause is obvious: Kids are watching too much TV when they need to be reading instead.

The increase in time spent watching TV is a likely contributor to a drop in scores on such standardized tests as the SAT. But insufficient evidence is provided for the conclusion that the time spent watching TV is the *sole* cause. Other factors may be at work, such as a decrease in parental involvement or deficiencies in the public school system.

---

### False Cause Fallacy

Occurs when one possible cause of a phenomenon
is assumed to be a (or the) cause *although reasons
are lacking for excluding other possible causes*

---

One special variety of the false cause fallacy is the *slippery slope* fallacy. This fallacy occurs when the arguer assumes that a chain reaction will occur but there is insufficient evidence that one (or more) events in the chain will cause the others. The chain of causes is supposedly like a steep slope—if you take one step on the slope, you'll slide all the way down. And since you don't want to slide all the way down, don't take the first step. Here is an example:

55. Never buy a lottery ticket. People who buy lottery tickets soon find that they want to gamble on horses. Next, they develop a strong urge to go to Las Vegas and bet their life savings in the casinos. The addiction to gambling gradually ruins their family life. Eventually, they die, homeless and lonely.

The links in this alleged causal chain clearly are weak. This is not to say that gambling is a risk-free practice. It is only to say that, logically speaking, when causal connections are claimed, there needs to be sufficient evidence that the connections are genuine. And to claim that buying a lottery ticket will cause one to die homeless and lonely is plainly to make a claim that is insufficiently supported by the evidence.

Slippery slope fallacies often play on our deepest fears. During the Vietnam War, it was frequently claimed that if Vietnam fell to communism, a chain reaction would occur, with the result that many countries would come under communist rule. From a historical perspective, it seems apparent that there was never any solid evidence that such a chain reaction would have occurred. Nevertheless, many Americans feared that it would. Thus, the slippery slope fallacy was persuasive because it played on people's fears.

Therapists sometimes call the slippery slope fallacy "catastrophizing." For example, a person's fears may lead him to think that a relatively minor incident will lead to utter catastrophe:

> 56. I told a joke at the party. It flopped. So, everyone there thought I was a loser. So, I'll never be invited again. In fact, if word gets out, I won't be invited anywhere. And I'm sure they're all talking about my stupid joke. So, I've completely ruined my chances for a decent social life. There's nothing left for me now but years of loneliness and misery. How I wish I'd never told that joke!

Although this example is extreme, it is a common human tendency to make rash assumptions about causal chains. The slippery slope fallacy is alive and well in the human heart.

In closing our discussion of the false cause fallacy, it may be helpful to note that in the English language there are many different ways to indicate a causal connection. For example, *depending on the context*, the following words and phrases may express a causal claim:

| | | |
|---|---|---|
| A produces B | A makes B | A leads to B |
| A creates B | A accounts for B | A brings about B |
| A generates B | A determines B | A is the source of B |
| A results in B | A is the origin of B | A gives birth to B |
| A gives rise to B | A brings B to pass | B occurs by A's influence |

The above list is by no means exhaustive. The key point to bear in mind is this: Since causal-claims can be expressed in many different ways in English, causal fallacies can occur when the word "cause" does not appear.

## 15. Complex Question

The fallacy of *complex question* consists in this: *asking a question that illegitimately presupposes some conclusion alluded to in the question.* Here's a classic example:

57. Have you stopped beating your wife?

If the respondent answers "Yes," he admits that he has beaten his wife in the past. If he answers "No," he seems to be admitting that he has beaten his wife in the past and that he continues to do so. To expose a fallacy of complex question, one must call into question what it presupposes. For instance, in this case, the response might be along these lines: "To put it mildly, your question is misleading; I have never beaten my wife."

It is important to notice that virtually any question has one or more presuppositions. Consider the following example:

58. Who is the governor of Ohio?

Question (58) presupposes that Ohio has a governor, but there is nothing illegitimate about this presupposition. Presuppositions are illegitimate when they are unwarranted by the evidence (and hence open to reasonable doubt).

In many cases, a fallacy of complex question involves two questions, the presupposition being that a single answer will satisfy both:

59. Will you please be kind and loan me $100?

Of course, the assumption here is that being kind involves lending the money. Again, an effective response will involve isolating the unwarranted presupposition and challenging it; for instance, "Being kind is one thing, lending the money is another. Let's not confuse the two."

---

### Fallacy of Complex Question

Asking a question that illegitimately presupposes
some conclusion alluded to in the question

---

Note that a complex question is not the same thing as a *leading* question. A leading question strongly suggests an answer the questioner wants to elicit, but a leading question need not involve an unwarranted assumption. For example, consider the following courtroom exchange:

*Attorney:* Is it true that on the afternoon of February 4 you saw the defendant enter the Starbucks Coffee Shop at the corner of Boston and Queen Anne Streets?

*Witness:* Yes.

*Attorney:* And is it true that you saw the defendant reach into his coat pocket and pull out a knife?

*Witness:* Yes.

*Attorney:* Did the knife have serrated edge?

*Witness:* Yes.

> *Attorney:*  Did the defendant point the knife at a man standing behind the cash register and say, "Open the cash register or die"?
>
> *Witness:*  Yes.

In asking such questions, the attorney may not be making any unwarranted assumptions. But a more open-ended question, such as, "Would you please describe what you saw on the afternoon of February 4?" would give the witness a chance to describe the events in his or her own words and would thus lessen the likelihood that the witness will simply provide coached answers.

Which of the following are complex questions?

60. Who is the King of France?

61. What time is it now?

62. Why is math so boring? Probably because it's so abstract.

Question (60) is complex because it illegitimately presupposes that France has a King. Question (62) is complex because it involves the unwarranted assumption that mathematics is very boring—an assumption that would certainly be rejected by anyone with a genuine interest in mathematics. Question (61) is not complex; it presupposes that there is some way to tell time and that "now" is a time, but these presuppositions are surely warranted.

---

### Summary of Fallacies Involving Unwarranted Assumptions

When these fallacies are committed, the arguer makes an illegitimate or unjustified assumption.

11. **Begging the Question** (or *petitio principii*)
    Assuming the point to be proved. The premises are similar in content to the conclusion *but not better known* than the conclusion.

12. **False Dilemma**
    Using a premise that unjustifiably reduces the number of alternatives to be considered

13. **Appeal to Unreliable Authority** (or *ad verecundiam* fallacy)
    Appealing to an authority when the reliability of the authority may reasonably be doubted. (The arguer assumes, without sufficient warrant, that the authority in question is reliable.)

14. **False Cause Fallacy**
    Illegitimately assuming that one possible cause of a phenomenon is a (or the) cause *although reasons are lacking for excluding other possible causes*

15. **Fallacy of Complex Question**
    Asking a question that illegitimately presupposes some conclusion alluded to in the question

The following exercises will give you an opportunity to apply the concepts introduced in this section.

## ◆ Exercise 4.3

**Part A:** Identifying Fallacies    Most of the following passages (but not all) exemplify fallacies. Many of the fallacies are fallacies involving unwarranted assumptions, but some are fallacies introduced in previous sections of this chapter. In some cases, a single passage exemplifies two or more fallacies. Identify all the fallacies that appear. In the case of fallacies involving an unwarranted assumption, identify the unwarranted assumption. If a passage does not contain a fallacy, simply write "not a fallacy."

* 1. In a recent speech, the president of General Motors asserted that our country has drifted dangerously away from its religious and ethical moorings. In light of this pronouncement, the cheery optimism of the liberals is no longer reasonable.

  2. Every American is either a Republican or a Democrat. Dr. Porter is an American, but she is not a Republican. So, she must be a Democrat.

  3. On Monday, Bill drank scotch and soda and noticed that he got drunk. On Tuesday, Bill drank whiskey and soda and noticed that he got drunk. On Wednesday, Bill drank bourbon and soda and noticed that he got drunk. Bill concluded that soda causes drunkenness. —Adapted from Wesley Salmon, *Logic*, 3rd ed. (Englewood Cliffs, NJ: Prentice-Hall, 1984), p. 112

* 4. If smoking is not harmful, then it is not wrong. And the tobacco companies say that smoking is not harmful. Therefore, smoking is not wrong.

  5. Sleeping pills work because they cause people to go to sleep.

  6. Left-turn signals frequently occur just before an automobile turns left. Right-turn signals frequently occur just before an automobile turns right. Consequently, turn signals cause automobiles to turn.

* 7. Either men are superior to women, or women are superior to men. Men are not superior to women. Hence, women are superior to men.

  8. Leonardo da Vinci's paintings are immoral if they incite rape. And the Reverend Posner states that da Vinci's paintings incite rape. Hence, da Vinci's paintings are immoral.

  9. Who's the fairest of them all, Daryl Hannah or Helen Hunt?

* 10. Obviously, humans have free will, since they have the power to make choices.

  11. Keegan is a reliable authority on military history. Keegan says that it was morally wrong for the Americans to fight in World War I. Hence, it was morally wrong for the Americans to fight in World War I.

  12. Day always follows night. The two are perfectly correlated. Therefore, night causes day.

* **13.** Last night we went to see *Hamlet*. The play was excellent since each scene was excellent. Plus, everybody who is anybody is raving about the play. I mean, the play was just excellent because it was really superb!

  **14.** Either God created everything (including human beings) in 6 days, or else human life evolved gradually out of lower life forms over a very long period of time apart from any divine activity. But you are not a religious fanatic, so you know about fossils. And hence, you know that human life evolved gradually out of lower life forms over a very long period of time. Thus, God did not create everything in 6 days. I mean, I hate to break the news, but you are just about the last person on Earth who believes that humans were created by God.

  **15.** Suicide is wrong for many reasons. First, because it involves killing. And killing is wrong because it is wrong to take a life. Second, suicide is wrong because it deeply wounds one's family and friends. And that is not cool— not cool at all. Third, suicide is the coward's way out. It's for weaklings who collapse the first time they run into a little adversity.

* **16.** Why was Warren G. Harding the best American president of the first half of the 20th century?

  **17.** We could get control of the crime problem in the United States if we would just punish criminals harshly. In Saudi Arabia, for example, thieves get their hands chopped off. Murderers are immediately put to death. And the rate of crime in Saudi Arabia is much lower than the rate of crime in the United States. Therefore, harsh punishments would greatly reduce the rate of crime in the United States.

  **18.** Time is composed of moments. Moments have no duration. Therefore, time has no duration. This rather surprising thesis is further supported by the following considerations: Time is illusory because time seems real but isn't real. Furthermore, down through the ages, the best and brightest people have always thought time was illusory.

* **19.** Without the discoveries of the great physicist Albert Einstein, the atomic bomb could not have been invented. And Einstein said that it was immoral for America to drop the atomic bomb on Hiroshima. Therefore, it was immoral for America to drop the atomic bomb on Hiroshima.

  **20.** The largest slave revolt in U.S. history was one that occurred near New Orleans in 1811. Four or five hundred slaves were involved, lightly armed with cane knives, axes, and clubs. They wounded a plantation owner and killed his son. The revolt was put down by the U.S. Army, which attacked the slaves, killing 66 of them. This is all true, for I read about it in Howard Zinn's *A People's History of the United States* (New York: HarperCollins, 1995). And Dr. Zinn is a well-known historian.

  **21.** What is the capital of Oregon?

* **22.** Folk dancing is bad because it leads to ballroom dancing, which in turn leads to modern dancing. And modern dancing leads to promiscuity, which causes a total breakdown in the moral fabric of a country and hence a lapse into primitive savagery.

23. Scientists have shown that a person loses a very small but measurable amount of weight at the time of death. This weight loss is probably due to the soul's leaving the body at that time. What else could account for this phenomenon? Here we have unexpected scientific evidence for the existence of an immaterial soul.

24. Violent crime has been on the increase for the past two decades. The quantity of violent movies has also increased during this time. Therefore, in all likelihood, the cause of the increase in violent crime is the increase in the quantity of violent movies.

* 25. I have worn these socks to the last five baseball games. Each time, I've gotten a base hit. So, these are my lucky socks. I play better when I wear them.

26. Why is California the best place to live? Well, of course, it's very beautiful. And there are many job opportunities. But most important of all, California is a very progressive state in every way—so many important new trends begin there!

27. I warned those boys not to stand on Prince Valdinsky's grave. He was murdered, you know. And when he was being buried, his mother put a curse on anyone who showed disrespect for his grave. I was there—it was a very eerie thing to watch. Anyway, those boys wouldn't listen, and now look at them, all broken up from that automobile crash. I tell you, that curse worked!

* 28. Why is murder wrong? Because it takes away everything the victim has and everything he or she will ever have, including all the interesting experiences, fulfilling activities, and rewarding personal relationships.

29. The will states that the painting of a beautiful woman in the storage bin shall be given to the brother of the deceased. But this is not a painting of a beautiful woman in a storage bin. It is a painting of a beautiful woman walking across a field. Therefore, this painting does not belong to the brother of the deceased. Yes, I realize that the brother *thinks* the painting is his by right, but his mind is clouded by greed, and so his arguments are without force.

30. Either you approve of legalizing drugs or you disapprove. You can't have it both ways. Those who want to legalize drugs claim that we are losing the war on drugs. Indeed, they claim that we cannot win that war—the demand for drugs is high, and when demand is high, supply is inevitable. But we must not be taken in by this pseudo-reasoning. If we legalize drugs, they will be cheaper and easier to obtain. If drugs are cheaper and easier to obtain, more and more people will use drugs. As more people use drugs, the rate of absenteeism and work-related injuries will increase, productivity in the workplace will decline, and schools will be less effective in preparing students for the workforce. Thus, the economy will lose momentum and eventually collapse. Goodbye, America!

**Part B:** Identifying Fallacies   Most of the following passages (but not all) exemplify fallacies. Many of the fallacies are fallacies involving unwarranted assumptions, but some are fallacies introduced in previous sections of this chapter. In some cases, a single passage exemplifies two or more fallacies. Identify all the fallacies that appear. In the case of fallacies involving an unwarranted assumption, identify the unwarranted assumption. If a passage does not contain a fallacy, simply write "not a fallacy."

* **1.** Would you please be a good boy and eat your spinach?

    **2.** Please don't tell me you think that human vegetables should be kept on respirators! After all, brain-dead humans are already dead. We know this because they are not alive.

    **3.** Here's how to win the lottery: Consult an astrologer. How do I know this? Well, I was watching a TV program recently, and there was an interview with this very intelligent man who said that astrology is based on scientific principles. So, astrology is based on science. Furthermore, last week I took the advice of an astrologer who gave me a number based on my astrological sign. Using the number, I won the lottery. So, obviously, astrology works on things like the lottery.

* **4.** When it comes to criminal punishment, one must favor either rehabilitation or deterrence. The rehabilitationists think criminals are sick and need treatment. The deterrence crowd wants harsh punishments that will put a stop to crime. Since it is just silly to suppose that every shoplifter or car thief is mentally ill, the rehabilitationists are mistaken. Hence, the deterrence view is correct. And by the way, here's another way to see the same point: Rehabilitationists hold that even the most hardened criminals can be cured in a few sessions with a psychotherapist. But hardened criminals cannot be cured so easily! Once again, then, we see that rehabilitationists are mistaken.

    **5.** How do we know that there is life in other galaxies? Actually, that's not a difficult question. It's simply a matter of probabilities. With so many millions of planets out there, it's overwhelmingly likely that life has evolved on some of them, just as it has here on Earth.

    **6.** I've heard that St. Andrew's Episcopal Church is very wealthy. You are a member of St. Andrew's, so you must be wealthy. Anyway, I can tell you're wealthy because you have a lot of money.

* **7.** My psychology professor says that religious experience is generated out of the deep human need for a father figure, not by an encounter with an actual deity. So, religious experience is not really an experience of God.

    **8.** Surely Anthony loves me. For he told me he loves me, and he wouldn't lie to someone he loves.

    **9.** That young man was just fine until he read Kierkegaard's *Fear and Trembling*. It wasn't but a week or so later that he began to walk in his sleep and to emit those awful moans. Therefore, *Fear and Trembling* is a dangerous book.

* **10.** How can anyone go on living in a world that contains 10 times as much misery as happiness?

    **11.** You either hate parties or you love them. So, since you say you don't hate parties, you must love them.

12. Some people don't believe the Bible, but I find that puzzling. Why would anyone not believe what God has said? After all, God is all-knowing and perfectly good, so God knows everything, and God would never lie.

\* **13.** My sociology professor says that monogamy is an unjust form of social organization. Therefore, monogamy is an unjust form of social organization.

14. According to Lillian Roxon's *Rock Encyclopedia*, it was an English band called the Zombies that came out with the hit record "She's Not There" in 1965. So, while you say "She's Not There" was by the Beatles, it was really by the Zombies.

15. Before television came along, we didn't have much of a problem with illegal drugs. But people learn about drugs on TV, and then they want the drugs. So, TV is ruining this country.

\* **16.** I was there, I tell you. I stood within 10 feet of the man. Either I was hallucinating, or he levitated. And I wasn't hallucinating. Therefore, he levitated.

17. According to the *Encyclopedia Britannica*, Mary Cassatt, who is often considered America's greatest woman painter, was born in 1844 and died in 1926. So, Cassatt lived from 1844 till 1926.

18. When it comes to morality, a person is either a cultural relativist or a dogmatist. Since you won't allow that infanticide is right for the Eskimos if they approve of it, you obviously aren't a cultural relativist. So, you must be a dogmatist.

\* **19.** We never lost a war prior to Vietnam. What had changed? Well, I'll tell you: The generation that went off to fight in the Vietnam War was the first generation in this country to grow up on rock music. It was rock music that brought about our downfall.

20. Either nonhuman animals are robots, or they have thoughts and feelings just like humans have. Nonhuman animals are not robots. Hence, they have thoughts and feelings just like humans have.

21. Religion is the opiate of the people. Therefore, religion is like a drug that can be used to make people forget or ignore the miserable conditions they live in.

\* **22.** Logic varies as languages vary. For logic is based on grammar. My chemistry professor said so. And any intelligent person will agree that different languages have different grammars. But if logic varies as languages vary, then logic is relative to cultures. Consequently, logic is relative to cultures.

23. People are either good or evil. And Doris is not good. Therefore, she is evil.

24. Would you please be a gentleman and refrain from talking politics?

\* **25.** Either you believe that the doctrine of reincarnation is true, or you believe that it is false. Clearly, you do not believe that the doctrine of reincarnation is true. Accordingly, you must believe that it is false.

26. Why do all philosophical problems turn out, in the final analysis, just to be a question of how to define terms?

27. You should stop reading your horoscope. Why? First, because reading your horoscope is a waste of time. After all, you could be reading great literature instead. Second, people will think you are superstitious if you read your horoscope. Third, you should quit reading your horoscope because horo-

scopes are for idiots. Fourth, you don't want to turn out like that weird guy at work, Bob Crombie. And Bob reads horoscopes! So, obviously, horoscopes produce weirdness. Hence, you've got to stop reading them.

\* **28.** When you get down to it, philosophers are just logic choppers who sit around trying to put reality into little boxes made of words. So, the philosophical arguments against time travel prove nothing. Hence, time travel is possible. Anyway, I know it's possible because it can happen. And besides, just about everyone *but* philosophers thinks that time travel is possible, so once again, time travel probably is possible.

**29.** Most Americans insist that terrorism is always wrong, but they are mistaken. Terrorism, after all, is simply the use of violence to further political ends. And no country on the face of the earth employs more violence to further its political ends than America does. So, Americans are in no position to condemn terrorism. Besides, one person's terrorist is another's freedom fighter. Why can't Americans see that their own revolutionary war heroes were all terrorists?

**30.** How do I know that mantras work? Consider this: Last week I said a mantra on Tuesday and on Friday. And guess what? Those days really went well for me. Furthermore, mantras work because they are effective. Finally, mantras are recommended by many great movie stars.

## Notes

1. *The Guide to American Law: Everyone's Legal Encyclopedia*, Vol. 4 (New York: West, 1984), p. 352.
2. Anthony Flew, A *Dictionary of Philosophy*, rev. 2nd ed. (New York: St. Martin's Press, 1979), p. 104. I have slightly altered the punctuation.
3. This example is borrowed from Robert Baum, *Logic*, 3rd ed. (New York: Holt, Rinehart and Winston, 1989), p. 485.
4. Not everyone agrees. See, for example, John Lamont, "Believing That God Exists Because the Bible Says So," *Faith and Philosophy* (Journal of the Society of Christian Philosophers) 13(1) (1966): 121–124.
5. I owe this example to Anthony Weston, A *Rulebook for Arguments* (Indianapolis, IN: Hackett, 1987), p. 88. I have elaborated the example somewhat.

*Chapter 5*

# Categorical Logic: Statements

In this chapter and the next, we will explore a traditional approach to logic that was first developed by Aristotle (384–322 B.C.E.). This approach to logic focuses on categorical arguments, that is, arguments whose validity depends centrally on the relationships among classes, sets, or categories. Historically, this approach to logic has been of tremendous importance in Western culture. It was the dominant approach to logic in the medieval and early modern periods and is still quite useful today.

## 5.1 Standard Forms of Categorical Statements

To understand categorical arguments, we must first understand categorical statements. A **categorical statement** is a statement that relates two classes or categories. A class is a collection or set of things. Here are some examples of categorical statements:

1. All ducks are animals.
2. No humans are horses.
3. Some soldiers are cowards.
4. Some subatomic particles are not electrons.

Statement (1) says that every member of the class of ducks is a member of the class of animals. Statement (2) says that the class of humans and the class of horses have no members in common. Statement (3) says that some (i.e., at least one) member of the class of soldiers is a member of the class of cowards. And statement (4) says that some (i.e., at least one) member of the class of subatomic particles is not a member of the class of electrons.

There are four different **standard forms** of categorical statements, traditionally labeled **A**, **E**, **I**, and **O**. This labeling stems from the medieval period when logic was studied in Latin. The letters are vowels from the Latin words *affirmo* and *nego*, meaning (respectively) "I affirm" and "I deny." To be in standard form, the elements of a categorical statement must appear in the following order:

1. quantifier (i.e., the word "all," "no," or "some")
2. subject term (i.e., a word or phrase that names a class or category)
3. copula ("are" or "are not")
4. predicate term (i.e., a word or phrase that names a class or category)

The four standard forms are as follows:

| Name | Form | Example |
|---|---|---|
| A | All S are P. | All trees are plants. |
| E | No S are P. | No plants are animals. |
| I | Some S are P. | Some trees are oaks. |
| O | Some S are not P. | Some trees are not oaks. |

The letter S stands for the subject term, and the letter P stands for the predicate term. For example, the word "trees" is the subject term in "All trees are plants," while the word "plant" is the predicate term. And in the statement "Some trees are not oaks," the word "trees" is the subject term, while the word "oaks" is the predicate term.

A term must denote (or refer to) a class or category; as such, a term is a noun or nounlike expression. Three brief comments may help clarify what counts as a term. First, it is important to realize that a term need not be a single word; indeed, it may be a rather long expression. For example, "All people who write best-selling novels are famous authors" is an **A** statement in standard form—the subject term is "people who write best-selling novels," and the predicate term is "famous authors." Second, note that a proper name is not a term, for a proper name denotes a specific individual rather than a class. Hence, "Some philosopher is Socrates" is not a standard-form categorical statement, since "Socrates" denotes a specific individual and not a class (i.e., collection of things). Third, adjectives are not terms. Thus, "All paintings are beautiful" is not in standard form because "beautiful," being an adjective, does not denote a class; however, "All paintings are beautiful things" is in standard form because "beautiful things" is a nounlike expression that denotes the class containing all the things that are beautiful.

To be in standard form, a statement must *strictly* possess one of the listed forms. For example, is "Every tree is a plant" an **A** statement in standard form? No. To put it into standard form, we must replace "Every" with "All," "is" with "are," "tree" with "trees," and so on, to arrive at "All trees are plants." We will discuss how to put statements into standard form shortly, but for now, note that the four forms are to be interpreted quite strictly.

## Quality and Quantity

Every categorical statement has a **quality**, affirmative or negative. If a statement affirms that one class is wholly or partially included in another class, then the statement's quality is *affirmative*. If a statement denies that one class is wholly or partially included in another, its quality is *negative*. Every categorical statement also has a **quantity**, universal or particular. *Universal* statements refer to all members of the class denoted by the subject term. *Particular* statements refer to only some members of the class denoted by the subject term.

An **A** statement ("All S are P") is a **universal affirmative** statement. A universal affirmative statement says that all members of class S are members of class P. Thus, "All wives are women" says that all members of the class of wives are also members of the class of women.

An **E** statement ("No S are P") is a **universal negative** statement. A universal negative statement says that no members of class S are members of class P. In other words, a universal negative says that classes S and P have no members in common. Thus, "No men are women" says that no members of the class of men are members of the class of women.

An **I** statement ("Some S are P") is a **particular affirmative** statement. A particular affirmative statement says that some members of class S are members of class P. Thus, "Some animals are carnivores" says that some members of the class of animals are also members of the class of carnivores. Here, it is important to note that for present purposes, the word "some" means "at least one." In ordinary English, "some" occasionally has the force of "some but not all." But this is not the meaning assigned to "some" in logic. It is especially important to bear in mind that "Some S are P" does not imply that "Some S are not P." (For example, "Some dogs are animals" does *not* imply that "Some dogs are not animals.")

An **O** statement ("Some S are not P") is a **particular negative** statement. A particular negative statement says that some members of class S are not members of class P. Thus, "Some mammals are not land animals" says that at least one member of the class of mammals is not a member of the class of land animals.

At this point we can sum up what has been said about categorical statements in the following table:

| Name | Form | Quantity | Quality |
|------|------|----------|---------|
| A | All S are P. | universal | affirmative |
| E | No S are P. | universal | negative |
| I | Some S are P. | particular | affirmative |
| O | Some S are not P. | particular | negative |

## Putting Categorical Statements into Standard Form

When categorical statements appear in ordinary English, they are often not in standard form. But the logical tools we will discuss here are designed to apply to statements in standard form. So, let us now consider some techniques for putting categorical statements into standard form.

First, as we have already noted, when a statement fails to be in standard form simply because its predicate is an adjective, we can add an appropriate noun. Thus, to put "All humans are rational" into standard form, we can write "All humans are rational animals" or "All humans are rational things."

Second, when the elements of a standard-form statement are all present but not in the right order, we merely rearrange the elements. Thus, to put "Rubies are all gems" into standard form, we simply write, "All rubies are gems."

Third, when a statement contains a verb other than "are," we can add "are" and shift the original verb into the predicate. For example, to put "All fish swim" into standard form, we can write, "All fish are swimmers." And to put "All criminals should be punished" into standard form, we may write, "All criminals are people who should be punished." Similarly, if the verb "to be" is in the past tense or future tense, we can add "are" and relocate the tensed verb in the predicate. Thus, to put "All workers were tired" into standard form, we may write, "All workers are people who were tired." And "No persons who confess will be prosecuted" may be rewritten as "No persons who confess are persons who will be prosecuted."

Fourth, each of the basic types of categorical statements has common stylistic variants. A **stylistic variant** of a categorical statement is just another way of saying the same thing. Let's first consider stylistic variants of **A** statements ("All S are P"). For example, each of the following is a stylistic variant of "All cats are mammals":

> Every cat is a mammal.
> Each cat is a mammal.
> Any cat is a mammal.
> If anything is a cat, then it is a mammal.
> Things are cats only if they are mammals.
> Only mammals are cats.

To put any of these statements into standard form, we simply write, "All cats are mammals."

Take special note of the word "only" in the preceding list. Be aware that "Only P are S" means "All S are P," but it does *not* mean "All P are S." For example, "Only mammals are cats" means "All cats are mammals" (which is true), but it does not mean "All mammals are cats" (which is false). By contrast, "Only cats are mammals" (which is false) means "All mammals are cats," but it does *not* mean "All cats are mammals" (which is true).

| *Summary of Stylistic Variants* | |
|---|---|
| **Universal Affirmative:**<br>**All S are P.** | **Universal Negative:**<br>**No S are P.** |
| Every S is a P.<br>Each S is a P.<br>Any S is a P.<br>If anything is an S, then it is a P.<br>Things are S only if they are P.<br>Only P are S. | Nothing that is an S is a P.<br>A thing is an S only if it is not a P.<br>If anything is an S, then it is not a P.<br>Nothing is an S unless it is not a P. |
| **Particular Affirmative:**<br>**Some S are P.** | **Particular Negative:**<br>**Some S are not P.** |
| There are S that are P.<br>At least one S is a P.<br>There exists an S that is a P.<br>Something is both an S and a P. | At least one S is not a P.<br>Not all S are P.<br>Not every S is a P.<br>Something is an S but not a P.<br>There is an S that is not a P. |

Next, consider stylistic variants of **E** statements ("No S are P"). For example, each of the following is a stylistic variant of "No whales are humans":

Nothing that is a whale is a human.
A thing is a whale only if it is not human.
If anything is a whale, then it is not a human.
Nothing is a whale unless it is not a human.

To put any of these into standard form, write, "No whales are humans."

Now, consider stylistic variants of **I** statements ("Some S are P"). For example, each of the following is a stylistic variant of "Some fish are sharks":

There are fish that are sharks.
At least one fish is a shark.
There exists a fish that is a shark.
Something is both a fish and a shark.

To put any of these into standard form, we simply write, "Some fish are sharks."

Finally, consider stylistic variants of O statements ("Some S are not P"). For example, each of the following is a stylistic variant of "Some fish are not sharks":

At least one fish is not a shark.
Not all fish are sharks.
Not every fish is a shark.
Something is a fish but not a shark.
There is a fish that is not a shark.

To put any of these into standard form, we simply write, "Some fish are not sharks."

Prior to the late 19th century, many logicians thought that all valid arguments could be analyzed in terms of classes or categories. From this perspective, the four standard forms of categorical statements are the basic elements of deductive logic. While logicians no longer hold that all valid arguments can be expressed in terms of categorical statements, many important logical insights still can be derived from the study of the logic of categorical statements.

The following exercise gives you some practice in working with categorical statements.

## ◆ Exercise 5.1

**Part A:** Categorical Statements   Name the form of each of the following categorical statements (**A, E, I,** or **O**). Identify the subject and predicate terms in each case. Then state the quantity (universal or particular) and quality (affirmative or negative).

* **1.** All hungry cannibals are dangerous people.

   **2.** No Ohioans are Texans.

   **3.** Some diamonds are not valuable objects.

* **4.** No green vegetables are minerals.

   **5.** Some outlaws are heroes.

   **6.** All equilateral triangles are geometrical figures.

* **7.** Some poems are not sonnets.

   **8.** No junk-food addicts are people with healthy diets.

   **9.** Some scoundrels are people who have been mistreated.

* **10.** Some numbers are not odd numbers.

   **11.** No pacifists are warmongers.

   **12.** All mammals are cats.

* **13.** Some celebrities are highly moral people.

   **14.** Some criminals are evil people.

   **15.** All people who intentionally direct violence at noncombatants for political purposes are terrorists.

* **16.** No odd numbers are even numbers.

17. Some bank robbers are well-trained professionals.

18. All unreported crimes are lamentable events.

* 19. Some art critics who like Picasso are snobs.

20. Some wealthy people are not nice people.

21. No sedimentary rocks are volcanic rocks.

* 22. All individuals who lie frequently are deeply unhappy people.

23. No losers are winners.

24. Some people who voted for Gore are intelligent people.

* 25. No photons are objects visible to the naked eye.

26. Some ancient gods are not morally perfect deities.

27. All people who worship money are lunatics.

* 28. Some literature professors who love Tolstoy are not good lecturers.

29. No created entities are things that have always existed.

30. No humans who are truly happy are people who never work.


**Part B: Standard Forms**   Which of the following are categorical statements in standard form? Which are not? (Remember, there are just four standard forms: "All S are P," "No S are P," "Some S are P," and "Some S are not P.") If a statement is already in standard form, simply name the form (**A, E, I,** or **O**) and indicate what the quantity and quality are. If a statement is not already in standard form, rewrite it so that it is; then name the form and indicate the quantity and quality.

* 1. No human being can swim across the Atlantic Ocean.

2. Every kangaroo is a marsupial.

3. At least one car is not a Ford.

* 4. At least one person is a nerd.

5. Nothing that is a spider is an insect.

6. All ancient Greeks worshiped Zeus.

* 7. There exists a poem that is not a sonnet.

8. There are saints who are reformed criminals.

9. Not all politicians are liars.

* 10. Some morally virtuous human beings are atheists.

11. Each patriotic American loves justice.

12. No Vikings were wimps.

* 13. Not every animal that can fly is a bird.

14. All people who have committed murder deserve death.

15. Some good-looking people are snobs.

* 16. Shawnees were all skillful trackers.

17. Nothing is a fool unless it is not a sage.

18. Masai warriors are all superb athletes.

* 19. No people who are unlucky are happy.

20. All college students who listened to Jimi Hendrix opposed the war in Vietnam.

21. Nothing is a snake unless it is not a mammal.

* 22. Only reptiles are lizards.

23. If anything is a chimpanzee, then it is not a fish.

24. Not every bright green stone is an emerald.

* 25. Things are birds only if they have feathers.

26. Only diamonds are gems.

27. World-class athletes all train vigorously.

* 28. Something is a painting but not a masterpiece.

29. Only physical objects are quarks.

30. The voters will all be disappointed.

* 31. There exists a mountain that is beautiful.

32. If anything is a slug, then it is not intelligent.

33. Soldiers who served under General George Patton all saw combat.

* 34. At least one tree is ugly.

35. Nothing that is an odd number is divisible by 2.

36. Things are beautiful only if they are pleasant to behold.

* 37. At least one animal is vicious.

38. If anything is a bad-tempered person, then it is a curmudgeon.

39. Only red things are scarlet.

* 40. If anything is a sibling that is female, then it is a sister.

41. Dogs over 15 years of age are all old.

42. A thing is a tragedy only if it is not a fortunate event.

* 43. Of the living survivors of the Nazi prison camps, some were tortured.

44. Hindus all believe in reincarnation.

45. No prisoners will be mistreated.

*  **46.** At least one soldier will be wounded.

   **47.** Whole numbers between 1 and 5 are in some cases even numbers.

   **48.** Of the living veterans of World War I, none were generals.

*  **49.** Not every person who chooses not to fight is a coward.

   **50.** There exists an animal that is a dog.

## 5.2 The Traditional Square of Opposition

We will now begin to discuss the logical relations between categorical state-ments. In this section and the next, we will focus on immediate inferences. An inference is said to be **immediate** when a conclusion is drawn from only one premise.

What are the logical relationships between standard-form categorical statements *having the same subject and predicate terms?* For example:

A   All dogs are collies.
E   No dogs are collies.
I   Some dogs are collies.
O   Some dogs are not collies.

Let us refer to categorical statements having the same subject term and the same predicate term as **corresponding statements**. Logicians in the Aristotelian tradi-tion offer the following theses regarding the logical relationships between corre-sponding statements.

First, corresponding **A** and **O** statements are contradictories. Two state-ments are **contradictories** if they cannot both be true and they cannot both be false. (In other words, if one is true, the other must be false; and if one is false, the other must be true.) For example, "All dogs are collies" contradicts "Some dogs are not collies." Therefore, given that all dogs are collies, we can immedi-ately conclude that it is false that some dogs are not collies. And given that some dogs are not collies, we can immediately conclude that not all dogs are collies.

Similarly, corresponding **E** and **I** statements are contradictories. For exam-ple, "No dogs are collies" contradicts "Some dogs are collies." Therefore, given that no dogs are collies, we can immediately conclude that it is false that some dogs are collies. And given that some dogs are collies, we can immediately con-clude that it is false that no dogs are collies.

Second, corresponding **A** and **E** statements are contraries. Two statements are **contraries** if they cannot both be true but they can both be false. (For instance, the following two statements are contraries: "The Taj Mahal is white all over" and "The Taj Mahal is blue all over." Although the Taj Mahal is, in fact, white, it could be painted, say, green, in which case both of these state-ments would be false.) For example, corresponding **A** and **E** statements such as

"All dogs are collies" and "No dogs are collies" are contraries. These statements can both be false if some (but not all) dogs are collies. But if one of these statements is true, the other must be false.

One exception to the Aristotelian view of contraries should be noted at this point, namely, the case in which **A** or **E** statements are necessary truths. A **necessary truth** is one that cannot be false under any possible circumstances, for example, "All triangles are three-sided figures" or "No triangles are circles." Clearly, if a statement is necessarily true, then it cannot be false; but two statements are contraries only if they can *both* be false. So, the Aristotelian thesis regarding contraries clearly does not hold in the special case in which an **A** or **E** statement is a necessary truth.

Third, corresponding **I** and **O** statements are subcontraries. Two statements are **subcontraries** if they cannot both be false but they can both be true. For example, "Some dogs are collies" and "Some dogs are not collies" are subcontraries.

One exception to the Aristotelian view of subcontraries should be noted at this point, namely, the case in which **I** or **O** statements are necessarily false. A statement is **necessarily false** if it cannot be true in any possible circumstances, for example, "Some circles are triangles" or "Some triangles are not three-sided figures." Clearly, if a statement is necessarily false, then it cannot be true, but two statements are subcontraries only if they both can be true. So, the Aristotelian thesis regarding subcontraries clearly does not hold in the special case in which an **I** or **O** statement is necessarily false.

Fourth, **A** statements logically imply their corresponding **I** statements. For example, the following argument is valid according to Aristotelians:

1. All ants are insects.
So, 2. Some ants are insects.

Similarly, **E** statements logically imply their corresponding **O** statements. For example, the following argument is valid according to Aristotelians:

1. No ants are antelopes.
So, 2. Some ants are not antelopes.

The logical relationship between a universal statement and its corresponding particular statement is called **subalternation**. The universal statement is called the **superaltern**, while the particular statement is called the **subaltern**. Thus, "All ants are insects" is a *superaltern* with "Some ants are insects" as its *subaltern*; and "No ants are antelopes" is a *superaltern* with "Some ants are not antelopes" as its *subaltern*. A *superaltern* implies its corresponding *subaltern*. This means that if the *superaltern* is true, the *subaltern* is true. But it also means that if the *subaltern* is false, then the *superaltern* is false (since any statement that implies a false statement is itself false). However, a *subaltern* does not imply its corresponding *superaltern* (e.g., "Some dogs are collies" does not imply "All dogs are collies").

All of these logical relationships can be pictured in a single diagram called the Traditional Square of Opposition, as shown here.

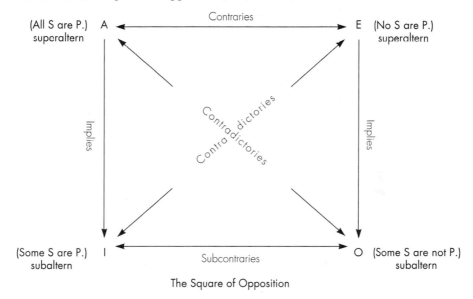

The Square of Opposition

The Traditional Square of Opposition forms a helpful picture of a number of important logical relationships between corresponding statements.

1. Suppose an **A** statement (All S are P) is true; then
   a. its corresponding **E** statement or contrary (No S are P) is false.
   b. its corresponding **I** statement or subaltern (Some S are P) is true.
   c. its corresponding **O** statement or contradictory (Some S are not P) is false.
2. Suppose an **E** statement (No S are P) is true; then
   a. its corresponding **A** statement or contrary (All S are P) is false.
   b. its corresponding **O** statement or subaltern (Some S are not P) is true.
   c. its corresponding **I** statement or contradictory (Some S are P) is false.

*Note:* When the truth or falsehood of one statement, X, logically implies *neither* the truth *nor* the falsehood of another statement, Y, let us say that the truth value of Y is *not guaranteed* by the truth value of X.

3. Suppose an **I** statement (Some S are P) is true; then
   a. its corresponding **E** statement or contradictory (No S are P) is false.
   b. the truth value of the corresponding **A** statement (All S are P) is not guaranteed.
   c. the truth value of the corresponding **O** statement (Some S are not P) is not guaranteed.

4. Suppose an **O** statement (Some S are not P) is true; then
   a. its corresponding **A** statement or contradictory (All S are P) is false.
   b. the truth value of the corresponding **E** statement (No S are P) is not guaranteed.
   c. the truth value of the corresponding **I** statement (Some S are P) is not guaranteed.

The following exercises provide you with an opportunity to deepen your understanding of the logical relationships embodied in the Traditional Square of Opposition.

## ◆ **Exercise 5.2**

**Part A:** Logical Relationships    Give the names of the logical relations that hold between the following pairs of corresponding categorical statements. (In the case of subalternation, indicate which statement is the superaltern and which is the subaltern, in the order in which they appear.) If the pair of statements does not exemplify any of the logical relations discussed in this section, simply write "None."

* 1. All roses are red flowers./No roses are red flowers.

2. All souls are immortal substances./Some souls are immortal substances.

3. Some people are jerks./Some people are not jerks.

* 4. No Apaches are Shawnees./Some Apaches are Shawnees.

5. No emeralds are plants./Some emeralds are not plants.

6. Some people who believe in ghosts are smart people./Some people who believe in ghosts are not smart people.

* 7. Some radical skeptics are profoundly miserable people./All radical skeptics are profoundly miserable people.

8. No truths are statements worth dying for./All truths are statements worth dying for.

9. All atoms are physical objects./Some atoms are not physical objects.

* 10. Some odd numbers are numbers that can be divided by 2 (without remainder)./Some odd numbers are not numbers that can be divided by 2 (without remainder).

11. Some gems are not amethysts./Some gems are amethysts.

12. All liars are harmful people./No liars are harmful people.

* 13. Some leaders are followers./Some leaders are not followers.

14. All positive whole numbers between 4 and 6 are odd numbers./No positive whole numbers between 4 and 6 are odd numbers.

15. Some dinosaurs are not rational animals./No dinosaurs are rational animals.

**Part B:** Immediate Inferences   Which of the following immediate inferences are valid according to Aristotelian logicians? Which are not valid?

* **1.** All cougars are carnivores. So, it is false that some cougars are not carnivores.

  **2.** All legal treaties are promises. Hence, it is not the case that no legal treaties are promises.

  **3.** Some mosquitoes are evil beings. Therefore, it is not true that no mosquitoes are evil beings.

* **4.** All self-absorbed people are boring people. It follows that some self-absorbed people are boring people.

  **5.** Some lawyers are shysters. So, all lawyers are shysters.

  **6.** No five-star generals are humble people. Consequently, it is false that some five-star generals are humble people.

* **7.** Some heavenly bodies are not planets. Thus, it is false that all heavenly bodies are planets.

  **8.** Some grapes are seedless fruit. So, some grapes are not seedless fruit.

  **9.** It is false that all geometrical figures are trapezoids. Accordingly, some geometrical figures are not trapezoids.

* **10.** No fossils are traces of the missing link. Therefore, it is not true that all fossils are traces of the missing link.

  **11.** No humans are morally perfect beings. It follows that some humans are not morally perfect beings.

  **12.** All boxers who admire Hurricane Carter are winners. So, some boxers who admire Hurricane Carter are winners.

* **13.** Some persons who have landed on the moon are not women. Hence, no persons who have landed on the moon are women.

  **14.** It is false that some grizzly bears are herbivores. It follows that some grizzly bears are not herbivores.

  **15.** It is false that some wealthy Americans are political radicals. Thus, no wealthy Americans are political radicals.

* **16.** It is false that all dinosaurs are animals that existed prior to the Cambrian explosion. Accordingly, some dinosaurs are not animals that existed prior to the Cambrian explosion.

  **17.** It is false that some Christians are not theists. Therefore, some Christians are theists.

  **18.** All bureaucrats are spies. So, some bureaucrats are spies.

* **19.** Some Senators are lovers of justice. It follows that some Senators are not lovers of justice.

  **20.** It is false that no astrologers are scientists. Consequently, some astrologers are scientists.

**Part C:** Generalizing   Recall that when the truth value of one statement X logically implies neither the truth nor the falsehood of another statement Y, we say the truth value of Y is *not guaranteed* by X.

* 1. Suppose an **A** statement is false. What can be logically inferred regarding the truth or falsehood of its corresponding **E, I,** and **O** statements?

  2. Suppose an **E** statement is false. What can be logically inferred regarding the truth or falsehood of its corresponding **A, I,** and **O** statements?

  3. Suppose an **I** statement is false. What can be logically inferred regarding the truth or falsehood of its corresponding **A, E,** and **O** statements?

* 4. Suppose an **O** statement is false. What can be logically inferred regarding the truth or falsehood of its corresponding **A, E,** and **I** statements.

**Part D:** Standard Form   Put the premise and conclusion of each of the following arguments into standard form. Then indicate whether each argument is valid.

* 1. If anything is a capitalist, then it is not a hero. So, at least one thing is a capitalist but not a hero.

  2. Only gods are immortal beings. Hence, there exist immortal beings that are gods.

  3. Every misguided moralist is a menace to society. Consequently, a thing is a menace to society only if it is a misguided moralist.

* 4. Things are positrons only if they are smaller than atoms. Therefore, not all positrons are smaller than an atom.

  5. If anything is a falsehood, then it is not beneficial. So, only beneficial things are falsehoods.

  6. There exists an athlete who can run the mile in under 4 minutes. Hence, not all athletes can run the mile in under 4 minutes.

* 7. Nothing is an acid unless it is not a base. Therefore, each acid is a base.

  8. Only acts that conform to the Ten Commandments are right acts. So, an act is right only if it does not conform to the Ten Commandments.

  9. Nothing that is a categorical argument is valid. Hence, not every categorical argument is valid.

* 10. Any person who is kept awake for over a week will go crazy. Thus, only persons who are kept awake for over a week will go crazy.

  11. A thing is a wicked act only if it is an act committed with malice aforethought. Therefore, at least one wicked act is an act committed with malice aforethought.

  12. Some people who defended slavery were plantation owners. Thus, not all persons who defended slavery were plantation owners.

* **13.** No person who invented the airplane died flying an airplane. It follows that only persons who died flying an airplane invented the airplane.

 **14.** Colonels are all authoritarian people. So, nothing that is a colonel is an authoritarian person.

 **15.** Only chemicals that turn blue litmus paper red are acids. Thus, there exists an acid that is a chemical that turns blue litmus paper red.

## 5.3  Further Immediate Inferences

In this section, we will discuss some important types of immediate inferences *beyond* those associated with the Traditional Square of Opposition. In particular, we will discuss conversion, obversion, and contraposition.

### Conversion

The **converse** of a standard-form categorical statement is formed simply by interchanging its subject and predicate terms. Here are four examples of statements together with their converses:

| Statement | Converse |
|---|---|
| A  All dogs are animals. | All animals are dogs. |
| E  No plants are animals. | No animals are plants. |
| I  Some plants are trees. | Some trees are plants. |
| O  Some plants are not trees. | Some trees are not plants. |

**Conversion** is the inference from a categorical statement to its converse. Conversion is valid for **E** and **I** statements. For example, both of the following arguments are valid:

 **5.** No plants are animals. So, no animals are plants.
 **6.** Some plants are trees. So, some trees are plants.

In fact, every **E** statement is logically equivalent to its converse. Two statements are **logically equivalent** if each validly implies the other. For example, "No plants are animals" implies (and is implied by) "No animals are plants." Similarly, every **I** statement is logically equivalent to its converse. For example, "Some plants are trees" implies (and is implied by) "Some trees are plants."

But, as regards **A** and **O** statements, conversion is not a valid form of argument. The following examples should suffice to indicate why:

 **7.** All dogs are animals. So, all animals are dogs.
 **8.** Some plants are not trees. So, some trees are not plants.

Both arguments move from a true premise to a false conclusion and hence are invalid.

However, logicians in the Aristotelian tradition have endorsed an inference called **conversion by limitation**. In conversion by limitation, we switch the subject and predicate terms of an **A** statement and change the quantity from universal to particular. Here is an example:

> 1. All seaweeds are plants.
> So, 2. Some plants are seaweeds.

The general pattern of the inference is as follows:

> 1. All S are P.
> So, 2. Some P are S.

To understand conversion by limitation, it may be helpful to note that we can move logically from "All S are P" to its subaltern "Some S are P," and then (since conversion is always valid for **I** statements) we can switch the subject and predicate terms to get "Some P are S." Thus, while *conversion* itself is not a valid argument form as applied to **A** statements, logicians in the Aristotelian tradition endorse conversion by limitation.

We can picture what has been said about conversion in the following table:

| Standard Form | Converse |
|---|---|
| **A** All S are P. | *All P are S. <br> *Converse by limitation:* Some P are S. |
| **E** No S are P. | No P are S. |
| **I** Some S are P. | Some P are S. |
| **O** Some S are not P. | *Some P are not S. |

The asterisk (*) indicates those cases in which the inference from the standard form statement to its converse is not a valid form of argument.

## Obversion

The concept of an obverse requires a bit of explanation. First, each class has a complement. The **complement** of a class X is the class containing all things that are not a member of X. For instance, the complement of the class of trees is the class containing all nontrees, that is, everything that is not a tree (horses, hawks, humans, hamburgers, and so on).

Second, each term has a term-complement. The **term-complement** is the word or phrase that denotes the class complement. For instance, the term-complement of "dogs" is "nondogs," which denotes the class containing everything that is not a dog. And the term-complement of "nondogs" is simply "dogs," which denotes the class containing everything that is not a nondog. (*Note:* Do not confuse term-complements with contrary terms. For instance, the term-complement of "winner" is not "loser" but "nonwinner," and the class of nonwinners includes players who tie, nonplayers, *and* losers.)

When a term consists of more than one word, care must be taken in forming the term-complement. For example, what is the term-complement of "wild dogs"? Is it, "non-wild dogs"? No. The term-complement must denote a class that includes *everything* outside the class denoted by the term. So, in this case the term-complement is "things that are not wild dogs," which denotes a class that includes both tame dogs and nondogs in general. (For example, it includes wild geese, since they are not wild dogs.) Similarly, the term-complement of "good gymnast" would not be "nongood gymnast" but "things that are not good gymnasts." And the class of *things that are not good gymnasts* includes not only all the mediocre and poor gymnasts but also all the nongymnasts (atoms, apples, airplanes, etc.).

The **obverse** of a statement is formed by (a) changing its quality (from affirmative to negative, or vice versa) and (b) replacing the predicate term with its term-complement. Here are four examples:

| | Statement | Obverse |
|---|---|---|
| **A** | All trees are plants. | No trees are nonplants. |
| **E** | No cats are trees. | All cats are nontrees. |
| **I** | Some trees are oaks. | Some trees are not nonoaks. |
| **O** | Some trees are not oaks. | Some trees are nonoaks. |

**Obversion** is the inference from a categorical statement to its obverse. Obversion is always valid. In fact, every standard-form categorical statement is logically equivalent to its obverse. For example, "No boxers are wimps" implies (and is implied by) "All boxers are nonwimps."

We can picture what has been said about obversion in the following table:

| | Standard Form | Obverse |
|---|---|---|
| **A** | All S are P. | No S are non-P. |
| **E** | No S are P. | All S are non-P. |
| **I** | Some S are P. | Some S are not non-P. |
| **O** | Some S are not P. | Some S are non-P. |

The inference from a standard-form categorical statement to its obverse is always valid, and vice versa.

## Contraposition

The **contrapositive** of a statement is formed by (a) replacing its subject term with the term-complement of its predicate term and (b) replacing the predicate term with the term-complement of its subject term. Here are four examples:

| Statement | Contrapositive |
|---|---|
| A   All cats are mammals. | All nonmammals are noncats. |
| E   No bats are elephants. | No nonelephants are nonbats. |
| I   Some plants are weeds. | Some nonweeds are nonplants. |
| O   Some plants are not weeds. | Some nonweeds are not nonplants. |

*Note:* In every case, we switch the subject and predicate terms, then replace each with its term-complement.

**Contraposition** is the inference from a statement to its contrapositive. Contraposition is valid for **A** and **O** statements. Thus, the following arguments are valid:

> 9. All rubies are stones. So, all nonstones are nonrubies.
>
> 10. Some trees are not elms. So, some nonelms are not nontrees.

It is interesting to note that these same results can be achieved by a sequence of obversions and conversions. For instance, consider the inference from an **A** statement to its contrapositive:

Step 1: All S are P.
Step 2: No S are non-P. [obverse of Step 1]
Step 3: No non-P are S. [converse of Step 2]
Step 4: All non-P are non-S. [obverse of Step 3]

*Note:* An **A** statement and its contrapositive are logically equivalent. Thus, "All collies are dogs" implies (and is implied by) "All nondogs are noncollies." Similarly, an **O** statement and its contrapositive are logically equivalent. Thus, "Some dogs are not collies" implies (and is implied by) "Some noncollies are not nondogs."

As regards **E** and **I** statements, contraposition is not a valid form of argument. For example, the following argument is invalid:

> 11. No dogs are trees. So, no nontrees are nondogs.

Argument (11) is plainly invalid. Its premise is true, but its conclusion is false. (Examples of nontrees include stones, steers, and stereoscopes; therefore, some nontrees are nondogs.) The following argument involves an inference from an **I** statement to its contrapositive and is also invalid:

> 12. Some animals are nondogs. So, some dogs are nonanimals.

Here, the premise is true. (The mere fact that there are cats is proof of that.) But the conclusion is false, so the argument is invalid.

While contraposition is not a valid form of argument as applied to **E** statements, Aristotelian logicians endorse an inference called **contraposition by limi-**

---

### Memory Device

1. OBVERSION is the **o**dd rule: It works on all four standard forms.

How about conversion and contraposition? Look at the *middle* vowels:

2. CONVERSION works on **E** and **I** statements.

3. CONTRAPOSITION works on **A** and **O** statements.

---

**tation**. To obtain the contrapositive *by limitation* of an **E** statement, we (a) replace the subject term with the term-complement of the predicate term, (b) replace the predicate term with the term-complement of the subject term, and (c) change the quantity from universal to particular. Here's an example:

1. No flags are rags.

So, 2. Some nonrags are not nonflags.

It is interesting to note that we can move from (1) to (2) by way of inferences previously discussed:

Step 1. No flags are rags.

Step 2. Some flags are not rags. [subaltern of Step 1]

Step 3. Some flags are nonrags. [obverse of Step 2]

Step 4. Some nonrags are flags. [converse of Step 3]

Step 5. Some nonrags are not nonflags. [obverse of Step 4]

The general pattern of inference in contraposition by limitation is as follows:

1. No S are P.

So, 2. Some non-P are not non-S.

We can sum up what has been said about contraposition in the following table:

| Standard Form | Contraposition |
|---|---|
| **A**  All S are P. | All non-P are non-S. |
| **E**  No S are P. | *No non-P are non-S.<br>*Contrapositive by limitation:* Some non-P are not non-S. |
| **I**  Some S are P. | *Some non-P are non-S. |
| **O**  Some S are not P. | Some non-P are not non-S. |

The asterisk (*) indicates those cases in which the inference from the standard-form statement to its contrapositive is not a valid form of argument.

The following exercises will test your understanding of immediate inferences.

## Summary Table: Conversion, Obversion, and Contraposition

| **Standard Form** | **Converse** |
|---|---|
| A All S are P. | *All P are S.<br>*Converse by limitation:* Some P are S. |
| E No S are P. | No P are S. |
| I Some S are P. | Some P are S. |
| O Some S are not P. | *Some P are not S. |

*Note:* An asterisk indicates that the form of argument is not valid.

| **Standard Form** | **Obverse** |
|---|---|
| A All S are P. | No S are non-P. |
| E No S are P. | All S are non-P. |
| I Some S are P. | Some S are not non-P. |
| O Some S are not P. | Some S are non-P. |

| **Standard Form** | **Contrapositive** |
|---|---|
| A All S are P. | All non-P are non-S. |
| E No S are P. | *No non-P are non-S.<br>*Contrapositive by limitation:*<br>Some non-P are not non-S. |
| I Some S are P. | *Some non-P are non-S. |
| O Some S are not P. | Some non-P are not non-S. |

*Note:* An asterisk indicates that the form of argument is not valid.

## ◆ Exercise 5.3

**Part A:** Term-Complements   Rewrite the following categorical statements, replacing each term with its term-complement.

* **1.** No brown bears are herbivores.
  **2.** All corporals are nongenerals.
  **3.** Some large birds are eagles.
* **4.** Some unhappy entities are not people.
  **5.** No things that are not humans are rational animals.
  **6.** All drinkers are nondrivers.
* **7.** No great women are men.
  **8.** Some athletes are poor losers.

   9. Some nonsmokers are not healthy people.
* 10. Some nonmetals are chemicals.

**Part B: Conversion**  Form the converse of each of the following statements. Then indicate whether conversion, as applied to the type of categorical statement in question, is a valid form of argument.

* **1.** No magnates are maggots.
   **2.** All miracles are acts of God.
   **3.** Some rectangles are nonsquares.
* **4.** Some explosives are not bombs.
   **5.** All demons are angels.
   **6.** No lovers are loners.
* **7.** All forgeries are copies.
   **8.** No roaches are coaches.
   **9.** Some Africans are not Kenyans.
* **10.** Some leopards are nontigers.

**Part C: Obversion**  Form the obverse of each of the following statements. (Recall that obversion always results in a valid inference.)

* **1.** All shar-peis are dogs.
   **2.** No platypi are vegetarians.
   **3.** Some prime ministers are women.
* **4.** Some heroes are not martyrs.
   **5.** All shamans are priests.
   **6.** No tulips are weeds.
* **7.** All colonels are objects weighing at least 100 pounds.
   **8.** Some logicians are septuagenarians.
   **9.** No giants are things less than 10 feet tall.
* **10.** No serigraphs are sculptures.

**Part D: Contraposition**  Form the contrapositive of each of the following statements. Then indicate whether contraposition, as applied to the type of categorical statement in question, is a valid form of argument.

* **1.** All cynics are pessimists.
   **2.** Some plants are nonroses.
   **3.** Some dramas are not comedies.
* **4.** Some noncollies are not nondogs.
   **5.** All photons are things that travel at the speed of light.
   **6.** No red oaks are elms.
* **7.** All things that can run at more than 50 miles an hour are cats.
   **8.** Some non-Fords are not nonautomobiles.
   **9.** All college students are entities having IQs of at least 100.
* **10.** All great white sharks are nonguppies.

**Part E:** Inferences from A Statements    Assuming that "All ideologues are fools" is true, what is implied regarding the truth or falsehood of the following statements? (If neither the truth nor the falsehood of the statement is implied, simply write "not guaranteed.") *Note:* To get the correct answer, you may need to make a series of inferences from the assumed statement.

* 1. All fools are ideologues.
   2. No ideologues are nonfools.
   3. Some ideologues are fools.
* 4. All nonfools are nonideologues.
   5. No nonfools are ideologues.
   6. Some fools are ideologues.
* 7. No fools are nonideologues.
   8. Some ideologues are not fools.
   9. No ideologues are fools.
* 10. Some ideologues are not nonfools.
  11. Some fools are not nonideologues.
  12. All nonideologues are nonfools.
* 13. Some nonfools are nonideologues.
  14. No fools are ideologues.
  15. No nonideologues are nonfools.

**Part F:** Inferences from E Statements    Assuming that "No psychiatrists are optimists" is true, what is implied regarding the truth or falsehood of the following statements? (If neither the truth nor the falsehood of the statement is implied, simply write "not guaranteed.") *Note:* To get the correct answer, you may need to make a series of inferences from the assumed statement.

* 1. All psychiatrists are nonoptimists.
   2. No optimists are psychiatrists.
   3. Some psychiatrists are not optimists.
* 4. No nonoptimists are nonpsychiatrists.
   5. All optimists are nonpsychiatrists.
   6. Some optimists are not psychiatrists.
* 7. All psychiatrists are optimists.
   8. All nonpsychiatrists are optimists.
   9. Some psychiatrists are optimists.
* 10. Some nonoptimists are not nonpsychiatrists.
  11. No nonpsychiatrists are optimists.
  12. Some optimists are nonpsychiatrists.
* 13. No nonoptimists are psychiatrists.
  14. Some optimists are psychiatrists.
  15. Some psychiatrists are nonoptimists.

**Part G:** Inferences from I Statements  Assuming that "Some chemicals are poisons" is true, what is implied regarding the truth or falsehood of the following statements? (If neither the truth nor the falsehood of the statement is implied, simply write "not guaranteed.") *Note:* To get the correct answer, you may need to make a series of inferences from the assumed statement.

*  1. Some poisons are chemicals.
  2. No chemicals are poisons.
  3. Some chemicals are not nonpoisons.
*  4. Some nonchemicals are nonpoisons.
  5. No poisons are chemicals.
  6. All chemicals are poisons.
*  7. Some nonpoisons are nonchemicals.
  8. No nonpoisons are nonchemicals.
  9. Some chemicals are not poisons.
* 10. Some nonchemicals are not nonpoisons.
 11. All poisons are chemicals.
 12. Some chemicals are nonpoisons.
* 13. Some nonchemicals are poisons.
 14. Some nonpoisons are chemicals.
 15. All chemicals are nonpoisons.

**Part H:** Inferences from O Statements  Assuming that "Some celebrities are not saints" is true, what is implied regarding the truth or falsehood of the following statements? (If neither the truth nor the falsehood of the statement is implied, simply write "not guaranteed.") *Note:* To get the correct answer, you may need to make a series of inferences from the assumed statement.

*  1. No celebrities are saints.
  2. All celebrities are saints.
  3. Some celebrities are nonsaints.
*  4. Some saints are not celebrities.
  5. Some nonsaints are not noncelebrities.
  6. Some celebrities are saints.
*  7. Some nonsaints are celebrities.
  8. All nonsaints are noncelebrities.
  9. No celebrities are nonsaints.
* 10. Some noncelebrities are not nonsaints.
 11. All celebrities are nonsaints.
 12. No saints are celebrities.
* 13. Some celebrities are not nonsaints.
 14. Some noncelebrities are saints.
 15. No nonsaints are celebrities.

## Chapter 6

# *Categorical Logic: Syllogisms*

**C**ategorical syllogisms are arguments composed entirely of categorical statements. Every categorical syllogism has two premises and one conclusion, and every categorical syllogism contains exactly three terms. For example:

1.      1. All human acts are behaviors caused by genes.
          2. All altruistic acts are human acts.
    So, 3. All altruistic acts are behaviors caused by genes.

"Human acts," "altruistic acts," and "behaviors caused by genes" are the terms in this syllogism. Categorical syllogisms are important and useful forms of argument. Many a long argument can be interpreted as a series of categorical syllogisms. And it is often revealing to try to express the main steps in a complex argument as a syllogism. Very often the attempt to "boil an argument down" into a categorical syllogism will reveal significant strengths and weaknesses.

## 6.1 Standard Form, Mood, and Figure

Before we can develop logical tools for evaluating categorical syllogisms, we must first develop a clear terminology for talking about them. Consider the following syllogism:

2.      1. All astronomers are scientists.
          2. Some astrologers are not scientists.
    So, 3. Some astrologers are not astronomers.

Note that one of the terms, namely, "scientists," occurs once in each premise. The **middle term** of a categorical syllogism is the term that occurs once in each premise. The **major term** of a categorical syllogism is the predicate term of the conclusion. Thus, "astronomers" is the major term of syllogism (2). The **minor term** of a categorical syllogism is the subject term of the conclusion. So, "astrologers" is the minor term of syllogism (2).

Just as there are standard forms for categorical statements, there is a standard form for categorical syllogisms. Our logical tools are designed to apply to syllogisms in standard form, so it is important to be able to put a syllogism into standard form. A categorical syllogism is in **standard form** when these conditions are met:

a. The premises and the conclusion are categorical statements in standard form ("All S are P," "No S are P," "Some S are P," or "Some S are not P").
b. The first premise contains the major term.
c. The second premise contains the minor term.
d. The conclusion is stated last.

The **major premise** of a categorical syllogism is the premise containing the major term, and the **minor premise** is the premise containing the minor term. So, when a categorical syllogism is in standard form, the first premise is the major premise and the second premise is the minor premise.

Which of the following categorical syllogisms are in standard form?

3.  1. All oaks are trees.
    2. All trees are plants.
So, 3. All oaks are plants.

4.  1. All trees are plants.
    2. All oaks are trees.
So, 3. All oaks are plants.

5.  1. All trees are plants.
    2. Only trees are oaks.
So, 3. All oaks are plants.

Only syllogism (4) is in standard form. Syllogism (3) is not in standard form because the minor premise comes first. And syllogism (5) is not in standard form because its second premise is not a categorical statement in standard form. We can put (5) into standard form by rewriting "Only trees are oaks" as "All oaks are trees."

The logical form of a categorical syllogism is determined by its mood and figure. The **mood** of a categorical syllogism *in standard form* is determined by the kinds of categorical statements involved and the order in which they appear. For example,

6.　　1. All psychiatrists are physicians.
　　　　2. Some psychologists are not physicians.
　So, 3. Some psychologists are not psychiatrists.

The mood of this syllogism is **AOO**. That is, the first premise is an **A** statement, the second premise is an **O** statement, and the conclusion is an **O** statement. What is the mood of the following syllogism?

7.　　1. No birds are mammals.
　　　　2. All bats are mammals.
　So, 3. No bats are birds.

The mood is **EAE**. That is, the first premise is an **E** statement, the second premise is an **A** statement, and the conclusion is an **E** statement. Since the mood involves the *sequence* of the statements as well as their types, be sure that a syllogism is in standard form when trying to identify its mood.

　　　Two syllogisms can have the same mood and yet differ in logical form. The following syllogism has the same mood as (7), but it differs in logical form:

8.　　1. No mammals are birds.
　　　　2. All mammals are bats.
　So, 3. No bats are birds.

We can bring out the difference in form by using letters to stand for terms. Let "S" stand for the minor term (the subject term of the conclusion), "P" for the major term (the predicate term of the conclusion), and "M" for the middle term. (Recall that the middle term occurs once in each premise but does not occur in the conclusion.) Then arguments (7) and (8) have the following forms, respectively:

　　　No P are M.　　　　No M are P.
　　　All S are M.　　　　All M are S.
　So, no S are P.　　So, no S are P.

In the Aristotelian scheme, (7) and (8) are said to differ in **figure**. Figure is specified by the position of the middle term. There are four possible figures, which can be diagrammed as follows:

| First Figure | Second Figure | Third Figure | Fourth Figure |
|:---:|:---:|:---:|:---:|
| M–P | P–M | M–P | P–M |
| S–M | S–M | M–S | M–S |
| So, S–P | So, S–P | So, S–P | So, S–P |

In the first figure, the middle term is the subject term of the major premise and the predicate term of the minor premise. In the second figure, the middle term is the predicate term of both premises. In the third figure, the middle term is the subject term of both premises. In the fourth figure, the middle term is the predicate term of the major premise and the subject term of the minor premise.

The form of a syllogism is completely specified by its mood and figure. The Aristotelian approach works out which combinations of mood and figure result in valid forms and which result in invalid forms. For example, argument (7) is a syllogism in the *second figure* having the mood **EAE**; this form is valid. On the other hand, argument (8) is a syllogism in the *third figure* having the mood **EAE**; this form is invalid. Thus, according to Aristotelian logic, validity is determined by mood and figure.

How many different forms of categorical syllogisms are there? Two hundred and fifty-six. As we have seen, there are four kinds of categorical statements and three categorical statements per categorical syllogism. Thus, there are $4^3 = 4 \times 4 \times 4 = 64$ possible moods (**AAA, AAE, AAI, AAO, AEA,** etc.). Moreover, there are four different figures, and $64 \times 4 = 256$. Out of all these possibilities, ancient and modern logicians agree that the following 15 forms are valid:

> First figure: **AAA, EAE, AII, EIO**
>
> Second figure: **EAE, AEE, EIO, AOO**
>
> Third figure: **IAI, AII, OAO, EIO**
>
> Fourth figure: **AEE, IAI, EIO**

It is not necessary to memorize this list of valid forms. It is much more important to learn how to test categorical syllogisms for validity, and we shall begin to do that in the next section. By the way, according to logicians in the Aristotelian tradition, an additional nine forms are valid:

> First figure: **AAI, EAO**
>
> Second figure: **AEO, EAO**
>
> Third figure: **AAI, EAO**
>
> Fourth figure: **AEO, EAO, AAI**

We will discuss why logicians in the Aristotelian tradition accept these additional nine forms as valid—and why many modern logicians do not—in section 6.4. For the moment, you may wish to note that all the forms in the additional set of nine involve an inference from two universal premises to a particular conclusion. These forms do not test valid using the method we shall discuss in the next two sections.

The following exercise will help you deepen your understanding of the concepts introduced in this section.

# ◈ *Exercise 6.1*

**Part A:** Standard Form   Which of the following categorical syllogisms are *in standard form?* Which are not? If a syllogism is not in standard form, rewrite it so that it is.

* **1.**    1. Some works of art are books.
          2. All novels are books.
  So, 3. Some works of art are novels.

  **2.**    1. Some poems are not masterpieces.
          2. No limericks are masterpieces.
  So, 3. Some limericks are not poems.

  **3.**    1. All movies are films.
          2. Some documentaries are not movies.
  So, 3. Some documentaries are not films.

* **4.**    1. All sculptures are beautiful.
          2. Some beautiful things are paintings.
  So, 3. Some sculptures are not paintings.

  **5.**    1. Some short stories are not interesting.
          2. Every famous short story is interesting.
  So, 3. Some short stories are not famous short stories.

  **6.**    1. Some artists are millionaires.
          2. No millionaires are poor.
  So, 3. At least one artist is not poor.

* **7.**    1. All sadists are mean.
          2. All art critics are mean.
  So, 3. All art critics are sadists.

  **8.**    1. All metaphors are figures of speech.
          2. All metaphors are words.
  So, 3. All figures of speech are words.

  **9.**    1. All opera singers are cool people.
          2. No rock singers are opera singers.
  So, 3. No rock singers are cool people.

* **10.**    1. Some ballerinas are clumsy dancers.
          2. All people who hate music are clumsy dancers.
  So, 3. Some people who hate music are ballerinas.

  **11.**    1. Some comedians are poets.
          2. Some comedians are prophets.
  So, 3. Some poets are prophets.

  **12.**    1. Every author is insightful.
          2. All novelists are authors.
  So, 3. All insightful people are novelists.

* **13.**     1. No aspiring actor is a saint.
        2. At least one aspiring actor is not an egoist.
   So, 3. Some egoists are saints.

  **14.**     1. Some musicians are not classically trained musicians.
        2. All jazz musicians are musicians.
   So, 3. Some jazz musicians are not classically trained musicians.

  **15.**     1. Only artists are alive.
        2. No ancient Greek poets are alive.
   So, 3. No artists are ancient Greek poets.

**Part B:** Mood and Figure    Specify the mood and figure of the following forms. Then use the list of valid forms provided in this section to determine whether the forms are valid.

* **1.**     1. Some P are M.
        2. All S are M.
   So, 3. Some S are P.

  **2.**     1. Some M are P.
        2. Some M are S.
   So, 3. Some S are P.

  **3.**     1. All P are M.
        2. No M are S.
   So, 3. No S are P.

* **4.**     1. No M are P.
        2. Some M are not S.
   So, 3. Some S are P.

  **5.**     1. No M are P.
        2. All S are M.
   So, 3. No S are P.

  **6.**     1. No P are M.
        2. All M are S.
   So, 3. No S are P.

* **7.**     1. All P are M.
        2. Some S are M.
   So, 3. Some S are P.

  **8.**     1. Some P are not M.
        2. Some S are not M.
   So, 3. Some S are not P.

  **9.**     1. Some M are not P.
        2. All M are S.
   So, 3. Some S are not P.

* **10.**     1. Some M are P.
        2. All S are M.
   So, 3. Some S are not P.

  **11.**     1. All P are M.
        2. Some S are not M.
   So, 3. Some S are not P.

  **12.**     1. No M are P.
        2. Some S are M.
   So, 3. Some S are not P.

* **13.**     1. All P are M.
        2. All S are M.
   So, 3. All S are P.

  **14.**     1. All M are P.
        2. All M are S.
   So, 3. All S are P.

  **15.**     1. All M are P.
        2. Some S are M.
   So, 3. Some S are P.

**Part C:** Putting Syllogisms into Standard Form    Put the following syllogisms into standard form. Then specify the mood and figure. Finally, use the list of valid forms to determine whether the syllogisms are valid.

* **1.** Every cowboy loves horses. Not all farmers love horses. It follows that at least one farmer is not a cowboy.

**2.** Nothing is a rodeo unless it is not an opera. Each opera includes singers. So, nothing that is a rodeo includes singers.

**3.** Not everyone who loves country music is a rodeo star. For at least one rock star loves country music; and no rock stars are rodeo stars.

* **4.** No cowards ride bulls; therefore, some fools are not cowards since at least one bull rider is a fool.

**5.** No cowgirls are city slickers; hence, no city slicker is a talented rider, because only talented riders are cowgirls.

**6.** There exists a drifter who is a sheriff; for at least one sheriff is a gunslinger, and a thing is a gunslinger only if it is a drifter.

* **7.** Only good guys are cowboys in white outfits. A thing is a cattle rustler only if it is not a good guy. It follows that no cowboys in white outfits are cattle rustlers.

**8.** Every barkeep who serves rotgut is a bad guy. Therefore, at least one person who won't live long is a bad guy since at least one barkeep who serves rotgut won't live long.

**9.** Only westerns are worth seeing because only good movies are worth seeing, and only westerns are good movies.

* **10.** At least one bronco is not hard to ride, for all bulls are hard to ride, and some broncos are not bulls.

**11.** Nothing is a wealthy landowner unless it is not a buckaroo. A thing is a cattle baron only if it is a wealthy landowner. Hence, nothing that is a buckaroo is also a cattle baron.

**12.** If anything is a bounty hunter, then it is not a sodbuster. At least one outlaw is a sodbuster; therefore, not every outlaw is a bounty hunter.

* **13.** A thing is a trail boss only if it is not a hired hand. There exists a rancher who is a hired hand. Consequently, at least one rancher is a trail boss.

**14.** Not all bandits will be hanged. After all, at least one bandit is not a horse thief, and every horse thief will be hanged.

**15.** Not all sheep ranchers are fast guns; hence, not all honest citizens are fast guns since only honest citizens are sheep ranchers.

**Part D:** Constructing Syllogisms   Write your own syllogisms with forms as specified below. Then use the list of valid forms provided in this section to determine whether the syllogisms are valid.

1. First figure: **EIO**
2. Second figure: **AEE**

3. Third figure: **IAI**

4. Fourth figure: **EAE**

5. First figure: **AAE**

6. Second figure: **EIO**

7. Third figure: **OAO**

8. Fourth figure: **IAI**

9. First figure: **EEA**

10. Second figure: **AOO**

## 6.2 Venn Diagrams and Categorical Statements

In this section and the next, we will examine a method for establishing the validity and invalidity of categorical arguments. This method was discovered around 1880 by the English logician John Venn. Venn's method involves the use of a special type of picture or diagram.

A Venn diagram consists of overlapping circles. Each circle stands for a class. Since each categorical statement has two terms, with each term denoting a class, the Venn diagram for a single categorical statement involves just two overlapping circles. For example, in the following diagram, the circle on the left denotes the class of dogs and the circle on the right denotes the class of animals. The numerals (1 through 4) are not normally part of the diagram but are added here temporarily to enable us to refer to the separate areas of the diagram.

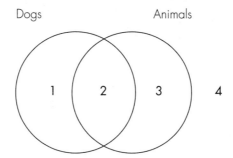

Area 1 stands for things that are dogs but not animals. Of course, in reality this area is empty since there are no dogs that are not animals. Area 2 (the area of overlap between the circles) stands for things that are both dogs and animals, that is, all the dogs. Area 3 stands for things that are animals but not dogs, such as cats, crickets, and kangaroos. Area 4 stands for things that are neither dogs nor animals, such as neutrons, nickels, and numbers.

To construct Venn diagrams, we indicate that the various areas of the diagram either contain objects or are empty. To show that an area contains at least one object, we use an "x." To show that an area is empty, we shade it in. If an area does not contain an "x" and is not shaded in, we simply have no information about it. Thus, to diagram a universal negative statement, such as "No dogs are cats," we indicate that the area of overlap between the two circles is empty by shading it in, as follows:

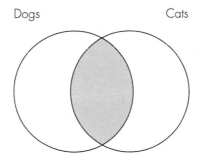

This sort of diagram, with shading in the area of overlap, is the sort you will always use for a universal negative statement. However, as previously noted, the English language provides various ways of saying that "No S are P," such as "If anything is an S, then it is not a P" and "Nothing that is an S is a P." When you encounter such stylistic variants in a syllogism, simply rewrite the statement in "No S are P" form and use a diagram similar to the one just shown. One last thing: Notice that the preceding diagram does not say that there are any dogs, nor does it say that there are any cats. It simply says that nothing belongs to the class (or set) of things that are both dogs and cats.

Universal affirmatives have the form "All S are P," and they say that the members of set S are also members of set P, or in other words, that S has no members that are not members of P. Thus, the diagram for "All dogs are animals" looks like this:

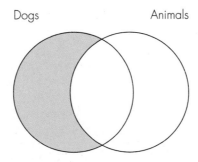

Notice that this diagram does not say that there are any dogs, nor does it say that there are any animals. It simply says, "If there are any dogs, then they are animals" (or "Anything you put in the dog-circle has to go in the animal-circle"). This is the sort of shading you will always use when diagramming a universal affirmative statement. However, as previously noted, the English language contains numerous stylistic variants for "All S are P," such as "Every S is a P," "If anything is an S, then it is a P," and "Only P are S." When you encounter these stylistic variants, rewrite the statement into "All S are P" form and use a diagram similar to the one just shown.

Particular affirmatives have the form "Some S are P," and these say that sets S and P have at least one member in common. The diagram for "Some dogs are collies" looks like this:

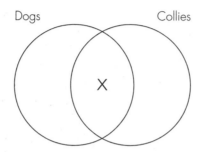

This diagram asserts that there exists at least one dog that is a collie. ("Something is in the dog-circle *and* in the collie-circle.") This is the type of diagram you will always use for particular affirmative statements. However, as previously noted, the English language contains a number of stylistic variants for "Some S are P," including "At least one S is a P" and "There are S that are P." When you encounter these variants, simply rewrite the statement into "Some S are P" form and use a diagram similar to the one just shown.

Particular negatives have the form "Some S are not P." These statements say that set S has at least one member that does not belong to set P. The diagram for "Some dogs are not collies" looks like this:

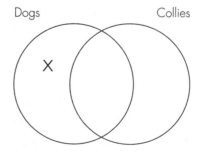

The diagram asserts that there exists at least one dog that is not a collie. ("Something is in the dog-circle but *not* in the collie-circle.") This is the type of diagram you will always use for particular negative statements. But as previously noted, the English language contains a number of stylistic variants for "Some S are not P," such as "Not all S are P" and "At least one S is not a P." When you encounter these variants, simply rewrite the statement in "Some S are not P" form and use a diagram similar to the one just shown.

Now that we know how to diagram the four relevant types of categorical statements, we can use Venn diagrams to evaluate arguments for validity. We begin with short arguments involving just one premise. To determine whether an argument is valid, we proceed as follows. First, we diagram the premise. Second, we look to see whether our diagram of the premise tells us that the conclusion is true. This works because if an argument is valid, the content of the conclusion is contained, at least implicitly, in the premise(s).

Let's start with some examples of conversion:

9.  1. No Namibians are Libyans.
    So, 2. No Libyans are Namibians.

To apply the Venn method, we draw two overlapping circles and label them. To cut down on writing, we will use capital-letter abbreviations to label our circles. In our current example, let's use "N" for "Namibians" and "L" for "Libyans." (Normally, we will use the first letter of the term to label the relevant circle.) As regards *single-premise* arguments, let us follow the convention of labeling the circle on the left with the *subject term* of the premise and the circle on the right with the *predicate term* of the premise, like this:

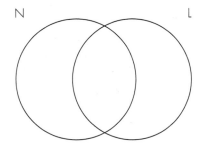

Now we diagram the premise:

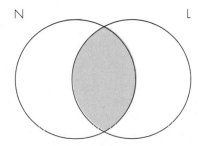

Next we look to see whether the diagram of the premise tells us that the conclusion is true. In this case, the answer is yes, for the shading indicates that no

Libyan is a Namibian. So, the diagram tells us that the argument is valid, which is as it should be since conversion is valid for **E** statements.

Let's consider a second short argument:

10.    1. All Liberians are Africans.
So, 2. All Africans are Liberians.

As before, we draw two overlapping circles, label them, and diagram the premise:

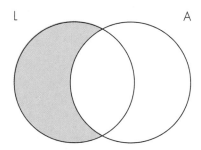

Now we look to see whether the diagram of the premise tells us that the conclusion is true. In this case, it does not. A diagram of the conclusion would have to shade in area 3, the part of the circle that stands for Africans who are not Liberians, like this:

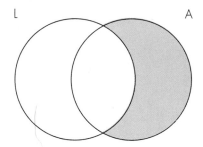

Thus, our diagram of the premise tells us that the argument is not valid. And this is as it should be since argument (10) is plainly invalid. In general, to determine whether premises make a conclusion true, it helps to compare a diagram of the premises with a separate diagram of the conclusion. For an argument to be valid, a diagram of the premises must contain the essential content of the conclusion, but this does not mean that the diagram of the premises will always look exactly like the diagram you would produce if you simply set out to diagram the conclusion.

Consider another example of conversion:

11.    1. Some Moroccans are Spanish speakers.
So, 2. Some Spanish speakers are Moroccans.

Again, we diagram the premise:

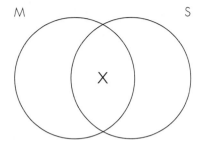

And now we look to see whether our diagram of the premise tells us that the conclusion of the argument is true. In this case, the answer is yes, the "x" tells us that some members of the class of Spanish speakers are also members of the class of Moroccans. So, our Venn diagram indicates that the argument is valid.

Consider one last example of conversion:

12.    1. Some Africans are not Nigerians.

So,  2. Some Nigerians are not Africans.

As before, we diagram the premise:

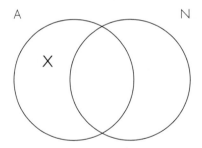

Does the diagram tell us that the conclusion is true? No, for this to be so, an "x" would have to appear in area 3, like this:

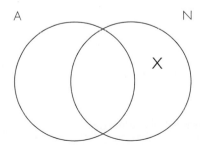

Consequently, the Venn method tells us that argument (12) is invalid.

Now let's consider an example of obversion:

13.  1. No Cameroonians are Zimbabweans.

So, 2. All Cameroonians are non-Zimbabweans.

The diagram of the premise is as follows:

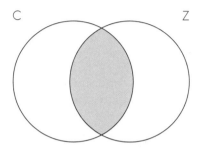

Does the diagram tell us that the conclusion is true? Yes, for it indicates that if there are any Cameroonians, they are not Zimbabweans (i.e., they must be in the part of the Cameroonian-circle that lies outside the Zimbabwean-circle). In the case of obversion, the conclusion of the argument is always logically equivalent to the premise, so a diagram of the premise is bound to contain the essential content of the conclusion.

The above diagram raises the issue of dealing with negative terms, such as "non-Zimbabweans." To avoid certain complications, we will *not* label the circles in our diagrams with negative terms. But we will be forced at times (as in the above case) to understand what sort of diagram is or would be needed where a negative term is involved. The essential question is, "In order for the statement to be true, where would the diagram need to be shaded or marked with an 'x'?" Sometimes it helps to experiment with a separate diagram on a sheet of scratch paper—do some shading or "x-ing" and ask, "Does that tell me that the statement is true?" A good working knowledge of obversion and contraposition is also helpful since it will help you identify statements that are (and are not) logically equivalent to the one containing a negative term. Let's consider some cases.

Here is an example of contraposition:

14.  1. All Ugandans are Africans.

So, 2. All non-Africans are non-Ugandans.

The diagram of the premise looks like this:

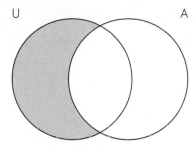

An **A** statement and its contrapositive are logically equivalent; so the diagram of the premise is bound to contain the essential content of the conclusion, but the term-complements ("non-Africans" and "non-Ugandans") may make this less than obvious. To understand the diagram, note that "All non-Africans are non-Ugandans" says that if anything is outside of the circle labeled "Africans," then it is outside the circle labeled "Ugandans." And the diagram does indeed contain this information.

Here's another example of contraposition:

15.    1. Some Africans are non-Kenyans.

So, 2. Some Kenyans are non-Africans.

The diagram of the premise is as follows:

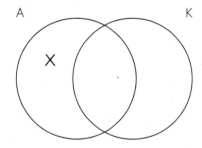

Does the diagram tell us that the conclusion is true? No, for there is no "x" in area 3, the area that stands for Kenyans who are non-Africans.

Now consider an especially difficult case involving negative terms, "No nonanimals are nondogs." (If you recall the table on contraposition, you know that this is *not* logically equivalent to "No dogs are animals.") To diagram "No nonanimals are nondogs," we have to shade in the area of overlap between "nonanimals" and "nondogs." In a diagram in which the circles are labeled "animals" and "dogs," the area of overlap is the area *outside* of the circles, so the diagram looks like this:

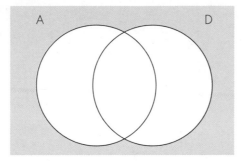

In closing this section, let's examine contradictories from the standpoint of the Venn method. Recall that if two statements are contradictories, then if one is true, the other must be false (and vice versa). Consider the following argument:

16.   1. Some Egyptians are not Moslems.
   So, 2. It's false that all Egyptians are Moslems.

The premise may be diagrammed as follows:

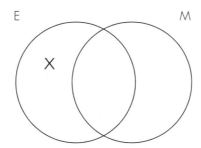

Does the diagram tell us that the conclusion of the argument is true? Yes. A diagram of "All Egyptians are Moslems" would declare area 1 of the diagram empty, but the "x" in area 1 tells us it isn't empty. Thus, given the content of the premise, it's false that all Egyptians are Moslems. Accordingly, the Venn method nicely confirms the Aristotelian view of contradictories.

The following exercise will give you some practice in using the Venn method.

## ◆ Exercise 6.2

**Part A:** Venn Diagrams and Standard Form   Put the following categorical statements into standard form, then construct a Venn diagram for each of them. Label the left circle of the diagram with an abbreviation of the subject term and the right circle with an abbreviation of the predicate term.

* **1.** At least one ancient philosopher believed in the unreality of change.

  **2.** Not every act of killing is an act of murder.

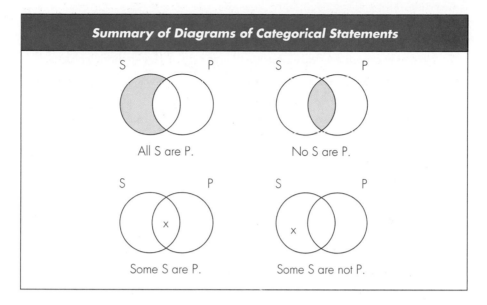

**Summary of Diagrams of Categorical Statements**

All S are P.

No S are P.

Some S are P.

Some S are not P.

3. If anything is a divine being, then it is not limited.

* 4. Only tax-dodgers deserve harsh treatment from the IRS.

5. At least one current musical hit will not be a hit next year.

6. Only people who believe in life after death are people who believe in reincarnation.

* 7. A thing is a chlorofluorocarbon only if it is not good for the ozone layer.

8. At least one corporation is cheating the government.

9. Only violent offenders should be incarcerated.

* 10. Nothing is a physical entity unless it is not spiritual.

**Part B:** Venn Diagrams and Arguments   Draw two Venn diagrams for each of the following arguments, one for the premise and one for the conclusion. First draw a Venn diagram of the premise, labeling the left circle with an abbreviation of the subject term and the right circle with an abbreviation of the predicate term. Second, draw a Venn diagram for the conclusion, but label the circles as before (with the left circle labeled by an abbreviation of the subject term of the *premise* and the right circle labeled with an abbreviation of the predicate term of the *premise*). Finally, indicate whether the argument is valid.

* 1. Some chairs are not thrones. So, some thrones are not chairs.

2. All scallops are mollusks. Hence, no scallops are nonmollusks.

3. All minds are brains. Therefore, all nonbrains are nonminds.

* 4. Some married persons are persons who have attachment disorders. Thus, some persons who have attachment disorders are married persons.

5. No laypersons are priests. It follows that all laypersons are nonpriests.

6. Some political philosophers are egalitarians. Accordingly, some non-egalitarians are things that are not political philosophers.

* 7. No elephants are beetles. Consequently, no nonbeetles are nonelephants.

8. No Pickwickian interpretations are obvious interpretations. So, no obvious interpretations are Pickwickian interpretations.

9. Some rays are devilfish. Hence, some devilfish are not nonrays.

* 10. Some wines are not merlots. Therefore, some nonmerlots are not nonwines.

11. All acts of torture are immoral acts. It follows that all immoral acts are acts of torture.

12. Some vipers are not copperheads. Consequently, some vipers are noncopperheads.

* 13. Some mammals are edentulous animals. Thus, all mammals are edentulous animals.

14. Some boring events are colloquia. Accordingly, some boring events are not colloquia.

15. Some theists are not predestinarians. Therefore, no theists are predestinarians.

## 6.3 Venn Diagrams and Categorical Syllogisms

The Venn method can be applied to categorical syllogisms. In fact, because the Venn method gives us a visual representation of the logic, many find it an especially insightful and intuitive way of testing syllogisms for validity.

To apply the Venn method to a categorical syllogism, we first check to see if the syllogism is in standard form. If it is, we can proceed immediately to construct a diagram. If the syllogism is not in standard form, we rewrite it so that it is. Next, since there are three terms in every categorical syllogism, with each term denoting a class, we need a diagram with three overlapping circles to represent the various possible relationships among the classes, as shown here:

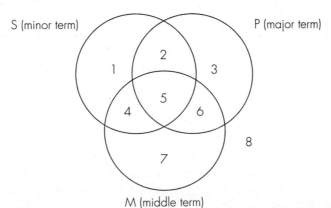

To ensure uniformity in our diagrams, we always let the circle in the middle stand for the class of things denoted by the *middle term* of the syllogism (the term that appears in both premises). To cut down on writing, we will ordinarily label this circle with an abbreviation of the middle term. The circle in the upper left stands for the class of things denoted by the *minor term* (the subject term of the conclusion). To cut down on writing, we will ordinarily label this circle with an abbreviation of the minor term. And the circle in the upper right stands for the set of things denoted by the *major term* (the predicate term of the conclusion). To cut down on writing, we will ordinarily label this circle with an abbreviation of the major term. The numerals (1 through 8) are not normally part of a Venn diagram, but they are added here temporarily to enable us to refer to the separate areas of the diagram. Notice that there are eight areas (counting the region outside the circles). Each area represents a possible relationship among the three sets or classes. For example, if we placed an "x" in area 5, we would be saying that at least one thing belongs to all three of the sets or classes. If we shaded in area 5, we would be saying that no object belongs to all three sets. If we placed an "x" in area 8, we would be saying that at least one thing is not a member of any of the three classes in question. If we shaded in areas 4 and 5, we would be saying that nothing that belongs to the set denoted by the middle term also belongs to the set denoted by the minor term.

To determine whether a syllogism is valid, we proceed as follows. First, we diagram the premises. Second, we look to see whether our diagram of the premises tells us that the conclusion is true. This works because if an argument is valid, the content of the conclusion is contained, at least implicitly, in the premises. Accordingly, we do not diagram the conclusion itself on these three circles (for doing so could easily confuse us about exactly what information was provided by the premises). Consider the following example:

17.   1. No rocks are sentient things.
     2. All animals are sentient things.
So, 3. No animals are rocks.

We set up our diagram and label the circles as just prescribed: An abbreviation of the middle term ("S" for "sentient things") labels the middle circle; an abbreviation of the minor term ("A" for "animals") labels the circle in the upper left; and an abbreviation of the major term ("R" for "rocks") labels the circle in the upper right. Next, we diagram the first premise:

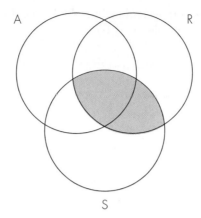

In diagramming the first premise, we focus on the two circles representing rocks and sentient things since only those classes are mentioned in the first premise. Next, we diagram the second premise:

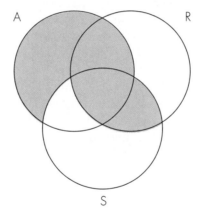

In diagramming the second premise, we need pay attention only to the circles representing animals and sentient things.

Having diagrammed the premises, we must now check to see whether the content of the conclusion has also been diagrammed in the process. In other words, does our diagram tell us that no animal is a rock? Yes, it does, for the areas of overlap between the circles representing these two classes are shaded in. Therefore, the argument is valid.

Our first example involved only universal statements. Let us now consider a syllogism involving a particular negative statement:

18.   1. All humans are rational beings.
      2. Some animals are not rational beings.
So, 3. Some animals are not humans.

First, we set up our diagram, label the three circles (as prescribed previously), and diagram the first premise:

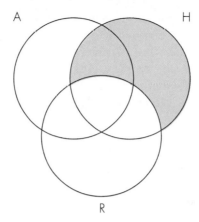

Once again, notice that we focus on only two circles at a time as we diagram the premises. Next, we diagram the second premise:

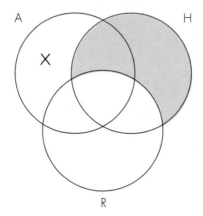

The "x" lies within the A-circle (which represents the class of animals) but outside the R-circle (which represents the class of rational beings). Why did we put our "x" in area 1 and not in area 2 of the diagram? We couldn't put it in area 2 because area 2 is shaded in. That is, the information in the first premise tells us that area 2 is empty. Thus, if we put an "x" in area 2, we would in effect be saying that the premises of the argument are logically inconsistent—that is, that the first premise says area 2 is empty, while the second premise says area 2 is not empty. Clearly, this would misrepresent the content of the two premises because they are consistent.

Now, we examine the diagram to see whether, in the process of diagramming the premises, we have diagrammed the content of the conclusion. Does the diagram tell us that some animals are not humans? Yes. The "x" lies within the animal-circle but outside the human-circle.

In diagramming argument (18), we diagrammed the universal premise before we diagrammed the particular premise. *When a syllogism contains both universal and particular premises, always diagram the universal premise first.* Otherwise, you may run into obstacles in constructing your diagram. To illustrate, try to diagram the particular premise of argument (18) prior to diagramming the universal premise. (You won't know whether to put the "x" in area 1 or area 2.)

How does the Venn diagram method apply to invalid arguments? Consider the following syllogism:

> 19.  1. All immoral persons are psychologically disturbed persons.
>      2. No saints are immoral persons.
> So, 3. No saints are psychologically disturbed persons.

We draw and label the circles and then diagram the first premise:

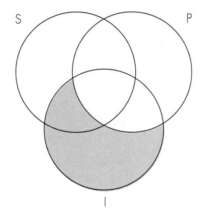

Next, we diagram the second premise:

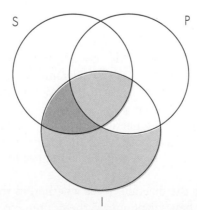

Notice that area 4 has been shaded in twice, since the diagram for each premise declares area 4 empty. This is not a problem; it merely means that our diagram is redundant as regards the emptiness of area 4.

Now that the premises are diagrammed, the crucial question is this: Does our diagram tell us that the conclusion of the argument is true? In other words, does it tell us that no saints are psychologically disturbed? The answer, of course, is that it does not. Area 2 has not been declared empty. Thus, the diagram leaves open the possibility that some saints are psychologically disturbed persons. This means that the premises do not guarantee the truth of the conclusion, and so the argument is invalid.

Let us now consider an example that brings out a slight complication in the Venn technique.

20.    1. All famous actors are highly successful people.

2. Some highly successful people are people of average intelligence.

So, 3. Some people of average intelligence are famous actors.

We diagram the universal premise first:

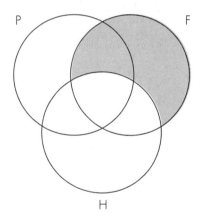

Now, when we try to diagram the second (or particular affirmative) premise, we see that the "x" could go in either area 4 or area 5. The premises do not contain more specific information than that. We indicate this by putting an "x" *precisely* on the line separating the two areas, like this:

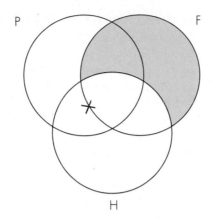

Now, for the argument to be valid, the premises must tell us that either area 2 or area 5 contains an object. But our diagram for the first premise declares that area 2 is empty. And our diagram for the second premise does not *assure* us that area 5 contains an object—it may or it may not. The "x" straddles areas 4 and 5, so the premises do not definitely say that the "x" belongs in area 4, nor do they say that the "x" belongs in area 5. Hence, the argument is invalid.

Obviously, the Venn method can be used to test argument forms as well as arguments. Can you construct a Venn diagram for the following form?

21.  1. All M are P.
     2. Some S are not M.
So,  3. Some S are not P.

The diagram looks like this:

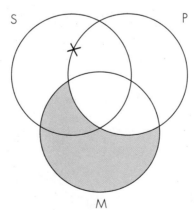

Note that the "x" straddles areas 1 and 2. The premises tell us that there is an "S" in at least one of these areas, but the premises do not tell us to place an "x" in area 1. And the argument form is valid *only if* the premises tell us to place an "x" within the S-circle but outside the P-circle. So, the argument form is not valid.

The following exercise provides you with an opportunity to use the Venn method on argument forms and categorical syllogisms.

## ◧ Exercise 6.3

**Part A:** Argument Forms   Construct Venn diagrams to determine whether the following argument forms are valid. In labeling the circles of your diagrams, remember that "M" labels the circle in the middle, "S" labels the circle in the upper left, and "P" labels the circle in the upper right.

*   **1.**   1. All M are P.
            2. Some M are not S.
     So, 3. Some S are not P.

    **2.**   1. No P are M.
            2. Some M are not S.
     So, 3. Some S are P.

    **3.**   1. No M are P.
            2. Some M are S.
     So, 3. Some S are not P.

*   **4.**   1. Some P are M.
            2. Some S are M.
     So, 3. Some S are P.

    **5.**   1. All P are M.
            2. Some M are not S.
     So, 3. Some S are not P.

    **6.**   1. All P are M.
            2. Some S are not M.
     So, 3. Some S are not P.

*   **7.**   1. No P are M.
            2. Some M are S.
     So, 3. Some S are P.

    **8.**   1. All P are M.
            2. No S are M.
     So, 3. No S are P.

    **9.**   1. No P are M.
            2. No S are M.
     So, 3. No S are P.

*   **10.**   1. All M are P.
             2. No S are M.
     So, 3. No S are P.

**Part B:** Categorical Syllogisms   Use Venn diagrams to determine the validity of the following categorical syllogisms. If a given syllogism is not in standard form, be sure to put it into standard form before constructing your diagram. In labeling the circles of your diagrams, use an abbreviation of the *middle term* to label the circle in the middle, use an abbreviation of the *minor term* to label the circle in the upper left, and use an abbreviation for the *major term* to label the circle in the upper right.

*   **1.** Only Greeks are Athenians. At least one human is not an Athenian. Therefore, not all humans are Greeks.

    **2.** Every animal is sentient. And each sentient thing is a rights-holder. Hence, if anything is an animal, then it is a rights-holder.

    **3.** No serial killer is good because every serial killer is evil, and no evil thing is good.

*   **4.** Every wicked person is self-deceived, for all liars are wicked, and every liar is self-deceived.

    **5.** Every person without a conscience is happy; hence, at least one criminal is happy since not every criminal has a conscience.

6. All those who have faith are virtuous. But there are highly moral people who do not have faith. Therefore, not all highly moral people are virtuous.

\* 7. No human is omniscient. Something is both divine and human. So, at least one divine being is not omniscient.

8. Only wars are great evils. Some wars are ordained by God. Hence, at least one great evil is ordained by God.

9. Not every hobby is worth doing well. But anything worth doing is worth doing well. Therefore, at least one hobby is not worth doing.

\* 10. If anything is a mental event, then it is not a brain event. For only physical events are brain events, and no mental events are physical.

11. Some philosophical views are not worth considering. Every philosophical view has been held by a genius. Thus, some views that have been held by geniuses are not worth considering.

12. No wicked person is utterly without a conscience. But all wicked persons are deeply confused individuals. Hence, no deeply confused individual is utterly without a conscience.

\* 13. Only metaphorical statements are similarity statements. And every statement is a similarity statement. Accordingly, a thing is a statement only if it is metaphorical.

14. Contrary to what traditional Western morality says, some acts of suicide are morally permissible. For all morally permissible acts are ones that conform to the categorical imperative, and some acts of suicide conform to the categorical imperative.

15. Only acts that maximize utility are obligatory. Not all acts that maximize utility are prescribed by the Ten Commandments. Therefore, at least one act prescribed by the Ten Commandments is not obligatory.

\* 16. Not every act is free, since every act foreknown by God is nonfree and some acts are foreknown by God.

17. Only acts approved of by God are moral. Some acts of killing are approved of by God. Hence, some acts of killing are moral.

18. No human is omnipotent. All divine beings are omnipotent. Therefore, no human is divine.

\* 19. Only persons who have inner conflicts are unhappy. At least one successful comedian is unhappy. We may conclude that some successful comedians are persons who have inner conflicts.

20. At least one tycoon is a person who has walked over others to get to the top. Every person who has walked over others to get to the top is evil. It follows that at least one tycoon is evil.

21. Some trees are maples. Some trees are oaks. So, some oaks are maples.

22. No balalaika is a banjo. Some balalaikas are beautiful. Hence, some beautiful things are not banjos.

23. Each tyrant is mendacious. If anything is a tyrant, then it is a liar. Consequently, all liars are mendacious.

24. Every aphorism is an apothegm. Each epigram is an aphorism. Accordingly, only apothegms are epigrams.

25. Every Saint Bernard is a large dog. Not all large dogs are brown. So, not all brown dogs are Saint Bernards.

## 6.4 The Modern Square of Opposition

We now come to some points of disagreement between the Aristotelian logical tradition and modern logic. By "modern logic" we here refer to the tradition of logic developed by 19th- and early 20th-century thinkers such as George Boole (1815–1864), John Venn (1834–1923), Charles Sanders Peirce (1839–1914), Gottlob Frege (1848–1925), and Bertrand Russell (1872–1970).

Consider the following argument:

22.    1. All Egyptians are Africans.

   So, 2. Some Egyptians are Africans.

The diagram of the premise looks like this:

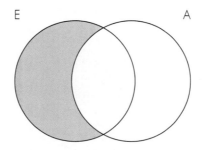

Does the diagram tell us the conclusion is true? No. An "x" would need to appear in the area of overlap between the two circles in order for the conclusion to be true. Note that argument (22) is an example of subalternation. Thus, our diagram in effect tells us that the Venn method (as presented in the two previous sections) does not confirm the Aristotelian view of subalternation. What's going on?

The Aristotelian and modern traditions agree that particular statements have existential import. Categorical statements have **existential import** if (and only if) they imply that their subject terms denote nonempty classes. For example, "Some Egyptians are Africans" implies that there *exists* at least one Egyptian (that is, the class of Egyptians has at least one member and so is not empty). Similarly, "Some Rwandans are not marathoners" implies that there *exists* at least one Rwandan. And since the Venn diagrams for particular statements require an "x" within the circle labeled by the subject term, the Venn method has built into it the view that particular statements have existential import.

But modern logicians understand universal statements to have a conditional (if-then) aspect. From this perspective, "All Egyptians are Africans" is equivalent to "If anything is an Egyptian, then it is an African." So understood, "All Egyptians are Africans" does not imply that there are any Egyptians. After all, "If anything is a unicorn, then it is an animal" is surely a true statement, but it does not imply that there actually are any unicorns. (If it did imply that there are unicorns, then it wouldn't be true.) Similarly, "No Namibians are Libyans" is equivalent to "If anything is a Namibian, then it is not a Libyan," and so understood, it does not imply that there are any Namibians. This modern understanding of universal statements is built into the Venn method as here presented. And this seemingly small point about universal statements has a series of ramifications for the Traditional Square of Opposition.

For example, consider the Aristotelian thesis that corresponding **A** and **E** statements are contraries (that is, they cannot both be true but can both be false). If the Aristotelians are right, the following argument is valid:

> **23.**    1. No Malawians are Tanzanians.
>
> So,  2. It is false that all Malawians are Tanzanians.

A Venn diagram of the premise is as follows:

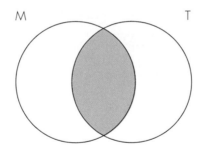

Does the diagram tell us that the conclusion is true? No. Think about it like this. First, mentally delete "It is false that" in the conclusion, so you have "All Malawians are Tanzanians," which would require shading in area 1, that is, declaring area 1 empty. Now, to make "All Malawians are Tanzanians" false, we need to do the opposite, that is, place an "x" in area 1 (thus declaring that some Malawians are not Tanzanians). So, the diagram tells us the conclusion is true only if an "x" appears in area 1, but no such "x" appears. Hence, the Venn method does not preserve the Aristotelian view that corresponding **A** and **E** statements are contraries.

What about subcontraries? Logicians in the Aristotelian tradition claim that corresponding **I** and **O** statements are subcontraries (that is, they can both be true but cannot both be false). If this Aristotelian claim about subcontraries is correct, the following argument is valid:

**24.**     1. It is false that some Chadians are Zambians.

So, 2. Some Chadians are not Zambians.

Now the premise here is equivalent to "It's false that something is both a Chadian and a Zambian," which requires us to shade in the area of overlap. (Think about it like this: "Some Chadians are Zambians" would require an "x" in the area of overlap, so to make that statement false, we do the opposite: shade the area in.) The Venn diagram of the premise looks like this:

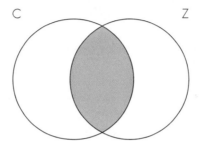

Does the diagram tell us that the conclusion is true? No, for there is no "x" in area 1. So, the Venn method does not preserve the Aristotelian view that corresponding **I** and **O** statements are subcontraries.

At this point, what's left of the Traditional Square of Opposition? Just the theses regarding contradictories, namely, *corresponding* **A** *and* **O** *statements are contradictories, and corresponding* **E** *and* **I** *statements are contradictories.* This is sometimes called the Modern Square of Opposition and may be represented pictorially as follows:

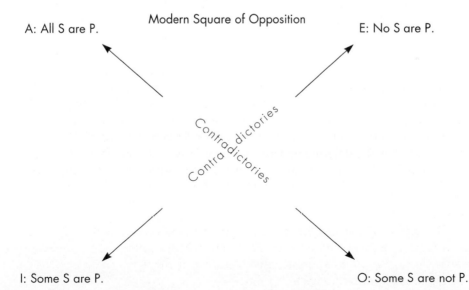

You may wish to stop a moment and compare this to the Traditional Square of Opposition discussed in section 5.2. The relationships along the sides of the Traditional Square have vanished (subalternation, contraries, subcontraries); only the diagonal relationships are retained (the contradictories).

The modern approach has at least one advantage over the Aristotelian approach that deserves special mention here. Consider the following pairs of statements:

25. All unicorns are animals. Some unicorns are not animals.

26. All ideal societies are perfectly just. Some ideal societies are not perfectly just.

27. No perfect vacuums are spaces through which sound can be transmitted.
    Some perfect vacuums are spaces through which sound can be transmitted.

Are these pairs contradictories? Oddly enough, they are not if we take an Aristotelian approach. For in each case, the subject term refers to an empty class. (Unicorns do not exist, and there are no ideal societies or perfect vacuums in existence.) It follows that the above pairs are not contradictories given the Aristotelian approach. For according to Aristotelians, all of the above statements have existential import. Thus, "All unicorns are animals" implies that at least one unicorn exists. And "Some unicorns are not animals" also implies that at least one unicorn exists. But any statement that implies a falsehood is itself false. Therefore, both "All unicorns are animals" and "Some unicorns are not animals" must be declared false by Aristotelians. But if two statements are contradictories, then if one is false, the other must be true. So, Aristotelians cannot preserve the thesis that corresponding **A** and **O** statements are always contradictories. And the same goes for corresponding **E** and **I** statements.

How does the modern approach differ? From this perspective, "All unicorns are animals" is equivalent to saying, "If anything is a unicorn, then it is an animal." This if-then statement seems to be true, and it doesn't imply that unicorns exist. But "Some unicorns are not animals" does imply that at least one unicorn exists, and so it is false. In this way, the modern approach preserves the thesis that corresponding **A** and **O** statements are contradictories *even when their subject terms refer to empty classes.* Similarly, if there are no unicorns, then "No unicorns are animals" is true, while "Some unicorns are animals" is false. So the modern approach also preserves the thesis that corresponding **E** and **I** statements are contradictories, *even when their subject terms refer to empty classes.*

Note that the differing understanding of universal statements affects the evaluation of conversion by limitation and contraposition by limitation. Consider conversion by limitation, which has this form:

28.    1. All S are P.
    So, 2. Some P are S.

A diagram of the premise looks like this:

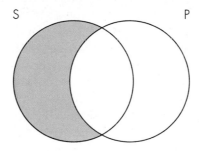

Does the diagram tell us that the conclusion is true? No, for there is no "x" in the area of overlap between the two circles. So, the Venn method tells us that conversion by limitation is not valid.

The differing understanding of universal statements also affects the assessment of certain syllogistic forms. In fact, nine syllogistic forms judged valid by Aristotelians are judged invalid via the modern approach. In every case, these syllogistic forms move from two universal premises to a particular conclusion. As an example, consider syllogisms in the first figure with the mood **AAI**:

29.　　1. All M are P (e.g., all perfect spouses are spouses).

　　　　2. All S are M (e.g., all perfect husbands are perfect spouses).

So, 3. Some S are P (e.g., some perfect husbands are spouses).

A Venn diagram for (29) looks like this:

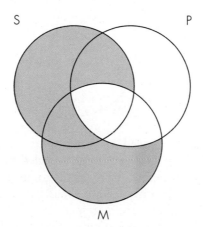

Does the diagram tell us that the conclusion is true? No, for there is no "x" in the area of overlap between the S-circle and the P-circle. Indeed, given the modern understanding of universal statements as having a conditional (if-then) aspect, no categorical syllogism with two universal premises and a particular conclusion is valid.

These disagreements between the Aristotelian and modern traditions in logic may seem a bit troubling. But note that the disagreement has its source in the very specific issue of whether universal categorical statements have existential import. Let us suppose that the modern logicians are correct in claiming that universal categorical statements do not have existential import. Still, in many actual cases, if an arguer appears to move from a universal categorical statement to a particular one, we can reasonably assume that the arguer has not stated all of his or her premises explicitly. (For practical purposes, it is often unnecessary to state every premise of an argument.) For example, the move from "All politicians are liars" to "Some politicians are liars" is valid if we add the premise "At least one politician exists." And in many cases, when someone asserts a premise of the form "All S are P," he or she is reasonably assuming that *there are some Ss.* Consider the following argument form:

30.    1. All S are P.
       2. At least one S exists.
   So, 3. Some S are P.

The second premise makes explicit the assumption that the class denoted by the subject term of the first premise is not empty. A diagram of the premises looks like this:

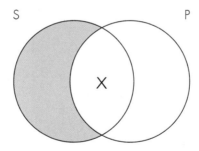

The second premise tells us we need an "x" within the S-circle, but the "x" can go only in the area of overlap between the two circles given our diagram of the first premise. (Here as elsewhere it is important to diagram universal premises before diagramming particular ones.) Thus, the diagram of the premises tells us that the conclusion is true and the argument is valid. By making unstated premises explicit, we can thus accept the modern view of universal statements while recognizing an insight in the traditional Aristotelian view. In this case, an inference akin to superalternation ("All S are P, so some S are P") is valid if we add that there are Ss (i.e., if we add that the subject term of "All S are P" denotes a nonempty class).

A similar point can be made about the syllogistic forms that Aristotelians regard as valid but modern logicians reject as invalid. For example, consider syllogisms in the second figure with **EAO** as their mood:

31.     1. No P are M.
        2. All S are M.
    So, 3. Some S are not P.

Here we need only add a premise to the effect that the subject term of the second premise denotes a nonempty class:

32.     1. No P are M.
        2. All S are M.
        3. At least one S exists.
    So, 4. Some S are not P.

Of course, (32) does not have the form of a categorical syllogism since it has three premises instead of two, but we can easily diagram it, as long as we remember to diagram the universal premises first:

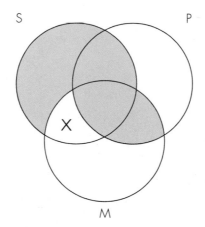

Premise 3 tells us to place an "x" within the S-circle, and the "x" can go only in area 4 given our diagrams for the universal premises. Clearly the diagram of the premises tells us that the conclusion is true, so argument form (32) is valid. Again, the point is that by adding unstated premises when it is reasonable to do so, we can in effect honor insights from both the Aristotelian and the modern traditions. Incidentally, arguments with unstated premises or conclusions are called *enthymemes*, and we shall take a closer look at them in the next section.

The following exercise gives you an opportunity to apply the concepts discussed in this section.

## ◆ **Exercise 6.4**

**Part A:** Argument Forms   Use Venn diagrams to test the following argument forms for validity. (Do not supply unstated premises.)

*   **1.**      1. No M are P.
          2. All S are M.
    So, 3. Some S are not P.

   **2.**      1. All P are M.
          2. No S are M.
    So, 3. Some S are not P.

   **3.**      1. All M are P.
          2. All M are S.
    So, 3. Some S are P.

*   **4.**      1. All M are P.
          2. All M are S.
          3. At least one M exists.
    So, 4. Some S are P.

   **5.**      1. No M are P.
          2. All M are S.
    So, 3. Some S are not P.

   **6.**      1. No M are P.
          2. All M are S.
          3. At least one M exists.
    So, 4. Some S are not P.

*   **7.**      1. No S are P.
    So, 2. Some non-P are not non-S.

   **8.**      1. All P are M.
          2. No M are S.
    So, 3. Some S are not P.

   **9.**      1. All P are M.
          2. All M are S.
    So, 3. Some S are P.

*   **10.**      1. No S are P.
          2. At least one S exists.
    So, 3. Some non-P are not non-S.

**Part B:** Testing Arguments   Use Venn diagrams to test the following arguments for validity. (Do not supply unstated premises.)

*   **1.**      1. All people who never make mistakes are admirable people.
          2. All ideal humans are people who never make mistakes.
    So, 3. Some ideal humans are admirable people.

**2.**     1. No plants are animals.
         2. All weeds are plants.
    So,  3. Some weeds are not animals.

**3.**     1. No perfect circles are perfect squares.
         2. Some perfect circles are objects of beauty.
    So,  3. Some objects of beauty are not perfect squares.

\*  **4.**     1. All persons who advocate the use of overwhelming nuclear force are persons who lack moral sensibility.
         2. All persons who advocate the use of overwhelming nuclear force are persons who should not serve as world leaders.
         3. At least one person who advocates the use of overwhelming nuclear force exists.
    So,  4. Some persons who should not serve as world leaders are persons who lack moral sensibility.

**5.**     1. All lions are cats.
         2. All cats are mammals.
    So,  3. Some mammals are lions.

**6.**     1. No terrorists who use nuclear weapons are good people.
         2. All terrorists who use nuclear weapons are people who mean well.
         3. At least one terrorist who uses nuclear weapons exists.
    So,  4. Some people who mean well are not good people.

\*  **7.**     1. All sycophants are flatterers.
         2. All flatterers are disgusting persons.
         3. At least one flatterer exists.
    So,  4. Some disgusting persons are sycophants.

**8.**     1. Some highly educated people are sybarites.
         2. All sybarites are poor role models.
    So,  3. Some poor role models are highly educated people.

**9.**     1. No oaks are elms.
         2. All oaks are trees.
         3. At least one elm exists.
    So,  4. Some trees are not elms.

\* **10.**     1. No members of the IRA are members of the IRS.
    So,  2. It is false that all members of the IRA are members of the IRS.

**11.**     1. All great inventors are slightly odd people.
         2. At least one great inventor exists.
    So,  3. Some slightly odd people are great inventors.

**12.**     1. No anarchists are Republicans.
         2. At least one anarchist exists.
    So,  3. Some non-Republicans are not nonanarchists.

\* **13.**     1. All scarlet things are red things.
    So,  2. It is false that no scarlet things are red things.

**14.**     1. No cities are nations.
      2. At least one city exists.
So,  3. Some cities are not nations.

**15.**     1. All people with perfect memories are people who remember
      everything.
So,  2. Some people with perfect memories are people who remember
      everything.

\* **16.**     1. It is false that some Germans are Zoroastrians.
So,  2. Some Germans are not Zoroastrians.

**17.**     1. It is false that some vampires are living things.
      2. At least one vampire exists.
So,  3. Some vampires are not living things.

**18.**     1. All people who do not care about social justice are heartless people.
So,  2. It is false that no people who do not care about social injustice are
      heartless people.

\* **19.**     1. No kangaroos are karate experts.
So,  2. Some kangaroos are not karate experts.

**20.**     1. It is false that some tyrants are not humans.
      2. At least one tyrant exists.
So,  3. Some tyrants are humans.

## 6.5 Enthymemes

An **enthymeme** is an argument with an unstated premise or an unstated conclusion. If we use the more general term "step" to refer to premises and/or conclusions, we can say that an enthymeme is an argument with one or more unstated steps. Unstated steps are also referred to as *missing* or *implicit* steps.

Enthymemes are common both in ordinary discourse and in academic writing. Why? Because many statements are presumed to be known to one's audience, and so it may be unnecessary to make these statements explicit. When evaluating an enthymeme, fairness and charity demand that we fill in the missing step(s). Here's an example:

> **33.** All Mozambicans are Africans. Hence, no Mozambicans are Asians.

A Venn diagram will show that (33), taken as it stands, is invalid. But obviously there is an unstated premise here, "No Africans are Asians" (or its converse, "No Asians are Africans"). And if we add this statement (or its converse) to the argument, we get a valid categorical syllogism:

> **34.**     1. No Africans are Asians.
>       2. All Mozambicans are Africans.
> So,  3. No Mozambicans are Asians.

Any kind of argument can have an unstated step, but we will here focus on categorical syllogisms. When we fill in missing steps in an argument, we must adhere to the principles of fairness and charity. This means that, to the extent possible, added steps should be true (or at least plausible) and should make the argument valid.

In order to evaluate an enthymematic categorical syllogism for validity, we proceed in three stages. First, identify the missing step. The missing step may be a major premise, a minor premise, or the conclusion. Second, put the syllogism into standard form. Third, apply the Venn method.

How do we identify the missing step? The missing step will contain two terms that have been used only once each in the enthymeme. If the missing step is a premise, the form (**A, E, I**, or **O**) and order of the terms should be chosen with an eye toward the information needed to arrive at the conclusion. If the missing step is a conclusion, the form and order of terms should be chosen with an eye toward what the information in the premises would show to be true. For example, consider the following argument:

> **35.** If anything is a moral judgment, then it is a subjective opinion. It follows that judgments about the wrongness of theft are subjective opinions.

The missing step here is a minor premise: "All judgments about the wrongness of theft are moral judgments." Putting the syllogism into standard form, we get:

> **36.**    1. All moral judgments are subjective opinions.
>
>    2. All judgments about the wrongness of theft are moral judgments.
>
> So, 3. All judgments about the wrongness of theft are subjective opinions.

And now we can readily apply the Venn method:

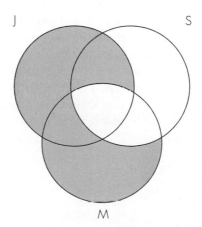

The diagram indicates that the argument is valid. The premise we have added seems to be true, but of course the first premise of the argument is highly controversial.

When adding steps to an enthymeme, it is not always possible to add a statement that is true (or plausible) and that makes the argument valid. Consider the following example:

37. All Ohioans are Americans. Hence, no Ohioans are socialists.

The missing step here is presumably "No Americans are socialists" (or its converse). Putting the syllogism into standard form, we get:

38.    1. No Americans are socialists.

      2. All Ohioans are Americans.

So, 3. No Ohioans are socialists.

Premise (1) is needed to make the argument valid, but (1) is false, since some Americans are socialists. When a false or doubtful premise is needed to make an argument valid, we bring out an important weakness in the argument by making the premise explicit, for in doing so we have identified an important reason for doubting the soundness of the argument.

In some cases, the context forces us to make a hard choice between adding a blatantly false premise and adding a premise that makes the argument invalid. For example, what is the missing step in the following argument?

39. All Lutherans are Christians. Therefore, all Protestants are Christians.

The missing step seems to be either "All Protestants are Lutherans" or "All Lutherans are Protestants." If we add "All Protestants are Lutherans" to the argument, then it is valid but has a blatantly false premise since not all Protestants are Lutherans (for example, Presbyterians and Baptists are Protestants). If we add "All Lutherans are Protestants" to the argument, then we add a true premise but one that makes the argument invalid. Obviously, the argument is deeply flawed. It is up to us to choose whether to present that flaw as a flaw in the logical structure or as a false premise. When faced with this sort of choice, let us adopt the practice of adding a step that makes the argument valid, leaving the truth value of the added step as a matter for discussion. So, in standard form, argument (39) looks like this:

40.    1. All Lutherans are Christians.

      2. All Protestants are Lutherans.

So, 3. All Protestants are Christians.

Sometimes the conclusion of an argument is left unstated.

41. Every politician who wants to win slings mud, and every politician wants to win!

When we put the argument into standard form, we make the conclusion explicit:

42.  1. All politicians who want to win are mudslingers.
     2. All politicians are politicians who want to win.
 So, 3. All politicians are mudslingers.

We add "All politicians are mudslingers" instead of "All mudslingers are politicians" because the former (unlike the latter) is guaranteed true by a diagram of the premises.

The following exercise will give you some practice in dealing with enthymemes.

## ◆ Exercise 6.5

**Part A:** Enthymemes   Identify the missing step in each of the following arguments. Then put the argument into standard form. Finally, use a Venn diagram to check the argument for validity.

* **1.** No certainty should be rejected. So, no self-evident propositions should be rejected.

 **2.** Every virtue is beneficial. Therefore, no vice is a virtue.

 **3.** Only rational animals are humans. It follows that no ducks are humans.

* **4.** Atoms are indestructible because every simple substance is indestructible.

 **5.** Every envious person wants others to fail. Consequently, no good person is envious.

 **6.** Nothing is a liar unless it is not praiseworthy. At least one liar is a human being. Draw your own conclusion!

* **7.** Only scientific statements are rational. It follows that aesthetic judgments are never rational.

 **8.** All verdicts rendered in courts of law are relative since all value judgments are relative.

 **9.** Perfect beings have every virtue. Therefore, at least one god is not a perfect being.

* **10.** Some beliefs about aliens are not rational, for all rational beliefs are proportioned to the available evidence.

11. No matter of faith is provable. At least one belief about life after death is a matter of faith. Draw your own conclusion!

12. No bears are wolves, so some grizzlies are not wolves.

* 13. Every vice is harmful. Accordingly, every vice is a form of laziness.

14. Every composite substance is a substance that has parts. Hence, no soul is a composite substance.

15. Every evil thing is to be avoided. But at least one evil thing is pleasurable. Draw your own conclusion.

**Part B:** More Enthymemes   The following enthymemes are paraphrased or slightly altered versions of arguments found in the writings of the philosopher Gottfried Wilhelm Leibniz. (These are arguments Leibniz *discusses*; some he endorses and some he does not.) Identify the missing step in each of the arguments. Then put the argument into standard form. Finally, use a Venn diagram to check the argument for validity.

*  1. Every event that is foreseen by God is predetermined. Consequently, every event is predetermined.

2. Every event that is predetermined is necessary. Every event is predetermined. Draw your own conclusion!

3. Every event is necessary. Hence, every sin is necessary.

*  4. No necessary event can be avoided. Only events that can be avoided are justly punished. Therefore, . . .

5. Every being that is omnipotent and perfectly good creates the best of all possible worlds. Hence, some deity creates the best of all possible worlds.

6. All composites are aggregates of simple substances. At least one composite exists. Draw your own conclusion.

*  7. Nothing that has no parts can come apart. So, nothing that has no parts can be annihilated.

8. If anything has the power to help everyone but helps only some, then it is not fair. Thus, some deity is not fair.

9. Any being who punishes people who do their best is an unjust being. No perfectly good being is an unjust being. Draw your own conclusion.

* 10. Every event is caused by a deity. It follows that every sin is caused by a deity.

## 6.6 Sorites and Removing Term-Complements

We have seen that ordinary language throws the logician many "curve balls" (i.e., complications). This section concerns two additional complications. First, we will discuss categorical syllogisms that are linked in a chain. Second, we will discuss categorical arguments that can be put into standard form through the elimination of term-complements.

## Sorites

The term "sorites" (so-rī-teez) comes from the Greek word *soros*, meaning "heap" or "pile." Roughly put, a sorites is a "heap" of syllogisms. More precisely, a **sorites** is a chain of syllogisms in which the final conclusion is stated but the subconclusions are unstated. Here is an example:

43.   1. All statements about beauty are statements known through the senses.

    2. All statements known through the senses are empirical statements.

    3. No mathematical statements are empirical statements.

    4. All geometrical statements are mathematical statements.

So,   5. No geometrical statements are statements about beauty.

Premises (1) and (2) validly imply the following subconclusion:

**Subconclusion 1**: All statements about beauty are empirical statements.

When combined with premise (3), subconclusion 1 validly implies:

**Subconclusion 2**: No mathematical statements are statements about beauty.

Premise (4) and subconclusion 2 validly imply (5), the conclusion of the argument. Thus, the sorites is a chain of three valid categorical syllogisms.

In general, sorites are easier to evaluate when they are in standard form. A sorites in **standard form** has these features:

    a. Each statement in the argument is in standard form ("All S are P," "No S are P," "Some S are P," or "Some S are not P").

    b. The predicate term of the conclusion occurs in the first premise.

    c. Each term appears twice, in two different statements.

    d. Each premise (except the first) has a term in common with the immediately preceding premise.

Is argument (43) in standard form? Yes. This is perhaps easier to see by looking at the form of the argument. Using obvious abbreviations, the form of the argument is this:

44.   1. All B are K.

    2. All K are E.

    3. No M are E.

    4. All G are M.

So,   5. No G are B.

When evaluating a sorites, we follow a three-step process. First, check to see if the sorites is in standard form. If it is, proceed to the next step. If it isn't, put it into standard form. To cut down on writing, we will freely use abbreviations for the terms as we put a sorites into standard form. Second, identify the subconclusions. Third, test each syllogism in the chain for validity, using a Venn diagram. If each syllogism in the chain is valid, the sorites is valid. If any of the syllogisms in the chain are invalid, the entire sorites is invalid on the principle that a chain is no stronger than its weakest link.

To illustrate this three-step process, let us evaluate the following sorites:

45. No cruel and unusual punishments are proportioned to the offense. Every just punishment is deserved. Moreover, all deserved punishments are proportioned to the offense. Therefore, no cruel and unusual punishment is a just punishment.

First, we put the sorites into standard form, using obvious abbreviations for the various terms (J: just punishments; D: deserved punishments; P: punishments that are proportioned to the offense; C: cruel and unusual punishments). Incidentally, it often helps to begin with the conclusion and then work backward, making sure that the first premise contains the predicate term of the conclusion:

46.     1. All J are D.
        2. All D are P.
        3. No C are P.
   So, 4. No C are J.

Premises (1) and (2) imply that all just punishments are punishments that are proportioned to the offense. Using our abbreviations:

Subconclusion 1: All J are P.

Let us adopt the practice of writing a subconclusion beside the last premise from which it is derived, like this:

47.     1. All J are D.
        2. All D are P.     Sub 1: All J are P.
        3. No C are P.
   So, 4. No C are J.

Subconclusion 1 and premise (3) combine to yield (4), the conclusion of the argument. So, this sorites is a chain of two categorical syllogisms. And we now apply the Venn method to each of the two categorical syllogisms:

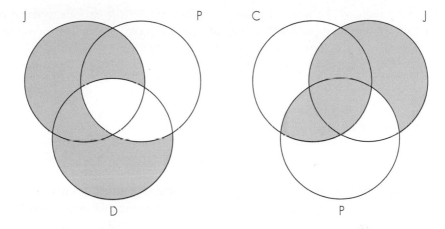

The diagram on the left evaluates the inference from premises (1) and (2) to subconclusion 1. The diagram on the right evaluates the inference from subconclusion 1 and premise (3) to the final conclusion of the argument, (4). Since both of these syllogisms are valid, the sorites itself is valid.

## Removing Term-Complements

Consider the following argument:

48.  1. All cats are nondogs.
  2. Some mammals are dogs.
So,  3. Some mammals are not cats.

This argument has four terms: "cats," "nondogs," "mammals," and "dogs." Hence, it is not a categorical syllogism in standard form. And if you try to evaluate this argument with a Venn diagram, questions arise regarding the label for the middle circle. You must label it either "dogs" or "nondogs." If you label the middle circle "dogs," then your diagram for the first premise cannot be the usual diagram for an **A** statement. If you label the middle circle "nondogs," then your diagram for the second premise cannot be the usual diagram for an **I** statement. (Try it!)

Note, however, that "dogs" and "nondogs" are term-complements. In arguments involving term-complements, we can often reduce the number of terms by applying conversion, obversion, and/or contraposition. For example, the obverse of "All cats are nondogs" is "No cats are dogs." Thus, we can rewrite argument (48) as:

49.  1. No cats are dogs.
  2. Some mammals are dogs.
So,  3. Some mammals are not cats.

We have reduced the number of terms in the argument from four to three by removing a term-complement. Argument (49) is a categorical syllogism in standard form, and the Venn diagram for it is entirely routine.

Consider yet another argument:

50.   1. No nonanimals are mammals.
      2. All nonmammals are nondogs.
So, 3. All dogs are animals.

Is this argument a categorical syllogism in standard form? No, it has six terms instead of three. But we can put it into standard form by a series of immediate inferences. First, we can convert the first premise to obtain "No mammals are nonanimals." Then, applying obversion, we get "All mammals are animals." Second, we can apply contraposition to premise (2) to get "All dogs are mammals." With these changes, the argument looks like this:

51.   1. All mammals are animals.
      2. All dogs are mammals.
So, 3. All dogs are animals.

Argument (51) is a categorical syllogism in standard form. Moreover, by removing the term-complements in argument (50), we have made it easier to understand.

We can often put an argument into standard form by removing term-complements via conversion, obversion, and/or contraposition. And we are free to remove term-complements as long as the changes we make to each statement produce a *logically equivalent* statement. (Remember, two statements are logically equivalent *if and only if* they validly imply each other.) However, if the changes we make produce any statement that is *not* logically equivalent to the original, then we have significantly changed the meaning of the statement—in which case we are working with a different argument from the original one. When removing term-complements, the permissible changes are as follows:

Conversion

No S are P.            No P are S.
Some S are P.          Some P are S.

Contraposition

All S are P.           All non-P are non-S.
Some S are not P.      Some non-P are not non-S.

Obversion

All S are P.           No S are non-P.
No S are P.            All S are non-P.
Some S are P.          Some S are not non-P.
Some S are not P.      Some S are non-P.

In each case, the statement on the left is logically equivalent to the statement on the right, and vice versa.

In attempting to remove term-complements, the most common error involves misapplications of conversion and contraposition. When you apply conversion to **A** and **O** statements, you do not in general wind up with logically equivalent statements. So, *never* use conversion on **A** and **O** statements when removing term-complements. Similarly, when you apply contraposition to **E** and **I** statements, you do not in general wind up with logically equivalent statements. So, *never* apply contraposition to **E** and **I** statements when removing term-complements. On the other hand, since a statement and its obverse are *always* logically equivalent, we are always free to apply obversion when we are removing term-complements.

It is often convenient to remove term-complements in order to put a sorites into standard form. Here's an example:

> 52.    1. No F are G.
>          2. All H are G.
>          3. All non-H are non-K.
>   So,  4. All K are non-F.

This sorites is not in standard form because the terms F, H, and K do not appear twice (the term-complements appear instead). But we can easily put this sorites into standard form by applying contraposition to premise (3) and obversion to the conclusion:

> 53.    1. No F are G.
>          2. All H are G.
>          3. All K are H.
>   So,  4. No K are F.

Again, by removing term-complements, we have not only put the argument into standard form but also made it easier to grasp and to evaluate.

The following exercise gives you practice in removing term-complements and in evaluating sorites.

## ◆ Exercise 6.6

**Part A:** Removing Term-Complements   The following categorical arguments (and argument forms) all have more than three terms. Reduce the terms to three in each case by removing term-complements via applications of conversion, obversion, and/or contraposition. To cut down on writing, use capital letters to abbreviate English terms.

> \*   1.    1. All M are non-P.
>                2. No S are non-M.
>      So,  3. No S are P.

2.    1. All logicians are nonpoets.
      2. Some logicians are not nondreamers.
   So, 3. Some dreamers are not poets.

3.    1. All non-P are non-M.
      2. Some S are M.
   So, 3. Some S are not non-P.

\*  4.    1. All nonphysicians are nonsurgeons.
         2. All physicians are nonchiropractors.
      So, 3. No chiropractors are surgeons.

5.    1. Some non-P are not non-M.
      2. No M are non-S.
   So, 3. Some S are not P.

6.    1. All mesomorphs are nonectomorphs.
      2. All nonectomorphs are things that are not slight persons.
   So, 3. No slight persons are mesomorphs.

\*  7.    1. No M are non-P.
         2. All non-M are non-S.
      So, 3. All S are P.

8.    1. No nonairplanes are jets.
      2. All nonjets are non-737s.
   So, 3. All 737s are airplanes.

9.    1. All M are non-P.
      2. Some S are M.
   So, 3. Some non-P are not non-S.

\* 10.    1. Some subatomic particles are mesons.
          2. No mesons are entities not subject to the strong nuclear force.
       So, 3. Some entities subject to the strong nuclear force are subatomic
              particles.

**Part B:** Standard Form    Put the following sorites into standard form, removing term-complements whenever possible. Then identify the unstated subconclusions and use Venn diagrams to test the sorites for validity.

\*  1.    1. Some A are B.
         2. All non-D are non-C.
         3. No B are non-C.
      So, 4. Some D are A.

2.    1. Some F are G.
      2. All non-H are non-G.
      3. All H are non-E.
   So, 4. Some non-E are not non-F.

   **3.**      1. Some K are non-L.
             2. No M are non-N.
             3. All N are L.
      So,   4. Some K are not M.

\*  **4.**      1. Some A are B.
             2. All non-E are non-D.
             3. All B are D.
             4. All E are non-C.
      So,   5. Some A are not C.

   **5.**      1. All F are non-M.
             2. All non-D are non-B.
             3. All D are M.
      So,   4. All F are non-B.

   **6.**      1. All U are non-T.
             2. All S are T.
             3. All non-S are non-R.
             4. All non-R are non-P.
      So,   5. All P are non-U.

\*  **7.**      1. All non-B are non-A.
             2. No C are B.
             3. Some D are non-C.
      So,   4. Some D are not A.

   **8.**      1. No R are non-S.
             2. All T are V.
             3. All non-R are non-Q.
             4. All P are Q.
             5. No T are S.
      So,   6. All V are non-P.

   **9.**      1. All F are G.
             2. No G are non-H.
             3. No J are H.
             4. Some K are J.
      So,   5. Some non-F are not non-K.

\* **10.**      1. Some B are A.
             2. All non-D are non-C.
             3. All B are C.
      So,   4. Some D are A.

**Part C:** Sorites   Put the following sorites into standard form. To cut down on writing, use capital letters as abbreviations for the various terms. Then identify the unstated subconclusions and use Venn diagrams to test the sorites for validity.

* **1.** No theorists who hold that life evolved from nonlife are people who have solid evidence for their views. Every advocate of chemical evolution is a theorist who holds that life evolved from nonlife. At least one Darwinian is a person who has solid evidence for his or her views. Consequently, not all Darwinians are advocates of chemical evolution.

   **2.** No voters who reject trickle-down economics are Republicans, for every voter who rejects trickle-down economics is a person who opposes tax cuts for the wealthy; all Democrats are non-Republicans; and only Democrats are persons who oppose tax cuts for the wealthy.

   **3.** All folks who know that the oil reserves are running low are people who favor the development of alternative sources of energy. Every person who favors the development of alternative sources of energy is a voter who favors a tax increase. All well-informed citizens are folks who know that the oil reserves are running low. Not every highly educated person is a voter who favors a tax increase. Therefore, not all highly educated people are well-informed citizens.

* **4.** Each and every dualist is a moral realist. Nothing is an emotivist unless it is not a moral realist. Only dualists are Zoroastrians. At least one positivist is an emotivist. It follows that some non-Zoroastrians are not nonpositivists.

   **5.** Every victim of sleep apnea is a sleep-deprived person. No sleep-deprived persons are nonunfortunates. At least one unfortunate is a college student. Therefore, some college students are victims of sleep apnea.

   **6.** No humans with a sense of justice are consumers who are willing to buy clothing made in sweatshops. But only shoppers are persons looking for good deals. Hence, not all shoppers are humans with a sense of justice because some persons looking for good deals are consumers who are willing to buy clothing made in sweatshops.

* **7.** Not all freethinkers are rational people. Every agnostic is a person who proportions his or her religious beliefs to the evidence. All people who proportion their religious beliefs to the evidence are rational people. Thus, not every freethinker is an agnostic.

   **8.** Only reasons that override mere prudence are ethical reasons. Some motives for laying down one's life are ethical reasons. No motives for laying down one's life are intentions that make sense if there's no life after death. It follows that not all reasons that override mere prudence are intentions that make sense if there's no life after death.

   **9.** There exist rapscallions that are human vermin. Only scalawags are moral freeloaders. All human vermin are moral freeloaders. Every scalawag is a nongangster. Hence, not every rapscallion is a gangster.

* **10.** No badly informed voters are responsible voters. Some folks who vote in every election are citizens who do not proportion their political beliefs to the evidence. Every citizen who does not proportion his or her political beliefs to the evidence is a badly informed voter. Only responsible voters are people

who ought to vote. Accordingly, not all folks who vote in every election are people who ought to vote.

## 6.7 Rules for Evaluating Syllogisms

Prior to the invention of Venn diagrams, categorical syllogisms were evaluated by means of a set of rules. Although the rules lack the visual intuitiveness of Venn diagrams, they are equally effective in testing syllogisms for validity. In this section, we will explore a set of rules for evaluating categorical syllogisms.

Our first rule is:

> **Rule 1:** A valid standard-form categorical syllogism must contain exactly three terms, and each term must be used with the same meaning throughout the argument.

A *fallacy of equivocation* occurs if a term is used with more than one meaning in a categorical syllogism. For example:

> 54. Only man is rational. But no woman is a man. Hence, no woman is rational.

Argument (54) violates Rule 1 because in the first premise, "man" means "human beings," while in the second premise, "man" means "male human."

The next two rules depend crucially on the concept of a term's being *distributed*. So, the rather technical concept of distribution must be explained in some detail before we proceed any further. A term is **distributed** in a statement if the statement says something about every member of the class that the term denotes. A term is **undistributed** in a statement if the statement does not say something about every member of the class the term denotes. For example:

> 55. All ants are insects.

Statement (55) says something about all members of the class of ants—namely, that every member of the class of ants belongs to the class of insects. Hence, the term "ants" is distributed in (55). But the term "insects" is undistributed, for the statement does not say anything about every member of the class of insects. In general, the subject term of a universal affirmative (or **A**) statement is distributed, while the predicate term is not.

Both terms are distributed in a universal negative (or **E**) statement. For instance:

> 56. No trumpets are flutes.

This says that every trumpet is excluded from the class of flutes and that every flute is excluded from the class of trumpets. Hence, both the subject term "trumpets" and the predicate term "flutes" are distributed.

Neither term is distributed in a particular affirmative (or **I**) statement. For example:

57. Some precious stones are diamonds.

This statement makes no assertion about all precious stones. Furthermore, it makes no assertion about all diamonds. Both the subject term and the predicate term of a particular affirmative statement are undistributed.

The predicate term of a particular negative (or **O**) statement is distributed, but its subject term is undistributed. For example:

58. Some precious stones are not diamonds.

Statement (58) does not say anything about *all* precious stones. But it does refer to all members of the class of diamonds, and it says that *all* diamonds are excluded from a portion of the class of precious stones.

To recap: Universal (**A** and **E**) statements distribute their subject terms, while negative (**E** and **O**) statements distribute their predicate terms. The following list summarizes our discussion of distribution:

| Letter Name | Form | Terms Distributed |
|---|---|---|
| A | All S are P. | S |
| E | No S are P. | S and P |
| I | Some S are P. | None |
| O | Some S are not P. | P |

We are now in position to state Rule 2.

Rule 2: In a valid standard-form categorical syllogism, the middle term must be distributed in at least one premise.

Here is an example of a syllogism that violates Rule 2:

59. All eagles are birds. All penguins are birds. So, all penguins are eagles.

The middle term, "birds," is not distributed in either premise since the predicate terms of **A** statements are not distributed. Within the Aristotelian scheme, a violation of Rule 2 is called a *fallacy of the undistributed middle*.

Why does the distribution of the middle term matter? Because the middle term has to serve as a link between the other terms. And if the middle term is undistributed, then neither premise makes an assertion about *all* the members of the class denoted by the middle term. Hence, it is possible that the minor term relates to one part of the class denoted by the middle term, while the major term relates to a different part of that class, with the result that there is no guaranteed link between the minor and major term.

Rule 3 also involves the concept of distribution.

Rule 3: In a valid standard-form categorical syllogism, a term must be distributed in the premises if it is distributed in the conclusion.

This rule can be broken in two basic ways, depending on whether the major or minor term is distributed in the conclusion but not in the premises. Consider the following examples:

60. All birds are animals. No bats are birds. So, no bats are animals.

61. All squares are rectangles. All squares are figures. So, all figures are rectangles.

In argument (60), the major term, "animals," is distributed in the conclusion but not in the premises. This sort of violation of Rule 3 is called a *fallacy of the illicit major.* In argument (61), the minor term, "figures," is distributed in the conclusion but not in the second premise. This type of violation of Rule 3 is called a *fallacy of the illicit minor.*

Why is it important for a term to be distributed in the premises if it is distributed in the conclusion? Well, suppose a term is distributed in the conclusion but not in the premises. Then the conclusion contains more information than the premises warrant because the conclusion says something about *all* members of the class denoted by the term, while the premises do *not* say something about all the members of that class. Therefore, if a term is distributed in the conclusion but not in the premises, the conclusion "goes beyond" the information contained in the premises, and hence the argument is invalid.

The next rule concerns the *quality* of the statements composing a categorical syllogism.

Rule 4: In a valid standard-form categorical syllogism, the number of negative premises must be equal to the number of negative conclusions.[1]

Since a syllogism has only one conclusion, this rule tells us that any categorical syllogism with two negative premises is invalid. For instance:

62. No dogs are cats. Some cats are not cocker spaniels. So, some cocker spaniels are not dogs.

The premises of argument (62) are true, while the conclusion is false, so (62) is clearly invalid.

Rule 4 also tells us that the conclusion of a categorical syllogism must be negative if one of the premises is negative. Thus, the following syllogism also violates Rule 4:

63. No tigers are wolves. Some felines are tigers. So, some felines are wolves.

---

### Summary of Rules for Determining the Validity of Categorical Syllogisms

**Rule 1:** A valid standard-form categorical syllogism must contain exactly three terms, and each term must be used with the same meaning throughout the argument.

**Rule 2:** In a valid standard-form categorical syllogism, the middle term must be distributed in at least one premise.

**Rule 3:** In a valid standard-form categorical syllogism, a term must be distributed in the premises if it is distributed in the conclusion.

**Rule 4:** In a valid standard-form categorical syllogism, the number of negative premises must be equal to the number of negative conclusions.

**Rule 5:** No valid standard-form categorical syllogism with a particular conclusion can have two universal premises.

---

Here again, the premises are true, while the conclusion is false, so the argument is invalid.

Finally, Rule 4 tells us that a categorical syllogism is invalid if it has a negative conclusion but no negative premises:

> **64.** All collies are dogs. Some animals are collies. So, some dogs are not animals.

Argument (64) has obviously true premises and an obviously false conclusion; therefore, it is plainly invalid. In fact, violations of Rule 4 are not common because the invalidity tends to be quite obvious.

At this point, our list of rules is complete from the traditional Aristotelian perspective. If we add the following rule, however, we can bring the Aristotelian system into agreement with modern systems of logic.

> **Rule 5:** No valid standard-form categorical syllogism with a particular conclusion can have two universal premises.[2]

Here is an example of a syllogism that violates Rule 5 but counts as valid in the traditional Aristotelian scheme:

> **65.** All Americans are humans. All morally perfect Americans are Americans. So, some morally perfect Americans are humans.

The conclusion asserts the existence of at least one morally perfect American. But from the standpoint of modern logic, we can assert that "all morally perfect Americans are Americans" without asserting that there actually *are* any morally perfect Americans. We can analyze the statement "All morally perfect Americans are Americans" as involving a conditional, along the following lines: "If anything is a morally perfect American, then it is an American." And such a statement can be true even if the term "employed" in the if-clause denotes an empty class.

Check your understanding of the Aristotelian theory of the syllogism by completing the following exercises.

## ◁▷ Exercise 6.7

**Part A:** Forms   Apply the five rules set forth in this section to determine whether the following forms are valid.

* **1.** No P are M. No M are S. So, no S are P.

 **2.** All M are P. No S are M. So, no S are P.

 **3.** All M are P. All M are S. So, all S are P.

* **4.** All P are M. All S are M. So, all S are P.

 **5.** No M are P. Some S are M. So, some S are not P.

 **6.** No M are P. All M are S. So, some S are not P.

* **7.** All P are M. Some S are not M. So, some S are not P.

 **8.** Some M are P. All S are M. So, some S are not P.

 **9.** All M are P. Some S are not M. So, some S are not P.

* **10.** Some P are not M. Some S are not M. So, some S are not P.

 **11.** All P are M. Some S are M. So, some S are P.

 **12.** No P are M. All M are S. So, no S are P.

* **13.** Some M are not P. All S are M. So, some S are not P.

 **14.** No M are P. Some M are not S. So, some S are not P.

 **15.** All P are M. No M are S. So, some S are not P.

* **16.** All M are P. All S are M. So, some S are P.

 **17.** All P are M. All M are S. So, all S are P.

 **18.** No P are M. All S are M. So, some S are not P.

* **19.** Some M are P. Some M are S. So, some S are P.

 **20.** Some P are M. All S are M. So, some S are P.

**Part B:** Valid or Invalid?   For each of the following categorical syllogisms, specify the form using "S" to stand for the minor term, "P" for the major term, and "M" for the middle term. (If the English argument itself is not in standard form, be sure your form puts the major premise first, the minor premise second, and the conclusion last.) Then apply the five rules set forth in this section to determine whether the syllogism has a valid form.

* **1.** Some great scientists are famous. No TV stars are great scientists. So, some TV stars are not famous.

  **2.** No deathly ill people are hypochondriacs. All hypochondriacs are dysfunctional people. Accordingly, some deathly ill people are dysfunctional people.

  **3.** Some books written by Kant are not great books. For no great books are books that put their readers to sleep. But some books written by Kant are books that put their readers to sleep.

* **4.** No humans are animals. All members of *homo sapiens* are animals. Therefore, no humans are members of *homo sapiens*.

  **5.** All values that can be quantified are important values. No human emotions are values that can be quantified. Consequently, no human emotions are important values.

  **6.** No great altruists are great thinkers. Some great thinkers are people who make life better for humanity in general. It follows that some people who make life better for humanity in general are not great altruists.

* **7.** All cars are vehicles. All Ford automobiles are cars. Hence, some Ford automobiles are vehicles.

  **8.** All banks are edges of rivers. Some banks are financial institutions. Thus, some financial institutions are edges of rivers.

  **9.** All acts that promote the general welfare are commanded by God. For all acts commanded by God are obligatory acts. And all acts that promote the general welfare are obligatory acts.

* **10.** All of the greatest human achievements are accomplishments that have come at a great price. Some accomplishments that have come at a great price are not brilliant discoveries. We may conclude that some of the greatest human achievements are not brilliant discoveries.

  **11.** All kleptomaniacs are troubled persons. No Bodhisattvas are troubled persons. So, some kleptomaniacs are not Bodhisattvas.

  **12.** All biologists are vivisectionists. Some vivisectionists are well-intentioned people. Therefore, some biologists are well-intentioned people.

  **13.** Every schipperke is a small dog. Some small dogs are not black. Hence, not all black dogs are schipperkes.

  **14.** No bagatelle is important. Some important things are pleasurable. It follows that at least one bagatelle is not pleasurable.

  **15.** All Mennonites are Protestants. No Mennonites are Roman Catholics. Accordingly, no Protestants are Roman Catholics.

## Notes

1. My formulation of Rule 4 is borrowed from Wesley C. Salmon, *Logic*, 3rd ed. (Englewood Cliffs, NJ: Prentice-Hall, 1984), p. 57.
2. My formulation of Rule 5 is borrowed from Irving Copi and Carl Cohen, *Introduction to Logic*, 9th ed. (Englewood Cliffs, NJ: Prentice-Hall, 1994), p. 266.

## Chapter 7

# Statement Logic:
# Truth Tables

The history of the discipline of logic is not a continuous, upward progression from one discovery to the next. Rather, it is characterized by episodes of discovery followed by lengthy periods in which little creative work was done. The philosopher Aristotle (384–322 B.C.E.) is generally considered the father of logic. His syllogistic logic was the first great systematic development in the field. The Stoic philosopher Chrysippus (279–206 B.C.E.) also made important contributions to logic by developing the rudiments of statement logic. For example, Chrysippus analyzed compound statements such as disjunctions and conditionals and identified the patterns of reasoning that we now refer to as *modus ponens* and *modus tollens*. But for over a thousand years after the death of Chrysippus, there were few significant advances in the field of logic. Most philosophers were content to write commentaries on the works of Aristotle and Chrysippus.

During the medieval period, there was a resurgence of interest in logic. Philosophers such as Peter Abelard (1079–1142) and William of Ockham (c. 1285–1349) made important contributions to the field. Some of the medieval logicians offered subtle insights into *modal logic* (roughly, the logic of possibility and necessity). However, at the end of the medieval period, logic again entered a time of relative neglect, so there was little creative work in the field from the middle of the 15th century until the time of the German philosopher Gottfried Wilhelm Leibniz (1646–1716). Leibniz stimulated interest in a more symbolic approach to logic.

Since the mid-19th century, the field of logic has developed at a rapid pace. We have already examined the work of John Venn (1834–1923), whose diagram method is perhaps the most intuitive means of evaluating categorical syllogisms. In this chapter, we will focus primarily on the truth table method developed by the American philosopher Charles Sanders Peirce (1839–1914).[1] However, before we can apply the truth table method, we must first learn how to translate English arguments into symbols.

# 7.1 Symbolizing English Arguments

In Chapter 1, we saw that arguments are valid by virtue of having a valid form. Modern logicians have developed very useful ways of symbolizing an argument's form. And as we will see, symbolizing an argument enables us to apply certain powerful techniques to determine its validity.

To symbolize statements properly, we must distinguish between atomic and compound statements. An **atomic statement** is one that does not have any other statement as a component. For example:

1. Shakespeare wrote *Hamlet*.

2. China has a large population.

3. Roses are red.

A **compound statement** is one that has at least one atomic statement as a component. For instance:

4. It is not the case that Ben Jonson wrote *Hamlet*.

5. China has a large population, and Luxembourg has a small population.

6. Either Palermo is the capital of Sicily, or Messina is the capital of Sicily.

7. If Sheboygan is in Wisconsin, then Sheboygan is in the U.S.A.

8. The Democrats win if and only if the Republicans quarrel.

We can symbolize the *atomic* statements in these compounds with capital letters, as follows:

B: Ben Jonson wrote *Hamlet*.
C: China has a large population.
L: Luxembourg has a small population.
P: Palermo is the capital of Sicily.
M: Messina is the capital of Sicily.
S: Sheboygan is in Wisconsin.
U: Sheboygan is in the U.S.A.
D: The Democrats win.
R: The Republicans quarrel.

The compounds themselves can then be written as follows (in order):

9. It is not the case that B.
10. C and L.
11. Either P or M.

12. If S, then U.
13. D if and only if R.

Note that statement (9) counts as a compound even though it has only one statement as a component. It is a compound consisting of an atomic statement and the phrase "it is not the case that."

Throughout this chapter and the next, we will use capital letters to stand for atomic statements. We will also use symbols to stand for the key logical words in our example compounds, namely, "it is not the case that," "and," "or," "if . . . then . . . ," and "if and only if." We will symbolize these English expressions by means of **logical operators**. We can sum up the symbol system as follows:*

| Operator | Name | Translates | Type of Compound |
|---|---|---|---|
| ~ | tilde | not | negation |
| • | dot | and | conjunction |
| ∨ | vee | or | disjunction |
| → | arrow | if-then | conditional |
| ↔ | double-arrow | if and only if | biconditional |

## Negations

The "~" symbol, called the **tilde**, is used to translate the English word "not" and its stylistic variants. Take the following example:

14. Roses are not blue. (R: Roses are blue)

The **scheme of abbreviation** on the right assigns a distinct capital letter to each atomic statement in the English. Using the tilde, we can then symbolize statement (14) as follows:

15. ~R

Of course, the English language provides a number of ways of negating a statement. For example:

a. It is not the case that roses are blue.
b. It is false that roses are blue.
c. It is not true that roses are blue.
d. Roses fail to be blue.

---

*From a historical point of view, symbolic logic is relatively new and its notation is not yet standardized. Thus, although the symbols provided in this text are in common use, they are not the only ones in common use. Many texts employ one or more of the following alternatives: "¬" to symbolize negations; "&" to symbolize conjunctions; "⊃" to symbolize conditionals, and "≡" to symbolize biconditionals. The lack of standard notation in logic is inconvenient, but it is not difficult to move from one notation to another once the basic principles have been mastered.

Statement (15) translates each of these English expressions into symbols.

---

Each of the statements below is a **negation**. The main operator is the *tilde*.

~C

~(A ∨ B)

~(F → G)

---

## Conjunctions

The "•" sign (called the **dot**) is used to translate the English word "and" as well as its stylistic variants. Take the following example:

16. Hobbes was born in 1588, *and* Descartes was born in 1596. (H: Hobbes was born in 1588; D: Descartes was born in 1596)

Using the scheme of abbreviation indicated, statement (16) translates into symbols as follows:

17. H • D

The statements composing a conjunction (*H* and *D* in this case) are called **conjuncts**. A partial list of stylistic variants for "and" is provided by the following set of sentences:

a. Hobbes was born in 1588, *but* Descartes was born in 1596.

b. Hobbes was born in 1588; *however*, Descartes was born in 1596.

c. *While* Hobbes was born in 1588, Descartes was born in 1596.

d. *Although* Hobbes was born in 1588, Descartes was born in 1596.

e. Hobbes was born in 1588, *yet* Descartes was born in 1596.

f. Hobbes was born in 1588; *nevertheless*, Descartes was born in 1596.

g. Hobbes was born in 1588 *even though* Descartes was born in 1596.

h. Hobbes was born in 1588 *though* Descartes was born in 1596.

(17) correctly symbolizes each of these variants. You may be thinking that such words as "but," "while," and "although" do not have quite the same connotation as "and" in ordinary English. Indeed, these words convey a sense of contrast that is lacking in "and." But bear in mind that some distortion often results when one language is translated into another. Moreover, *for the purpose of evaluating arguments for validity*, the expressions in the previous list can usually be translated adequately by means of the dot.

It should be noted, however, that the dot does not correctly translate *every* use of the English word "and." Consider the following statements:

18. Jane became pregnant and got married. (P: Jane became pregnant; M: Jane got married)
19. Jane got married and became pregnant.[2]

In ordinary conversation, these two statements do not mean the same thing. Here, the word "and" has the force of "and then." In other words, it indicates a temporal order. But the dot does not indicate any such temporal order, so the dot cannot adequately translate statements (18) and (19). Can the dot provide an adequate translation of the following statements?

20. Jack and Jill are married. (J: Jack is married; M: Jill is married)
21. Jack and Jill are persons. (J: Jack is a person; P: Jill is a person)

Statement (20) would normally be taken to mean that Jack and Jill are married *to each other*. But if we translate (20) via the dot, we get a statement that could be true even if Jack and Jill are *not* married to each other, namely, $J \cdot M$. On the other hand, (21) *can* be adequately translated by means of the dot: $J \cdot P$.

Parentheses must often be used as a form of punctuation. To understand why, consider the following statement:

22. It is not true that both Carla and Bill won. (C: Carla won; B: Bill won)

The correct symbolization is as follows:

23. $\sim(C \cdot B)$

If we remove the parentheses, we get this:

24. $\sim C \cdot B$

(24) says, "Carla did not win, and Bill won," which is not at all the meaning of (22). So, the placement of parentheses is important when translating English into symbols.

In longer statements, we may alternate parentheses and brackets, since multiple sets of parentheses can become confusing. For instance:

25. The statement "Al is old, but he is strong and healthy" is false. (O: Al is old; S: Al is strong; H: Al is healthy)

The comma indicates how the conjuncts are to be grouped:

26. $\sim[O \cdot (S \cdot H)]$

---

Each of the statements below is a **conjunction**. The main operator is the *dot*.

E • ~F

(G v H) • K

(L → M) • (N v O)

---

## Disjunctions

The "v" sign (called the **vee**) is used to symbolize disjunctions. (This symbol is borrowed from the first letter of the Latin word *vel*, meaning "or.") The vee means "either . . . or . . . or *both*," which is commonly referred to as the *inclusive* sense of the word "or." The vee does *not* mean "either . . . or . . . *but not both*," which is commonly referred to as the *exclusive* sense of the word "or."[3] Consider this example:

> 27. Either Carol attends college or she gets a job (or both). (C: Carol attends college; J: Carol gets a job)

Statement (27) can be translated into symbols this way:

> 28. C v J

(28) also translates the stylistic variants of (27), such as the following:

> a. Carol attends college *and/or* she gets a job.
> b. Carol attends college *or* she gets a job.
> c. *Either* Carol attends college *or* she gets a job.
> d. Carol attends college *unless* she gets a job.

As a general rule, when symbolizing arguments containing disjunctions, assume that the word "or" is used in the inclusive sense unless this assumption renders the argument invalid. For example, consider the following argument, which has the form of a *disjunctive syllogism*:

> 29. Lassie is either a cat or a dog. Lassie is not a cat. So, Lassie is a dog.
> (C: Lassie is a cat; D: Lassie is dog)

This argument is correctly symbolized as follows:

> 30. C v D,  ~C  ∴ D

Several things should be noted here. First, a comma is used to punctuate (or separate) the premises. Second, the vee is used in the first premise even though C and D cannot in fact both be true. The argument form is valid even if the "or" is inclusive: "Either *C* or *D* (or both) are true. It is not true that C. So, *D* is true." Third, note the use of the triple-dot symbol to mark the conclusion. This is customary among logicians.

What if we need the exclusive "or" to represent an argument fairly? For example:

> 31. Either the Sonics won or the Bulls won. The Sonics won. So, the Bulls did not win. (S: The Sonics won; B: The Bulls won)

Intuitively, the argument is valid, but the following symbolized version is invalid:

> 32. S ∨ B, S ∴ ~B

Here's a counterexample: "Either trees are plants or flowers are plants (or both are plants). Trees are plants. So, flowers are not plants." To present the argument fairly, we need to interpret the first premise as follows:

> 33. Either the Sonics won or the Bulls won, but it is not true that both the Sonics won and the Bulls won.

The comma indicates that the main logical connective in (33) is the word "but," which is symbolized by the dot. The left conjunct is a disjunction ("Either the Sonics won or the Bulls won"), and the right conjunct is the negation of a conjunction ("It is not true that both the Sonics won and the Bulls won"). So, in symbols, (33) looks like this:

> 34. (S ∨ B) • ~(S • B)

This example draws attention once again to the importance of parentheses. For example, if we omit the set of parentheses on the left, we have: $S \lor B \cdot \sim(S \cdot B)$. But this expression is ambiguous—it might be taken to mean (34), but it could also be taken to mean this: $S \lor [B \cdot \sim(S \cdot B)]$. Note that the main operator in the latter statement is the vee rather than the dot. Thus, parentheses are often needed to prevent ambiguity.

With (34) as its first premise, argument (31) as a whole is symbolized as follows:

> 35. (S ∨ B) • ~(S • B), S ∴ ~B

This argument is intuitively valid, and we will prove that it is valid later in this chapter.

Before leaving disjunctions, let us note that statements of the form "Neither *A* nor *B*" can be symbolized in two ways. For instance:

> 36. Neither Sue nor Fred is happy. (S: Sue is happy; F: Fred is happy)

We can symbolize statement (36) by means of the vee, as follows:

37.  ~(S ∨ F)

But we can also symbolize it by means of the dot, like this:

38.  ~S • ~F

---

Each of the statements below is a **disjunction**. The main operator is the *vee*.
~P ∨ Q
(R • S) ∨ ~T
(U → W) ∨ ~(X • Y)

---

## Conditionals

The "→" sign (called the **arrow**) is used to symbolize conditionals. For example:

39.  If Fido is a dog, then he is an animal. (D: Fido is a dog; A: Fido is an animal)

(39) can be symbolized as follows:

40.  D → A

As we observed in Chapter 1, there are many stylistic variants for if-then state-ments. We will use the arrow to symbolize all of them. For example, expression (40) symbolizes not only (39) but also each of the following:

a. *Given that* Fido is a dog, Fido is an animal.

b. Fido is an animal *given that* he is a dog.

c. *Assuming that* Fido is a dog, he is an animal.

d. Fido is an animal *assuming that* he is a dog.

e. *Provided that* Fido is a dog, he is an animal.

f. Fido is an animal *provided that* he is a dog.

g. *On the condition that* Fido is a dog, he is an animal.

h. Fido is an animal *on the condition that* he is a dog.

i. Fido is an animal *if* he is a dog.

j. Fido is a dog *only if* he is an animal.

k. Fido's being a dog *is a sufficient condition for* Fido's being an animal.

l. Fido's being an animal *is a necessary condition for* Fido's being a dog.

Items (k) and (l) merit comment. A *sufficient condition* is a condition that guarantees that a statement is true (or that a phenomenon will occur). For instance, *Fido's being a dog* guarantees that he is an animal. By contrast, *Fido's being an animal* does not guarantee that he is a dog, for he might be some other kind of animal. The *antecedent* (if-clause) of a true conditional statement provides a sufficient condition for the truth of the *consequent* (then-clause).

A *necessary condition* is a condition that, if lacking, guarantees that a statement is false (or that a phenomenon will not occur). Thus, *Fido's being an animal* is a necessary condition for *Fido's being a dog*, for if Fido is not an animal, then he is not a dog. The consequent (then-clause) of a true conditional statement provides a necessary condition for the truth of the antecedent (if-clause).

---

Each of the statements below is a **conditional**. The main operator is the *arrow*.

$\sim X \to Y$

$Z \to (A \lor B)$

$(C \cdot \sim D) \to (E \lor \sim F)$

---

Let us now symbolize an argument involving a conditional statement:

41. If humans have souls, then immaterial things can evolve from matter. Immaterial things cannot evolve from matter. So, humans do not have souls. (H: Humans have souls; M: Immaterial things can evolve from matter)

Using the scheme of abbreviation provided, argument (41) can be symbolized like this:

42. $H \to M$, $\sim M$ $\therefore \sim H$

Again, we use the triple-dot symbol to mark the conclusion. Can you identify the form employed in argument (42)? It is *modus tollens*.

Before leaving our discussion of conditionals, let us note that the word "unless" can be translated by means of the arrow as well as the vee. For example:

43. We will lose unless we do our best. (L: We will lose; B: We will do our best)

As we have already seen, (43) can be symbolized as follows:

44. $L \lor B$

But it can also be symbolized by a combination of the arrow and the tilde, like this:

45. $\sim B \to L$

In other words, (43) has the same meaning as "If we do not do our best, then we will lose."

## Biconditionals

The "↔" sign (called the **double-arrow**) is used to symbolize biconditionals. For example:

46. Mary is a teenager *if and only if* she is from 13 to 19 years of age. (M: Mary is a teenager; Y: Mary is from 13 to 19 years of age)

This statement may be symbolized as follows:

47. M ↔ Y

And (47) symbolizes not only (46) but also its stylistic variants, such as these:

a. Mary is a teenager *just in case* she is from 13 to 19 years of age.

b. Mary's being a teenager is *a necessary and sufficient condition for* Mary's being from 13 to 19 years of age.

---

Each of the following statements is a **biconditional**. The main operator is the *double-arrow*.

~H ↔ J

~K ↔ (P ∨ Q)

(L • M) ↔ (N → T)

---

Let us now consider an example that illustrates some of the finer points of translating arguments into symbols:

48. If Dostoyevsky was right, then everything is permissible if God does not exist. But it is not true that if God does not exist, everything is permissible. Therefore, Dostoyevsky was not right. (D: Dostoyevsky was right; E: Everything is permissible; G: God exists)

The first premise may be symbolized as follows:

49. D → (~G → E)

Note that we cannot remove the parentheses from (49), for if we did, we would alter the meaning:

50. D → ~G → E

Statement (50) is ambiguous because it could be interpreted as (49) or as follows:

51. (D → ~G) → E

And these two statements have different meanings. (51) translates sentences that are difficult to put gracefully into English, such as the following:

52. If Dostoyevsky was right only if God does not exist, then everything is permitted.

53. If God doesn't exist given that Dostoyevsky was right, then everything is permitted.

This should make it clear that (51) is not an accurate translation of the first premise of the argument.

Now, let us symbolize the second premise of argument (48), that is, "It is not true that if God does not exist, everything is permissible":

54.  ~(~G → E)

Note that there must be a tilde *outside* the parentheses in this case because "it is not true that" precedes the word "if" in the English statement. Moreover, we cannot drop the parentheses. If we did, we would get this:

55.  ~~G → E

Statement (55) says, "If it is not true that God does not exist, then everything is permissible." In other words, since the two "nots" cancel each other out, it says, "If God exists, everything is permissible," which is not at all the meaning of the English.

Finally, let us symbolize the conclusion of argument (48), that is, "Dostoyevsky was not right":

56.  ~D

Note that we use no parentheses in symbolizing the conclusion. For example, do *not* write ~(D). We do not put parentheses around a single statement letter because this only adds clutter. Nor do we write (~D). *Parentheses may be used with the dot, the vee, the arrow, and the double-arrow, but not with the tilde itself.*

Now, let's put all the pieces together. Here is the original argument and our symbolization of it:

If Dostoyevsky was right, then everything is permissible if God does not exist. But it is not true that if God does not exist, everything is permissible. Therefore, Dostoyevsky was not right. (D: Dostoyevsky was right; E: Everything is permissible; G: God exists)

*In symbols:* D → (~G → E),  ~(~G → E)  ∴ ~D

In closing this section, let us describe our symbolic language more precisely. The vocabulary consists of parentheses, the logical operators (namely, ~, v, •, →, and ↔), and statement letters (that is, capital letters A through Z). An *expression* of statement logic is *any* sequence of symbols in this vocabulary, such as ($\rightarrow S \lor \leftrightarrow (N\sim)$). A grammatically correct symbolic expression is called a **well-formed formula** (WFF for short). To sum up what counts as a WFF, let us use the italicized, lowercase letters *p* and *q* as **statement variables**, which can stand for any statement. For instance, in the following summary, the statement variable *p* could stand for A, for $\sim$B, for (C $\lor$ $\sim$D), for (E $\bullet$ F), for (G $\rightarrow$ H), and so on. A symbolic expression is a WFF under the following conditions:

1. Capital letters (which stand for atomic statements) are WFFs.
2. If *p* is a WFF, then so is $\sim p$.
3. If *p* and *q* are WFFs, then so is $(p \bullet q)$.
4. If *p* and *q* are WFFs, then so is $(p \lor q)$.
5. If *p* and *q* are WFFs, then so is $(p \rightarrow q)$.
6. If *p* and *q* are WFFs, then so is $(p \leftrightarrow q)$.

*Nothing counts as a WFF unless it can be demonstrated to be one by applications of the above conditions.* Consider a symbolic expression that violates the above conditions:

57. (A $\lor$ B $\bullet$ C)

We cannot tell whether the main operator in (57) is the vee or the dot. Thus, (57) is ambiguous between the following:

58. ((A $\lor$ B) $\bullet$ C)
59. (A $\lor$ (B $\bullet$ C))

Both of these formulas are WFFs. Let us examine (58) in detail. Its main operator is the dot. To apply condition (3) above, replace *p* with (A $\lor$ B) and *q* with C. Thus, (58) is a WFF given that (A $\lor$ B) and C are WFFs. Condition (1) assures us that C is a WFF. Condition (4) assures us that (A $\lor$ B) is a WFF if A is a WFF and B is a WFF; and of course A and B are WFFs according to condition (1). Hence, (58) is itself a WFF.

Please note that the six conditions above are to be taken quite strictly. For example, condition (2) does not tell us to place parentheses around negations, so we should not do so. Thus, $\sim$A is a WFF, but ($\sim$A) is not a WFF. Also, the above conditions tell us to use parentheses along with the dot, vee, arrow, and double-arrow. So, strictly speaking, our rules tell us to write (F $\rightarrow$ G) rather than F $\rightarrow$ G. And whenever there is a question about whether a given expression is a WFF, we can use the above conditions strictly to obtain a definitive answer. *That said, for the sake of convenience, certain abbreviations are permitted and will be routinely employed.* For example, we can drop parentheses in many cases without creating ambiguity, and we will do so to avoid clutter. Thus, we will routinely write $F \rightarrow G$ rather than $(F \rightarrow G)$, and $(A \vee B) \bullet C$ rather than $((A \vee B) \bullet C)$. Also, even though our rules make no mention of brackets, we will often alternate parentheses with brackets in long expressions, as this makes the statements a bit easier to read. For example, we will routinely write $\sim[F \bullet (G \vee H)]$ rather than $\sim(F \bullet (G \vee H))$.

The symbolic language we have developed in this section is extremely useful as a means of representing the forms of arguments. But, as with any language, practice is essential to facility. The following exercises provide you with an opportunity to practice translating English into symbols.

## ◆ Exercise 7.1

**Part A:** Well-Formed Formulas?   Which of the following symbolic expressions are well-formed formulas (WFFs)? Which are not? (In answering these questions, use the six conditions for WFFs strictly, making no allowances for routine abbreviations.)

* 1. $(A \rightarrow B \rightarrow C)$
  2. $(\sim B)$
  3. $(\sim(C) \rightarrow F)$
* 4. $(E \rightarrow (\sim F \rightarrow G)$
  5. $\sim((H \rightarrow J) \rightarrow (K \rightarrow L)$
  6. $(M \rightarrow \sim\sim N)$
* 7. $(O \rightarrow \sim(P \rightarrow R))$
  8. $((Q \rightarrow S) \rightarrow T)$
  9. $(\sim U \rightarrow (W))$
* 10. $\sim Z$

  11. $\sim(B \bullet C)$
  12. $\sim(\sim W \vee \sim Z)$
* 13. $\sim(m \leftrightarrow \sim h)$
  14. $(\sim E \bullet \sim F \bullet \sim\sim G)$
  15. $\sim(\sim A \rightarrow \sim R)$
* 16. $(\sim S \vee \sim R \vee \sim(T \bullet U))$
  17. $(\sim P \vee Q \vee \sim R)$
  18. $((L \vee M) \rightarrow \sim S)$
* 19. $(\sim(D \bullet E) \leftrightarrow (F \vee \sim G))$
  20. $((\sim H \bullet \sim\sim F) \rightarrow \sim(\sim K \leftrightarrow \sim N))$

**Part B:** Permissible Departures from Strict Grammar   What counts as a WFF is defined strictly in terms of six conditions, but in some cases, parentheses can be dropped without changing the meaning and without causing ambiguity. Also, in some cases, alternating brackets with parentheses makes a formula easier to read. Which of the following are examples of formulas that permissibly depart from a strict application of the six conditions by dropping a set of parentheses or by an appropriate use of brackets?

* 1. $E \vee \sim F$
  2. $\sim G \bullet \sim H$
  3. $\sim J \leftrightarrow \sim K$
* 4. $\sim L \vee [(M \rightarrow N) \rightarrow \sim O]$
  5. $(\sim Q \vee \sim R \vee \sim\sim S)$

  6. $(A \vee B) \leftrightarrow (C \leftrightarrow D)$
* 7. $\sim U \rightarrow \sim X$
  8. $[\sim Z \bullet \sim W \vee \sim\sim Y]$
  9. $\sim A \rightarrow (\sim C \rightarrow F)$
* 10. $(B \bullet E) \bullet [(G \vee H) \bullet (J \bullet K)]$

**Part C: Symbolizing** Translate the following statements into symbols, using the schemes of abbreviation provided.

* 1. The crops will fail unless it rains. (C: The crops will fail; R: It rains)

2. Humans are animals if they are mammals. (A: Humans are animals; M: Humans are mammals)

3. The statement "If humans are rational, then they are not animals" is false. (R: Humans are rational; A: Humans are animals)

* 4. Bats are mammals only if they nourish their young with milk. (M: Bats are mammals; N: Bats nourish their young with milk)

5. Coffee isn't good if it isn't fresh-brewed. (G: Coffee is good; F: Coffee is fresh-brewed)

6. Assuming that your test scores are high and you get your paper in on time, you will do well. (T: Your test scores are high; P: You get your paper in on time; W: You will do well)

* 7. Roberto lacks wisdom. (R: Roberto has wisdom)

8. The statement "Humans lack rationality" is false. (H: Humans have rationality)

9. Polly fails to be a parrot provided that she cannot talk and does not want a cracker. (P: Polly is a parrot; T: Polly can talk; C: Polly wants a cracker)

* 10. Neither birds nor snakes are mammals. (B: Birds are mammals; S: Snakes are mammals)

11. Given that Linda is both smart and diligent, she will do well; but Linda is not diligent. (S: Linda is smart; D: Linda is diligent; W: Linda will do well)

12. Al wins only if Ed does not win, and Ed wins only if Al does not win. (A: Al wins; E: Ed wins)

* 13. If Smith fails to win, then either Jones wins or Smith and Jones are tied. (S: Smith wins; J: Jones wins; T: Smith and Jones are tied)

14. Assuming that Julio is a bachelor, he is a man who is unmarried. (B: Julio is a bachelor; M: Julio is a man; J: Julio is married)

15. Erin's being penniless is a sufficient condition for her being miserable. (P: Erin is penniless; M: Erin is miserable)

* 16. Kareem's being tall is a necessary condition for his being on the team. (K: Kareem is tall; T: Kareem is on the team)

17. The statement "Santa does not exist" is false. (S: Santa exists)

18. We will be evicted unless we pay the rent. (E: We will be evicted; P: We pay the rent)

* 19. Although reindeer exist, Santa does not exist; but adults are not honest if Santa does not exist. (R: Reindeer exist; S: Santa exists; H: Adults are honest)

20. Paula will pass the test just in case she studies diligently. (P: Paula will pass the test; S: Paula studies diligently)

**Part D:** More Symbolizing  Translate the following statements into symbols, using the schemes of abbreviation provided.

* **1.** The picture frame is square only if it is rectangular. (S: The picture frame is square; R: The picture frame is rectangular)

  **2.** You will not succeed if you lack common sense. (S: You will succeed; C: You have common sense)

  **3.** If Sammy is a penguin, then Sammy is a bird that cannot fly. (P: Sammy is a penguin; B: Sammy is a bird; F: Sammy can fly)

* **4.** Either you work hard or you have fun, but not both. (W: You work hard; F: You have fun)

  **5.** Given that Bozo has a bill, Bozo is either a duck or a platypus. (B: Bozo has a bill; D: Bozo is a duck; P: Bozo is a platypus)

  **6.** Neither penguins nor ostriches can fly. (P: Penguins can fly; O: Ostriches can fly)

* **7.** If Alvin has a bill, then he is not a platypus if he has feathers. (B: Alvin has a bill, P: Alvin is a platypus; F: Alvin has feathers)

  **8.** Neither Smith nor Jones wins if there is a tie, but Jones does not win given that Smith wins. (S: Smith wins; J: Jones wins; T: There is a tie)

  **9.** While Miriam is both competent and hard-working, she is not interested in the job. (C: Miriam is competent; H: Miriam is hard-working; J: Miriam is interested in the job)

* **10.** Given that Murphy is a bat only if he can fly, Murphy is not a bat. (B: Murphy is a bat; F: Murphy can fly)

  **11.** Sally will pass unless her mind goes blank. (P: Sally will pass; M: Sally's mind goes blank)

  **12.** Either Tyson wins or Holyfield wins, but not both. (T: Tyson wins; H: Holyfield wins)

  **13.** Stella's being in Arkansas is a sufficient condition for her being in the U.S.A. (A: Stella is in Arkansas; U: Stella is in the U.S.A.)

  **14.** Humberto's being competent is a necessary and sufficient condition for his being hired. (C: Humberto is competent; H: Humberto is hired)

  **15.** Solomon's growing older is a necessary condition for his becoming wiser, but it is not a sufficient condition for his becoming wiser. (S: Solomon grows older; W: Solomon becomes wiser)

  **16.** Dan's being in Pennsylvania is a necessary condition for his being in Philadelphia. (D: Dan is in Pennsylvania; P: Dan is in Philadelphia)

  **17.** It is always wrong to kill the innocent only if it is wrong to kill an insane person in self-defense. (K: It is always wrong to kill the innocent; S: It is wrong to kill an insane person in self-defense)

  **18.** It is not the case that if the Seahawks win, the Cowboys win. (S: The Seahawks win; C: The Cowboys win)

**19.** It is not always wrong to kill the innocent just in case it is not wrong to kill an insane person in self-defense. (K: It is always wrong to kill the innocent; S: It is wrong to kill an insane person in self-defense)

**20.** Plato's being a rational animal is a necessary and sufficient condition for his being human. (R: Plato is rational; A: Plato is an animal; H: Plato is human)

**Part E:** More Symbolizing   Symbolize the following statements, using the schemes of abbreviation provided.

&ast; **1.** Fido is a dog only if Fido is an animal. (D: Fido is a dog; A: Fido is an animal)

**2.** Josey is a mammal if Josey is a cat. (M: Josie is a mammal; C: Josey is a cat)

**3.** Physical laws cannot be changed given that they are either necessary or eternal. (C: Physical laws can be changed; N: Physical laws are necessary; E: Physical laws are eternal)

&ast; **4.** Snakes are mammals only if snakes nourish their young with milk, but snakes do not nourish their young with milk. (M: Snakes are mammals; N: Snakes nourish their young with milk)

**5.** The statement "If evil exists, then God does not exist" is false. (E: Evil exists; G: God exists)

**6.** If Smith is guilty only if Smith's blood is on the murder weapon, then Smith is not guilty if Smith's blood is not on the murder weapon. (G: Smith is guilty; B: Smith's blood is on the murder weapon)

&ast; **7.** It is not true that if the Eiffel Tower is in Ohio, then it is in Europe. (O: The Eiffel Tower is in Ohio; E: The Eiffel tower is in Europe)

**8.** The defendant's having a motive is not a sufficient condition for his being guilty. (M: The defendant has a motive; G: The defendant is guilty)

**9.** Jane will fail unless she studies. (F: Jane will fail; S: Jane studies)

&ast; **10.** Assuming Fred is both rational and an animal, Fred is human; but Fred is not rational. (R: Fred is rational; A: Fred is an animal; H: Fred is human)

**11.** Senator Crockett's approval of the war is not a necessary condition for her re-election. (W: Senator Crockett approves of the war; R: Senator Crockett will be re-elected)

**12.** Unless we stop using fossil fuels, the earth will continue to get warmer. (S: We stop using fossil fuels; E: The earth will continue to get warmer)

&ast; **13.** Marie Curie's being a scientist is a necessary condition, but not a sufficient condition, for her being a physicist. (S: Marie Curie is a scientist; P: Marie Curie is a physicist)

**14.** If God exists, then evil does not exist unless God has a good reason for allowing evil. (G: God exists; E: Evil exists; R: God has a good reason for allowing evil)

**15.** Aaron Eckhart's being a movie star is a sufficient condition, but not a necessary condition, for his being famous. (M: Aaron Eckhart is a movie star; F: Aaron Eckhart is famous)

## 7.2 Truth Tables

Truth tables can be used to determine the validity (or invalidity) of a large class of arguments. In this section, we will examine the truth tables for the five basic types of compounds formed via the operators introduced in the previous section: the tilde, the dot, the vee, the arrow, and the double-arrow.

The main idea behind truth tables is that the truth value of certain compound statements is a function of the truth value of the atomic statements that make them up. A compound statement is said to be **truth-functional** if its truth value is completely determined by the truth value of the atomic statements that compose it. Let us now examine a series of truth-functional compounds.

We will again use the italicized, lowercase letters *p* and *q* as statement variables that can stand for any statement. For instance, the statement variable *q* can stand for A, for ~B, for ~C ∨ D, for E ↔ F, and so on.

### Negations

*A negation has the opposite truth value of the statement negated.* For example, the statement "Bertrand Russell was born in 1872" is true; so its negation, "Bertrand Russell was not born in 1872," is false. And "John F. Kennedy was born in 1872" is false; so its negation, "John F. Kennedy was not born in 1872," is true. Thus, negations are *truth-functional* compounds. We can present this in a kind of diagram, called a **truth table**, as follows:

| *p* | ~*p* |
|---|---|
| T | F |
| F | T |

This truth table has two vertical **columns**, one on the left and one on the right. The column on the left gives the possible truth values for any statement *p*, namely, T (true) and F (false). The column on the right gives the corresponding truth values for the negation, ~*p*. The table also has two horizontal **rows**. In the first (or top) row, *p* is true, so its negation is false. In the second (or bottom) row, *p* is false, so its negation is true.

### Conjunctions

*A conjunction is true if both its conjuncts are true; otherwise, it is false.* Thus, one false conjunct renders an entire conjunction false. For example, "St. Augustine and Abraham Lincoln were both born in 354" is false, for although

St. Augustine was born in 354, Lincoln was not. We can sum up the relationship between the truth value of a conjunction and the truth value of its conjuncts as follows:

| $p$ | $q$ | $p \cdot q$ |
|-----|-----|:-----------:|
| T | T | T |
| T | F | F |
| F | T | F |
| F | F | F |

Here, the two columns on the left list all the possible truth value assignments for any two statements. Row 1 represents the situation in which both statements are true. Rows 2 and 3 represent the *two* situations in which the statements *differ* in truth value ($p$ true, $q$ false; and $p$ false, $q$ true). Finally, row 4 represents the situation in which both statements are false. The column under the dot indicates that the conjunction as a whole is true *only if* both conjuncts are true (namely, in row 1); otherwise, the conjunction as a whole is false.

## Disjunctions

*A disjunction (represented by the vee) is false if both its disjuncts are false; otherwise, it is true.* Consider the following examples:

60. Either George Washington or John F. Kennedy was born in 2003 (or both were).
61. Either Abraham Lincoln or Andrew Jackson was born in 1809 (or both were).
62. Either Franklin D. Roosevelt or Jimmy Carter was a Democrat (or both were).

Statement (60) is false because both its disjuncts are false. (61) is true since Lincoln was born in 1809. (The statement as a whole is true even though Jackson was born not in 1809 but in 1767.) And (62) is true because both Roosevelt and Carter were Democrats. We can present these possibilities succinctly in a truth table as follows:

| $p$ | $q$ | $p \vee q$ |
|-----|-----|:----------:|
| T | T | T |
| T | F | T |
| F | T | T |
| F | F | F |

Again, the columns on the left represent the four possible combinations of truth values for any two statements. The column under the vee indicates that the disjunction is false only when both disjuncts are false (namely, in row 4); otherwise, the disjunction as a whole is true.

## Material Conditionals

A *material conditional (represented by the arrow) is false if its antecedent is true and its consequent is false; otherwise, it is true*. However, English conditionals are rather complicated, and so we need to discuss the relationship between the arrow and the English if-then in some detail. Consider the following examples:

63. If some dogs are collies, then no dogs are collies.
64. If George Washington was born before Jimmy Carter, then Jimmy Carter was born before George Washington.
65. If physical objects exert a gravitational attraction on each other, then a fist-sized chunk of lead released 3 feet from the surface of the earth will always float in midair.

Each of these conditionals has a true antecedent and a false consequent, and each conditional *is itself* false. Indeed, *an English conditional is always false when its antecedent is true and its consequent is false*. As it turns out, this fact is so important as regards the validity of arguments that logicians have defined a special type of conditional, called the **material conditional**, that is false *only* when its antecedent is true and its consequent is false. The truth table for the material conditional, which is represented by the arrow, is as follows:

| $p$ | $q$ | $p \rightarrow q$ |
|-----|-----|-------------------|
| T | T | T |
| T | F | F |
| F | T | T |
| F | F | T |

Again, note that the material conditional is false *only* in the situation in which the antecedent is true and the consequent is false (row 2).

Now consider the following four English sentences, which correspond to the four rows in the truth table for the material conditional:

a. If the Eiffel Tower is in France, then the Eiffel Tower is in Europe.
b. If the Eiffel Tower is in France, then the Eiffel Tower is in the U.S.A.
c. If the Eiffel Tower is in Germany, then the Eiffel Tower is in Europe.
d. If the Eiffel Tower is in Ohio, then the Eiffel Tower is in the U.S.A.

With the exception of (b), each of these conditionals is true. In (a), both antecedent and consequent are true. In (c), the antecedent is false, while the consequent is true; however, the conditional itself is true, since if the Eiffel Tower *is* in Germany, it is certainly in Europe. It may seem odd that a conditional could be true when both antecedent and consequent are false, but (d) illustrates that this can be so: If the Eiffel Tower *is* in Ohio, then of course it is in the U.S.A.

At this point, it may seem that the English if-then is truth-functional and that the truth table for the material conditional is also a truth table for the English if-then. Unfortunately, things are not that simple. Consider the following conditionals:

a. If $1 + 1 = 2$, then the Eiffel Tower is in France.
b. If the Eiffel Tower is in Ohio, then it is in Europe.
c. If the Eiffel Tower is in Germany, then it is in the U.S.A.

In (a), both antecedent and consequent are true, yet the conditional as a whole seems false. At any rate, most people would hesitate to pronounce it true, since there is no relevance between the antecedent and the consequent. But if (a) is false, then English conditionals are not in general truth-functional. Obviously, if they *are* truth-functional, then any conditional with a true antecedent *and* a true consequent must be true. It appears, then, that there is a significant difference between the material conditional, defined by the preceding truth table, and ordinary English conditionals. This is borne out if we examine rows 3 and 4 of the truth table in the light of (b) and (c). (b) corresponds to row 3, since it has a false antecedent and true consequent. If we went by the truth table, we would say that (b) is true, but from the standpoint of common sense, it is false. If the Eiffel Tower *is* in Ohio, then it certainly is not in Europe. Similarly, (c) seems false. If the Eiffel Tower *is* in Germany, then it certainly is not in the U.S.A. Yet, if we go by the truth table for the material conditional, we must pronounce (c) true, since both antecedent and consequent are false.

Why are logicians so interested in the material conditional if it doesn't correspond to English conditionals? What good does it do to have a truth table for conditionals if we can see that the truth table does not give an accurate picture of the relationship between the truth value of English conditionals (in general) and the truth value of their constituent parts? As it turns out, when the truth table method is applied to arguments, it nicely corroborates our belief in the validity of such intuitive inference rules as those introduced in Chapter 1—*modus ponens, modus tollens,* hypothetical syllogism, disjunctive syllogism, and constructive dilemma. Moreover, it confirms our belief in the *invalidity* of such common, formal fallacies as denying the antecedent and affirming the consequent. In short, the material conditional captures that part of the meaning of the English conditional that is essential for the validity of the basic argument forms of statement logic.

## Material Biconditionals

A *material biconditional (represented by the double-arrow) is true when its two constituent statements have the same truth value, and it is false if the two statements differ in truth value.* Thus, the truth table for the material biconditional is as follows:

| $p$ | $q$ | $p \leftrightarrow q$ |
|-----|-----|-----------------------|
| T   | T   | T                     |
| T   | F   | F                     |
| F   | T   | F                     |
| F   | F   | T                     |

Notice that the material biconditional is true when its constituent parts are both *false* (row 4) as well as when they are both true (row 1).

The truth table for the biconditional is perhaps more readily understandable if one realizes that a biconditional is in effect a conjunction of two conditionals. Consider an example:

**66.** Lincoln won the election *if and only if* Douglas lost the election.

Statement (66) can be broken down into two conditional statements, as follows:

**67.** Lincoln won the election *if* Douglas lost the election.
**68.** Lincoln won the election *only if* Douglas lost the election.

In standard form, (67) and (68) look like this (respectively):

**69.** If Douglas lost the election, then Lincoln won the election.
**70.** If Lincoln won the election, then Douglas lost the election.

So, (66) can be rewritten as a conjunction of two conditionals:

**71.** If Lincoln won the election, then Douglas lost the election; and if Douglas lost the election, then Lincoln won the election. (L: Lincoln won the election; D: Douglas lost the election)

Similar remarks could be made about any biconditional. Let us symbolize (66) and (71) and then check to see if the truth tables for these statements are alike. In symbols, (66) and (71) look like this (respectively):

**72.** $L \leftrightarrow D$
**73.** $(L \rightarrow D) \bullet (D \rightarrow L)$

| Summary of Truth Tables for the Five Compounds | | | | | | | | | | | | | |
|---|---|---|---|---|---|---|---|---|---|---|---|---|---|

| Negation | | Conjunction | | | Disjunction | | | Conditional | | | Biconditional | | |
|---|---|---|---|---|---|---|---|---|---|---|---|---|---|
| $p$ | $\sim p$ | $p$ | $q$ | $p \cdot q$ | $p$ | $q$ | $p \vee q$ | $p$ | $q$ | $p \rightarrow q$ | $p$ | $q$ | $p \leftrightarrow q$ |
| T | F | T | T | T | T | T | T | T | T | T | T | T | T |
| F | T | T | F | F | T | F | T | T | F | F | T | F | F |
|   |   | F | T | F | F | T | T | F | T | T | F | T | F |
|   |   | F | F | F | F | F | F | F | F | T | F | F | T |

Let us work out the truth table for (73). The first row looks like this:

$$\begin{array}{cc|ccc} L & D & (L \rightarrow D) & \cdot & (D \rightarrow L) \\ \hline T & T & T & T & T \end{array}$$

When $L$ and $D$ are both true, then of course $L \rightarrow D$ is true, and so is $D \rightarrow L$. Hence, we place a "T" under the main operator, the dot, because both conjuncts are true. (Strictly speaking, we only need the "T" under the dot; the others are merely "scratch work" to ensure accuracy.) Now let us add the second row to the truth table:

$$\begin{array}{cc|ccc} L & D & (L \rightarrow D) & \cdot & (D \rightarrow L) \\ \hline T & T & T & T & T \\ T & F & F & F & T \end{array}$$

With $L$ true and $D$ false, $(L \rightarrow D)$ is false, while $(D \rightarrow L)$ is true. (Remember, the material conditional is false *only when* its antecedent is true and its consequent is false.) So, we have a conjunction with one false conjunct and one true conjunct. We place an "F" under the dot, since one false conjunct makes the entire conjunction false.

Next, we fill in truth values for the third row:

$$\begin{array}{cc|ccc} L & D & (L \rightarrow D) & \cdot & (D \rightarrow L) \\ \hline T & T & T & T & T \\ T & F & F & F & T \\ F & T & T & F & F \end{array}$$

With $L$ false and $D$ true, $L \rightarrow D$ is true; however, $D \rightarrow L$ is false. So, we again place an "F" under the dot, since we have one false conjunct. We can now add the fourth and final row to the truth table:

| L D | $(L \rightarrow D) \cdot (D \rightarrow L)$ | | |
|-----|-----|-----|-----|
| T T | T | T | T |
| T F | F | F | T |
| F T | T | F | F |
| F F | T | T | T |

With $L$ and $D$ both false, $L \rightarrow D$ is true, and so is $D \rightarrow L$. We place a "T" under the dot, since both conjuncts are true.

The column under the dot gives us the truth value of the entire statement, row by row. (As mentioned previously, the columns under the arrows are merely scratch work and, as such, are not essential to the truth table.) And the column under the dot is exactly like the column under the double-arrow in the truth table for the biconditional:

| L D | $L \leftrightarrow D$ |
|-----|-----|
| T T | T |
| T F | F |
| F T | F |
| F F | T |

To check your understanding of the truth-functional compounds discussed in this section, complete the following exercises.

## ◆ **Exercise 7.2**

**Part A:** True or False?   Determine the truth value of the following compound statements. Make the following assumptions: $A$ is true, $B$ is true, $C$ is false, and $D$ is false.

* **1.** $A \cdot C$
  **2.** $A \lor C$
  **3.** $\sim A$
* **4.** $B \rightarrow D$
  **5.** $D \rightarrow B$
  **6.** $A \leftrightarrow B$
* **7.** $C \leftrightarrow D$
  **8.** $\sim(A \cdot B)$
  **9.** $C \lor D$
* **10.** $\sim(C \lor D)$
  **11.** $\sim C \rightarrow D$
  **12.** $\sim(D \rightarrow A)$
* **13.** $(A \cdot C) \rightarrow B$

**14.** $C \rightarrow (A \rightarrow D)$
**15.** $(C \rightarrow A) \rightarrow D$
* **16.** $\sim(A \leftrightarrow D)$
**17.** $\sim C \cdot \sim D$
**18.** $\sim(\sim A \leftrightarrow \sim B)$
* **19.** $(A \cdot C) \lor (B \cdot D)$
**20.** $(C \lor A) \cdot (D \lor B)$
**21.** $\sim[A \rightarrow (C \lor B)]$
* **22.** $(D \leftrightarrow A) \lor (C \rightarrow B)$
**23.** $(\sim C \rightarrow A) \leftrightarrow (\sim A \lor D)$
**24.** $\sim B \leftrightarrow (A \cdot C)$
* **25.** $\sim(D \lor C) \rightarrow B$

**Part B: More True or False**    Determine the truth value of the following compound statements.

* **1.** It is not the case that Abraham Lincoln was born in 1997.

   **2.** If water is $H_2O$, then water is not wet.

   **3.** Either New York City is the capital of Montana, or Seattle is the capital of Montana.

* **4.** Hillary Clinton is a married man if and only if Hillary Clinton is a husband.

   **5.** If Reno is in Nevada, then Reno is in the U.S.A.

   **6.** Either Alabama is a southern state (of the U.S.A.), or Maine is a southern state.

* **7.** It is not the case that both Charlie Chaplin and George Washington are past presidents of the U.S.A.

   **8.** If either Mozart or Beethoven was born in Korea, then it is false that both Mozart and Beethoven were born in Australia.

   **9.** If the Taj Mahal is green, then the Taj Mahal is not invisible.

* **10.** If Paris is the capital of France, then neither Seattle nor Spokane is the capital of France.

   **11.** Samuel Clemens wrote *Huckleberry Finn* if and only if Samuel Clemens is Mark Twain.

   **12.** If Reno is in Nevada, then Reno is in Canada.

* **13.** If the Statue of Liberty is in Kentucky, then the Statue of Liberty is in the U.S.A.

   **14.** Either Bruce Willis or Clint Eastwood is president of the U.S.A.

   **15.** If Reno is in Nevada, then either Reno is in Canada, or Reno is in the U.S.A.

**Part C: Assigning Truth Values**    What truth values must be assigned to the atomic statements in order to make the following compounds *false*?

* **1.** $\sim P \vee Q$

   **2.** $\sim R \rightarrow S$

   **3.** $\sim(E \cdot G)$

* **4.** $\sim(A \rightarrow B) \rightarrow C$

   **5.** $(T \leftrightarrow \sim W) \vee T$

   **6.** $\sim(\sim G \vee H) \rightarrow \sim K$

* **7.** $(Y \rightarrow \sim Z) \vee \sim Y$

   **8.** $(L \leftrightarrow M) \rightarrow \sim M$

   **9.** $\sim A \rightarrow \sim(\sim B \cdot C)$

* 10.  ~(N ↔ P) ∨ ~P
   11.  ~(~A ∨ ~B) ∨ ~A
   12.  (~C ∨ E) → ~(E • C)
* 13.  ~(H • J) ∨ (K → L)
   14.  (M • N) → ~P
   15.  (R • ~S) → (R ↔ Q)

## 7.3  Using Truth Tables to Evaluate Arguments

We are now in a position to use truth tables to establish the validity and invalidity of arguments. Let's begin by examining an argument having the form *modus tollens*:

> 74.  If Lincoln is 8 feet tall, then Lincoln is over 7 feet tall. But it is not the case that Lincoln is over 7 feet tall. It follows that Lincoln is not 8 feet tall. (L: Lincoln is 8 feet tall; S: Lincoln is over 7 feet tall)

The argument may be symbolized as follows:

> 75.  L → S,  ~S  ∴ ~L

First, we generate all the possible truth-value assignments for $L$ and $S$. Since there are two truth values (truth and falsehood), our truth table must have $2^n$ rows, where $n$ is the number of statement letters in the symbolic argument. In this case, we have just two statement letters, $L$ and $S$, so our truth table will have $2^2$ rows ($2^2 = 2 \times 2 = 4$). The truth-value assignments can be generated in a completely mechanical way; indeed, it is important to generate them mechanically both to avoid error and to facilitate communication. In the column nearest to the vertical line (in this case, the column under $S$), simply alternate Ts and Fs. In the next column to the left (in this case, the column under $L$), alternate couples (two Ts, followed by two Fs). Like this:

| L | S | |
|---|---|---|
| T | T | |
| T | F | |
| F | T | |
| F | F | |

We then write the steps of the argument out on the line at the top of the table and fill in the columns under each step of the argument, row by row. Row 1 looks like this:

| L  S | L → S, | ~S | ∴ ~L |
|------|--------|----|------|
| T  T | T      | F  | F    |

As we have seen, $L \to S$ is true when $L$ and $S$ are both true. Of course, $\sim S$ is false when $S$ is true, and $\sim L$ is false when $L$ is true.

Next, we fill in truth values in row 2:

| L  S | L → S, | ~S | ∴ ~L |
|------|--------|----|------|
| T  T | T      | F  | F    |
| T  F | F      | T  | F    |

With its antecedent true and consequent false, $L \to S$ is false in this row of the table. Since $S$ is false, $\sim S$ must be true. And since $L$ is true, $\sim L$ must be false.

Now we add row 3:

| L  S | L → S, | ~S | ∴ ~L |
|------|--------|----|------|
| T  T | T      | F  | F    |
| T  F | F      | T  | F    |
| F  T | T      | F  | T    |

The conditional premise is true when its antecedent is false and its consequent is true. Obviously, $\sim S$ is false when $S$ is true, and $\sim L$ is true when $L$ is false.

To complete the table, we add the fourth and final row.

| L  S | L → S, | ~S | ∴ ~L |
|------|--------|----|------|
| T  T | T      | F  | F    |
| T  F | F      | T  | F    |
| F  T | T      | F  | T    |
| F  F | T      | T  | T    |

The conditional premise is true in row 4. (The material conditional is false *only when* its antecedent is true and its consequent is false; otherwise, it is true.) Since $L$ and $S$ are both false in this row, $\sim S$ and $\sim L$ are true.

Now, what does the truth table tell us about the argument? Each row in the table describes a possible situation in very abstract terms. For example, row 1 describes a situation in which both *L* and *S* are true. *L* and *S* could be about any topic—science, sorcery, celery, whatever. As long as the statements are both true, row 1 tells us that the first premise is true, the second premise is false, and the conclusion is false. *What we are looking for is a row, and hence a possible situation, in which the premises are all true but the conclusion is false.* If we can find such a row (or situation), then the argument form is invalid. Recall that validity preserves truth—if you start with truth and reason validly, you'll get a true conclusion. So, if a form of argument *can* lead from true premises to a false conclusion, that form of argument is invalid. As we look at the table for the symbolic argument (75), which has the form *modus tollens*, we see that there is no row in which all of the premises are true and the conclusion is false. This means that the argument has a valid form; hence, the argument itself is valid. And because the English argument (74) has the same form, it too is valid.

Now let's see what happens when we apply the truth table method to one of the formal fallacies. Here is an argument having the form of the fallacy of denying the antecedent:

76. If society approves of genetic engineering, then genetic engineering is morally permissible. But society does not approve of genetic engineering. Therefore, genetic engineering is not morally permissible. (S: Society approves of genetic engineering; G: Genetic engineering is morally permissible)

We translate the argument into symbols as follows:

77. $S \rightarrow G$, $\sim S$ $\therefore$ $\sim G$

The truth table looks like this:

| S  G | $S \rightarrow G$, | $\sim S$ | $\therefore$ $\sim G$ |
|------|------|------|------|
| T  T | T | F | F |
| T  F | F | F | T |
| F  T | T | T | F |
| F  F | T | T | T |

Is there a row in which the premises are all true and the conclusion is false? Yes, row 3. This shows that the argument form is invalid, for it does not preserve truth. The table gives us the additional bit of information that the invalidity of the form is revealed in situations in which the antecedent of the conditional premise (i.e., *S*) is false and its consequent (i.e., *G*) is true. This gives us a strong hint about how to write an English **counterexample** that will connect what we have learned from the truth table with our intuitions as speakers of English. As you will recall from Chapter 1, a good counterexample has the following features: (a) It has the same form as the original argument, (b) its premises are *well-known* truths, and (c) its conclusion is a *well-known* falsehood. Here is a counterexample to argument (77):

> 78. If George Washington was 8 feet tall, then he was over 2 feet tall. But Washington was not 8 feet tall. So, he was not over 2 feet tall.

Note that the conditional premise has a false antecedent but a true consequent: Washington wasn't 8 feet tall, but he was certainly over 2 feet tall. Moreover, the conditional premise as a whole is plainly true: Anyone who is 8 feet tall is certainly over 2 feet tall. And, of course, the second premise is true, while the conclusion is false. So, this English example illustrates the sort of situation described by the third row of the truth table. The pattern of reasoning is *always* invalid, since it allows for true premises and a false conclusion.

Of course, not all truth tables are as short as those we've examined thus far. Let us see what happens when we apply the truth table method to arguments having three statement letters.

> 79. If the equatorial rain forests produce oxygen used by Americans, then either Americans ought to pay for the oxygen, or they ought to stop complaining about the destruction of the rain forests. But either it is false that Americans ought to pay for the oxygen, or it is false that Americans ought to stop complaining about the destruction of the rain forests. Therefore, it is false that the equatorial rain forests produce oxygen used by Americans. (E: The equatorial rain forests produce oxygen by Americans; P: Americans ought to pay for the oxygen; S: Americans ought to stop complaining about the destruction of the rain forests)

Using the scheme of abbreviation provided, the argument translates into symbols as follows:

> 80. $E \rightarrow (P \vee S)$, $\sim P \vee \sim S$ $\therefore$ $\sim E$

Now we are ready to construct a truth table. We list the statement letters *in the order in which they appear* in our symbolization: $E, P, S$. Since a truth table must have $2^n$ rows, where $n$ is the number of statement letters, in this case we need a table with eight rows ($2^3 = 2 \times 2 \times 2 = 8$). To generate every possible combination of truth values for the three statement letters *mechanically*, we alternate Ts and Fs in the column nearest the vertical line, under $S$. Then we alternate couples (two Ts, followed by two Fs, etc.) in the next column to the left, under $P$. Finally, we alternate quadruples (four Ts followed by four Fs) in the column on the far left, under $E$, like this:

| E | P | S |   |
|---|---|---|---|
| T | T | T | |
| T | T | F | |
| T | F | T | |
| T | F | F | |
| F | T | T | |
| F | T | F | |
| F | F | T | |
| F | F | F | |

It's important to generate the possible truth-value combinations *in the manner indicated,* for two reasons. First, doing so will enable you to construct truth tables quickly and accurately. Second, for purposes of communication, a *standard method* of generating truth-value combinations is needed. Without a standard method, truth tables cannot readily be compared or checked for accuracy.

Next, we fill in the truth values for the premises and conclusion row by row. Check out each row of the following table. Only the circled columns are absolutely essential. The other columns are scratch work done to guarantee accuracy. For example, because the first premise is a conditional, only the column under the arrow is essential to the table. But filling in some other columns often helps one avoid errors.

| E | P | S | E → (P ∨ S), | ~P ∨ ~S | ∴ ~E |
|---|---|---|---|---|---|
| T | T | T | T    T | F F F | F |
| T | T | F | T    T | F T T | F |
| T | F | T | T    T | T T F | F |
| T | F | F | F    F | T T T | F |
| F | T | T | T    T | F F F | T |
| F | T | F | T    T | F T T | T |
| F | F | T | T    T | T T F | T |
| F | F | F | T    F | T T T | T |

Once the table is complete, we examine it to see if there are any rows in which the premises are all true while the conclusion is false. Rows 2 and 3 meet this condition, so the argument is invalid. (An argument is invalid as long as *at least one* row meets this condition.)

Using the hints provided by row 3 of the truth table, we can construct a counterexample to argument (80):

81. If George Washington was born before Harry Truman, then either Abraham Lincoln was born before George Washington, or Abraham Lincoln was born before Harry Truman. Either it is false that Abraham Lincoln was born before

George Washington, or it is false that Abraham Lincoln was born before Harry Truman. So, it is false that George Washington was born before Harry Truman. (E: George Washington was born before Harry Truman; P: Abraham Lincoln was born before George Washington; S: Abraham Lincoln was born before Harry Truman)

Note that the counterexample matches the scenario described in row 3 of the truth table perfectly: *E* (i.e., Washington was born before Truman) is true, *P* (i.e., Lincoln was born before Washington) is false, and *S* (i.e., Lincoln was born before Truman) is true.

Truth tables can be used to evaluate for validity even when our English intuitions fail us. For example, is the following argument valid? Most people find it difficult to answer simply on the basis of logical intuition.

82. If Socrates works hard, he gets rich. But if Socrates doesn't work hard, he enjoys life. Moreover, if Socrates does not get rich, then he does not enjoy life. Hence, Socrates gets rich. (H: Socrates works hard; R: Socrates gets rich; L: Socrates enjoys life)

Using the scheme of abbreviation provided, the argument can be symbolized as follows:

83. H → R,  ~H → L,  ~R → ~L  ∴ R

The truth table looks like this:

| H | R | L | H → R | ~H → L | ~R → ~L | ∴ R |
|---|---|---|-------|--------|---------|-----|
| T | T | T | T | T | T | T |
| T | T | F | T | T | T | T |
| T | F | T | F | T | F | F |
| T | F | F | F | T | T | F |
| F | T | T | T | T | T | T |
| F | T | F | T | F | T | T |
| F | F | T | T | T | F | F |
| F | F | F | T | F | T | F |

*There is no row in which the premises are true and the conclusion is false*; therefore, the argument form is valid. Since argument (82) is one that most people find difficult to assess through unaided logical intuition, the fact that a truth table enables us to achieve a definitive evaluation illustrates the power of this method.

The truth table method does have an important limitation: It becomes unwieldy as arguments become longer. For instance, suppose we wish to evaluate an argument having the form of a constructive dilemma. In symbols, we have the following:

84. A ∨ B, A → C, B → D ∴ C ∨ D

Here, we have four statement letters, so we need $2^4$ rows in our truth table ($2^4 = 2 \times 2 \times 2 \times 2 = 16$). The truth table looks like this:

| A B C D | A ∨ B, | A → C, | B → D | ∴ C ∨ D |
|---------|--------|--------|-------|---------|
| T T T T | T | T | T | T |
| T T T F | T | T | F | T |
| T T F T | T | F | T | T |
| T T F F | T | F | F | F |
| T F T T | T | T | T | T |
| T F T F | T | T | T | T |
| T F F T | T | F | T | T |
| T F F F | T | F | T | F |
| F T T T | T | T | T | T |
| F T T F | T | T | F | T |
| F T F T | T | T | T | T |
| F T F F | T | T | F | F |
| F F T T | F | T | T | T |
| F F T F | F | T | T | T |
| F F F T | F | T | T | T |
| F F F F | F | T | T | F |

The argument is valid, for there are no rows in which all the premises are true and the conclusion is false. Note that the initial truth-value assignments on the left are generated in the mechanical way previously described: alternate Ts and Fs under the letter closest to the vertical line (*D* in the table); alternate couples under the next letter to the left (*C*); alternate quadruples under the next letter (*B*); finally, alternate groups of eight. How many rows would be needed for a truth table involving five statement letters? Thirty-two ($2^5 = 2 \times 2 \times 2 \times 2 \times 2 = 32$). And if six statement letters were involved, we would need a truth table with 64 rows. So, the truth table method is cumbersome when applied to arguments involving many statement letters. Nevertheless, it is a powerful method that is useful in many cases.

   Check your understanding by completing the following exercises.

## ◆ Exercise 7.3

**Part A: Truth Tables**   Construct truth tables to determine whether the following arguments are valid. Make initial truth-value assignments in the mechanical fashion described in this section. That is, list statement letters *in the order in which they appear* in the argument; then alternate Ts and Fs in the column under the letter *closest* to the vertical line; alternate couples (two Ts, two Fs, etc.) under the next letter on the left; and so on.

* 1.  A ∨ B, ~A ∴ B
  2.  F → G, F ∴ G
  3.  ~A ∨ ~B, ~B ∴ ~~A
* 4.  ~P → ~R ∴ ~(P → R)
  5.  ~(X → Y) ∴ ~X → ~Y
  6.  E ∴ D ∨ E
* 7.  A • B ∴ B
  8.  ~(N • L) ∴ ~N → ~L
  9.  (A ∨ B) • ~(A • B), A ∴ ~B
* 10. ~F • ~G ∴ ~F ↔ ~G
  11. ~(S • ~R), ~R ∴ ~S

  12.  A ↔ B ∴ A • B
* 13.  D ↔ (E ∨ C), ~D ∴ ~C
  14.  A → (B → C) ∴ A → (B • C)
  15.  N ↔ (M • L), ~L ∴ ~N
* 16.  A → B, B → C ∴ A → C
  17.  (Q • U) → Z, ~Z ∴ ~Q
  18.  (E ↔ G) → H, ~H ∴ ~E ∨ ~G
* 19.  A ∨ B, A → C, B → C ∴ C
  20.  A → C, B → D, ~C ∨ ~D
       ∴ ~A ∨ ~B

**Part B:** More Truth Tables   Construct truth tables to determine whether the following arguments are valid.

* 1.  A • ~B ∴ ~(A → B)
  2.  F → G ∴ ~F → ~G
  3.  ~E → ~G ∴ G → E
* 4.  ~(H • K) ∴ ~H • ~K
  5.  A → B, B ∴ A
  6.  X ∨ Y, Y ∴ ~X
* 7.  A ∴ (A ∨ B) • ~(A • B)
  8.  ~(T ↔ ~S) ∴ ~T ∨ S
  9.  ~F ∨ ~G ∴ ~(F ∨ G)
* 10. ~(H ↔ J) ∴ ~H ↔ ~J
  11.  ~(A → B) ∴ A • ~B
  12.  ~(N ↔ P) ∴ N → ~P
  13.  ~(A ↔ B) ∴ (A • ~B) ∨ (B • ~A)
  14.  (H • B) → S ∴ B → S
  15.  P → Q, S → Q, ~Q ∴ ~P • ~S
  16.  Z → (S ∨ G), Z ∴ S
  17.  ~(L ∨ M), ~M ↔ ~N ∴ ~N
  18.  P → (~Q ∨ R), P • ~R ∴ ~Q
  19.  A → (B → C) ∴ (A • B) → C
  20.  ~[~(D • E) ∨ (F ∨ ~D)] ∴ D • (E • ~F)

**Part C: English Arguments** Symbolize the following arguments. Then use truth tables to determine whether they are valid.

* **1.** Not having exceeded our natural resources is a necessary condition for its being appropriate to expand our city. Unfortunately, we have exceeded our natural resources. Consequently, it is not appropriate to expand our city. (E: We have exceeded our natural resources; A: It is appropriate to expand our city)

 **2.** Humans evolved from lower life forms given that either human life evolved from inanimate matter apart from divine causes, or God created human life via the long, slow process we call evolution. God created human life via the long, slow process we call evolution. It follows that humans evolved from lower life forms. (H: Humans evolved from lower life forms; M: Human life evolved from inanimate matter apart from divine causes; G: God created human life via the long, slow process we call evolution)

 **3.** American foreign policy is bankrupt unless it is based on clear moral principles. American foreign policy is not based on clear moral principles just in case it is based primarily on the national interest. Unfortunately, American foreign policy is based primarily on the national interest. We may infer that American foreign policy is bankrupt. (B: American foreign policy is bankrupt; M: American foreign policy is based on clear moral principles; N: American foreign policy is based primarily on the national interest)

* **4.** You won't get an A unless you do well on all the exams. Therefore, if you do well on all the exams, you will get an A. (A: You will get an A; W: You do well on all the exams)

 **5.** There are necessary truths (i.e., truths that cannot be false under any possible circumstances). For assuming that there are no necessary truths, there are no necessary connections between premises and conclusions. But there are no valid arguments if there are no necessary connections between premises and conclusions; and there are valid arguments. (N: There are necessary truths; C: There are necessary connections between premises and conclusions; V: There are valid arguments)

 **6.** On the condition that land mines are designed to inflict horrible suffering, they ought to be banned unless inflicting horrible suffering is sometimes justified. It is not true that inflicting horrible suffering is sometimes justified, but it is true that land mines are designed to inflict horrible suffering. Accordingly, land mines ought to be banned. (L: Land mines are designed to inflict horrible suffering; B: Land mines ought to be banned; S: Inflicting horrible suffering is sometimes justified)

* **7.** The reduction of violence is a necessary and sufficient condition for making drugs legal. But more people will use drugs if drugs are made legal. And violence is not reduced if more people will use drugs. Hence, drugs are not made legal. (V: Violence is reduced; L: Drugs are made legal; P: More people will use drugs)

8. Augustine achieves heaven if Augustine is virtuous. But Augustine is happy provided that he is not virtuous. Augustine does not achieve heaven only if he is not happy. Therefore, Augustine achieves heaven. (A: Augustine achieves heaven; V: Augustine is virtuous; H: Augustine is happy)

9. Not all living things are able to feel pain. For all living things are able to feel pain only if all living things have nervous systems. But not all living things have nervous systems given that plants do not have nervous systems. And plants do not have nervous systems. (L: All living things are able to feel pain; N: All living things have nervous systems; P: Plants have nervous systems)

10. It is morally permissible for mentally superior extraterrestrials to eat humans on the condition that it is morally permissible for humans to eat animals. But either it is not morally permissible for mentally superior extraterrestrials to eat humans, or human life lacks intrinsic value. However, human life has intrinsic value. We are forced to conclude that it is not morally permissible for humans to eat animals. (E: It is morally permissible for mentally superior extraterrestrials to eat humans; H: It is morally permissible for humans to eat animals; V: Human life has intrinsic value)

## 7.4 Abbreviated Truth Tables

As we have seen, the truth table method is rather cumbersome when applied to arguments having more than three statement letters. But there are ways to make it less cumbersome, and we will explore one of them in this section, namely, the **abbreviated truth table method**. The essential insight behind abbreviated truth tables is this: If we can construct *one* row of a truth table, *making all the premises true while the conclusion is false*, then we have shown that the argument form in question is invalid. Here's an example:

85. If I am thinking, then my neurons are firing. Hence, if my neurons are firing, then I am thinking. (A: I am thinking; N: My neurons are firing)

Using the scheme of abbreviation provided, we may symbolize the argument as follows:

86. $A \rightarrow N$ $\therefore N \rightarrow A$

We begin by hypothesizing that all the argument's premises are true while its conclusion is false:

| | $A \rightarrow N$ | $\therefore$ $N \rightarrow A$ |
|---|---|---|
| | T | F |

Now we work backward. If the conclusion is false, then $N$ must be true and $A$ must be false. We fill in these values uniformly throughout the argument:

$$
\begin{array}{c|cc}
& A \rightarrow N \quad \therefore \quad N \rightarrow A \\
\hline
& \text{F T T} \qquad \text{T F F}
\end{array}
$$

This truth assignment does indeed make the conclusion false and the premise true. We have in effect constructed a row in the truth table that shows the argument to be invalid: It is the row in which $A$ is false and $N$ is true. We add this information at the left to complete our abbreviated truth table:

$$
\begin{array}{cc|cc}
A & N & A \rightarrow N \quad \therefore \quad N \rightarrow A \\
\hline
F & T & \text{F T T} \qquad \text{T F F}
\end{array}
$$

We have thus shown the argument to be invalid. And as before, our truth-functional assessment of the argument gives a strong hint about how to construct an English counterexample:

87. If Thomas Jefferson was 500 years old when he died, then he lived to be more than a year old. Therefore, if Jefferson lived to be more than a year old, then he was 500 years old when he died.

The premise of argument (87) is plainly true even though its antecedent is false. And, of course, the conclusion of the argument is false, too.

Let's try a more complicated example. Consider the following symbolic argument:

88. $E \vee S$, $E \rightarrow (B \bullet U)$, $\sim S \vee \sim U$ $\therefore$ $B$

Again, we hypothesize that all the premises can be true while the conclusion is false:

$$
\begin{array}{c|cccc}
& E \vee S, & E \rightarrow (B \bullet U), & \sim S \vee \sim U & \therefore & B \\
\hline
& \text{T} & \text{T} & \text{T} & & \text{F}
\end{array}
$$

Then we work backward to determine the truth value of each constituent statement letter. Since we have assigned "F" to $B$ in the conclusion, we must assign "F" to $B$ uniformly throughout the argument. (Remember, we are in effect constructing a single row in a truth table.) This means that $B \bullet U$ is also false. Hence, we must assign "F" to $E$; otherwise, the second premise will be false, which contradicts our hypothesis. Now, if $E$ is false, we must make $S$

true; otherwise, the first premise will be false, which contradicts our hypothesis. And if S is true, then ~S is false, so we must make ~U true (and hence U
false) to make the third premise true. Thus, we arrive at our abbreviated truth
table:

| E  S  B  U | E ∨ S, E → (B • U), ~S ∨ ~U  ∴ B |
|------------|--------------------------------|
| F  T  F  F | FTT FT FFF  FTTTF     F |

In this case, an argument that would require a 16-row truth table can be dealt
with quickly by means of an abbreviated truth table.

The abbreviated truth table method can also be used to show that an argument is valid. Let's try it out on an old friend, disjunctive syllogism. Again,
we begin by hypothesizing that the conclusion can be false while the premises
are true:

| | A ∨ B, ~A ∴ B |
|---|---|
| | T   T     F |

If ~A is true, then A is false. But since B is also false, A ∨ B is false, contrary to
our hypothesis. Thus, in trying to assign values so that the premises are all true
and the conclusion is false, we are forced to contradict ourselves. This means the
argument is valid. We indicate that we were forced to assign truth values incon-
sistently by writing "T/F" under the first premise:

| | A ∨ B, ~A ∴ B | |
|---|---|---|
| | F(T/F)F  TF     F | Valid |

Using an abbreviated truth table is a bit more complicated when the conclusion of the argument is false on *more than one* assignment of truth values—for
example, when the conclusion is a conjunction or a biconditional. In such cases,
the following principles will suffice:

**Principle 1:** If there is *any* assignment of values in which the premises are all true
and the conclusion is false, then the argument is invalid.

**Principle 2:** If more than one assignment of truth values will make the conclusion
false, then consider each such assignment; if each assignment that makes the conclusion false makes *at least one* premise false, then the argument is valid.

For instance, consider the following symbolic argument:

**89.** F → G,  G → H  ∴ ~F • H

There are three ways to make the conclusion false: (a) make both conjuncts false, (b) make the left conjunct false and the right one true, or (c) make the left conjunct true and the right one false. If we neglect this complexity, we can easily fall into error, for not every assignment that makes the conclusion false makes the premises true. For instance:

| | F → G,  G → H  ∴ ~F • H |
|---|---|
| | T T/F F   F T F     FTFF |

With this assignment, the first premise is false. (We could make the first premise true by assigning "T" to G, but then the second premise would be false.) If we overlook the fact that other truth value assignments render the *conclusion* false, we might suppose that this abbreviated truth table shows that the argument is valid. But it does not because there is a way of assigning "F" to the conclusion that makes all the premises true, namely:

| F G H | F → G,  G → H  ∴ ~F • H |
|---|---|
| F F F | F T F   F T F     TFFF |

And this proves that the argument form is invalid.

To show that an argument is valid, we must consider every truth-value assignment in which its conclusion is false. Consider the following example:

**90.** P → Q,  Q → P  ∴ P ↔ Q

A biconditional is false whenever its two constituent statements *differ* in truth value. So in this case, we must consider the assignment in which P is true and Q is false, *and also* the assignment in which P is false and Q is true.

| | P → Q,  Q → P  ∴  P ↔ Q | |
|---|---|---|
| | T (T/F) F   F T T     T F F | |
| | F T T   T (T/F) F     F F T     Valid |

Here, each assignment that makes the conclusion false also makes one of the premises false (which contradicts our hypothesis that all the premises can be true while the conclusion is false). Thus, we have shown the argument to be valid.

The following exercise gives you an opportunity to practice the abbreviated truth table method.

## ◆ Exercise 7.4

**Part A:** Abbreviated Truth Tables   Use abbreviated truth tables to show that the following arguments are invalid.

* 1. A → (B → C) ∴ B → C
  2. ~(E ↔ F) ∴ ~E • ~F
  3. ~(G ↔ H) ∴ ~G → ~H
* 4. J → ~K ∴ ~(J ↔ K)
  5. (P • Q) → R, ~R ∴ ~P
  6. ~(Z • H), ~Z → Y, W → H ∴ ~W → Y
     How many rows would be needed in a complete truth table for argument 6?
* 7. ~(S • H), (~S • ~H) → ~U ∴ ~U
  8. (F • G) ↔ H, ~H ∴ ~G
  9. ~(B → C), (D • C) ∨ E ∴ ~B
* 10. (P → ~Q) ↔ ~R, R ∴ ~P
  11. S → (T → V) ∴ (S → T) → V
  12. A → (B → C) ∴ A → (B • C)
* 13. (Z • Y) → W ∴ Z → (Y • W)
  14. ~(C ∨ D), (~C • ~E) ↔ ~D, ~E → (C ∨ F), S ∨ F ∴ S
     How many rows would be needed in a complete truth table for argument 14?
  15. (F ↔ G) ↔ H, ~H ∴ ~F • ~G
* 16. P → Q, P → R, Q ↔ R, S, S → R ∴ P • Q
  17. S → (A • O), ~P ∨ ~R, P → (S ∨ Z), Z → (O → R) ∴ Z ∨ ~P
  18. A ∨ (B • C), ~A ∴ (A • B) ∨ (A • C)
* 19. ~(Q ∨ S), ~T ∨ S, (U • W) → Q ∴ (~T • ~U) • W
  20. ~J • ~K, L → J, M → K, (M → ~L) → ~(N • O) ∴ ~N

**Part B:** More Abbreviated Truth Tables   Use abbreviated truth tables to show that the following arguments are invalid.

* 1. ~(A • B), ~A → C, ~B → D ∴ C • D
  2. L ↔ (M • N), M ∨ N, ~L ∴ ~M
  3. (O ↔ P) → R, ~R ∴ ~O ∨ P
* 4. ~(V • X) → ~Y ∴ ~[(V • X) → Y]

   5. ~(Z • H), ~Z → Y, W → H ∴ ~W → Y
   6. ~X ∨ (C • A), ~Y ∨ ~B, ~Y ∨ (X ∨ T), T → (A → B) ∴ T ∨ ~Y
* 7. ~(Z → A), Z → B, ~A → C ∴ C • ~B
   8. B → (C • D), ~E ∨ ~F, E → (B ∨ G), G → (D → F) ∴ G ∨ ~E
      How many rows would be needed in a complete truth table for item 8?
   9. ~(D ↔ E), ~D → F, E → G ∴ F • G
* 10. H ∨ ~S, H → Z, ~S → P ∴ P ↔ Z
   11. ~[(J • K) → (M ∨ N)] ∴ K • N
   12. A → B, C → ~D, ~B ∨ D ∴ ~A ↔ ~C
   13. ~E → (G • A), ~(P ↔ ~L) ∨ E, ~(P • L) ∨ Q, ~N → ~G ∴ Q • A
   14. (G → E) ↔ S, ~(S ∨ H), ~(P • ~H) ∴ G • E
   15. ~(C ↔ ~D) ∨ E, ~E → (G • H), (C • D) → K, ~N → ~G ∴ K • H
      How many rows would be needed in a complete truth table for item 15?

**Part C:** Valid or Invalid?    Some of the following arguments are valid, and some
are invalid. Use abbreviated truth tables to determine which are valid and which are
invalid.

* 1. ~A ∨ B ∴ A → B
   2. F → (G ↔ H), ~F • ~H ∴ ~G
   3. ~M ∴ ~N ∨ ~M
* 4. A ∨ (B • C) ∴ (A • B) ∨ (A • C)
   5. P → ~(Q • R), P • R ∴ ~Q
   6. X → Z, Y → Z, ~Z ∴ X ↔ Y
   7. ~(S → R), S → J, ~R ↔ W ∴ W → ~J
   8. ~M → O, ~N → O, ~O ↔ ~P, ~P ∴ M • N
      How many rows would be needed in a complete truth table for item 8?
   9. (A ∨ B) • (A ∨ C) ∴ A • (B ∨ C)
   10. R ↔ ~Q, R ∨ Q, R ∨ P ∴ (P • Q) → R

**Part D:** English Arguments    Translate the following English arguments into symbols, using the schemes of abbreviation provided. Use abbreviated truth tables to
determine whether the arguments are valid.

* 1. If you want to mess up your life, you should drink a lot of booze. Therefore,
      if you don't want to mess up your life, you should not drink a lot of booze.
      (W: You want to mess up your life; B: You should drink a lot of booze)

   2. Being undetermined is a necessary but not a sufficient condition for human
      behavior's being free. The laws of subatomic physics are statistical only if

human behavior is not determined. And the laws of subatomic physics are statistical. It follows that human behavior is free. (D: Human behavior is determined; F: Human behavior is free; L: The laws of subatomic physics are statistical)

3. Given that nuclear energy is needed if and only if solar energy cannot be harnessed, nuclear energy is not needed. For solar energy can be harnessed provided that funds are available; and funds are available. (N: Nuclear energy is needed; S: Solar energy can be harnessed; F: Funds are available)

* 4. If the Gulf War was about oil, and if human life is more valuable than oil, then the Gulf War was immoral. Human life is more valuable than oil, but the Gulf War was not about oil. Therefore, the Gulf War was not immoral. (G: The Gulf War was about oil; H: Human life is more valuable than oil; I: The Gulf War was immoral)

5. The rate of teenage drunk driving will decrease just in case the taxes on beer increase. The taxes on beer increase only if either the federal government or the state government will resist the liquor lobby. The state government will resist the liquor lobby, but the federal government will not. Accordingly, the rate of teenage drunk driving will not decrease. (R: The rate of teenage drunk driving will decrease; B: The taxes on beer increase; F: The federal government will resist the liquor lobby; S: The state government will resist the liquor lobby)

6. Erik attains Valhalla given that he is valiant. And Erik is depressed assuming that he is not valiant. Furthermore, Erik fails to attain Valhalla only if he is not depressed. Thus, Erik is depressed. (E: Erik attains Valhalla; V: Eric is valiant; D: Eric is depressed)

* 7. If society is the ultimate source of moral authority, then if society approves of polygamy, polygamy is right. But it is not true either that society is the ultimate source of moral authority or that society approves of polygamy. Hence, polygamy is not right. (S: Society is the ultimate source of moral authority; P: Society approves of polygamy; R: Polygamy is right)

8. Either the earth is millions of years old, or it is only 6000 years old. If the earth is millions of years old, then the traditional story of creation is a myth, and ultimate reality is nothing but atoms in motion. Now, either it is false that the earth is only 6000 years old, or it is false that ultimate reality is nothing but atoms in motion. Therefore, the traditional story of creation is a myth. (E: The earth is millions of years old; S: The earth is only 6000 years old; B: The traditional story of creation is a myth; U: Ultimate reality is nothing but atoms in motion)

9. Wittgensteinians are right if logic is embedded in language. But logic is embedded in language if and only if logic varies as language varies. And logic is language-relative if logic varies as language varies. Moreover, given that logic is language-relative, contradictions may be true in some languages.

Therefore, Wittgensteinians are right only if contradictions may be true in some languages. (W: Wittgensteinians are right; E: Logic is embedded in language; V: Logic varies as language varies; R: Logic is language-relative; C: Contradictions may be true in some languages)

10. Although most Americans approve of gun control, gun control is neither wise nor moral. For gun control is wise if and only if it prevents criminals from obtaining weapons. And gun control is moral if and only if it preserves our liberty. But it is not the case that gun control both preserves our liberty and prevents criminals from obtaining weapons. (W: Gun control is wise; M: Gun control is moral; P: Gun control prevents criminals from obtaining weapons; L: Gun control preserves our liberty)

## 7.5 Tautology, Contradiction, Contingency, and Logical Equivalence

Truth tables can be used to sort statements into logically significant categories: tautologies, contradictions, and contingent statements. This section explains how to identify tautologies, contradictions, and contingent statements; it also describes their main logical properties.

The atomic components of a statement are simply the atomic statements within it. For example, the atomic components of $\sim P \rightarrow Q$ are $P$ and $Q$. (In the special case of an atomic statement, the atomic component is simply the statement itself. So, the atomic component of $R$ is simply $R$.) A statement is a **tautology** if *it is true regardless of the truth values of its atomic components*. Equivalently, a statement is a tautology if there is a "T" beneath its main operator in every row of its truth table. The tautologies of statement logic belong to a class of statements that are true simply by virtue of their form.* Here are some examples:

91. Either it is raining or it is not raining. (R: It is raining)
92. If trees are plants, then trees are plants. (P: Trees are plants)
93. If neither atoms nor molecules exist, then atoms do not exist. (A: Atoms exist; M: Molecules exist)

These statements can be translated into symbols as follows, in order:

94. $R \lor \sim R$
95. $P \rightarrow P$

---

*Not all statements that are true by virtue of their form are tautologies in the sense here defined. For example, the following statement is not a tautology, but it is true by virtue of its form: "If everything is human, then something is human." We will examine statements of this type in Chapter 9, "Predicate Logic." According to many philosophers, statements that are true by virtue of their form (including tautologies) belong to a larger class of statements called *necessary truths*. Necessary truths are truths that cannot be false under any possible circumstances. Here is an example of a necessary truth that does not appear to be true simply by virtue of its form: "If Al is older than Bob, then Bob is younger than Al."

96. ~(A ∨ M) → ~A

If we construct truth tables for these statements, then every row under the main logical operator will contain a "T":

| R | R ∨ ~R |
|---|--------|
| T | T |
| F | T |

| P | P → P |
|---|-------|
| T | T |
| F | T |

| A | M | ~(A ∨ M) → ~A |
|---|---|-----------------|
| T | T | T |
| T | F | T |
| F | T | T |
| F | F | T |

Tautologies have some interesting and paradoxical properties. For example, every argument whose conclusion is a tautology is valid—regardless of the content of the premises. Consider the following example:

97. The moon is made of green cheese. So, either Santa is real or Santa is not real. (M: The moon is made of green cheese; S: Santa is real)

Here is a symbolization and truth table for argument (97):

| M | S | M | ∴ S ∨ ~S |
|---|---|---|----------|
| T | T | T | T |
| T | F | T | T |
| F | T | F | T |
| F | F | F | T |

As you can see, there is no row in which the premise is true while the conclusion is false, and so the argument is valid. This may seem puzzling because intuitively the premise is irrelevant to the conclusion. But the argument does satisfy our definition of validity, for since the conclusion is a tautology, it is impossible for the conclusion to be false while the premise is true.

A statement is a **contradiction** if *it is false regardless of the truth values of its atomic components*. Equivalently, a statement is a contradiction if there is an "F" beneath its main operator in every row of its truth table. The contradictions of statement logic belong to a class of statements that are false simply by virtue of their form. Here are two examples:

98. Ants exist, and yet they do not exist. (A: Ants exist)

99. If lemons are yellow, then they are not blue; but lemons are both blue and yellow. (Y: Lemons are yellow; B: Lemons are blue)

In symbols, we have this:

100. A • ~A
101. (Y → ~B) • (B • Y)

If we construct a truth table for a contradiction, then every row under the main logical operator will contain an "F":

| A | A • ~A |   | Y B | (Y → ~B) • (B • Y) |
|---|--------|---|-----|-------------------|
| T | F      |   | T T | F                 |
| F | F      |   | T F | F                 |
|   |        |   | F T | F                 |
|   |        |   | F F | F                 |

Like tautologies, contradictions have some interesting logical properties. For example, any argument that has a contradiction among its premises is a valid argument. For instance:

102. Atoms exist, and yet they do not exist. So, God exists. (A: Atoms exist; G: God exists)

Here is the truth table:

| A G | A • ~A ∴ G |
|-----|-----------|
| T T | F      T  |
| T F | F      F  |
| F T | F      T  |
| F F | F      F  |

Note that there is no row in which the premise is true and the conclusion is false; hence, the argument is valid. This may seem strange, but the argument does satisfy our definition of validity. It is impossible for the conclusion to be false while the premise is true (because it is impossible for the premise to be true). Notice, however, that all arguments having a contradiction among their premises are *unsound*, since contradictions are always false.

We can go a step further here: Any argument with logically inconsistent premises will be valid yet unsound. If the premises of an argument are inconsistent, then if we form a conjunction of the premises, that conjunction will be a contradiction. Here is an example:

103. P → Q, ~P → Q, ~Q ∴ R

If we form a conjunction of the premises, the argument looks like this:

| P Q R | (P → Q) • [(~P → Q) • ~Q] ∴ R |
|-------|---------------------------------|
| T T T | T F F T |
| T T F | T F F F |
| T F T | F F T T |
| T F F | F F T F |
| F T T | T F F T |
| F T F | T F F F |
| F F T | T F F T |
| F F F | T F F F |

The truth table reveals that the conjunction is a contradiction. Again, the point is that, paradoxically, every argument with inconsistent premises is valid. (Of course, all such arguments are *unsound* due to having one or more false premises.) How will you know if the premises of an argument are inconsistent? Here's how: There will be no row in the truth table in which all of the premises are true. For instance:

| M N L | M ↔ N, M • ~N ∴ L |
|-------|---------------------|
| T T T | T F T |
| T T F | T F F |
| T F T | F T T |
| T F F | F T F |
| F T T | F F T |
| F T F | F F F |
| F F T | T F T |
| F F F | T F F |

Because there is no row in which all the premises are true, the premises are inconsistent and the argument is valid.

A statement is **contingent** if *it is true on some assignments of truth values to its atomic components and false on others*. Equivalently, a statement is contingent if there is a "T" beneath its main operator in at least one row of its truth table *and* an "F" beneath its main operator in at least one row of its truth table. Here is an example:

104. P • (P → R)

The truth table looks like this:

| P R | P • (P → R) |
|-----|-------------|
| T T | T |
| T F | F |
| F T | F |
| F F | F |

Contingent statements have important logical relations to both tautologies and contradictions. For example, any argument that has a tautology as its premise but a contingent statement as its conclusion is invalid. (The premise will be true in every row of the truth table, while the conclusion will be false in at least one row.) And suppose that the premises of an argument, when made into a conjunction, form a contingent statement. Then, if the conclusion of the argument is a contradiction, the argument is invalid. (The conclusion will be false in every row, while the premise will be true in at least one row.)

Notice that tautologies and contradictions place limitations on the method of abbreviated truth tables that was introduced in the previous section. For instance, if an argument has a tautology as its conclusion, then there is no way to assign truth values so that the conclusion is false. One way to deal with such a case is to use a complete truth table to prove that the conclusion is a tautology (which simultaneously proves that the argument is valid). Similarly, if at least one premise is a contradiction (or if the premises are inconsistent), then there is no way to assign values so that the premises are all true, and a complete truth table may be needed to establish this, as in the case of argument (102). However, a complete truth table is not always needed in such cases, for consider the following (admittedly odd) argument:

105. B • ~B ∴ B

We can deal with this argument by means of an abbreviated truth table:

| | B • ~B ∴ B | | |
|---|------------|---|---|
| | F(T/F)T | F | Valid |

Since there is only one way to make B false, and it forces an assignment of "F" to the premise, the abbreviated truth table works in this case.

Logically equivalent statements, such as $P \vee \sim Q$ and $\sim Q \vee P$, validly imply each other. More formally, two statements are **logical equivalent** if *they agree in truth value regardless of the truth values assigned to their atomic components*. In other words, two statements are logically equivalent if, in a truth table constructed for both statements, the same truth value occurs beneath the main operators of the two statements in each row. For example:

| A B | A → B | ~A ∨ B |
|-----|-------|--------|
| T T | T | T |
| T F | F | F |
| F T | T | T |
| F F | T | T |

Note that the columns under the arrow and the vee are exactly the same, row by row.

The concept of logical equivalence has an important relationship to the concept of a tautology—namely, if a biconditional statement is a tautology, then its two constituent statements (joined by the double-arrow) are logically equivalent. For instance, consider the following tautology:

| F G | (F → G) ↔ (~G → ~F) |
|-----|---------------------|
| T T | T    T    T |
| T F | F    T    F |
| F T | T    T    T |
| F F | T    T    T |

From the fact that $(F \rightarrow G) \leftrightarrow (\sim G \rightarrow \sim F)$ is a tautology, we may infer that the following two statements are logically equivalent:

106.  F → G
107.  ~G → ~F

Note also that in the truth table, the same truth value occurs beneath the main operators of the two statements (i.e., the arrows) in each row.

To sum up, truth tables can be used to sort statements into logically significant categories: tautologies, contradictions, and contingent statements. And, as we have seen, each of these types of statements has important logical properties. In addition, we have seen how truth tables can be used to show that statements are logically equivalent.

To check your understanding of these concepts, complete the following exercises.

## ◆ Exercise 7.5

**Part A:** Tautologies, Contradictions, and Contingent Statements   Use truth tables to determine whether the following statements are tautologies, contradictions, or contingent statements.

* 1. ~A → (A → B)
  2. ~F → G
  3. ~S ↔ S
* 4. B → (A → B)
  5. F → [~(F • G) → ~G]
  6. A → [(A → B) → B]
* 7. P → (P → Q)
  8. (A ↔ B) → (~A • ~B)
  9. ~P • ~(~P ∨ ~Q)
*10. (R • ~R) → S
 11. B → [~(A • B) → A]
 12. ~(F → G) • G
 13. ~(N ↔ M) → (N • ~M)
 14. [A → (B ∨ C)] → [(A → B) ∨ (A → C)]
 15. (~P ↔ P) → Q
 16. ~(K → L) → (K • ~L)
 17. [A → (B → C)] → [(A → B) → (A → C)]
 18. (H → J) → ~(H • ~J)
 19. (~Z • ~W) → (Z ↔ W)
 20. [(A → B) → A] → A

**Part B: Logical Equivalence** Use truth tables to prove that the following pairs of statements are logically equivalent. It will be useful to know these particular equivalences as we move on to the material in the next chapter.

* 1. ~(A • B)                ~A ∨ ~B
  2. ~(F ∨ G)                ~F • ~G
  3. P • (Q ∨ R)             (P • Q) ∨ (P • R)
* 4. S → U                   ~S ∨ U
  5. Q                       ~~Q
  6. P ∨ (Q • R)             (P ∨ Q) • (P ∨ R)
  7. F ↔ G                   (F • G) ∨ (~F • ~G)
  8. A ∨ B                   B ∨ A
  9. K • K                   K
 10. U ↔ Z                   (U → Z) • (Z → U)

**Part C:** English Arguments   Symbolize the following arguments. Then use truth tables to determine whether they are valid. Most of these arguments illustrate important logical properties of tautologies, contradictions, or contingent statements.

*  **1.** Grass is green. So, if Clinton wins, then Clinton wins. (G: Grass is green; W: Clinton wins)

   **2.** Light is both a wave and a particle. But if light is a wave, then it is not a particle. So, physicists are profoundly mistaken. (W: Light is a wave; P: Light is a particle; M: Physicists are profoundly mistaken)

   **3.** Either unicorns exist or unicorns do not exist. Therefore, trees exist. (U: Unicorns exist; T: Trees exist)

*  **4.** Pain is an illusion if and only if it is not an illusion. It follows that everything is an illusion. (P: Pain is an illusion; E: Everything is an illusion)

   **5.** If it is wet, then it is wet if it is raining. Consequently, either Sasquatch exists or Sasquatch fails to exist. (W: It is wet; R: It is raining; S: Sasquatch exists)

   **6.** Human behavior is determined only if human behavior is not free. Human behavior is determined; nevertheless, it is free. Therefore, life is but a dream. (D: Human behavior is determined; F: Human behavior is free; L: Life is but a dream)

   **7.** The sky's being colored is a necessary condition for its being blue. It follows that the sky's being blue is a sufficient condition for its being colored. (C: The sky is colored; B: The sky is blue)

   **8.** It is not the case both that electrons exist and that electrons do not exist. Hence, electrons exist. (E: Electrons exist)

   **9.** If ultimate reality is divine, then it can be described in human language if and only if it cannot be described in human language. So, ultimate reality is not divine. (U: Ultimate reality is divine; L: Ultimate reality can be described in human language)

   **10.** If you do not accept me as I am, then you do not love me. You accept me as I am if and only if you accept me as a violent criminal. You love me, but you do not accept me as a violent criminal. Consequently, you do not love me. (A: You accept me as I am; L: You love me; C: You accept me as a violent criminal)

## Notes

1. C. S. Peirce, "On the Algebra of Logic: A Contribution to the Philosophy of Notation," *American Journal of Mathematics* 7 (1885): 180–202. The credit for the invention and development of truth tables should probably be spread around a bit. The idea occurs informally in Gottlob Frege's *Begriffsschrift* (Halle, Germany: L. Nebert, 1879). And the Austrian philosopher Ludwig Wittgenstein developed truth tables independently in his famous *Tractatus Logico-philosophicus* (London: Routledge & Kegan Paul, 1922).

2. The example is borrowed from Wesley Salmon, *Logic*, 3rd ed. (Englewood Cliffs, NJ: Prentice-Hall, 1984), p. 39.

3. Some logicians deny that the word "or" has two meanings. These logicians hold that the word "or" always means "either . . . or . . . *or both*," but they would agree that in many contexts both disjuncts cannot in fact be true—for instance, "Either all trees are plants or some trees are not plants." I do not wish to enter into the dispute about whether "or" has two meanings. I will only venture to say that I have found it pedagogically useful to speak of an *inclusive* and *exclusive* sense of the word "or," and thus I have freely done so in this book.

*Chapter 8*

# Statement Logic: Proofs

In the previous chapter, we used truth tables to evaluate arguments in statement logic (the part of logic in which atomic statements are the basic units). We saw, however, that truth tables are cumbersome when applied to arguments involving numerous statement letters. In this chapter, we will develop a system of natural deduction that has certain advantages over the truth table method. In a system of *natural deduction*, one uses a set of inference rules to prove that the conclusion of an argument follows from its premises. And for the purpose of proving arguments valid, a system of natural deduction has at least two advantages over the truth table method. First, it is less cumbersome. Second, such systems more clearly mirror our intuitive patterns of reasoning (the ways we ordinarily argue) than do truth tables. The German logician and mathematician Gerhard Gentzen (1909–1945) was the first to develop a system of natural deduction.[1]

Our system of natural deduction will be introduced in stages. Section 8.1 gives us 8 initial rules of inference that permit us to construct a limited variety of proofs. Sections 8.2 and 8.3 each introduce 5 more rules, bringing the total to 18 rules. In section 8.4, we add a special rule called "conditional proof." With the addition of conditional proof, our system of natural deduction can prove as valid any argument that is valid according to the truth table method. And since each of our rules of inference is itself valid, *any argument that can be proved valid in our system of natural deduction is indeed valid*. In section 8.5, we add one more rule, called "*reductio ad absurdum*," that makes many proofs either shorter or more intuitive. Finally, in section 8.6, we discuss proving theorems.

## 8.1 Implicational Rules of Inference

Let us use the word "proof" in a technical sense to refer to a series of steps that leads from the premises of a symbolic argument to its conclusion. The fundamental idea is to show that the premises lead, by way of valid rules of inference, to the conclusion. The underlying principle is this: *Whatever follows from a set of statements by means of valid inferences is true if all the statements in the set are true.*

Our first set of inference rules is mostly familiar. The first five were introduced as argument forms in Chapter 1. Once again, we use italicized, lowercase letters as variables that stand for any given statement: *p*, *q*, *r*, and *s*.

**Rule 1**: *Modus ponens* (MP):    $p \to q$
$$p$$
$$\therefore q$$

**Rule 2**: *Modus tollens* (MT):    $p \to q$
$$\sim q$$
$$\therefore \sim p$$

**Rule 3**: Hypothetical syllogism (HS):    $p \to q$
$$q \to r$$
$$\therefore p \to r$$

**Rule 4**: Disjunctive syllogism (DS), in two forms:

$$p \lor q \qquad\qquad p \lor q$$
$$\sim p \qquad\qquad\quad \sim q$$
$$\therefore q \qquad\qquad\quad \therefore p$$

**Rule 5**: Constructive dilemma (CD):    $p \lor q$
$$p \to r$$
$$q \to s$$
$$\therefore r \lor s$$

*Note that each rule is given an abbreviation designed to cut down on the amount of writing involved in constructing proofs.* To these familiar forms we add three additional patterns of inference, two involving conjunctions and one involving disjunctions.

**Rule 6**: Simplification (Simp), in two forms:

$$p \cdot q \qquad\qquad p \cdot q$$
$$\therefore p \qquad\qquad \therefore q$$

Simplification says, in effect, that if you have a conjunction, then you may infer either conjunct. Here is an English example:

1. Both Pierre Curie and Marie Curie were physicists. Therefore, Marie Curie was a physicist.

This type of inference may seem so obvious as to be trivial, but it is nonetheless valid. And one aspect of the power of logic is its capacity to break complex reasoning down into easy steps.

The next rule tells us that if we have two statements as steps in an argument, we may conjoin them.

**Rule 7:** Conjunction (Conj):     $p$
                                    $q$
                                    $\therefore p \cdot q$

Again, this rule is obviously valid. Here is an example:

2. Thomas Aquinas died in 1274. William Ockham died in 1349. Consequently, Aquinas died in 1274, *and* Ockham died in 1349.

The rule of addition is perhaps a bit less obvious than the rules we have considered so far.

**Rule 8:** Addition (Add) in two forms:

$$p \qquad\qquad p$$
$$\therefore p \vee q \qquad \therefore q \vee p$$

This schema tells us that from any given statement $p$, one may infer a disjunction that has $p$ as one of its disjuncts—and the other disjunct may be anything you please. For instance:

3. Thomas Paine wrote *Common Sense*. Hence, either Thomas Paine wrote *Common Sense* or Patrick Henry wrote *Common Sense* (or both did).

This type of inference may seem odd, but it is valid. Recall that only one disjunct must be true for an inclusive disjunction to be true. Thus, "Either $1 + 1 = 2$ or $2 + 2 = 22$ (or both)" is true, even though "$2 + 2 = 22$" is false. And hence, every instance of addition is valid since it is impossible for the conclusion of an argument of this form to be false *given that its premise is true*.

Is the following argument an example of addition?

4. Adam stole the money. It follows that either Adam stole the money or Betty stole the money, but not both. (A: Adam stole the money; B: Betty stole the money)

No. Argument (4) has the following invalid form:

5. A  $\therefore$ $(A \vee B) \cdot {\sim}(A \cdot B)$

And it is easy to construct a counterexample to this pattern of reasoning. For instance:

6. Four is an even number. So, either 4 is even or 6 is even, *but not both*.

Because the premise is obviously true but the conclusion is obviously false, the counterexample proves that form (5) is invalid. So, it is important not to confuse form (5) with the rule of addition.

The italicized, lowercase letters in the previous argument schemas play a special role. They can be replaced by any symbolic sentence *as long as the replacement is uniform throughout the argument*. For example, both of the following count as instances of *modus ponens*:

$$\begin{array}{ll} {\sim}F \to G & L \to (M \to N) \\ {\sim}F & L \\ \therefore\ G & \therefore\ M \to N \end{array}$$

In the inference on the left, $\sim$F is substituted for the letter *p*, while G is substituted for the letter *q* in the original schema: $p \to q, p \therefore q$. Note that we have replaced *p* with $\sim$F throughout the argument schema; substitutions must be uniform in this sense. In the example on the right, L is substituted for *p*, while $(M \to N)$ is substituted for *q* in the original schema. In both cases, the pattern of reasoning is *modus ponens* because one premise is a conditional, the other is the antecedent of the conditional, and the conclusion is the consequent of the conditional.

In substituting symbolic formulas for lowercase letters, precision is required. Consider the following argument. Is it an instance of *modus tollens*?

$$\begin{array}{l} C \to {\sim}D \\ D \\ \therefore\ {\sim}C \end{array}$$

No, it is not. The schema for *modus tollens* is $p \to q, \sim q \therefore \sim p$. If we replace the letter *q* with $\sim$D in the first premise, we must replace *q* with $\sim$D in the second premise as well, in which case we obtain the following argument:

$$\begin{array}{l} C \to {\sim}D \\ {\sim}{\sim}D \\ \therefore\ {\sim}C \end{array}$$

This *is* an instance of *modus tollens*. To apply *modus tollens*, we need a conditional *and* the negation of its consequent. If the consequent of the conditional is itself a negation, such as $\sim$D, the other premise will be a double-negation, such as $\sim\sim$D above.

To ensure an understanding of our new inference rules, let us consider a series of examples. Which rules of inference, if any, are exemplified by the following arguments?

$$\begin{array}{ll} {\sim}P \to (Q \bullet R) & X \vee (Y \leftrightarrow Z) \\ (Q \bullet R) \to S & {\sim}(Y \leftrightarrow Z) \\ \therefore\ {\sim}P \to S & \therefore\ X \end{array}$$

The argument on the left is an example of hypothetical syllogism. Note that ~P replaces p, (Q • R) replaces q, and S replaces r in the original schema: $p \rightarrow q$, $q \rightarrow r \therefore p \rightarrow r$. The argument on the right is an example of disjunctive syllogism. Here, X replaces p and (Y ↔ Z) replaces q in the second form of disjunctive syllogism: $p \lor q$, $\sim q \therefore p$.

Which rules of inference, if any, are exemplified by the following arguments?

~M v ~N

~M → ~O

~N → ~P         ~(B • ~C)

∴ ~O v ~P       ∴ ~(B • ~C) v ~D

The argument on the left is an example of constructive dilemma. Here, ~M replaces p, ~N replaces q, ~O replaces r, and ~P replaces s in the schema for constructive dilemma: $p \lor q, p \rightarrow r, q \rightarrow s \therefore r \lor s$. The argument on the right is an example of addition. Note that ~(B • ~C) replaces p, while ~D replaces q in the first form of addition: $p \therefore p \lor q$.

Which rules of inference, if any, are exemplified by the following arguments?

                  A v ~B

(C → D) • (E v F)     B

∴ E v F            ∴ A

The argument on the left is an example of simplification. Here, (C → D) replaces p, while (E v F) replaces q in the second form of simplification: $p • q \therefore q$. The argument on the right, however, does *not* exemplify any of our inference rules. But if we changed the second premise to ~~B, then we would have an instance of the second form of disjunctive syllogism: $p \lor q, \sim q \therefore p$. (Substitute A for p and ~B for q.)

Let us now use our new inference rules to construct some proofs. We begin with an English argument:

7. If some employees deserve 5 times the wages of others, then some employees are 5 times more valuable than others. It is not true that some employees are 5 times more valuable than others. So, it is not true that some employees deserve 5 times the wages of others. (D: Some employees deserve 5 times the wages of others; V: Some employees are 5 times more valuable than others)

Using the scheme of abbreviation provided, the argument should be symbolized as follows:

1. D → V

2. ~V        ∴ ~D

The first lines of our proof contain the premises of the argument. To the right of the last premise we write the conclusion, marked by the three-dot symbol. This serves as a reminder of what we are trying to derive from the premises. (Thus, the expression ∴ ~D is not really a part of the proof but merely a reminder of what we need to prove.) What we want to do is to arrive at the conclusion, ~D, by means of our inference rules. We have a conditional premise, and we also have the negation of its consequent. That is, we have here the makings of a *modus tollens*–type argument. To see this, substitute D for *p* and substitute V for *q* in the original diagram for *modus tollens*: *p* → *q*, ~*q* ∴ ~*p*. Proper proof procedure requires that *we list the lines to which we are applying the rule of inference, as well as the abbreviation of the inference rule*. Accordingly, our completed proof looks like this:

> 1. D → V
> 2. ~V            ∴ ~D
> 3. ~D            1, 2, MT

Line (3) tells us that ~D follows from lines (1) and (2) by *modus tollens*. We have shown that the premises of the argument lead to the conclusion by way of a valid rule of inference. Notice that the only lines in the proof without annotation (without an explicit indication of how we arrived at them) are the premises. *Let us adopt the convention that any step in an argument without annotation will be understood to be a premise.*

Consider a slightly more complicated example:

> 8.  If the workplace is a meritocracy, then the most qualified person always gets the job. But the most qualified person does not always get the job if networking plays a role in who gets most jobs. Furthermore, networking does play a role in who gets most jobs. Therefore, the workplace is not a meritocracy. (W: The workplace is a meritocracy; M: The most qualified person always gets the job; N: Networking plays a role in who gets most jobs)

Using the scheme of abbreviation provided, the argument should be symbolized as follows:

> 1. W → M
> 2. N → ~M
> 3. N             ∴ ~W

As before, the first lines of our proof contain the premises of the argument, with the conclusion written off to the right of the last premise. The completed proof runs as follows:

> 1. W → M
> 2. N → ~M
> 3. N             ∴ ~W
> 4. ~M            2, 3, MP
> 5. ~W            1, 4, MT

Lines (2) and (3) imply ~M by the rule *modus ponens*. To see this, replace *p* with N and *q* with ~M in the schema for *modus ponens*: $p \rightarrow q, p \therefore q$. Lines (1) and (4) imply ~W by the rule *modus tollens*: $p \rightarrow q, \sim q \therefore \sim p$ (replacing *p* with W and *q* with M).

Let us now consider a proof that employs our inference rules involving conjunctions:

> 9. Women earn only 75¢ for every dollar earned by men. If women earn only 75¢ for every dollar earned by men, and 90% of children who live with one parent live with their mothers, then men are better off than women, and women are victims of injustice. Ninety percent of children who live with one parent live with their mothers. Feminists are right if women are victims of injustice. So, feminists are right. (W: Women earn only 75¢ for every dollar earned by men; C: 90% of children who live with one parent live with their mothers; M: Men are better off than women; V: Women are victims of injustice; F: Feminists are right)

Using the scheme of abbreviation provided, the translation into symbols looks like this:

> 1. W
> 2. $(W \cdot C) \rightarrow (M \cdot V)$
> 3. C
> 4. $V \rightarrow F$        $\therefore$ F

The proof may be completed thus:

> 5. $W \cdot C$        1, 3, Conj
> 6. $M \cdot V$        2, 5, MP
> 7. V        6, Simp
> 8. F        4, 7, MP

Note that line (5) comes from lines (1) and (3) by substituting W for *p* and C for *q* in the schema for conjunction: $p, q \therefore p \cdot q$. And line (7) comes from line (6) by substituting M for *p* and V for *q* in the second form of simplification: $p \cdot q \therefore q$.

One last example will demonstrate some of the inference rules involving disjunctions.

> 10. If Pierre is an assassin, then either he should be put to death, or he should be given a life sentence. He should be put to death only if murderers deserve death. He should be given a life sentence only if murderers forfeit their right to liberty. Pierre is an assassin, but murderers do not deserve death. Therefore, murderers forfeit their right to liberty. (A: Pierre is an assassin; D: Pierre should be put to death; L: Pierre should be given a life sentence; M: Murderers deserve death; F: Murderers forfeit their right to liberty)

Using the scheme of abbreviation provided, the argument may be symbolized like this:

    1. $A \rightarrow (D \vee L)$
    2. $D \rightarrow M$
    3. $L \rightarrow F$
    4. $A \cdot \sim M$      $\therefore$ F

The proof may be completed as follows:

    5. A           4, Simp
    6. $D \vee L$      1, 5, MP
    7. $M \vee F$      6, 2, 3, CD
    8. $\sim M$         4, Simp
    9. F           7, 8, DS

Note that line (7) derives from the steps indicated by substituting $D$ for $p$, $L$ for $q$, $M$ for $r$, and $F$ for $s$ in the original schema for constructive dilemma: $p \vee q$, $p \rightarrow r, q \rightarrow s \therefore r \vee s$. And line (9) derives from lines (7) and (8) by substituting $M$ for $p$ and $F$ for $q$ in the first form of disjunctive syllogism: $p \vee q$, $\sim p \therefore q$.

    Our first eight inference rules are called **implicational rules** to set them apart from equivalence rules, which will be introduced in the next section. When using an equivalence rule, one always moves from a single statement (such as $\sim H \cdot J$) to another statement that is logically equivalent to the first (such as $J \cdot \sim H$). (Recall that logically equivalent statements validly imply each other. They agree in truth value regardless of the truth values assigned to their atomic components.) But implicational rules lack this feature. For example, we may move from $F \cdot G$ to $F$ by simplification, but obviously $F$ is not logically equivalent to $F \cdot G$. Because of this difference between implicational and equivalence rules, implicational rules must be applied to entire lines in a proof and not merely to parts of lines. To illustrate, consider the following inference:

    1. $F \rightarrow (G \rightarrow H)$
    2. $\sim H$              $\therefore F \rightarrow \sim G$
    3. $F \rightarrow \sim G$        ???

Does line (3) follow from lines (1) and (2) by *modus tollens*? No. *Modus tollens* must be applied to entire lines in a proof. So, in order to have an instance of *modus tollens*, we need two things:

    ■   A conditional statement that is an entire line in a proof

    ■   Another line that is *the negation of the consequent* of that conditional

In the preceding example, the first is satisfied but the second is not. Line (1) *is* a conditional that represents an entire line in the proof. But the negation of its consequent is ~(G → H), not ~H. So, line (3) does not follow from lines (1) and (2) by *modus tollens*.

Notice that we construct our proofs by means of *one* application of *one* rule of inference per line, as indicated in the annotation listed to the right. We do this to ensure that each step in every proof is explicit and clearly justified by a rule in our system of logic. Which of the following proofs is properly constructed?

| | | | | |
|---|---|---|---|---|
| 1. A → ~B | | | 1. A → ~B | |
| 2. A • C | ∴ ~B | | 2. A • C | ∴ ~B |
| 3. ~B | 1, 2, MP | | 3. A | 2, Simp |
| | | | 4. ~B | 1, 3, MP |

The proof on the right is correct; the proof on the left skips a required application of simplification and misapplies *modus ponens*. To apply *modus ponens*, we need (a) a conditional that is an entire line in the proof and (b) another line that is *precisely* the antecedent of that conditional. Clause (a) is satisfied in line (1) of the above proofs, but clause (b) is not satisfied in the proof on the left because A never appears by itself on any line.

The following hints or rules of thumb may help you as you construct proofs:

> **Rule of Thumb 1:** It usually helps to work backward. So, start by looking at the conclusion, and then try to find the conclusion (or elements thereof) in the premises.

For example:

1. A → [B → (C ∨ D)]
2. B • A
3. ~D                    ∴ C

The conclusion here is C. Does it appear anywhere in the premises? Yes, it is embedded in the consequent of premise (1). And if we could obtain C ∨ D from premise (1), we could combine it with ~D—that is, premise (3)—to get C, by disjunctive syllogism. But how can we obtain C ∨ D? Consider a second rule of thumb:

> **Rule of Thumb 2:** Apply the inference rules to break down the premises.

We could get A from line (2) by simplification and use it together with line (1) to obtain B → (C ∨ D), by *modus ponens*. Then we could get B from line (2) (by simplification) and apply *modus ponens* again, to obtain C ∨ D. The whole proof would then look like this:

1. A → [B → (C ∨ D)]
2. B • A
3. ~D                          ∴ C
4. A                           2, Simp
5. B → (C ∨ D)                 1, 4, MP
6. B                           2, Simp
7. C ∨ D                       5, 6, MP
8. C                           3, 7, DS

Let's consider another example:

1. E ∨ F
2. E → G
3. F → H
4. (G ∨ H) → J          ∴ J ∨ K

Using rule of thumb 1, we start by examining the conclusion. We look to see if the conclusion (or parts thereof) appear in the premises, noting that *J* is the consequent of premise (4). Now, is there any way to break premise (4) down, as rule of thumb 2 suggests? Yes, we can use the rule of constructive dilemma to obtain G ∨ H from premises (1), (2), and (3), and then use *modus ponens* to get *J*. But where do we go from there? In particular, how can we obtain *K* when it appears nowhere in the premises? At this point, it will be helpful to bear in mind an additional rule of thumb:

> **Rule of Thumb 3:** If the conclusion contains a statement letter that does not appear in the premises, use the rule of addition.

The whole proof looks like this:

1. E ∨ F
2. E → G
3. F → H
4. (G ∨ H) → J          ∴ J ∨ K
5. G ∨ H                1, 2, 3, CD
6. J                    4, 5, MP
7. J ∨ K                6, Add

These rules of thumb are helpful in many cases, but a certain amount of ingenuity is required when doing proofs. Furthermore, to gain facility in constructing proofs, one must practice. Hence, the following exercises are provided.

| Summary of Implicational Rules |
| :--- |

1. *Modus ponens* (MP):

$$p \rightarrow q$$
$$p$$
$$\therefore q$$

2. *Modus tollens* (MT):

$$p \rightarrow q$$
$$\sim q$$
$$\therefore \sim p$$

3. Hypothetical syllogism (HS):

$$p \rightarrow q$$
$$q \rightarrow r$$
$$\therefore p \rightarrow r$$

4. Disjunctive syllogism (DS), in two forms:

$$p \lor q \qquad\qquad p \lor q$$
$$\sim p \qquad\qquad\quad \sim q$$
$$\therefore q \qquad\qquad\quad \therefore p$$

5. Constructive dilemma (CD):

$$p \lor q$$
$$p \rightarrow r$$
$$q \rightarrow s$$
$$\therefore r \lor s$$

6. Simplification (Simp), in two forms:

$$p \cdot q \qquad\qquad p \cdot q$$
$$\therefore p \qquad\qquad \therefore q$$

7. Conjunction (Conj):

$$p$$
$$q$$
$$\therefore p \cdot q$$

8. Addition (Add), in two forms:

$$p \qquad\qquad\qquad p$$
$$\therefore p \lor q \qquad\qquad \therefore q \lor p$$

## ◆ *Exercise 8.1*

**Part A: Annotating**   For each of the following proofs, indicate from which steps each inference is drawn and by which rule the inference is made. (See the Answer Key for an illustration.)

\*  **1.**  1. $F \rightarrow G$
  2. $G \rightarrow H$  $\therefore F \rightarrow H$
  3. $F \rightarrow H$

  **2.**  1. $\sim S \rightarrow \sim P$
  2. $\sim S$  $\therefore K \lor \sim P$
  3. $\sim P$
  4. $K \lor \sim P$

  **3.**  1. $E \rightarrow (T \rightarrow S)$
  2. $\sim (T \rightarrow S)$
  3. $\sim R \lor E$  $\therefore \sim R$
  4. $\sim E$
  5. $\sim R$

* **4.** 1. H ∨ ~C
   2. H → ~B
   3. ~C → D
   4. (~B ∨ D) → (K • J)  ∴ J
   5. ~B ∨ D
   6. K • J
   7. J

**5.** 1. D
   2. ~H
   3. (D • ~H) → (E ∨ H)  ∴ E
   4. D • ~H
   5. E ∨ H
   6. E

**6.** 1. ~A → ~B
   2. ~~B • C  ∴ ~~A • C
   3. ~~B
   4. ~~A
   5. C
   6. ~~A • C

* **7.** 1. ~(P • Q) ∨ R
   2. (~E • ~R) → (A • B)
   3. E → (P • Q)
   4. ~R  ∴ B ∨ (F • G)
   5. ~(P • Q)
   6. ~E
   7. ~E • ~R
   8. A • B
   9. B
   10. B ∨ (F • G)

**8.** 1. F ∨ S
   2. G
   3. [G • (F ∨ S)] → ~T
   4. ~B → T  ∴ ~~B
   5. G • (F ∨ S)
   6. ~T
   7. ~~B

**9.** 1. F → B
   2. ~D
   3. (~D • G) → (B → S)
   4. G
   5. ~S  ∴ G • ~F
   6. ~D • G
   7. B → S
   8. F → S
   9. ~F
   10. G • ~F

* **10.** 1. W → (X ∨ ~Y)
   2. ~~Y • W  ∴ X ∨ ~Z
   3. W
   4. X ∨ ~Y
   5. ~~Y
   6. X
   7. X ∨ ~Z

**Part B:** Correct or Incorrect?   Some of the following inferences are correct applications of the eight rules introduced in this section, and some are not. If an inference is a correct application of a rule, name the rule. If an inference is not a correct application of a rule, explain why it is not. (The question is whether the conclusion in each case can be reached *in a single step* from the premise(s) by an application of one of the rules.)

* **1.**    K → L
         ~L
      ∴ ~K

**2.**    G → F
         E → G
      ∴ E → F

**3.**    M → N
         ~M
      ∴ ~N

* **4.**    ~B ∨ ~Y
         ~B → ~X
         ~Y → Z
      ∴ ~X ∨ Z

5.  $(E \cdot F) \vee G$
    $\sim(E \cdot F)$
    $\therefore G$

6.  $(N \cdot P) \rightarrow (O \vee S)$
    $O \vee S$
    $\therefore N \cdot P$

\* 7.  $\sim E \vee \sim F$
    $\sim\sim F$
    $\therefore \sim E$

8.  $A \rightarrow \sim\sim B$
    $\sim B$
    $\therefore \sim A$

9.  $(P \rightarrow Q) \vee R$
    $P$
    $\therefore Q \vee R$

\* 10.  $(R \cdot S) \rightarrow T$
    $\therefore S \rightarrow T$

11.  $(K \vee L) \rightarrow M$
    $\sim M$
    $\therefore \sim(K \vee L)$

12.  $(H \vee \sim S) \rightarrow \sim W$
    $H \vee \sim S$
    $\therefore \sim W$

\* 13.  $T \rightarrow \sim U$
    $U$
    $\therefore \sim T$

14.  $P \cdot Q$
    $\therefore (R \rightarrow S) \vee (P \cdot Q)$

15.  $R \rightarrow \sim S$
    $\sim\sim S$
    $\therefore \sim R$

\* 16.  $\sim C \vee \sim D$
    $X \rightarrow C$
    $Y \rightarrow D$
    $\therefore \sim X \vee \sim Y$

17.  $\sim G \vee \sim P$
    $G$
    $\therefore \sim P$

18.  $A \rightarrow (B \rightarrow C)$
    $B$
    $\therefore A \rightarrow C$

\* 19.  $(\sim B \vee D) \rightarrow E$
    $\sim\sim B$
    $\therefore D \rightarrow E$

20.  $\sim T \rightarrow \sim N$
    $\sim\sim N$
    $\therefore \sim\sim T$

**Part C: Proofs**  Construct proofs to show the following symbolic arguments valid. Commas mark the breaks between premises. (See the Answer Key for an illustration.)

\*  1. $H \rightarrow \sim B$, $D \rightarrow B$, $H$ $\therefore \sim D$

2. $F \rightarrow (G \rightarrow H)$, $\sim F \rightarrow J$, $\sim(G \rightarrow H)$ $\therefore J$

3. $(F \vee E) \rightarrow \sim D$, $S \vee D$, $E$ $\therefore S$

\*  4. $\sim A \rightarrow F$, $A \rightarrow D$, $\sim D$, $F \rightarrow S$ $\therefore S \vee X$

5. $(A \cdot E) \rightarrow F$, $E$, $F \rightarrow (D \cdot \sim C)$, $A$ $\therefore \sim C$

6. $\sim F \vee \sim G$, $\sim F \rightarrow Z$, $\sim G \rightarrow \sim R$, $(Z \vee \sim R) \rightarrow (U \rightarrow P)$, $\sim P$ $\therefore \sim U$

\*  7. $\sim(S \vee R)$, $B \rightarrow (S \vee R)$, $B \vee P$, $\sim Q \vee B$ $\therefore P \cdot \sim Q$

8. $C \rightarrow (T \rightarrow L)$, $\sim L$, $\sim E \rightarrow C$, $L \vee \sim E$ $\therefore \sim T$

9. $\sim\sim A$, $B \rightarrow \sim A$ $\therefore \sim B$

* 10. $(B \cdot A) \rightarrow C$, $\sim D \rightarrow (B \cdot A)$, $\sim C$ $\therefore$ $\sim \sim D$

  11. $(\sim B \cdot \sim C) \rightarrow (D \rightarrow C)$, $\sim B$, $C \rightarrow B$ $\therefore$ $\sim D$

  12. $(D \cdot H) \rightarrow R$, $S \rightarrow (D \cdot H)$ $\therefore$ $S \rightarrow R$

* 13. $(T \rightarrow C) \rightarrow \sim F$, $S \rightarrow C$, $T \rightarrow S$, $F \vee \sim P$ $\therefore$ $\sim P$

  14. $(A \vee \sim B) \rightarrow (F \vee (R \cdot G))$, $A$, $F \rightarrow L$, $(R \cdot G) \rightarrow T$, $(L \vee T) \rightarrow S$ $\therefore$ $S$

  15. $P \vee Q$, $(Q \cdot \sim R) \rightarrow S$, $R \rightarrow P$, $\sim P$ $\therefore$ $S$

* 16. $(E \vee F) \rightarrow \sim G$, $\sim H$, $H \vee K$, $(K \vee L) \rightarrow E$ $\therefore$ $\sim G$

  17. $(M \vee N) \rightarrow \sim S$, $T \rightarrow (M \vee N)$, $\sim S \rightarrow \sim (M \vee N)$ $\therefore$ $T \rightarrow \sim (M \vee N)$

  18. $(E \vee \sim B) \rightarrow (\sim S \vee T)$, $E$, $\sim S \rightarrow L$, $T \rightarrow \sim C$, $(L \vee \sim C) \rightarrow A$ $\therefore$ $A$

* 19. $\sim \sim B$, $\sim C \rightarrow \sim B$, $(\sim \sim C \vee T) \rightarrow P$ $\therefore$ $P$

  20. $B \vee \sim C$, $B \rightarrow E$, $\sim \sim C$ $\therefore$ $\sim B \vee E$

**Part D:** More Proofs   Construct proofs to show that the following arguments are valid. Commas mark the breaks between premises.

* 1. $P \rightarrow Q$, $R \rightarrow \sim S$, $P \vee R$, $(Q \vee \sim S) \rightarrow (\sim T \vee \sim W)$, $\sim \sim T$ $\therefore$ $\sim W$

  2. $(A \vee G) \rightarrow K$, $K \rightarrow (B \rightarrow F)$, $A \cdot B$ $\therefore$ $F$

  3. $\sim M$, $(\sim M \cdot \sim N) \rightarrow (Q \rightarrow P)$, $\sim N$, $P \rightarrow R$ $\therefore$ $Q \rightarrow R$

* 4. $\sim (R \vee S)$, $\sim (T \cdot V) \rightarrow (R \vee S)$, $\sim \sim (T \cdot V) \rightarrow W$ $\therefore$ $W \vee \sim R$

  5. $\sim W \cdot \sim \sim Z$, $(\sim W \cdot X) \rightarrow Y$, $\sim Z \vee X$ $\therefore$ $Y$

  6. $F \rightarrow A$, $\sim J \cdot \sim K$, $H \rightarrow (G \rightarrow F)$, $\sim K \rightarrow (\sim J \rightarrow H)$ $\therefore$ $G \rightarrow A$

* 7. $\sim F \rightarrow J$, $\sim F \vee \sim G$, $\sim G \rightarrow \sim H$, $(J \vee \sim H) \rightarrow \sim K$, $\sim L \rightarrow K$ $\therefore$ $\sim \sim L$

  8. $Y \rightarrow W$, $(Z \rightarrow W) \rightarrow (V \cdot \sim T)$, $Z \rightarrow Y$, $Q \rightarrow T$ $\therefore$ $\sim Q$

  9. $(\sim N \cdot M) \rightarrow T$, $\sim O \rightarrow M$, $\sim O \cdot \sim N$ $\therefore$ $T \vee S$

* 10. $\sim A \cdot \sim C$, $\sim C \rightarrow D$, $(D \cdot \sim A) \rightarrow (E \rightarrow \sim H)$, $E \cdot (\sim F \rightarrow H)$ $\therefore$ $\sim \sim F$

  11. $R \rightarrow D$, $B \rightarrow R$, $(B \rightarrow D) \rightarrow (E \vee F)$, $\sim E$ $\therefore$ $F$

  12. $\sim F \rightarrow \sim G$, $P \rightarrow \sim Q$, $\sim F \vee P$, $(\sim G \vee \sim Q) \rightarrow (L \cdot M)$ $\therefore$ $L$

* 13. $(Z \cdot A) \vee \sim Y$, $(Z \cdot A) \rightarrow U$, $W \vee \sim U$, $\sim W$ $\therefore$ $\sim Y$

  14. $(D \cdot E) \vee F$, $F \rightarrow C$, $(D \cdot E) \rightarrow \sim B$, $(\sim B \vee C) \rightarrow (A \rightarrow P)$, $\sim P$ $\therefore$ $\sim A$

  15. $O \rightarrow N$, $\sim M$, $S \rightarrow R$, $P \rightarrow O$, $R \rightarrow P$, $(S \rightarrow N) \rightarrow (M \vee L)$ $\therefore$ $\sim P \vee L$

* 16. $(\sim M \vee L) \rightarrow (\sim A \rightarrow B)$, $\sim S \rightarrow T$, $R \rightarrow \sim S$, $\sim M \cdot J$, $R \vee \sim A$ $\therefore$ $T \vee B$

  17. $F \rightarrow \sim G$, $\sim \sim G \cdot O$, $(\sim F \cdot \sim \sim G) \rightarrow [(\sim H \rightarrow E) \cdot (C \rightarrow F)]$, $C \vee \sim H$ $\therefore$ $E$

  18. $\sim N \cdot \sim M$, $\sim P \rightarrow N$, $\sim N \rightarrow Z$, $(Z \cdot \sim \sim P) \rightarrow K$ $\therefore$ $K \cdot \sim M$

* 19. $A \vee D$, $\sim D$, $(C \vee A) \rightarrow \sim E$ $\therefore$ $\sim E$

20. $(C \rightarrow Q) \cdot (\sim L \rightarrow \sim R)$, $(S \rightarrow C) \cdot (\sim N \rightarrow \sim L)$, $\sim Q \cdot J$,
$\sim Q \rightarrow (S \vee \sim N)$ $\therefore \sim R$

21. $\sim(Z \vee Y) \rightarrow \sim W$, $\sim U \rightarrow \sim(Z \vee Y)$, $(\sim U \rightarrow \sim W) \rightarrow (T \rightarrow S)$,
$S \rightarrow (R \vee P)$, $[T \rightarrow (R \vee P)] \rightarrow [(\sim R \vee K) \cdot \sim K]$ $\therefore \sim R$

* 22. $\sim A$, $[\sim A \vee (B \cdot C)] \rightarrow (D \rightarrow \sim E)$, $\sim E \rightarrow \sim F$, $(D \rightarrow \sim F) \rightarrow G$
$\therefore (G \cdot \sim A) \vee \sim H$

23. $(S \vee U) \cdot \sim U$, $S \rightarrow [T \cdot (F \vee G)]$, $[T \vee (J \cdot P)] \rightarrow (\sim B \cdot E)$ $\therefore S \cdot \sim B$

24. $\sim X \rightarrow (\sim Y \rightarrow \sim Z)$, $X \vee (W \rightarrow U)$, $\sim Y \vee W$, $\sim X \cdot T$, $(\sim Z \vee U) \rightarrow \sim S$
$\therefore (R \vee \sim S) \cdot T$

* 25. $(D \vee C) \rightarrow (F \vee H)$, $(H \cdot G) \rightarrow (F \vee E)$, $(D \vee B) \rightarrow (\sim F \rightarrow G)$,
$(F \vee D) \cdot (\sim F \cdot A)$ $\therefore E$

**Part E: English Arguments** Symbolize the following arguments using the schemes of abbreviation provided. Then construct proofs to show that the arguments are valid.

* 1. No one can know anything, for every piece of reasoning must start somewhere. And if every piece of reasoning must start somewhere, then every piece of reasoning begins with an unsupported premise. Now, if every piece of reasoning begins with an unsupported premise, then all human thinking is based on mere assumption. And if all human thinking is based on mere assumption, no one can know anything. (S: Every piece of reasoning must start somewhere; U: Every piece of reasoning begins with an unsupported premise; A: All human thinking is based on mere assumption; K: No one can know anything)

2. Theists say that God created the world. They say that the world must have a cause. But why? The world must have a cause only if everything must have a cause. But if everything must have a cause, then God has a cause. However, God isn't God if God has a cause. And if God isn't God, God doesn't exist. So, if the world must have a cause, there is no God. (W: The world must have a cause; E: Everything must have a cause; H: God has a cause; G: God is God; X: God exists)

3. Either we should stop going places, or we should develop hydrogen-powered cars, or we should go on driving gasoline-powered cars. We should go on driving gasoline-powered cars only if we should destroy the ozone layer. We should not stop going places and we should not destroy the ozone layer. Therefore, we should develop hydrogen-powered cars. (P: We should stop going places; H: We should develop hydrogen-powered cars; G: We should go on driving gasoline-powered cars; O: We should destroy the ozone layer)

* 4. Dinosaurs are extinct. And given that dinosaurs are extinct, they suffered some catastrophe if they died suddenly. The dinosaurs died suddenly, assuming that they froze due to a sudden drop in temperature or were attacked by a lethal virus. The dinosaurs froze due to a sudden drop in temperature

provided that the sun's rays were blocked. The earth's atmosphere was filled with dust due to the impact of a comet, and the sun's rays were blocked. Therefore, the dinosaurs suffered some catastrophe. (E: Dinosaurs are extinct; C: The dinosaurs suffered some catastrophe; D: The dinosaurs died suddenly; F: The dinosaurs froze due to a sudden drop in temperature; V: The dinosaurs were attacked by a lethal virus; S: The sun's rays were blocked; A: The earth's atmosphere was filled with dust due to the impact of a comet)

5. In spite of the fact that advocates of suicide and euthanasia often claim that every right—including the right to life—can be waived, I think it's absurd to suggest that every right can be waived. (To waive a right is to agree, for good moral reasons, not to exercise it.) For if every right can be waived, then if I announce that I am waiving my right to liberty, you are morally permitted to enslave me. But obviously, it is not true that if I announce that I am waiving my right to liberty, then you are morally permitted to enslave me. (E: Every right can be waived; A: I announce that I am waiving my right to liberty; P: You are morally permitted to enslave me)

6. If morality is not subjective, then either morality is relative to cultures, or God is the source of all moral values. If morality is subjective, then if I approve of racism, racism is right. Plainly, it's false that if I approve of racism, racism is right. Furthermore, if morality is relative to cultures, then the cannibalism in New Guinea is right, and the caste system in India is right. The statement "The cannibalism in New Guinea is right, and the caste system in India is right" is false. God exists if God is the source of all moral values. Accordingly, God exists. (S: Morality is subjective; M: Morality is relative to cultures; V: God is the source of all moral values; A: I approve of racism; R: Racism is right; C: The cannibalism in New Guinea is right; I: The caste system in India is right; G: God exists)

* 7. Al has precognition. And assuming that Al has precognition, Al experiences events prior to their occurrence. But if Al experiences events prior to their occurrence, then either events exist prior to their occurrence, or Al predicts the future on the basis of what he knows about the past and present. It is simply nonsense to say that events exist prior to their occurrence. We may infer that Al predicts the future on the basis of what he knows about the past and present. (P: Al has precognition; A: Al experiences events prior to their occurrence; E: Events exist prior to their occurrence; F: Al predicts the future on the basis of what he knows about the past and present)

8. God's existence is either necessary or impossible, if it is not contingent. God's existence is a matter of metaphysical luck if it is contingent. God's existence is emphatically not a matter of metaphysical luck. God's existence is not impossible if the concept of an omnipotent and perfectly good being is coherent. The concept of an omnipotent and perfectly good being is coherent. Therefore, God's existence is necessary. (N: God's existence is necessary; I: God's existence is impossible; C: God's existence is contingent; M: God's

existence is a matter of metaphysical luck; T: The concept of an omnipotent and perfectly good being is coherent)

9. Either the "eye for an eye" principle is interpreted literally, or it is interpreted figuratively. If it is interpreted literally, then the state must do to criminals what they have done to their victims. If the state must do to criminals what they have done to their victims, then the state must torture torturers. On the other hand, if the "eye for an eye" principle is interpreted figuratively, the state need only mete out punishments that are proportional to the crime. If the state need only mete out punishments that are proportional to the crime, then the state is free to give murderers life imprisonment rather than the death penalty. Now, the state must not torture torturers if such acts are immoral. And it is indeed immoral to torture torturers. Hence, the state is free to give murderers life imprisonment rather than the death penalty. (L: The "eye for an eye" principle is interpreted literally; F: The "eye for an eye" principle is interpreted figuratively; C: The state must do to criminals what they have done to their victims; T: The state must torture torturers; P: The state need only mete out punishments that are proportional to the crime; S: The state is free to give murderers life imprisonment rather than the death penalty; I: It is immoral to torture torturers)

10. Either Mary is in much pain or she isn't in much pain. And Mary lacks a capacity to make a rational decision about ending her life if she is in a lot of pain. On the other hand, given that Mary isn't in much pain, she is in no position to know what she will want when she is in much pain. Furthermore, Mary has no right to end her life if either she lacks a capacity to make a rational decision about ending her life or she is in no position to know what she will want when she is in much pain. But Mary has no right to "die with dignity" if she has no right to end her life. Therefore, Mary has no right to "die with dignity." (M: Mary is in much pain; R: Mary lacks a capacity to make a rational decision about ending her life; K: Mary is in no position to know what she will want when she is in much pain; E: Mary has no right to end her life; D: Mary has no right to "die with dignity")

## 8.2  *Five Equivalence Rules*

In developing a system of natural deduction, the logician is pulled in two directions. On the one hand, it is possible to develop a system with a small number of inference rules. But in systems with only a few rules, the proofs are often quite long and require much ingenuity. Moreover, the proof strategies tend to depart substantially from those employed in ordinary reasoning. On the other hand, it is possible to develop a system with a very large number of rules. Such systems allow for relatively short proofs, but most people find it difficult to remember a large number of rules. The present system of statement logic is a compromise that includes 20 rules altogether—8 implicational rules, 10 equivalence rules (introduced in this section and the next), conditional proof, and *reductio ad absurdum*.

Recall that two statements are *logically equivalent* if they validly imply each other. So, it is a valid inference to move from one statement to another that is logically equivalent to it. We can also say that two statements are logically equivalent if they agree in truth value regardless of the truth values assigned to their atomic components.[2] For example, $P \vee Q$ is logically equivalent to $Q \vee P$, and the inference from $P \vee Q$ to $Q \vee P$ is valid. Now, an equivalence rule, as the name suggests, is based on a logical equivalence. And our use of the equivalence rules depends on this further principle: *Within truth-functional logic, if we replace part of a compound statement with anything logically equivalent to that part, the resulting statement will have the same truth value as the original compound.* For example, if we start with $(P \vee Q) \to R$ and replace $(P \vee Q)$ with $(Q \vee P)$, we get a statement that has the same truth value as the first, namely, $(Q \vee P) \to R$. *And the inference from $(P \vee Q) \to R$ to $(Q \vee P) \to R$ is clearly valid because the two statements must have the same truth value.*

Five equivalence rules are introduced in this section and five more in the next section. Using the four-dot symbol (: :) to indicate logical equivalence, we can state our first equivalence rule, the rule of **double-negation**, as follows:

Rule 9: Double-negation (DN): $p :: \sim\sim p$

The four-dot symbol tells us that we may move validly from $\sim\sim p$ to $p$, as well as from $p$ to $\sim\sim p$. All our equivalence rules are two-directional in this sense, unlike the implicational rules introduced in the previous section. For example, the rule of addition allows one to move from $p$ to $p \vee q$, but it does not allow one to move from $p \vee q$ to $p$. Indeed, the latter move is invalid; here is a counterexample: "Either the number 3 is even, or the number 2 is even. So, the number 3 is even."

The rule of double-negation formalizes the intuition that any statement implies, and is implied by, the negation of its negation. Here are two English examples:

11. It is not true that Booth did not kill Lincoln. So, Booth killed Lincoln.

12. Booth killed Lincoln. So, it is not true that Booth did not kill Lincoln.

The usefulness of this rule is illustrated in constructing a proof for the following short argument:

13. If humans do not have free will, then they are not responsible for their actions. But obviously, humans are responsible for their actions. Thus, humans have free will. (F: Humans have free will; R: Humans are responsible for their actions)

Using the scheme of abbreviation provided, argument (13) translates into symbols as follows:

1. ~F → ~R
2. R                    ∴ F

The proof must include two applications of the double-negation rule:

3. ~~R      2, DN
4. ~~F      1, 3, MT
5. F        4, DN

Note that we cannot obtain *F* from the premises in one step by applying MT. MT tells us that if we have a conditional in one line of a proof and *the negation of the conditional's consequent* in another line of the proof, then we can infer the negation of the antecedent. But line (2) of the proof does not give us the negation of the consequent of line (1). The negation of ~*R* is ~~*R*, and hence we must use the double-negation rule prior to applying MT.

As mentioned in the previous section, there is an important difference between implicational and equivalence rules as regards the construction of proofs. *We can apply equivalence rules to parts of lines in a proof and to entire lines.* We can do this because we never change the truth value of a statement by replacing some part of it with a logically equivalent expression. By contrast, *we can apply implicational rules only to entire lines in a proof.* The need for this restriction is illustrated by the following fallacious argument:

14. If Harry Truman was president in 1950, and Dwight Eisenhower was president in 1950, then America had two presidents in 1950. Therefore, if Truman was president in 1950, then America had two presidents in 1950. (T: Truman was president in 1950; E: Eisenhower was president in 1950; A: America had two presidents in 1950)

Without our restriction on implicational inference rules, we could construct the following proof:

1. (T • E) → A      ∴ T → A
2. T → A            1, *incorrect use of Simp* [not permitted]

Plainly, we do not want to allow this type of move. (An abbreviated truth table quickly reveals that the argument is invalid.) The proper use of both implicational and equivalence rules is illustrated in the following proof:

1. (A → B) → (A → ~~C)
2. A
3. A → D
4. D → B        ∴  C

At this point, if we tried to apply MP to lines (1) and (2) to derive *B* or ~~*C*, we would be misapplying MP. An implicational rule such as MP cannot be applied to a *part* of line (1); it must be applied to the whole line. So, we would need A → B to get A → ~~C from line (1) by MP. On the other hand, since double-negation is an equivalence rule, we can, if we wish, apply double-negation to a part of a line. Thus, we can complete our proof as follows:

     5. (A → B) → (A → C)     1, DN
     6. A → B     3, 4, HS
     7. A → C     5, 6, MP
     8. C     2, 7, MP

The fact that equivalence rules can be applied to parts of lines makes them very flexible tools to work with. But error will result if one fails to keep the distinction between implicational and equivalence rules firmly in mind. To repeat: The eight rules introduced in the previous section are all implicational rules (*modus ponens*, *modus tollens*, hypothetical syllogism, disjunctive syllogism, constructive dilemma, simplification, conjunction, and addition). The 10 rules introduced in this section and the next are all equivalence rules. For easy reference, a table of inference rules is provided on the inside front cover of this book.

    Our second equivalence rule is **commutation**, which applies to both disjunctions and conjunctions:

    Rule 10: Commutation (Com): $(p \vee q) :: (q \vee p)$
                                 $(p \cdot q) :: (q \cdot p)$

Here are two English examples of commutation:

15. Either Sarah loves psychology, or Harlan hates history. So, either Harlan hates history, or Sarah loves psychology.

16. Frege is a logician, and Russell is a logician. So, Russell is a logician, and Frege is a logician.

The utility of the rule of commutation is revealed in constructing a proof for the following argument:

17. If pointless suffering occurs, then God is not both benevolent and omnipotent. But God is both omnipotent and benevolent. So, pointless suffering doesn't occur. (P: Pointless suffering occurs; B: God is benevolent; O: God is omnipotent)

     1. P → ~(B • O)
     2. O • B            ∴ ~P
     3. B • O           2, Com
     4. ~~(B • O)     3, DN
     5. ~P            4, 1, MT

To underscore the difference between implicational and equivalence rules, it may be helpful to note that the following alternative proof is also correct:

3.  P → ~(O • B)         1, Com
4.  ~~(O • B)            2, DN
5.  ~P                   3, 4, MT

Here, the rule of commutation is applied to *part* of line (1) to obtain line (3).

The rule of **association** is so obvious that you may not have thought of it as involving an inference. It comes in two forms, one governing disjunctions and one governing conjunctions:

Rule 11:  Association (As):  $(p \lor (q \lor r)) :: ((p \lor q) \lor r)$
$(p \bullet (q \bullet r)) :: ((p \bullet q) \bullet r)$

In English, this sort of inference would normally be signaled by a shift in punctuation. Here is an example of the first form of association:

18.  Either the alleged eyewitnesses of UFO landings are telling the truth, or they are lying or they've been duped. So, either the alleged eyewitnesses of UFO landings are telling the truth or they are lying, or they've been duped.

In our symbolic language, the parentheses play the role that the commas play in the English example. The practical value of the rule of association is illustrated in constructing a proof for the following short argument:

19.  Either cigarette manufacturers are greedy or they are ignorant of cancer research, or they dislike young people. But it is not true that either cigarette manufacturers are ignorant of cancer research or they dislike young people. Therefore, cigarette manufacturers are greedy. (C: Cigarette manufacturers are greedy; R: Cigarette manufacturers are ignorant of cancer research; D: Cigarette manufacturers dislike young people)

1.  (C ∨ R) ∨ D
2.  ~(R ∨ D)          ∴ C
3.  C ∨ (R ∨ D)       1, As
4.  C                 2, 3, DS

Our next rule was first made explicit by the English logician Augustus De Morgan (1806–1871) and so is named after him. It comes in two forms. **De Morgan's laws** delineate the logical relations of negated conjunctions and negated disjunctions.

Rule 12:  De Morgan's laws (DeM):  $\sim(p \bullet q) :: (\sim p \lor \sim q)$
$\sim(p \lor q) :: (\sim p \bullet \sim q)$

Here is an English example of an inference endorsed by the first of De Morgan's laws:

20.  Spot is not both a dog and a cat. So, either Spot is not a dog or Spot is not a cat.

The first law also tells us that we may reverse this reasoning and infer the *premise* of argument (20) from its conclusion. (This should make sense, as the premise and conclusion are logically equivalent.) Here is an English example of the second law:

21. It's not true that either hydrogen or oxygen is a metal. So, hydrogen is not a metal and oxygen is not a metal.

The second law also tells us that we may reverse this reasoning and infer the premise from the conclusion. As the following example illustrates, De Morgan's laws are quite useful in constructing proofs.

22. Either people are equal and deserve equal pay for equal work, or else people are not equal and do not deserve equal pay for equal work. People are not equal. So, people do not deserve equal pay for equal work. (E: People are equal; D: People deserve equal pay for equal work)

    1. $(E \cdot D) \lor (\sim E \cdot \sim D)$
    2. $\sim E$                              $\therefore \sim D$
    3. $\sim E \lor \sim D$                  2, Add
    4. $\sim(E \cdot D)$                     3, DeM
    5. $\sim E \cdot \sim D$                 1, 4, DS
    6. $\sim D$                              5, Simp

The strategy required in this proof is a bit indirect. The basic insight is that the second premise, $\sim E$, is clearly incompatible with the left disjunct of the first premise, $E \cdot D$. This means that an application of disjunctive syllogism is in the offing. But we have to use addition and one of De Morgan's laws before we can apply disjunctive syllogism.

Our next rule of inference relies on the logical equivalence between a conditional and its contrapositive. To form the contrapositive of a conditional, switch the antecedent and consequent and negate both. To illustrate, the contrapositive of "If Bob is an uncle, then Bob is male" is "If Bob is not male, then Bob is not an uncle." Let us call the inference rule itself **contraposition**.

Rule 13: Contraposition (Cont): $(p \rightarrow q) :: (\sim q \rightarrow \sim p)$

The utility of this rule becomes apparent in evaluating the following argument:

23. If it is wrong to use drugs only if they impair the user's mental functions, then it is not wrong to use caffeine. And if drugs do not impair the user's mental functions, then it is not wrong to use drugs. Hence, it is not wrong to use caffeine. (W: It is wrong to use drugs; D: Drugs impair the user's mental functions; C: It is wrong to use caffeine)

    1. $(W \rightarrow D) \rightarrow \sim C$
    2. $\sim D \rightarrow \sim W$           $\therefore \sim C$

> 3. W → D                  2, Cont
> 4. ~C                     1, 3, MP

To emphasize the point that equivalence rules can be applied to *part* of a line, let us note that the proof could also be completed as follows:

> 3. (~D → ~W) → ~C         1, Cont
> 4. ~C                     2, 3, MP

Here, contraposition is applied to *part* of line (1) to obtain line (3).

The five rules introduced in this section may seem obvious or even trivial, but some logicians have rejected one or more of them. This results from skepticism about the **law of the excluded middle**, which says that for any given statement, either it or its negation is true. Using statement variables, we can state the law of the excluded middle as follows: $p \lor \sim p$. One group of logicians who reject the law of the excluded middle is the intuitionists. The intuitionists hold that the truth of a statement consists in there being a proof of it. Thus, to prove that any statement of the form $p \lor q$ is true, we must either prove that $p$ is true or prove that $q$ is true. Now, consider Goldbach's conjecture, which states that every even number greater than 2 is equal to the sum of two primes. No one has proved that this conjecture is true, and no one has proved that it is not true. Let us symbolize Goldbach's conjecture with the letter "G". According to the intuitionists, then, the statement G ∨ ~G is not true because neither disjunct has been proved, and so the law of the excluded middle is not true.[3]

However, given the rules introduced in this section, we cannot deny the law of the excluded middle unless we are prepared to deny the **law of noncontradiction**, which states that contradictions are never true. Using statement variables, the law of noncontradiction can be expressed as follows: $\sim(p \cdot \sim p)$. And all logicians endorse the law of noncontradiction. Now, consider the following proof:

> 1. ~(G • ~G)      ∴ G ∨ ~G
> 2. ~G ∨ ~~G       1, DeM
> 3. ~G ∨ G         2, DN
> 4. G ∨ ~G         3, Com

The premise says that Goldbach's conjecture is not both true and false (or that Goldbach's conjecture and its negation are not *both* true). And the conclusion says that Goldbach's conjecture is either true or false (or that either Goldbach's conjecture or its negation is true). It appears, then, that if we wish to reject the law of the excluded middle, we must also reject at least one of the following: De Morgan's laws, double-negation, commutation, or the law of noncontradiction. But each of these is very hard to deny.

| | |
|---|---|
| **Summary of the First Set of Equivalence Rules** | |

**9.** Double-negation (DN):       $p :: \sim\sim p$

**10.** Commutation (Com):       $(p \lor q) :: (q \lor p)$
                                $(p \cdot q) :: (q \cdot p)$

**11.** Association (As):         $(p \lor (q \lor r)) :: ((p \lor q) \lor r)$
                                $(p \cdot (q \cdot r)) :: ((p \cdot q) \cdot r)$

**12.** De Morgan's laws (DeM):   $\sim(p \cdot q) :: (\sim p \lor \sim q)$
                                $\sim(p \lor q) :: (\sim p \cdot \sim q)$

**13.** Contraposition (Cont):    $(p \to q) :: (\sim q \to \sim p)$

As you complete the exercises that follow, keep in mind that the three rules of thumb provided in the previous section still apply: Start with the conclusion and work backward; break premises down into simpler components using MP, MT, Simp, DS, and so on; and if a "new" statement letter appears in the conclusion, use addition. To these three rules of thumb, we now add the following:

> Rule of Thumb 4: It is often useful to consider logically equivalent forms of the conclusion.

For example, suppose the conclusion is $\sim(A \cdot B)$. Then it may help to notice that the conclusion is logically equivalent to $\sim A \lor \sim B$, according to De Morgan's laws. Or if the conclusion is $\sim D \to \sim C$, it may be helpful to note that the conclusion is equivalent to $C \to D$, by contraposition.

> Rule of Thumb 5: Both conjunction and addition can lead to useful applications of De Morgan's laws.

Consider the following examples:

| | | | | | |
|---|---|---|---|---|---|
| 1. $\sim E$ | | | 1. $\sim G$ | | |
| 2. $\sim F$ | | | 2. $\sim G \lor \sim H$ | 1, Add | |
| 3. $\sim E \cdot \sim F$ | 1, 2, Conj | | 3. $\sim(G \cdot H)$ | 2, DeM | |
| 4. $\sim(E \lor F)$ | 3, DeM | | | | |

As before, rules of thumb are to be taken as helpful hints. They do not automatically provide a solution in every case. A summary of rules of thumb for constructing proofs appears in section 8.5 on page 349.

## ◇ *Exercise 8.2*

**Part A:** Annotating   Annotate the following short proofs. (In each case, the argument has only one premise.)

*  **1.** 1. ~~A → B ∴ A → B
      2. A → B

   **2.** 1. ~C → ~D ∴ D → C
      2. D → C

   **3.** 1. ~(E • ~D) ∴ D ∨ ~E
      2. ~E ∨ ~~D
      3. ~E ∨ D
      4. D ∨ ~E

*  **4.** 1. ~(E ∨ D) ∴ ~D
      2. ~E • ~D
      3. ~D

   **5.** 1. ~A • [(A ∨ B) ∨ C] ∴ B ∨ C
      2. ~A
      3. (A ∨ B) ∨ C
      4. A ∨ (B ∨ C)
      5. B ∨ C

   **6.** 1. F • (G • R) ∴ G • F
      2. (F • G) • R
      3. F • G
      4. G • F

*  **7.** 1. [(P → Q) → R] • (~Q → ~P) ∴ ~~R
      2. ~Q → ~P
      3. P → Q
      4. (P → Q) → R
      5. R
      6. ~~R

   **8.** 1. [~(S • T) ∨ ~~U] • (T • S) ∴ U
      2. T • S
      3. S • T
      4. ~(S • T) ∨ ~~U
      5. ~~(S • T)
      6. ~~U
      7. U

   **9.** 1. ~W ∨ (~X ∨ ~Y) ∴ ~Y ∨ ~(W • X)
      2. (~W ∨ ~X) ∨ ~Y
      3. ~(W • X) ∨ ~Y
      4. ~Y ∨ ~(W • X)

* **10.** 1. [~O → (~M → ~N)] • ~(N → M)  ∴ O
  2. ~O → (~M → ~N)
  3. ~(N → M)
  4. ~(~M → ~N)
  5. ~~O
  6. O

 **11.** 1. ~~P • ~P  ∴ W
  2. ~~P
  3. ~~P ∨ W
  4. P ∨ W
  5. ~P
  6. W

 **12.** 1. ~T  ∴ ~(T • ~~S)
  2. ~T ∨ ~S
  3. ~(T • S)
  4. ~(T • ~~S)

* **13.** 1. ~A  ∴ ~[(B • C) • A]
  2. ~(B • C) ∨ ~A
  3. ~[(B • C) • A]

 **14.** 1. (S → G) • (G → T)  ∴ ~T → ~S
  2. S → G
  3. G → T
  4. S → T
  5. ~T → ~S

 **15.** 1. ~R → ~S  ∴ ~P ∨ (S → ~~R)
  2. S → R
  3. S → ~~R
  4. ~P ∨ (S → ~~R)

**Part B: Correct or Incorrect?**   Some of the following inferences are correct applications of our rules, and some are not. If an inference is a correct application of our rules, name the rule. If an inference is not a correct application of our rules, explain why it is not. (The question is whether the conclusion in each case can be reached *in a single step* from the premise(s) by an application of one of our rules.)

* **1.**   ~(~E ∨ B)
  ∴ ~~E • ~B

 **2.**   ~B → ~C
  ∴ C → B

 **3.**   ~(F ∨ G)
  ∴ ~F ∨ ~G

* **4.**   ~W ∨ ~Z
  ∴ ~(W • Z)

 **5.**   A • ~B
  ∴ ~B • A

 **6.**   ~D → ~E
  ∴ ~~E → ~~D

* **7.**   ~S ∨ T
  ∴ ~(S • ~T)

 **8.**   ~J ∨ ~~K
  ∴ ~(J • ~K)

9.　　P → ~Q
　　　∴ Q → ~P

* 10.　　O → R
　　　∴ ~R → ~O

11.　　[B ∨ (C ∨ A)] ↔ D
　　　∴ [(C ∨ B) ∨ A] ↔ D

12.　　~(D • C) → E
　　　∴ (~D ∨ ~C) → E

* 13.　　~(L • ~M)
　　　∴ ~(~M • L)

14.　　~(U • ~Z)
　　　∴ ~U ∨ ~~Z

15.　　(~~N ∨ ~M) ↔ (L • K)
　　　∴ ~(~N • M) ↔ (L • K)

* 16.　　~[(O • ~P) • W]
　　　∴ ~[O • (~P • W)]

17.　　~(R ∨ ~Q)
　　　∴ ~R • ~~Q

18.　　~~S ↔ T
　　　∴ S ↔ T

* 19.　　~~(U ∨ W)
　　　∴ ~(~U • ~W)

20.　　~(X → Y)
　　　∴ ~X → ~Y

**Part C: Proofs**   Construct proofs for each of the following symbolic arguments. Commas are used to mark the breaks between premises. (Each proof can be completed in fewer than 10 steps, including premises.)

* **1.** ~(C • D), ~C → S, ~D → T ∴ S ∨ T

**2.** (W → U) • ~X ∴ ~U → ~W

**3.** F → ~G, G ∴ ~F

* **4.** ~(~A ∨ B) ∴ A

**5.** (~P → Q) • ~Q ∴ P

**6.** ~(N ∨ M), ~L → (M ∨ N) ∴ L

* **7.** (A ∨ B) ∨ C, ~A ∴ C ∨ B

**8.** (W • ~X) ∨ (Y • Z), (~X • W) → U, (Y • Z) → T ∴ U ∨ T

**9.** ~(S ∨ R), P → R ∴ ~P

* **10.** F → (G • H), (H • G) → J ∴ F → J

**11.** K ∨ (L ∨ S), ~(K ∨ L) ∴ S

**12.** ~P, ~(P ∨ Q) → ~R, ~Q ∴ ~R

* **13.** ~S → (T • U), (~S → X) → ~Z, (U • T) → X ∴ ~Z

**14.** ~(~B → A), C → (~A → B) ∴ ~C

**15.** ~E, F → (D ∨ E), ~D ∴ ~F

* **16.** (K ∨ P) ∨ X, K → ~O, (P ∨ X) → ~L ∴ ~(O • L)

**17.** (G ∨ H) → (J ∨ K) ∴ ~(J ∨ K) → ~(H ∨ G)

**18.** ~A → ~~R, G → ~U, ~A ∨ G ∴ ~(~R • U)

* **19.** ~(L • M) → ~(N ∨ O) ∴ (O ∨ N) → (M • L)

**20.** B → E, (B ∨ C) ∨ D, (D ∨ C) → F ∴ E ∨ F

21. W → ~U, W ∨ X, ~T → (Z • U), X → ~Z ∴ T
* 22. ~(~P • Q), ~Q → R, P → ~S ∴ R ∨ ~S
23. ~B, A → (B • C) ∴ ~A
24. [S → (J • Q)] • ~Q ∴ ~S
* 25. ~B, ~(C • B) → C, ~F → ~C ∴ F

**Part D: Longer Proofs** Construct proofs to show that the following arguments are valid. Commas are used to mark the breaks between premises.

* 1. ~~T ∨ ~R, ~(S ∨ ~R), (T • ~S) → ~Q, W → Q ∴ ~W
2. ~(J • L), (~J ∨ ~L) → ~M, ~E ∨ (M ∨ ~S) ∴ ~(S • E)
3. E → [~(H ∨ K) → R], ~~E • (~H • ~K) ∴ ~~R
* 4. B → E, ~F ∨ G, (B • C) • D, (D • C) → F ∴ E • G
5. P ∨ (Q ∨ R), (Q ∨ P) → ~S, R → ~T, U → (S • T) ∴ ~U ∨ Z
6. ~~W • [(X ∨ W) → Y], H → ~Y ∴ ~H
* 7. ~(B • ~C), ~B → D, C → ~E ∴ ~E ∨ D
8. (F • G) → (H • J), (J • H) → (K ∨ L), (L ∨ K) → M ∴ (G • F) → M
9. ~Y ∨ N, (Y • ~N) ∨ (Y • Z), (Z • Y) → ~~U ∴ U ∨ ~V
* 10. ~A → ~B, D → E, (B → A) → (C ∨ D), C → F ∴ E ∨ F
11. ~(H ↔ G) ∨ ~J, K → (H ↔ G), ~L → J ∴ ~(K • ~L)
12. (X • Q) → (Z • ~T), R • (T ∨ ~Z) ∴ (~X ∨ ~Q) • R
* 13. ~[(M ∨ N) ∨ O], (P • R) → N, ~P → T, ~R → S ∴ T ∨ S
14. Z → (U • X), ~[(U • W) • X], W ∴ ~Z
15. ~(~A • B) ↔ ~(C ∨ ~D) ∴ (~B ∨ A) ↔ (D • ~C)
* 16. ~[(E • F) ∨ G], (H ∨ ~E) → G ∴ ~(F ∨ H)
17. ~(R → S) → ~(~T → ~U), ~W → T, U → ~W, ~S ∴ ~R
18. ~[(L ∨ M) • N], (P → ~Q) → N, Q → ~P ∴ ~M
* 19. [(A • B) ∨ ~C] → (~X • ~Y), ~(Y ∨ X) → Z, ~C ∨ (A • B)
∴ ~~Z
20. H ∨ G, ~(~D → E), (F ∨ G) → (~E → D) ∴ ~J ∨ H
21. ~(~P • ~Q), Q → (X ∨ R), P → Y ∴ X ∨ (Y ∨ R)
* 22. A ∨ (B ∨ C), ~A • ~C ∴ [(B ∨ C) • ~(A ∨ C)] • (A ∨ B)
23. ~F, ~(F • ~S) → ~P, (~S • F) ∨ ~T ∴ ~(P ∨ T)
24. O → (H • M), (O → G) → (H → ~M), ~G → (~H ∨ ~M)
∴ H → ~M
* 25. Z • Y, T → X, ~Y → ~S, ~(X ∨ Y) ∨ ~Z ∴ ~(T ∨ S) • Y

## 8.3 *Five More Equivalence Rules*

To this point, our system of natural deduction includes 8 implicational rules and 5 equivalence rules. With these 13 rules, we can construct proofs for many valid arguments in statement logic. But we need 5 more equivalence rules (plus a rule called "conditional proof") if our system of natural deduction is to be able to *prove valid* every argument that is valid according to the truth table method. So, in this section, we add 5 more equivalence rules to our system.

The rule of **distribution** tells us how certain combinations of the dot and the vee interrelate. It comes in two forms.

> **Rule 14:**  Distribution (Dist): $(p \cdot (q \vee r)) :: ((p \cdot q) \vee (p \cdot r))$
> $(p \vee (q \cdot r)) :: ((p \vee q) \cdot (p \vee r))$

To grasp these inferences, think about them truth functionally. For example, consider the first form of distribution: Suppose $(p \cdot (q \vee r))$ is true; then $p$ is true and $(q \vee r)$ is true; so either $(p \cdot q)$ is true or $(p \cdot r)$ is true (or both). Similarly, suppose $((p \cdot q) \vee (p \cdot r))$ is true. If $(p \cdot q)$ is true, then $(p \cdot (q \vee r))$ must be true, too; but if $(p \cdot r)$ is true, then, again, $(p \cdot (q \vee r))$ must be true. Notice that when distribution is applied correctly, the main logical operator changes (either from the dot to the vee or from the vee to the dot). Here are some English examples of distribution:

24. "Bats are animals, and they are either mammals or birds" implies (and is implied by) "Either bats are animals and mammals, or bats are animals and birds."

25. "Either Bill lost the lottery, or Bill won and he is rich" implies (and is implied by) "Either Bill lost the lottery or he won, and either Bill lost the lottery or he is rich."

The utility of the rule of distribution is brought out when we construct a proof of the following argument:

26. Either Fiona is insane, or she is guilty and a liar. But if Fiona is either insane or a liar, then she is dangerous. It follows that Fiona is dangerous. (F: Fiona is insane; G: Fiona is guilty; L: Fiona is a liar; D: Fiona is dangerous)

    1. $F \vee (G \cdot L)$
    2. $(F \vee L) \rightarrow D$      $\therefore$ D
    3. $(F \vee G) \cdot (F \vee L)$      1, Dist
    4. $F \vee L$      3, Simp
    5. D      2, 4, MP

Perhaps because distribution appears a bit complex, there is some tendency to overlook occasions for its use when constructing proofs, but it is often quite useful.

The rule of **exportation** tells us that statements of the form "If $p$ and $q$, then $r$" are logically equivalent to statements of the form "If $p$, then if $q$, then $r$." In symbols, we have the following:

Rule 15: Exportation (Ex): $((p \cdot q) \to r) :: (p \to (q \to r))$

Here is an English example:

27. "If Sue is intelligent and she studies hard, then she gets good grades" implies (and is implied by) "If Sue is intelligent, then if she studies hard, she gets good grades."

A proof of the following argument will illustrate a typical usage of exportation.

28. If World War I was not a war in defense of the U.S.A., and only wars of defense are just, then the American participation in World War I was not just. World War I was not a war in defense of the U.S.A. It follows that if only wars of defense are just, then the American participation in World War I was not just. (W: World War I was a war in defense of the U.S.A.; D: Only wars of defense are just; J: American participation in World War I was just)

1. $(\sim W \cdot D) \to \sim J$
2. $\sim W$              $\therefore$ $D \to \sim J$
3. $\sim W \to (D \to \sim J)$      1, Ex
4. $D \to \sim J$          2, 3, MP

The **redundancy** rule is obviously valid, and as the name suggests, it allows us to eliminate certain types of redundancy.

Rule 16: Redundancy (Re): $p :: (p \cdot p)$
$\qquad\qquad\qquad\qquad p :: (p \vee p)$

A proof of the following argument reveals a typical use of this rule.

29. Either pain is real or it is an illusion. If pain is real, then pain is bad. And if pain is an illusion, then pain is bad. Accordingly, pain is bad. (R: Pain is real; I: Pain is an illusion; B: Pain is bad)

1. $R \vee I$
2. $R \to B$
3. $I \to B$        $\therefore$ $B$
4. $B \vee B$      1, 2, 3, CD
5. $B$          4, Re

Note that the rule allows us to introduce redundancy as well as to eliminate it. For example, the redundancy rule allows us to move from $\sim A$ to $\sim A \cdot \sim A$ and from $R$ to $R \vee R$.

The rule of **material equivalence** gives us a way of handling biconditionals. It comes in two forms. The first form tells us that a biconditional is logically equivalent to a *conjunction* of two conditionals. The second form tells us that a biconditional is logically equivalent to a *disjunction* of two conjunctions. The second form makes sense if you remember the truth table for the biconditional:

$(p \leftrightarrow q)$ is true if either $p$ and $q$ are both true or $p$ and $q$ are both false; otherwise, $(p \leftrightarrow q)$ is false.

Rule 17: Material equivalence (ME): $(p \leftrightarrow q) :: ((p \rightarrow q) \cdot (q \rightarrow p))$
$(p \leftrightarrow q) :: ((p \cdot q) \vee (\sim p \cdot \sim q))$

A proof of the following argument will illustrate a typical usage of material equivalence.

30. Withholding medical treatment is wrong if and only if either the patient has a valuable future life or the family insists on medical treatment. But the patient is brain dead. And if the patient is brain dead, then he has not got a valuable future life. Furthermore, it is not the case that the family insists on medical treatment. It follows that withholding medical treatment is not wrong. (W: Withholding medical treatment is wrong; L: The patient has a valuable future life; F: The family insists on medical treatment; B: The patient is brain dead)

1. $W \leftrightarrow (L \vee F)$
2. $B$
3. $B \rightarrow \sim L$
4. $\sim F$            $\therefore \sim W$
5. $\sim L$           2, 3, MP
6. $[W \rightarrow (L \vee F)] \cdot [(L \vee F) \rightarrow W]$     1, ME
7. $W \rightarrow (L \vee F)$        6, Simp
8. $\sim L \cdot \sim F$          5, 4, Conj
9. $\sim (L \vee F)$         8, DeM
10. $\sim W$           7, 9, MT

The last of our equivalence rules is called **material implication**. It is based on the logical equivalence between statements of the form $(p \rightarrow q)$ and a *disjunction* whose disjuncts are the consequent of the conditional and the negation of its antecedent. This equivalence can easily be demonstrated with a truth table.

Rule 18: Material implication (MI): $(p \rightarrow q) :: (\sim p \vee q)$

Without material implication, our proof system would lack the capacity to prove valid every argument that is valid according to the truth table method. But it is important to remember that $\sim p \vee q$ and $p \rightarrow q$ are equivalent because of the truth-functional definition we have given the arrow. As we saw in Chapter 7, not every English statement of the form "If $p$, then $q$" is equivalent to "Either not $p$ or $q$." For example, "If the Eiffel Tower is in Ohio, then it is in France" is intuitively false; but the disjunction "Either the Eiffel Tower is not in Ohio, or the Eiffel Tower is in France" is true, since the Eiffel Tower is in fact in France (and not in Ohio). Accordingly, we include the rule of material implication in our system, but with the realization that if a proof relies on this rule, it may fail to mirror our intuitive logical convictions about English conditionals.

Our proof of the following argument makes a strategic use of both material implication and the rule of distribution.

31. If either humans do not need meat or eating meat is unhealthy, then humans should not eat meat. Hence, if humans do not need meat, then humans should not eat meat. (N: Humans need meat; E: Eating meat is unhealthy; S: Humans should eat meat)

   1. $(\sim N \vee E) \to \sim S$          $\therefore \sim N \to \sim S$
   2. $\sim(\sim N \vee E) \vee \sim S$      1, MI
   3. $\sim S \vee \sim(\sim N \vee E)$      2, Com
   4. $\sim S \vee (\sim\sim N \bullet \sim E)$      3, DeM
   5. $(\sim S \vee \sim\sim N) \bullet (\sim S \vee \sim E)$    4, Dist
   6. $\sim S \vee \sim\sim N$            5, Simp
   7. $\sim\sim N \vee \sim S$            6, Com
   8. $\sim N \to \sim S$             7, MI

This proof is rather complex, and it suggests the following rules of thumb (to be added to the five rules of thumb introduced previously):

Rule of Thumb 6: Material implication can lead to useful applications of distribution.

This is illustrated by lines (2) through (5) in the previous proof. But here is a simpler case:

   1. $A \to (B \bullet C)$
   2. $\sim A \vee (B \bullet C)$       1, MI
   3. $(\sim A \vee B) \bullet (\sim A \vee C)$       2, Dist

Rule of Thumb 7: Distribution can lead to useful applications of simplification.

This rule of thumb is illustrated in lines (4) through (6) in the previous proof, but here is another example:

   1. $(D \bullet E) \vee (D \bullet F)$
   2. $D \bullet (E \vee F)$       1, Dist
   3. $D$            2, Simp

At least one more rule of thumb (not suggested by the previous proof) may be helpful as you complete the exercises at the end of this section:

Rule of Thumb 8: Addition can lead to useful applications of material implication.

Here are two examples:

| **Summary of the Second Set of Equivalence Rules** | |
|---|---|
| 14. Distribution (Dist): | $(p \bullet (q \lor r)) :: ((p \bullet q) \lor (p \bullet r))$<br>$(p \lor (q \bullet r)) :: ((p \lor q) \bullet (p \lor r))$ |
| 15. Exportation (Ex): | $((p \bullet q) \to r) :: (p \to (q \to r))$ |
| 16. Redundancy (Re): | $p :: (p \bullet p)$<br>$p :: (p \lor p)$ |
| 17. Material equivalence (ME): | $(p \leftrightarrow q) :: ((p \to q) \bullet (q \to p))$<br>$(p \leftrightarrow q) :: ((p \bullet q) \lor (\sim p \bullet \sim q))$ |
| 18. Material implication (MI): | $(p \to q) :: (\sim p \lor q)$ |

| | | | | |
|---|---|---|---|---|
| 1. B | | | 1. ~F | |
| 2. ~A ∨ B | 1, Add | | 2. ~F ∨ G | 1, Add |
| 3. A → B | 2, MI | | 3. F → G | 2, MI |

A summary of rules of thumb for constructing proofs is provided in section 8.5 on page 349.

In closing this section, let us reflect briefly on the value of proofs. What good are they? First, many valid arguments are sufficiently complex to dazzle one's logical intuitions. In such cases, our proof system comes into its own by enabling us to show how we can get from the premises to the conclusion *using only the rules we have explicitly adopted.* So, unless we have doubts about our system of rules, a proof should settle all doubts about the validity of even very complicated arguments. Second, suppose you claim that an argument is valid and someone else claims that it isn't. What can you do? Well, if the argument can be shown to be valid by means of a proof, then this should settle the matter (unless the other person rejects one or more of the rules in our system). The power of logic consists partly in the fact that in so many cases, it can settle the question of an argument's validity. And once we determine that an argument is valid, the question of its soundness turns entirely on whether its premises are true.

## ◆ Exercise 8.3

**Part A: Annotating**   Annotate the following short proofs. (In each case, the argument has only one premise.)

* 1. 1. B ↔ E  ∴ E → B
     2. (B → E) • (E → B)
     3. E → B
  2. 1. (B • C) ∨ (~B • ~C)  ∴ B ↔ C
     2. B ↔ C

   **3.** 1. ~(A • A) ∨ (B ∨ B)  ∴ A → B
      2. ~(A • A) ∨ B
      3. (A • A) → B
      4. A → B

\* **4.** 1. H → (J → ~H)  ∴ H → ~J
      2. H → (~~H → ~J)
      3. (H • ~~H) → ~J
      4. (H • H) → ~J
      5. H → ~J

   **5.** 1. P • ~Q  ∴ P • (~Q ∨ R)
      2. (P • ~Q) ∨ (P • R)
      3. P • (~Q ∨ R)

   **6.** 1. F ∨ (~G • H)  ∴ G → F
      2. (F ∨ ~G) • (F ∨ H)
      3. F ∨ ~G
      4. ~G ∨ F
      5. G → F

\* **7.** 1. M → ~N  ∴ N → ~M
      2. ~M ∨ ~N
      3. ~N ∨ ~M
      4. N → ~M

   **8.** 1. ~S ↔ T  ∴ (~S • T) ∨ (S • ~T)
      2. (~S • T) ∨ (~~S • ~T)
      3. (~S • T) ∨ (S • ~T)

   **9.** 1. (B • B) ∨ (C • D)  ∴ B ∨ D
      2. B ∨ (C • D)
      3. (B ∨ C) • (B ∨ D)
      4. B ∨ D

\* **10.** 1. (U → U) ∨ (~U → U)  ∴ ~U ∨ U
      2. (~U ∨ U) ∨ (~U → U)
      3. (~U ∨ U) ∨ (~~U ∨ U)
      4. (~U ∨ U) ∨ (U ∨ U)
      5. (~U ∨ U) ∨ U
      6. ~U ∨ (U ∨ U)
      7. ~U ∨ U

  **11.** 1. ~(T ∨ T)  ∴ T → ~T
      2. ~T • ~T
      3. ~T
      4. ~T ∨ ~T
      5. T → ~T

**12.**  1. X • (Y ∨ Z)  ∴ (X • Y) ∨ Z
     2. (X • Y) ∨ (X • Z)
     3. [(X • Y) ∨ X] • [(X • Y) ∨ Z]
     4. (X • Y) ∨ Z

**\* 13.**  1. ~P → P  ∴ ~P → Q
     2. ~~P ∨ P
     3. ~~P ∨ ~~P
     4. ~~~P
     5. ~~P ∨ Q
     6. ~P → Q

**14.**  1. [(~R ∨ ~S) • ~S] ∨ [R • (~R ∨ ~S)]  ∴ ~R → ~S
     2. [(~R ∨ ~S) • ~S] ∨ [(~R ∨ ~S) • R]
     3. (~R ∨ ~S) • (~S ∨ R)
     4. ~S ∨ R
     5. S → R
     6. ~R → ~S

**15.**  1. Q ∨ (~P • T)  ∴ (~Q → ~P) • (~Q → T)
     2. (Q ∨ ~P) • (Q ∨ T)
     3. Q ∨ ~P
     4. ~P ∨ Q
     5. P → Q
     6. ~Q → ~P
     7. Q ∨ T
     8. ~~Q ∨ T
     9. ~Q → T
     10. (~Q → ~P) • (~Q → T)

**Part B:** Correct or Incorrect?   Some of the following inferences are correct applications of our rules, and some are not. If an inference is a correct application of our rules, name the rule. If an inference is not a correct application of our rules, explain why it is not. (The question is whether the conclusion in each case can be reached *in a single step* from the premise by an application of one of our rules.)

**\* 1.**   (~B ∨ ~B) ↔ A
    ∴ ~B ↔ A

**2.**   N ∨ M
    ∴ ~N → M

**3.**   ~~P ∨ Q
    ∴ ~P → Q

**\* 4.**   (C • ~L) ∨ (C • S)
    ∴ C • (~L ∨ S)

**5.**   (~M • N) → ~L
    ∴ ~M → (N → ~L)

**6.**   S → (R • R)
    ∴ S → R

**\* 7.**   K ∨ (X • R)
    ∴ (K • X) ∨ (K • R)

**8.**   ~H → P
    ∴ H ∨ P

9.  $X \rightarrow (Y \rightarrow Z)$
    $\therefore (X \cdot Y) \rightarrow Z$

* 10.  $(\sim U \vee S) \rightarrow Q$
      $\sim \sim U$
      $\therefore S \rightarrow Q$

11.  $(\sim W \vee \sim U) \rightarrow (\sim F \vee \sim F)$
     $\therefore (\sim W \vee \sim U) \rightarrow \sim F$

12.  $\sim A \rightarrow \sim B$
     $\therefore \sim \sim A \vee \sim B$

* 13.  $\sim A \vee (N \cdot Z)$
      $\therefore (\sim A \vee N) \cdot (\sim A \vee Z)$

14.  $F \rightarrow (G \cdot H)$
     $\therefore F \rightarrow (G \rightarrow H)$

15.  $(\sim J \cdot \sim K) \vee (\sim J \cdot \sim L)$
     $\therefore \sim J \cdot (\sim K \vee \sim L)$

* 16.  $M \cdot (O \vee U)$
      $\therefore (M \cdot O) \vee (M \cdot U)$

17.  $(S \vee T) \cdot (S \vee \sim W)$
     $\therefore S \vee (T \cdot \sim W)$

18.  $A \cdot (\sim B \vee C)$
     $\therefore (A \vee \sim B) \cdot (A \vee C)$

* 19.  $(E \cdot H) \rightarrow V$
      $\therefore E$

20.  $(B \rightarrow C) \vee K$
     $B$
     $\therefore C \vee K$

**Part C: Short Proofs**    Construct proofs for each of the following symbolic arguments.

* 1. $\sim M \vee N \quad \therefore \sim N \rightarrow \sim M$

2. $\sim B \leftrightarrow C, \ \sim B \quad \therefore C$

3. $\sim S \vee (R \cdot T), \ \sim R \quad \therefore \sim S$

* 4. $\sim A \vee \sim A, \ A \vee P \quad \therefore P$

5. $(D \rightarrow C) \cdot (C \rightarrow D), \ E \rightarrow \sim (D \leftrightarrow C) \quad \therefore \sim E$

6. $F \cdot (G \vee H), \ \sim F \vee \sim H \quad \therefore F \cdot G$

* 7. $(\sim J \cdot K) \rightarrow L, \ \sim J \quad \therefore \sim L \rightarrow \sim K$

8. $(\sim N \vee M) \cdot (\sim N \vee O) \quad \therefore \sim (M \cdot O) \rightarrow \sim N$

9. $P \cdot P, \ Q \rightarrow \sim P \quad \therefore \sim Q$

* 10. $\sim R, \ (R \rightarrow S) \rightarrow T \quad \therefore T$

11. $U \rightarrow (X \rightarrow W), \ Z \rightarrow \sim [(U \cdot X) \rightarrow W] \quad \therefore \sim Z$

12. $\sim D \quad \therefore C \rightarrow \sim D$

* 13. $E \rightarrow H, \ [(E \vee F) \cdot (E \vee G)], \ [(F \cdot G) \rightarrow H] \quad \therefore H$

14. $(\sim J \cdot K) \vee (\sim J \cdot L), \ M \rightarrow J \quad \therefore \sim M$

15. $\sim N \leftrightarrow \sim O, \ (\sim O \rightarrow \sim N) \rightarrow P \quad \therefore P$

* 16. $\sim \sim (R \cdot S), \ T \rightarrow (R \rightarrow \sim S) \quad \therefore \sim T$

17. $\sim C, \ (\sim A \cdot B) \vee (\sim A \cdot C) \quad \therefore B$

18. $(\sim D \vee E) \cdot (\sim D \vee \sim F), \ (E \cdot \sim F) \rightarrow \sim G, \ \sim D \rightarrow \sim G \quad \therefore \sim G$

* 19. $H \vee H, \ H \leftrightarrow \sim J \quad \therefore \sim J$

20. $X \leftrightarrow Y$, $\sim\sim(X \vee Y)$ $\therefore X \cdot Y$
21. $[(L \cdot M) \vee \sim L] \cdot [(L \cdot M) \vee \sim M]$ $\therefore L \leftrightarrow M$
*22. $P \cdot Q$ $\therefore [(R \vee P) \cdot R] \vee [(R \vee P) \cdot Q]$
23. $R \cdot \sim R$ $\therefore S \cdot \sim S$
24. $\sim O$ $\therefore \sim Q \to \sim(O \cdot P)$
*25. $(A \to B) \leftrightarrow C$, $\sim(A \to B) \vee \sim C$ $\therefore \sim C$

**Part D:** Longer Proofs Construct a proof for each of the following symbolic arguments.

* 1. $(Z \vee \sim Y) \cdot (Z \vee W)$, $Z \to \sim\sim U$, $\sim Y \to (W \to U)$ $\therefore U$
2. $\sim U \to \sim B$, $S \to \sim B$, $\sim(U \cdot \sim S)$, $T \vee B$ $\therefore T$
3. $(Q \cdot R) \vee (\sim Q \cdot \sim R)$, $N \to \sim(Q \leftrightarrow R)$, $E \vee N$ $\therefore E$
* 4. $\sim H \vee (G \vee F)$, $\sim F$, $S \to \sim(H \to G)$ $\therefore \sim S$
5. $\sim(J \cdot L)$, $(J \to \sim L) \to (\sim M \cdot \sim X)$, $E \vee (M \vee X)$ $\therefore E$
6. $(L \vee M) \cdot (L \vee \sim S)$, $A \to \sim L$, $A \to (\sim M \vee S)$ $\therefore \sim A$
* 7. $B \vee (C \cdot \sim D)$, $(D \to B) \leftrightarrow P$ $\therefore P$
8. $(G \cdot S) \vee (G \cdot \sim T)$, $\sim R \to \sim G$, $(T \to S) \to Q$ $\therefore R \cdot Q$
9. $\sim X \leftrightarrow \sim Y$, $\sim X \vee \sim Y$, $Z \leftrightarrow Y$ $\therefore \sim Z$
*10. $(B \cdot C) \to D$, $B$, $Q \to \sim(\sim C \vee D)$, $\sim Q \leftrightarrow T$ $\therefore T$
11. $(F \cdot G) \vee (F \cdot \sim H)$, $(H \to G) \to L$, $L \to (P \to \sim F)$ $\therefore \sim P$
12. $\sim X \vee (M \cdot O)$, $(X \to O) \to \sim M$ $\therefore \sim X$
13. $(\sim Z \cdot W) \to Q$, $\sim Z$, $R \leftrightarrow (W \cdot \sim Q)$ $\therefore \sim R$
14. $A \leftrightarrow B$, $\sim\sim(A \vee B)$ $\therefore B$
15. $(A \vee B) \cdot (A \vee G)$, $M \to \sim A$, $\sim Q \to (\sim B \vee \sim G)$ $\therefore M \to Q$
16. $Y \cdot (\sim N \vee A)$, $\sim Y \vee N$, $(A \cdot Y) \to \sim\sim K$ $\therefore K$
17. $\sim G \to \sim F$, $(\sim F \vee G) \to (H \vee J)$, $H \to Z$, $J \to \sim P$ $\therefore P \to Z$
18. $(D \cdot E) \vee (\sim D \cdot \sim E)$, $(H \cdot J) \to \sim(D \leftrightarrow E)$, $\sim\sim H \vee J$ $\therefore J \leftrightarrow \sim H$
19. $(\sim E \vee Z) \cdot (\sim E \vee W)$, $\sim K \to E$, $\sim K \to (\sim Z \vee \sim W)$, $K \leftrightarrow U$ $\therefore R \to U$
20. $(R \cdot S) \vee (R \cdot \sim E)$, $(Y \cdot O) \to (E \cdot \sim S)$, $(O \to \sim Y) \to L$ $\therefore L$
21. $\sim E$, $\sim(E \cdot D) \to F$, $(\sim F \vee B) \cdot (\sim F \vee C)$ $\therefore A \vee (B \cdot C)$
22. $T \to R$, $R \to S$, $\sim R \leftrightarrow S$ $\therefore \sim T \cdot S$
23. $(\sim K \to K) \to \sim L$, $\sim(\sim L \to \sim M) \to L$, $M$ $\therefore K \leftrightarrow \sim L$
24. $W$, $\sim Y \to (\sim W \cdot \sim X)$ $\therefore Y \cdot [(\sim W \cdot \sim X) \to Z]$
25. $F \vee \sim I$, $I \vee H$, $\sim(G \leftrightarrow J) \to \sim H$ $\therefore [(\sim G \vee \sim J) \cdot (G \vee J)] \to F$

**Part E: English Arguments**   Symbolize the following arguments, and then construct proofs to show that they are valid.

* **1.** If workers should be paid, then either they should be paid according to their needs (as Marx asserted), or they should be paid for services rendered. If workers should be paid according to their needs, then single mothers should be paid more (other things being equal) than their co-workers, and so should workers who have large families. If workers should be paid for services rendered, then workers should receive equal pay for equal work. Workers should be paid, but it is not the case that workers having large families should be paid more (other things being equal) than their co-workers. Hence, workers should receive equal pay for equal work. (P: Workers should be paid; N: Workers should be paid according to their needs; S: Workers should be paid for services rendered; M: Single mothers should be paid more (other things being equal) than their co-workers; F: Workers who have large families should be paid more (other things being equal) than their co-workers; E: Workers should receive equal pay for equal work)

**2.** If either the defendant refuses to take the stand or he confesses, then he is guilty. We may infer that the defendant is guilty if he refuses to take the stand. (R: The defendant refuses to take the stand; C: The defendant confesses; G: The defendant is guilty)

**3.** If beauty is in the eye of the beholder, then beauty is not objective. But beauty is objective if it is observable. And beauty can be seen, can't it? Furthermore, beauty can be seen if and only if beauty is observable. Therefore, popular opinion to the contrary, beauty is not in the eye of the beholder. (E: Beauty is in the eye of the beholder; B: Beauty is objective; O: Beauty is observable; S: Beauty can be seen)

* **4.** Either sex is for procreation, or it is for interpersonal union and pleasure. If sex is for either procreation or interpersonal union, then societal rules are needed to regulate sex. It follows that societal rules are needed to regulate sex. (S: Sex is for procreation; U: Sex is for interpersonal union; P: Sex is for pleasure; R: Societal rules are needed to regulate sex)

**5.** Young smokers either identify with their future selves or fail to identify with their future selves. If young smokers identify with their future selves, then they are irrational if they know smoking causes cancer. If young smokers fail to identify with their future selves, then they act without due regard for another person (namely, their future self), assuming that they know smoking causes cancer. And given that young smokers act without due regard for another person, they are immoral. But while young smokers do know that smoking causes cancer, they are not immoral. Therefore, young smokers are irrational, and they identify with their future selves. (I: Young smokers identify with their future selves; R: Young smokers are irrational; K: Young smok-

ers know that smoking causes cancer; A: Young smokers act without due
regard for another person; M: Young smokers are immoral) —This argument
makes use of material in Derek Parfit, *Reasons and Persons* (New York:
Oxford University Press, 1986), pp. 319–320

6. It is a biological fact that animals in most species will make greater sacrifices
   for near relatives than for others. (For instance, a calf's mother will defend it
   to the death but will not defend the calf of another cow.) Given this fact,
   there is a general law that animals act so as to preserve genes similar to their
   own. But if there is a general law that animals act so as to preserve genes similar to their own, then sociobiologists are right and it is biologically impossible to treat all people equally. Now, if it is biologically impossible to treat all
   people equally, then it is futile to preach the ideal of equality and futile to
   preach the ideal of universal love. Hence, it is futile to preach universal love
   if sociobiologists are right. [*Hint:* In symbolizing the argument, ignore the
   parenthetical remark.] (B: It is a biological fact that animals in most species
   will make greater sacrifices for near relatives than for others; G: There is a
   general law that animals act so as to preserve genes similar to their own;
   S: Sociobiologists are right; E: It is biologically impossible to treat all people
   equally; P: It is futile to preach the ideal of equality; U: It is futile to preach
   the ideal of universal love)

7. You can walk to the door only if you can walk to the halfway point between
   yourself and the door. But unfortunately, you can walk to the halfway point
   between yourself and the door only if you can walk to a point *halfway* to the
   halfway point! Now, if you cannot walk halfway to the halfway point only if
   you cannot walk to the door, then you can walk to the door only if you can
   perform an infinite number of acts in a finite period of time. Obviously, you
   cannot perform an infinite number of acts in a finite period of time. So, as
   Zeno of Elea concluded, in spite of what your senses may tell you, you cannot
   walk to the door. (D: You can walk to the door; H: You can walk to the
   halfway point between yourself and the door; P: You can walk halfway to the
   halfway point; F: You can perform an infinite number of acts in a finite
   period of time)

8. This is the best of all possible worlds. For God exists; and if God is not both
   morally perfect and omnipotent, then God does not exist. Now, if God is
   omnipotent, God can create just any possible world. And if God is morally
   perfect, God will create the best possible world if He can create it. And God
   can create the best of all possible worlds if and only if God can create just
   any possible world. Moreover, this is the best of all possible worlds given that
   God will create the best of all possible worlds. (G: God exists; M: God is
   morally perfect; O: God is omnipotent; A: God can create just any possible
   world; W: God will create the best possible world; C: God can create the best
   possible world; B: This is the best of all possible worlds)

9. God cannot know the future free acts of his creatures if God is in time. For if God is in time, God's knowledge of the future is a prediction based on the past and present. However, if humans have free will, then their future acts are not infallibly predictable based on the past and the present. If the future acts of humans are not infallibly predictable based on the past and the present, then God cannot know the future free acts of his creatures if God is in time. Finally, if humans do not have free will, then God's knowledge of the future is not a prediction based on the past and the present. (T: God is in time; P: God's knowledge of the future is a prediction based on the past and present; F: Humans have free will; I: The future acts of humans are infallibly predictable based on the past and present; K: God can know the future free acts of his creatures)

10. All inductive arguments presuppose that the unobserved resembles the observed. (For example, "All observed emeralds have been green; therefore, the next emerald to be found will be green.") Given that all inductive arguments presuppose that the unobserved resembles the observed, induction is unjustified unless we have good reason to believe that the unobserved resembles the observed. If we have good reason to believe that the unobserved resembles the observed, then we have either a good deductive argument or a good inductive argument. We have a good inductive argument only if not all inductive arguments presuppose that the unobserved resembles the observed. We have a good deductive argument only if valid reasoning can begin with the observed and end with the unobserved. Sad to say, valid reasoning cannot begin with the observed and end with the unobserved. It thus appears that David Hume's skeptical conclusion is inescapable: Induction is unjustified. [*Hint:* In symbolizing the argument, ignore the parenthetical remark.] (P: All inductive arguments presuppose that the unobserved resembles the observed; J: Induction is justified; R: We have good reason to believe that the unobserved resembles the observed; D: We have a good deductive argument; I: We have a good inductive argument; V: Valid reasoning can begin with the observed and end with the unobserved)

## 8.4 Conditional Proof

Consider the following argument.

32. If Hank is a horse, then Hank is not a bird. So, if Hank is a horse, then Hank is a horse and not a bird. (H: Hank is a horse; B: Hank is a bird)

This argument may seem a bit odd, but it is plainly valid. Its form is as follows:

33. H → ~B ∴ H → (H • ~B)

Unfortunately, we cannot prove that the argument is valid using only the 18 rules we have in hand so far.[4] In fact, to make our system of statement logic complete, we need to add one further element, a rule called "conditional proof" (CP for short). Without this rule (or some equivalent addition to our system), we would be unable to construct proofs for many valid arguments. CP also greatly simplifies many proofs that in principle could be done without it.

The basic idea behind CP is that *we can prove a conditional true by assuming that its antecedent is true and showing that its consequent can be derived from this assumption* (together with whatever premises are available). For example, take argument (33). We have $H \rightarrow \sim B$ as a premise. We need to show that the premise validly implies the conclusion, which is a conditional statement: $H \rightarrow (H \cdot \sim B)$. We assume $H$, the antecedent of the conclusion. Now, from the assumption $H$ and the premise $H \rightarrow \sim B$, we can derive $\sim B$ by *modus ponens*. From $\sim B$ and the assumption $H$, we can obtain $H \cdot \sim B$ by conjunction. This shows that the antecedent, $H$, of the conditional conclusion leads logically to its consequent, $H \cdot \sim B$, given the premise. Therefore, the argument is valid.

Now, we need to formalize this intuitive proof technique. This means we need a way to include assumptions in our proofs, bearing in mind that an assumption is not a premise. In fact, since conditionals are hypothetical, the antecedent of a conditional may be false (and may be admitted to be false by the arguer) even though the conditional itself is true. So, we need a way of using assumptions temporarily—a way that keeps it clear that we are not treating them as premises. As an example, the formal proof of argument (33) would look like this:

1. H → ~B      ∴ H → (H • ~B)
2. H      Assume
3. ~B      1, 2, MP
4. H • ~B      2, 3, Conj
5. H → (H • ~B)      2–4, CP

The word "Assume" indicates the special status of $H$. The box indicates the *scope* of the assumption (i.e., the part of the proof in which the assumption is made). The steps from line (2) to line (4) do not prove that $H \cdot \sim B$ follows from the argument's premise. (They *would* prove this if $H$ were a premise and not a mere assumption.) Rather, lines (2) through (4) show only that $H \cdot \sim B$ is true *on the assumption that H is true*. We box in the steps and enter line (5) to make it clear that only a conditional conclusion has been established. The annotation of line (5) mentions the steps falling within the scope of the assumption, as well as the type of proof used (CP). It is crucial to note that line (5) follows logically from the premise of the argument, namely, $H \rightarrow \sim B$. We haven't added a premise to the argument in line (2). We have merely introduced a temporary assumption for the purpose of proving that the *conditional* conclusion follows from the premise.

Using lowercase letters as statement variables, we can make a diagram of conditional proof as follows:

Premises

The vertical dots here stand for inferences from the premises and the assumption. In the typical case, $(p \rightarrow q)$ is the conclusion of the argument, though as we will see, this is not necessarily the case.

Let's consider another example:

34. If most Americans favor gun control, then if lobbies block gun control proposals, democracy is hindered. If most Americans favor gun control, then lobbies do block gun control proposals. Therefore, if most Americans favor gun control, democracy is hindered. (M: Most Americans favor gun control; L: Lobbies block gun control proposals; D: Democracy is hindered)

    1. $M \rightarrow (L \rightarrow D)$              
    2. $M \rightarrow L$            $\therefore M \rightarrow D$
    3. $M$               Assume
    4. $L \rightarrow D$          1, 3, MP
    5. $L$               2, 3, MP
    6. $D$               4, 5, MP
    7. $M \rightarrow D$         3–6, CP

Notice that it would be a mistake to suppose that the statements within the box have been shown to follow from the premises alone. We box in the statements precisely to remind ourselves of their tentative status, dependent as they are on the assumption in line (3). We stop making our assumption at line (7). And our proof shows that line (7) follows logically from the premises—that is, lines (1) and (2).

When you are making an assumption for the purpose of conditional proof, always select the *antecedent* of the conditional statement that you are trying to obtain. CP is often useful when the conclusion of an argument is a conditional statement. So, we can state the following rule of thumb:

> **Rule of Thumb 9:** If the conclusion of an argument is a conditional statement, use CP.

For instance, consider the following symbolic argument:

35. $\sim S \rightarrow W$,   $\sim R \rightarrow U$,   $(U \vee W) \rightarrow T$   $\therefore$ $\sim(S \bullet R) \rightarrow (T \vee Z)$

Because the conclusion of this argument is a conditional statement, CP is a good method to try. And we should assume the *antecedent* of the conclusion, $\sim(S \bullet R)$. Accordingly, the proof looks like this:

```
1. ~S → W
2. ~R → U
3. (U ∨ W) → T          ∴ ~(S • R) → (T ∨ Z)
4. ~(S • R)             Assume
5. ~S ∨ ~R              4, DeM
6. W ∨ U                5, 1, 2, CD
7. U ∨ W                6, Com
8. T                    3, 7, MP
9. T ∨ Z                8, Add
10. ~(S • R) → (T ∨ Z)  4–9, CP
```

Again, we box in the lines of the proof that fall within the *scope* of the assumption (the part of the proof in which the assumption is made). These lines tell us that if we have $\sim(S \bullet R)$, then we can obtain $T \vee Z$. The boxed-in steps are *hypothetical* in nature, for they depend on the assumption in line (4). We stop making our assumption at line (10). And our proof shows that line (10) follows validly from the premises—that is, lines (1), (2), and (3).

So far, we have considered cases in which only one assumption is introduced. But sometimes it is helpful to introduce more than one assumption—for example, when you are trying to prove a conditional whose *consequent* is a conditional. Here is an example:

36. If space travelers from another galaxy visit Earth, then aliens will rule us if our technology is inferior. But if our technology is inferior and aliens will rule us, then our liberty will decrease. So, if space travelers from another galaxy visit Earth, then our liberty will decrease if our technology is inferior. (S: Space travelers from another galaxy visit Earth; A: Aliens will rule us; T: Our technology is inferior; L: Our liberty will decrease)

We symbolize the argument and begin a conditional proof in line (3).

```
1. S → (T → A)
2. (T • A) → L          ∴ S → (T → L)
3. S                    Assume
4. T → A                1, 3, MP
```

Having derived line (4), we could turn our attention to premise (2), applying commutation, exportation, and so on, but with CP another strategy is possible. Note that the conclusion, $S \rightarrow (T \rightarrow L)$, is a conditional with another conditional (namely, $T \rightarrow L$) as its consequent. Thus, we can usefully introduce a second assumption (again, the antecedent of a conditional), as follows:

$$
\begin{array}{lll}
1.\ S \rightarrow (T \rightarrow A) & & \\
2.\ (T \cdot A) \rightarrow L & \therefore\ S \rightarrow (T \rightarrow L) & \\
3.\ S & \text{Assume} & \\
4.\ T \rightarrow A & 1,\ 3,\ \text{MP} & \\
\quad 5.\ T & \text{Assume} & \\
\quad 6.\ A & 4,\ 5,\ \text{MP} & \\
\quad 7.\ T \cdot A & 5,\ 6,\ \text{Conj} & \\
\quad 8.\ L & 2,\ 7,\ \text{MP} & \\
\quad 9.\ T \rightarrow L & 5\text{–}8,\ \text{CP} & \\
\end{array}
$$

Now, at this point, we have shown that if $T$, then $L$, for by assuming $T$, we were able to obtain $L$. But all of this occurs within the scope of our first assumption (i.e., $S$), and *a proof is always incomplete as long as we are still making an assumption*. Furthermore, we have not yet reached the conclusion of the argument, so we need one additional step:

$$
\begin{array}{lll}
1.\ S \rightarrow (T \rightarrow A) & & \\
2.\ (T \cdot A) \rightarrow L & \therefore\ S \rightarrow (T \rightarrow L) & \\
3.\ S & \text{Assume} & \\
4.\ T \rightarrow A & 1,\ 3,\ \text{MP} & \\
\quad 5.\ T & \text{Assume} & \\
\quad 6.\ A & 4,\ 5,\ \text{MP} & \\
\quad 7.\ T \cdot A & 5,\ 6,\ \text{Conj} & \\
\quad 8.\ L & 2,\ 7,\ \text{MP} & \\
\quad 9.\ T \rightarrow L & 5\text{–}8,\ \text{CP} & \\
10.\ S \rightarrow (T \rightarrow L) & 3\text{–}9,\ \text{CP} & \\
\end{array}
$$

Lines (3) through (9) indicate that if we have $S$, we can obtain $T \rightarrow L$. In other words, the proof shows that line (10) follows logically from the premises—that is, lines (1) and (2). So, the argument is valid.

Here is the place to issue two important warnings: First, because the statements within the boxes are dependent on assumptions, we cannot make use of boxed-in statements in later parts of a proof. For example, in the previous proof, it may appear that we could write $L$ on line (9) by applying *modus ponens* to lines (7) and (2), but line (7) is available only because of the assumption in line (5). And the box indicates that we *discharged* (i.e., ceased to make) that assumption when we got to line (9). So, we cannot make use of line (7) in subsequent parts of the proof. In general, boxed-in lines cannot be used to justify later steps in a proof, for the boxes indicate that we have ceased to make the assumption in question. Second, no proof involving CP is complete until all assumptions are discharged.

It should be noted that CP is sometimes useful even when the conclusion of the argument is not a conditional. Here is an example:

> 37. If God stops people from performing acts that cause unnecessary suffering, then *either* God denies creatures a choice between good and evil, or God can cause the free acts of his creatures. If God can cause the free acts of his creatures, then the concept of free will is empty. The concept of free will is not empty. So, either God does not stop people from performing acts that cause unnecessary suffering, or else God denies creatures a real choice between good and evil. (S: God stops people from performing acts that cause unnecessary suffering; G: God denies creatures a choice between good and evil; F: God can cause the free acts of his creatures; W: The concept of free will is empty)

We symbolize the argument and begin a conditional proof in line (4). This makes sense if one realizes that the conclusion, ~S ∨ G, is logically equivalent to S → G.

$$
\begin{array}{lll}
1. & S \rightarrow (G \lor F) & \\
2. & F \rightarrow W & \\
3. & \sim W & \therefore \ \sim S \lor G \\
\hline
4. & S & \text{Assume} \\
5. & G \lor F & 1, 4, \text{MP} \\
6. & \sim F & 2, 3, \text{MT} \\
7. & G & 5, 6, \text{DS} \\
\hline
8. & S \rightarrow G & 4\text{--}7, \text{CP} \\
9. & \sim S \lor G & 8, \text{MI}
\end{array}
$$

Note that *by CP we always obtain a conditional*, and this case is no exception. Lines (4) through (7) establish S → G. We then apply MI to obtain the conclusion of the argument.

CP can be used when the conclusion of an argument is a biconditional. For example:

> 38. (B ∨ A) → C, A → ~C, ~A → B ∴ B ↔ C

The basic strategy is to prove two conditionals, conjoin them, and then use ME:

$$
\begin{array}{lll}
1. & (B \lor A) \rightarrow C & \\
2. & A \rightarrow \sim C & \\
3. & \sim A \rightarrow B & \therefore \ B \leftrightarrow C \\
\hline
4. & B & \text{Assume} \\
5. & B \lor A & 4, \text{Add} \\
6. & C & 1, 5, \text{MP} \\
\hline
7. & B \rightarrow C & 4\text{--}6, \text{CP}
\end{array}
$$

| | |
|---|---|
| 8. C | Assume |
| 9. ~~C | 8, DN |
| 10. ~A | 2, 9, MT |
| 11. B | 3,10, MP |
| 12. C → B | 8–11, CP |
| 13. (B → C) • (C → B) | 7, 12, Conj |
| 14. B ↔ C | 13, ME |

Note that although two assumptions are made in this proof, neither falls within the scope of the other. So, at line (13), we are free to conjoin lines (7) and (12).

It is possible to construct a direct proof for the previous argument, a **direct proof** being one that makes no use of assumptions. (Try it!) The direct proof is slightly longer than the one just presented, but more important, the direct proof is less intuitive, as it involves the use of MI. We have noted more than once that MI is not an intuitive rule when applied to some English conditionals. Accordingly, it is reassuring that we can often construct a conditional proof without MI when a direct proof would require an application of MI.

Conditional proof renders our system of statement logic complete. Whatever can be proved valid through the truth tables can be proved valid using our 8 implicational rules, 10 equivalence rules, and CP. It is interesting to note that some systems achieve completeness in a different way, by adding the rule of *absorption*, which countenances inferences from $p → q$ to $p → (p • q)$. However, CP tends to make proofs both shorter and more intuitive than does absorption.[5]

*Note:* As you complete the following exercises, it may be helpful to refer to the summary of rules of thumb that appears on page 349.

## ◆ *Exercise 8.4*

**Part A:** Conditional Proofs   Use CP to show that each of the following symbolic arguments is valid.

* 1. $Z → (~Y → X)$, $Z → ~Y$ ∴ $Z → X$

 2. $P → Q$ ∴ $P → (Q ∨ R)$

 3. $(F ∨ ~G) → ~L$ ∴ $L → G$

* 4. $A → B$, $A → C$ ∴ $A → (B•C)$

 5. $(H ∨ E) → K$ ∴ $E → K$

 6. $(B → ~C) → D$ ∴ $B → (~C → D)$

* 7. $P$ ∴ $(P → Q) → Q$

 8. $S$ ∴ $~(S•R) → ~R$

 9. $(G → H) → J$ ∴ $H → J$

* 10. $C → (~D → E)$, $(D → ~D) → (E → G)$ ∴ $C → (~D → G)$

 11. $H → (J•K)$, $~L → (J•M)$ ∴ $(~L ∨ H) → J$

12. $\sim X \vee (O \cdot W)$, $(X \to O) \to (W \to X)$ $\therefore W \to X$

*13. $(A \vee N) \to \sim S$, $M \to [N \to (S \cdot T)]$ $\therefore \sim(\sim M \vee \sim N) \to (S \cdot \sim A)$

14. $\sim P \vee (Q \cdot \sim R)$ $\therefore (R \vee R) \to \sim P$

15. $(S \vee T) \leftrightarrow \sim E$, $S \to (F \cdot \sim G)$, $A \to W$, $T \to \sim W$ $\therefore (\sim E \cdot A) \to \sim G$

*16. $A \to (B \to C)$ $\therefore (A \to B) \to (A \to C)$

17. $(G \cdot P) \to K$, $E \to Z$, $\sim P \to \sim Z$, $G \to (E \vee L)$ $\therefore (G \cdot \sim L) \to K$

18. $S \to (\sim T \to U)$, $\sim T \to (U \to O)$ $\therefore \sim S \vee [(T \to \sim T) \to O]$

*19. $A \to (B \cdot C)$, $B \to D$, $C \to \sim D$ $\therefore A \to X$

20. $B \to [(E \cdot \sim G) \to M]$, $\sim(\sim E \vee G) \to (M \to R)$
    $\therefore B \to [\sim(\sim G \to \sim E) \to R]$

21. $P \to (Q \to R)$ $\therefore Q \to (P \to R)$

22. $Q \to R$ $\therefore (P \vee Q) \to (P \vee R)$

23. $A \leftrightarrow B$ $\therefore \sim B \leftrightarrow \sim A$

24. $C \leftrightarrow D$, $D \leftrightarrow \sim E$ $\therefore C \leftrightarrow \sim E$

25. $\sim A$ $\therefore [(A \cdot B) \vee (C \cdot D)] \leftrightarrow [(A \vee C) \cdot (A \vee D)]$


**Part B:** English Arguments Symbolize the following arguments, using the schemes of abbreviation provided. Then use CP to show that the arguments are valid.

*  1. If Jones doesn't vote, then he shouldn't vote. For after all, if Jones doesn't vote, then either he lacks intelligence or he lacks a proper value system. And Jones shouldn't vote if he lacks intelligence. Furthermore, Jones shouldn't vote if he lacks a proper value system. (V: Jones does vote; I: Jones has intelligence; P: Jones has a proper value system; S: Jones should vote)

   2. Euthanasia is wrong if either the patient prefers to go on living or she still maintains her higher faculties. Therefore, if the patient still maintains her higher faculties, then euthanasia is wrong. (P: The patient prefers to go on living; F: The patient maintains her higher faculties; E: Euthanasia is wrong)

   3. If we should forgive our enemies, then it is wrong to punish criminals. For if we should forgive our enemies, then we should forget the offense and behave as if the offense never occurred. And we should punish criminals if and only if we should not behave as if the offense never occurred. Furthermore, it is wrong to punish criminals if and only if we should not punish criminals. (F: We should forgive our enemies; W: It is wrong to punish criminals; O: We should forget the offense; B: We should behave as if the offense never occurred; S: We should punish criminals)

   4. If God believes on Monday that I'll tell a lie on Tuesday, then either I have the power to make one of God's past beliefs false, or I cannot refrain from lying on Tuesday. I do not have the power to make one of God's past beliefs

false if either God is infallible or the past is unalterable. The past is unalterable. It follows that if God believes on Monday that I'll tell a lie on Tuesday, then I cannot refrain from lying on Tuesday. (B: God believes on Monday that I'll tell a lie on Tuesday; F: I have the power to make one of God's past beliefs false; R: I can refrain from lying on Tuesday; I: God is infallible; P: The past is unalterable)

5. If humans lack free will, then there is no moral responsibility. Materialism is true if and only if only matter exists. Assuming that only matter exists, every event is the result of past states of the world plus the operation of natural laws. Now, if every event is the result of past states of the world plus the operation of natural laws, then human acts are under human control only if either humans have control over the past or humans have control over the natural laws. Humans do not have control over the past, and they do not have control over the natural laws. Finally, if human acts are not under human control, then humans do not have free will. We may conclude that if materialism is true, then there is no moral responsibility. (F: Humans have free will; R: There is moral responsibility; M: Materialism is true; O: Only matter exists; E: Every event is the result of past states of the world plus the operation of natural laws; C: Human acts are under human control; P: Humans have control over the past; N: Humans have control over the natural laws)

**Part C:** Valid or Invalid?    Symbolize the following arguments. If an argument is invalid, prove this by means of an abbreviated truth table. If an argument is valid, construct a proof to demonstrate its validity.

1. If either moral judgments are products of biological causes or moral judgments are not based on empirical evidence, then morality is not objective. But if moral judgments are not products of biological causes, then moral judgments are not based on empirical evidence. Hence, morality is not objective. (M: Moral judgments are products of biological causes; E: Moral judgments are based on empirical evidence; O: Morality is objective)

2. It is false that if we continue to use gasoline, then the air will not be polluted. Either we do not continue to use gasoline or we use solar power. If we continue to use gasoline and air-pollution control devices are perfected, then the air will not be polluted. Therefore, we use solar power if and only if air-pollution control devices are perfected. (G: We continue to use gasoline; A: The air will be polluted; S: We use solar power; P: Air-pollution control devices are perfected)

3. Given that Henri Rousseau's *The Dream* is pornographic if and only if Rousseau painted it with the intention of inciting lust in the viewers, Rousseau's *The Dream* is not pornographic. For Rousseau painted it with the intention of inciting lust in the viewers only if every nude painting is painted with the intention of inciting lust in the viewers. And the latter suggestion is wildly false! (P: Henri Rousseau's *The Dream* is pornographic; L: Rousseau painted *The Dream* with the intention of inciting lust in the

viewers; N: Every nude painting is painted with the intention of inciting lust in the viewers)

4. If Boethius is morally virtuous, then he achieves heaven. But if he isn't morally virtuous, then his longings are satisfied. On the other hand, if Boethius doesn't achieve heaven, then his longings are not satisfied. So, Boethius's longings are satisfied. (M: Boethius is morally virtuous; H: Boethius achieves heaven; L: Boethius's longings are satisfied)

5. Either God has a reason for his commands, or morality is ultimately arbitrary. If God has a reason for his commands, then reasons that are independent of God's will make actions right. Consequently, reasons that are independent of God's will make actions right provided that morality is not ultimately arbitrary. (R: God has a reason for his commands; M: Morality is ultimately arbitrary; I: Reasons that are independent of God's will make actions right)

## 8.5 Reductio ad Absurdum

Although our system of statement logic is already complete, we will add one more rule that simplifies proofs in many cases, namely, *reductio ad absurdum* (RAA for short). The basic principle behind RAA is this: *Whatever implies a contradiction is false*. Using the italicized, lowercase letters *p* and *q* as statement variables (which can stand for any statement), we can see that RAA is closely related to *modus tollens*. Suppose we know that a given statement $\sim p$ implies a contradiction:

39. $\sim p \rightarrow (q \cdot \sim q)$

Now, we know that contradictions are false. So, we also know this:

40. $\sim (q \cdot \sim q)$

But, then if we apply *modus tollens* to (39) and (40), we get $\sim\sim p$ and, hence, *p* by DN. This is the essential logic underlying *reductio ad absurdum*. Since $\sim p$ leads to (or "reduces" to) a logical absurdity (i.e., a contradiction), $\sim p$ must be false, and hence *p* is true. Now, in practice, the contradiction does not usually follow from a single statement all by itself. Rather, the contradiction usually follows from the premises of the argument (which are taken as true for the purpose of establishing validity) *together with* the temporary assumption, $\sim p$, where *p* is the conclusion of the argument.

Look at it this way. Suppose we have three statements that together imply a contradiction. For instance:

$\sim A \rightarrow (B \cdot \sim C)$
$B \rightarrow C$
$\sim A$

Using MP, Simp, and Conj, one can derive C • ~C from these statements in only a few steps. Because these statements imply a contradiction, we know that at least one of them is false. Now, given that the first two statements are true, we can conclude that ~A is false and hence that A is true. This reasoning shows the following argument to be valid:

41. ~A → (B • ~C), B → C ∴ A

The formal proof runs as follows:

```
1. ~A → (B • ~C)
2. B → C                ∴ A
3. ~A                   Assume
4. B • ~C               1, 3, MP
5. B                    4, Simp
6. C                    2, 5, MP
7. ~C                   4, Simp
8. C • ~C               6, 7, Conj
9. A                    3–8, RAA
```

For the purpose of establishing the *validity* of an argument, the truth of the premises is a given. So, since the premises, together with ~A, imply a contradiction, we may conclude that ~A is false, and hence that A is true. As with CP, we box in the lines that fall within the scope of the assumption and add line (9) to indicate that A follows not from our assumption but from the premises of the argument. The annotation for line (9) mentions the lines falling within the scope of the assumption and adds "RAA" for *reductio ad absurdum*.

When the conclusion of an argument is the *negation* of a statement, (e.g., ~B), your assumption line should usually be the statement itself (in this case, B) rather than a double-negation. This procedure will usually save some steps. For example, consider the following proof:

```
1. B ↔ ~A
2. ~A → ~C
3. C ∨ D
4. ~C → ~D               ∴ ~B
5. B                     Assume
6. (B → ~A) • (~A → B)   1, ME
7. B → ~A                6, Simp
8. ~A                    5, 7, MP
9. ~C                    8, 2, MP
10. D                    3, 9, DS
11. ~D                   4, 9, MP
12. D • ~D               10, 11, Conj
13. ~B                   5–12, RAA
```

Note that in line (5), we assume $B$ rather than $\sim\sim B$. It wouldn't be a logical error to assume $\sim\sim B$, but it would add an unnecessary step. (We'd have to apply DN to drop the double-negation prior to performing a *modus ponens* step.)

Thus, a proof involving RAA may proceed in two ways. When we are trying to prove a negation, we obtain our assumption line simply by dropping the tilde. When we are trying to prove a statement that is not a negation, we obtain our assumption line by *adding* a tilde. Using lowercase letters as statement variables, we can make a diagram of these two forms of RAA as follows:

To Prove a Negation: $\sim p$

To Prove a Statement
That Is Not a Negation: $p$

Premises

Premises

```
 ⌈ p                 Assume        ⌈ ~p               Assume
 |   .                             |   .
 |   .                             |   .
 |   .                             |   .
 | (q • ~q)                        | (q • ~q)
 ⌊ ~p                RAA           ⌊ p                RAA
```

The procedure is essentially the same in both cases: We show that a statement (together with the premises) implies a contradiction and conclude that the statement is false. Note: As with CP, no proof involving RAA is complete until all assumptions have been discharged.

When should one use RAA? There is usually no way to know for sure, apart from experiment, whether RAA will prove useful, but here are some points to keep in mind. First, RAA will always work (assuming, of course, that the argument is valid), but RAA may unnecessarily complicate a proof. Second, when direct proof seems difficult or impossible and the conclusion of the argument is not a conditional, try RAA. (If the conclusion is a conditional, CP is usually preferable to RAA.) Consider an example:

**42.** $(F \lor \sim F) \to G$ $\therefore$ $G$

Applying MI to the premise, we get $\sim(F \lor \sim F) \lor G$. By DeM we can then obtain $(\sim F \cdot \sim\sim F) \lor G$. Com will give us $G \lor (\sim F \cdot \sim\sim F)$. And Dist will yield $(G \lor \sim F) \cdot (G \lor \sim\sim F)$. Now we can simplify to obtain $G \lor \sim F$ as well as $G \lor \sim\sim F$. But where do we go from here? Maybe it would help to have an assumption to work with. And since the conclusion is not a conditional, let's try RAA:

```
  1. (F ∨ ~F) → G        ∴ G
 ⌈ 2. ~G                 Assume
 | 3. ~(F ∨ ~F)          1, 2, MT
 | 4. ~F • ~~F           3, DeM
 ⌊ 5. G                  2–4, RAA
```

In this case, RAA makes the proof short and easy. Let us now add a tenth rule of thumb:

> **Rule of Thumb 10:** If direct proof is difficult and the conclusion of the argument is not a conditional, try RAA.

RAA and CP are closely related from a theoretical standpoint. For example, we can always use CP whenever we use RAA. To illustrate, consider the following proofs:

```
 1. ~P → (Q • R)
 2. R → ~Q                ∴  P
┌ 3. ~P                   Assume
│ 4. Q • R                1, 3, MP
│ 5. R                    4, Simp
│ 6. ~Q                   2, 5, MP
│ 7. Q                    4, Simp
│ 8. Q v P                7, Add
└ 9. P                    6, 8, DS
10. ~P → P                3–9, CP
11. ~~P v P               10, MI
12. P v P                 11, DN
13. P                     12, Re
```

```
 1. ~P → (Q • R)
 2. R → ~Q                ∴  P
┌ 3. ~P                   Assume
│ 4. Q • R                1, 3, MP
│ 5. R                    4, Simp
│ 6. ~Q                   2, 5, MP
│ 7. Q                    4, Simp
└ 8. Q • ~Q               6, 7, Conj
 9. P                     3–8, RAA
```

Note that the CP proof is exactly like the RAA proof down to line (7). The remaining steps are characteristic of ones we could employ *whenever we have derived a contradiction from an assumption*. So, there is a close theoretical relationship between CP and RAA. RAA proofs, however, will typically be shorter *except when* the conclusion of the argument is a conditional.

It is also worth noting that in principle, we could dispense with CP and use RAA to complete our system of statement logic, for RAA works whenever CP works. To illustrate, consider the following RAA proof for an argument having a conditional as its conclusion:

---

**Summary of Rules of Thumb for Constructing Proofs**

1. It usually helps to work backward. So, start by looking at the conclusion. Try to find the conclusion (or elements thereof) in the premises.
2. Apply the inference rules to break down the premises.
3. If the conclusion contains a statement letter that does not appear in the premises, use the rule of addition.
4. It is often useful to consider logically equivalent forms of the conclusion.
5. Both conjunction and addition can lead to useful applications of De Morgan's laws.
6. Material implication can lead to useful applications of distribution.
7. Distribution can lead to useful applications of simplification.
8. Addition can lead to useful applications of material implication.
9. If the conclusion of an argument is a conditional statement, use CP.
10. If direct proof is difficult and the conclusion of the argument is not a conditional, try RAA.

---

1. $Z \rightarrow (\sim Y \rightarrow X)$
2. $Z \rightarrow \sim Y$      $\therefore\ Z \rightarrow X$
3. $\sim(Z \rightarrow X)$      Assume
4. $\sim(\sim Z \vee X)$      3, MI
5. $\sim\sim Z \cdot \sim X$      4, DeM
6. $\sim\sim Z$      5, Simp
7. $Z$      6, DN
8. $\sim Y$      2, 7, MP
9. $\sim Y \rightarrow X$      1, 7, MP
10. $X$      8, 9, MP
11. $\sim X$      5, Simp
12. $X \cdot \sim X$      10, 11, Conj
13. $Z \rightarrow X$      3–12, RAA

While from a purely theoretical standpoint we do not need both CP *and* RAA, both rules are intuitive and both are quite useful. Thus, it is important to be able to employ both of them. In this regard, we can note that it is easy to construct a *seven*-step CP proof for the previous argument, a fact that underscores rule of thumb 9: If the conclusion of an argument is a conditional, use CP.

It is possible to combine RAA and CP. Here is an example:

```
    1. ~(S • ~R) ∨ (S → T)   ∴ S → (R ∨ T)
 ┌─ 2. S                      Assume (for CP)
 │┌─ 3. ~(R ∨ T)              Assume (for RAA)
 ││  4. ~R • ~T               3, DeM
 ││  5. ~R                    4, Simp
 ││  6. S • ~R                2, 5, Conj
 ││  7. ~~(S • ~R)            6, DN
 ││  8. S → T                 1, 7, DS
 ││  9. T                     2, 8, MP
 ││ 10. ~T                    4, Simp
 │└─11. T • ~T                9, 10, Conj
 │  12. R ∨ T                 3–11, RAA
 └─ 13. S → (R ∨ T)          2–12, CP
```

In line (2), we begin a conditional proof. Having begun a CP proof, we need to obtain the consequent of the conditional in question, namely, $R \vee T$. If we assume $\sim(R \vee T)$ and derive a contradiction, we will have shown that $R \vee T$ must be true given that $S$ is true. The preceding proof spells out the details. Note that in this case, an RAA proof falls within the scope of a CP proof.

As we have seen, when using RAA, one typically derives a contradiction from the assumption that the *conclusion* of the argument is false. But other assumptions can be useful. Here's an example:

```
    1. L → H
    2. L → ~H
    3. ~L → (S ∨ R)
    4. ~R                     ∴ S
 ┌─ 5. L                      Assume
 │  6. H                      1, 5, MP
 │  7. ~H                     2, 5, MP
 └─ 8. H • ~H                 6, 7, Conj
    9. ~L                     5–8, RAA
   10. S ∨ R                  9, 3, MP
   11. S                      10, 4, DS
```

Why assume $L$ at line (5)? This assumption makes sense for two reasons. First, if we can obtain $\sim L$, then obviously we can derive $S$ from premises (3) and (4). Second, given premises (1) and (2), if we assume $L$, we can easily derive a contradiction.

Note: as with CP, because the statements within the boxes of an RAA proof are dependent on one or more assumptions, we cannot make use of boxed-in statements in *later* parts of a proof. For example, could we enter $\sim L \cdot H$ at line (10) in the above proof, using "6, 9, Conj" as our annotation? No. For at that point in the proof, line (6) is off limits—we obtained H by making an assumption, and (as the box indicates) we stopped making that assumption when we got to line (9).

As you complete the exercises for this section, you may find the summary of rules of thumb helpful.

## ⟨⟩ Exercise 8.5

**Part A:** Proofs  Construct proofs to show that the following symbolic arguments are valid. Use RAA but not CP.

* 1. A → B ∴ ~(A • ~B)
  2. P → Q, ~P → J, ~Q → ~J ∴ Q
  3. F → G, F ∨ G ∴ G
* 4. (H ∨ R) • (H ∨ ~R) ∴ H
  5. (M → L) → M ∴ M
  6. ~P ↔ Q, ~(Q ∨ R), (P • ~R) → S ∴ S
* 7. Z → (X ∨ Y), X → ~W, Y → ~W, ~W → ~Z ∴ ~Z
  8. E ∨ T, T → (B • H), (B ∨ E) → K ∴ K
  9. (O ∨ N) → (O • N) ∴ N ↔ O
* 10. ~A • ~B ∴ A ↔ B
  11. ~W ∨ (Z → Y), ~X → (W ∨ Y), W → Z ∴ Y ∨ X
  12. ~P → (R • S), ~Q → (R • T), ~(S ∨ T) ∴ P • Q
* 13. D → ~(A ∨ B), ~C → D ∴ A → C
  14. E ∴ (E • H) ∨ (E • ~H)
  15. ~Q → (L → F), Q → ~A, F → B, L ∴ ~A ∨ B
* 16. W → (X ∨ G), G → M, ~M ∴ ~W ∨ X
  17. (~H ∨ K) • (~H ∨ L), ~N → H, ~N → (~L ∨ ~K), P ↔ N ∴ S → P
  18. C → (D → H), D • ~H, H ∨ T ∴ ~C • T
* 19. ~S → (T • U), ~R → ~(T ∨ U), (T ↔ U) → (~~S • R) ∴ R • S
  20. (A → B) → (C → A) ∴ C → A
  21. (S ∨ T) ∨ (V ∨ W) ∴ (V ∨ T) ∨ (S ∨ W)
  22. S → T ∴ (U ∨ S) → (U ∨ T)
  23. X → Y ∴ (Y ∨ X) → Y
  24. R • P, R → (S ∨ Q), ~(Q • P) ∴ S
  25. K, D → E, D → F, D → G, J → ~K, E → H, H → [I → (~J → ~G)], F → (K → I) ∴ ~D

**Part B:** Valid or Invalid?   For each of the following pairs of arguments, one is valid and one is invalid. Use an abbreviated truth table to determine which argument is invalid. Then construct a proof to show that the other member of the pair is valid, using either RAA or CP.

\*  1. $(F \rightarrow G) \rightarrow H$  $\therefore$ $F \rightarrow (G \rightarrow H)$

\*  2. $F \rightarrow (G \rightarrow H)$  $\therefore$ $(F \rightarrow G) \rightarrow H$

3. $\sim L \rightarrow L$, $\sim L \leftrightarrow N$  $\therefore$ $\sim N$

4. $(E \cdot F) \rightarrow G$  $\therefore$ $F \rightarrow G$

5. $(\sim D \vee H) \cdot (\sim D \vee \sim P)$, $\sim D \rightarrow S$, $(H \cdot P) \rightarrow \sim U$  $\therefore$ $S \vee \sim U$

6. $\sim(S \rightarrow R)$  $\therefore$ $S \cdot \sim R$

7. $(Z \vee Y) \cdot (Z \vee W)$  $\therefore$ $Z \cdot (Y \vee W)$

8. $P \rightarrow \sim Q$  $\therefore$ $Q \rightarrow \sim P$

9. $\sim S \rightarrow (F \rightarrow L)$, $F \rightarrow (L \rightarrow P)$  $\therefore$ $\sim S \rightarrow (F \rightarrow P)$

10. $A \rightarrow (B \vee C)$  $\therefore$ $(A \rightarrow B) \cdot (\sim A \vee C)$

**Part C:** English Arguments   Symbolize the following arguments using the schemes of abbreviation provided. Then construct proofs to show that the arguments are valid. Use only RAA.

\*  1. If the rate of literacy has declined, then either TV or parental neglect is the cause. If TV is the cause, then we can't increase literacy unless we can get rid of TV. If parental neglect is the cause, then we can't increase literacy unless we are willing to support early childhood education with our tax dollars. The rate of literacy has declined, but we can't get rid of TV and we certainly aren't willing to support early childhood education with our tax dollars. So, we can't increase literacy. (R: The rate of literacy has declined; T: TV is the cause of the decline in the rate of literacy; P: Parental neglect is the cause of the decline in the rate of literacy; L: We can increase literacy; C: We can get rid of TV; W: We are willing to support early childhood education with our tax dollars)

2. Either vegetarians are misguided, or factory farming is cruel and the grain fed to animals could save thousands of starving people. Vegetarians are misguided only if feeding grain to animals is an efficient way to make protein. And if the grain fed to animals could save thousands of starving people, then American consumers are insensitive if they insist on eating meat at the current rate. American consumers insist on eating meat at the current rate. Therefore, either American consumers are insensitive, or feeding grain to animals is an efficient way to make protein. (V: Vegetarians are misguided; F: Factory farming is cruel; G: The grain fed to animals could save thousands of starving people; E: Feeding grain to animals is an efficient way to make pro-

tein; A: American consumers are insensitive; M: American consumers insist on eating meat at the current rate)

3. We should maximize the general welfare if and only if utilitarianism is true. If we should maximize the general welfare, we should promote the greatest sum of pleasure. If we should promote the greatest sum of pleasure, then we are morally obligated to increase the size of the population provided that we can increase the size of the population without reducing the standard of living. We can increase the size of the population without reducing the standard of living, but we are not morally obligated to increase the size of the population if either increasing the size of the population will destroy the environment or no individual experiences the sum of pleasure. Obviously, no individual experiences the sum of pleasure. It follows that utilitarianism is not true. (W: We should maximize the general welfare; U: Utilitarianism is true; P: We should promote the greatest sum of pleasure; M: We are morally obligated to increase the size of the population; R: We can increase the size of the population without reducing the standard of living; E: Increasing the size of the population will destroy the environment; N: No individual experiences the sum of pleasure)

4. According to some Hindu traditions, reincarnation is true, but reality is undifferentiated being. However, it is not the case that *both* reincarnation is true *and* reality is undifferentiated being. For reincarnation is true if and only if a person's soul transfers to another body at death. But if a person's soul transfers to another body at death, then each individual soul is real and each individual soul differs from all other souls. But if reality is undifferentiated being, then all apparent differences are illusory. And if each individual soul is real, then souls are not illusory. However, if each individual soul differs from all other souls and souls are not illusory, then not all apparent differences are illusory. (R: Reincarnation is true; U: Reality is undifferentiated being; T: A person's soul transfers to another body at death; E: Each individual soul is real; D: Each individual soul differs from all other souls; S: Souls are illusory; A: All apparent differences are illusory)

5. Some hold the view that while contradictions *could* be true, we happen to know that they are always false. This view is mistaken. For if contradictions could be true, then if the evidence for some statements is counterbalanced by equally strong evidence for their negations, some contradictions are true for all we know. Now, if there are areas of controversy among scholars, then the evidence for some statements is counterbalanced by equally strong evidence for their negations. And it almost goes without saying that there are areas of controversy among scholars. Finally, some contradictions are true for all we know if and only if we do not know that contradictions are always false. (C: Contradictions could be true; K: We know that contradictions are always false; E: The evidence for some statements is counterbalanced by equally strong evidence for their negations; S: Some contradictions are true for all we know; A: There are areas of controversy among scholars)

**Part D:** Valid or Invalid?  Symbolize the following arguments using the schemes of abbreviation provided. If an argument is invalid, demonstrate this by means of an abbreviated truth table. (Only one of the arguments is invalid.) If an argument is valid, demonstrate this by constructing a proof. You can use CP, RAA, or direct proof.

1. If Smith works hard, then he gets elected. But if he doesn't work hard, then he is happy. Moreover, if he doesn't get elected, then he isn't happy. We may infer that Smith gets elected. (W: Smith works hard; E: Smith gets elected; H: Smith is happy)

2. If either mathematical laws are due to arbitrary linguistic conventions or mathematical laws are not based on empirical evidence, then math is merely a game played with symbols. If mathematical laws are not based on empirical evidence, then they are not due to arbitrary linguistic conventions. So, math is merely a game played with symbols. (M: Mathematical laws are due to arbitrary linguistic conventions; E: Mathematical laws are based on empirical evidence; G: Math is merely a game played with symbols)

3. God is not outside of time if time is real. For, as St. Thomas Aquinas pointed out, if God is outside of time, then God sees all of time (past, present, and future) at a glance. But if God sees all of time at a glance, then all of time (past, present, and future) already exists. Now, if all of time already exists, then the future already exists. However, if the future already exists, then I have already committed sins that I will commit in the future. But if time is real, I have emphatically *not* already committed sins that I will commit in the future. (O: God is outside of time; S: God sees all of time at a glance; A: All of time already exists; F: The future already exists; I: I have already committed sins that I will commit in the future; T: Time is real)

4. Television has destroyed the moral fiber of our country if it has both stifled creativity and substantially interfered with communication between children and parents. Of course, television has not destroyed the moral fiber of our country, assuming that our country still has moral fiber. However, one must admit that television has substantially interfered with communication between children and parents. Furthermore, the statement "Television has stifled creativity if and only if television is a good thing" is false. It follows that television is a good thing given that our country still has moral fiber. (T: Television has destroyed the moral fiber of our country; S: Television has stifled creativity; C: Television has substantially interfered with communication between children and parents; M: Our country still has moral fiber; G: Television is a good thing)

5. There is life after death if and only if there is a God. For either God exists or only matter exists. And if only matter exists, then when we die our bodies simply decay and we cease to exist permanently. Of course, if we cease to exist permanently, then there is no life after death. But God exists if and only if God is both perfectly good and omnipotent. If God is

omnipotent, God is able to raise humans from the dead. If God is perfectly good, then God wants to raise humans from the dead if resurrection is necessary for their fulfillment. Resurrection is necessary for human fulfillment if most people die with their deepest longings unsatisfied; and as a matter of fact most people do die in that condition. If God is able *and* wants to raise humans from the dead, then there is life after death. (L: There is life after death; G: God exists; M: Only matter exists; D: When we die our bodies simply decay; E: We cease to exist permanently; P: God is perfectly good; O: God is omnipotent; A: God is able to raise humans from the dead; W: God wants to raise humans from the dead; R: Resurrection is necessary for human fulfillment; U: Most people die with their deepest longings unsatisfied)

## 8.6 Proving Theorems

A **theorem** is a statement that can be proved independently of any premises. The theorems of statement logic are identical with the tautologies of statement logic. (Recall that a *tautology* is a statement that is true in every row of its truth table.) Theorems belong to a class of statements that are true by virtue of their logical form. Many philosophers regard theorems as one type of necessary truth. A **necessary truth** is a truth that cannot be false under any possible circumstances.

Theorems have some rather paradoxical logical properties. For instance, any argument that has a theorem as its conclusion is valid, regardless of the information in the premises. This is so because it is impossible for a theorem to be false, and hence it is impossible for the conclusion of such an argument to be false while the premises are true. Note that this implies that each theorem is validly implied by any other theorem.

To prove a theorem, use either CP or RAA. If the theorem is itself a conditional statement, it is usually best to use CP. Here is an example:

$$\therefore \ \sim A \rightarrow [(A \lor B) \rightarrow B]$$

| | |
|---|---|
| 1. $\sim A$ | Assume |
| 2. $A \lor B$ | Assume |
| 3. $B$ | 1, 2, DS |
| 4. $(A \lor B) \rightarrow B$ | 2–3, CP |
| 5. $\sim A \rightarrow [(A \lor B) \rightarrow B]$ | 1–4, CP |

The theorem itself is indicated by the triple-dot symbol. This proof shows that if we have $\sim A$, then if we have $A \lor B$, we can derive $B$. In other words, the proof shows that the statement beside the triple-dot symbol is indeed a theorem: It can be proved without appealing to any premises.

In some cases, RAA is the best approach. Here is a simple example:

$$\therefore\ P \lor \sim P$$

| | | |
|---|---|---|
| 1. $\sim(P \lor \sim P)$ | Assume | |
| 2. $\sim P \cdot \sim\sim P$ | 1, DeM | |
| 3. $P \lor \sim P$ | 1–2, RAA | |

In other cases, a combination of CP and RAA works best. For instance:

$$\therefore\ [(F \to G) \to F] \to F$$

| | |
|---|---|
| 1. $(F \to G) \to F$ | Assume (for CP) |
| 2. $\sim F$ | Assume (for RAA) |
| 3. $\sim(F \to G)$ | 1, 2, MT |
| 4. $\sim(\sim F \lor G)$ | 3, MI |
| 5. $\sim\sim F \cdot \sim G$ | 4, DeM |
| 6. $\sim\sim F$ | 5, Simp |
| 7. $\sim F \cdot \sim\sim F$ | 2, 6, Conj |
| 8. $F$ | 2–7, RAA |
| 9. $[(F \to G) \to F] \to F$ | 1–8, CP |

Sometimes it is necessary to introduce multiple assumptions to prove a theorem. Here is an example:

$$\therefore\ [A \to (B \to C)] \to [(A \to B) \to (A \to C)]$$

| | |
|---|---|
| 1. $A \to (B \to C)$ | Assume |
| 2. $A \to B$ | Assume |
| 3. $A$ | Assume |
| 4. $B$ | 2, 3, MP |
| 5. $B \to C$ | 1, 3, MP |
| 6. $C$ | 4, 5, MP |
| 7. $A \to C$ | 3–6, CP |
| 8. $(A \to B) \to (A \to C)$ | 2–7, CP |
| 9. $[A \to (B \to C)] \to [(A \to B) \to (A \to C)]$ | 1–8, CP |

There is an important connection between valid arguments and theorems. To understand this connection, we first need the concept of a **corresponding conditional**. In the case of an argument with a single premise, one forms the corresponding conditional simply by connecting the premise and conclusion with an arrow. Here is an example:

*Argument:* $\sim(A \lor \sim B)$  $\therefore$ B

*Corresponding conditional:* $\sim(A \lor \sim B) \to B$

In the case of an argument with multiple premises, forming the corresponding conditional is a two-step process. First, one conjoins the premises—that is, one forms a conjunction of the premises. Second, one connects this conjunction with the conclusion of the argument by means of an arrow. To illustrate:

*Argument:* P → Q, ~Q ∴ ~P
*Conjunction of premises:* (P → Q) • ~Q
*Corresponding conditional:* [(P → Q) • ~Q] → ~P

Note that in this case, the form of the argument is *modus tollens*. Of course, the argument is valid, and the corresponding conditional is a theorem. This is a relationship that can be counted on for every symbolic argument of statement logic: A symbolic argument is valid if and only if its corresponding conditional is a theorem.

Consider a second example. The argument form is traditionally known as *destructive dilemma*:

*Argument:* ~A ∨ ~B, C → A, D → B ∴ ~C ∨ ~D

To form the corresponding conditional, we first make a conjunction out of the premises, like this:

(~A ∨ ~B) • [(C → A) • (D → B)]

Next, we connect this conjunction to the conclusion of the argument with an arrow, to obtain the corresponding conditional:

((~A ∨ ~B) • [(C → A) • (D → B)]) → (~C ∨ ~D)

Now, we can prove that the argument is valid by proving that its corresponding conditional is a theorem:

∴ ((~A ∨ ~B) • [(C → A) • (D → B)]) → (~C ∨ ~D)

| | |
|---|---|
| 1. (~A ∨ ~B) • [(C → A) • (D → B)] | Assume |
| 2. ~A ∨ ~B | 1, Simp |
| 3. (C → A) • (D → B) | 1, Simp |
| 4. C → A | 3, Simp |
| 5. D → B | 3, Simp |
| 6. ~(~C ∨ ~D) | Assume |
| 7. ~~C • ~~D | 6, DeM |
| 8. ~~C | 7, Simp |
| 9. C | 8, DN |
| 10. A | 4, 9, MP |
| 11. ~~A | 10, DN |
| 12. ~B | 2, 11, DS |
| 13. ~~D | 7, Simp |
| 14. D | 13, DN |
| 15. B | 5, 14, MP |
| 16. B • ~B | 15, 12, Conj |
| 17. ~C ∨ ~D | 6–16, RAA |
| 18. ((~A ∨ ~B) • [(C → A) • (D → B)]) → (~C ∨ ~D) | 1–17, CP |

The following exercises will provide you with practice in constructing proofs for theorems.

## ◆ *Exercise 8.6*

**Part A:** Theorems    Prove the following theorems using either CP or RAA.

* 1. $\sim(P \to Q) \to (P \cdot \sim Q)$
  2. $\sim(A \cdot \sim A)$
  3. $[(S \lor R) \cdot \sim R] \to S$
* 4. $(X \to Y) \to \sim(X \cdot \sim Y)$
  5. $(\sim F \cdot \sim G) \to (F \leftrightarrow G)$
  6. $\sim(H \cdot [(H \to J) \cdot (H \to \sim J)])$
* 7. $K \to [(K \to L) \to L]$
  8. $\sim(M \leftrightarrow \sim M)$
  9. $(\sim N \to O) \lor (N \to O)$
* 10. $(P \cdot \sim Q) \to \sim(P \leftrightarrow Q)$
  11. $[(\sim B \to \sim A) \to A] \to A$
  12. $\sim[(X \leftrightarrow Y) \cdot \sim(X \lor \sim Y)]$
  13. $\sim F \to (F \to G)$
  14. $[\sim H \lor (\sim J \lor K)] \to [(\sim H \lor J) \to (\sim H \lor K)]$
  15. $[(\sim M \lor M) \to M] \to M$
  16. $[(P \to Q) \cdot (R \to \sim Q)] \to \sim(P \cdot R)$
  17. $D \to (C \to D)$
  18. $\sim[(E \lor F) \cdot ((E \to G) \cdot [(F \to G) \cdot \sim G])]$
  19. $(\sim X \to Y) \lor (X \to Z)$
  20. $[(A \to B) \lor (A \to C)] \to [A \to (B \lor C)]$

**Part B:** Challenging Theorems    Prove the following theorems using either CP or RAA.

* 1. $(T \to U) \lor (U \to T)$
  2. $(D \to E) \to [(F \to E) \to ((D \lor F) \to E)]$
  3. $[(H \to I) \to H] \to H$
* 4. $[P \lor (\sim P \cdot Q)] \leftrightarrow (P \lor Q)$
  5. $(R \leftrightarrow S) \to [((T \to R) \leftrightarrow (T \to S)) \cdot ((R \to T) \leftrightarrow (S \to T))]$
  6. $[(S \lor T) \cdot (Q \lor R)] \to [((S \cdot Q) \lor (S \cdot R)) \lor ((T \cdot Q) \lor (T \cdot R))]$

* 7. $[((L \cdot M) \vee (L \cdot N)) \vee ((P \cdot M) \vee (P \cdot N))] \rightarrow [(L \vee P) \cdot (M \vee N)]$
  8. $[(K \rightarrow J) \cdot (Q \rightarrow R)] \rightarrow [((\sim K \cdot \sim Q) \vee (\sim K \cdot R)) \vee ((J \cdot \sim Q) \vee (J \cdot R))]$
  9. $[((\sim E \cdot \sim G) \vee (\sim E \cdot H)) \vee ((F \cdot \sim G) \vee (F \cdot H))] \rightarrow [(E \rightarrow F) \cdot (G \rightarrow H)]$
* 10. $[(A \cdot B) \vee (C \cdot D)] \rightarrow [((A \vee C) \cdot (A \vee D)) \cdot ((B \vee C) \cdot (B \vee D))]$

**Part C:** Corresponding Conditionals   Form the corresponding conditional for each of the following symbolic arguments. Then construct a proof to show that each of the conditionals is a theorem.

* 1. $\sim A \vee \sim B,\ B \therefore \sim A$
  2. $C \leftrightarrow D,\ C \therefore D$
  3. $\sim E \therefore E \rightarrow F$
  4. $G \rightarrow J,\ \sim K \rightarrow \sim H,\ G \vee H \therefore J \vee K$
  5. $\sim M \vee \sim S,\ \sim L \therefore (\sim L \cdot \sim M) \vee (\sim L \cdot \sim S)$
  6. $N \cdot O \therefore P \rightarrow N$
  7. $\sim R,\ Q \therefore \sim(Q \rightarrow R)$
  8. $\sim S \vee T,\ \sim T \vee U \therefore U \vee \sim S$
  9. $\sim(W \rightarrow X),\ Z \rightarrow X \therefore \sim Z$
  10. $A \leftrightarrow \sim A \therefore B$

## Notes

1. The relevant work is Gerhard Gentzen, "Untersuchungen über das logische Schliessen," *Mathematische Zeitschrift* 39 (1934): 176–210, 405–431.
2. For more on logical equivalence, see section 7.5.
3. The most famous intuitionist is the Dutch mathematician Luitzen Egbertus Jan Brouwer (1881–1966). See Anthony Flew, *A Dictionary of Philosophy* (New York: St. Martin's Press, 1979), p. 178.
4. The form of the argument and the observation that it cannot be proved directly from the rules of inference adopted thus far are borrowed from Howard Kahane, *Logic and Philosophy: A Modern Introduction*, 6th ed. (Belmont, CA: Wadsworth, 1990), p. 88.
5. This observation is borrowed from Kahane, *Logic and Philosophy*, p. 88. A popular text that uses absorption instead of CP is Irving M. Copi and Carl Cohen, *Introduction to Logic*, 8th ed. (New York: Macmillan, 1990), chap. 9.

## Chapter 9

# *Predicate Logic*

**M**any arguments cannot be evaluated properly via the tools of statement logic. Take the following example:

1. All skeptics are depressed. Some logicians are skeptics. So, some logicians are depressed.

Argument (1) is obviously valid, but suppose we try to symbolize it, using the techniques of statement logic. Our scheme of abbreviation would look something like this:

S: All skeptics are depressed; L: Some logicians are skeptics; D: Some logicians are depressed.

Using this scheme of abbreviation, (1) translates into symbols as follows:

2. S, L ∴ D

But argument (2) is invalid. We can easily show this with an abbreviated truth table. (Simply assign falsehood to *D* and truth to *S* and *L*.) So, the validity of (1) is not revealed through the techniques of statement logic.

As we learned in Chapter 6, argument (1) is a categorical syllogism.* In this chapter, we will see how categorical logic can be developed by adding elements to our system of statement logic. From a historical point of view, the connections between statement logic and categorical logic were poorly understood until quite recently. In fact, it was Gottlob Frege (1848–1925), a German professor of mathematics, who first demonstrated the conceptual links between them.[1] This chapter on predicate logic, which depends heavily on Frege's pioneering

---

*Categorical syllogisms are arguments composed entirely of categorical statements. Categorical statements come in four basic forms: "All S are P," "No S are P," "Some S are P," and "Some S are not P" (where S and P are terms denoting classes). Every categorical syllogism has two premises and one conclusion, and every categorical syllogism contains exactly three terms.

work, covers not only forms of argument that can be evaluated via the methods of Aristotle and Venn (see Chapter 6) but also forms that lie well beyond the range of these earlier methods.

## 9.1 Predicates and Quantifiers

To apply the most powerful methods available to arguments within categorical logic, we must first learn how to symbolize categorical statements. For example, before we can evaluate categorical syllogisms, such as argument (1), we must learn how to symbolize the four types of categorical statements that play a central role in Aristotelian logic. By way of review, here is an example of each of the four main types of categorical statements:

| Name | Form | Example |
|------|------|---------|
| Universal affirmative | All S are P. | All trees are plants. |
| Universal negative | No S are P. | No trees are animals. |
| Particular affirmative | Some S are P. | Some dogs are collies. |
| Particular negative | Some S are not P. | Some dogs are not collies. |

This section explains how to symbolize not only these types of statements but also a much wider range of categorical statements.

Consider this atomic sentence:

3. Aristotle is a logician.

We need a way of symbolizing this sentence that reveals its subject-predicate structure. Sentence (3) says that a particular thing or entity, namely, Aristotle, has a certain property or attribute, namely, the property or attribute of being a logician. If we let the lowercase letter *a* name the individual, Aristotle, and let the capital letter *L* stand for the predicate "is a logician," we can symbolize (3) as follows.

4. La

And if we use the lowercase letter *b* to name the Roman philosopher Boethius, the statement "Both Aristotle and Boethius are logicians" translates as follows:

5. La • Lb

In this chapter, we will use capital letters A through Z to designate properties (such as being human, being mortal, being rational, etc.). When so used, we will call these symbols **predicate letters**. (Note that capital letters can still be used to stand for statements as needed, but we are here expanding their use.) Lowercase letters *a* through *u* will be used to name individuals. We will call these symbols **individual constants**. "Individuals" in this context refers not only to individual persons, such as Boethius and Aristotle, but also more generally to things or objects *as opposed to properties*. For example, in the statement "Seattle is beautiful," the name "Seattle" denotes an individual, a particular city, while the predicate "is beautiful" attributes a property to that city. And in the statement "Mount Rainier is snow-covered," the name "Mount Rainier" denotes an individual, a particular mountain, while the predicate "is snow-covered" attributes a property to that mountain.

The remaining lowercase letters—*v*, *w*, *x*, *y*, and *z*—will serve as **individual variables**. Variables do not name individuals but rather serve primarily as placeholders. To grasp the idea of a placeholder, consider the following expression:

6. _____ is Greek.

The blank space here can be filled with the name of any individual. If we place a name denoting the ancient Greek philosopher Socrates or Plato in the blank, a true statement results. If we place a name denoting the American president George Washington or Abraham Lincoln in the blank, a false statement results. Now, if we use G to stand for "is Greek," the following expression, which contains a variable, says the same thing as expression (6):

7. Gx

(We could just as well have written Gy or Gz.) The expression "x is Greek" is neither true nor false, just as "_____ is Greek" is neither true nor false. So, Gx is not a statement (i.e., a sentence that is either true or false). Rather, we will call it a **statement function**, for if we replace x with an individual constant, we get a statement. For example:

8. Gs

(8) is true if *s* denotes the ancient Greek philosopher Socrates. So, it is important to keep in mind the distinction between individual constants and individual variables. Whereas the individual constants (*a* through *u*) are always used to name specific individuals, the individual variables (*v* through *z*) are primarily used as placeholders. (We will consider other uses of individual variables shortly, but for now think of them simply as placeholders.)

When is a capital letter used as a predicate letter? As a statement letter? When a capital letter is coupled with an individual constant or an individual variable, it is a predicate letter, used to designate a property or attribute. For example, in the following expressions, the capital letters are used as predicate letters: *Fa*, *Gd*, and *Px*. When a capital letter is not coupled with an individual constant or an individual variable, then in our symbol system, it is used to stand for a statement—for instance, *F*, *G*, and *P*.

Suppose we want to symbolize the statement "Everything is human." How do we go about this? Of course, we need a scheme of abbreviation to tell us what capital letter stands for the predicate "is human." We indicate the scheme of abbreviation in parentheses following the statement to be symbolized, like this:

> **9.** Everything is human. (Hx: x is human)

Now, to symbolize this statement, we must employ a **quantifier**. A quantifier is used to indicate how many things have the property (or properties) in question. For example, the words "all" and "some" are quantifiers in English. To get at the concept of a quantifier, let us note that statement (9) bears a close relationship to the following expression:

> **10.** _____ is human.

Everything is human if and only if (10) is true regardless of which "fillers" we place in the blank. Therefore, we could express (9) this way:

> **11.** For any individual thing x, x is human. (Hx: x is human)

For the sake of brevity, we will use a variable enclosed in parentheses to stand for the phrase "for any individual thing x." Thus, we can symbolize statement (11) as follows:

> **12.** (x)Hx

(12) correctly symbolizes both (11) and (9). The symbol (x) is called a **universal quantifier**. It may be read variously as "for any x," "for all x," "for each x," and "for any individual thing x." By the way, we could use a variable other than x to translate statement (9), "Everything is human," for the variables in the scheme of abbreviation are merely placeholders. So, the following is also a correct symbolization of (9):

> **13.** (y)Hy

Now, suppose we wish to symbolize a **universal affirmative** statement, such as the following:

> **14.** All humans are mortal. (Hx: x is human; Mx: x is mortal)

Let us begin by rephrasing this universal affirmative. Statement (14) says, in effect, that *if anything is human, then it is mortal.* In other words, it says that the following expression is true *for any "filler"* we place in the blank spaces: "If _____ is human, then _____ is mortal." Consequently, we can rewrite "All humans are mortal" in rather technical logical language, as follows:

> **15.** For any individual thing x, if x is human, then x is mortal.

The advantage of this technical logical language, which we will call "logicese," is that it is easily translated into symbols. Using the scheme of abbreviation provided, we can translate statement (15), and hence (14), into symbols, as follows:

16. (x)(Hx → Mx)

Note that *universal affirmative statements involve the arrow.* This analysis of universal statements partially in terms of *conditionals* provides one of the crucial links between statement logic and categorical logic. Shortly, we will provide a similar analysis of universal negatives, particular affirmatives, and particular negatives. Each of these analyses essentially involves elements of statement logic. These Frege-style analyses of Aristotelian categorical statements enable us to develop a system of proof for predicate logic that builds on and is an extension of the system of proof for statement logic.

Note that it would be quite wrong to symbolize "All humans are mortal" as follows:

17. (x)(Hx • Mx)

This says that everything in the entire universe is both human and mortal! So, obviously, (17) is not equivalent to (16): $(x)(Hx \rightarrow Mx)$. *We need the arrow rather than the dot when symbolizing universal affirmatives.*

Universal affirmatives can be expressed in a variety of ways in English. For example, each of the following is a stylistic variant of "All humans are mortal":

a. Every human is mortal.

b. Each human is mortal.

c. Humans are mortal.

d. Any human is mortal.

e. If anything is a human, then it is mortal.

f. Anything that is a human is a mortal.

g. A thing is human only if it is mortal.

h. Only mortals are humans.

Each of (a) through (h) is correctly symbolized by (16): $(x)(Hx \rightarrow Mx)$. Note that in (h), the order of the terms is reversed. The word "only" often causes confusion. For example, "All trees are plants," which is a true statement, is *not* equivalent to "Only trees are plants," which is a false statement. Rather, "All trees are plants" is equivalent to "Only plants are trees" because "Only plants are trees" is equivalent to "If a thing is not a plant, then it is not a tree," which, in turn, is equivalent to "If a thing is a tree, then it is a plant."

Let us now consider **universal negative** statements. How will we symbolize them? For example:

18. No trees are animals. (Tx: x is tree; Ax: x is an animal)

This says, in effect, that if anything is a tree, then it is not an animal. In logicese, statement (18) looks like this:

19. For any x, if x is a tree, then x is not an animal.

So, we can symbolize (18) by means of a universal quantifier, the arrow, and the tilde:

20. (x)(Tx → ~Ax)

There are various ways of expressing universal negatives in English. For example, (18) has the following stylistic variants:

a. Nothing that is a tree is an animal.

b. All trees are nonanimals.

c. If anything is a tree, then it is not an animal.

d. A thing is a tree only if it is not an animal.

e. Nothing is a tree unless it is not an animal.

(20) symbolizes each of (a) through (e).

Our examination of universal negative statements raises questions about the placement of tildes. How would you translate the following statements into symbols?

21. Nothing is human. (Hx: x is human)

22. Not everything is human. (Hx: x is human)

23. Not every human is a hero. (Hx: x is a human; Ox: x is a hero)

In logicese, (21) becomes "For all $x$, $x$ is not human." In symbols, we have $(x)\sim Hx$. We can rephrase (22) as "It is not the case that, for every $x$, $x$ is human." In symbols, we have $\sim(x)Hx$. And (23) translates into "It is not true that for every $x$, if $x$ is a human, then $x$ is a hero." In symbols, we have $\sim(x)(Hx \rightarrow Ox)$. These examples underscore the fact that the placement of tildes requires careful attention.

A second quantifier, called the **existential quantifier**, is used to assert that at least one thing has a specified property. Our symbol for the existential quantifier looks like this: $(\exists x)$. (The "E" is backwards so it won't be confused with a predicate letter.) This symbol is read, "There is at least one $x$ such that" or "There exists an $x$ such that" or simply "There is an $x$ such that." Consider the following statement:

24. Something is mortal. (Mx: x is mortal)

In logicese, (24) looks like this: "There exists an $x$ such that $x$ is mortal." In symbols, we have this:

25. $(\exists x)Mx$

With the existential quantifier in hand, we can symbolize **particular affirmatives**, such as:

26. Some dogs are collies. (Dx: x is a dog; Cx: x is a collie)

"Some" means "at least one." So, in logicese, statement (26) looks like this: "There is at least one $x$ such that $x$ is both a dog and a collie." In symbols, we have this:

27. $(\exists x)(Dx \cdot Cx)$

Note that (27) is *not* equivalent to either of the following:

28. There is an x such that *if* x is a dog, *then* x is a collie.
29. $(\exists x)(Dx \rightarrow Cx)$.

Both (28) and (29) tell us merely that something is such that *if* it is a dog, *then* it is a collie. Applying the rule MI, we see that (29) is logically equivalent to $(\exists x)(\sim Dx \lor Cx)$. But this statement is true given that something is *either* not a dog *or* a collie. So, the mere existence of one thing that is not a dog—say, a desk or a duck—is sufficient to ensure the truth of (29). Hence, (29) is a far cry from "Some dogs are collies." *Therefore, when symbolizing particular affirmatives, we need to combine the existential quantifier with the dot rather than the arrow.*

Stylistic variants of "Some dogs are collies" include the following:

a. At least one dog is a collie.
b. There are dogs that are collies.
c. Something is both a dog and a collie.
d. There exists a dog that is a collie.

Each of these is correctly symbolized as follows: $(\exists x)(Dx \cdot Cx)$.

The symbolization for **particular negative** statements is now apparent. Consider:

30. Some dogs are not collies. (Dx: x is a dog; Cx: x is collie)

Statement (30) translates into logicese as follows: "There is an $x$ such that $x$ is a dog and $x$ is not a collie." In symbols, we have this:

31. $(\exists x)(Dx \cdot \sim Cx)$

There are numerous ways of expressing particular negatives in English. For example, stylistic variants of "Some dogs are not collies" include the following:

a. At least one dog is not a collie.

b. There are dogs that are not collies.

c. Something is a dog but not a collie.

d. Not all dogs are collies.

e. Not every dog is a collie.

Note that (d) and (e) can be translated using either the existential quantifier or the universal quantifier:

32. $(\exists x)(Dx \cdot \sim Cx)$

33. $\sim (x)(Dx \rightarrow Cx)$

Later in the chapter, we will be able to prove that these two statements are logically equivalent.

To this point, our use of the language of predicate logic has been informal. But for the sake of clarity, we must now have a formal description of that language. This description may seem needlessly technical, but it is required if we are to avoid serious misunderstandings. In particular, we must have a clear grasp of what counts as a well-formed formula of predicate logic.

The vocabulary of predicate logic consists of statement letters (capital letters A through Z), individual constants (lowercase letters *a* through *u*), individual variables (*v*, *w*, *x*, *y*, and *z*), predicate letters (capital letters A through Z when coupled with individual constants or variables, e.g., *Fa*, *Gx*, and *Hxy*), the logical operators ($\sim$, $\vee$, $\cdot$, $\rightarrow$, and $\leftrightarrow$), the quantifier symbols, and parentheses. An *expression* of predicate logic is *any* sequence of symbols in this vocabulary, such as $(B \rightarrow Fy \vee (\exists z)\sim$. An *atomic formula* of predicate logic is either a statement letter or a predicate letter coupled with individual constants or variables.

In what follows, we will use the capital, cursive letters $\mathcal{P}$ and $\mathcal{Q}$ to stand for any expressions in the language of predicate logic. And we will use the bold letter **x** to stand for any individual variable (*v*, *w*, *x*, *y*, and *z*). The **well-formed formulas** (WFFs) of predicate logic can be characterized as follows:

Any atomic formula is a WFF. *Examples:* A, Ba, Cx, and Dxb.

If $\mathcal{P}$ is a WFF, then so is $\sim \mathcal{P}$. *Examples:* $\sim$M, $\sim$Ga, and $\sim$Hx.

If $\mathcal{P}$ and $\mathcal{Q}$ are WFFs, then so are $(\mathcal{P} \cdot \mathcal{Q})$, $(\mathcal{P} \vee \mathcal{Q})$, $(\mathcal{P} \rightarrow \mathcal{Q})$, and $(\mathcal{P} \leftrightarrow \mathcal{Q})$. *Examples:* (Fa · Gb), (Hx ∨ Kd), (Sy → Ry), and (Lb ↔ Mc).

If $\mathcal{P}$ is a WFF that contains at least one occurrence of **x** and no **x**-quantifier, then $(\mathbf{x})\mathcal{P}$ and $(\exists \mathbf{x})\mathcal{P}$ are both WFFs. *Examples:* (y)Ny, ($\exists$z)Az, (x)(Sx → Ra), and (x)(y)Fxy.

Nothing counts as a WFF of predicate logic unless it can be demonstrated to be one by application of the above conditions.[2] (The meaning of some of the previous examples may be unclear at the moment, but it will be explained later in this chapter.)*

Although nothing counts as a WFF unless it can be demonstrated to be one via the previous conditions, we continue to allow some informal uses for the sake of convenience; for example, we permit the omission of parentheses when no ambiguity results. Thus, we may write $Fa \vee (y)Gy$ instead of $(Fa \vee (y)Gy)$. Similarly, brackets may be employed to increase readability; accordingly, we may write $(x)[(Ax \cdot Bx) \rightarrow Cx]$ instead of $(x)((Ax \cdot Bx) \rightarrow Cx)$.

Which of the following are WFFs? Which are not WFFs?

$((x)Fx \vee (x)Gx)$

$(x)(Hx \cdot (\exists y)Ly)$

$(x)Fb$

$(a)Ta$

$(x)(Ax \rightarrow (x)Bx)$

The first expression is a WFF. $Fx$ is an atomic formula, so it is a WFF. Also, $Fx$ contains at least one occurrence of $x$ and no $x$-quantifier, so $(x)Fx$ is a WFF. For similar reasons, $(x)Gx$ is a WFF. And the disjunction of any two WFFs is itself a WFF. The second expression is also a WFF. $Hx$ and $Ly$ are atomic formulas; $Ly$ contains an occurrence of $y$ and no $y$-quantifier, so $(\exists y)Ly$ is a WFF. Thus, $(Hx \cdot (\exists y)Ly)$, being the conjunction of two WFFs, is itself a WFF. Moreover, it contains at least one occurrence of $x$ and no $x$-quantifier; therefore, $(x)(Hx \cdot (\exists y)Ly)$ is a WFF.

The third expression is not a WFF. $Fb$ is an atomic formula, but it contains no occurrences of $x$, so $(x)Fb$ does not satisfy our definition of a WFF. The fourth expression is not a WFF because $a$ is an individual constant, not a variable, and a quantifier must contain a variable: $v$, $w$, $x$, $y$, or $z$. The expression $(a)Ta$ is nonsense, like saying, "For all Abraham Lincoln, Abraham Lincoln is tall." The fifth expression is not a WFF. It should now be clear that $(Ax \rightarrow (x)Bx)$ is a WFF, but it contains an x-quantifier, and therefore $(x)(Ax \rightarrow (x)Bx)$ does not satisfy our definition of a WFF.

Given an understanding of what counts as a WFF of predicate logic, we can easily grasp the important concepts of the *scope* of a quantifier, and of *free* and *bound* variables. The **scope** of a quantifier within a formula is the shortest WFF immediately to the right of the quantifier. Here is an example:

---

*The notation for predicate logic (like the notation for statement logic) is not yet standardized. Although "$(x)$" is the most frequently used symbol for the universal quantifier, "$(\forall x)$" is not uncommon. And in place of "$(\exists x)$" for the existential quantifier, some systems employ "$Vx$".

**34.** $(x)Hx \rightarrow Mx$

In (34), the scope of the quantifier $(x)$ is $Hx$. And (34) must not be confused with:

**35.** $(x)(Hx \rightarrow Mx)$

In (35), the scope of the quantifier is the conditional, $(Hx \rightarrow Mx)$. Here it may help to note that $(Hx$ is not a WFF. Applying the conditions for being a WFF strictly—as we must—a parenthesis may appear only with the dot, the vee, the arrow, the double-arrow, or as part of a quantifier.

An occurrence of a variable **x** is **bound** if (and only if) that occurrence lies within the scope of an **x**-quantifier. To clarify, by this definition, $(z)$ or $(\exists z)$ can bind only occurrences of $z$-variables; $z$-quantifiers cannot bind occurrences of, for example, y-variables. An occurrence of a variable is **free** if it is not bound. Now, ignoring the variable contained in the quantifier, which variables in (34) are bound? Which are free? The $x$ in "$Hx$" is bound, for it lies within the scope of the $(x)$ quantifier; the $x$ in "$Mx$" is free because it does not lie within the scope of any quantifier. By contrast, in (35), the quantifier binds both the $x$ in "$Hx$" and the $x$ in "$Mx$," for both fall within the scope of the quantifier.

Why does it matter whether a variable is bound or free? Let $Hx$ mean "$x$ is human" and $Mx$ mean "$x$ is mortal." Then (34) says,

**36.** If everything is human, then ___ is mortal.

Note that (36) is not a statement but a statement function, for "___ is mortal" has no truth value. Accordingly, (34) has a very different meaning than (35). Given our scheme of abbreviation, (35) means:

**37.** If anything is human, then *it* is mortal.

And as we have seen, (37) is a stylist variant of "All humans are mortal."

To ensure clarity regarding the concept of the scope of a quantifier, consider a slightly more complicated example:

**38.** $(\exists y)(Ny \rightarrow (x)Rx) \cdot Sw$

What is the scope of $(\exists y)$? The shortest WFF immediately to the right of $(\exists y)$ is the conditional, $(Ny \rightarrow (x)Rx)$. And the y in "$Ny$" is bound by the $(\exists y)$ quantifier. What is the scope of $(x)$? Answer: $Rx$. And the $x$ in "$Rx$" is bound by the quantifier $(x)$. Note that $(\exists y)$ does not bind the $x$ in "$Rx$." Since quantifiers can bind only occurrences of the variables they contain, $(\exists y)$ can bind only occurrences of y. Finally, because the occurrence of the variable $w$ in (38) does not fall within the scope of any quantifier, the $w$ in "$Sw$" is free.

We now have a fairly precise understanding of the language of predicate logic. We also have in hand a grasp of the concept of the scope of a quantifier and of the concept of free and bound variables. Thus equipped, let us return to our discussion of translating English sentences into symbols. The following list of examples should serve as a helpful guide in symbolizing English sentences. To avoid mistakes when symbolizing, it often helps to translate English into logicese first, and then into symbols. This process is made explicit in the examples below. Examine each of the items closely.

| English | Logicese | Symbols |
|---|---|---|
| 1. All ruffians are dangerous. (Rx: x is a ruffian; Dx: x is dangerous) | For any x (if x is a ruffian, then x is dangerous). | $(x)(Rx \rightarrow Dx)$ |
| 2. No plants are minerals. (Px: x is a plant; Mx: x is a mineral) | For all x (if x is a plant, then x is not a mineral). | $(x)(Px \rightarrow \sim Mx)$ |
| 3. Some people are stingy. (Px: x is a person; Sx: x is stingy) | There is an x such that (x is a person and x is stingy). | $(\exists x)(Px \cdot Sx)$ |
| 4. Some students are not bored. (Sx: x is a student; Bx: x is bored) | There exists an x such that (x is a student and x is not bored). | $(\exists x)(Sx \cdot \sim Bx)$ |
| 5. Electrons exist. (Ex: x is an electron) | There exists a y such that y is an electron. | $(\exists y)Ey$ |
| 6. Everything is an electron. (Ex: x is an electron) | For any z, z is an electron. | $(z)Ez$ |
| 7. Vampires do not exist. (Vx: x is a vampire) | For all x, it is not the case that x is a vampire. | $(x)\sim Vx$ |
| 8. Something is a logician. (Lx: x is a logician) | There is an x such that x is a logician. | $(\exists x)Lx$ |
| 9. Someone is a logician. (Px: x is a person; Lx: x is a logician) | There is a y such that (y is a person and y is a logician). | $(\exists y)(Py \cdot Ly)$ |
| 10. If Aristotle is a logician, then there is at least one logician. (Lx: x is a logician; a: Aristotle) | If Aristotle is a logician, then there is an x such that x is a logician. | $La \rightarrow (\exists x)Lx$ |
| 11. Either Abelard is a logician or no one is a logician.(Lx: x is a logician; a: Abelard; Px: x is a person) | Either Abelard is a logician, or for all x (if x is a person, then x is not a logician). | $La \lor (x)(Px \rightarrow \sim Lx)$ |

| | | |
|---|---|---|
| 12. If everything is beautiful, then nothing is ugly. (Bx: x is beautiful; Ux: x is ugly) | If for all x, x is beautiful, then for all x, x is not ugly. | (x)Bx → (x)~Ux |
| 13. Only women are mothers. (Wx: x is a woman; Mx: x is a mother) | For any y (if y is a mother, then y is a woman). | (y)(My → Wy) |
| 14. If anything is either red or blue, then it has a color. (Rx: x is red; Bx: x is blue; Cx: x has a color) | For any x [if (either x is red or x is blue), then x has a color]. | (x)[(Rx ∨ Bx) → Cx] |
| 15. Some but not all humans are rational. (Hx: x is human; Rx: x is rational) | There is an x such that (x is human and x is rational) and it is not the case that for every x (if x is human, then x is rational). | (∃x)(Hx • Rx) • ~(x)(Hx → Rx) |

The following exercises will give you practice in using quantifiers, predicate letters, individual variables, and individual constants.

## ◆ Exercise 9.1

**Part A:** Well-Formed Formulas?    Which of the following are well-formed formulas (WFFs)? Which are not?

*1. (x)Ax
 2. (x)(Ax)
 3. ~(∃y)By
*4. (a)Ca
 5. (z)~Tz
 6. (~x)Hx
*7. ~(x)~Jx
 8. Cx
 9. (z)P~z

*10. (∃z)(Sx • Rz)
 11. (∃u)Gu
 12. (w)(~Dw)
*13. (P • (x)Fx)
 14. ((x)Gx → (x)Nx)
 15. (y)(My → ~Oy)
*16. ~b
 17. (y)(Hy ∨ (∃y)Fy)
 18. ((y)Ry ∨ (∃z)~Sz)

*19. (x)((Fx ∨ Gx) → Hx)
 20. (Q • (Rg ∨ (x)Ex))
 21. (∃x)Ba
*22. (z)M
 23. (∃y)Gx
 24. (∃x)(∃x)Fx
*25. (y)(∃x)Sxy

**Part B:** Free and Bound Variables    Ignoring the variables contained in the quantifiers, determine which occurrences of variables are free and which are bound in the following formulas.

* 1. (x)(Hx ∨ Gy)
  2. (x)(y)(Ax ↔ By) ∨ ~Bz
  3. (∃y)(Cy ∨ Db) • Ed
* 4. (z)[(Fz ∨ Gz) → Jx]

5. $(\exists x)Kx \cdot (x)Lx$

6. $(x)(Mx \vee (y)\sim Ny)$

* 7. $(x)(y)Pxy \cdot Qx$

8. $(\exists y)(R \cdot Sy)$

9. $(x)[(Tx \vee Ux) \rightarrow \sim Ax]$

*10. $(x)[(Bx \cdot (y)Dy) \leftrightarrow (z)Ez]$

11. $(x)(\exists y)[(\exists z)Fxz \vee (z)Fyz]$

12. $(z)[\sim Ge \rightarrow (Hz \vee Ky)]$

*13. $(\exists x)Lx \cdot (\exists x)Nx$

14. $(y)[(Ox \vee (x)Px) \leftrightarrow Wy]$

15. $(x)[(y)(Abz \vee By) \rightarrow Cyx]$

**Part C: Symbolizing**  Symbolize the following statements using the schemes of abbreviation provided.

* 1. No Zoroastrians are Moslems. (Zx: x is a Zoroastrian; Mx: x is a Moslem)

2. All kangaroos are marsupials. (Kx: x is a kangaroo; Mx: x is a marsupial)

3. Peter Abelard is a logician, but Jacob Boehme is not. (Lx: x is a logician; a: Peter Abelard; b: Jacob Boehme)

* 4. Not every marsupial is a kangaroo. (Mx: x is a marsupial; Kx: x is a kangaroo)

5. Nothing is right. (Rx: x is right)

6. Not everything is right. (Rx: x is right)

* 7. Something is right. (Rx: x is right)

8. Something is not right. (Rx: x is right)

9. Only dogs are animals. (Dx: x is a dog; Ax: x is an animal)

*10. At least one mortal is human. (Mx: x is mortal; Hx: x is human)

11. A thing is a logician only if it is rational. (Lx: x is a logician; Rx: x is rational)

12. All trees are nonanimals. (Tx: x is tree; Ax: x is an animal)

*13. Some people are good and some people are not good. (Px: x is a person; Gx: x is good)

14. Something is both good and evil. (Gx: x is good; Ex: x is evil)

15. There exists a person who is good. (Px: x is a person; Gx: x is good)

*16. Only blue things are sky-blue. (Bx: x is blue; Sx: x is sky-blue)

17. If Socrates is not a philosopher, then Aristotle is not a philosopher. (s: Socrates; Px: x is a philosopher; a: Aristotle)

18. Not all animals are rational. (Ax: x is an animal; Rx: x is rational)

*19. There exists an animal that has a soul. (Ax: x is an animal; Sx: x has a soul)

20. If all bats are mammals, then some mammals have wings. (Bx: x is a bat; Mx: x is a mammal; Wx: x has wings)

21. All birds except penguins can fly. (Bx: x is a bird; Px: x is a penguin; Fx: x can fly)

*22. All and only circles are perfect. (Cx: x is a circle; Px: x is perfect)

23. One fails the course when blowing off the final exam. (Px: x is a person; Fx: x fails the course; Bx: x blows off the final exam)

24. If any explorer discovers gold, then he or she will become famous. (Ex: x is an explorer; Dx: x discovers gold; Fx: x will become famous)

*25. Humans are featherless bipeds. (Hx: x is human; Fx: x is featherless; Bx: x is a biped)

**Part D:** More Symbolizing  Symbolize the following statements using the schemes of abbreviation provided.

* 1. A thing is a cat only if it is an animal. (Cx: x is cat; Ax: x is an animal)

2. Some people are wicked. (Px: x is a person; Wx: x is wicked)

3. Some diseases are not fatal. (Dx: x is a disease; Fx: x is fatal)

* 4. Every logic student is wise. (Lx: x is a logic student; Wx: x is wise)

5. No soldier is a sailor. (Sx: x is a soldier; Ax: x is a sailor)

6. Only animals are wolves. (Ax: x is an animal; Wx: x is wolf)

* 7. Everything is an illusion. (Ix: x is an illusion)

8. Not everything is an illusion. (Ix: x is an illusion)

9. Either something is an illusion or nothing is an illusion. (Ix: x is an illusion)

*10. Nothing is right unless it is not wrong. (Rx: x is right; Wx: x is wrong)

11. If neither Aristotle nor Boole is a logician, there are no logicians. (Lx: x is a logician; a: Aristotle; b: Boole)

12. Some but not all paintings are forgeries. (Px: x is a painting; Fx: x is a forgery)

*13. If everything is mental, then nothing is physical. (Mx: x is mental; Px: x is physical)

14. If nothing is mortal, then nothing is human. (Mx: x is mortal; Hx: x is human)

15. If everyone is sad, then no one is happy. (Sx: x is sad; Px: x is a person; Hx: x is happy)

*16. If anyone is sad, then he or she is not happy. (Sx: x is sad; Px: x is a person; Hx: x is happy)

17. If Cudworth is a logician and all logicians are bores, then he is a bore. (Lx: x is a logician; Bx: x is a bore; c: Cudworth)

18. Something is red all over and something is green all over, but it is not true that something is both red all over and green all over. (Rx: x is red all over; Gx: x is green all over)

* **19.** If ghosts do not exist, then no houses are haunted. (Gx: x is ghost; Hx: x is a house; Nx: x is haunted)

  **20.** If any number is odd, then not every number is even. (Nx: x is a number; Ox: x is odd; Ex: x is even)

  **21.** No bears, with the exception of teddy bears, are safe. (Bx: x is a bear; Tx: x is a teddy bear; Sx: x is safe)

* **22.** Only large rodents are capybaras. (Lx: x is large; Rx: x is a rodent; Cx: x is a capybara)

  **23.** Among sports, only football is painful. (Sx: x is a sport; Fx: x is football; Px: x is painful)

  **24.** All and only hip cats play jazz. (Hx: x is hip; Cx: x is a cat; Jx: x plays jazz)

* **25.** None but surfers are cool. (Sx: x is a surfer; Cx: x is cool)

**Part E: Quiz on Symbolizing** Symbolize the following statements using the schemes of abbreviation provided.

1. Every wombat is a marsupial. (Wx: x is a wombat; Mx: x is a marsupial)
2. No wombat is a duck. (Wx: x is a wombat; Dx: x is a duck)
3. Some rectangles are squares. (Rx: x is a rectangle; Sx: x is square)
4. At least one rectangle is not a square. (Rx: x is a rectangle; Sx: x is square)
5. Not every person is a vegetarian. (Px: x is a person; Vx: x is a vegetarian)
6. Something is both green and not green. (Gx: x is green)
7. Only cats are mammals. (Cx: x is a cat; Mx: x is mammal)
8. A thing is a sphere only if it is not a cube. (Sx: x is sphere; Cx: x is a cube)
9. There exists a tree that is an oak. (Tx: x is tree; Ox: x is an oak)
10. If everything is blue, then nothing is red. (Bx: x is blue; Rx: x is red)

**Part F: Challenging Translations** Translate the following statements into symbols using the schemes of abbreviation provided. (*Note:* Some of these are rather difficult.)

* **1.** No rectangle is a square unless it is equilateral. (Rx: x is a rectangle; Sx: x is a square; Ex: x is equilateral)

  **2.** Not all murderers deserve capital punishment, but Smith is a murderer who deserves capital punishment. (Mx: x is a murderer; Dx: x deserves capital punishment; s: Smith)

  **3.** If Darwin is not a biologist, then no one is a biologist. (d: Darwin; Bx: x is a biologist; Px: x is a person)

* **4.** None but citizens can vote. (Cx: x is citizen; Vx: x is a thing that can vote)

  **5.** Only citizens can vote. (Cx: x is citizen; Vx: x is a thing that can vote)

  **6.** If everything is a human, then Fido is a human. (Hx: x is a human; f: Fido)

* **7.** If all humans are mortal but Socrates is not mortal, then Socrates is not human. (Hx: x is human; Mx: x is mortal; s: Socrates)

  **8.** If everyone is wise, then no one is a fool. (Px: x is a person; Wx: x is wise; Fx: x is a fool)

  **9.** If anyone is wise, then he or she is not a fool. (Px: x is person; Wx: x is wise; Fx: x is a fool)

* **10.** Fetuses lack a right to life if they are neither humans nor moral agents. (Fx: x is a fetus; Rx: x has a right to life; Hx: x is human; Mx: x is a moral agent)

  **11.** None but men are fathers. (Mx: x is a man; Fx: x is a father)

  **12.** If anyone is either courageous or just, then he is virtuous. (Px: x is a person; Cx: x is courageous; Jx: x is just; Vx: x is virtuous)

* **13.** If Bob is a dog and all dogs are animals, then Bob is an animal. (b: Bob; Dx: x is a dog; Ax: x is an animal)

  **14.** Either no one is wise or Solomon is wise. (Px: x is a person; Wx: x is wise; s: Solomon)

  **15.** All and only married men are husbands. (Mx: x is married; Nx: x is a man; Hx: x is a husband)

* **16.** If anyone is both happy and sad, then he is confused. (Px: x is a person; Hx: x is happy; Sx: x is sad; Cx: x is confused)

  **17.** At least one nonphysical thing exists given that God exists. (Px: x is physical; G: God exists)

  **18.** Only benevolent deities are worthy of worship. (Bx: x is benevolent; Dx: x is a deity; Wx: x is worthy of worship)

* **19.** Nothing is good unless something is evil. (Gx: x is good; Ex: x is evil)

  **20.** No animal is a dog unless it is a mammal. (Ax: x is an animal; Dx: x is a dog; Mx: x is a mammal)

  **21.** When it rains, it pours, and an old man snores. (R: It is raining; P: It is pouring; Mx: x is a man; Ox: x is old; Sx: x snores)

* **22.** The whale is neither a killer nor a fish. (Wx: x is a whale; Kx: x is a killer; Fx: x is a fish)

  **23.** Some artists are not painters but dancers. (Ax: x is an artist; Px: x is a painter; Dx: x is a dancer)

  **24.** No shark attacks unless provoked. (Sx: x is a shark; Ax: x attacks; Px: x is provoked)

* **25.** If anyone can play chess, Kasparov can. (Px: x is a person; Cx: x can play chess; k: Kasparov)

## 9.2 *Demonstrating Invalidity*

An **algorithm** is a precisely described and finite procedure for solving a problem. The truth tables we studied in Chapter 7 are an algorithm for statement logic. If we follow the correct procedures for constructing a truth table, we can determine the validity of any argument within statement logic. Unfortunately, there is no such algorithm for predicate logic. This was proved in 1936 by the American logician Alonzo Church.[3] Nevertheless, there are methods similar to truth tables that can be used to evaluate many arguments in predicate logic. We will examine one such method in this section, the **finite universe method**.

An argument is invalid if it is *possible* for its conclusion to be false while its premises are true. Thus, if we can describe a possible situation in which the conclusion of an argument is false while its premises are true, then we have shown the argument to be invalid. This is the essential principle underlying the finite universe method. And the finite universe method enables us to describe such situations simply and abstractly by imagining universes with a small number of objects.

To understand the finite universe method, we must first understand the meaning of quantified statements in universes containing a small number of objects. For instance, let us imagine a universe containing only two objects— *a* and *b*. We can picture it like this:

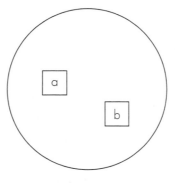

Two-Object Universe

Let us first consider the meaning of universally quantified statements in a two-object universe. A **universally quantified statement** is a WFF of the form $(\mathbf{x})\mathcal{P}$, where the bold **x** stands for any variable. Example:

39. Everything is red. (Rx: x is red)
    *In symbols:* (x)Rx

Since *a* and *b* are the only items in this universe, $(x)Rx$ is equivalent *in this universe* to the following conjunction:

Ra • Rb

In general, in a finite universe, a universally quantified statement is equivalent to a certain conjunction.

We also need to consider the meaning of existentially quantified statements. An **existentially quantified statement** is a WFF of the form $(\exists x)\mathcal{P}$, where the bold **x** stands for any variable. Example:

40. Something is red. (Rx: x is red)
    *In symbols:* (∃x)Rx

This statement is equivalent, in our two-object universe, to the following disjunction:

Ra ∨ Rb

In general, in a finite universe, an existentially quantified statement is equivalent to a certain disjunction.

To ensure understanding, let us consider a slightly larger universe containing three objects—*a*, *b*, and *c*:

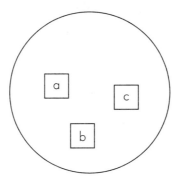

Three-Object Universe

In this universe, $(x)Rx$ is equivalent to the following conjunction:

Ra • (Rb • Rc)

And in this universe, $(\exists x)Rx$ is equivalent to the following disjunction:

Ra ∨ (Rb ∨ Rc)

Obviously, we could continue working out these equivalences for universes of larger (but finite) sizes. However, the general principle should be clear at this point: Universally quantified statements become conjunctions; existentially quantified statements become disjunctions.

A special case worth noting is that of a universe with only one object:

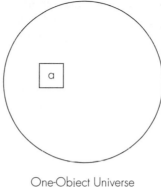

One-Object Universe

In this universe, "Everything is red" is equivalent to "*a* is red" (in symbols, *Ra*). But "Something is red" is also equivalent (in our one-object universe) to "*a* is red" (in symbols, *Ra*). Thus, in a one-object universe, (*x*)*Rx* is equivalent to (∃*x*)*Rx*. If (*x*)*Rx* is true, then (∃*x*)*Rx* must be true; and if (∃*x*)*Rx* is true, then (*x*)*Rx* must be true.

Let us now consider the meaning of *universal affirmative* and *particular affirmative* statements in a two-object universe. Here is a universal affirmative statement in both English and symbols:

**41.** All collies are dogs. (Cx: x is a collie; Dx: x is a dog)
   *In symbols:* (x)(Cx → Dx)

In a universe containing just two objects, *a* and *b*, this universal affirmative statement is equivalent to the following conjunction:

(Ca → Da) • (Cb → Db)

As before, universally quantified statements become conjunctions, but note that an arrow appears in each conjunct.

Here is a particular affirmative statement in both English and symbols:

**42.** Some dogs are collies. (Dx: x is a dog; Cx: x is a collie)
   *In symbols:* (∃x)(Dx • Cx)

In a universe containing only two objects, *a* and *b*, this particular affirmative statement is equivalent to the following disjunction:

(Da • Ca) ∨ (Db • Cb)

Note that the dot appears in each disjunct.

The process of translating universally quantified statements into conjunctions, and existentially quantified statements into disjunctions, should now be clear. To apply the finite universe method, we first translate the premises and conclusion of an argument into conjunctions and disjunctions, as we have been doing. We then apply the method of abbreviated truth tables to determine whether the conclusion can be false while the premises are true. The basic idea is that the validity of an argument does not depend on there being a large number of objects in the universe. For instance, if a pattern of reasoning allows for true premises and a false conclusion in a two-object universe, then that pattern of reasoning is invalid. No further proof is needed.

Let's try the method out on a short argument:

43. Nothing red is blue. Something is not blue. So, something is red. (Rx: x is red; Bx: x is blue)

    *In symbols:* (x)(Rx → ~Bx), (∃x)~Bx ∴ (∃x)Rx

To keep things as simple as we can, we first translate the premises and conclusion for a one-object universe, like this:

Ra → ~Ba, ~Ba ∴ Ra

Now, we apply the method of abbreviated truth tables. If we can find a truth value assignment in which the premises are true while the conclusion is false, we have shown the argument to be invalid:

| Ra Ba | Ra → ~Ba, ~Ba ∴ Ra |
|-------|---------------------|
| F  F  | F T T F  T F   F     |

This assignment does the job. We have shown that it is possible for an argument of the preceding pattern to have true premises and a false conclusion. Hence, the form is invalid. (We could obtain the same result by translating the premises and conclusion for a two-object universe, a three-object universe, and so on, but there is no need to do so.)

A one-object universe will not always be adequate for our purposes. Consider the following argument:

44. Nothing good is evil. Something is good. So, nothing is evil. (Gx: x is good; Ex: x is evil)

    *In symbols:* (x)(Gx → ~Ex), (∃x)Gx ∴ (x)~Ex

For a one-object universe, the argument translates as follows:

Ga → ~Ea, Ga ∴ ~Ea

Now, we apply the abbreviated truth table method:

| Ga Ea | Ga → ~Ea, Ga ∴ ~Ea |
|---|---|
| T  T | T T/F F T   T    F T |

Although we hypothesized that the premises could be true (while the conclusion is false), we were forced to contradict the hypothesis, as the symbol "T/F" indicates. So, let's try a two-object universe:

| Ga Ea Gb Eb | (Ga → ~Ea) • (Gb → ~Eb), Ga ∨ Gb ∴ ~Ea • ~Eb |
|---|---|
| T  F  F  T | T T T F T  F  T F T    T T F    T F F F T |

Here, the premises are true and the conclusion is false. This shows that the argument form is invalid, for there are circumstances in which it leads from true premises to a false conclusion.

To show that certain kinds of arguments are invalid, we need to consider a universe containing at least three objects. Here is an example:

45. (∃x)(Ax • ~Bx), (∃x)(Bx • ~Ax) ∴ (x)(Ax ∨ Bx)

| Aa Ba Ab Bb Ac Bc | (Aa • ~Ba) ∨ [(Ab • ~Bb) ∨ (Ac • ~Bc)], |
|---|---|
| F  F  T  F  F  T | F F T F  T  T T T F  T  F F F T |

| (Ba • ~Aa) ∨ [(Bb • ~Ab) ∨ (Bc • ~Ac)] | ∴ (Aa ∨ Ba) • [(Ab ∨ Bb) • (Ac ∨ Bc)] |
|---|---|
| F F T F  T  F F F T  T  T T T F | F  F  F   T T F T F T T |

Obviously, this method becomes rather unwieldy as we consider universes with more than two members. The good news is that in many cases, a one- or two-object universe will be sufficient to reveal the invalidity of an argument.

The bad news here is multiple. First, there are invalid arguments within predicate logic whose invalidity *cannot* be shown via the finite universe method. These arguments belong to the logic of relations, the more advanced part of predicate logic (see section 9.5).[4] Second, there are cases in which a large (though finite) universe would be needed to apply the finite universe method, making it impractical without a computer. For instance, some invalid arguments can be shown to be invalid only in a universe with at least $2^n$ objects, where $n$ is the number of predicate letters. So, if such an argument has only three predicate letters, then the finite universe method would require a universe with eight objects.

In spite of these limitations, the finite universe method can deepen our understanding of the meaning of quantified statements by revealing a great many invalid inferences. In practice, it is usually best to consider a one-object universe first and then try a two- or three-object universe as needed. Of course, if an argument is valid, it cannot be shown to be invalid by means of the finite universe method.

Using the finite universe method, we can now sort out some issues that arose in Chapter 5 as we discussed the Aristotelian Square of Opposition. Recall that *corresponding* categorical statements have the same subject and predicate terms. And from an Aristotelian perspective, a universal affirmative statement implies its corresponding particular affirmative—for example, "All unicorns are animals" implies "Some unicorns are animals." Similarly, a universal negative statement implies its corresponding particular negative—for example, "No unicorns are horses" implies "Some unicorns are not horses." Modern logicians, following George Boole, deny that these inferences are valid. Let's examine the inference from a universal affirmative to its corresponding particular affirmative, using the finite universe method.

> **46.** All unicorns are animals. So, some unicorns are animals. (Ux: x is a unicorn; Ax: x is an animal)
>
> *In symbols:* $(x)(Ux \rightarrow Ax)$  $\therefore$ $(\exists x)(Ux \cdot Ax)$

The invalidity is demonstrable in a one-object universe:

| Ua Aa | Ua → Aa $\therefore$ Ua · Aa |
|-------|------------------------------|
| F  T  | F  T  T        F F T          |

In general, the inference from a universal affirmative to its corresponding particular affirmative will move from truth to falsehood when the subject terms denote an empty class. The inference from universal negative statements to their corresponding particular negatives is invalid for the same reason.

Here is a related point. In the Aristotelian scheme, corresponding universal affirmative and universal negative statements are said to be **contraries**. Contraries cannot both be true, but they can both be false. To illustrate, "All unicorns are animals" and "No unicorns are animals," according to Aristotelians, are contraries. But according to modern logicians, these statements are not contraries because they can both be true. Now, if the Aristotelians are right, the following argument should be valid:

> **47.** All unicorns are animals. So, it is false that no unicorns are animals. (Ux: x is a unicorn; Ax: x is an animal)

That is, if "All unicorns are animals" and "No unicorns are animals" are contraries, then if "All unicorns are animals" is true, "No unicorns are animals" must be false. Here's the argument in symbols:

$(x)(Ux \rightarrow Ax)$  $\therefore$  $\sim(x)(Ux \rightarrow \sim Ax)$

We translate for a one-object universe and assign truth values as follows:

| Ua Aa | Ua → Aa ∴ ~(Ua → ~Aa) |
|-------|------------------------|
| F T   | F T T     F F T F T    |

On this truth-value assignment, the premise is true and the conclusion is false, so the inference is invalid. The reason is this: The conditionals Ua → Aa and Ua → ~Aa are both true when Ua is false. And, of course, Ua is false assuming the class of unicorns is empty. We can generalize this point as follows: *Whenever the subject term of corresponding universal affirmative and universal negative statements denotes an empty class, both statements are true.* This is why modern logicians deny the Aristotelian thesis that corresponding universal affirmative and universal negative statements are contraries.

Before bringing our discussion of the finite universe method to a close, let us consider a special complication that arises when one quantifier falls within the scope of another. For example:

(∃x)(Sx → (y)Ry) ∴ (y)[(∃x)Sx → Ry]

Note that in the premise, the scope of (∃x) is (Sx → (y)Ry) so that the (y) quantifier falls within the scope of (∃x). The situation is reversed in the conclusion, where the scope of (y) is [(∃x)Sx → Ry], and the (∃x) quantifier lies within the scope of (y). How do we translate such formulas for a two-object universe? It may help to translate them in two stages, one quantifier at a time. Let's start with the premise:

Stage 1: (Sa → (y)Ry) ∨ (Sb → (y)Ry)
Stage 2: (Sa → [Ra • Rb]) ∨ (Sb → [Ra • Rb])

In stage 1, we translated the existential quantifier and in stage two the universal quantifier. (The order doesn't matter.) The translation of the conclusion is as follows:

Stage 1: [(∃x)Sx → Ra] • [(∃x)Sx → Rb]
Stage 2: [(Sa ∨ Sb) → Ra] • [(Sa ∨ Sb) → Rb]

In stage 1, we translated the universal quantifier and in stage two the existential quantifier. The following truth-value assignment reveals the invalidity of the argument:

| Sa Ra Rb Sb | (Sa → [Ra • Rb]) ∨ (Sb → [Ra • Rb]) |
|-------------|--------------------------------------|
| F F F T     | F T FFF  T T F  FFF                  |

| ∴ [(Sa ∨ Sb) → Ra] • [(Sa ∨ Sb) → Rb] |
|----------------------------------------|
| F TT  F F F  FTT  F F                   |

The fact that the argument is invalid underscores the importance of the scope of the quantifiers, from the standpoint of logic.

Although we have mentioned some limitations of the finite universe method, the following exercises will help you understand the power of the method. It is indeed useful in a wide range of cases. Incidentally, all of the arguments in these exercises can be shown to be invalid in either a one-object or a two-object universe.

## ◆❯ Exercise 9.2

**Part A:** Demonstrating Invalidity   Use the finite universe method to show that the following symbolic arguments are invalid.

*  1. (x)(Ax → Bx) ∴ (∃x)(Ax • Bx)
   2. (∃x)Cx ∴ (x)Cx
   3. (z)(Fz → ~Gz), (∃z)(Fz • ~Hz) ∴ (∃z)(Gz • Hz)
*  4. (∃y)Ky → (∃y)Ly ∴ (y)(Ky → Ly)
   5. (∃x)(Ax → Bx) ∴ (x)(Ax → Bx)
   6. (∃x)(Rx → Sx) ∴ (x)Rx → (x)Sx
*  7. (x)Hx → (x)~Jx ∴ (x)(Jx → ~Hx)
   8. (∃z)Mz, (∃z)Nz ∴ (∃z)(Mz • Nz)
   9. (x)(Ax → Bx), (∃x)Bx ∴ (∃x)Ax
* 10. (∃y)(Ry → Sy) ∴ (∃y)Ry → (∃y)Sy
  11. (x)(Cx → ~Dx) ∴ ~(x)(Cx → Dx)
  12. (∃z)(Nz ↔ Pz) ∴ (z)(Nz ↔ Pz)
* 13. (y)(Ay → By), Bd ∴ Ad
  14. (x)Fx → (x)Gx ∴ (x)(Fx → Gx)
  15. (∃x)Dx, (∃x)Cx ∴ (x)(Dx • Cx)
* 16. (x)(Mx → Nx), (∃x)Mx ∴ (x)Nx
  17. ~(∃y)(Sy • Py) ∴ (∃y)(Sy • ~Py)
  18. (x)Tx ↔ (x)Ux ∴ (x)(Tx ↔ Ux)
* 19. (∃z)(Az • Bz), (∃z)(Cz • Bz) ∴ (∃z)(Az • Cz)
  20. (x)(Ox ∨ Px) ∴ (x)Ox ∨ (x)Px
  21. ~[(∃x)Hx → (y)Ny] ∴ (∃x)(Hx → (y)Ny)
* 22. ~(x)(Ax → (∃y)By) ∴ (x)Ax → (∃y)By
  23. (∃x)(Lx → (z)Mz) ∴ (∃x)Lx → (z)Mz
  24. (y)Fy → (∃x)Gx ∴ (x)[(y)Fy → Gx]
* 25. (x)Sx → (∃y)Ry ∴ (x)(Sx → (∃y)Ry)

26. $(x)(Lx \rightarrow Nx)$ ∴ $(\exists x)Lx \rightarrow (x)Nx$

27. $(x)Fx \rightarrow (y)Gy$ ∴ $(x)[Fx \rightarrow (y)Gy]$

* 28. $\sim(x)(Ax \rightarrow Bx)$ ∴ $(x)Ax \rightarrow (x)Bx$

29. $(x)[(\exists y)Uy \cdot Zx]$ ∴ $(x)(Ux \cdot Zx)$

30. $(\exists x)[(y)Ry \rightarrow Tx]$ ∴ $(y)Ry \rightarrow (x)Tx$

**Part B:** English Arguments   Translate the following English arguments into symbols. Then use the finite universe method to show that the arguments are invalid.

* **1.** All students who take logic are courageous. Therefore, some students who take logic are courageous. (Sx: x is a student; Lx: x takes logic; Cx: x is courageous)

**2.** All human beings are moral agents. Hence, all moral agents are human beings. (Hx: x is a human being; Mx: x is a moral agent)

**3.** Every general is arrogant. There are lieutenants who are not generals. It follows that at least one lieutenant is not arrogant. (Gx: x is a general; Ax: x is arrogant; Lx: x is a lieutenant)

* **4.** All saints are good people. Some bankers are good people. Consequently, some bankers are saints. (Sx: x is saint; Gx: x is a good person; Bx: x is a banker)

**5.** Nothing is a lover unless it is not a fighter. If anything is a fighter, then it is not a peacemaker. Accordingly, no lovers are peacemakers. (Lx: x is a lover; Fx: x is a fighter; Px: x is a peacemaker)

**6.** There is an x such that if x is a tycoon, then x is a rapscallion. Thus, some tycoons are rapscallions. (Tx: x is a tycoon; Rx: x is a rapscallion)

**7.** If everything is a circle, then everything is a square. Therefore, if anything is a circle, then it is square. (Cx: x is a circle; Sx: x is a square)

**8.** Something is guilty. We may infer that Bob Smith is guilty. (Gx: x is guilty; b: Bob Smith)

**9.** Nothing that is a ghost is also a vampire. So, there exists a ghost who is not a vampire. (Gx: x is a ghost; Vx: x is a vampire)

**10.** All anarchists are fanatics. All communists are fanatics. We may infer that all communists are anarchists. (Ax: x is an anarchist; Fx: x is a fanatic; Cx: x is a communist)

**11.** If anything is a human, then it is a sinner. Dracula is not a human. Hence, Dracula is not a sinner. (Hx: x is a human; Sx: x is a sinner; d: Dracula)

**12.** Everything that is fully caused by material antecedents is determined. Some determined events are not free. Consequently, some things that are fully caused by material antecedents are not free. (Cx: x is fully caused by material antecedents; Dx: x is a determined event; Fx: x is free)

**13.** Only acts that promote the general happiness are morally obligatory. Not all acts that promote the general happiness are socially acceptable. Therefore, at least one act that is socially acceptable is not morally obligatory. (Ax: x is an act; Px: x promotes the general happiness; Mx: x is morally obligatory; Sx: x is socially acceptable)

14. All scientists who are engaged in cancer research are vivisectionists. Some vivisectionists are well intentioned but misguided. Therefore, some scientists who are engaged in cancer research are well intentioned but misguided. (Sx: x is a scientist; Cx: x is engaged in cancer research; Vx: x is a vivisectionist; Wx: x is well intentioned; Mx: x is misguided)

15. Only things approved of by either God or society are morally permissible. Some acts of violence are approved of by either God or society. Hence, some acts of violence are morally permissible. (Gx: x is approved of by God; Sx: x is approved of by society; Mx: x is morally permissible; Vx: x is an act of violence)

## 9.3 Constructing Proofs

In this section and the next, we will extend our practice of employing proofs to establish validity. Let us begin by observing that all the rules of statement logic still apply within predicate logic. For example, consider the following argument:

48. If Gretchen is not rational, then she is not a moral agent. But Gretchen is a moral agent. So, she is rational. (g: Gretchen; Rx: x is rational; Mx: x is a moral agent)

We can symbolize this argument and prove it valid as follows:

| | | |
|---|---|---|
| 1. ~Rg → ~Mg | | ∴ Rg |
| 2. Mg | | |
| 3. ~~Mg | 2, DN | |
| 4. ~~Rg | 1, 3, MT | |
| 5. Rg | 4, DN | |

Because *Rg* and *Mg* are statements, they can be moved about in accordance with all the rules of statement logic, just as statement letters can. Here's another example:

49. For all x, it is not the case that *either* x is red *or* x is blue. So, for all x, x is not red *and* x is not blue. (Rx: x is red; Bx: x is blue)

1. (x)~(Rx ∨ Bx)    ∴ (x)(~Rx • ~Bx)
2. (x)(~Rx • ~Bx)    1, DeM

This inference is permitted because De Morgan's laws are equivalence rules, and equivalence rules, unlike implicational rules, can be applied to parts of lines in a proof (as well as to entire lines).

## Universal Instantiation

We will now add four implicational rules of inference for predicate logic.[5] Our first new rule is called **universal instantiation** (UI for short). The following simple argument illustrates the need for this new rule:

50. All humans are mortal. Socrates is human. Therefore, Socrates is mortal.
    (Hx: x is human; Mx: x is mortal; s: Socrates)
    1. (x)(Hx → Mx)
    2. Hs     ∴ Ms

Now, one might be tempted to apply *modus ponens* to lines (1) and (2), but this would be a mistake. The raw materials for a *modus ponens*–type inference are not present. We need a conditional, namely, Hs → Ms, to apply *modus ponens*. And our first premise is not a conditional (though it contains an arrow) but a universally quantified statement. However, the first premise tells us that for every x, if x is human, then x is mortal. And what's true of every individual thing must also be true of Socrates, right? So, from line (1), we can infer the following:

    3. Hs → Ms     1, UI

We call the rule of inference that permits this move "universal instantiation" (UI) because it allows us to derive a specific instance from a universally quantified statement. The remainder of the proof is now merely statement logic:

    1. (x)(Hx → Mx)
    2. Hs              ∴ Ms
    3. Hs → Ms         1, UI
    4. Ms              3, 2, MP

While the basic idea behind UI is quite intuitive, the formal statement of the rule is a bit complex. The rule is designed to permit such inferences as the following:

    A.  1. (x)Tx
        2. Ta                        1, UI
    B.  1. (x)Tx
        2. Tx                        1, UI
    C.  1. (x)Tx
        2. Ty                        1, UI
    D.  1. (y)(Pa → Fy)
        2. Pa → Fb                   1, UI
    E.  1. (z)~[(Az • Bz) v Cz]
        2. ~[(Aa • Ba) v Ca]         1, UI
    F.  1. (x)(Bx v (z)Cz)
        2. Ba v (z)Cz                1, UI

Take a close look at these inferences. In each case, a universal quantifier is dropped and the variables to which it is bound are replaced by an individual constant or individual variable. Notice that variables *not bound* by the quantifier must be left alone—see inference (F). Note also that a variable can be replaced by itself—see inference (B).

We must now attempt a more precise and technical statement of the rule of universal instantiation. In order to do this, we must first be clear about the concept of an *instance* of a quantified statement. Consider the following WFF:

A. $(x)[Lx \lor (\exists y)(Ny \bullet Px)]$

Here the scope of $(x)$ is $Lx \lor (\exists y)(Ny \bullet Px)$. Of course, with the $(x)$ quantifier removed, both occurrences of the $x$-variable are free, while the $y$ in "$Ny$" remains bound by $(\exists y)$. Suppose we replace both of the free $x$-variables in $Lx \lor (\exists y)(Ny \bullet Px)$ with a constant, such as $d$. Then we have:

B. $Ld \lor (\exists y)(Ny \bullet Pd)$

We might also replace both of the free $x$-variables in $Lx \lor (\exists y)(Ny \bullet Px)$ with another variable, like this:

C. $Lz \lor (\exists y)(Ny \bullet Pz)$

(B) and (C) are *instances* of formula (A). They result from substituting constants or variables for the variables that become free when $(x)$ is removed from (A); *however, to count as instances, these substitutions must be carried out under certain restrictions, to be specified momentarily.* But first consider the following WFFs, which are NOT instances of (A):

D. $Lz \lor (\exists y)(Ny \bullet Px)$
E. $Ly \lor (\exists y)(Ny \bullet Py)$

How does (D) differ from (C)? Note that only one of the free $x$-variables in $Lx \lor (\exists y)(Ny \bullet Px)$ has been replaced by $z$. To count as an instance, *each* of the free $x$-variables would have to be replaced. In other words, the replacement needs to be *uniform*, and since it isn't, (D) does not count as an instance of (A).

How does (E) differ from (C)? To see the crucial difference, note that in (E), the $y$ in "$Py$" is bound by $(\exists y)$. The $x$-variables in $Lx \lor (\exists y)(Ny \bullet Px)$ have been uniformly replaced with $y$-variables, but while both $x$-variables in $Lx \lor (\exists y)(Ny \bullet Px)$ are free, only one of the $y$-variables is free in $Ly \lor (\exists y)(Ny \bullet Py)$. For this reason, (E) does not count as an instance of (A).

With the above examples in mind, we can grasp a formal definition of an *instance* of a quantified WFF. Let $(x)\mathcal{P}$ and $(\exists x)\mathcal{P}$ stand for quantified WFFs ($\mathcal{P}$ stands for the scope of the quantifier in question). Let the bold letter **c** stand for any constant and the bold letter **y** stand for any variable.

---

### Universal Instantiation (UI), in Two Forms

$(\mathbf{x})\mathcal{P}$
$\therefore \mathcal{P}\mathbf{c}$

Where the bold letter **c** is any constant and $\mathcal{P}\mathbf{c}$ is an instance of $(\mathbf{x})\mathcal{P}$.

$(\mathbf{x})\mathcal{P}$
$\therefore \mathcal{P}\mathbf{y}$

Where the bold letter **y** is any variable and $\mathcal{P}\mathbf{y}$ is an instance of $(\mathbf{x})\mathcal{P}$.

**Correct Applications**

1. (z)Az
2. Ab          1, UI

1. (x)(Bx → Cx)
2. Bx → Cx     1, UI

**Errors to Avoid**

1. ~(x)Ax
2. ~Ax            1, *incorrect use of UI*

1. (x)Dx → (y)Ey
2. Dx → (y)Ey    1, *incorrect use of UI*

The incorrect applications on the right both involve the same basic error—that is, applying UI to universally quantified *parts* of statements instead of to whole statements that are universally quantified, that is, of the form $(\mathbf{x})\mathcal{P}$.

---

An **instance** of a quantified WFF $(\mathbf{x})\mathcal{P}$ or $(\exists\mathbf{x})\mathcal{P}$ is any WFF obtained by the following steps:

Step 1: Remove the initial quantifier, $(\mathbf{x})$ or $(\exists\mathbf{x})$ as the case may be.

Step 2: In the WFF resulting from step 1, either:

(a) Uniformly replace all free occurrences of the variable **x** in $\mathcal{P}$ with occurrences of **c**. Here we signify the resulting instance by $\mathcal{P}\mathbf{c}$ (and **c** is referred to as the *instantial constant*). Or,

(b) Uniformly replace all free occurrences of the variable **x** in $\mathcal{P}$ with *free* occurrences of the variable **y**. Here we signify the resulting instance by $\mathcal{P}\mathbf{y}$ (and **y** is referred to as the *instantial variable*).

Note that (b) allows us to replace occurrences of *x*-variables with *x*-variables, occurrences of *y*-variables with *y*-variables, and so on. For example, *Fx* is an instance of (x)Fx.

To ensure understanding, consider the following WFF:

F. (∃x)[(z)(Az • Bx) → Cx]

Which of the following are instances of (F)? Which are not instances?

$(z)(Az \cdot Bx) \rightarrow Cx$
$(z)(Az \cdot Bn) \rightarrow Cn$
$(z)(Az \cdot By) \rightarrow Cy$
$(z)(Az \cdot Bz) \rightarrow Cz$
$(z)(Az \cdot By) \rightarrow Cx$

The first three WFFs are instances of (F). The fourth WFF is not an instance of (F) because the $x$ in "Bx" is free in $(z)(Az \cdot Bx) \rightarrow Cx$, but the $z$ in "Bz" is not free in $(z)(Az \cdot Bz) \rightarrow Cz$. The fifth WFF is not an instance of (F) because the $x$-variables in $(z)(Az \cdot Bx) \rightarrow Cx$ have not been *uniformly* replaced—only one has been replaced with a $y$-variable.

Now that we have a definition of "instance" in hand, we can give a precise formulation of the rule of universal instantiation. Letting $(\mathbf{x})\mathcal{P}$ stand for any universally quantified WFF, we can formulate the UI rule as follows:

**Universal Instantiation (UI)**

First form:           $(\mathbf{x})\mathcal{P}$

$\therefore \mathcal{P}\mathbf{c}$ (where the bold letter **c** is any constant
and $\mathcal{P}\mathbf{c}$ is an instance of $(\mathbf{x})\mathcal{P}$)

Second form:       $(\mathbf{x})\mathcal{P}$

$\therefore \mathcal{P}\mathbf{y}$ (where the bold letter **y** is any variable
and $\mathcal{P}\mathbf{y}$ is an instance of $(\mathbf{x})\mathcal{P}$)

Which of the following are correct applications of UI? Which are incorrect?

A. 1. $(x)(Lx \vee \sim Mx)$
   2. $Lc \vee \sim Mc$          1, UI
B. 1. $(y)(Ac \cdot By)$
   2. $Ac \cdot By$             1, UI
C. 1. $(y)(Ac \cdot By)$
   2. $Ac \cdot Bc$            1, UI
D. 1. $(x)[Fx \vee (\exists z)(Gz \leftrightarrow Hx)]$
   2. $Fy \vee (\exists z)(Gz \leftrightarrow Hy)$    1, UI
E. 1. $(x)[Kx \rightarrow (y)(Ly \cdot Nx)]$
   2. $Ky \rightarrow (y)(Ly \cdot Ny)$      1, UI

All are correct *except* for (E). The problem with (E) is that $Ky \rightarrow (y)(Ly \cdot Ny)$ is not an instance of $(x)[Kx \rightarrow (y)(Ly \cdot Nx)]$, for the $x$ in "Nx" is free in $Kx \rightarrow (y)(Ly \cdot Nx)$, but the $y$ in "Ny" is not free in $Ky \rightarrow (y)(Ly \cdot Ny)$.

To ensure understanding, let us highlight three moves that are not permitted by UI. First, UI does *not* permit this:

1. ~(y)Gy
2. ~Gs 1, *incorrect use of UI*

This is like arguing, "Not everything is Greek; therefore, Socrates is not Greek," which is plainly invalid. Our formulation of the rule of UI does not permit this inference because according to our formulation, UI can be applied only to statements that are universally quantified (i.e., of the form $(\mathbf{x})\mathcal{P}$), not to universally quantified *parts* of statements. Line (1) in the preceding erroneous proof is not a universally quantified statement but the *negation* of a universally quantified statement.

Second, UI does *not* permit the following sort of inference:

1. (x)Ex → (y)Dy
2. Es → (y)Dy     1, *incorrect use of UI*

This is like arguing, "If everything is an even number, then everything is divisible by 2 (without remainder). Hence, if 6 is an even number, then everything is divisible by 2 (without remainder)." The premise of this argument is true, but the conclusion is false. (The conclusion is false because it has a true antecedent and false consequent.) So, the argument is invalid. In this erroneous proof, the error consists in applying UI to a universally quantified *part* of a statement—in this case, the antecedent of a conditional—rather than to an entire statement that is universally quantified, that is, of the form $(\mathbf{x})\mathcal{P}$.

Third, UI does *not* permit the following inference:

1. (x)(Ex → Dx)
2. Es → Dn     1, *incorrect use of UI*

This is like arguing, "All even numbers are exactly divisible by 2. So, if 6 is even, then 9 is exactly divisible by 2." Since this argument has a true premise but a false conclusion, it is invalid. The problem is that we failed to replace all free occurrences of $x$ in $Ex → Dx$ uniformly, with *the same* individual constant.

## Existential Instantiation

Our second new inference rule is called **existential instantiation** (EI). Just as UI allows us to drop universal quantifiers, EI allows us to drop existential quantifiers. EI is commonly used in mathematics. Here's an example: "Something when added to 13 equals 29. So, $x + 13 = 29$." EI allows us to move logically from a general statement that something has a certain property to the claim that a particular entity has that property—so long as nothing has been assumed about that entity. Here are some typical inferences permitted by existential instantiation:

A. 1. (∃x)Fx
   2. Fy               1, EI
B. 1. (∃x)Fx
   2. Fx               1, EI
C. 1. (∃y)(Sy • (x)Rx)
   2. Sz • (x)Rx     1, EI
D. 1. (∃z)(Pz → Tz)
   2. Px → Tx       1, EI

To avoid fallacies, however, we need a careful formulation of the EI rule. Let $(\exists x)\mathcal{P}$ stand for any statement that is existentially quantified. Then we can formulate the rule of existential instantiation as follows:

**Existential Instantiation (EI)**

    (∃**x**)$\mathcal{P}$

∴ $\mathcal{P}$**y** (where $\mathcal{P}$**y** is an instance of (∃**x**)$\mathcal{P}$ and **y** is any
       variable not occurring free previously in the proof)

Note that **y** stands for variables, not for constants. Also note the special restriction: **y** must be a variable that has NOT occurred free previously in the proof. Without this restriction, we could (in effect) make unwarranted assumptions about **y**.

Here is a simple proof involving an application of EI:

1. (x)(Ax → (y)By)
2. (∃x)Ax     ∴ (y)By
3. Ax          2, EI
4. Ax → (y)By  1, UI
5. (y)By       3, 4, MP

Using EI, we can move to Ax at line (3) because x does not occur *free* previously in the proof.

Now, consider the following erroneous proof:

1. (∃x)Sx
2. (∃x)Cx     ∴ Sx • Cx
3. Sx          1, EI (correct)
4. Cx          2, *incorrect use of EI*
5. Sx • Cx   3, 4, Conj

This is like arguing, "Something is a square. Something is a circle. So, x is a square circle." Because no individual thing can be a square circle, there can be no such x. Yet, the premises of the argument are true. So, it is invalid. The error results from our failure to honor the restriction that we cannot existen-

---

### *Existential Instantiation (EI)*

$(\exists x)\mathcal{P}$

$\therefore \mathcal{P}y$

Where $\mathcal{P}y$ is an instance of $(\exists x)\mathcal{P}$ and **y** is a variable not occurring free previously in the proof.

**Correct Applications**                    **Errors to Avoid**

1. $(\exists z)Fz$                          1. $(\exists y)Ay$
2. $Fz$              1, EI                   2. $Ab$              1, *incorrect use of EI*

1. $(\exists x)(Dx \cdot Ex)$               1. $(x)Gx$
2. $Dy \cdot Ey$     1, EI                   2. $(\exists x)Hx$
                                            3. $Gx$              1, UI
                                            4. $Hx$              2, *incorrect use of EI*

The incorrect uses on the right involve two distinct errors: (a) existentially instantiating to an individual constant and (b) existentially instantiating to a variable that has occurred free earlier in the proof.

---

tially instantiate to a variable *if that variable occurs free earlier in the proof*. The variable $x$ occurs free in line (3), so we may not existentially instantiate to $x$ in line (4).

Consider a second abuse of EI:

1. $(\exists y)Ey$
2. $En$          1, *incorrect use of EI*

This is like arguing, "Something is an even number. So, 9 is an even number." The invalidity is obvious. The problem here is that we have employed an *individual constant rather than a variable* in our application of EI. We have to use variables because they serve, in this case, as names of unknowns. As noted previously, this use of variables is common in math. For example, in "$x - 23 = 49$," $x$ is used as the name of an unknown quantity.

Finally, note that EI must be applied to existentially quantified statements, not to existentially quantified *parts* of statements. Existentially quantified statements are of the form $(\exists x)\mathcal{P}$. Consider the following misapplication of EI:

1. $Na \rightarrow (\exists x)Lx$
2. $Na \rightarrow Lx$          1, *incorrect use of EI*

The problem here is that the premise is not an existentially quantified statement but a conditional. Thus, to apply EI in this way is to apply EI to the consequent of a conditional, and so to part of a statement. If we translate the above formulas for a two-object universe (with $x$ and $a$ as the objects), the invalidity is apparent:

| Na Lx La | Na $\rightarrow$ (Lx $\vee$ La) $\therefore$ Na $\rightarrow$ Lx |
|---|---|
| T  F  T | T  T  F TT         T  F  F |

## Universal Generalization

UI and EI allow us to drop quantifiers. But when the conclusion of an argument is a quantified statement, we may need to introduce a quantifier into a proof. Our third new inference rule, **universal generalization** (UG), permits us to introduce a universal quantifier under certain conditions. Consider the following argument and the accompanying proof, which illustrates a typical use of UG.

51. All trees are plants. All plants are living things. So, all trees are living things.
    (Tx: x is a tree; Px: x is a plant; Lx: x is a living thing)
    1. (x)(Tx $\rightarrow$ Px)
    2. (x)(Px $\rightarrow$ Lx)        $\therefore$ (x)(Tx $\rightarrow$ Lx)
    3. Tx $\rightarrow$ Px         1, UI
    4. Px $\rightarrow$ Lx         2, UI
    5. Tx $\rightarrow$ Lx         3, 4, HS
    6. (x)(Tx $\rightarrow$ Lx)     5, UG

The addition of the universal quantifier in line (6) is legitimate because the validity of the earlier steps in the proof did not require any specific lowercase letter. We instantiated to $x$, but we could have instantiated to any lowercase letter: $y$, $z$, $a$, $b$—you name it. In fact, we could have instantiated to every letter (one at a time) had we so desired.

The inference from line (5) to (6) is similar to certain types of inferences made in mathematics. For example, a geometer may prove that all rectangles have such-and-such a property by arguing that a certain figure, X, about which we assume *only* that it is a rectangle, has that property. If one makes no assumption about X other than that it is a rectangle, the conclusion about X may be generalized to all rectangles.

Using $(\mathbf{x})\mathcal{P}$ to stand for any universally quantified statement, we may formulate the rule of universal generalization (UG) as follows:

Universal Generalization (UG)

$\mathcal{P}\mathbf{y}$

$\therefore (\mathbf{x})\mathcal{P}$    (where **y** stands for any variable, $\mathcal{P}\mathbf{y}$ is an instance of $(\mathbf{x})\mathcal{P}$, **y** is not free in any line derived by an application of EI, and **y** does not occur free in $(\mathbf{x})\mathcal{P}$)

---

### Universal Generalization (UG)

$\mathcal{P}$**y**
∴ **(x)**$\mathcal{P}$

Where **y** stands for any variable, $\mathcal{P}$**y** is an instance of **(x)**$\mathcal{P}$, **y** is not free in any line derived by an application of EI, and **y** does not occur free in **(x)**$\mathcal{P}$.

| **Correct Applications** | | **Errors to Avoid** | |
|---|---|---|---|
| 1. (x)Fx | | 1. Ba | |
| 2. Fx | 1, UI | 2. (x)Bx | 1, *incorrect use of UG* |
| 3. (y)Fy | 2, UG | | |
| | | 1. (x)(Hx → Lx) | |
| 1. (x)Sx | | 2. Hx → Lx | 1, UI |
| 2. (x)Tx | | 3. (x)Hx → Lx | 2, *incorrect use of UG* |
| 3. Sx | 1, UI | | |
| 4. Tx | 2, UI | 1. (∃x)Ax | |
| 5. Sx • Tx | 3, 4, Conj | 2. (x)(Ax → Bx) | |
| 6. (x)(Sx • Tx) | 5, UG | 3. Ax | 1, EI |
| | | 4. Ax → Bx | 2, UI |
| | | 5. Bx | 3, 4, MP |
| | | 6. (x)Bx | 5, *incorrect use of UG* |

The incorrect uses on the right involve three distinct errors: (a) universally generalizing on the basis of a statement about a single individual, (b) applying UG to part of a line, and (c) applying UG when the instantial variable, **y**, is free in a line derived by an application of EI.

---

Here is a proof that illustrates the use of UG:

1. (y)(~Ay • Bd)      ∴ (x)~Ax
2. ~Ay • Bd           1, UI
3. ~Ay                2, Simp
4. (x)~Ax             3, UG

Since ~Ay is an instance of (x)~Ax, y is not free in any line derived by EI, and y does not occur free in (x)~Ax, the move from line (3) to line (4) is correct.

We must immediately highlight four important restrictions on UG. First, note that **y** in $\mathcal{P}$**y** stands for individual variables, not for individual constants. Otherwise, the rule would endorse such blatantly invalid inferences as the following:

1. Os
2. (x)Ox      1, *incorrect use of UG*

This is like arguing, "Seven is an odd number. So, everything is an odd number."

A second important restriction on UG stems from the fact that UG is an implicational rule, and as such it must be applied to entire lines in a proof, not to parts of lines. Consider the following proof. Are all the steps correct?

1. (x)(Cx ∨ ~Cx)      ∴ (x)Cx ∨ (x)~Cx
2. Cx ∨ ~Cx      1, UI
3. (x)Cx ∨ ~Cx      2, UG
4. (x)Cx ∨ (x)~Cx      3, UG

Both applications of UG are *incorrect*. In line (3), UG has been applied to part of line (2), specifically, to the left disjunct of line (2). And in line (4), UG is applied to the right disjunct of line (3). So, the proof is flawed. The finite universe method readily shows that the argument is in fact invalid:

| Ca Cb | (Ca ∨ ~Ca) • (Cb ∨ ~Cb) | ∴ (Ca • Cb) ∨ (~Ca • ~Cb) |
|-------|--------------------------|----------------------------|
| T   F | T T   F   T F T   T | T F F   F   F F T |

Again, the point to remember is that UG must be applied to an entire line in a proof, never to part of a line.

A third important restriction on UG is this: To avoid fallacies, **y** must not be free in any line derived by an application of EI. Without this restriction, we could argue as follows:

1. (∃x)Rx
2. Rx      1, EI
3. (x)Rx      2, *incorrect use of UG*

Clearly, this is invalid—like arguing, "Something is red. So, everything is red."

The fourth restriction on UG is this: The instantial variable must not occur free in (**x**)$\mathcal{P}$. Without this restriction, we could argue as follows:

1. (y)(Ay → By)
2. Ay → By      1, UI
3. (x)(Ay → Bx)      2, *incorrect use of UG*

If we translate (1) and (3) above for a two-object universe (using *x* and *y* as the objects), it is apparent that we cannot move logically from (1) as a premise to (3) as a conclusion:

| Ax Bx Ay By | (Ax → Bx) • (Ay → By) ∴ (Ay → Bx) • (Ay → By) |
|---|---|
| F F  T T | F  T  F  T  T  T       T  F  F  F  T  T |

The move from (1) to (2) is a correct application of UI; the problem occurs in the move from (2) to (3); specifically, the instantial variable, y, occurs free in (x)(Ay → Bx). We could have derived, for example, (x)(Ax → Bx) by UG at line (3), but the move to (x)(Ay → Bx) is a rule violation.

The UG rule is the most complicated of our rules of inference for predicate logic. Getting clear on the restrictions is important, since it will enable you to use the rule with confidence. Incidentally, one additional restriction on UG will be discussed in section 9.4, as we consider how conditional proof and RAA may be used in predicate logic.

UG and UI can be combined to prove the validity of many categorical syllogisms. Here is a typical example:

52. No scientists are astrologers. All biologists are scientists. So, no biologists are astrologers. (Sx: x is scientist; Ax: x is an astrologer; Bx: x is a biologist)

   1. (x)(Sx → ~Ax)
   2. (x)(Bx → Sx)      ∴ (x)(Bx → ~Ax)
   3. Sy → ~Ay          1, UI
   4. By → Sy           2, UI
   5. By → ~Ay          3, 4, HS
   6. (x)(Bx → ~Ax)     5, UG

Here, we instantiated to y in lines (3) and (4), but we could have instantiated to any of our variables and then applied UG in line (6).

## Existential Generalization

The need for our fourth new inference rule, **existential generalization** (EG), is illustrated by the following argument and proof:

53. All rock stars are musicians. Sheryl Crow is a rock star. So, there is at least one musician. (Rx: x is a rock star; Mx: x is a musician; c: Sheryl Crow)
   1. (x)(Rx → Mx)
   2. Rc                ∴ (∃x)Mx
   3. Rc → Mc           1, UI
   4. Mc                2, 3, MP
   5. (∃x)Mx            4, EG

The move from line (4) to (5) is intuitive: "Sheryl Crow is a musician; therefore, there is at least one musician."

There are two forms of EG. Using $(\exists x)\mathcal{P}$ to stand for any existentially quantified statement, we can formulate the EG rule as follows:

Existential Generalization (EG)

First form:      $\mathcal{P}\mathbf{c}$

    ∴ $(\exists \mathbf{x})\mathcal{P}$ (where **c** is any constant and $\mathcal{P}\mathbf{c}$ is an instance of $(\exists \mathbf{x})\mathcal{P}$)

Second form:  $\mathcal{P}\mathbf{y}$

    ∴ $(\exists \mathbf{x})\mathcal{P}$ (where **y** is any variable and $\mathcal{P}\mathbf{y}$ is an instance of $(\exists \mathbf{x})\mathcal{P}$)

Which of the following are correct applications of EG? Which are incorrect?

A. 1. Fa
   2. $(\exists x)Fx$        1, EG

B. 1. Ac • Bc
   2. $(\exists z)(Az \bullet Bz)$   1, EG

C. 1. Gx
   2. $(\exists x)Gx$      1, EG

D. 1. Tz ∨ Rz
   2. $(\exists y)(Ty \lor Ry)$   1, EG

E. 1. Ma • Sa
   2. $(\exists x)(Mx \bullet Sa)$   1, EG

F. 1. Ha • ~Hb
   2. $(\exists x)(Hx \bullet {\sim}Hx)$   1, EG

All are correct *except* (F): $Ha \bullet {\sim}Hb$ is not an instance of $(\exists x)(Hx \bullet {\sim}Hx)$, since the free *x*-variables in $Hx \bullet {\sim}Hx$ have not been replaced *uniformly*. And the inference in question is invalid, like arguing, "Jane Addams is a human being and Bear Mountain is not a human being; therefore some entity is both a human being and not a human being."

Examine (E) closely. It is correct because $Ma \bullet Sa$ is an instance of $(\exists x)(Mx \bullet Sa)$. And though (E) may look a bit odd, the inference is valid, like arguing, "Al is mad and Al is sad; hence, there is an *x* such that (*x* is mad and Al is sad)." (The conclusion must be true if the premise is true.)

EG, like the other rules introduced in this section, is an implicational rule. Thus, it may not be applied to part of a line. Consider the following proof—are all the steps correct?

1. $(\exists x)(Lx \rightarrow Na)$     ∴ $(\exists x)Lx \rightarrow Na$
2. $Lx \rightarrow Na$           1, EI
3. $(\exists x)Lx \rightarrow Na$     2, EG

No, this use of EG is incorrect—it has been applied to part of a line, specifically, EG has been applied to the antecedent of the conditional $Lx \to Na$. The finite universe method reveals that the argument is in fact invalid.

| La Lb Na | $(La \to Na) \lor (Lb \to Na)$ | $\therefore (La \lor Lb) \to Na$ |
|---|---|---|
| T F F | T F F T F T F | T T F F F |

The point to keep in mind is that EG must be applied to an entire line in a proof, never to part of a line.

It is noteworthy that the following proof is correct, given our rules:

1. $(x)Rx$     $\therefore (\exists x)Rx$
2. $Ry$     1, UI
3. $(\exists x)Rx$     2, EG

In other words, given that everything has property $R$, we may conclude that something has $R$. The fact that this proof is valid in our system shows that our system contains an assumption that is standard in classical systems of logic— namely, at least one thing exists. Without this assumption, we could not instantiate to $y$ in line (2).[*]

With the addition of EG, we can now handle syllogisms having particular affirmative (or negative) statements as conclusions. For instance:

**54.** All artists are highly creative. Some photographers are artists. So, some photographers are highly creative. (Ax: x is an artist; Cx: x is highly creative; Px: x is a photographer)

1. $(x)(Ax \to Cx)$
2. $(\exists x)(Px \cdot Ax)$     $\therefore (\exists x)(Px \cdot Cx)$
3. $Px \cdot Ax$     2, EI
4. $Ax \to Cx$     1, UI
5. $Ax$     3, Simp
6. $Cx$     4, 5, MP
7. $Px$     3, Simp
8. $Px \cdot Cx$     7, 6, Conj
9. $(\exists x)(Px \cdot Cx)$     8, EG

---

[*]Not all systems of logic involve the assumption that at least one thing exists. Those that do not make this assumption are called "Free Logics." ("Free Logic" means "Logic free of assumptions about existence.") For an excellent discussion of Free Logics, see Stephen Read, *Thinking About Logic: An Introduction to the Philosophy of Logic* (New York: Oxford University Press, 1995), pp. 131–144.

---

### Existential Generalization (EG), in Two Forms

$\mathcal{P}c$
$\therefore (\exists x)\mathcal{P}$

Where **c** is any constant and
$\mathcal{P}c$ is an instance of $(\exists x)\mathcal{P}$.

$\mathcal{P}y$
$\therefore (\exists x)\mathcal{P}$

Where **y** is any variable and
$\mathcal{P}y$ is an instance of $(\exists x)\mathcal{P}$.

**Correct Applications**

1. Ka
2. (∃y)Ky          1, EG

1. Lx • Nx
2. (∃x)(Lx • Nx)     1, EG

1. My ∨ Oy
2. (∃x)(Mx ∨ Oy)  1, EG

**Errors to Avoid**

1. Az → (y)By
2. (∃z)Az → (y)By     1, *incorrect use of EG*

1. (x)(Dx → Eb)
2. (x)(Dx → (∃y)Ey)   1, *incorrect use of EG*

The incorrect uses on the right involve the same basic error: applying EG to part of a line instead of to an entire line. Like all of the other inference rules introduced in this section, EG is an implicational rule, not an equivalence rule.

---

Note that we applied EI before UI. What if we had reversed these inferences? Consider:

1. (x)(Ax → Cx)
2. (∃x)(Px • Ax)        $\therefore$ (∃x)(Px • Cx)
3. Ax → Cx          1, UI
4. Px • Ax          2, *incorrect use of EI*

Line (4) violates one of the restrictions on EI. We may not existentially instantiate to a variable that occurs free earlier in a proof. As we noted, without this restriction, our EI rule would permit fallacies. This leads to our first rule of thumb for predicate logic:

Rule of Thumb 1: Apply EI before you apply UI.

Consider the following alternative attempt to prove argument (54). Can we apply MP to lines (6) and (4) to obtain Cx?

1. (x)(Ax → Cx)
2. (∃x)(Px • Ax)        ∴ (∃x)(Px • Cx)
3. Py • Ay              2, EI
4. Ax → Cx             1, UI
5. Py                  3, Simp
6. Ay                  3, Simp
7. ¿¿¿

No. To apply MP, we need a conditional on one line and the antecedent of that conditional on another line. And the antecedent of line (4) is Ax, not Ay. This suggests a second rule of thumb for predicate logic:

> **Rule of Thumb 2:** Universally instantiate to free variables or individual constants and apply the rules of statement logic.

Is the following alternative proof for argument (54) correct?

1. (x)(Ax → Cx)
2. (∃x)(Px • Ax)        ∴ (∃x)(Px • Cx)
3. Py • Ay              2, EI
4. Ay → Cy             1, UI
5. Ay                  3, Simp
6. Py                  3, Simp
7. Cy                  4, 5, MP
8. Py • Cy             6, 7, Conj
9. (∃x)(Px • Cx)       8, EG

Yes. First, existentially instantiate to the variable $y$. Next, universally instantiate to $y$ and apply the rules of statement logic. Line (8) tells us that $y$ has attributes $P$ and $C$; so, we may conclude in line (9) that *something* has attributes $P$ and $C$.

   The following exercises will give you some practice in applying the four rules of inference introduced in this section.

## ◆ Exercise 9.3

**Part A:** Annotating    Annotate the following proofs.

\* 1. 1. (x)(Rx → Tx)
      2. ~Tc  ∴ ~Rc
      3. Rc → Tc
      4. ~Rc

**2.** 1. Km
2. (∃x)Kx → (x)Lx ∴ Lm
3. (∃x)Kx
4. (x)Lx
5. Lm

**3.** 1. (z)(Az → Bz)
2. (∃y)Ay ∴ (∃y)By
3. Ay
4. Ay → By
5. By
6. (∃y)By

\* **4.** 1. Hn ∴ (∃x)Hx
2. (∃x)Hx

**5.** 1. (x)(Rx → ~Ox)
2. (∃y)(Sy • Ry) ∴ (∃z)(Sz • ~Oz)
3. Sy • Ry
4. Ry → ~Oy
5. Ry
6. ~Oy
7. Sy
8. Sy • ~Oy
9. (∃z)(Sz • ~Oz)

**6.** 1. (z)(Mz • Lz)
2. (z)Mz → Kd ∴ (∃y)Ky
3. Mz • Lz
4. Mz
5. (z)Mz
6. Kd
7. (∃y)Ky

\* **7.** 1. (y)(Ry → Ny)
2. ~Ng ∴ (∃y)~Ry
3. Rg → Ng
4. ~Rg
5. (∃y)~Ry

**8.** 1. Ab ∨ (Bb • Cb)
2. (x)~Cx ∴ (∃x)Ax
3. (Ab ∨ Bb) • (Ab ∨ Cb)
4. Ab ∨ Cb
5. ~Cb
6. Ab
7. (∃x)Ax

   **9.** 1. (x)(Fx → Gx)
     2. (x)(Gx → Fx)   ∴ (x)(Fx ↔ Gx)
     3. Fx → Gx
     4. Gx → Fx
     5. (Fx → Gx) • (Gx → Fx)
     6. Fx ↔ Gx
     7. (x)(Fx ↔ Gx)

 *  **10.** 1. (∃y)Py → (z)(~Nz ∨ Oz)
     2. Pn
     3. ~Om   ∴ (∃x)~Nx
     4. (∃y)Py
     5. (z)(~Nz ∨ Oz)
     6. ~Nm ∨ Om
     7. ~Nm
     8. (∃x)~Nx

   **11.** 1. (x)(Kx → Lx)
     2. (x)(Lx → Mx)   ∴ (x)(Kx → Mx)
     3. Kx → Lx
     4. Lx → Mx
     5. Kx → Mx
     6. (x)(Kx → Mx)

   **12.** 1. (x)[(Ax ∨ Bx) → Cx]
     2. (x)~Cx   ∴ (x)~Bx
     3. (Ax ∨ Bx) → Cx
     4. ~Cx
     5. ~(Ax ∨ Bx)
     6. ~Ax • ~Bx
     7. ~Bx
     8. (x)~Bx

 *  **13.** 1. (y)(Dy • Ey)   ∴ (y)Dy • (y)Ey
     2. Dy • Ey
     3. Dy
     4. (y)Dy
     5. Ey
     6. (y)Ey
     7. (y)Dy • (y)Ey

   **14.** 1. (∃x)(Jx • Kx)   ∴ (∃x)Jx • (∃x)Kx
     2. Jy • Ky
     3. Jy
     4. (∃x)Jx
     5. Ky
     6. (∃x)Kx
     7. (∃x)Jx • (∃x)Kx

15. 1. (x)[Ma ∨ (Lx • Nx)]
    2. ~Ma ∴ (x)Nx
    3. Ma ∨ (Ly • Ny)
    4. Ly • Ny
    5. Ny
    6. (x)Nx

**Part B:** Correct or Incorrect?　Which of the following inferences are permitted by our inference rules? Which are not permitted?

\*   **1.** 1. (x)Ax → (x)Bx
      2. Ax → (x)Bx         1, UI

  **2.** 1. (∃x)(Dx • Fx)
      2. (∃x)Gx
      3. Dx • Fx          1, EI
      4. Dx               3, Simp
      5. (x)Dx           4, UG
      6. Fx               3, Simp
      7. (∃x)Fx         6, EG
      8. Gx               2, EI

  **3.** 1. (∃y)Hy → (∃y)Jy
      2. Hy → (∃y)Jy     1, EI

\*   **4.** 1. (∃z)(Kz • Lz)
      2. (∃z)Kz          1, Simp

  **5.** 1. (∃y)(Ry • Sy)
      2. Rb • Sb         1, EI

  **6.** 1. (x)(Mx → Nx)
      2. (x)(Nx → Ox)
      3. Mx → Nx      1, UI
      4. Nx → Ox      2, UI
      5. Mx → Ox      3, 4, HS
      6. (x)(Mx → Ox)   5, UG
      7. Md → Od      6, UI
      8. (∃y)(My → Oy)  7, EG

\*   **7.** 1. (x)(y)(My ↔ Nx)
      2. (y)(My ↔ Ny)    1, UI

  **8.** 1. ~(x)(Tx ∨ Ax)
      2. ~(Tx ∨ Ax)     1, UI

  **9.** 1. (x)[(y)Fy ∨ Hx]
      2. (y)Fy ∨ Hx      1, UI
      3. (y)Fy ∨ (∃z)Hz  2, EG

* 10.  1. (x)(Bx → (z)Cz)
    2. (x)Bx
    3. (z)Cz                 1, 2, MP

11.  1. (x)(Px → Sx)
    2. Px → Sc           1, UI
    3. Pc → Sc           1, UI
    4. (y)(Sy → Sy)      3, UG

12.  1. (x)[(Fx • (∃y)Gy) → Hx]
    2. (Fa • (∃y)Gy) → Hx   1, UI

* 13.  1. (x)(Ax ∨ Bx)
    2. Ax ∨ Bx           1, UI
    3. (y)(Ax ∨ By)      2, UG

14.  1. (∃x)(Px • Sx)
    2. Py • Sy             1, EI
    3. (∃z)(Pz • Sy)       2, EG
    4. Pz • Sy             3, EI
    5. (∃z)(Pz • Sz)       4, EG

15.  1. (x)[Cx → (∃y)((Fy • My) • Kx)]
    2. (∃z)Cz
    3. Cx                      2, EI
    4. Cx → (∃y)((Fy • My) • Kx)     1, UI
    5. (∃y)((Fy • My) • Kx)        3, 4, MP
    6. (Fy • My) • Kx              5, EI
    7. Fy • My                 6, Simp
    8. (y)(Fy • My)            7, UG

**Part C: Proofs** Construct proofs to show that the following symbolic arguments are valid. Use direct proof rather than CP or RAA.

*  1. Ja → Hb, (y)~Hy  ∴ (∃x)~Jx

  2. (x)(~Tx → ~Hx), Ha  ∴ Ta

  3. (x)Mx → (y)Ny, (x)~~Mx  ∴ Nd

*  4. (z)(Nz → ~Ez), (z)(Sz → Nz)  ∴ (z)(Sz → ~Ez)

  5. (∃x)(Ax • Bx)  ∴ (∃x)Ax • (∃x)Bx

  6. (y)(Fy → Gy), Fb  ∴ (∃y)(Fy • Gy)

*  7. (x)(Dx → Lx), (∃x)Dx  ∴ (∃x)(Dx • Lx)

  8. (z)(Hz → Jz), (∃z)(Hz • Kz)  ∴ (∃z)(Jz • Kz)

  9. (x)[(Ax ∨ Bx) → Cx], (∃x)Bx  ∴ (∃x)Cx

* 10. (y)(~Py → ~Ly), Lc ∨ Ld  ∴ Pd ∨ Pc

 11. (∃x)(Dx • ~Rx), (x)(Dx → Wx)  ∴ (∃x)(Wx • ~Rx)

12. $(z)[Uz \rightarrow (Kz \vee Sz)]$, $(z)Uz$, $(\exists z)\sim Sz$ ∴ $(\exists z)Kz$

* **13.** $(x)(Ax \leftrightarrow \sim Ax)$ ∴ $Bc$

14. $(x)[Cx \rightarrow (Dx \cdot (\exists y)Ey)]$, $\sim Db$ ∴ $(\exists x)\sim Cx$

15. $(x)[(Ax \cdot Bx) \rightarrow Cd]$, $(x)(Ax \rightarrow \sim Bx) \rightarrow (x)Ex$, $\sim Cd$ ∴ $Ed$

* **16.** $(z)\sim[\sim(x)Jx \vee \sim Kz]$ ∴ $Jc \cdot Kc$

17. $(x)(Fx \cdot Gx)$, $\sim(x)Gx \vee Ha$ ∴ $(\exists x)Hx$

18. $(x)[(Bx \rightarrow (z)Az) \rightarrow \sim P]$, $(\exists x)\sim Bx$ ∴ $\sim P$

* **19.** $(y)\sim(Ly \rightarrow My)$, $(y)Ly \rightarrow (\exists x)Dx$ ∴ $(y)\sim My \cdot (\exists x)Dx$

20. $(x)[(Sx \cdot \sim(z)Rz) \rightarrow Nd]$, $(x)\sim Nx$, $(\exists x)Sx$ ∴ $Rc$

**Part D: Proofs** Construct proofs to show that the following symbolic arguments are valid. Use direct proof rather than CP or RAA.

* **1.** $(x)[Px \rightarrow (\exists y)Oy]$, $(\exists z)Pz$ ∴ $(\exists y)Oy$

2. $(\exists x)(Jx \cdot Kx)$ ∴ $(\exists x)Jx \cdot (\exists x)Kx$

3. $(x)(Gx \rightarrow Hx)$, $(\exists x)(\sim Fx \cdot Gx)$ ∴ $(\exists x)(\sim Fx \cdot Hx)$

* **4.** $(\exists y)Fy \rightarrow (y)My$, $Fg$ ∴ $Mg$

5. $(x)(Jx \rightarrow \sim Ex)$, $(\exists x)(Jx \vee Jd)$ ∴ $(\exists y)(Ey \rightarrow \sim Ed)$

6. $(x)(Lx \rightarrow Mx) \rightarrow (x)(Nx \rightarrow Lx)$, $(x)\sim Lx$ ∴ $(x)\sim Nx$

* **7.** $(x)(Sx \rightarrow Tx)$, $(\exists y)(Ry \cdot \sim Ty)$ ∴ $(\exists z)(Rz \cdot \sim Sz)$

8. $(x)(Bx \rightarrow Cx)$, $(x)(Ax \rightarrow Bx)$, $(x)(Cx \rightarrow Dx)$, $(\exists x)\sim Dx$ ∴ $(\exists x)\sim Ax$

9. $(x)(Rx \leftrightarrow Sx)$ ∴ $(x)(Rx \rightarrow Sx) \cdot (x)(Sx \rightarrow Rx)$

* **10.** $(x)[(Bx \vee Ax) \leftrightarrow Cx]$, $(x)\sim Cx$ ∴ $(x)(Ax \leftrightarrow Bx)$

11. $(x)(Dx \rightarrow \sim Kx)$, $(\exists x)(Ex \cdot Hx)$, $(x)(Hx \rightarrow Dx)$, $(x)(Jx \rightarrow Kx)$
∴ $(\exists x)(Ex \cdot \sim Jx)$

12. $(x)[Fx \leftrightarrow (Hx \cdot \sim(y)Gy)]$, $(\exists x)\sim Fx$, $(z)Hz$ ∴ $Gc$

* **13.** $(x)[Bx \rightarrow (Cx \cdot Dx)]$, $(\exists x)Bx$ ∴ $(\exists x)\sim(\sim Cx \vee \sim Dx)$

14. $(x)[Mx \rightarrow (\exists y)(Ny \cdot Px)]$, $(x)(Nx \rightarrow \sim G)$, $(\exists x)Mx$ ∴ $\sim G$

15. $(x)[Rx \rightarrow (Sx \vee (y)Ty)]$, $(x)(Rx \rightarrow Sx) \rightarrow Pb$, $\sim(y)Ty$ ∴ $Pb$

**Part E: English Arguments** Symbolize the following arguments using the schemes of abbreviation provided. Then construct proofs to show that the arguments are valid. Use direct proof rather than CP or RAA.

* **1.** Only humans have inherent value. No chimps are humans. So, no chimps have inherent value. (Hx: x is a human; Ix: x has inherent value; Cx: x is a chimp)

2. Every fetus has an immortal soul. A thing has an immortal soul only if it has a right to life. Hence, each and every fetus has a right to life. (Fx: x is fetus; Sx: x has an immortal soul; Rx: x has a right to life)

3. There are rights that cannot be waived. But alienable rights can be waived. It follows that some rights are inalienable. (Rx: x is right; Wx: x can be waived; Ax: x is an alienable right)

\* **4.** God is a perfect being. Nothing perfect is unreal. Therefore, God is real. (g: God; Px: x is a perfect being; Rx: x is real)

5. At least one instance of intentional killing is not wrong. But every murder is wrong. Hence, some instances of intentional killing are not murder. (Kx: x is an instance of intentional killing; Mx: x is murder; Wx: x is wrong)

6. Some wars are just. No war of aggression is just. Accordingly, there are wars that are not wars of aggression. (Wx: x is a war; Jx: x is just; Ax: x is a war of aggression)

\* **7.** A person deserves the death penalty if and only if he is a serial killer. Bundy is a serial killer, but Oswald is not. Both Bundy and Oswald are persons. Hence, Bundy deserves the death penalty, but Oswald does not. (Px: x is a person; Dx: x deserves the death penalty; Sx: x is a serial killer; b: Bundy; o: Oswald)

8. All contingent beings are causally dependent. No necessary beings are causally dependent. Every physical entity is contingent. All atoms are physical entities. We may conclude that no atom is a necessary being. (Cx: x is a contingent being; Dx: x is causally dependent; Nx: x is a necessary being; Px: x is a physical entity; Ax: x is an atom)

9. At least one instance of killing an innocent human is not wrong. For some instances of killing an innocent human are either accidental or in self-defense. But neither accidental killing nor killing in self-defense is wrong. (Kx: x is an instance of killing an innocent human; Wx: x is wrong; Ax: x is an accidental killing; Sx: x is a case of killing in self-defense)

10. Only things having human bodies are human. No unembodied soul has a human body. Only unembodied souls survive the death of the body. Thus, no humans survive the death of the body. (Bx: x has a human body; Hx: x is human; Ux: x is an unembodied soul; Sx: x survives the death of the body)

## 9.4 Quantifier Negation, RAA, and CP

In this section, we add two equivalence rules to our system of proof and explain how to use conditional proof and *reductio ad absurdum* within predicate logic. Consider the following pair of statements:

**55.** Everything is nonred (or nothing is red).

**56.** It is not the case that something is red.

It should be obvious that each of these statements validly implies the other. In symbols, these intuitive inferences would look like this (using *R* to stand for "is red"):

$$(x){\sim}Rx \qquad\qquad\qquad {\sim}(\exists x)Rx$$
$$\therefore\ {\sim}(\exists x)Rx \qquad\qquad\qquad \therefore\ (x){\sim}Rx$$

In both cases, one begins with a quantifier having a tilde on one side. One then switches the tilde to the opposite side and changes the type of quantifier.

It should also be obvious that the following two statements validly imply each other:

**57.** Something is not red.

**58.** Not everything is red.

In symbols, the inferences would look like this:

$$(\exists x){\sim}Rx \qquad\qquad {\sim}(x)Rx$$
$$\therefore\ {\sim}(x)Rx \qquad\qquad \therefore\ (\exists x){\sim}Rx$$

Such inferences are permitted by the rule of **quantifier negation** (QN). To state this rule, we will use the cursive letter $\mathscr{P}$ to stand for any WFF and the bold **x** to stand for any variable. QN comes in two forms, as follows:

$$\sim(\exists\mathbf{x})\mathscr{P}\ ::\ (\mathbf{x}){\sim}\mathscr{P}$$
$$\sim(\mathbf{x})\mathscr{P}\ ::\ (\exists\mathbf{x}){\sim}\mathscr{P}$$

The four-dot symbols indicate that both of these rules are equivalence rules. In each case, we can move logically from the formula on the left to the formula on the right, *and vice versa*. In each case, one begins with a quantifier having a tilde on one side. One then switches the tilde to the opposite side and changes the type of quantifier.

Here are some typical examples of inferences permitted by the QN rule:

```
A. 1. (x)~Fx
   2. ~(∃x)Fx            1, QN
B. 1. ~(∃x)(Sx v Rx)
   2. (x)~(Sx v Rx)      1, QN
C. 1. ~(y)(Ay → By)
   2. (∃y)~(Ay → By)     1, QN
D. 1. (∃z)~(Cz • Dz)
   2. ~(z)(Cz • Dz)      1, QN
```

Because QN is an *equivalence* rule, it can be applied to *parts* of a line. For example:

E. 1. $(x){\sim}Hx \rightarrow (y)Ky$
   2. ${\sim}(\exists x)Hx \rightarrow (y)Ky$        1, QN
F. 1. $(y)By \rightarrow {\sim}(x)Ax$
   2. $(y)By \rightarrow (\exists x){\sim}Ax$        1, QN

Note that in example (E), QN is applied to the antecedent of a conditional, while in example (F), it is applied to the consequent of a conditional.

The following argument and proof illustrate the utility of the quantifier negation rule:

59. Not all animals are moral agents. Only moral agents have rights. Hence, some animals do not have rights. (Ax: x is an animal; Mx: x is a moral agent; Rx: x has rights)

  1.  ${\sim}(x)(Ax \rightarrow Mx)$
  2.  $(x)(Rx \rightarrow Mx)$        $\therefore (\exists x)(Ax \bullet {\sim}Rx)$
  3.  $(\exists x){\sim}(Ax \rightarrow Mx)$     1, QN
  4.  ${\sim}(Ax \rightarrow Mx)$        3, EI
  5.  ${\sim}({\sim}Ax \vee Mx)$        4, MI
  6.  ${\sim}{\sim}Ax \bullet {\sim}Mx$       5, DeM
  7.  ${\sim}Mx$            6, Simp
  8.  $Rx \rightarrow Mx$          2, UI
  9.  ${\sim}Rx$            8, 7, MT
10.  ${\sim}{\sim}Ax$          6, Simp
11.  $Ax$              10, DN
12.  $Ax \bullet {\sim}Rx$         11, 9, Conj
13.  $(\exists x)(Ax \bullet {\sim}Rx)$    12, EG

When a tilde appears on the left side of a quantified statement, it is often useful to apply QN so that one can apply EI or UI. Lines (1), (3), and (4) illustrate this type of sequence, which suggests a third rule of thumb for predicate logic:

> **Rule of Thumb 3:** When a tilde appears on the left side of a quantifier, it is often useful to apply QN and instantiate. (But keep in mind that EI and UI are implicational rules and cannot be applied to parts of a statement.)

Using QN, we can prove the equivalence of statements such as these:

60. Not all animals are cats. (Ax: x is an animal; Cx: x is a cat)

61. Some animals are not cats. (Ax: x is an animal; Cx: x is a cat)

The following proofs show that we can move logically from either one of these statements to the other; hence, they are logically equivalent.

1. ~(x)(Ax → Cx)          ∴ (∃x)(Ax • ~Cx)
2. (∃x)~(Ax → Cx)         1, QN
3. (∃x)~(~Ax ∨ Cx)        2, MI
4. (∃x)(~~Ax • ~Cx)       3, DeM
5. (∃x)(Ax • ~Cx)         4, DN

1. (∃x)(Ax • ~Cx)          ∴ ~(x)(Ax → Cx)
2. (∃x)(~~Ax • ~Cx)       1, DN
3. (∃x)~(~Ax ∨ Cx)        2, DeM
4. (∃x)~(Ax → Cx)         3, MI
5. ~(x)(Ax → Cx)          4, QN

Sometimes, the QN rule enables us to make use of statement logic rules without instantiating. Here is an example:

1. (x)~Ax → (z)Bz
2. (∃z)~Bz               ∴ (∃x)Ax
3. ~(z)Bz                2, QN
4. ~(x)~Ax               1, 3, MT
5. (∃x)~~Ax              4, QN
6. (∃x)Ax                5, DN

The QN rule is often useful when employing the *reductio ad absurdum* (RAA) method. For example:

1. (x)(Lx → Mx)
2. (∃x)Lx               ∴ (∃x)Mx
3. ~(∃x)Mx              Assume
4. (x)~Mx               3, QN
5. Lx                   2, EI
6. Lx → Mx              1, UI
7. Mx                   6, 5, MP
8. ~Mx                  4, UI
9. Mx • ~Mx             7, 8, Conj
10. (∃x)Mx              3–9, RAA

But while RAA and CP can be used in predicate logic as well as in statement logic, *the use of these methods demands an additional restriction on universal general-ization* (UG). We previously stated the UG rule as follows:

$$\mathcal{P}\mathbf{y}$$
$$\therefore (\mathbf{x})\mathcal{P}$$

Where **y** stands for any variable, $\mathcal{P}\mathbf{y}$ is an instance of $(\mathbf{x})\mathcal{P}$, **y** is not free in any line derived by an application of EI, and **y** does not occur free in $(\mathbf{x})\mathcal{P}$.

Now, we must add the following:

> *Restriction:* UG cannot be used within the scope of an assumption for RAA or CP if **y** occurs *free* in the assumption.

To understand the need for this restriction, consider the following invalid argument and erroneous proof:

**62.** If everything is red, then everything is blue. So, all red things are blue. (Rx: x is red; Bx: x is blue)

*In symbols:* (x)Rx → (x)Bx  ∴ (x)(Rx → Bx)

| | |
|---|---|
| 1. (x)Rx → (x)Bx | ∴ (x)(Rx → Bx) |
| 2. Rx | Assume |
| 3. (x)Rx | 2, *incorrect use of UG* [violates the new restriction] |
| 4. (x)Bx | 1, 3, MP |
| 5. Bx | 4, UI |
| 6. Rx → Bx | 2–5, CP |
| 7. (x)(Rx → Bx) | 6, UG |

To see that the argument is invalid, consider this: The premise is true because its antecedent is false—not everything is red. But the conclusion, "All red things are blue," is obviously false. And, of course, any argument with a true premise and a false conclusion is invalid. The invalidity of the argument is also revealed if we apply the finite universe method:

| Ra Rb Ba Bb | (Ra • Rb) → (Ba • Bb)  ∴ (Ra → Ba) • (Rb → Bb) |
|---|---|
| T  F  F  T | TFF  T  FFT      T  F  F  F  FT T |

Our new restriction on UG prevents us from "proving" that such invalid arguments are valid.

Let us consider some further examples of CP and RAA in predicate logic. Here is a correct use of CP:

| | |
|---|---|
| 1. (x)(Rx → Bx) | ∴ (x)Rx → (x)Bx |
| 2. (x)Rx | Assume |
| 3. Rx → Bx | 1, UI |
| 4. Rx | 2, UI |
| 5. Bx | 3, 4, MP |
| 6. (x)Bx | 5, UG |
| 7. (x)Rx → (x)Bx | 2–6, CP |

Here, we have *not* violated the new restriction on UG because the variable *x* does not occur free in the assumption in line (2). Note that this proof shows that one can move logically from the *conclusion* of argument (62) to its *premise*. The following use of CP is also permissible:

```
 1. (x)(Fx → Gx)
 2. (x)(Fx → Hx)              ∴ (x)[Fx → (Gx • Hx)]
 3. Fx                        Assume
 4. Fx → Gx                   1, UI
 5. Fx → Hx                   2, UI
 6. Gx                        3, 4, MP
 7. Hx                        3, 5, MP
 8. Gx • Hx                   6, 7, Conj
 9. Fx → (Gx • Hx)            3–8, CP
10. (x)[Fx → (Gx • Hx)]       9, UG
```

This proof does *not* violate our new restriction on UG because UG is not used *within the scope of the assumption*. Rather, we apply UG after we have discharged the assumption. Here, we may add a fourth rule of thumb for predicate logic:

> **Rule of Thumb 4**: If the conclusion is a universally quantified statement containing an arrow, use CP to prove the relevant conditional and then apply UG.

When the conclusion of an argument is an existentially quantified statement, RAA is often useful. For example:

```
 1. (x)(Px → Sx)
 2. Pa ∨ Pb                   ∴ (∃x)Sx
 3. ~(∃x)Sx                   Assume
 4. (x)~Sx                    3, QN
 5. Pa → Sa                   1, UI
 6. ~Sa                       4, UI
 7. ~Pa                       5, 6, MT
 8. Pb                        2, 7, DS
 9. Pb → Sb                   1, UI
10. Sb                        9, 8, MP
11. ~Sb                       4, UI
12. Sb • ~Sb                  10, 11, Conj
13. (∃x)Sx                    3–12, RAA
```

This argument illustrates our fifth and final rule of thumb for predicate logic:

> **Rule of Thumb 5**: When the conclusion of an argument is an existentially quantified statement, RAA is often useful.

As in statement logic, it is sometimes useful to employ more than one assumption in the same proof. In the following proof, CP and RAA are combined:

---

### Summary of Rules of Thumb for Predicate Logic

1. Apply EI before you apply UI.
2. Universally instantiate to free variables or individual constants and apply the rules of statement logic.
3. When a tilde appears on the left side of a quantifier, it is often useful to apply QN and instantiate. (But keep in mind that EI and UI are implicational rules and cannot be applied to parts of a statement.)
4. If the conclusion is a universally quantified statement containing an arrow, use CP to prove the relevant conditional and then apply UG.
5. When the conclusion of an argument is an existentially quantified statement, RAA is often useful.

---

| | |
|---|---|
| 1. (x)Ax ∨ (x)Bx | ∴ (x)(~Ax → Bx) |
| 2. ~Ax | Assume (for CP) |
| 3. (x)Ax | Assume (for RAA) |
| 4. Ax | 3, UI |
| 5. Ax • ~Ax | 4, 2, Conj |
| 6. ~(x)Ax | 3–5, RAA |
| 7. (x)Bx | 1, 6, DS |
| 8. Bx | 7, UI |
| 9. ~Ax → Bx | 2–8, CP |
| 10. (x)(~Ax → Bx) | 9, UG |

This proof does not violate our new restriction on UG because UG is not used within the scope of the assumption in line (2). We could also construct a proof for this argument using RAA alone, but it would be longer.

These exercises provide you with practice in using QN, RAA, and CP.

## ◆ Exercise 9.4

**Part A:** Proofs  Construct proofs to show that the following arguments are valid. You may use direct proof, CP, or RAA.

* **1.** (x)Ax → (x)Bx,  ~(x)Bx ∴ (∃x)~Ax

   **2.** ~(∃y)Cy,  (y)~Cy → (z)Dz ∴ Db

   **3.** ~(x)~Fx ∴ (∃x)Fx

* **4.** ~(∃x)~Gx ∴ (x)Gx

   **5.** (∃y)Hy → (∃y)Jy,  (y)~Jy ∴ ~Ha

  6. $(z)[(Kz \lor Lz) \to Mz]$ $\therefore$ $(z)(Lz \to Mz)$
* 7. $(x)(Nx \to Ox)$ $\therefore$ $\sim(x)Ox \to \sim(x)Nx$
  8. $\sim(\exists x)\sim Px$, $\sim(\exists y)Sy \lor \sim(x)Px$ $\therefore$ $\sim Sd$
  9. $(x)\sim Rx \to (\exists x)\sim\sim Tx$ $\therefore$ $(x)\sim Tx \to (\exists x)Rx$
*10. $(x)(Ax \to \sim Bx)$, $(y)Ay$ $\therefore$ $(z)\sim Bz$
 11. $\sim(\exists x)(Fx \cdot \sim Gx)$ $\therefore$ $(x)(Fx \to Gx)$
 12. $(x)(Jx \to Kx)$ $\therefore$ $(x)[Jx \to ((y)(Ky \to Ly) \to Lx)]$
*13. $(\exists x)[Bx \to (y)\sim Cy]$, $\sim(\exists y)Cy \to \sim(\exists z)Dz$ $\therefore$ $(x)Bx \to (z)\sim Dz$
 14. $(\exists x)[Fx \cdot (y)(Gy \to Hx)]$, $(x)[Fx \to (y)(By \to \sim Hx)]$ $\therefore$ $(x)(Gx \to \sim Bx)$
 15. $(x)[Dx \to (\exists y)(Fy \cdot Gy)]$ $\therefore$ $(x)\sim Fx \to \sim(\exists y)Dy$
*16. $\sim(x)Mx \lor (\exists x)\sim Mx$, $(\exists x)Sx \to (x)Mx$, $Sb \lor (x)\sim Px$ $\therefore$ $\sim Pa$
 17. $[(x)Hx \to (\exists x)Gx] \to \sim(\exists y)(Fy \lor (\exists z)Tz)$, $\sim(x)Fx \to (\exists x)Gx$,
     $(x)Hx \to (\exists x)\sim Fx$ $\therefore$ $(\exists x)\sim Tx$
 18. $(x)Hx \lor [(x)Kx \cdot (\exists x)\sim Lx]$, $(x)Hx \to \sim(x)Nx$, $\sim(x)Lx \to (\exists x)\sim Nx$,
     $(x)Mx \lor (x)Nx$ $\therefore$ $Mc$
*19. $(x)(Lx \leftrightarrow (y)My)$ $\therefore$ $(x)Lx \lor (x)\sim Lx$
 20. $(x)Ax \lor (x)Bx$ $\therefore$ $(x)(Ax \lor Bx)$ [*Hint:* Use two assumptions.]

**Part B: Proofs**   Construct proofs to show that the following symbolic arguments are valid. You may use direct proof, CP, or RAA.

* 1. $(\exists x)Fx \to (\exists x)(Gx \cdot Hx)$, $(\exists x)Hx \to (x)Jx$ $\therefore$ $(x)(Fx \to Jx)$
  2. $(x)(Wx \to Sx)$ $\therefore$ $(\exists x)Wx \to (\exists x)Sx$
  3. $(x)\sim Kx \lor (\exists x)Lx$, $(x)\sim Lx$ $\therefore$ $\sim Kb$
* 4. $\sim(\exists x)Mx \to (\exists x)(Nx \cdot Px)$, $(x)\sim Px$ $\therefore$ $(\exists x)Mx$
  5. $\sim(\exists x)(Rx \lor Sx) \lor (x)Tx$, $(\exists x)\sim Tx$ $\therefore$ $\sim(\exists x)Sx$
  6. $(x)(Ax \to (y)By)$ $\therefore$ $(x)Ax \to (x)Bx$
* 7. $(x)(Cx \to Dx)$, $\sim(\exists x)Cx \to (\exists x)Dx$ $\therefore$ $\sim(x)\sim Dx$
  8. $(z)(Ez \to (\exists x)Fx)$, $(z)Gz \to (\exists z)Ez$ $\therefore$ $(z)Gz \to (\exists z)Fz$
  9. $\sim(x)\sim Ax$, $(\exists x)Ax \to (x)Bx$, $(x)[(Bx \lor Cx) \to Dx]$ $\therefore$ $(x)Dx$
*10. $(\exists x)\sim Kx \to \sim(\exists x)Dx$, $\sim(x)Kx$, $Db \leftrightarrow Qa$ $\therefore$ $\sim Qa$
 11. $\sim[(x)Fx \lor (\exists x)Gx]$, $(\exists x)\sim Fx \to (y)Hy$, $(x)\sim Gx \to (z)Jz$ $\therefore$ $(x)(Hx \cdot Jx)$
 12. $\sim(x)Kx \to (\exists x)Lx$, $(\exists x)\sim Kx \to (x)(Lx \to Mx)$ $\therefore$ $\sim(x)Kx \to (\exists x)Mx$
*13. $\sim[(x)Ax \to (\exists x)Bx]$, $(\exists x)\sim Cx \to (\exists x)Bx$, $(x)[(Ax \cdot Cx) \to Da]$ $\therefore$ $Da$
 14. $\sim[(y)Zy \cdot (y)Wy]$, $(\exists y)\sim Zy \to (y)Uy$, $(\exists y)Ry \to (y)Wy$ $\therefore$ $(y)(Uy \lor \sim Ry)$
 15. $Ba \leftrightarrow \sim(\exists x)Cx$, $(\exists x)Ax \lor (x)Bx$, $(x)\sim Ax$ $\therefore$ $\sim Ce$

* **16.** (x)[(Ax → ~Bx) ∨ Cb], ~(∃x)Cx, (∃y)By ∴ ~(y)Ay

  **17.** (∃x)Sx → (y)(~Ty → Uy), (∃x)Rx → (∃x)~Tx
    ∴ (∃x)(Sx • Rx) → (∃z)Uz

  **18.** (x)(~Gx ∨ ~Hx), (x)[(Jx → Fx) → Hx] ∴ ~(∃x)(Fx • Gx)

* **19.** [~(x)(R • Px) → (R → ~(x)Px)] → (∃x)[Ax • (y)(~Ay ∨ ~By)]
    ∴ ~(x)Bx

  **20.** (x)Px ∴ (∃x)[Px • (Qx → (y)Qy)]

**Part C:** Logical Equivalents  Construct proofs to show that the following are valid. By constructing these proofs, you will show that each pair of statements is logically equivalent. Take special note of the fourth and fifth pairs, as these indicate the somewhat surprising behavior of quantifiers that bind variables in the antecedent of a conditional.

*  **1.** (x)(Ax • Bx) ∴ (x)Ax • (x)Bx
  **2.** (x)Ax • (x)Bx ∴ (x)(Ax • Bx)
  **3.** (∃x)(Ax ∨ Bx) ∴ (∃x)Ax ∨ (∃x)Bx
*  **4.** (∃x)Ax ∨ (∃x)Bx ∴ (∃x)(Ax ∨ Bx)
  **5.** (x)(P → Ax) ∴ P → (x)Ax
  **6.** P → (x)Ax ∴ (x)(P → Ax)
*  **7.** (x)(Ax → P) ∴ (∃x)Ax → P

  **8.** (∃x)Ax → P ∴ (x)(Ax → P)
  **9.** (∃x)(Ax → P) ∴ (x)Ax → P
 **10.** (x)Ax → P ∴ (∃x)(Ax → P)
 **11.** (∃x)(P → Ax) ∴ P → (∃x)Ax
 **12.** P → (∃x)Ax ∴ (∃x)(P → Ax)
 **13.** (x)Ax ∨ P ∴ (x)(Ax ∨ P)
 **14.** (x)(Ax ∨ P) ∴ (x)Ax ∨ P

**Part D:** English Arguments  Symbolize the following arguments, using the schemes of abbreviation provided. Then construct proofs to show that the arguments are valid. You may use either direct proof, CP, or RAA.

*  **1.** Every act of terrorism is deplorable. If there is an act of terrorism that either promotes the general welfare or corrects an injustice, then some acts of terrorism are not deplorable. So, no act of terrorism corrects an injustice. (Tx: x is an act of terrorism; Dx: x is deplorable; Wx: x promotes the general welfare; Cx: x corrects an injustice)

  **2.** All brain processes are physical processes. No mental processes are tangible. Therefore, every brain process that is a mental process is also an intangible physical process. (Bx: x is a brain process; Px: x is a physical process; Mx: x is a mental process; Tx: x is tangible)

  **3.** Either Smith is a criminally insane person, or all kleptomaniacs are criminally insane persons. But it is not the case that there are persons who are criminally insane. We may infer that Smith is not a kleptomaniac. (Cx: x is criminally insane; Px: x is a person; Kx: x is a kleptomaniac; s: Smith)

*  **4.** An act of killing is wrong if and only if it eliminates the prospect of future valuable life. To kill a potential person is to kill. To kill a fetus is to kill a

potential person. To kill a potential person is to eliminate the prospect of future valuable life. It follows that killing a fetus is wrong. (Kx: x is an act of killing; Wx: x is wrong; Ex: x eliminates the prospect of future valuable life; Px: x is an act of killing a potential person; Fx: x is an act of killing a fetus)

5. If there are any gods, then all free creatures are predestined. If there are any free creatures, then whatever is predestined is morally responsible. Accordingly, if there are any gods, then all free creatures are morally responsible. (Gx: x is a god; Fx: x is a free creature; Px: x is predestined; Mx: x is morally responsible)

6. No absolute right can be denied. Every right can be denied if one person's right to life can conflict with another person's right to life. Unfortunately, one person's right to life can conflict with another person's right to life. Therefore, no rights are absolute rights. (Ax: x is an absolute right; Rx: x is a right; Dx: x can be denied; P: One person's right to life can conflict with another person's right to life)

* 7. Some reprobates are boring. Some highly moral individuals are humorous. If there are any reprobates, then highly moral individuals are fascinating if they are humorous. We may conclude that there are highly moral individuals who are fascinating. (Rx: x is a reprobate; Bx: x is boring; Mx: x is highly moral; Hx: x is humorous; Fx: x is fascinating)

8. If some poltergeists are not ghosts, then some haunted houses are dangerous. But it is not the case that there are any ghosts or haunted houses. Therefore, it is not the case that there are any poltergeists. (Px: x is a poltergeist; Gx: x is a ghost; Hx: x is a haunted house; Dx: x is dangerous)

9. Contraception is not right if it violates the purpose of sex or obviates valuable life. Some acts of contraception obviate valuable life. If a thing is not right, then it is wrong. Hence, some acts of contraception are wrong. (Cx: x is an act of contraception; Rx: x is right; Vx: x violates the purpose of sex; Ox: x obviates valuable life; Wx: x is wrong)

10. If some acts of torturing the innocent are not wrong, then all acts of torturing the innocent are right. Some acts of torturing the innocent are approved by society. Consequently, if no acts of torturing the innocent are right, then some things approved by society are wrong. (Tx: x is an act of torturing the innocent; Wx: x is wrong; Rx: x is right; Sx: x is approved by society)

**Part E:** Ready for a Challenge?   Try the following proof. It's a bit on the long side: (x)Px  ∴  ~(∃x)Qx  ↔  ~[(∃x)(Px • Qx) • (y)(Qy → Py)]

## 9.5  The Logic of Relations: Symbolizations

Thus far, we have considered only **monadic** (one-place) predicate letters, such as Ax, By, and Cz. Monadic predicate letters are adequate for ascribing an attribute (e.g., being human) to an individual. But individuals not only have attributes, they also bear relations to one another. For example, we can say that Smith *is older than* Jones or that Elizabeth *is a sister of* John. Modern predicate logic encompasses the logic of relations, but to symbolize relations, we need predicate letters with more than one place. These are called **polyadic** predicate letters. For instance, we can use *Oxy* to stand for "*x* is older than *y*" or *Sxy* to stand for "*x* is a sister of *y*."

Here is a simple example of an argument that involves a relational predicate:

> 63. Al is taller than Bob. Bob is taller than Chris. If one thing is taller than a second and the second is taller than a third, then the first is taller than the third. So, Al is taller than Chris.

We need a polyadic predicate letter to symbolize the relation "*x* is taller than *y*," so here is a scheme of abbreviation for argument (63):

> Txy: x is taller than y; a: Al; b: Bob; c: Chris

Using this scheme of abbreviation, "Al is taller than Bob" becomes simply *Tab*, and "Bob is taller than Chris" becomes *Tbc*. To symbolize the third premise, we first translate it into logicese: "For all *x*, for all *y*, and for all *z*, if *x* is taller than *y* and *y* is taller than *z*, then *x* is taller than *z*." The complete symbolization looks like this:

> 64. Tab, Tbc, (x)(y)(z)[(Txy • Tyz) → Txz] ∴ Tac

And the proof runs as follows:

1. Tab
2. Tbc
3. (x)(y)(z)[(Txy • Tyz) → Txz]     ∴ Tac
4. (y)(z)[(Tay • Tyz) → Taz]     3, UI
5. (z)[(Tab • Tbz) → Taz]     4, UI
6. (Tab • Tbc) → Tac     5, UI
7. Tab • Tbc     1, 2, Conj
8. Tac     6, 7, MP

Although we already have the inference rules needed for constructing proofs that involve relations, we will delay a detailed discussion of such proofs until the next section. For now, let us turn our attention to symbolizing statements involving relations.

Statements involving relations can be rather difficult to symbolize, but much of the difficulty can be removed by working through a series of well-chosen examples. Perhaps the most important skill to develop here is that of translating English into logicese. How would you symbolize the following sentence?

> 65. Someone loves everyone. (Px: x is a person; Lxy: x loves y)

First, let's rewrite it in logicese: "There exists an $x$ such that $x$ is a person, and for every $y$, if $y$ is a person, then $x$ loves $y$." Once we have the logicese, symbolizing is easy:

66. $(\exists x)[Px \bullet (y)(Py \rightarrow Lxy)]$

Now, examine the following closely related sentences, along with their symbolic translations. (The scheme of abbreviation remains the same.)

67. Everyone loves someone.

In logicese, we have "For any $x$, if $x$ is a person, then there exists a $y$ such that $y$ is a person and $x$ loves $y$." In symbols:

68. $(x)[Px \rightarrow (\exists y)(Py \bullet Lxy)]$

How would you symbolize the following sentence?

69. No one loves everyone.

In logicese, we have "For every $x$, if $x$ is a person, then it is not true that for every $y$, if $y$ is a person, $x$ loves $y$." In symbols:

70. $(x)[Px \rightarrow \sim(y)(Py \rightarrow Lxy)]$

Statement (69) can also be translated into logicese as follows: "It is not the case that there is an $x$ such that $x$ is a person and for all $y$, if $y$ is a person, then $x$ loves $y$." So, we can also symbolize (69) this way:

71. $\sim(\exists x)[Px \bullet (y)(Py \rightarrow Lxy)]$

We can prove that statements (70) and (71) are logically equivalent. To do this, we must show that (70) implies (71), and vice versa. The following proof shows that (71) implies (70). That (70) implies (71) is left as an exercise.

| | |
|---|---|
| 1. $\sim(\exists x)[Px \bullet (y)(Py \rightarrow Lxy)]$ | $\therefore (x)[Px \rightarrow \sim(y)(Py \rightarrow Lxy)]$ |
| 2. $Px$ | Assume (for CP) |
| 3. $(x)\sim[Px \bullet (y)(Py \rightarrow Lxy)]$ | 1, QN |
| 4. $(y)(Py \rightarrow Lxy)$ | Assume (for RAA) |
| 5. $\sim[Px \bullet (y)(Py \rightarrow Lxy)]$ | 3, UI |
| 6. $\sim Px \vee \sim(y)(Py \rightarrow Lxy)$ | 5, DeM |
| 7. $\sim\sim(y)(Py \rightarrow Lxy)$ | 4, DN |
| 8. $\sim Px$ | 6, 7, DS |
| 9. $Px \bullet \sim Px$ | 2, 8, Conj |
| 10. $\sim(y)(Py \rightarrow Lxy)$ | 4–9, RAA |
| 11. $Px \rightarrow \sim(y)(Py \rightarrow Lxy)$ | 2–10, CP |
| 12. $(x)[Px \rightarrow \sim(y)(Py \rightarrow Lxy)]$ | 11, UG |

Now, try to symbolize the following sentence:

> **72.** No one loves anyone.

In logicese, we have "For any *x*, if *x* is a person, then for any *y*, if *y* is a person, *x* does not love *y*." In symbols:

> **73.** (x)[Px → (y)(Py → ~Lxy)]

Statement (72) can also be translated into logicese as follows: "It is not the case that there is an *x* such that *x* is a person and there is a *y* such that *y* is a person, and *x* loves *y*." In symbols:

> **74.** ~(∃x)[Px • (∃y)(Py • Lxy)]

Predicate letters can be of more than two places. For example, the following sentence involves the three-place relation "*x* steals *y* from *z*":

> **75.** Every thief steals something valuable from someone. (Tx: x is a thief, Sxyz: x steals y from z; Vx: x is valuable; Px: x is a person)

In logicese, we have "For any *x*, if *x* is a thief, then there is a *y* such that *y* is valuable, and there is a *z* such that *z* is a person, and *x* steals *y* from *z*." The symbolization looks like this:

> **76.** (x)(Tx → (∃y)[Vy • (∃z)(Pz • Sxyz)])

Again, our symbolization brings out the logical complexity that can be present in rather ordinary English sentences.

As mentioned previously, the best way to ensure accuracy of translation into symbols within predicate logic is first to translate English into logicese and then to translate logicese into symbols. The following short list of examples should serve as a useful guide for this process.

| English | Logicese | Symbols |
|---|---|---|
| 1. No woman is smarter than Eve. (Wx: x is a woman; Sxy: x is smarter than y; e: Eve) | For all x (if x is woman, then it is not the case that x is smarter than e). | (x)(Wx → ~Sxe) |
| 2. If Adam is taller than Eve, then someone is taller than Eve. (a: Adam; c: Eve; Txy: x is taller than y; Px: x is a person) | If a is taller than e, then there is an x such that (x is a person and x is taller than e). | Tae → (∃x)(Px • Txe) |

| 3. | No one is shorter than himself. (Px: x is a person; Sxy: x is shorter than y) | For all x (if x is a person, then it is not the case that x is shorter than x). | (x)(Px → ~Sxx) |
|----|----|----|----|
| 4. | No one is shorter than everyone. (Px: x is a person; Sxy: x is shorter than y) | For all x [if x is a person, then it is not the case that for all y (if y is a person then x is shorter than y)]. | (x)[Px → ~(y)(Py → Sxy)] |
| 5. | Everyone is shorter than someone. (Px: x is a person; Sxy: x is shorter than y) | For any x [if x is a person, then there is a y such that (y is a person and x is shorter than y)]. | (x)[Px → (∃y)(Py • Sxy)] |
| 6. | Every adult gives a present to some child. (Ax: is an adult; Gxyz: x gives y to z; Px: x is a present; Cx: x is a child) | For all x [if x is an adult, then there is a y such that (y is a present and there is a z such that (z is a child, and x gives y to z)]. | (x)[Ax → (∃y)(Py • (∃z)(Cz • Gxyz)] |

In closing this section, let us take note of certain general characteristics of relations. Some relations are **symmetrical**. If a relation R is symmetrical, then if *a* bears R to *b*, *b* bears R to *a*. For example, the relation "being a sibling of" is symmetrical, for if Jeff is a sibling of Jane, then Jane must be a sibling of Jeff. On the other hand, the relation "being a mother of" is **asymmetrical**, for if Thelma is the mother of Sharlene, then Sharlene is not the mother of Thelma. To generalize: If a relation R is asymmetrical, then if *a* bears R to *b*, *b* does not bear R to *a*. Note that some relations are **nonsymmetrical**—that is, they are neither symmetrical nor asymmetrical. The relation "being a sister of" is nonsymmetrical, for if Jane is a sister of Chris, Chris may or may not be a sister of Jane—it all depends on whether Chris is male or female.

A relation R is **reflexive** if things must bear R to themselves. For example, each thing is identical with itself. So, identity is a reflexive relation. An **irreflexive** relation is one an entity cannot bear to itself. For example, since nothing can be larger than itself, "being larger than" is an irreflexive relation. And a **nonreflexive** relation is one that is neither reflexive nor irreflexive. "Being proud of" is nonreflexive because a person may or may not be proud of him- or herself.

If a relation R is **transitive**, then if *a* bears R to *b* and *b* bears R to *c*, *a* bears R to *c*. "Being taller than" is transitive. To illustrate: If Al is taller than Bob, and Bob is taller than Chris, then Al must be taller than Chris. On the other hand, "being father of" is an **intransitive** relation, for if Earl is the father of John and John is the father of Drew, then Earl cannot be the father of Drew. To generalize: If a relation R is intransitive, then if *a* bears R to *b* and *b* bears R to *c*, *a* does not bear R to *c*. Finally, a relation is **nontransitive** if it is neither transitive nor intransitive. The relation "being an acquaintance of" is nontransitive. If Rick is an acquaintance of Dawn and Dawn is an acquaintance of Pete, then Rick may or may not be an acquaintance of Pete.

The following exercises will give you some practice in applying the concepts introduced in this section.

## ◆ *Exercise 9.5*

**Part A:** Matching  Match the item on the left with the appropriate characteristic on the right.

| | |
|---|---|
| ____ | 1. If x is older than y and y is older than z, then x is older than z. |
| ____ | 2. Nothing is bigger than itself. |
| ____ | 3. If x is shorter than y, then y is not shorter than x. |
| ____ | 4. Everything is the same size as itself. |
| ____ | 5. If x is married to y, then y is married to x. |
| ____ | 6. If x is greater than y, then y is not greater than x. |
| ____ | 7. If x is equal to y, then y is equal to x. |
| ____ | 8. If x is the mother of y and y is the mother of z, then x is not the mother of z. |
| ____ | 9. If x loves y and y loves z, then x may or may not love z. |
| ____ | 10. If x admires y, then y may or may not admire x. |
| ____ | 11. A person may or may not hate himself. |
| ____ | 12. If x is obligated to y and y is obligated to z, then x may or may not be obligated to z. |

**A.** Symmetrical
**B.** Asymmetrical
**C.** Nonsymmetrical
**D.** Reflexive
**E.** Irreflexive
**F.** Nonreflexive
**G.** Transitive
**H.** Intransitive
**I.** Nontransitive

**Part B:** Symbolizing  Symbolize the following statements using the schemes of abbreviation provided.

* 1. Nothing stands to the left of itself. (Lxy: x stands to the left of y)

 2. No human is taller than Goliath. (Hx: x is human; Txy: x is taller than y; g: Goliath)

 3. No human is taller than himself. (Hx: x is human; Txy: x is taller than y)

* 4. Some financier is richer than everyone. (Fx: x is a financier; Rxy: x is richer than y; Px: x is a person)

 5. Someone gives everyone something. (Px: x is a person; Gxyz: x gives to y [object] z)

6. Someone gives someone everything. (Px: x is a person; Gxyz: x gives to y [object] z)

* 7. No deity is weaker than some human. (Dx: x is a deity; Hx: x is human; Wxy: x is weaker than y)

8. No one gives anyone anything. (Px: x is a person; Gxyz: x gives to y [object] z)

9. Everyone gives someone something. (Px: x is a person; Gxyz: x gives to y [object] z)

* 10. No one who is poor is richer than someone who is wealthy. (Ox: x is a person; Px: x is poor; Rxy: x is richer than y; Wx: x is wealthy)

11. No one is more fun than Chris. (Px: x is person; Fxy: x is more fun than y; c: Chris)

12. No cat is smarter than some horse. (Cx: x is cat; Sxy: x is smarter than y; Hx: x is a horse)

* 13. No mouse is mightier than himself. (Mx: x is a mouse; Mxy: x is mightier than y)

14. Every woman is stronger than some man. (Wx: x is a woman; Sxy: x is stronger than y; Mx: x is a man)

15. If Apollo is better than Hera and Hera is better than Cronos, then Apollo is better than Cronos. (Bxy: x is better than y; a: Apollo; h: Hera; c: Cronos)

* 16. Every moviegoer admires Bogart. (Mx: x is moviegoer; Axy: x admires y; b: Bogart)

17. Some moviegoers admire themselves as well as Bogart. (Mx: x is a moviegoer; Axy: x admires y; b: Bogart)

18. Some saints help someone everyday. (Sx: x is a saint; Hxyz: x helps y on z; Px: x is person; Dx: x is a day)

* 19. No saint helps everyone everyday. (Sx: x is a saint; Hxyz: x helps y on z; Px: x is person; Dx: x is a day)

20. Everyone falls in love with someone at some enchanted moment. (Px: x is a person; Lxyz: x falls in love with y at z; Ex: x is enchanted; Mx: x is a moment)

21. The relation "being older than" is asymmetrical. (Oxy: x is older than y)

* 22. The relation "being the father of" is intransitive. (Fxy: x is the father of y)

23. The relation "being larger than" is irreflexive. (Lxy: x is larger than y)

24. The relation "being south of" is transitive. (Sxy: x is south of y)

* 25. The relation "being near to" is symmetrical. (Nxy: x is near to y)

**Part C:** More Matching    Match the item on the left with the appropriate characteristic on the right.

___ 1. Nothing is smaller than itself.

___ 2. If x hates y, then y may or may not hate x.

___ 3. If x is the same size as y, then y is the same size as x.

___ 4. Everything is the same weight as itself.

___ 5. If x is near y, then y is near x.

___ 6. If x is less than y, then y is not less than x.

___ 7. If x likes y and y likes z, then x may or may not like z.

___ 8. If x is the father of y and y is the father of z, then x is not the father of z.

___ 9. If x is taller than y, then y is not taller than x.

___ 10. If x is younger than y and y is younger than z, then x is younger than z.

A. Symmetrical

B. Asymmetrical

C. Nonsymmetrical

D. Reflexive

E. Irreflexive

F. Nonreflexive

G. Transitive

H. Intransitive

I. Nontransitive

**Part D: More Symbolizing** Symbolize the following statements using the schemes of abbreviation provided.

\* 1. Someone gets angry at everyone. (Px: x is a person; Axy: x gets angry at y)

2. Everyone laughs at someone. (Px: x is a person; Lxy: x laughs at y)

3. Everything is either colorless or the same color as itself. (Cx: x has a color; Sxy: x has the same color as y)

\* 4. Some people like themselves, but some people do not like themselves. (Px: x is a person; Lxy: x likes y)

5. No one laughs at anyone. (Px: x is a person; Lxy: x laughs at y)

6. Some students find Kant boring, but Amy is a student who does not find Kant boring. (Sx: x is a student; Bxy: x finds y boring; k: Kant; a: Amy)

\* 7. Everything is caused by something (or other). (Cxy: x is caused by y)

8. Nothing causes everything. (Cxy: x causes y)

9. Something causes everything. (Cxy: x causes y)

\* 10. Nothing causes anything. (Cxy: x causes y)

11. Everyone gets angry at someone about something. (Px: x is a person; Axyz: x gets angry at y about z)

12. Everything has a cause; but for all x and y, if x precedes y, then y does not cause x. (Cxy: x causes y; Pxy: x precedes y)

13. Every entity is either necessary or dependent on a necessary entity. (Nx: x is necessary; Dxy: x is dependent on y)

14. No logician argues about every subject with everyone. (Lx: x is a logician; Sx: x is a subject; Px: x is a person; Axyz: x argues about y with z)

15. Either nothing is dependent on anything or everything is dependent on something. (Dxy: x is dependent on y)

16. No one is obligated to everyone. (Px: x is a person; Oxy: x is obligated to y)

17. Everyone is obligated to someone. (Px: x is a person; Oxy: x is obligated to y)

18. The relation "being to the north of" is transitive. (Nxy: x is north of y)

19. The relation "being next to" is symmetrical. (Nxy: x is next to y)

20. The relation "being the same shape as" is reflexive. (Sxy: x is the same shape as y)

21. Some number is greater than itself. (Nx: x is a number; Gxy: x is greater than y)

22. God will punish the wicked. (g: God; Wx: x is wicked; Pxy: x will punish y)

23. Some philosopher studies every book with some teacher. (Px: x is a philosopher; Sxyz: x studies y with z; Bx: x is a book; Tx: x is a teacher)

24. Every philosopher studies some book with every teacher. (Px: x is a philosopher; Sxyz: x studies y with z; Bx: x is a book; Tx: x is a teacher)

25. No philosopher studies any book with any teacher. (Px: x is a philosopher; Sxyz: x studies y with z; Bx: x is a book; Tx: x is a teacher)

**Part E: Ready for a Challenge?** Symbolize the following sentences. Some of these are rather difficult.

\* 1. Someone is having her cake and eating it too. (Hxy: x is having y; Px: x is a person; Cx: x is a cake; Exy: x is eating y)

2. There is some particular thing that is between any two things. (Bxyz: x is between y and z)

3. Between any two things there is something or other. (Bxyz: x is between y and z)

\* 4. All metaphysicians except idealists postulate the existence of at least one corporeal entity. (Mx: x is a metaphysician; Ix: x is an idealist; Pxy: x postulates the existence of y; Cx: x is a corporeal entity)

5. Some guys have all the luck. (Gx: x is a guy; Hxy: x has y; Lx: x is a bit of luck)

6. Everybody needs somebody sometime. (Px: x is a person; Tx: x is a time; Nxyz: x needs y at z)

\* 7. Everyone who hates someone hates herself. (Px: x is a person; Hxy: x hates y)

8. There is someone who loves and is loved by Brit. (Px: x is a person; Lxy: x loves y; b: Brit)

9. No bank is without at least some money. (Bx: x is a bank; Pxy: x is in y; Mx: x is a unit of money)

* **10.** Some planets' moons are Jupiter's moons. (Px: x is a planet; Mxy: x is a moon of y; j: Jupiter)

11. Nobody weds anyone to anyone, unless she meets them both. (Px: x is a person; Wxyz: x weds y to z; Mxy: x meets y)

12. Once upon a time in a place far away, there lived a mighty warrior. (Tx: x is a time; Px: x is a place; Fx: x is far away; Wx: x is a mighty warrior; Lxyz: x lived at y during z)

* **13.** There was a time when nobody lived anywhere. (Tx: x is a time; Rx: x is a person; Px: x is a place; Lxyz: x lived at y during z)

14. A dog's bark is worse than his bite. (Dx: x is a dog; Bxy: x is a bark of y; Wxy: x is worse than y; Txy: x is a bite of y)

15. Every even number has a successor. (Ex: x is even; Nx: x is a number; Hxy: x has y; Sx: x is a successor)

* **16.** A rolling stone gathers no moss. (Rx: x rolls; Sx: x is a stone; Gxy: x gathers y; Mx: x is moss)

17. If anything can kill a fast-moving mammal, the cheetah can. (Kxy: x can kill y; Fx: x is fast-moving; Mx: x is a mammal; Cx: x is a cheetah)

18. An Italian's dinner is spicier than a Norweigian's. (Ix: x is an Italian; Dxy: x is a dinner of y; Sxy: x is spicier than y; Nx: x is a Norwegian)

* **19.** If anyone is married to anyone, then someone wed them both. (Px: x is a person; Mxy: x is married to y; Wxyz: x wed y to z)

20. You can fool some of the people all of the time and all of the people some of the time, but you can't fool all of the people all of the time. (Fxyz: x can fool y at z; Px: x is a person; Tx: x is a time)

## 9.6  *The Logic of Relations: Proofs*

The inference rules for predicate logic introduced in sections 9.3 and 9.4 are sufficient for the logic of relations. But it will be helpful to highlight some new types of situations that can arise and to issue some important reminders regarding restrictions on our inference rules.

First, if you have a premise with more than one quantifier, apply UI or EI to remove the quantifiers one at a time, from left to right. Here is an example:

| | |
|---|---|
| 1. $(\exists x)(y)Hxy$ | $\therefore (\exists x)Hxx$ |
| 2. $(y)Hxy$ | 1, EI |
| 3. $Hxx$ | 2, UI |
| 4. $(\exists x)Hxx$ | 3, EG |

In this connection, remember that UI and EI are implicational rules, and hence they cannot be applied to *parts* of statements. For this reason, the following use of UI is incorrect:

1. (∃x)(y)Hxy                     ∴ (∃x)Hxx
2. (∃x)Hxy                        1, *incorrect use of UI*

We can apply UI only to *universally* quantified statements, and (∃x)(y)Hxy is not a universally quantified statement. Similarly, we can apply EI only to *existentially* quantified statements. Consider the following proof:

1. (∃x)(∃y)Fxy → Gb
2. (x)(y)Fxy                      ∴ Gb
3. (y)Fxy                         2, UI
4. Fxy                            3, UI
5. (∃y)Fxy                        4, EG
6. (∃x)(∃y)Fxy                    5, EG
7. Gb                             1, 6, MP

May we infer (∃y)Fxy → Gb from premise (1) by EI? No, for in doing so, we would be applying EI to *part* of a statement (specifically, to the antecedent of a conditional). In the first premise, (∃x) has scope over only (∃y)Fxy. Incidentally, notice that just as we removed the quantifiers on premise (2) one at a time, we put quantifiers back on one at a time also, at lines (5) and (6).

Second, remember that EG and UG are implicational rules. Is the following application of EG correct?

1. (x)Ax → Bac        ∴ (x)Ax → (∃y)Byc
2. (x)Ax → (∃y)Byc    1, EG

No. Here EG has been applied to part of a statement, specifically to the consequent of a conditional. However, the following proof is correct:

1. (x)Ax → Bac        ∴ (x)Ax → (∃y)Byc
2. (x)Ax              Assume
3. Bac                1, 2, MP
4. (∃y)Byc            3, EG
5. (x)Ax → (∃y)Byc    2–4, CP

Is the following use of UG correct?

1. (x)[(y)Lxy → Ma]   ∴ (x)(y)Lxy → Ma
2. (y)Lxy → Ma        1, UI
3. (x)(y)Lxy → Ma     2, UG

No. We cannot apply UG to part of a statement, and here we have applied UG to the antecedent of a conditional. We can, however, show that the argument is valid using CP:

$$
\begin{array}{lll}
& 1.\ (x)[(y)Lxy \rightarrow Ma] & \therefore\ (x)(y)Lxy \rightarrow Ma \\
& 2.\ (x)(y)Lxy & \text{Assume} \\
& 3.\ (y)Lxy \rightarrow Ma & 1,\ \text{UI} \\
& 4.\ (y)Lxy & 2,\ \text{UI} \\
& 5.\ Ma & 3,\ 4,\ \text{MP} \\
& 6.\ (x)(y)Lxy \rightarrow Ma & 2\text{--}5,\ \text{CP}
\end{array}
$$

Third, when applying UI, take care that the instantial variable is free. The second form of UI allows us to move from $(x)\mathscr{P}$ to $\mathscr{P}\mathbf{y}$, where the bold letter $\mathbf{y}$ stands for any variable and $\mathscr{P}\mathbf{y}$ is an instance of $(x)\mathscr{P}$. The following inference violates this rule:

$$
\begin{array}{lll}
1.\ (x)(\exists y)Gyx & & \\
2.\ (\exists y)Gyy & & 1,\ \textit{incorrect use of UI}
\end{array}
$$

Note that $(\exists y)Gyy$ is not an instance of $(x)(\exists y)Gyx$ because the $x$ in $(\exists y)Gyx$ is free, but if we replace the $x$ with a $y$, the $y$ is not free. The move from $(x)(\exists y)Gyx$ to $(\exists y)Gyy$ is like arguing, "For every natural number $x$, there is a natural number $y$ such that $y$ is greater than $x$. So, there is a natural number $y$ such that $y$ is greater than $y$." Since no number is greater than itself, we have moved from a true premise to a false conclusion, and the inference is invalid.

Now, consider the following proof. Is it correct?

$$
\begin{array}{lll}
1.\ (\exists y)(\exists x)Syx \rightarrow\ \sim Rc & & \\
2.\ (x)(\exists y)Sxy & & \therefore\ \sim Rc \\
3.\ (\exists y)Szy & & 2,\ \text{UI} \\
4.\ Szy & & 3,\ \text{EI} \\
5.\ (\exists x)Szx & & 4,\ \text{EG} \\
6.\ (\exists y)(\exists x)Syx & & 5,\ \text{EG} \\
7.\ \sim Rc & & 1,\ 6,\ \text{MP}
\end{array}
$$

Yes. However, in order to obtain the antecedent of line (1), we might have been tempted to instantiate to $y$ at line (3)—by UI, from line (2). But had we done so, we would have obtained $(\exists y)Syy$, and our UI rule will not permit such an inference.

Fourth, as with UI, when using EI, be sure that the instantial variable is free. For example, the following application of EI is incorrect:

$$
\begin{array}{lll}
1.\ (\exists y)(\exists x)Byx & & \\
2.\ (\exists x)Bxx & & 1,\ \textit{incorrect use of EI}
\end{array}
$$

Our EI rule tells us that we must replace the y free in $(\exists x)Byx$ with a *free* variable; but of course none of the xs in $(\exists x)Bxx$ are free.

Fifth, when using UI, remember that variables and constants must be substituted *uniformly*. Here are some correct and incorrect applications of UI:

1. $(x)[Mx \cdot (Lx \vee (y)Kxy)]$
2. $Mb \cdot (Lb \vee (y)Kby)$        1, UI (correct)
3. $Mz \cdot (Lz \vee (y)Kzy)$        1, UI (correct)
4. $Mb \cdot (Lb \vee (y)Kxy)$        1, UI (incorrect)
5. $Mx \cdot (Lc \vee (y)Kxy)$        1, UI (incorrect)

Similarly, when using EI, variables must be substituted *uniformly*. Here are some correct and incorrect applications:

1. $(\exists x)(y)(Pxy \leftrightarrow \sim Oxy)$
2. $(y)(Pxy \leftrightarrow \sim Oxy)$        1, EI (correct)
3. $(y)(Pwy \leftrightarrow \sim Owy)$        1, EI (correct)
4. $(y)(Pzy \leftrightarrow \sim Oxy)$        1, EI (incorrect)

Now, is the following proof correct?

1. $(\exists y)[Ny \cdot (x)(Nx \rightarrow Lyx)]$        $\therefore (\exists x)(\exists y)Lxy$
2. $Nz \cdot (x)(Nx \rightarrow Lzx)$        1, EI
3. $Nz$        2, Simp
4. $(x)(Nx \rightarrow Lzx)$        2, Simp
5. $Nz \rightarrow Lzz$        4, UI
6. $Lzz$        5, 3, MP
7. $(\exists y)Lzy$        6, EG
8. $(\exists x)(\exists y)Lxy$        7, EG

Yes. Note that in moving from line (1) to line (2), all free y-variables in $Ny \cdot (x)(Nx \rightarrow Lyx)$ are replaced with z-variables free in $Nz \cdot (x)(Nx \rightarrow Lzx)$, in accordance with our EI rule. Look closely at the move from line (6) to line (7). This is permitted because $Lzz$ is an instance of $(\exists y)Lzy$ (after removing the $(\exists y)$ quantifier, simply replace the y in $Lzy$ with a z). Suppose line (6) says that z loves z, then line (7) simply says that *something* is such that z loves it.

Sixth, remember that we may never EI to a variable that occurs free previously in the proof. For example:

1. $(x)(\exists y)Gyx$
2. $(\exists y)Gyx$        1, UI
3. $Gxx$        2, *incorrect use of EI*
4. $(\exists x)Gxx$        3, EG

This is like arguing, "For every natural number $x$, there is a natural number $y$ such that $y$ is greater than $x$. So, some natural number is greater than itself." Clearly, the argument is invalid. From a technical standpoint, the error consists in existentially instantiating to an $x$-variable in line (3), when an $x$-variable is free in line (2).

Seventh, recall the special restrictions on variables in connection with UG. UG lets us move from $\mathscr{P}y$ to $(x)\mathscr{P}$, where $y$ is a variable and $\mathscr{P}y$ is an instance of $(x)\mathscr{P}$, but only on the following conditions: First, $y$ must not be free in any line derived by an application of EI. Second, $y$ must not occur free in $(x)\mathscr{P}$. And third, UG cannot be used within the scope of an assumption for CP or RAA if $y$ occurs *free* in the assumption. Is the following use of UG correct?

1. (y)Eyy
2. Eyy             1, UI
3. (x)Exy          2, UG???
4. (∃y)(x)Exy      3, EG

Moving from (1) to (4) is like arguing, "Every number is equal to itself. Therefore, there is a number such that all numbers are equal to it." (Since the premise is true and the conclusion is false, the argument is invalid.) The proof goes wrong at step 3, where UG is misapplied, for $y$, the instantial variable, is free in $(x)Exy$.

The logic of relations enables us to see the subtlety of many rather ordinary-looking English sentences. For example, consider the following argument:

77. Each thing causes at least one thing. So, something causes something.
    (Cxy: x causes y)
    *In symbols:* (x)(∃y)Cxy   ∴ (∃x)(∃y)Cxy

Note that it would be wrong to switch the order of the quantifiers in the premise as follows: $(∃y)(x)Cxy$. This formula says that *at least one thing is such that everything causes it,* which is quite different from the premise of argument (77). The proof for (77) is short and simple:

1. (x)(∃y)Cxy       ∴ (∃x)(∃y)Cxy
2. (∃y)Cxy          1, UI
3. (∃x)(∃y)Cxy      2, EG

Now, compare argument (77) to the following fallacious argument:

78. Each thing causes at least one thing. So, at least one thing is such that
    everything causes it. (Cxy: x causes y)
    *In symbols:* (x)(∃y)Cxy   ∴ (∃y)(x)Cxy

Even if each thing causes at least one thing, we cannot infer that something is caused by everything. So, we shouldn't be able to construct a (correct) proof for argument (78). Which of the following steps cannot be justified by our rules?

1. (x)(∃y)Cxy      ∴ (∃y)(x)Cxy
2. (∃y)Cxy      ?
3. Cxy      ?
4. (x)Cxy      ?
5. (∃y)(x)Cxy      ?

Line (2) follows from line (1) by UI, and line (3) follows from line (2) by EI. The problem comes at line (4). It may seem that line (4) derives from line (3) by UG, but this is not so. UG allows us to move from $\mathcal{P}\mathbf{y}$ to $(\mathbf{x})\mathcal{P}$, but $\mathbf{y}$ must not be free in any line derived by an application of EI. In this proof, the role of $\mathcal{P}\mathbf{y}$ is played by Cxy in line (3), while the role of $(\mathbf{x})\mathcal{P}$ is played by $(x)$Cxy in line (4). Since the $x$ in Cxy is free and line (3) is arrived at by EI, we cannot apply UG in line (4).

In closing, let us consider an argument that involves a grammatically complicated conclusion:

79. The *Mona Lisa* is beautiful. So, anyone who steals the *Mona Lisa* steals something beautiful. (a: The *Mona Lisa*; Bx: x is beautiful; Px: x is a person; Sxy: x steals y)

The symbolization is as follows:

80. Ba  ∴ (x)[(Px • Sxa) → (∃y)(By • Sxy)]

Here is a proof for argument (80). Note the use of two assumptions.

| | |
|---|---|
| 1. Ba | ∴ (x)[(Px • Sxa) → (∃y)(By • Sxy)] |
| 2. Px • Sxa | Assume (for CP) |
| 3. ~(∃y)(By • Sxy) | Assume (for RAA) |
| 4. (y)~(By • Sxy) | 3, QN |
| 5. ~(Ba • Sxa) | 4, UI |
| 6. ~Ba v ~Sxa | 5, DeM |
| 7. ~~Ba | 1, DN |
| 8. ~Sxa | 6, 7, DS |
| 9. Sxa | 2, Simp |
| 10. Sxa • ~Sxa | 9, 8, Conj |
| 11. (∃y)(By • Sxy) | 3–10, RAA |
| 12. (Px • Sxa) → (∃y)(By • Sxy) | 2–11, CP |
| 13. (x)[(Px • Sxa) → (∃y)(By • Sxy)] | 12, UG |

The following exercises will give you an opportunity to explore the logic of relations.

# ◆ Exercise 9.6

**Part A:** Correct or Incorrect?  Which of the following inferences are permitted by our inference rules? Which are not?

* **1.**  1. (x)(y)(Mx • Nxy)
    2. (y)(My • Nyy)  1, UI

**2.**  1. (x)(y)Axy
    2. (y)Axy  1, UI
    3. Axx  2, UI
    4. (y)Ayy  3, UG

**3.**  1. (x)Fx ↔ Gab
    2. (x)Fx ↔ (∃x)Gxb  1, EG

* **4.**  1. (x)[(∃y)Lxy → Kx]
    2. (∃y)Lby → Kb  1, UI

**5.**  1. (∃x)Bax → (y)Cyb
    2. Bax → (y)Cyb  1, EI

**6.**  1. (∃x)Dxb
    2. Dab  1, EI

* **7.**  1. Eab → Fab
    2. (x)(Exb → Fxb)  1, UG

**8.**  1. ~(x)Jxd
    2. ~Jxd  1, UI

**9.**  1. (x)(Gxb → Hxb)
    2. Gyb → Hyb  1, UI
    3. (x)Gxb → Hyb  2, UG

* **10.**  1. (∃x)(y)(Kyx ∨ ~Lxy)
    2. (y)(Kyy ∨ ~Lyy)  1, EI

**11.**  1. (x)[(∃y)Ayx ∨ ~Bx]
    2. (∃y)Ayc ∨ ~Bc  1, UI

**12.**  1. (x)(y)Pxy
    2. (x)Pxy  1, UI

* **13.**  1. (x)[Sxb → (y)Rxy]
    2. Szb → (y)Rzy  1, UI

**14.**  1. (∃x)(Hxb • ~Hab)
    2. Hyb • ~Hab  1, EI
    3. (∃y)(Hyb • ~Hyb)  2, EG

**15.**  ⌈1. Nxd  Assume
    ⌊2. (x)Nxd  1, UG
    3. Nxd → (x)Nxd  1–2, CP

* **16.**  1. (x)(∃y)Jyx
     2. (∃y)Jyx            1, UI
     3. Jyx               2, EI
     4. (x)Jyx            3, UG

  **17.**  1. (x)Mxd
     2. Mxd               1, UI
     3. (∃y)Mxy           2, EG
     4. (z)(∃y)Mzy        3, UG

  **18.**  1. (z)(∃y)Pzy
     2. (∃y)Pzy           1, UI
     3. Pzz               2, EI

* **19.**  1. ~Lnn
     2. (∃x)~Lxx          1, EG
     3. (∃x)~Lxn          1, EG
     4. (∃x)~Lnx          1, EG

  **20.**  1. (∃x)(y)Axy
     2. (y)Axy            1, EI
     3. Axy               2, UI
     4. (x)Axx            3, UG

  **21.**  1. (x)[~~Jxb • (~Jxb ∨ Kxx)]
     2. ~~Jab • (~Jab ∨ Kaa)   1, UI
     3. ~~Jab             2, Simp
     4. ~Jab ∨ Kaa        2, Simp
     5. Kaa               3, 4, DS

* **22.**  1. (∃x)Fxd
     2. Fxd               1, EI
     3. (x)Fxd            2, UG

  **23.**  1. (∃x)[Ax • (y)(Ay → Bxy)]
     2. Ax • (y)(Ay → Bxy)    1, EI
     3. Ax                2, Simp
     4. (y)(Ay → Bxy)     2, Simp
     5. Ax → Bxx          4, UI
     6. Bxx               5, 3, MP
     7. (x)Bxx            6, UG

  **24.**  1. (x)(Cxb • Dxb)
     2. Cab • Dcb         1, UI

  **25.**  1. (y)Fby
     2. (x)(y)Fxy         1, UG

**Part B:** Proofs   Construct proofs to show that the following arguments are valid. You may use direct proof, CP, or RAA.

* **1.** (x)(y)(Rxy → Ryx), Rab ∴ Rba
  **2.** (∃x)~Rxx, ~(x)Rxx → (x)(y)~Txy ∴ ~Tba
  **3.** (x)(y)(z)[(Wxy • Wyz) → Wxz], Wab, Wbc ∴ Wac
* **4.** (y)(Bay ∨ Bya) ∴ Baa
  **5.** Meb → Nbb, (z)~Nzz ∴ ~Meb
  **6.** (x)(Tx → (y)[Vy → (∃z)(Pz • Sxyz)]), Tb • Ve ∴ (∃z)(Pz • Sbez)
* **7.** (∃x)[Hx • (y)(Hy → Lyx)] ∴ (∃x)(Hx • Lxx)
  **8.** (x)[Px → ~(y)(Py → Lxy)] ∴ ~(∃x)[Px • (y)(Py → Lxy)]
  **9.** (x)[Px → (y)(Py → ~Lxy)] ∴ ~(∃x)[Px • (∃y)(Py • Lxy)]
* **10.** ~(∃x)[Px • (∃y)(Py • Lxy)] ∴ (x)[Px → (y)(Py → ~Lxy)]
  **11.** (∃y)(z)~Kzy ∴ (y)(∃z)~Kyz
  **12.** (x)(y)(Sxy → ~Syx) ∴ (x)~Sxx
  **13.** (x)[Px → ~(∃y)Mxy] ∴ ~(∃x)(Px • Mxb)
  **14.** (∃x)(y)(Jx • Ny), (∃x)(Jx • Nx) → ~(∃x)Ux ∴ ~Ud
  **15.** (x)(Kbx → Gxc), (∃x)Gxc → (∃y)Gcy ∴ (∃x)Kbx → (∃y)Gcy
  **16.** (∃x)(∃y)(z)Pxyz ∴ (z)(∃x)(∃y)Pxyz
  **17.** (x)(y)(Rxy → ~Ryx) ∴ (x)(y)[(~Sxy • Rxy) → ~Ryx]
  **18.** (∃y)(x)(Lxy → Mxy) ∴ (∃x)(y)Lxy → (∃y)(∃x)Mxy
  **19.** (x)(Gx → Fx), (∃x)Fx → ~(∃y)(∃z)Hyz ∴ (∃x)Gx → ~Hbc
  **20.** (x)[Fx → (y)(Sy → Rxy)], (x)[Px → (y)(Rxy → Ty)],
  ∴ (∃x)(Fx • Px) → (y)(Sy → Ty)
  **21.** (x)(~Rx ∨ Nx), ~(∃x)Nx ∨ (∃y)(z)Szy ∴ ~(∃x)Rx ∨ (z)(∃y)Szy
  **22.** (∃x)(Mx • Nx), (∃x)[Mx • (y)(Ny → ~Lxy)]
  ∴ (∃x)[Mx • ~(y)(My → Lyx)]
  **23.** (x)(y)(Hxy → ~Ia), (∃x)Hbx • (x)(y)(z)Jxyz ∴ ~(Jabc → Ia)
  **24.** (x)(y)[~Cxy ∨ (Dx → Dy)], (x)(~Dx → ~Ax),
  (x)[Ax → (∃y)(By • Cxy)], (∃x)Ax ∴ (∃x)(Bx • Dx)
  **25.** (x)(y)(Rxy → (∃z)Szxy), (x)(y)(z)[Szxy → (Tzx • Tzy)], (x)Rxa
  ∴ (x)(∃y)(Syxa • Tya)

**Part C: English Arguments** Symbolize and construct proofs to show that the following arguments are valid.

* **1.** Ormazd is morally superior to Ahriman. For all x, for all y, if x is morally superior to y, then y is not morally superior to x. Hence, Ahriman is not morally superior to Ormazd. (o: Ormazd; a: Ahriman; Sxy: x is morally superior to y)

2. There is an entity that is more powerful than all entities. Therefore, at least one entity is more powerful than itself. (Mxy: x is more powerful than y)

3. There is at least one person. For all x, for all y, x loves y if and only if x loves x. Mad Dog MacKenzie loves no one. It follows that Mad Dog does not love himself. (Px: x is a person; Lxy: x loves y; m: Mad Dog MacKenzie)

* 4. Any rational animal is of greater intrinsic value than any nonrational animal. Karen is a rational animal, but she is not of greater intrinsic value than George. So, if George is an animal, then he is rational. (Rx: x is rational; Ax: x is an animal; Gxy: x is of greater intrinsic value than y; k: Karen; g: George)

5. Something is such that everything was created by it. We may infer that everything was created by something. (Cxy: x was created by y)

6. Carl is not on the team. For Carl is a sprinter, and Carl is faster than any sprinter on the team. But no sprinter is faster than himself. (c: Carl; Sx: x is a sprinter; Fxy: x is faster than y; Tx: x is on the team)

* 7. All horses are animals. Therefore, every tail of a horse is a tail of an animal. (Hx: x is a horse; Ax: x is animal; Txy: x is a tail of y)

8. It is not the case that there exists a nation more just than Norway. Every utopia is more just than Norway. Hence, no utopia is a nation. (Nx: x is a nation; Jxy: x is more just than y; n: Norway; Ux: x is a utopia)

9. God does not cause any free act that he wants to occur. Moreover, if there are any free acts that God does not want to occur, God does not cause them. Hence, God does not cause any free acts. (g: God; Cxy: x causes y; Fx: x is a free act; Wxy: x wants y to occur)

* 10. There are sets. Hence, it is not the case that there is a set that contains all and only those sets that do not contain themselves. (Sx: x is a set; Cxy: x contains y)

11. If God is greater than Gabriel and Gabriel is greater than Eve, then God is greater than Eve. Gabriel is an angel. God is greater than every angel. Eve is a human. Every angel is greater than every human. Consequently, God is greater than Eve. (Gxy: x is greater than y; g: God; Ax: x is an angel; b: Gabriel; Hx: x is human; e: Eve)

12. Every physical event has a physical cause. Every brain event is a physical event. If any brain event has a physical cause, then it lacks a mental cause. It follows that no brain event has a mental cause. (Px: x is physical; Ex: x is an event; Cxy: x causes y; Bx: x occurs in the brain; Mx: x is mental)

13. Whatever is not observable by both Einstein and Feynman is outside the realm of science. If an electron is observable by Feynman, then it is observable by Einstein. Accordingly, if any electron is not observable by Einstein, then it is outside the realm of science. (Oxy: x is observable by y; e: Einstein; f: Feynman; Sx: x is outside the realm of science; Ex: x is an electron)

14. If Cameron Diaz has greater intrinsic worth than Lassie and Lassie has greater intrinsic worth than every insentient creature, then Cameron Diaz has greater intrinsic worth than every insentient creature. Lassie is a merely sentient creature. Cameron Diaz has greater intrinsic worth than every merely sentient creature. Every plant is an insentient creature. Every merely sentient creature has greater intrinsic worth than every insentient creature. So, Cameron Diaz has greater intrinsic worth than every plant. (d: Cameron Diaz; Gxy: x has greater intrinsic worth than y; s: Lassie; Ix: x is an insentient creature; Sx: x is a merely sentient creature; Px: x is a plant)

15. Every act is caused by a desire. Every desire is caused by a brain process. For all x, y, and z, if x is caused by y and y is caused by z, then x is caused by z. Thus, every act is caused by a brain process. (Ax: x is an act; Dx: x is a desire; Cxy: x is caused by y; Bx: x is brain process)

**Part D:** A System Without UG and EG?   The rules UG and EG are standard in systems of predicate logic because these rules mirror intuitive inferences. However, the special restrictions on these rules make them relatively difficult to master. So, you may be interested to know that our system of predicate logic is complete without these rules. That is, any proof we can complete using our statement logic rules (including CP and RAA), UI, EI, UG, EG, and QN, *can also be completed without* using UG and EG. However, the price we would pay for doing without UG and EG is that most proofs must be completed by CP and RAA, which tends to make the proofs longer. Symbolize the following arguments, then construct two proofs for each argument—one that uses neither UG nor EG and one that uses at least one of these rules. Compare the length of the proofs.

1. Every number is divisible by itself. Some even number is a number. So, some even number is divisible by itself. (Nx: x is a number; Dxx: x is divisible by x; Ex: x is an even number)

2. All even numbers are divisible by 2. Nothing divisible by 2 is odd. So, no even number is odd. (Ex: x is an even number; Dxy: x is divisible by y; t: 2; Ox: x is odd)

## 9.7 Identity: Symbolizations

Among the many different types of relations, one is particularly important for logic, namely, identity. For instance, consider the following argument:

81. George Orwell wrote *1984*. George Orwell is identical with Eric Blair. Therefore, Eric Blair wrote *1984*. (o: George Orwell; Wxy: x wrote y; n: *1984*; Ixy: x is identical with y; b: Eric Blair)

This argument is obviously valid, but we cannot prove it valid given the inference rules introduced thus far. Using the scheme of abbreviation provided, the symbolization looks like this:

1. Won

2. Iob ∴ Wbn

Now what do we do? We have no useful moves to make because as yet we have no inference rules concerning the identity relation.

To introduce identity into our system of logic, we will borrow a symbol from arithmetic—namely, the equality sign—but we will refer to it as the **identity sign**. Except for the addition of the identity sign, the language for predicate logic with identity is exactly like the language for predicate logic. So, we can symbolize the statement "George Orwell is identical with Eric Blair" as follows:

82. o = b

Here are some additional examples of identity claims, together with their symbolizations:

83. Thomas Edward Lawrence was Lawrence of Arabia. (t: T. E. Lawrence; a: Lawrence of Arabia)

    *In symbols:* t = a

84. Kareem Abdul-Jabbar is Lew Alcindor. (k: Kareem Abdul-Jabbar; a: Lew Alcindor)

    *In symbols:* k = a

85. Muhammed Ali is the same individual as Cassius Clay. (m: Muhammed Ali; c: Cassius Clay)

    *In symbols:* m = c

And we can symbolize negations of identity statements by means of the negation sign, as follows:

86. Sarah Jessica Parker is not identical with Clint Eastwood. (s: Sarah Jessica Parker; c: Clint Eastwood)

    *In symbols:* ~s = c

87. John Milton is distinct from William Shakespeare. (m: John Milton; s: William Shakespeare)

    *In symbols:* ~m = s

Note that statements or statement functions are formed by placing a *constant* or a *variable* on each side of the identity sign; for example, $a = b$, $x = y$, and $a = y$. Also note that in order to negate an identity statement, we simply attach a tilde to it—no parentheses are employed. Thus, to negate $x = y$, we simply write $\sim x = y$, which is read as, "It is not the case that $x$ is identical with $y$." To clarify how the new symbols work, consider the following English sentence together with its symbolization:

**88.** Everything identical with the number 7 is an odd number. (s: the number 7; Ox: x is an odd number)

*In symbols:* (x)(x = s → Ox)

Here the parentheses indicate that the scope of the quantifier is $x = s \rightarrow Ox$. Without the parentheses, we would have $(x)x = s \rightarrow Ox$, in which case the scope of the quantifier would be $x = s$.

By means of the identity sign we can symbolize many complicated types of statements. The following list provides you with a guide for moving from English to logicese to symbols. Since these translations often involve lengthy conjunctions or disjunctions, we will allow some informal abbreviations to reduce the number of parentheses; for example, a long conjuction such as $(Fa \cdot (Gb \cdot Hc))$ can be abbreviated like this: $Fa \cdot Gb \cdot Hc$. After all, the rule of association tells us that, however we group these conjuncts, the resulting statement will be logically equivalent to the original.

### Only

*English:* Only Edison invented the phonograph. (e: Edison; Px: x invented the phonograph)

*Logicese:* e invented the phonograph, and for all x, if x invented the phonograph, then x is identical with e.

*Symbols:* Pe • (x)(Px → x = e)

### The Only

*English:* The only person who is guilty is David. (Px: x is person; Gx: x is guilty; d: David)

*Logicese:* d is a person and d is guilty, and for all x, if x is a person and x is guilty, then x is identical with d.

*Symbols:* Pd • Gd • (x)[(Px • Gx) → x = d]

### No . . . Except

*English:* No one except Bell invented the telephone. (Px: x is a person; b: Bell; Tx: x invented the telephone)

*Logicese:* b is a person and b invented the telephone, and for all x, if x is a person and x invented the telephone, then x is identical with b.

*Symbols:* Pb • Tb • (x)[(Px • Tx) → x = b]

### All . . . Except

*English:* All European countries except Switzerland declared war. (Ex: x is a European country; s: Switzerland; Dx: x declared war)

*Logicese:* s is a European country and s did not declare war, and for all x, if x is a European country and x is not identical with s, then x declared war.

*Symbols:* Es • ~Ds • (x)[(Ex • ~x = s) → Dx]

### Superlatives

*English:* The tallest mountain is Mount Everest. (Mx: x is a mountain; Txy: x is taller than y; e: Mount Everest)

*Logicese:* e is a mountain, and for all x, if x is a mountain and x is not identical with e, then e is taller than x.

*Symbols:* Me • (x)[(Mx • ~x = e) → Tex]

*Note:* The strategy regarding superlatives is to say, first, that a certain individual x falls into a class and, second, that x has a certain property in greater degree than anything else that falls into that class.

### At Most

*English:* There is at most one god. (Gx: x is a god)

*Logicese:* For all x, for all y, if x is a god and y is a god, then x is identical with y.

*Symbols:* (x)(y)[(Gx • Gy) → x = y]

*English:* There are at most two gods. (Gx: x is a god)

*Logicese:* For all x, for all y, for all z, if x is a god and y is a god and z is a god, then either x is identical with y or x is identical with z or y is identical with z.

*Symbols:* (x)(y)(z)[(Gx • Gy • Gz) → (x = y ∨ x = z ∨ y = z)]

*Note:* These "at most" statements do not assert that there are any gods. The first merely states that if there are any gods, then the maximum number is one. And the second states that if there are any gods, then the maximum number is two.

### At Least

*English:* There is at least one god. (Gx: x is a god)

*Logicese:* There exists an x such that x is a god.

*Symbols:* (∃x)Gx

*English:* There are at least two gods. (Gx: x is a god)

*Logicese:* There exists an x and there exists a y such that x is a god and y is a god and x is distinct from y.

*Symbols:* (∃x)(∃y)(Gx • Gy • ~x = y)

*Note:* If we had omitted ~x = y from our symbolization of "There are at least two gods," we would have left open the possibility that x and y are one and the same thing.

### Exactly One

*English:* There is exactly one God. (Gx: x is a god)

*Logicese:* There is an x such that x is a god, and for all x, for all y, if x is a god and y is a god, then x is identical with y.

*Symbols:* (∃x)Gx • (x)(y)[(Gx • Gy) → x = y]

*Note:* Here "exactly one" is viewed as a conjunction of "at least one" and "at most one." However, there is a more elegant way of symbolizing "exactly one." To illustrate, "There is exactly one God" can be written in logicese as "There is an $x$ such that $x$ is a god and for all $y$, if $y$ is a god, then $y = x$." In symbols:

$$(\exists x)[Gx \bullet (y)(Gy \rightarrow y = x)]$$

Similarly, "There are exactly two gods" can be symbolized as follows:

$$(\exists x)(\exists y)[Gx \bullet Gy \bullet {\sim}x = y \bullet (z)(Gz \rightarrow (z = x \vee z = y))]$$

The identity sign has been used to provide an important analysis of *definite descriptions*. A definite description is an expression of the form "the so-and-so," such as "the smallest prime number," "the discoverer of polonium," or "the author of *War and Peace*." Such expressions seem intended to denote exactly one object or person. But consider the following example, which Bertrand Russell discussed in "On Denoting":[6]

89.  The present King of France is bald.

Since France presently has no king, the expression "the present King of France" apparently fails to refer to anyone or anything. How then can (89) be a meaningful sentence (as it appears to be)? Russell suggested that statements involving definite descriptions, such as (89), make three claims:

    a.  A thing of a certain type exists (in this case, a present King of France).
    b.  It is unique.
    c.  It has a certain property (in this case, it is bald).

From Russell's perspective, then, we can rewrite (89) in logicese as follows: There is an $x$ such that $x$ is a present King of France, and for all $y$, if $y$ is a present King of France, then $y$ is identical with $x$, and $x$ is bald. Letting $Kx$ stand for "$x$ is a present King of France" and $Bx$ stand for "$x$ is bald," the symbolization looks like this:

90.  $(\exists x)[Kx \bullet (y)(Ky \rightarrow y = x) \bullet Bx]$

This analysis of (89) does not invite the question, "To what object, if any, does 'the present King of France' refer?" Rather, this analysis simply invites us to ask whether there are any actual objects having the property of being a present King of France. Of course, the answer is no. Thus, the meaning of the sentence is clear; indeed, we can see clearly that it is false. Because Russell's analysis of statements involving definite descriptions has been very influential, we will adopt it on a provisional basis. Let us consider one further example of a statement involving a definite description, together with its symbolization:

### Definite Descriptions

*English:* The discoverer of polonium is Polish. (Dx: x discovered polonium; Px: x is Polish)

*Logicese:* There is an x such that x discovered polonium, and for all y, if y discovered polonium, y is identical with x, and x is Polish.

*Symbols:* (∃x)[Dx • (y)(Dy → y = x) • Px]

The following exercises provide you with an opportunity to symbolize statements involving identity.

## ◆ Exercise 9.7

**Part A: Symbolizing** Symbolize the following sentences using the schemes of abbreviation provided.

* **1.** Cameron Diaz is not identical with Linda Fiorentino. (d: Cameron Diaz; f: Linda Fiorentino)

  **2.** Samuel Clemens is identical with Mark Twain. (s: Samuel Clemens; m: Mark Twain)

  **3.** Everything is identical with something.

* **4.** Nothing is distinct from itself.

  **5.** Everything differs from something.

  **6.** Nothing differs from everything.

* **7.** Each thing is identical with itself.

  **8.** If two things are identical to a third thing, then they are identical to each other.

  **9.** Only Faraday discovered electromagnetic induction. (f: Faraday; Dx: x discovered electromagnetic induction)

* **10.** At least two people invented the airplane. (Px: x is a person; Ax: x invented the airplane)

  **11.** No one except Dostoyevsky wrote *Crime and Punishment*. (Px: x is a person; d: Dostoyevsky; Wxy: x wrote y; c: *Crime and Punishment*)

  **12.** Goliath is the tallest human. (g: Goliath; Hx: x is human; Txy: x is taller than y)

  **13.** At most two persons invented the airplane. (Px: x is a person; Ax: x invented the airplane)

  **14.** There is exactly one dollar in my wallet. (Dx: x is a dollar in my wallet)

  **15.** At least two physicists discovered polonium. (Px: x is a physicist; Dx: x discovered polonium)

  **16.** Eddie Murphy is the funniest comedian. (m: Eddie Murphy; Cx: x is a comedian; Fxy: x is funnier than y)

17. Every star except the sun is outside our solar system. (Sx: x is a star; s: The sun; Ox: x is outside our solar system)

18. The most brilliant physicist is Einstein. (Px: x is a physicist; Bxy: x is more brilliant than y; e: Einstein)

19. There is at most one mountain in Ohio. (Mx: x is a mountain; Ox: x is in Ohio)

20. There are at most two wizards. (Wx: x is a wizard)

**Part B:** More Symbolizing Symbolize the following sentences, using the schemes of abbreviation provided.

* 1. If something is distinct from itself, then nothing makes sense. (Mx: x makes sense)

2. If anything is distinct from itself, then it is strange. (Sx: x is strange)

3. Everything is identical with itself if and only if nothing is distinct from itself.

* 4. There are exactly two entities.

5. There are at least two honest politicians. (Hx: x is honest; Px: x is a politician)

6. Everything but God is created. (g: God; Cx: x is created)

* 7. Exactly one person shot Abraham Lincoln. (Px: x is a person; Sxy: x shot y; a: Abraham Lincoln)

8. The author of *The Brothers Karamazov* is Russian. (Wxy: x wrote y; Rx: x is Russian; b: *The Brothers Karamazov*)

9. The star of the movie *Patton* is George C. Scott. (Sxy: x is a star of y; p: *Patton*; g: George C. Scott)

* 10. No Dane except Kierkegaard is gloomy. (Dx: x is a Dane; k: Kierkegaard; Gx: x is gloomy)

11. No movie star is identical with both Jennifer Lopez and Jennifer Aniston. (Mx: x is a movie star; j: Jennifer Lopez; a: Jennifer Aniston)

12. If Meriwether Lewis is an explorer and William Clark is an explorer, then there are at least two explorers. (m: Meriwether Lewis; c: William Clark; Ex: x is an explorer)

13. The whole number between 6 and 8 is an odd number. (Wxyz: x is a whole number between y and z; s: 6; e: 8; Ox: x is an odd number)

14. Everyone who loves someone else also loves herself. (Px: x is a person; Lxy: x loves y)

15. At least one person is angry at everyone except himself. (Px: x is a person; Axy: x is angry at y)

## 9.8 Identity: Proofs

To construct proofs involving the identity relation, we will add three new rules of inference.[7] The first of these is called **Leibniz' law** (LL), after the philosopher who first made it explicit, Gottfried Wilhelm Leibniz (1646–1716). Leibniz' law is the principle that if $x$ and $y$ are identical, then every property of $x$ is a property of $y$, and vice versa. Here are some typical inferences permitted by Leibniz' law:

A. 1. $a = b$
   2. Fa
   3. Fb                1, 2, LL
B. 1. $x = y$
   2. Fx • Gx
   3. Fy • Gy         1, 2, LL
C. 1. $x = d$
   2. Wxn
   3. Wdn            1, 2, LL
D. 1. $y = e$
   2. ~Lxy
   3. ~Lxe            1, 2, LL

In each case, we substitute an individual variable or individual constant for another that denotes the same entity. To state our inference rules in a general fashion, we will use the bold letters **m** and **n** to stand for any individual constant *or* individual variable. And we will use $\mathcal{P}$**m** and $\mathcal{P}$**n** to stand for WFFs containing **m** and **n**, respectively. Leibniz' law comes in two forms, as follows:

    **m = n**       **n = m**
    $\mathcal{P}$**m**         $\mathcal{P}$**m**
 ∴ $\mathcal{P}$**n**     ∴ $\mathcal{P}$**n**

Here, we obtain $\mathcal{P}$**n** by replacing *one or more* free occurrences of **m** in $\mathcal{P}$**m** with free occurrences of **n** in $\mathcal{P}$**n**. *Note:* To grasp this rule, it is important to understand that individual constants (unlike individual variables) are always free because they cannot be bound by quantifiers. Which of the following are correct applications of LL? Which are incorrect?

A.  1. $b = c$
    2. (x)(Ax → Bx)
    3. Ab → Bb       2, UI
    4. Ac → Bc       1, 3, (?)
B.  1. Cx • Dx
    2. $y = x$
    3. Cy • Dy       1, 2, (?)

C.  1. (y)(My ∨ Ny)
    2. x = d
    3. Mx ∨ Nx           1, UI
    4. Md ∨ Nx         2, 3, (?)

D.  1. (y)Gyo
    2. o = y
    3. (y)Gyy           1, 2, (?)

All are correct except for application (D). Regarding (D), the problem is that $o$ is free in line (1) but is replaced by $y$, which is bound in line (3). The inference in (D) is like arguing, "Every positive number is greater than zero, and zero is equal to $y$; therefore, every positive number is greater than itself." The invalidity is obvious. Note that in (C), only one occurrence of $x$ in line (3) is replaced by $d$ in line (4). This is permitted by Leibniz' law.

Armed with Leibniz' law, we can easily prove the validity of the argument that appears at the beginning of the previous section: "George Orwell wrote *1984*. George Orwell is identical with Eric Blair. Therefore, Eric Blair wrote *1984*." The symbolization and proof are as follows:

    1. Won
    2. o = b       ∴ Wbn
    3. Wbn         1, 2, LL

The following argument and proof illustrate another application of LL:

91. William Ockham died of the black plague. Billy the Kid did not die of the black plague. So, William Ockham is not Billy the Kid. (o: William Ockham; Dx: x died of the black plague; b: Billy the Kid)

    1. Do
    2. ~Db            ∴ ~o = b
    3. o = b         Assume
    4. Db             1, 3, LL
    5. Db • ~Db     4, 2, Conj
    6. ~o = b       3–5, RAA

This proof illustrates the general principle that if $x$ has a certain property and $y$ lacks that property, then $x$ is not identical to $y$.

Our next inference rule is called **symmetry** (Sm). Where the bold **m** and **n** stand for either individual constants or individual variables, the rule may be stated as follows. It comes in two forms:

    **m = n**          **~m = n**

   ∴ **n = m**     ∴ **~n = m**

Symmetry justifies such intuitive inferences as these:

92. Lewis Carroll was Charles Lutwidge Dodgson. Therefore, Charles Lutwidge Dodgson was Lewis Carroll. (c: Lewis Carroll; d: Charles Lutwidge Dodgson)

93. Woody Allen is not Gottfried Wilhelm Leibniz. So, Gottfried Wilhelm Leibniz is not Woody Allen. (a: Woody Allen; g: Gottfried Wilhelm Leibniz)

The proofs are short and simple:

| | | | | |
|---|---|---|---|---|
| 1. c = d | ∴ d = c | | 1. ~a = g | ∴ ~g = a |
| 2. d = c | 1, Sm | | 2. ~g = a | 1, Sm |

Our third and final rule of inference governing the logic of identity is the principle that *each thing is identical with itself*. We will call this simply the **identity** (Id) rule. It differs from all our previous rules in that it does not involve a premise. We may represent it as follows:

∴ **n = n**

Here, the bold **n** stands for any individual constant or individual variable. The Id rule allows us to enter statements of self-identity, such as $b = b$, as lines in a proof. This rule isn't used very often in constructing proofs, but our system of logic would not be complete without it. Here are an argument, symbolization, and proof that illustrate an application of Id:

94. Everything that is identical with Bill Cosby is a comedian. So, Bill Cosby is a comedian. (b: Bill Cosby; Cx: x is a comedian)

*In symbols:* $(x)(x = b \rightarrow Cx)$ ∴ Cb

| | |
|---|---|
| 1. $(x)(x = b \rightarrow Cx)$ | ∴ Cb |
| 2. $b = b \rightarrow Cb$ | 1, UI |
| 3. $b = b$ | Id |
| 4. Cb | 2, 3, MP |

*Note:* The parentheses in premise (1) indicate that the *scope* of the quantifier is $x = b \rightarrow Cx$. Without the parentheses, we would have $(x)x = b \rightarrow Cx$, in which case the scope of the quantifier would be $x = b$ and we could not apply UI at step 2.

With the addition of Id, our system of predicate logic with identity is complete. The following exercise gives you an opportunity to make use of the new inference rules.

## ◆ *Exercise 9.8*

**Part A:** Proofs    Construct proofs to show that the following arguments are valid.

\* 1. Na • ~Nb ∴ ~a = b

2. ~a = b ∴ $(\exists x)(\exists y)$~x = y

   **3.** Rab • (∃x)~Rxb ∴ (∃x)~x = a

\* **4.** c = d → e = g, d = c, Fg ∴ Fe

   **5.** (x)x = a → ~b = b ∴ ~a = x

   **6.** (x)(~Gx → ~x = d) ∴ Gd

\* **7.** (y)(Ay → By), Ab, b = c ∴ Bc

   **8.** (z)(Cz → Dz), ~Dg • Ca ∴ ~g = a

   **9.** (x)(~Fx → ~Ex), (x)(Fx → Gx), ~Gb • Ea ∴ ~a = b

\* **10.** (x)(Hx → Jx), (x)(Kx → Lx), Hd • Kc, c = d ∴ Jc • Ld

  **11.** (x)(Gx → x = d), (∃x)(Fx • Gx) ∴ Fd

  **12.** (x)(y)[Cyx → ~(z)Dz], (x)n = x, (∃x)[Ax • (y)(Ay → Cxy)] ∴ ~Dn

\* **13.** (∃x)Hx, (x)(y)[(Hx • Hy) → x = y] ∴ (∃x)[Hx • (y)(Hy → x = y)]

  **14.** (x)(y)y = x, (x)Mxx ∴ Mab

  **15.** (x)[(∃y)Kxy → (∃z)Kzx], (x)(Kxg • x = b) ∴ (∃z)Kzb

\* **16.** (∃x){[(Ax • Bxa) • (y)((Ay • Bya) → y = x)] • Dxb}, Ac • Bca ∴ Dcb

  **17.** (x)x = a ∴ (x)(y)x = y

  **18.** (∃x)Wx • (x)(y)[(Wx • Wy) → x = y] ∴ (∃x)[Wx • (y)(Wy → x = y)]

  **19.** (x)[Mx → (x = a ∨ x = b)], (∃x)(Mx • Nx) ∴ Ma ∨ Mb

  **20.** (∃x)[Fx • (y)(Fy → x = y)] → ~(x)(∃y)x = y, Fb ∴ (∃y)(Fy • ~b = y)

**Part B: English Arguments**   Symbolize the following arguments using the schemes of abbreviation provided. Then construct proofs to show that the arguments are valid.

\* **1.** No one antedates himself. Augustine antedates Boethius. Augustine and Boethius are both persons. Therefore, Augustine is not identical with Boethius. (Px: x is a person; Axy: x antedates y; a: Augustine; b: Boethius)

  **2.** I am not my body. The clump of cells in the corner of the room is my body. It follows that I am not identical with the clump of cells in the corner of the room. (i: I; b: my body; c: the clump of cells in the corner of the room)

  **3.** Every mental state is identical with some brain state or other. All mental states are introspectible. There is at least one mental state. Hence, some brain state is introspectible. (Mx: x is a mental state; Bx: x is a brain state; Nx: x is introspectible)

\* **4.** There are exactly two omniscient beings. Apollo is omniscient. We may infer that there is an omniscient being distinct from Apollo. (Ox: x is omniscient; a: Apollo)

  **5.** The only suspect who confessed is Benjamin Bondurant. The only suspect with a motive is Charles Ashworth. At least one suspect who confessed also has a motive. Consequently, Benjamin Bondurant is one and the same individual as Charles Ashworth. (Sx: x is suspect; Cx: x confessed; b: Benjamin Bondurant; c: Charles Ashworth; Mx: x has a motive)

6. The perfect triangle is not a material object. Hence, there is a perfect triangle. (Px: x is perfect; Tx: x is a triangle; Mx: x is a material object)

7. There are at least two physical objects. Jupiter is a physical object. Accordingly, there is at least one physical object other than Jupiter. (Px: x is a physical object; j: Jupiter)

8. The perfect being is divine. All divine beings are benevolent. We may conclude that the perfect being is benevolent. (Px: x is a perfect being; Dx: x is a divine being; Bx: x is benevolent)

9. The greatest painter is Rembrandt. Michelangelo is greater than Rembrandt. Michelangelo is not the same individual as Rembrandt. If one thing is greater than another, then the latter is not greater than the former. Therefore, Michelangelo is not a painter. (Px: x is a painter; Gxy: x is greater than y; r: Rembrandt; m: Michelangelo)

10. The most powerful person is God. The most powerful person is not morally weak. If one thing is more powerful than another, then the latter is not more powerful than the former. If God is not morally weak, then God is morally good. It follows that God is morally good. (Mxy: x is more powerful than y; Px: x is a person; g: God; Wx: x is morally weak; Gx: x is morally good)

## Notes

1. See A. N. Prior, "History of Logic," in Paul Edwards, ed., *The Encyclopedia of Philosophy*, Vol. 4 (New York: Macmillan Free Press, 1967), p. 520; and Anthony Flew, "Logic," *A Dictionary of Philosophy*, 2nd ed. (New York: St. Martin's Press, 1979), pp. 208–212. Flew remarks, "The advance in Frege's system . . . is the introduction of quantifiers. . . . This enabled him to unify the logic of propositions [i.e. statement logic] . . . with the study of those logical relationships which had previously been treated in the theory of the syllogism" (p. 211). Gottlob Frege's *Begriffsschrift* was first published in 1879; an English translation is available in J. van Heijnoort, ed., *From Frege to Gödel: A Source Book in Mathematical Logic, 1879–1931* (Cambridge, MA: Harvard University Press, 1967).
2. The recursive definition of "well-formed formulas" provided here is borrowed in its essentials from Merrie Bergmann, James Moor, and Jack Nelson, *The Logic Book*, 4th ed. (Boston: McGraw-Hill, 2004), 289.
3. See Flew, *A Dictionary of Philosophy*, p. 63. The relevant work is Alonzo Church, "A Note on the *Entscheidungsproblem*," *Journal of Symbolic Logic* I (1936): pp. 40–41.
4. See Donald Kalish, Richard Montague, and Gary Mar, *Logic: Techniques of Formal Reasoning*, 2nd ed. (New York: Harcourt Brace Jovanovich, 1980), p. 238. These authors give the following example: $(x)(y)(z)[(Fxy \cdot Fyz) \rightarrow Fxz]$, $(x)(\exists y)Fxy$ $\therefore (\exists x)Fxx$.
5. The system of rules here employed for predicate logic is borrowed from Christopher Menzel, co-developer of *The Logic Tutor*, www.mhhe.com.
6. Bertrand Russell, "On Denoting," *Mind*, Vol. 14 (Oxford University Press, 1905), pp. 479–493.
7. The system of rules here employed for the logic of identity is based on a system developed by Kalish, Montague, and Mar, *Logic*, chap. 5.

## Chapter 10

# *Induction*

So far, we have focused primarily on deductive logic, and hence on tests for the validity and invalidity of arguments. But as we saw in Chapter 1, the premises of some *invalid* arguments provide a significant degree of support for their conclusions. We will now look into some of these types of arguments in greater detail. In short, we will take up the subject of inductive logic. **Inductive logic** is the part of logic that is concerned with tests for the strength and weakness of arguments. To date, logicians have made far more headway in deductive logic than in inductive logic so that inductive logic is relatively less developed. For example, effective tests for strength and weakness have so far proven more elusive than tests for validity and invalidity. Our approach will be to examine common forms of argument that can be strong and to describe some of the main evaluative techniques available.

## 10.1 Inductive and Deductive Logic: Contrasts and Clarifications

Recall that a **strong argument** has the following essential feature: It is probable (but not necessary) that if the premises are true, then the conclusion is true. For example:

> 1. Ninety percent of 40-year-old American women live to be at least 50. Helen is a 40-year-old American woman. So, Helen will live to be at least 50.

Argument (1) is not valid, but its premises do provide some support for its conclusion. Just consider this: If you have to place a bet, and the premises of (1) sum up the relevant information you have in hand, then you should bet on the conclusion of (1) rather than on its negation.

A **weak argument** has the following essential feature: It is not probable that if its premises are true, then its conclusion is true. For example:

> **2.** Fifty percent of 30-year-old American women live to be 80. Alice is a 30-year-old American woman. So, Alice will live to be 80.

Is it probable that if the premises of this argument were true, then its conclusion would be true? Let us assume for the moment that the premises are true. If 50 percent of 30-year-old American women will live to be 80, then 50 percent of 30-year-old American women will *not* live to be 80. So, given only the information provided in the premises, we could just as well conclude that *Alice will not live to be 80*. In short, the premises give us no reason to prefer the conclusion of the argument to its negation. Thus, it is *not* probable that if the premises were true, then the conclusion would be true. Hence, the argument is weak.

A **cogent argument** is one that has two essential features: (a) It is strong and (b) all its premises are true. An **uncogent argument** is one that is either (a) weak or (b) strong, with at least one false premise. Note that "uncogent argument" is *not* defined as an argument that either is weak or has a false premise. This latter definition is too broad because it would classify *valid arguments with false premises* as uncogent. It is unhelpful to classify valid arguments as uncogent since they meet a higher logical standard than strength.

## Cogent Arguments Can Have False Conclusions

Let us now contrast deduction and induction. First, note that a sound argument cannot have a false conclusion, but a cogent argument can have a false conclusion. A sound argument cannot have a false conclusion because if an argument is valid and has only true premises, then it must have a true conclusion. But if an argument is strong and has only true premises, it is still possible (though unlikely) that its conclusion is false. To illustrate, suppose the premises of the following argument are true:

> **3.** Ninety percent of the cars in the parking lot were vandalized last night. My car was in the parking lot. So, my car was vandalized last night.

But suppose I go to the parking lot and discover that my car was not vandalized. Does that mean the argument is weak? No, it simply means that my car was among the 10 percent not vandalized. Again, the main point is that the conclusion of a cogent argument can be false.

## Form Does Not Ensure Strength

Second, while every argument with a valid form is valid, the strength of an argument is not ensured by its form. To grasp this point, let us consider a form of argument that can be strong under certain conditions: **statistical syllogism**. Here is an example:

> **4.** Ninety-five percent of women over 30 years of age cannot run the mile in under 5 minutes. Rebekah is a woman over 30 years of age. Hence, Rebekah cannot run the mile in under 5 minutes.

The form of a statistical syllogism can be represented as follows:

> 1. ____ percent of A is B.
> 2. c is an A.
> So, 3. c is a B.

In our example, A stands for the set of women over 30, while B stands for the set of things that cannot run the mile in under 5 minutes. The lowercase letter c stands for a particular person, Rebekah. (In another case, c might stand for a particular thing, event, or situation.) The blank space is to be filled with numbers greater than 50 and less than 100. If we place the number 50 in the blank, we get a weak argument. If we place the number 100 in the blank, we get a valid argument—it is as if we had said, "All A is B." So, we will stipulate that the numbers filling the blank in a statistical syllogism must lie between 50 and 100 *exclusive*. By the way, in ordinary English, a statistical syllogism may be formulated without the use of specific percentages. For instance, the following counts as a statistical syllogism: "The vast majority of violent criminals are unhappy. Jones is a violent criminal. So, Jones is unhappy."

Now, consider argument (4) in light of the following statistical syllogism:

> **5.** Eighty percent of women over 30 who are world-class marathoners can run the mile in under 5 minutes. Rebekah is a woman over 30 who is a world-class marathoner. Therefore, Rebekah can run the mile in under 5 minutes.

The premises of arguments (4) and (5) could all be true. But their conclusions contradict each other (assuming "Rebekah" names the same person in both arguments). This situation cannot arise in the case of valid arguments. If the premises of two *valid* arguments can be combined to form a consistent set of statements, then the conclusions of those arguments must be consistent as well.

What is going on? Assuming one is fully aware of the information contained in the premises of argument (5), one cannot rightly pronounce argument (4) strong. Yet, (4), like (5), has the form of a statistical syllogism. So, while it is obvious that arguments having the form of a statistical syllogism *can* be strong, it is also clear that having that form is not a guarantee of strength.

Logicians are not agreed on how to characterize what is wrong with argument (4) *given that* the premises of both arguments are true. Perhaps the best we can say is this: If someone were to advance (4) *while aware* of the information contained in the premises of (5), that person would be leaving out relevant evidence, evidence that has a bearing on the truth of the conclusion of (4). We might call such a culpable omission the **fallacy of incomplete evidence**.[1] And, in general, when one seeks to meet the standard of strength but *knowingly omits relevant evidence*, one is apt to fall short of the standard. The main point for the moment, however, is simply that form does not ensure strength. This fact greatly complicates the process of testing arguments for strength and weakness. Let us amplify this point briefly.

We have already seen that a knowledge of valid argument forms is a powerful tool in evaluating arguments for validity. But when evaluating arguments for strength, the identification of form only serves to rule out certain types of errors. For example, consider the following argument:

6. Five percent of adults can do 50 push-ups. John Barton is an adult. So, John Barton can do 50 push-ups.

This argument may appear to be a statistical syllogism, but it is not really of that form because the percentage is too low. The percentage must lie between 50 and 100 (exclusive) to meet the requirements for a statistical syllogism. And given only the information provided in the premises of (6), we have more reason to deny the conclusion than to affirm it. ("Ninety-five percent of adults cannot do 50 push-ups. John is an adult. So, John cannot do 50 push-ups.") Accordingly, the form of argument (6) is flawed.

As we have just seen, however, *given only the information provided in the premises*, arguments having a certain form will appear strong, and yet they may be weak, if relevant information has been omitted. This is so, for example, whenever the argument has the form of a statistical syllogism. And this leaves us with the question, "When does the omission of relevant evidence count as a logical error?" It is clearly an error to omit evidence (or information) when one knows full well that it reduces the strength of one's argument. But consider the following cases:

- The relevant evidence is readily available, and most people are aware of it. The arguer is not aware of it, but his ignorance is excusable for some reason (e.g., due to illness or other circumstances beyond his control, he has been isolated from the ordinary sources of information).

- The relevant evidence is readily available, and most people are aware of it. The arguer is not aware of it, but her ignorance is culpable (i.e., she should be aware of it).

- The relevant evidence is available but only through some investigation (e.g., a trip to the library), and the arguer is not aware of the evidence.

Do we want to say that a fallacy of incomplete evidence has been committed in some or all of these kinds of cases? This issue is under dispute among logicians, and we cannot attempt to resolve it here. But the very nature of the issue underscores the fact that induction is far less tidy than deduction.

## Strength Comes in Degrees

Here is a third important contrast between deduction and induction. Validity is an all-or-nothing affair; it does not come in degrees. For instance, if two arguments are valid, it makes no sense to say that one of them is more valid than the other. But strength does come in degrees. Statistical syllogisms nicely illustrate this fact. An argument of the form "___ percent of A are B; c is an A; so, c is a B" will be stronger as the number in the blank nears 100, and it will be less strong as the number nears 50 (assuming that no fallacy of incomplete evidence has been committed). Accordingly, if two arguments are strong, one of them may well be stronger than the other.

## A Clarification

One often hears it said that "deductive arguments proceed from the general to the specific, while inductive arguments proceed from the specific to the general." There are problems with this thesis.[2]

Some valid arguments move from general premises to a general conclusion:

> 7. All Shiites are Moslems. All Moslems are monotheists. Hence, all Shiites are monotheists.

Some valid arguments go from particular premises to a particular conclusion:

> 8. William of Ockham died in 1349. Bertrand Russell did not die in 1349. Therefore, William of Ockham is not identical with Bertrand Russell.

Perhaps surprisingly, some valid arguments even go from particular to general:

> 9. Franklin Roosevelt was a Democrat. So, anyone who voted for Roosevelt voted for a Democrat.

Furthermore, some strong arguments have a general premise but a particular conclusion:

> 10. All lemons previously tasted have been sour. Therefore, the next lemon to be tasted will be sour.

Note that the premise here concerns only *previously* tasted lemons, while the conclusion concerns a lemon as yet untasted. So, the argument is not valid, but it is nevertheless strong. And certain types of strong arguments move from particular premises to particular conclusions:

> 11. Jeff Lyle is similar to Jim Gossett in that each weighs 150 pounds. My CD player broke when Jeff sat on it. So, my CD player will break if Jim sits on it.

By some fluke, or perhaps because the CD player is on a softer surface, the conclusion of this argument could be false even if the premises are true. So, the argument is not valid, but it does appear to be strong. Finally, some strong arguments have general premises and a general conclusion:

> 12. All five starters on the basketball team performed well throughout the season. All five starters have shown a willingness to sacrifice personal glory for the sake of the team throughout the season. All five starters are experienced competitors. All five starters are rested and in good health. All five starters are highly motivated to do their best. So, all five starters on the basketball team will perform well in the competition tomorrow.

Note that the conclusion of argument (12) could be false even if the premises are true. For instance, one of the players may perform poorly due to receiving some dismaying news just prior to the game. So, the argument is not valid, but it seems to be strong.

To sum up, it is a mistake to suppose that strong arguments always move from particular statements to general statements. And it is equally erroneous to suppose that valid arguments always move from general statements to particular ones. These characterizations are at best gross oversimplifications. The key point to keep in mind, then, is that a strong argument has this essential feature: It is probable (but not necessary) that if its premises are true, then its conclusion is true.

The following exercises will test your understanding of the material in this section.

## ◖◗ Exercise 10.1

**Part A: True or False?**   Which of the following statements are true? Which are false?

* 1. If an argument is cogent, then it has true premises.
  2. If an argument is cogent, then it is strong.
  3. If an argument is cogent, then it is invalid.
* 4. If an argument is strong and has only true premises, then it is cogent.
  5. If an argument is weak, then it is probable that if its premises are true, its conclusion is false.
  6. If an argument is strong, then it is possible that its conclusion is false even if its premises are true.
* 7. If an argument is weak, then it is uncogent.
  8. If an argument has a false premise, then it must be uncogent.
  9. If an argument has true premises and a false conclusion, then it is weak.
* 10. If an argument is valid, then it is strong.
  11. If an argument is strong, then it is valid.
  12. If an argument is uncogent, then it is weak.

* **13.** If an argument is weak, then it must be invalid.

  **14.** If the conclusion of an argument is *exactly as probable* as its negation, given the premises of the argument, then the argument is weak.

  **15.** If an argument is uncogent, then it is strong but has at least one false premise.

* **16.** Strong arguments always proceed from the specific to the general.

  **17.** Valid arguments always proceed from the general to the specific.

  **18.** Some valid arguments proceed from the general to the general.

* **19.** If an argument is valid and has at least one false premise, then it is uncogent.

  **20.** If an argument is weak, then it is not likely that if its premises are true, then its conclusion is true.

**Part B:** Identifying and Evaluating Statistical Syllogisms   Which of the following arguments have the form of a statistical syllogism? Which do not? Some of the arguments contain information that suggests a possible fallacy of incomplete evidence. Explain why.

*   **1.** Fifty percent of the marbles in container 3 are green. The next marble to be drawn is a marble from container 3. Hence, the next marble to be drawn is green.

  **2.** Two-thirds of the students at Seattle Pacific University are women. Chris is a student at Seattle Pacific. Consequently, Chris is a woman.

  **3.** The vast majority of Americans approved of the Gulf War. John Montgomery is an American. So, John Montgomery approved of the Gulf War even though he belongs to a religious group most of whose members are pacifists.

*   **4.** More than half of all voters in the state of Washington favor campaign reform. Gordon Johnark, a U.S. senator, is a voter in the state of Washington. Accordingly, Gordon Johnark favors campaign reform.

  **5.** Philosophy 301 is similar to Philosophy 101 in that both are philosophy courses. Philosophy 101 is a course Diana dislikes. So, Philosophy 301 is a course Diana dislikes.

  **6.** Most college students do not work full-time. Jane is a college student. Therefore, Jane does not work full-time.

*   **7.** Seventy percent of the citizens of Salt Lake City do not drink coffee. Phil Goggans is a citizen of Salt Lake City. So, even though Phil owns and operates the Caffeine Club Coffee House, he probably does not drink coffee.

  **8.** One hundred percent of Texans love Texas. Jeanine Diller is a Texan. Therefore, Jeanine loves Texas.

  **9.** Eighty-two percent of those in a randomly chosen sample of 4000 Americans eat meat. Therefore, about 82 percent of Americans eat meat.

* **10.** Nearly all Mennonites are (were, and will be) pacifists. John Howard Yoder was a Mennonite. Accordingly, John Howard Yoder was a pacifist.

  **11.** According to the *National Enquirer*, last week a woman gave birth to a baby whose father came from Mars. Therefore, last week a woman gave birth to a baby whose father came from Mars.

  **12.** Fifty-one percent of Marines are under 19 years old. Captain Lawrence is a Marine. So, Captain Lawrence is under 19 years old.

* **13.** Jack is 65 years old. So, Jack is not currently making a living as a professional boxer.

  **14.** Ninety percent of abortions in the 1980s were performed in the first 12 weeks of pregnancy. Ms. Brown's abortion occurred in the 1980s. Thus, Ms. Brown's abortion was performed in the first 12 weeks of her pregnancy.

  **15.** Ninety-nine percent of lemons are sour. The fruit I am about to eat is a lemon. Therefore, the fruit I am about to eat is sour.

## 10.2 Arguments from Authority and Induction by Enumeration

In this section, we will examine two common types of arguments that are strong when properly constructed. In this context, a "properly constructed" argument is not merely one that conforms to a certain pattern or form but also one that avoids any fallacy of incomplete evidence.

### Arguments from Authority

Let us begin with **arguments from authority**, which have the following form:

> 1. *R* is a reliable authority regarding *S*.
> 2. *R* sincerely asserts that *S*.
> So, 3. *S*.

Here, *R* stands for any reliable source of information (e.g., an acknowledged expert, a group of experts, or a reference work), while *S* stands for any statement. We use arguments from authority when we appeal to dictionaries, encyclopedias, maps, or experts in any field. For instance:

> 13. In his *Dictionary of Philosophy,* Anthony Flew defines "logicism" as the view that "mathematics, in particular arithmetic, is part of logic." So, that is what logicism is.[3]

Arguments from authority are strong given that the authority in question is reliable, and the more reliable the authority, the stronger the argument. An authority is reliable to the extent that he or she can be counted on to provide true statements on the subject at issue. However, even reliable authorities can make mistakes, and for this reason arguments from authority are not valid. (Incidentally, an appeal to an *infallible* authority would be a special type of valid argument, for an infallible cognitive authority is one that cannot make mistakes. Thus, "R is an infallible authority regarding S, and R sincerely asserts S; therefore, S" is a valid form. Of course, it is one thing to observe that this form of argument is valid and another thing altogether to claim to know that there is an infallible authority who has sincerely asserted such-and-such statements.)

Note that the word "authority" is ambiguous. In this context, "authority" means "cognitive authority." A *cognitive* authority is a person or group possessing a special fund of knowledge. In other contexts, however, "authority" means "organizational authority." An *organizational* authority is a person or group whose particular office or role involves the responsibility of making certain decisions that affect others in the organization (e.g., school, corporation, or nation). It is vital that these two meanings of "authority" not be confused, for the following form of argument is weak: "An organizational authority asserts that S is true; therefore, S is true." Except when organizational authorities happen also to be cognitive authorities regarding S, the fact that they assert S does not provide good evidence that S is true. While this is obvious on reflection, the trust placed in organizational authorities often leads to a confusion between the two types of authority in ordinary life.

The *ad verecundiam* fallacy (or appeal to unreliable authority) is an argument from authority with a false or doubtful first premise: "R is a reliable authority regarding S." For example, if a breakfast cereal is endorsed as nutritious by a celebrity but there are no grounds for thinking the celebrity has expertise regarding nutrition, then an *ad verecundiam* fallacy has occurred. Such arguments are uncogent if the premise in question is false, but even when we cannot rightly claim that the premise is false, we may still rightly claim that the premise is open to reasonable doubt, and hence that the cogency of the argument is in doubt.[4]

As regards arguments from authority, the *fallacy of incomplete evidence* typically arises when the arguer fails to note that an equally reliable authority (or a more reliable authority) denies the conclusion (either explicitly or implicitly). For example, suppose you look up a historical personage, such as Thomas Aquinas, in a reliable source and reason as follows:

14. In Cahn's *Classics of Western Philosophy*, we read that Thomas Aquinas was born in 1225. So, Aquinas was born in 1225.[5]

However, you later find another reliable source stating that Aquinas was born in 1224.[6] The difference may simply be due to honest error (e.g., a printer's error or a mistake on the part of the author). Alternatively, it may be due to a difference of opinion among historians. Assuming the authorities *are* both *generally reliable* on the subject in question, the premises of the original argument remain true (i.e., Cahn is a reliable authority on the subject in question, and he does assert that Aquinas was born in 1225), but the strength of the inference is called into doubt by the conflict between reliable authorities. In such a case, one can often avoid a fallacy of incomplete evidence simply by drawing on a wider range of reliable authorities. If nearly all of the most reliable authorities agree on a point, then the appeal to authority can still render a conclusion probable. Or one may appeal to an authority with a specialized expertise in the issue in question.[7] However, it may happen that the more one looks into the matter, the more it appears that the authorities are not basing their assertions on solid evidence. In such a case, the appeal to authority is weak.

Arguments from authority often fail in another way. The authority may be misquoted or misinterpreted. When this occurs, the second premise of the argument, "R sincerely asserts that S," is false. The reliable authority didn't really assert S; rather, the reliable authority asserted some other statement P, which may (or may not) be easily confused with S. In this case, the argument is uncogent because it has a false second premise.

To sum up, arguments from authority can be cogent, but several errors must be avoided. For example, fallacies of incomplete evidence can occur if the relevant authorities disagree. Moreover, arguments from authority often fail to be cogent because the arguer misquotes (or misinterprets) the relevant authorities. In this case, the argument has a false premise of the form "R sincerely asserts that S." Finally, if there is reasonable doubt about the reliability of the alleged authority, an *ad verecundiam* fallacy is committed.

## Induction by Enumeration

Let us now consider another type of argument that is strong when properly constructed. This type of argument is called **induction by enumeration**, and the form is as follows:

1. ____ percent of a sample of A is B.
So, 2. Approximately ____ percent of A is B.

The **sample** consists of the members of set A that have been observed. Thus, the sample is a subset of set A. Set A itself is called the **population**. The blanks may be filled by numbers from 0 to 100, inclusive. For instance:

15. Twenty-five percent of a sample of the students at St. Ambrose College are members of the Republican Party. So, approximately 25 percent of the students at St. Ambrose College are members of the Republican Party.

Here, "twenty-five" fills the blanks, the set of students at St. Ambrose College replaces A, and the set of persons belonging to the Republican Party replaces B. Argument (15) is correct in form, but it may still be weak. The *fallacy of incomplete evidence* arises if our sample is too small or if it is biased. For instance, if our sample consists of only 4 students, and St. Ambrose has 3000 students enrolled, then our sample is just too small to warrant the inference. Or suppose our sample is large but biased—it was taken at a meeting of the Young Democrats Club. Then, again, the argument will be weak. Our sample must be *representative* of set A, or else the premise will not support the conclusion.

How large does a sample need to be? How can one avoid biased samples? These are important questions that we cannot explore in great detail. But even a small amount of information about sampling errors can help one avoid them. Let us here consider three features of a good sample. A good sample is *random*, of *appropriate size*, and not distorted by *psychological factors*.[8]

## Random Samples

A good sample is *random* as opposed to *biased*. "Random" here has a technical meaning. A sample is **random** if (and only if) each member of the population has an equal chance of being selected for observation. A famous case of a biased sample illustrates the need for random samples. In 1936, *Literary Digest* magazine conducted a poll to determine who would win the presidential election— Republican Alf Landon or Democrat Franklin D. Roosevelt. The *Digest* sent out 10 million questionnaires, of which roughly 2 million were returned. A sample of 2 million is a very large sample compared to those used in a Gallup poll, so there was no problem with the size of the sample. And based on the sample, the *Digest* predicted that Landon would win the election, but in fact Roosevelt won by a landslide. What went wrong? At least in part, this: The names of those to be polled had been taken mainly from lists of telephone subscribers and lists of automobile registrations. However, the election occurred during the Great Depression, when many people could not afford a telephone or an automobile. And a very large percentage of those on government relief voted for Roosevelt.

How can a random sample be obtained? In some cases, the randomness of a sample is fairly easy to obtain. This is especially so when the members of a population are known to have a high degree of uniformity. To take an extreme case, suppose our argument concerns hydrogen atoms. Hydrogen atoms are exceedingly similar to one another, each having one proton and one electron. So, although the total number of hydrogen atoms is very large (according to physicists, there are about $10^{80}$ hydrogen atoms!), a relatively small sample would support an inference about the total population. Similarly, police detectives can learn much from a few strands of hair or a few drops of blood at the scene of a crime. A person's hairs tend to be very similar to one another, and one drop of a victim's (or suspect's) blood will be very similar to another.

However, if we are concerned with human opinions about, say, which foods taste best, our population will have a very low degree of uniformity, for humans have widely varying views about which foods taste best. And thus, we will need to take elaborate precautions to ensure a random sample. Bias can creep into a sample in many ways, some of them rather subtle. To cite just one common problem, when a sample consists of questionnaires that must be voluntarily returned, people on one side of an issue may have much stronger feelings than those on the other side, and those with stronger feelings may be more likely to return the questionnaire, which skews the result.

To avoid such biased samples, researchers use elaborate methods to obtain a genuinely random sample. In essence, a city, state, or country is divided into geographical areas (taking population density into account), and then, within each area, those to be interviewed are selected on a chance basis:

> The most common procedure is to divide the overall population into separate categories (or "strata") according to the size of the locality the people live in. Specific geographical areas are then determined on a systematic (or on a random) basis in which a specified number of interviews are to be conducted. The people actually interviewed fall into the sample on a chance basis. They are not interviewed because they are representative of any particular population characteristic. Rather, they are interviewed solely because the area in which they live has fallen into the sample.[9]

Here is a rough, oversimplified illustration: Suppose the total population of a country is about 250 million. And suppose we divide the country into 250 geographical areas with 1 million people in each area. If six persons are then chosen randomly from each area, we have a sample of 1500.[10]

### Appropriate Sample Size

A good sample is of the appropriate size. It would be nice if a simple mathematical formula could be applied to determine the appropriate sample size in any given case. Unfortunately, no such formula is available. As we have just seen, the appropriate size of the sample depends on such factors as the degree of uniformity within the population. It also depends on (a) the size of the population and (b) the acceptable degree of error.

**Size of the Population**   To some extent, the size of the sample depends on the size of the population. This is especially true when the population is relatively small. For instance, if we are taking an opinion poll at a small college with only a few hundred students enrolled, our sample can be smaller than it would need to be if we were polling students at a university with 20,000 enrolled. However, one common misconception about samples is that the larger the population, the larger the sample should be. The fact is that problems with samples depend

> only slightly upon the size of the population under study if it is a large population. To achieve a sampling error of plus or minus three percentage points requires a sample of 1500 interviews—regardless of whether one is surveying a city, a state, or the nation.[11]

We can perhaps best understand this point by means of an illustration. Suppose we are drawing a sample of 500 marbles from a barrel containing 10,000 marbles, half of them red and half blue. And let us stipulate that our sample is chosen randomly so that each marble in the barrel has an equal chance of being selected. Our sample likely will contain approximately 250 red marbles (give or take a few), and approximately 250 blue ones (give or take a few). Now, suppose the barrel contains 1 million marbles instead of 10,000. If we select 500 marbles at random, we should still get approximately 250 red and 250 blue. Thus, a larger population does not necessarily require a larger sample.[12]

***Acceptable Degree of Error***    The **sampling error** is the difference between the percentage of the sample that has the attribute in question and the percentage of the population that has it. For instance, suppose we take a random sample of 10 marbles from a population of 100: 6 marbles in our sample are red, 4 are blue. We conclude that 60 percent of the marbles in the population are red. In fact, let us suppose, exactly 50 percent of the marbles in the population are red. The sampling error in this case is 10 percent.

Based on experience with the Gallup polls, the relationship between sample size and sampling error can be stated with remarkable precision for studies of large populations. Consider the following data:[13]

| Number of Interviews | Margin of Error (in percentage points) |
| --- | --- |
| 4000 | ± 2 |
| 1500 | ± 3 |
| 1000 | ± 4 |
| 750 | ± 4 |
| 600 | ± 5 |
| 400 | ± 6 |
| 200 | ± 8 |
| 100 | ±11 |

Let us suppose that we are conducting a poll, and our (randomly selected) sample contains 1000 registered voters, of whom 700 say they currently favor Smith for president. We conclude that 70 percent of the registered voters currently favor Smith for president, with a sampling error of ±4 percent. In other words, given our evidence, it is probable that between 66 and 74 percent of the registered voters currently favor Smith for president. And, as the data indicate, we can reduce the margin of error by increasing the size of our sample. Of course, it takes more time and effort to obtain larger samples (and hence more money), so we may rest content with a smaller sample if we do not have a strong need for greater accuracy.

### Psychological Factors

One last potential problem with samples should be noted: distortion due to psychological factors. Even if a sample is randomly chosen and of the appropriate size, an induction by enumeration can still be weak if psychological factors enter the picture in certain ways. For instance, the nature of the questions asked in a survey may be such as to produce inaccuracies. If people are asked, "How often have you driven your car while intoxicated?" or "Have you stolen anything in the past year?" they may not wish to answer truthfully. Furthermore, the answers may be influenced by the interviewer. For instance, a frown or a shocked tone of voice may cause the interviewee to modify his or her answers.

To sum up, arguments having the form of an induction by enumeration can be strong, but several errors must be avoided. Most important, the sample must be sufficiently large and random. Furthermore, care must be taken to ensure that psychological factors do not produce an inaccurate sample.

The following exercise gives you practice in evaluating both arguments from authority and inductions by enumeration.

## ◆ Exercise 10.2

**Identifying Inductive Arguments**   Which of the following arguments are examples of the types of inductive argument introduced in this section? Which are not? (a) If an argument is not an example of any of the types of arguments introduced in this section, simply write "incorrect form." (b) If an argument is an example of a type of argument introduced in this section, identify the type. (c) Specify the sampling error wherever possible. (d) Identify any fallacies of incomplete evidence, and briefly indicate why a fallacy has been committed.

* **1.** One hundred percent of the dogs that have been dissected have had kidneys. Hence, 100 percent of the members of the class of dogs have kidneys.

  **2.** In a recent study, a randomly chosen sample of 1500 American husbands were asked how many times they had had extramarital affairs. Eighty-four percent of those in the sample stated that they had never had an extramarital affair. Hence, approximately 84 percent of American husbands have never had an extramarital affair.

  **3.** The word "obviate" means "to do away with or prevent" because that is what *Webster's Dictionary* says it means.

* **4.** According to a recent poll, 50 percent of a random sample of 1500 voters in Ohio favor Quigley for governor. Thus, roughly 50 percent of voters in Ohio favor Quigley for governor.

  **5.** Bertrand Russell, a noted logician, states that the social mores concerning sex outside of marriage are harmful and oppressive. So, the social mores concerning sex outside of marriage are harmful and oppressive.

  **6.** According to a recent poll, 65 percent of a randomly chosen sample of 1000 voters in San Francisco are Democrats. Thus, 65 percent of American voters are Democrats.

* **7.** The *Bantam Medical Dictionary* says that an *ectopic pregnancy* is "the development of a fetus at a site other than the womb" (e.g., the fallopian tube). So, an ectopic pregnancy is the development of a fetus at a site outside the womb.

8. According to a recent poll, zero percent of a randomly chosen sample of five U.S. voters favor Mack Smith for president. So, zero percent of U.S. voters favor Mack Smith for president.

9. According to a recent poll, only 15 percent of a randomly chosen sample of 750 Oregon voters favor McKay for senator. Thus, approximately 15 percent of Oregon voters favor McKay for senator.

\* 10. The noted astrologer Vashti Zinia states that the stars determine the course of human history. So, our fate is in the hands of the stars.

11. The following information is gleaned from Howard Zinn, *A People's History of the United States* (New York: HarperCollins, 1995), p. 585: In February 1991, U.S. aircraft dropped bombs on an air raid shelter in Baghdad. Between 400 and 500 people were killed. The Pentagon claimed the shelter was a military target. But reporters who were allowed to inspect the site asserted that there was no evidence of any military presence. Now, given this information from Zinn, we may conclude that the Pentagon was right: The shelter was a military target.

12. In a recent study involving 600 male prison inmates in Georgia, 80 percent of those in the sample indicated disapproval of the death penalty. Hence, 80 percent of men in Georgia disapprove of the death penalty.

\* 13. Sixty-seven percent of those in a randomly chosen sample of 4000 Americans are overweight. Therefore, about 67 percent of Americans are overweight.

14. In a recent study, a randomly chosen sample of 400 clergymen were asked whether they have had sexual fantasies involving same-sex partners. Only 4 of the clergymen answered in the affirmative. Thus, only about 1 percent of clergymen have had sexual fantasies involving same-sex partners.

15. Eighty-two percent of a randomly chosen sample of 600 American college students are sleep-deprived. Therefore, approximately 82 percent of American college students are sleep-deprived.

\* 16. According to a recent poll, 80 percent of a randomly chosen sample of 10 Americans prefer football to soccer. Hence, about 80 percent of Americans prefer football to soccer.

17. Of a randomly selected sample of 1000 Americans, only 140 had red hair. So, about 14 percent of Americans have red hair.

18. In a recent study involving a randomly chosen sample of 200 college sophomores, none of those polled planned to take a course in symbolic logic. Hence, no college sophomores plan to take a course in symbolic logic.

\* 19. According to Dee Brown, *Bury My Heart at Wounded Knee* (New York: Washington Square Press, 1981), 153 Native Americans are known to have been killed in the massacre at Wounded Knee, although the actual number may well be as high as 300. Only 25 U.S. soldiers were killed, most of them by "friendly fire" from other soldiers. According to Brown, the soldiers ordered the Native Americans to give up their rifles, but a young Minneconjou named Black Coyote did not give up his rifle. Some eyewitnesses say that Black Coyote opened fire on the soldiers; others say he was deaf and did not understand the soldiers. Therefore, based on this information, we may conclude that Black Coyote started the incident at Wounded Knee by firing on the soldiers.

20. According to a recent poll, 90 percent of a randomly chosen sample of 4000 women in Mississippi reported that they believe that God exists. Hence, approximately 90 percent of American women believe that God exists.

## 10.3 Mill's Methods and Scientific Reasoning

Mill's methods provide us with patterns of reasoning to use in reaching conclusions of the form "A causes B." These patterns of reasoning are not valid, but the premises can provide significant support for their conclusions. Mill's methods are useful in many kinds of situations, from mundane cause-and-effect issues to the rarefied and technical areas of modern science. Because Mill's methods are used routinely by scientists, a discussion of Mill's methods leads naturally to a consideration of scientific reasoning.

### Mill's Methods

We often want to know what has caused some event or phenomenon. For example, when one is ill, one may visit a physician to discover the cause. When one's automobile will not run, one tries to find a competent mechanic to identify the cause. And when a friendship ceases to be enjoyable, one may speculate on the cause(s).

Unfortunately, the word "cause" is ambiguous. Sometimes, it is used to refer to a **sufficient condition** for some event or phenomenon: If X is a sufficient condition for Y, then if X occurs, Y occurs. In other cases, the word "cause" may be used to refer to a **necessary condition** for some event or phenomenon: If X is a necessary condition for Y, then Y occurs *only if* X occurs. Consider some examples:

16. For humans, being beheaded is a sufficient condition for death.
17. For flowers, water is a necessary condition for growth.

If a person is beheaded, he or she dies. So, being beheaded is a sufficient condition for death. But other conditions are also sufficient for death—for example, having one's air supply cut off for a day. By contrast, water is a necessary condition for the growth of flowers, but it is not a sufficient condition—light is also necessary, as are the proper nutrients in the soil. When an event or phenomenon occurs, all the necessary conditions must be present. (They wouldn't be necessary conditions if the event could occur without them.) And "cause" is often ambiguous—it may denote either a necessary or a sufficient condition. Furthermore, "cause" is sometimes used to refer to a condition that is neither sufficient nor necessary. For example, a forest ranger may tell us that lightning caused a forest fire. The lightning immediately preceded the fire, but it wouldn't have caused the fire if the weather had been wet and cold. So, the lightning is not by itself a sufficient condition. Nor is it a necessary condition, for a carelessly discarded cigarette might also have ignited the forest fire (in the absence of any lightning). So, in this case, the lightning is simply the most obvious or salient condition in a group of conditions that, *taken together, form a sufficient condition*—for example, (a) lightning strikes timber, (b) the timber is dry, and (c) oxygen is present.

In his book *A System of Logic*, the English philosopher John Stuart Mill (1806–1873) developed five methods for establishing conclusions of the form "A causes B." Let us now examine Mill's methods.

First, Mill proposed the **method of agreement**. To apply this method, one attempts to identify a common factor in a range of cases. For example, suppose five students at Vernon Elementary School become nauseated shortly after lunch. The school nurse makes a list of what each student ate for lunch:

> Student 1: Milk, tuna salad, candy bar
> Student 2: Tuna salad, Coke, potato chips
> Student 3: Milk, tuna salad, chocolate cake
> Student 4: Apple, orange juice, tuna salad
> Student 5: Tuna salad, milk, carrots, cupcake

The nurse observes that all of these students ate the tuna salad in the school cafeteria. Thus, eating the tuna salad is a factor common to all five cases. Of course, this is not enough, by itself, to prove that the tuna salad caused the nausea, but the search for a common factor gives us a good place to start in identifying the cause.

Second, Mill proposed the **method of difference**. To apply this method, we compare two cases, one in which the effect is present and one in which the effect is absent. To continue with our school lunch example, the "effect" is the nausea. To apply this method, the school nurse would find out what one or more students *who didn't become nauseated* ate for lunch. For example, suppose students (6) and (7) didn't become nauseated:

> Student 6: Pizza, Coke, tossed salad
> Student 7: Hot dog, milk, potato chips

Since the effect (nausea) is absent, the cause is absent as well. And since students (6) and (7) did not eat the tuna salad, the nurse gains an additional line of evidence in favor of the tuna salad as the cause of the nausea. (Of course, it could be that those who became ill just happen to have an intolerance of tuna. Then the common factor is more subtle and complex—a combination of the material ingested and the conditions specific to the students who became ill, such as food allergies.)

Mill's third method, his so-called **joint method**, is simply a combination of the method of agreement and the method of difference. And, as we have just seen, it is entirely natural to combine the two.

Mill's fourth method is called the **method of concomitant variation**. To employ this method, we show that as one factor varies, another varies in a corresponding way. A simple example would be the speed of a car and the extent to which the accelerator is pressed down. The more you press down on the accelerator, the faster the car goes. In the case of the nauseated schoolchildren, the nurse may find that some students are sicker than others and that the more tuna salad a student ate, the sicker he or she is. This would give the nurse yet further evidence that eating the tuna salad caused the nausea.

Mill's fifth method is called the **method of residues**. The method of residues is applied when some of the causes of a phenomenon have already been verified; we then conclude that a remaining factor completes the causal account. For example, suppose a room in your house is very cold in the winter. You identify three possible causes: (a) a broken windowpane, (b) a hole in the ceiling, and (c) a clogged furnace duct. You replace the windowpane and unclog the furnace duct; the room is not as cold as it was, but it is still relatively cool. You conclude that the hole in the ceiling accounts for the *residual* coldness. To generalize, in applying the method of residues, we "subtract out" those aspects of the effect whose causes are known and conclude that the rest of the effect ("the residue") is due to an additional cause.

It should be obvious that arguments employing Mill's methods are not valid, for even if the premises are true, it is possible that the conclusion is false. The following example (which we first encountered in Chapter 4) illustrates this point:

18. On Monday, Bill drank scotch and soda and noticed that he got drunk. On Tuesday, Bill drank whiskey and soda and noticed that he got drunk. On Wednesday, Bill drank bourbon and soda and noticed that he got drunk. Bill concluded that soda causes drunkenness.[14]

Here, Bill applies the method of agreement. Soda is indeed a common factor in the three cases. And yet Bill has arrived at a false conclusion. The problem is that Bill failed to recognize another, very important common factor, namely, alcohol. In this case, Bill's oversight is outlandish. But in the history of science, there are many cases in which the most important common factor was something that most people did not even regard as a possible cause. For example, prior to Louis Pasteur's famous experiments in 1881, virtually no one thought that vaccination could produce immunity to anthrax. And until 1900, when

Walter Reed proved that mosquitoes can transmit yellow fever, most people had never even regarded mosquito bites as a possible cause of the disease.

The soda and alcohol example illustrates something very important about Mill's methods: To make effective use of the methods, we have to make intelligent guesses about which conditions are causally relevant in a given case. For example, just prior to Bill's getting intoxicated, he may have been wearing a white shirt, breathing regularly, thinking about summer vacation, and eating a sandwich. Why do we ignore these prior conditions as we consider possible causes of Bill's inebriated state? Well, our background knowledge gives us some ideas about the kinds of conditions that might produce the effect in question. Accordingly, out of the myriad conditions present in any given case, we hypothesize that only some of them are causally relevant. Thus, our discussion of Mill's methods leads naturally to a discussion of the formation and testing of hypotheses. In other words, our discussion of Mill's methods leads naturally to a discussion of scientific reasoning.

## Scientific Reasoning

Boiled down to its essentials, scientific reasoning involves (a) describing the problem, (b) formulating hypotheses, and (c) testing the hypotheses. To illustrate this process, let us consider the work of one scientist, Ignaz Semmelweis, a physician who worked in the Vienna General Hospital. In the 1840s, he made an important discovery concerning the cause of childbed (puerperal) fever. At that time, childbed fever was a frequent cause of death among pregnant women in Europe.[15]

### Describing the Problem

The Vienna General Hospital had two maternity divisions. In one of these divisions, the First Maternity Division, 8.2 percent of the mothers died of childbed fever in 1844, 6.8 percent died in 1845, and 11.4 percent died in 1846. In the Second Maternity Division, however, the death rate was much lower: 2.3, 2.0, and 2.7 during the same years.

### Formulating and Testing Hypotheses

Semmelweis formulated a number of hypotheses. Because some people thought that the crowded conditions in the First Maternity Division might be the cause of the problem, Semmelweis formulated the following hypothesis:

> $H_1$: Childbed fever is caused by the crowded conditions in the First Maternity Division.

Semmelweis tested this hypothesis by considering its implications. He observed that the Second Division was actually more crowded than the First. (Due to the notorious reputation of the First Division, women understandably went to great lengths to avoid being assigned to it.) Thus, he reasoned that if $H_1$ were true, then the rate of childbed fever should be at least as high in the Second Division as in the First. But, as noted previously, the rate was in fact lower in the Second Division. So, Semmelweis concluded that $H_1$ is false. (*Note:* In rejecting $H_1$, Semmelweis made use of Mill's method of difference. Since the *effect*—that is, the higher rate of mortality due to childbed fever—was lacking in the Second Division, the cause should also have been absent. But the crowded conditions were present; therefore, they must not have been the cause.)

Semmelweis observed that the women in the two divisions delivered their babies in different positions; those in First Division delivered lying on their backs, while those in the Second Division delivered lying on their sides. Accordingly, Semmelweis formulated the following hypothesis:

> $H_2$: Childbed fever is caused by the position of delivery (specifically, by the mother lying on her back rather than on her side).

To test this hypothesis, Semmelweis instructed the First Division to use the same method of delivery as that used in the Second Division. But this change did not affect the rates of mortality, so Semmelweis concluded that $H_2$ is false.

Desperate for answers, Semmelweis tried a psychological hypothesis. He noted that the priest who administered the sacraments to the dying women was readily visible to the women in the First Division, so he formulated this hypothesis:

> $H_3$: The appearance of the priest terrifies the patients, making them more susceptible to childbed fever.

To test this hypothesis, Semmelweis instructed the priest to come by a different route so that he would not be seen or heard except by those who were already gravely ill. But this made no difference in the rate of childbed fever or the rate of death; accordingly, Semmelweis inferred that $H_3$ is false.

At length, a tragic accident led Semmelweis to an insightful hypothesis. A colleague of Semmelweis's named Kolletschka was accidentally cut by an assistant's scalpel while performing an autopsy. Shortly thereafter, Kolletschka died of an illness whose symptoms were the same as those of childbed fever. Semmelweis intuited that Kolletschka's death had been caused by the "cadaveric matter" introduced into his bloodstream during the autopsy. Furthermore, Semmelweis knew that the doctors and medical students often examined the women in the First Division immediately after performing dissections in the autopsy room, and although the medical personnel washed their hands, an unmistakable odor indicated that some of the cadaveric matter was still present. This led Semmelweis to the following hypothesis:

> $H_4$: Childbed fever is caused by cadaveric matter on the hands of medical examiners.

Again, Semmelweis tested the hypothesis by considering its implications. If $H_4$ was correct, then childbed fever could be prevented by removing the infectious material from the hands of those examining the pregnant women. Accordingly, he required all those who participated in such examinations to wash their hands in a solution containing chlorinated lime. As a result of this measure, the rate of childbed fever dropped dramatically in the First Division; indeed, it became lower than the rate in the Second Division.

Semmelweis also noted that $H_4$ explained why the rates of disease and mortality had differed between the two divisions, for the patients in the Second Division had been cared for by midwives rather than by those whose training involved the dissection of cadavers. (Note the use of Mill's method of difference here: The effect is absent in the Second Division, and so is the cause.) Semmelweis concluded that $H_4$ is true.

Let us now consider the general principles involved in testing hypotheses. Let us use $H$ to stand for a hypothesis and $I$ to stand for an implication of the hypothesis. You may have noticed that Semmelweis employed the following pattern of reasoning in rejecting hypotheses:

1. If $H$, then $I$.
2. It is not the case that $I$.
So, it is not the case that $H$.

This is the general pattern for rejecting an empirical hypothesis as a result of an unfavorable test outcome (i.e., one that conflicts with the predictions made on the basis of the hypothesis). Note that the form is *modus tollens*, which meets the standard of deductive logic, namely, validity. For this reason, and also because valid forms may be employed in deriving test implications from a hypothesis, this picture of scientific hypothesis testing is often called the "hypothetico-deductive method."

It would, however, be a gross oversimplification to suggest that rejecting a scientific hypothesis is simply a matter of applying *modus tollens*. In a typical case, one must make many background assumptions to obtain the premises. For example, suppose an astronomical hypothesis implies that a planet will be in a certain location at a certain time. An astronomer uses her telescope to observe whether the planet is present at the location and time implied by the hypothesis, but she does not see the planet. Has the hypothesis been disproved? Not necessarily. The astronomer may have made an error in aiming the telescope. The telescope may have malfunctioned. And note that using the telescope presupposes that the various hypotheses concerning optics, which are employed in the design and construction of the telescope, are true. So, in testing one hypothesis, we may need to assume that another hypothesis or theory is true. The point is that while *modus tollens* may be employed in testing hypotheses, applying it in scientific situations involves making many background assumptions that may be open to question in a given case (e.g., the telescope did not malfunction, the astronomer used the telescope properly, and so on).

How is a hypothesis confirmed? It may seem that Semmelweis used the following pattern of reasoning (where *H* stands for the hypothesis and *I* stands for an implication of the hypothesis):

1. If *H*, then *I*.
2. *I*.
So, *H*.

("If cadaveric matter causes childbed fever, then the patients currently being treated in the First Division do not get childbed fever when the cadaveric matter is absent. The patients currently being treated in the First Division do not get childbed fever when the cadaveric matter is absent. So, cadaveric matter causes childbed fever.") But the form of argument here is the fallacy of affirming the consequent. Are we saying, then, that scientific reasoning rests on a fallacy? No. It would indeed be a fallacy to argue that if one specific implication of a hypothesis holds true, then the hypothesis holds true. But if we can identify many specific implications of a hypothesis, and observation (or experiment) indicates that all the implications are true, we can accumulate a significant amount of support for the hypothesis. Each instance in which an implication of a hypothesis is observed to be true is called a **confirming instance**. And at some point, as the number (and/or kind) of confirming instances for a hypothesis increases, scientists find it unreasonable to attribute this to chance or mere coincidence. However, it is extremely difficult to specify clear and general logical principles for determining when a hypothesis is strongly supported by the evidence, and we cannot enter into a discussion of these complicated issues here.[16]

What do scientists look for in a hypothesis?[17] At least four things. First, generally speaking, a hypothesis should be logically consistent with hypotheses or theories that are already well established. There are exceptions to this general rule, however. For example, Einstein's theories were not consistent with Newton's, and yet they came to be accepted because they explained things Newton's theories could not explain.

Second, a hypothesis should have explanatory power. A hypothesis has explanatory power to the extent that known facts can be inferred from it. And, of course, the "known facts" mentioned here must include those we are seeking to explain; otherwise, the hypothesis is irrelevant. To illustrate, Semmelweis's hypothesis that cadaveric material (when introduced into the bloodstream) causes childbed fever has explanatory power. From it, we can infer that persons who have had cadaveric material introduced into their bloodstreams are apt to contract childbed fever, which explains the high rate of childbed fever in the First Maternity Division.

Third, a good scientific hypothesis should be liable to empirical tests. Suppose Semmelweis had hypothesized that the higher rate of childbed fever in the First Division was caused by ghosts who haunt the First Division (but not the

Second Division). Is there any way to test this hypothesis? There might be. Perhaps the ghosts can be seen or heard at certain times, or perhaps their influences can be thwarted by the work of an exorcist. But suppose no tests are allowed. The alleged ghosts, it is asserted, cannot be seen or heard. No traces of them can be found, not even in principle. Nor are they the type of ghosts who will respond to the work of exorcists. And so on. Such an untestable hypothesis is not acceptable within any scientific discipline.

But at least two cautionary remarks are warranted here. First, scientists routinely form hypotheses concerning entities that are not directly observable, such as electrons and protons. Nevertheless, many observable events can be explained in terms of these unobserved entities. For instance, if a hypothesis states that electrons behave in such-and-such a way, implications concerning observable events can be derived from the hypothesis. Scientists can then check to see if these events occur. Second, it is one thing to say that an untestable hypothesis is unscientific and another to say that it is untrue. There may well be things that cannot be explained scientifically—for example, the very existence of physical reality—and such things may have to be explained via untestable hypotheses or else not explained at all.

Finally, other things being equal, scientists generally prefer a simpler hypothesis to one that is more complicated. But consider an example outside of science for a moment. When investigating a murder, police do not typically begin with a complicated hypothesis to the effect that the victim was assassinated as part of an international conspiracy. Rather, it seems best to start with a relatively simple hypothesis and complicate it only as necessary to explain the phenomenon.

To take a scientific case, suppose we are testing a steel spring that hangs from the ceiling.[18] We place a 1-pound weight on the spring, and it extends 1 inch; we place a 2-pound weight on the spring, and it extends 2 inches; we place a 3-pound weight on the spring, and it extends 3 inches; and so on. We hypothesize that the behavior of the spring conforms to the formula $x = y$ (where $x$ is the force in pounds and $y$ is the extension in inches).

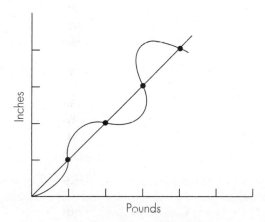

> ### Summary of Mill's Methods
>
> The **method of agreement** involves identifying a "common factor," that is, one that is present whenever the effect is present.
>
> The **method of difference** involves comparing two cases, one in which the effect is present and one in which it is absent. If when the effect is absent the possible cause C is also absent, the test lends support to C as the cause.
>
> The **joint method** involves combining the first two methods.
>
> The **method of concomitant variation** involves showing that as one factor varies, another varies in a corresponding way.
>
> The **method of residues** is applied when multiple, partial causes account for the effect: "Subtract out" those aspects of the effect whose causes are known and conclude that the rest of the effect ("the residue") is due to an additional cause.

In the graphical representation, our hypothesis is represented by the straight diagonal line. The dots stand for specific observations we have made—for example, "A 2-pound weight extends the spring 2 inches." The curvy line represents an alternative hypothesis that is far more complicated but that still accounts for each of the observations. The point, once again, is that a good scientific hypothesis avoids unnecessary complications. If a relatively simple hypothesis works, one should not complicate it.

To sum up, Mill's methods provide us with some helpful strategies for reaching conclusions of the form "A causes B." But in order to use Mill's methods effectively, we have to make intelligent guesses about which conditions are apt to cause the phenomenon in question. That is, we have to formulate hypotheses. Scientific reasoning involves describing a problem, formulating hypotheses, and testing them. Hypotheses are tested by drawing out their implications and checking to see if the implications are true. A good scientific hypothesis is consistent with well-established hypotheses, has explanatory power, can be tested, and is relatively simple.

The following exercises give you some practice in applying the concepts introduced in this section.

## ◆ Exercise 10.3

**Part A:** Mill's Methods   Which of Mill's methods is illustrated in each of the following examples? If, in your opinion, the conclusion reached indicates that an inadequate hypothesis was employed, formulate a better hypothesis.

* **1.** By his third shot of whiskey, Robert noticed that he was feeling intoxicated. He drank another shot of whiskey and found that the feeling increased.

Curious, he drank yet another shot, and his head really began to spin. Robert concluded that the whiskey was making him drunk.

2. Dick and Jane took a history exam. Both did poorly, although both studied for many hours. Both had pulled an "all-nighter." They concluded that the cause of their poor performance on the exam was a lack of sleep.

3. Tom, Tanya, and Teri ate dinner at a Japanese restaurant. Tom had rice, squid, and salad. Tanya had rice, octopus, and salmon. Teri had rice, squid, and cucumber rolls. After the meal, Tom and Teri had upset stomachs, but Tanya did not. They concluded that the squid caused their upset stomachs.

\* 4. Alonzo has done well on his last three math exams. In each case, he studied very intensely for 3 hours the night before the exam. Also, in each case, he departed from his usual informal style of dress and wore a tie to the exam. Alonzo concluded that wearing a tie increases the quality of his performance on examinations.

5. Joe is weighing cargo on trucks, using a drive-on scale. A truck pulls onto the scale, and Joe records the total weight of 6000 pounds. He subtracts the weight of the truck, which is 4500 pounds, to determine the weight of the cargo, 1500 pounds.

6. An economist noted a correlation between the length of women's skirts and the price of stocks. As fashion trends moved in the direction of shorter skirts, stock prices increased. But as fashion trends moved in the direction of longer skirts, stock prices fell. The economist concluded that fashion trends regarding the length of women's skirts cause stock prices to rise and fall.

\* 7. A certain physics professor got into his car to drive home from work. As he backed out of the parking place, he noticed a large oil spot. The next day he parked in a different parking place, one that had no oil spot. But as he backed out of the parking place at the end of the day, he once again noticed a large oil spot. He concluded that an oil leak from his car had caused the oil spots.

8. Pasteur gave each of 25 farm animals a vaccination for anthrax. These animals, as well as 25 who had not been vaccinated, were subsequently given a large dose of anthrax germs. None of the vaccinated animals came down with the disease, but all of the others died of anthrax. Pasteur concluded that his vaccine produced immunity to anthrax.

9. A mechanic is trying to fix a car that leaks a small puddle of oil every day. Looking under the hood, he notices oily stains in two places: (a) near the back of the valve cover at the top of the engine and (b) near the bottom of the engine, where the oil pan is attached. The mechanic replaces the gasket in the valve cover, and the leaking decreases by about half, but a puddle of oil still appears whenever the car is parked for several hours. The mechanic concludes that the remaining leakage is coming from the bottom of the engine, where the oil pan is attached.

* **10.** A doctor had 10 patients suffering from a rare form of cancer. By investigating the life histories of his patients, he found that each of them had worked for several years at a nuclear power plant and each had been exposed to significantly high amounts of radiation on at least one occasion. The doctor concluded that the radiation was the cause of cancer in each of the 10 cases.

**11.** Bobby pulled the lever on the little black box. His electric train began to move forward. He pulled the lever a bit further. The train went faster. He pulled the lever further, and the train went so fast that it flew off the track. Bobby concluded that pulling the lever caused the train to go faster.

**12.** A psychiatrist treated five soldiers who wished to stop stuttering. He discovered that each of the soldiers had begun to stutter shortly after undergoing a frightening experience in combat. The psychiatrist concluded that the stuttering was caused by extreme fear.

* **13.** Galvani was dissecting a dead frog. By chance, he touched the nerves of the frog's leg with an instrument that conveyed an electrical impulse. The frog's leg muscles contracted suddenly. Galvani touched the frog's nerves many times with the instrument, and each time the frog's leg muscles contracted sharply. Galvani then touched the frog's nerves with a metal instrument that did not convey an electrical impulse. The frog's leg did not contract. Galvani concluded that an electrical impulse had caused the dead frog's muscles to contract.

**14.** A Martian visited a large city in North America. While walking the streets incognito, he observed the traffic closely. He noted that when lights blinked on the left side of a vehicle, it nearly always turned left; and when lights blinked on the right side of a vehicle, it nearly always turned right. The Martian concluded that the blinking lights caused the vehicles to turn.

**15.** Mary is trying to determine the source of water in her basement. Possible causes include a leaky pipe and water seeping through the basement walls. Mary fixes the leaky pipe, and the amount of water in the basement decreases substantially but still remains at a significant level. She concludes that the rest of the problem is due to water seeping through the basement walls.

* **16.** On Wednesday night, Fran had shrimp, fries, and a salad with blue cheese dressing. She broke out in hives. The following Sunday, she ate the same meal, and again she broke out in hives. She suspected that the blue cheese dressing was the problem. So, a few days later, she ate shrimp, fries, and a salad with Italian dressing. She did not break out in hives. Fran concluded that the blue cheese dressing had indeed caused the hives.

**17.** Sharon drank one cup of coffee with cream on an empty stomach. She began to feel more alert. So, she had a second cup of coffee, again with cream. She noticed that she felt a bit jittery, but the coffee was delicious, so she had a third cup, adding a generous portion of cream. Suddenly, Sharon began to feel very nervous and to talk excitedly. She concluded that the cream was making her feel nervous.

18. A psychiatrist treated six men who wanted to be married but always wound up in profoundly unsatisfying relationships with women. He found that all of the men had been neglected as children by their parents. He concluded that parental neglect had left the men without resources for maintaining satisfying relationships with women.

* 19. At one point in his research on the causes of yellow fever, Walter Reed confined some volunteers to a carefully sealed room. The room contained a number of mosquitoes that were known to have bitten persons having yellow fever. All the volunteers were bitten by the mosquitoes, and all contracted yellow fever. In another room, mosquitoes were carefully sealed out, and the people staying in that room did not contract yellow fever. Reed concluded that the mosquitoes were spreading yellow fever.

20. "On one occasion, . . . [Semmelweis] and his associates, having carefully disinfected their hands, examined first a woman in labor who was suffering from a festering cervical cancer; then they proceeded to examine twelve other women in the same room, after only routine washing without renewed disinfection. Eleven of the twelve patients died of puerperal fever. Semmelweis concluded that childbed fever can be caused not only by cadaveric material, but also by 'putrid matter derived from living organisms.'" —Carl G. Hempel, *Philosophy of Science* (Englewood Cliffs, NJ: Prentice-Hall, 1966), p. 6

21. Colette took one Benadryl capsule and felt a bit drowsy. She took a second Benadryl capsule and began to feel very sleepy. She took a third Benadryl capsule and could scarcely keep her eyes open. She concluded that Benadryl causes sleepiness.

* 22. Betty, a department store manager, seeks an explanation for a register that often shows a shortage of cash at the end of the day. Betty suspects that one of the employees, Frank, is dipping from the till. But she also suspects that another employee, Jon, is making frequent mistakes in counting change. Betty confronts Frank about the matter; he admits to stealing and is fired. The frequency and amounts of the shortfall decrease sharply but are still nontrivial. Betty concludes that the persisting problem is likely due to Jon's mistakes in counting change.

23. Marla ate some cookies that she obtained from a vending machine. Shortly after she ate the cookies, her lips began to tingle, and then they swelled up. Because the swelling didn't last very long, she quickly forgot about the incident. But a few weeks later, she again ate some cookies from a vending machine, and once again her lips swelled up immediately. She concluded that something in the cookies was causing her lips to swell up.

24. The chief of police is trying to account for a recent upsurge in violent crime in the subways. He suspects that two causes are operating: first, a reduction in allocation of funds to the police department, which leads to fewer police on duty in the subways, and second, the appearance of the subway cars— specifically, they are covered with graffiti and often full of trash. (The chief suspects that the appearance of the subway cars tends to make people feel

that no one cares what goes on in the subways.) A discussion with the mayor solves the funding problem. The number of police on duty in the subways doubles, and the rate of violence drops significantly but does not return to the same level as before the recent upsurge. The chief concludes that the appearance of the subway cars accounts for what remains of the higher-than-usual rate of violence in the subways.

25. A sociologist closely observed correlations between demographics and the rate of violent crime. He noted that the rate of violent crime rose as the percentage of young men (15 to 25 years of age) *relative to the rest of the population* increased. For example, he noted that about 15 years after each baby boom, there is an increase in the rate of violent crime and the rate remains high for approximately 10 years. After about 10 years, the rate of violent crime falls off. The sociologist concluded that increases in the rate of violent crime are largely caused by an increase in the number of young men (as a percentage of the population).

**Part B:** Hypotheses   In the following arguments, identify any hypotheses that fail to meet the four criteria for good scientific hypotheses. State which criterion is violated, and explain your answer.

\* 1. Frederick has been having trouble with his watch. It keeps losing time. He had the battery replaced, but that didn't help. So, Frederick hypothesized that an invisible demon had possessed his watch, slowing down the mechanism. He took the watch to a priest for an exorcism, but that didn't help either. Frederick concluded that the demon must be the type of demon that cannot be exorcised.

2. Robert was behind in his lab work in Chemistry 101. He heated some chemicals in a test tube. A gas was generated, and Robert filled a balloon with the gas. The balloon floated upward when released. Robert concluded that boiling the chemicals had somehow produced a situation in which the law of gravity was temporarily suspended. He excitedly wrote up his lab reports, expecting an A for his remarkable discovery.

3. Jennifer has been having trouble with her computer. For example, occasionally a few letters in a document get misplaced (without any action on her part). In an effort to account for these glitches, Jennifer hypothesizes that the computer has developed free will and is now occasionally making its own choices.

\* 4. A certain biology professor noted a correlation between increased activity among bees and the beginning of spring. He hypothesized that as bees flap their wings, their body heat increases, which warms the air around them, thus bringing about the changes in seasons from winter to spring.

5. A mechanic is trying to discover why your car won't start. He hypothesizes that the trouble is due to poltergeistic activity. When you state your intention of obtaining a second opinion, he indicates that this will do you no

good, since he is the only mechanic who can intuit the presence of poltergeists in cars and no observational checks are possible.

6. A certain professor got into his car to drive home from work. As he backed out of the parking place, he noticed a large oil spot. The next day he parked in a different parking place, one that had no oil spot. But as he backed out of the parking place at the end of the day, he once again noticed a large oil spot. He concluded that a group of pranksters had lifted his car up via blimp and poured oil under it on both days.

\* 7. A detective is trying to explain two murders that are remarkably similar in detail yet happened at the same time in very different locations—one in Florida and one in Alaska. The detective hypothesizes that the murderer has somehow learned to travel faster than the speed of light.

8. A biologist is trying to account for the extinction of the dinosaurs. He hypothesizes that the dinosaurs simply decided to stop having sex.

9. A detective is assigned to a murder case. The victim has been shot six times with a large-caliber handgun. Forensic tests indicate that the bullets all came from the same gun. With virtually no other facts to go on, the detective hypothesizes that there were six murderers who took turns shooting the victim, each of them firing one shot.

10. Martha has received her logic exam back from the instructor. She did well but lost a few points on one item. Specifically, on the exam, an inference of the form "If A, then B; not A; so not B" is identified as *modus tollens*. The answer is in Martha's handwriting. But since Martha knows that the inference form is in fact the fallacy of denying the antecedent, she hypothesizes that the CIA stole her exam from the instructor, erased her original answer, and wrote an incorrect answer in her handwriting.

**Part C:** For Discussion   Suppose you are a detective trying to solve a burglary. The specific evidence under consideration is:

*Evidence:* Ms. Vogel's TV is missing. It's a small TV set easily carried by one person. McGraw was seen lurking about Vogel's house while she was on vacation, and McGraw's fingerprints are on the table where Vogel kept her TV.

As a detective, you happen to have some relevant background information:

*Background information:* McGraw and Kingston both have a record of petty theft, and both live within easy walking distance of Vogel's house.

Now, based on these givens, which of the following hypotheses is preferable, and why?

Hypothesis 1: McGraw stole the TV.
Hypothesis 2: Kingston stole the TV.

Hypothesis 3: Spies from a foreign country stole the TV, and they framed McGraw (forcing him to walk around Vogel's house while she was on vacation and forcing him to touch her TV table).

Hypothesis 4: McGraw and Kingston both stole the TV.

Which hypotheses have the most explanatory power? Which accord best with the background information? Which, if any, are preferable on grounds of simplicity?

## 10.4 Arguments from Analogy

Another type of argument that can be strong, when properly constructed, is the argument from analogy. **Arguments from analogy** have the following form:

1. *A* is similar to *B* in relevant respects.
2. *B* has property *P.*
So, 3. *A* has property *P.*

Here, A and B can stand for many different things. They may stand for a specific object or person (e.g., my car or Socrates). They may stand for a type or kind of object (e.g., cars in general or human beings). They may stand for specific events or situations (e.g., the situation in which your car has broken down). *P* stands for any sort of property (e.g., the property of being fast, the property of being intelligent, or the property of being dangerous). Let's consider an example:

19. *The Tempest* and *A Midsummer Night's Dream* are both plays written by William Shakespeare. These two plays are very similar in length. I was able to read *A Midsummer Night's Dream* in the space of an evening. So, I am able to read *The Tempest* in the space of an evening.

Here, "*The Tempest*" replaces A and "*A Midsummer Night's Dream*" replaces B in the original schema. *P* is the property of being readable (by me) in the space of an evening.

How, in general, do we go about evaluating the strength of an argument from analogy? Basically, we have to evaluate to what degree (if any) A's similarity to B provides support for the statement that A has property P. Unfortunately, there is no formula or mechanical method for evaluating arguments from analogy. But in assessing the logical connection between the premises and the conclusion, it usually helps to ask the following three questions:

**Question 1:** What are the relevant respects in which A and B are similar? Ideally, the one who offers the argument supplies this information, but often the information is provided only in part. Similarities are relevant if they increase the likelihood of A's having property P. And, generally speaking, the more relevant respects A and B share, the stronger the argument.

**Question 2:** Are A and B dissimilar in any relevant respects? That is, does the analogy between A and B break down at any relevant points? Dissimilarities are relevant if they decrease the likelihood of A's having property P. Relevant differences between A and B tend to weaken the argument.

**Question 3:** Are there things (other than A) that are similar to B in the relevant respects? If so, do these things have property P? To the extent that there are things relevantly similar to B that lack P, the analogy breaks down. To the extent that there are things relevantly similar to B that have P, the analogy holds up.

Let us evaluate argument (19) in terms of these three questions.

*Question 1:* In what relevant respects are A (*The Tempest*) and B (*A Midsummer Night's Dream*) similar? They are similar in length, and both are written in Elizabethan English. The style of writing is also similar.

*Question 2:* Are A (*The Tempest*) and B (*A Midsummer Night's Dream*) dissimilar in any relevant respects? *The Tempest* is a more serious play than *A Midsummer Night's Dream*, and in places *The Tempest*, unlike *A Midsummer Night's Dream*, is rather pessimistic in tone. So, it might take a little longer to read *The Tempest*.

*Questions 3:* Are there things other than A (*The Tempest*) that are similar to B (*A Midsummer Night's Dream*) in the relevant respects and that have property P (i.e., can be read by me in an evening)? Yes, I once read another of Shakespeare's plays, *As You Like It*, in an evening. And it is similar in length, type of English, and style to *A Midsummer Night's Dream*.

To sum up, the answer to Question 1 indicates that there are several relevant respects in which *The Tempest* and *A Midsummer Night's Dream* are similar. The answer to Question 2 notes a relevant dissimilarity, but the dissimilarity does not seem to weaken the analogy much. The answer to Question 3 indicates that as we consider related examples, the analogy holds up. Accordingly, the argument appears to be strong.

Let's consider a second argument from analogy:

20. Parrots and humans can both talk. Humans can think rationally. Therefore, parrots can think rationally.

Here, "parrots" replaces A and "humans" replaces B in the original schema. P is the property of being able to think rationally.

*Question 1:* What are the relevant similarities between parrots and humans? The chief relevant similarity is the ability to talk. Of course, it is true that both parrots and humans can talk. And there is *some* sort of linkage between the ability to talk and the ability to think rationally, since it is primarily in the linguistic behavior of humans that their capacity for rational thought is exhibited.

*Question 2:* Are parrots dissimilar to humans in any relevant respects? Yes, in at least two relevant respects. First, as far as we can tell, parrots merely *mimic* what they hear. They do not produce their own sentences in a spontaneous, creative fashion. And, of course, mimicking is not a reliable indication of rational thought. Second, the brain of a parrot is much smaller than that of a human. And this raises a legitimate doubt as to whether parrots are capable of the kind of thinking of which humans are capable.

Incidentally, it must be understood that not all dissimilarities are relevant ones. For example, parrots have feathers and humans do not. But this dissimilarity has no apparent bearing on the issue at hand (i.e., can parrots think rationally?), and so it is irrelevant for present purposes. Relevant dissimilarities are those that affect the likelihood of A's having property P.

*Question 3:* Are there any examples of things (other than parrots) that can talk but cannot think rationally? Apparently so, for some deranged persons are able to talk but only in a highly disconnected and illogical fashion. So, apparently, there are things that talk but do not think rationally. This observation again draws attention to a weakness in the analogy between parrots and humans (in general).

To sum up, our answer to Question 1 indicates that there are *some* relevant similarities between parrots and humans but not many. Our answers to Questions 2 and 3 indicate that these similarities are *not* sufficient to make it likely that if the premises of argument (20) are true, then its conclusion is true. Therefore, argument (20) is weak.

Arguments from analogy are often used in moral and legal reasoning. Let us consider an argument from analogy on a very controversial issue, not with a view to settling the issue but simply to illustrate the process of evaluating such arguments.

21. The prohibition of so-called hard drugs such as cocaine and heroin is similar to the prohibition of alcohol. The prohibition of alcohol was well intentioned and based on legitimate concerns about the dangers of alcohol consumption. The prohibition of alcohol also led to a highly profitable black market ruled by organized crime and marked by violence. Now, we can all agree that the prohibition of alcohol was, in the last analysis, a mistake. Therefore, the prohibition of hard drugs is also a mistake—hard drugs should be legalized.

Here, A is the prohibition of hard drugs and B is the prohibition of alcohol. Property P is that of being a mistake. Again, we use our three questions as tools for analyzing the argument.

*Question 1:* In what ways are A and B relevantly similar? The premises spell out a number of relevant similarities between the prohibition of hard drugs and the prohibition of alcohol—certainly enough relevant similarities to give the argument some initial plausibility.

> ### Summary of Arguments from Analogy
>
> **Form**
>
>     1. *A* is similar to *B* in relevant respects.
>
>     2. *B* has property *P.*
>
> So,  3. *A* has property *P.*
>
> **Questions to Ask**
>
> 1. What are the relevant respects in which *A* and *B* are similar? In general, the more relevant respects *A* and *B* share, the stronger the argument.
>
> 2. Are *A* and *B* dissimilar in any relevant respects?
>
> 3. Are there things (other than *A*) that are similar to *B* in the relevant respects? If so, do these things have property *P*? To the extent that there are things relevantly similar to *B* that lack *P,* the analogy breaks down. To the extent that there are things relevantly similar to *B* that have *P,* the analogy holds up.

*Question 2:* Are *A* and *B* dissimilar in any relevant respects? Critics of argument (21) might claim that prohibiting hard drugs is relevantly different from prohibiting alcohol in at least two ways. For instance:

    a. Drugs such as cocaine and heroin are more addictive than alcohol and, hence, are in some respects potentially more harmful to individuals and society than alcohol is.

    b. The current social context is different from that in which alcohol was legalized. When alcohol was legalized, drug abuse was not a serious social problem in America. But now it is. Therefore, legalizing hard drugs will probably add to currently severe problems such as death and injury resulting from traffic accidents, babies born with health problems because their mothers abuse chemical substances, and workplaces that are less efficient because of the number of people who use drugs while working.

Surely, these alleged dissimilarities, if accurate, are relevant and weaken the analogy at least to some degree.

*Question 3:* Are there things other than *A* (the prohibition of hard drugs) that are similar to *B* (the prohibition of alcohol) in the relevant respects but that lack *P* (the property of being a mistake)? Critics of argument (21) may point out that there are many drugs that cannot be used legally without a doctor's prescription. Surely, then, it is not in general a mistake to prohibit the use of a drug (except under doctor's orders). Proponents of argument (21) might reply, however, that prescription drugs are not in general relevantly similar to cocaine and heroin, for prescription drugs are not being sold in large quantities through black markets, and they are not under the control of organized criminals.

Our purpose at present is the limited one of illustrating the appropriate method of evaluating an argument from analogy. So, we will make no effort to render a final judgment on the strength of argument (21). But in a case such as this, where highly controversial claims are at issue, we may learn valuable truths and become aware of important questions by exploring an analogy to the best of our ability, even if it is difficult or impossible to reach a clear verdict on the strength of the argument. Thus, an argument from analogy can be useful even when its strength is in dispute.

The following exercise provides you with an opportunity to evaluate a series of arguments from analogy.

## ◆ Exercise 10.4

**Part A: Analyzing and Evaluating Analogies** Analyze the following arguments in terms of the schema for arguments from analogy, identifying A and B (the things being compared) and property P. Below each argument is a suggested criticism or reply. Does the reply point to an important weakness in the analogy? Why or why not? Wherever possible, briefly state at least one additional criticism that calls the strength of the argument into question.

* **1.** Mars is similar to the earth in that both are planets that orbit the sun. The earth is inhabited by living things. Therefore, Mars is inhabited by living things.
  *Reply:* The moon also orbits the sun, but we know that the moon is not inhabited by living things.

**2.** Having an abortion is like using contraception. In both cases, the intent is the same: to avoid having a baby. And plainly, contraception is morally permissible. Thus, abortion is morally permissible also.
  *Reply:* Abortion involves taking life, while contraception prevents life from occurring.

**3.** Marijuana is as much a gift from God as lettuce. Therefore, since it is not wrong to enjoy lettuce, it is not wrong to enjoy marijuana.
  *Reply:* Marijuana is usually smoked, while lettuce is eaten.

* **4.** Logic, like whiskey, loses its beneficial effects when taken in very large quantities. Therefore, very large quantities of logic should be avoided. —Lord Dunsany, *My Ireland,* as quoted in H. L. Mencken (ed.), *A New Dictionary of Quotations* (New York: Knopf, 1978), p. 705 (*Note:* This quotation is slightly altered—I've made the conclusion explicit, and the original has "too" where I've used "very.")
  *Reply:* Whereas whiskey has alcohol in it, logic does not.

**5.** Suppose Buddhists became politically powerful in America and succeeded in having Buddhism taught in the public schools. Would that be morally

acceptable? Of course not. Therefore, it is not morally acceptable to have Christianity taught in the public schools.
*Reply:* Until recently, Buddhism has not been very influential in America, while Christianity has been influential in America from the beginning.

6. Can nonhuman animals feel pain? Well, the higher mammals have nervous systems that are similar to human nervous systems. Furthermore, higher mammals behave in ways similar to humans when damage is inflicted. (For example, just as a human is apt to cry out and withdraw his finger if it is stabbed with a pin, so a dog is apt to yelp and withdraw its paw if it is stabbed with a pin.) Therefore, higher mammals can feel pain.
*Reply:* Animals cannot talk to us and explain how they feel, but humans can.

7. Taxation of earnings from labor is on a par with forced labor . . . it is like forcing the person to work *n* hours for another's purpose. Therefore, since it is wrong to force one person to work for another's purpose, it is wrong for the government to tax our earnings. —Robert Nozick, *Anarchy, State, and Utopia* (New York: Basic Books, 1974), p. 169 (*Note:* I have made the conclusion explicit.)
*Reply:* All governments tax their citizens, but only corrupt or tyrannical governments have programs of forced labor.

8. If at times force can be used to counter force, why should lies never be used to counter lies? . . . just as someone forfeits his rights to noninterference by others, when he threatens them forcibly, so a liar has forfeited the ordinary right to be dealt with honestly. —Sissela Bok, *Lying: Moral Choice in Public and Private Life* (New York: Random House, 1979), p. 133 (*Note:* Bok states the argument in order to discuss it, not to endorse it.)
*Reply:* Lying involves the use of language, whereas force need not involve the use of language.

9. For the first six to eight weeks of pregnancy, the fetus has no brain waves. So, during this period, the fetus is similar to a brain-dead adult. Therefore, if a brain-dead adult is not living, neither is a fetus during the first six to eight weeks of pregnancy. —Adapted from Baruch Brody, "Fetal Humanity and the Theory of Essentialism," in Robert Baker and Frederick Elliston, eds., *Philosophy and Sex* (Buffalo: Prometheus Books, 1975), pp. 348–352
*Reply:* A brain-dead adult is not growing and gaining new powers, but a fetus is growing and gaining new powers.

10. Belief in God is like belief in electrons. For example, no one has ever seen an electron, just as no one has ever seen God. Similarly, the concept of an electron plays an important role in physical theory, just as the concept of God plays an important role in theology. Furthermore, one can reasonably believe that electrons exist even if one cannot summarize the evidence for their existence, for one can reasonably believe in electrons on the basis of authority (e.g., a physics textbook). Thus, one can reasonably believe in God even if one cannot summarize the evidence for God's existence.

*Reply:* Whereas electrons are physical objects, God (if God exists) is not physical.

**Part B:** More Analogies   Analyze the following arguments in terms of the schema for arguments from analogy, identifying *A* and *B* (the things being compared) and property *P*. Below each argument is a suggested criticism or reply. Does the reply point to an important defect in the analogy? Why or why not?

\*  1. People often mistreat dogs. But dogs are just mentally deficient people. And a mentally deficient person is still a person. Now, obviously, it is wrong to kill a mentally deficient person *merely on the grounds* that caring for him is inconvenient. Accordingly, it is wrong to kill a dog *merely on the grounds* that caring for it is inconvenient.
   *Reply:* Dogs do not look very much like people.

2. Surrogate motherhood is slave owning, for both slave owning and surrogate motherhood involve the buying and selling of human beings. (The only difference is that in the case of surrogate motherhood, the humans who are bought and sold are always babies.) And yet everyone will agree that slave-owning is immoral. We may therefore conclude that surrogate motherhood is immoral also.
   *Reply:* Surrogate mothers do not sell their babies; rather, surrogate mothers "rent" the use of their own reproductive capacities.

3. The United States of America is a gentleman's club. The various states freely agree to join the United States, just as gentlemen freely join a club. And take note: In the case of a club, one is free to withdraw at one's own discretion. Thus, any state in the United States is free to withdraw (secede) at its own discretion.
   *Reply:* The analogy is weak since only men join gentlemen's clubs, but both men and women are citizens of states.

\*  4. A computer, like the human brain, is capable of responding to stimuli in astonishingly complex ways. Computers can play chess, enter into dialogues, and solve extremely difficult mathematical problems. Now, humans are aware of their own thoughts and feelings. Therefore, computers are aware of their own thoughts and feelings also.
   *Reply:* Computers are made mostly of metal and plastic, but humans are not.

5. Suppose a wicked tyrant threatens to kill 10 innocent people unless you give him all your discretionary income. If you refuse to give the money, you will not be harmed, but the 10 innocent people will be put to death. If you give the money, both you and the 10 innocent people will go unharmed. (Assume that you have no other options such as overthrowing the tyrant or helping the 10 people escape.) Clearly, in such circumstances, you are morally obligated to give up your discretionary income to save the 10 people. Now, you are in fact in a situation quite like this. World hunger is the wicked tyrant. The 10 innocent people are the starving poor of the Third World. Therefore,

you are morally obligated to give up your discretionary income to save the starving poor. —Adapted from Louis Pascal, "Judgement Day," in Peter Singer, ed., *Applied Ethics* (New York: Oxford University Press, 1986), pp. 105–111

*Reply:* In the wicked tyrant case, you can identify exactly who will die, but in the case of world hunger, you cannot identify the individuals who will die.

6. Suppose you have been kidnapped by the Society of Music Lovers and your kidneys have been connected to the circulatory system of a famous violinist who lies unconscious beside you. You know that if you detach yourself from his circulatory system, the violinist will die. You also know that if you stay attached to the violinist for nine months, he'll regain his health (and your health will not suffer). In such circumstances, would you be morally obligated to remain connected to the violinist? Surely not. It would be very nice of you to remain connected, but it is not your moral duty to do so. Therefore, it is not wrong for a woman to have an abortion in the case of pregnancy through rape. —Adapted from Judith Jarvis Thomson, "A Defense of Abortion," in Peter Singer, ed., *Applied Ethics* (New York: Oxford University Press, 1986), pp. 37–56

*Reply:* Detaching yourself from the famous violinist is not killing—it is not like shooting him in the head with a gun. In other words, detaching yourself from the violinist is merely letting him die. By contrast, abortion involves killing the fetus.

7. How do I know that other people have inner mental lives of their own? Well, I know that I have such an inner life—I feel pain, I worry, I think thoughts, and I dream dreams. And I know that other people have a central nervous system very similar to mine. Therefore, other people have inner mental lives of their own.

*Reply:* Chimps also have a central nervous system similar to yours.

8. Rich nations are tiny lifeboats surrounded by masses of drowning people. Thus, it is impossible for rich nations to save many of those living in the poorest nations. —Adapted from Garrett Hardin, "Lifeboat Ethics: The Case Against Helping the Poor," in Stephen Satris, ed., *Taking Sides: Clashing Views on Controversial Moral Issues*, 4th ed. (Guilford, CT: Dushkin, 1994), pp. 350–357

*Reply:* Rich nations such as the United States own vast amounts of land. So, obviously, they can hold a lot more people than a lifeboat can.

9. When the technique of *in vitro* fertilization is employed, eggs are withdrawn from the woman by laparoscopy and fertilized in a petri dish (usually by the husband's sperm but sometimes by a donor's sperm). A number of eggs are removed at one time and fertilized, for various reasons. For one thing, women who seek *in vitro* fertilization typically have a history of difficulties in achieving pregnancy. Thus, multiple attempts at inserting embryos (i.e., fertilized eggs) into the womb are often required. Also, the pain and expense of multiple surgeries are saved by removing more than one egg per laparoscopy.

Now, after the eggs are fertilized, they must be frozen, and if the woman becomes pregnant, there may be unneeded or superfluous frozen embryos. These embryos are simply thawed and discarded if the pregnancy results in the birth of a baby. And obviously, there is nothing immoral about discarding such superfluous frozen embryos. But note that this has implications for the abortion debate. Since discarding a frozen embryo is not and cannot reasonably be equated with murder, early abortions cannot reasonably be equated with murder either.

*Reply:* Frozen embryos cannot grow; but under normal circumstances, a zygote can.

10. The experiences of a clairvoyant person are similar to the experiences of a sighted person. Both types of experience involve vivid images. And both types of experience *seem* to tell us about events in the real world. Now, admittedly, not everyone is clairvoyant, but not everyone is sighted either. Furthermore, while the experiences of clairvoyant persons sometimes prove illusory, the experiences of sighted persons sometimes prove to be illusory, too. After all, optical illusions are common enough. Nevertheless, it is reasonable to believe that the experience of seeing is a source of truth about the world. Hence, it is reasonable to believe that the experiences of clairvoyant persons are a source of truth about the world.

*Reply:* Most people are sighted, but at best only a small minority are clairvoyant.

## Notes

1. I have borrowed this label from Wesley Salmon, *Logic*, 3rd ed. (Englewood Cliffs, NJ: Prentice-Hall, 1984), p. 97.
2. My discussion of this common misconception is heavily indebted to Brian Skyrms, *Choice and Chance*, 3rd ed. (Belmont, CA: Wadsworth, 1986), pp. 13–15.
3. Anthony Flew, *Dictionary of Philosophy*, rev. ed. (New York: St. Martin's Press, 1979), p. 215.
4. For a review of the *ad verecundiam* fallacy, see section 4.3.
5. Steven M. Cahn, ed., *Classics of Western Philosophy*, 2nd ed. (Indianapolis, IN: Hackett, 1977), p. 279.
6. For example, James F. Ross, *Introduction to the Philosophy of Religion* (London: Macmillan, 1969), p. 29. Yet another authority states that Aquinas was born in 1225 *or* 1226; see Bertrand Russell, *A History of Western Philosophy* (New York: Simon & Schuster, 1945), p. 452.
7. For example, Frederick Copleston, a well-known authority on Aquinas, states that Aquinas was born *either* at the end of 1224 *or* at the beginning of 1225. See Copleston, *A History of Philosophy*, Vol. 2, *Mediaeval Philosophy*, Part II, *Albert the Great to Duns Scotus* (New York: Image Books, 1962), p. 20.
8. My discussion of the features of a good sample is heavily influenced by the discussion in Hurley, *A Concise Introduction to Logic*, pp. 548–552.
9. Charles W. Roll, Jr., and Albert H. Cantril, *Polls: Their Use and Misuse in Politics* (New York: Basic Books, 1972), p. 67.
10. See Roll and Cantril, *Polls*, pp. 82–89, for a detailed discussion of the elaborate methods used to obtain a random sample.
11. Roll and Cantril, *Polls*, p. 74.

12. The illustration is borrowed from Roll and Cantril, *Polls*, p. 75.
13. Roll and Cantril, *Polls*, p. 72.
14. This example is borrowed from Salmon, *Logic*, p. 112. I have paraphrased freely.
15. My account of Semmelweis's work borrows heavily from Carl G. Hempel, *Philosophy of Natural Science* (Englewood Cliffs, NJ: Prentice-Hall, 1966), pp. 3–6.
16. For an accessible discussion of the complexities involved in the confirmation of scientific hypotheses, see Del Ratzsch, *Philosophy of Science* (Downers Grove, IL: InterVarsity Press, 1986), pp. 41–96.
17. My brief summary of criteria for good scientific hypotheses is indebted to the discussion in Irving M. Copi and Carl Cohen, *Introduction to Logic*, 9th ed. (Englewood Cliffs, NJ: Prentice-Hall, 1994), pp. 534–539.
18. This example is borrowed from Salmon, *Logic*, p. 134.

## Chapter 11

# *Probability*

In Chapter 10, we examined a series of types of arguments that are strong when properly constructed. We defined a strong argument as one having this feature: It is *probable* (but not necessary) that if its premises are true, then its conclusion is true. In this chapter, we will take a closer look at the concept of probability, which is a main ingredient in our concept of strength. First, we examine three theories regarding the nature of probability. Second, we consider the elementary rules of probability. Finally, we focus on Bayes' theorem as a tool for determining the probability of a hypothesis given the evidence.

## 11.1 Three Theories of Probability

Consider the following statements:

1. The probability that *you will select a king from an ordinary deck of playing cards on the next draw* is 4 out of 52.
2. The probability that *a 20-year-old woman will live to be 30* is .913.
3. The probability that *Tom and Sue will like each other* is high.

These three statements correspond to three different understandings of the nature of probability: the classical theory, the relative frequency theory, and the subjectivist theory.[1]

### The Classical Theory

This theory stems from the work of two French mathematicians, Blaise Pascal (1623–1662) and Pierre de Fermat (1601–1665). According to the **classical**

**theory**, the probability of an event (or of a statement's being true) is determined by the following formula:

$$P(s) = f/n$$

Here, $P$ is read as "the probability of," $s$ stands for any event or for any statement's being true, $f$ stands for the number of favorable outcomes, and $n$ stands for the number of possible outcomes. For instance, what is the probability that *you will select a king from an ordinary deck of playing cards on the next draw*? The number of favorable outcomes is 4 because there are 4 kings, but the number of possible outcomes is 52 because there are 52 cards in the deck. So, the probability that you will select a king on the next draw is 4/52, or 1/13.

The classical theory involves two noteworthy assumptions:

**Assumption 1:** All possible outcomes are equally probable.

**Assumption 2:** All possible outcomes are taken into account.

Assumption 1 is also known as the **principle of indifference**. In our playing card example, this assumption could be false under certain circumstances. For instance, suppose the person drawing the card wants to draw a king and knows the location of one or more of the kings (e.g., on top of the deck). Or suppose the cards have been marked by someone who intends to cheat. The classical theory assumes that one card is just as likely to be drawn as another. Assumption 2 could also be false under certain circumstances—for example, if a card has been removed from the deck or if some cards have been added.

Take another example. What is the probability that *you will get "heads" on the next toss of a fair coin*? There are two possible outcomes: heads or tails. The favorable outcome is heads. So, the probability that you will get heads on the next toss is one out of two, or 1/2 (or .5). Now, you might question whether the two assumptions hold true in this type of case. Is it not possible—however unlikely—that a coin will remain balanced on its edge, in which case we have more than two possible outcomes? The answer, strictly speaking, is yes, but for practical purposes we may reasonably ignore such remote possibilities. Similarly, any given coin is likely to have imperfections that may affect the outcomes (e.g., it may be slightly out of balance). In this case, the *principle of indifference* is violated, strictly speaking, but again, for practical purposes, it may be reasonable to ignore this.

In some cases, however, the two assumptions of the classical theory clearly do not hold even as rough approximations. How probable is it, for instance, that a 50-year-old man will die of lung cancer within 10 years? What are the possible outcomes here? The outcomes include all the possible ways to die—automobile accident, heart attack, murder, shark attack, nuclear war, and so on—as well as the possibility of not dying within 10 years. There seems to be no way to take all the possible outcomes into account in this sort of case. Furthermore, it does not seem reasonable to suppose that the possible outcomes are equally likely. Surely, for example, most people are more likely to die of a heart attack than of a shark attack.

## The Relative Frequency Theory

This theory was developed from the study of mortality records used by life insurance companies. (Life insurance companies obviously have a stake in knowing the probability that persons of any given age will live for a specified period of time, e.g., 10, 20, or 30 years.) According to the **relative frequency theory**, the probability of an event (or of a statement's being true) is given by the following formula:

$$P(s) = f_o / n_o$$

Here, $f_o$ is the number of observed favorable outcomes and $n_o$ is the total number of observed outcomes. For example, suppose we wish to discover the probability that a 20-year-old woman will live 10 more years. We observe a sample of 20-year-old women over a 10-year period. If our sample contains 1000 women and 913 are alive 10 years later, we conclude that the probability that a 20-year-old woman will live 10 more years equals 913/1000, or .913.

The relative frequency theory can also be applied to coin tossing. Suppose you toss a coin 100 times and record that it came up tails 48 times. What is the probability that you will get "tails" on the next toss? By our formula, the probability is 48/100, or 12/25 (or .48). Note that this approach enables us to determine that a coin is loaded or off balance. For example, if after 100 tosses you get tails only 13 times, then you would presumably be justified in concluding that the coin is loaded or off balance.

The relative frequency theory can be applied only if an appropriate sample can be identified. And, sometimes, this appears to be impossible. For instance, what sample would one use to calculate the probability that Tom and Sue—two people who have never met—will like each other? So many subtle factors contribute to the phenomenon of mutual liking that there is no clear way to identify a sample in this case and hence no clear way to apply the relative frequency theory.

Can we apply the classical theory in this sort of case? Well, we can identify the possible outcomes: (a) Tom likes Sue and Sue likes Tom, (b) Tom likes

Sue but Sue does not like Tom, (c) Tom does not like Sue but Sue likes Tom, and (d) Tom does not like Sue and Sue does not like Tom. But is there good reason to assume that these four possible outcomes are equally probable? Certainly, we cannot in general make such an assumption when two people meet for the first time. Temperament and personal bias often render liking more (or less) probable. So, the principle of indifference is apt to be violated in such cases.

Since, in some cases, the classical and relative frequency theories appear inapplicable, let us consider an additional theory.

## The Subjectivist Theory

According to the **subjectivist theory**, probability is interpreted as an individual's confidence that an event will occur (or that a statement is true). That confidence (or degree of belief) can be stated in terms of the odds that the individual would accept on a bet. The odds are the probability that an event will happen *divided by* the probability that it will not happen (or the probability of a statement's being true *divided by* the probability of its not being true). For example, you might be willing to give 3-to-1 odds that *Speedsteed will win the Derby*, in which case you have assigned a probability of $3/(3 + 1) = 3/4$ to that statement. Or you might be willing to give 2-to-1 odds that *Tom and Sue will like each other*, in which case you have assigned a probability of $2/(2 + 1) = 2/3$ to that statement.

In general, if you give $x$-to-$y$ odds for a statement $s$, then you assign the following probability to it: $x/(x + y)$. Thus, a subjectivist approach to probability can be given a quantitative interpretation as follows:

$$P(s) = x/(x + y)$$

Here, $x$-to-$y$ odds are given for $s$'s occurring or being true. For instance, if you give 3-to-5 odds that Speedsteed will win, you assign a probability of $3/(3 + 5) = 3/8$. If you give 7-to-3 odds that Speedsteed will win, you assign a probability of $7/(7 + 3) = 7/10$. And if you give *even* odds that Speedsteed will win (such as 1-to-1 odds), you assign a probability of $1/(1 + 1) = 1/2$.

In assigning odds, it is necessary for an individual to be consistent. For instance, if I lay 3-to-2 odds that Speedsteed will win, then I am assigning that statement a probability of $3/(3 + 2) = 3/5$. I cannot then consistently give the same odds that Speedsteed will not win. In fact, for reasons that will be discussed in the next section, if I lay 3-to-2 odds that Speedsteed will win, I must lay 2-to-3 odds that Speedsteed will not win if I am to be consistent.

One problem with the subjectivist theory is suggested by its name: Different people may assign different probabilities to the same statement. This problem can be mitigated, to some extent, by taking the average of the various probabilities individuals ascribe to a statement or by applying the theory only when individuals agree about the odds.

The classical, relative frequency, and subjectivist theories give us alternative methods for assigning probability to a statement. In a given case, one of these theories may be easier to apply than another, and in some cases, we may find it difficult to apply any of the theories. However, given that we can assign probabilities to statements F and G, the probability calculus, which we will examine in the next section, tells us how to determine the probabilities of *compounds* involving F and G (e.g., disjunctions and conjunctions). In this way, the probability calculus is similar to truth tables. A truth table does not tell us the truth value of noncompound statements such as F, G, and H, but a truth table does tell us the value of (F ∨ G), for example, given truth-value assignments for F and for G. Similarly, the probability calculus does not tell us the probability of noncompound statements, but it does enable us to determine the probability of compound statements whenever we can assign probabilities to the noncompound statements involved.

## ◆ Exercise 11.1

**Part A:** Classical Theory  Use the classical theory to determine the probability of each of the following statements. Assume you are drawing from an ordinary deck of playing cards and that each card drawn is replaced so that there are always 52 cards in the deck. (If you are not a cardplayer, the following information may be of use: Each deck of 52 playing cards comes in four suits: hearts, diamonds, clubs, and spades. Each suit contains 13 cards: an ace, a two, a three, a four, a five, a six, a seven, an eight, a nine, a ten, a jack, a queen, and a king. Hearts and diamonds are red; clubs and spades are black.)

* **1.** You select the jack of diamonds on the next draw.
 **2.** You select a queen on the next draw.
 **3.** You select a red card on the next draw.
* **4.** You select a heart on the next draw.
 **5.** You select a black card on the next draw.
 **6.** You select the ace of spades on the next draw.
* **7.** You select the three of diamonds on the next draw.
 **8.** You select an ace on the next draw.
 **9.** You select the five of hearts on the next draw.
 **10.** You select a club on the next draw.

**Part B:** Relative Frequency Theory  Use the relative frequency theory to answer each of the following questions. If the classical theory provides a different answer or is inapplicable, explain why.

* **1.** You toss a coin 1000 times, and it turns up heads 503 times. What is the probability that the coin will turn up heads on the next toss?

**2.** You toss a coin 100 times, and it turns up tails 51 times. What is the probability that the coin will turn up tails on the next toss?

**3.** You roll a die 60 times, getting a five 10 times. What is the probability of getting a five on the next roll?

**4.** You roll a die 600 times, getting a three 400 times. What is the probability of getting a three on the next roll? Is the die loaded or off balance?

**5.** An urn contains 50 red marbles and 50 blue marbles. You draw marbles one at a time, *replacing each one* after recording the outcome. Between each draw, you shake the urn in an effort to ensure that each marble has an equal chance of being selected. Out of 100 selections, you draw 46 blue marbles. What is the probability of drawing a blue marble on the next draw?

**Part C:** Subjectivist Theory   Use the subjectivist theory to answer each of the following questions.

* **1.** If you give odds of 4 to 1 that *Andretti will win the Indianapolis 500*, what probability have you assigned to this statement?

**2.** If you give odds of 7 to 4 that *Jack and Jill will marry*, what probability have you assigned this statement?

**3.** If you give odds of 2 to 3 that *you will sink your next free throw*, what probability have you assigned this statement?

* **4.** If you lay odds of 17 to 2 that *it will rain today*, what probability have you assigned this statement?

**5.** If you lay odds of 11 to 14 that *Ken Griffey, Jr., will hit a homer his next time at bat*, what probability have you assigned this statement?

**6.** If you lay odds of 1 to 6 that *Earth has been visited by extraterrestrials*, what probability have you assigned this statement?

* **7.** If you give odds of 2 to 5 that *Smith will win the election*, what probability have you assigned this statement?

**8.** If you give odds of 8 to 3 that *Jones will win the election*, what probability have you assigned this statement?

**9.** If you lay odds of 2 to 1 that *you will pass your next logic exam*, what probability have you assigned this statement?

**10.** If you give even odds that a fair coin will turn up heads on the next toss, does your assignment of probability differ from that of the classical theory?

**Part D:** For Discussion   Which theory of probability would you use to determine the probability of each of the following statements given the information available?

Why? If more than one theory is applicable in a given case, explain why one theory is more applicable than the others (if possible). If two or more theories are equally applicable, explain why.

* **1.** You roll a die 100 times and get a six 40 times. What is the probability that you will get a six on the next roll?

  **2.** You give 100-to-1 odds that you will drive across town tonight without getting into an accident. What is the probability that you will drive across town tonight without getting into an accident?

  **3.** The Sonics have played the Bulls 10 times this season. The Sonics have won four games and lost six. What is the probability that the Sonics will win tonight's game against the Bulls?

  **4.** You roll a die 120 times, and get a three 20 times. What is the probability that you will get a three on the next roll?

  **5.** Smith and Jones have raced against each other in the 100-yard dash 10 times this season. Smith has won five of these races, and Jones has won five. Smith, however, slightly injured her right ankle in practice yesterday, leading you to give 6-to-4 odds that Jones will win tonight's race between Smith and Jones. What is the probability that Jones will win tonight's race against Smith?

## 11.2 The Rules of Probability

Pascal and Fermat discovered the basic rules of probability. Oddly, their work was a response to a question about gambling asked by Chevalier de Mere, a friend of Pascal's.[2]

In this section and the next, our discussion of probability presupposes the truth-functional logic introduced in Chapter 7. Accordingly, we will employ the symbols for statement logic first introduced in that chapter—specifically, "$\sim$" for negation, "$\vee$" for disjunctions, "$\cdot$" for conjunctions, "$\rightarrow$" for the material conditional, and "$\leftrightarrow$" for the material biconditional.

Probability values are expressed as numbers from 0 to 1. Zero is the lowest degree of probability; 1 is the highest. It is customary to assign the tautologies of statement logic (which are true in every row of the truth table) the highest probability, namely, 1. So, for example, $P(A \vee \sim A) = 1$. Hence, we may state our first rule of probability theory as follows:

> Rule 1: If a statement $p$ is a tautology, then $P(p) = 1$.

Here the italicized, lowercase $p$ stands for any statement whatever, including compound statements such as $[B \rightarrow (B \vee C)]$. And since a truth table reveals that $[B \rightarrow (B \vee C)]$ is a tautology, Rule 1 tells us that $P[B \rightarrow (B \vee C)] = 1$.

By contrast, contradictions, which are false in every row of the truth table, receive the lowest probability, namely, 0. This gives us our second rule of probability theory:

Rule 2:   If a statement $p$ is a contradiction, then P($p$) = 0.

For example, Rule 2 tells us that P(H • ~H) = 0 and that P(B ↔ ~B) = 0.

Two statements are **mutually exclusive** if they cannot both be true. For example:

4. Julian Lennon is exactly 25 years old today.
5. Julian Lennon is exactly 55 years old today.

A set of statements is **exhaustive** if one of the statements must be true. For example:

6. Jodie Foster is 35.
7. Jodie Foster is 40.
8. It is not the case that either Jodie Foster is 35 or Jodie Foster is 40.

Note that any statement and its negation are mutually exclusive as well as jointly exhaustive.

Now, suppose two statements, $p$ and $q$, are mutually exclusive. For example, perhaps we are rolling a single six-sided die of the type used in ordinary board games. Let $T$ stand for "The die will turn up three," and let $S$ stand for "The die will turn up six." Now, assuming the die is not loaded, there is one chance in six that it will turn up on any given side. So, P(T) = 1/6 and P(S) = 1/6. And our chances of rolling *either three or six* on the next roll are two out of six. In other words, we add the probabilities: P(T ∨ S) = 1/6 + 1/6 = 2/6 = 1/3. Examples such as this give us an intuitive grasp of the **restricted disjunction rule**:

Rule 3:   If $p$ and $q$ are mutually exclusive, then P($p$ ∨ $q$) = P($p$) + P($q$).

(This is called the *"restricted* disjunction rule" because it governs only the case in which two statements are mutually exclusive.) The following two examples are designed to enable you to see the intuitive plausibility of the restricted disjunction rule for yourself.

Suppose we are about to draw 1 card from an ordinary, well-shuffled deck of 52 playing cards. What is the probability that we will select either the ace of clubs or the ace of diamonds? Assuming each of the 52 cards has an equal chance of being drawn, P(draw ace of clubs) = 1/52, and P(draw ace of diamonds) = 1/52. So, intuitively, we have 2 chances out of 52 of selecting either the ace of clubs or the ace of diamonds (on the next draw), and this is just what the restricted disjunction rule tells us:

P(draw ace of clubs ∨ ace of diamonds) = P(draw ace of clubs) + P(draw ace of diamonds) = 1/52 + 1/52 = 2/52 = 1/26

What is the probability of drawing a queen from a well-shuffled deck (on the next draw)? Since there is one queen per suit and four suits, the intuitively correct answer is 4 out of 52, and again this is just what the restricted disjunction rule tells us:

P(draw queen of clubs ∨ draw queen of hearts ∨ draw queen of diamonds ∨ draw queen of spades) = P(draw queen of clubs) + P(draw queen of hearts) + P(draw queen of diamonds) + P(draw queen of spades) = 1/52 + 1/52 + 1/52 + 1/52 = 4/52 = 1/13

The restricted disjunction rule tells us something important about the probability of negations. Namely, it enables us to calculate the probability of a negation from the probability of the statement negated. Take the statement S. By the restricted disjunction rule, we can conclude:

$$P(S \vee \sim S) = P(S) + P(\sim S)$$

(A statement and its negation are mutually exclusive.) And since S ∨ ∼S is a tautology, by Rule 1 we may write:

$$P(S \vee \sim S) = 1$$

Now, it is a general principle of mathematics that two quantities equal to a third quantity are equal to each other. (If $x = z$ and $y = z$, then $x = y$.) So, from the two prior equations, we may draw the following conclusion:

$$P(S) + P(\sim S) = 1$$

At this point, we subtract the $P(S)$ from both sides of the equation:

$$P(\sim S) = 1 - P(S)$$

Using the lowercase letter $p$ to stand for any statement whatever, we can now generalize this reasoning and state the **negation rule**:

> **Rule 4:**  $P(\sim p) = 1 - P(p)$

The negation rule is very useful. For example, if we know that the probability of rolling a four on the next throw of the die is 1/6, then the negation rule allows us to immediately calculate the probability that a four will not turn up on the next throw:

> $P(\text{not roll } 4) = 1 - P(\text{roll } 4) = 1 - 1/6 = 5/6$

Since there are 13 cards in each suit, the probability that I will select a spade on the next draw from a well-shuffled deck is 13/52. What is the probability that I will *not* select a spade on the next draw? As follows:

> $P(\text{not select spade}) = 1 - P(\text{select spade}) = 52/52 - 13/52 = 39/52 = 3/4$

Obviously, not every pair of statements is mutually exclusive. So, we need a more general disjunction rule to take care of cases in which the disjuncts can both be true. For example, suppose we want to know the probability of getting either a king or a club on the next draw. Since there is a king of clubs, these two possibilities are not mutually exclusive. How shall we proceed? We have to subtract the probability of drawing a king that is also a club:

> $P(\text{draw king} \lor \text{club}) = P(\text{draw king}) + P(\text{draw club}) - P(\text{draw king} \cdot \text{club})$

If we do not subtract this quantity, in effect, we count the king of clubs twice—once as a king and once as a club, which skews the result. Now, since there is one king per suit, the probability that we will draw a king (on the next draw) is 4/52. The probability that we will draw a club is 13/52, since there are 13 cards in each suit. But what is the probability that we will draw both a king *and* a club? Because there is only one king that is also a club, the probability that we will draw a king and a club is simply the probability that we will draw the king of clubs, that is, 1/52. Plugging these values into our formula, we get:

> $P(\text{draw king} \lor \text{club}) = 4/52 + 13/52 - 1/52 = 16/52 = 4/13$

This sort of example gives us an intuitive grasp of the **general disjunction rule**:

> **Rule 5:**  $P(p \lor q) = P(p) + P(q) - P(p \cdot q)$

We can apply the general disjunction rule even when $p$ and $q$ are mutually exclusive, for in such a case, $P(p \cdot q)$ will always be 0. For example, what is the probability that the next card to be drawn will be either a club or a diamond? Applying Rule 5 we get:

P(club ∨ diamond) = P(club) + P(diamond) − P(club • diamond)

And since a card cannot be both a club and a diamond, we may write:

P(club ∨ diamond) = 13/52 + 13/52 − 0 = 26/52 = 1/2

The following examples should enable you to see the intuitive plausibility of the general disjunction rule for yourself. What is the probability of selecting either the jack of hearts or a red card (on the next draw)? There is one jack of hearts and 26 red cards. So, one might be tempted to say P(jack of hearts ∨ red) = 27/52, but this answer ignores the fact that the jack of hearts is itself red (and hence has been counted twice). The general disjunction rule gives the correct formula to employ:

P(jack of hearts ∨ red) = P(jack of hearts) + P(red) − P(jack of hearts • red)

And since the only card that is both the jack of hearts and red is the jack of hearts, we plug in values as follows:

P(jack of hearts ∨ red) = 1/52 + 26/52 − 1/52 = 26/52 = 1/2

What is the probability of drawing either a red card or an eight (on the next draw)? Because half the cards (i.e., 26) are red, and there are 4 eights (1 in each suit), one might be tempted to answer 30/52. But this would be a mistake because 2 of the eights are red and they've been counted twice. The general disjunction rule gives the correct answer:

P(red ∨ eight) = 26/52 + 4/52 − 2/52 = 28/52 = 7/13

Before leaving our discussion of the general disjunction rule, let us note that it enables us to handle the material conditional, for $p \rightarrow q$ is logically equivalent to $\sim p \vee q$, and hence P($p \rightarrow q$) is equal to P ($\sim p \vee q$). However, as we noted in Chapter 7, the material conditional does not adequately capture the meaning of the English "if-then" in every context. For this reason, logicians have developed a rule of probability that is designed to capture the meaning of English conditionals as they are used in contexts involving judgments about probability. Accordingly, we turn now to a rule of probability designed to capture a different sense of "if-then" than the material conditional.

Suppose we want to know the probability that $q$ is true *given that p* is true. Following standard notation in probability theory, we will write "The probability of $q$ given that $p$" as: P($q/p$). This notation is read variously as "The probability of $q$ *on the condition that p*," "The probability of $q$ on $p$," or "The probability of $q$ given $p$." The **conditional rule** is as follows:

Rule 6: $P(q/p) = \dfrac{P(p \cdot q)}{P(p)}$

Stated in the abstract, this rule may not seem at all obvious to you. Why suppose that the probability of a conditional equals the probability of the conjunction of its antecedent and consequent *divided by* the probability of its antecedent? The correctness of this rule is best seen through the lens of specific examples. Suppose I am about to draw exactly one card from a well-shuffled deck. Consider the probability that I will draw a club *given that* I will draw the ace of clubs. Intuitively, the probability is 1, since if the card drawn is the ace of clubs, it must be a club. And this is exactly what Rule 6 tells us:

$$P(\text{club/ace of clubs}) = \frac{P(\text{ace of clubs} \cdot \text{club})}{P(\text{ace of clubs})}$$

The probability of drawing the ace of clubs is 1/52. The probability of drawing a club *that is also the ace of clubs* is simply the probability of drawing the ace of clubs. So, we write:

$$P(\text{club/ace of clubs}) = \frac{1/52}{1/52} = 1$$

Consider a second example. What is the probability that I will draw a spade *given that* I will draw a heart? (Remember, I am drawing just one card from a well-shuffled deck.) Intuitively, the probability is 0, since if I draw just one card and it is a heart, I certainly do not draw a spade. Let's see if the conditional rule bears this out:

$$P(\text{spade/heart}) = \frac{P(\text{heart} \cdot \text{spade})}{P(\text{heart})}$$

The probability of drawing a heart on a given draw is 13/52. Because a card cannot be both a heart and a spade, the probability of drawing a heart *and* a spade (on a given draw) is 0. Plugging in these values, we get:

$$P(\text{spade/heart}) = \frac{0}{13/52} = 0$$

Thus, the conditional rule once again gives us the intuitively correct answer.

A third example: What is the probability that I will draw the king of hearts from a well-shuffled deck *given that* I will draw a king? Since there are four kings altogether, but only one king of hearts, this probability is intuitively 1/4. Applying the conditional rule, we get:

$$P(\text{king of hearts/king}) = \frac{P(\text{king} \cdot \text{king of hearts})}{P(\text{king})}$$

The probability of drawing a king on a single draw from a well-shuffled deck is 4/52. The probability of drawing a king that is also the king of hearts is, of course, simply the probability of drawing the king of hearts, that is, 1/52. Therefore:

$$P(\text{king of hearts}/\text{king}) = \frac{1/52}{4/52} = 1/52 \times 52/4 = 52/208 = 1/4$$

Once again, the conditional rule accords with our intuitions.*

One last example: What is the probability that I will draw a club *given that* I will draw a black card? Since half the black cards are clubs and half are spades, the answer is intuitively 1/2. The conditional rule tells us:

$$P(\text{club}/\text{black}) = \frac{P(\text{black} \bullet \text{club})}{P(\text{black})}$$

Now, half the cards in a deck are black and half are red. So, P(black) = 1/2. And the probability of drawing a card that is both black *and* a club is simply the probability of drawing a club, namely, 13/52, or 1/4. Once again, the conditional rule gives us the intuitively correct answer:

$$P(\text{club}/\text{black}) = \frac{1/4}{1/2} = 1/4 \times 2/1 = 2/4 = 1/2$$

Now, the conditional rule is important, not only for what it tells us about the probability of conditionals but also because from it we can immediately deduce the **general conjunction rule**:

**Rule 7:**  $P(p \bullet q) = P(p) \times P(q/p)$

To prove this, we begin with the conditional rule:

$$P(q/p) = \frac{P(p \bullet q)}{P(p)}$$

Next, we multiply both sides of the equation by P(*p*):

$$P(p) \times P(q/p) = P(p) \times \frac{P(p \bullet q)}{P(p)}$$

---

*Since math skills can become "rusty" with disuse, this note explains how to divide complex fractions, that is, fractions in which the numerator and/or denominator involve fractions. To get right to the point: a/b divided by c/d = a/b times d/c. For example, 1/3 divided by 4/5 = 1/3 times 5/4 = 5/12. Thus, the division of a fraction may be interpreted as multiplication by the reciprocal of its *divisor*. (In the above formula, the divisor is c/d.)

Now, since $a \times \dfrac{b}{a} = \dfrac{a \times b}{a} = \dfrac{a}{a} \times b = 1 \times b = b$, we can transform the right-hand side of the equation as follows:

$$P(p) \times P(q/p) = P(p \bullet q)$$

And this is just what the general conjunction rule says. For example, consider the situation in which one draws a card from a well-shuffled deck and, *without* replacing it, draws a second card. What is the probability of drawing the ace of spades on the first draw *and* the ace of spades on the second draw? The answer is 0, since there is only one ace of spades and it was removed on the first draw. This is exactly the answer given by the general conjunction rule:

P(ace of spades on 1 • ace of spades on 2) = P(ace of spades on 1) × P(ace of spades on 2 *given* ace of spades on 1) = 1/52 × 0 = 0

What is the probability of drawing a red card on the first draw and a red card on the second draw? Of course, P(red on 1) = 1/2. But if we do select a red card on the first draw, only 51 cards will be left, 25 of them red. So, our chances of getting a red card the second time will be 25/51. How do we ascertain P(red on 1 • red on 2)? The general conjunction rule gives the answer:

P(red on 1 • red on 2) = P(red on 1) × P(red on 2 *given* red on 1) = 1/2 × 25/51 = 25/102.

In other words, the probability is just a bit shy of 1/4. Of course, the numerically precise answer is something virtually no one can directly intuit. But since the general conjunction rule follows from the conditional rule, and we have seen that the conditional rule accords with our intuitions about probability, we can trust the answer given by the general conjunction rule.

What is the probability of drawing an ace on the first draw *and* (without replacing the first card drawn) another ace on the second draw?

P(ace on 1 • ace on 2) = P(ace on 1) × P(ace on 2 *given* ace on 1)

Now, the probability of getting an ace on the first draw is only 4/52. But if we do draw an ace and lay it aside, 51 cards remain in the deck, 3 of them aces. So, the probability of selecting an ace on the second draw, given that we drew an ace on the first draw, is 3/51. Therefore:

P(ace on 1 • ace on 2) = 4/52 × 3/51 = 12/2652 = 1/221

In other words, the probability of drawing two consecutive aces is quite low. Here again, although virtually no one can directly intuit the precise numerical probability, the answer is reliable assuming the conditional rule (from which we derived the general conjunction rule) is reliable.

If two statements, *p* and *q*, are such that neither one affects the probability of the other, they are said to be **independent**. In such a case, $P(q/p) = P(q)$ and $P(p/q) = P(p)$. For example, "The German philosopher Gottfried Wilhelm Leibniz died in 1716" and "The next card to be drawn will be a jack" are independent. Thus, the probability that "The next card to be drawn will be a jack *given that* Leibniz died in 1716" is simply the probability that the next card to be drawn will be a jack, namely, 4/52. In such cases, we can apply the **restricted conjunction rule**:

Rule 8: If *p* and *q* are independent, $P(p \cdot q) = P(p) \times P(q)$.

For example, consider the probability of selecting an ace twice by drawing from a well-shuffled deck, replacing the card, reshuffling, and drawing a second time. Because, in this sort of case, what one gets on the first draw has no effect on what one gets on the second draw, it is convenient to apply the restricted conjunction rule:

P(ace on 1 • ace on 2) = P(ace on 1) x P(ace on 2)

Plugging in numerical values, we get:

P(ace on 1 • ace on 2) = 4/52 x 4/52 = 1/13 x 1/13 = 1/169

It is instructive to compare this with the probability calculated previously of drawing two aces consecutively *without* replacing the card selected on the first draw.

The restricted conjunction rule provides us with an important logical insight. Suppose we have a conjunction of independent statements, each of which has a probability of less than 1 but greater than 1/2. For example, suppose $P(A) = 7/10$, $P(B) = 7/10$, and $P(C) = 7/10$. What is the probability of the whole conjunction?

P[A • (B • C)] = 7/10 x 7/10 x 7/10 = 343/1000

Note that although each conjunct is more probable than not, the entire conjunction has a probability of less than 1/2. So, the negation of this conjunction is more probable than the conjunction itself. Therefore, when we conjoin *probably true but independent* statements—think, for example, of a creed in which some of the statements may be independent—the probability of the compound may sink below 1/2, even though each conjunct is more probable than not. (Of course, it may still be true that the entire creedal statement is more probable than any interesting alternative creed.)

To check your understanding of the basic rules of probability theory, complete the following exercises.

| **Summary of the Rules of Probability** |
| --- |

1. If a statement $p$ is a tautology, then $P(p) = 1$.
2. If a statement $p$ is a contradiction, then $P(p) = 0$.
3. **Restricted disjunction rule:** If $p$ and $q$ are mutually exclusive, then $P(p \lor q) = P(p) + P(q)$.
4. **Negation rule:** $P(\sim p) = 1 - P(p)$
5. **General disjunction rule:** $P(p \lor q) = P(p) + P(q) - P(p \cdot q)$
6. **Conditional rule:** $P(q/p) = \dfrac{P(p \cdot q)}{P(p)}$
7. **General conjunction rule:** $P(p \cdot q) = P(p) \times P(q/p)$
8. **Restricted conjunction rule:** If $p$ and $q$ are independent, $P(p \cdot q) = P(p) \times P(q)$.

## ◆ Exercise 11.2

**Part A:** Disjunctions    Suppose you have an ordinary deck of playing cards. Assuming that you are as likely to draw one card as another, what is the probability that on your next draw you will select each of the following?

*   **1.** A spade or a diamond?

    **2.** A jack or a queen?

    **3.** A king or a nonking?

*   **4.** The queen of diamonds or a heart?

    **5.** A king or a spade?

    **6.** A club or a red card?

*   **7.** A red card or an ace?

    **8.** A black card or the 10 of hearts?

    **9.** A black card or the 10 of spades?

  **10.** A black card or a 10?

**Part B:** Conjunctions and Conditionals    You have an ordinary deck of cards. You draw one card, do *not* replace it, and then draw a second card. Assuming you are as likely to draw one card as another, find the following probabilities.

*   **1.** P(jack on first draw • queen on second draw)

    **2.** P(ace on first draw • ace on second draw)

    **3.** P(ace of hearts on first • red on second)

*   **4.** P(club on first • club on second)

   **5.** P(club on first • diamond on second)

   **6.** P(black on first • black on second)

\* **7.** P(queen of hearts on first • queen of hearts on second)

   **8.** P(spade on first • black on second)
   [*Note:* Because the conditional rule and the general conjunction rule are interdependent, you must answer the last two items by thinking intuitively. For example, regarding #9, if you select an ace on the first draw and do not put it back in the deck, what are your chances of selecting a king on the second draw?]

   **9.** P(king on second draw *given* ace on first draw)

   **10.** P(red on second *given* jack of spades on first)

**Part C:** Various Compound Statements   Let G be "God exists," M be "Miracles occur," *T* be "A → A," and *D* be "Ducks exist." Assume that $P(G) = 3/5$, $P(M) = 3/10$, $P(D) = 9/10$, and $P(G/M) = 9/10$. Also assume that $D$ and $M$ are independent. Determine the following probabilities.

| | |
|---|---|
| \* **1.** P(~G) | **9.** P(D/M) |
| **2.** P(~M) | \* **10.** P[D → (G → D)] |
| **3.** P(G • ~G) | **11.** P(M/D) |
| \* **4.** P(M ∨ ~M) | **12.** P(~D) |
| **5.** P(T) | **13.** P(D • M) |
| **6.** P(~T) | **14.** P(D ∨ M) |
| \* **7.** P(M • G) | **15.** P[G → (M ∨ G)] |
| **8.** P(M ∨ G) | |

**Part D:** The Strength of Arguments   Use the rules of probability to determine the strength of the following arguments. In other words, given that the premises are true, how likely is the conclusion?

\* **1.** The odds are 5 to 1 that Team A will beat Team B in the quarter-finals. The odds are 4 to 1 that Team C will beat Team D in the quarter-finals. Therefore, Team A will play Team C in the semifinals.

   **2.** The odds are 6 to 1 that Chris is lying. Therefore, it is not the case that Chris is lying.

   **3.** The odds are 1 to 3 that Mad Dog Mike killed Jones. The odds are 2 to 1 that Bad Dog Bob killed Jones. There is a probability of zero that Mad Dog

Mike and Bad Dog Bob *both* killed Jones. Therefore, either Mad Dog Mike or Bad Dog Bob killed Jones.

* **4.** The die is fair (not loaded or off balance), and I roll it twice. Therefore, I roll a five twice.

 **5.** The odds are 1 to 4 that Bill stole the TV. The odds are 1 to 3 that Jack stole the TV. The odds are 1 to 9 that Jack and Bill both stole the TV. Therefore, either Jack or Bill stole the TV.

 **6.** Jack and Jill are married, and they are both 30 years of age. The probability that a 30-year-old man will live to age 80 is .63, while the probability that a 30-year-old woman will live to age 80 is .71. Therefore, Jack and Jill will both live to age 80.

* **7.** The odds are 15 to 1 that Ted was at the party. Moreover, it is very likely that if Ted was at the party, Sue was also; in fact, the odds are 20 to 1. So, Ted and Sue were both at the party.

 **8.** The odds are 2 to 1 that Radical Jack Jones will defeat Buster Bonzo in the semifinal bout. The odds are even that Crocker Crunch will defeat The Blue Basher in the semifinal bout. Therefore, Radical Jack Jones will meet Crocker Crunch in the championship bout.

 **9.** The odds are 2 to 1 that Zeus exists. And the odds are 2 to 1 that wisdom is a virtue. "Zeus exists" is logically independent of "Wisdom is a virtue." Hence, Zeus exists and wisdom is a virtue.

 **10.** The odds are 9 to 1 that trees are real. And the odds are 0 to 1 that life is but a dream *given that* trees are real. So, trees are real and life is nothing but a dream.

## 11.3 Bayes' Theorem

Thomas Bayes (1702–1761) was an English theologian and mathematician who made an important contribution to the theory of probability. According to many philosophers, Bayes' theorem gives us an important insight into the relationship between the evidence for a hypothesis and the hypothesis itself. Assuming this is so, Bayes' theorem provides us with important information relative to assessing inductive arguments. Let us see how we can derive Bayes' theorem from the basic rules of probability theory.

Let us use the italicized, lowercase letter *h* to stand for any hypothesis and *e* to stand for a statement that summarizes the observational evidence for that hypothesis. We begin with the conditional rule:[3]

$$P(h/e) = \frac{P(e \cdot h)}{P(e)}$$

This tells us that the probability of a hypothesis *given* the evidence is equal to the probability of the conjunction of the evidence and the hypothesis *divided by* the probability of the evidence.

A proof or truth table will reveal that *e* is logically equivalent to $(e \cdot h) \vee (e \cdot {\sim}h)$. Therefore, we may replace *e* with $(e \cdot h) \vee (e \cdot {\sim}h)$ wherever we wish, and it is useful to do so in the denominator:

$$P(h/e) = \frac{P(e \cdot h)}{P[(e \cdot h) \vee (e \cdot {\sim}h)]}$$

Now, by the restricted disjunction rule, $P[(e \cdot h) \vee (e \cdot {\sim}h)]$ is equal to $P(e \cdot h) + P(e \cdot {\sim}h)$. Therefore, we may write:

$$P(h/e) = \frac{P(e \cdot h)}{P(e \cdot h) + P(e \cdot {\sim}h)}$$

Next, we apply the rule of commutation to the three conjunctions on the right side of the equation, as follows:*

$$P(h/e) = \frac{P(h \cdot e)}{P(h \cdot e) + P({\sim}h \cdot e)}$$

Finally, we apply the general conjunction rule three times, to arrive at **Bayes' theorem**:

$$P(h/e) = \frac{P(h) \times P(e/h)}{[P(h) \times P(e/h)] + [P({\sim}h) \times P(e/{\sim}h)]}$$

Now, in order to use Bayes' theorem to discover the degree to which a given hypothesis is supported by the evidence, we need just three pieces of information: $P(h)$, $P(e/h)$, and $P(e/{\sim}h)$. (Remember, if we have $P(h)$, we can

---

*According to the rule of commutation, statements of the form $(p \cdot q)$ and $(q \cdot p)$ are logically equivalent and, hence, may be exchanged whenever it is convenient to do so. In other words, from a logical point of view, it is always permissible to interchange the conjuncts in a conjunction. The rule of commutation also applies to disjunctions, since $(p \vee q)$ is logically equivalent to $(q \vee p)$.

calculate P($\sim h$) using the negation rule.) P($h$) stands for the **prior** or **antecedent probability** of the hypothesis—that is, the likelihood of the hypothesis independent of the evidence $e$. Normally, $e$ is a statement summarizing the latest observational evidence so that we have some background evidence to appeal to in estimating P($h$).* P($e/h$) is the likelihood that the evidence (or phenomenon in question) would be present, assuming the hypothesis is true. P($e/\sim h$) is the likelihood that the evidence (or phenomenon in question) would be present, assuming the hypothesis is false. An example will help make these abstractions concrete.

Suppose a doctor has diagnosed a patient as having *either* some minor stomach troubles *or* stomach cancer. And let us assume that the doctor knows that the patient does not have *both* minor stomach troubles *and* stomach cancer. The doctor also knows that, given the symptoms, 30 percent of patients have stomach cancer; the rest have minor stomach troubles. Accordingly, the doctor initially suspects that the patient has only minor stomach troubles. But the doctor proceeds to conduct a test. Experience indicates that 90 percent of cases of stomach cancer yield a positive result when this test is applied, but only 10 percent of cases of minor stomach troubles yield a positive result. What is the probability that the patient has stomach cancer *given that the test turns out positive?*

Following our practice of using capital letters to stand for specific statements, here's a scheme of abbreviation that will help us apply Bayes' Theorem:

H: The patient has stomach cancer

E: The test is positive.

We want to find P(H/E), that is, the probability that the hypothesis is true given the evidence. To do this, we need three bits of information. First, we need P(H), that is, the prior or antecedent probability of the hypothesis. Second, we need P(E/H), that is, the probability of a positive test result *assuming that* the hypothesis is true. Finally, we need to know P(E/$\sim$H), that is, the probability of a positive test result *assuming that* the hypothesis is not true. It is built into the case that if the patient does not have cancer, then he or she has minor stomach troubles. So, given the parameters of the case, information about $\sim$H is given by way of information about "minor stomach troubles."

The doctor's background knowledge provides the prior or antecedent probability that the patient has stomach cancer, for given the symptoms, 30 percent of patients have stomach cancer. In other words, P(H) = 30/100 = 3/10. We can obtain P($\sim$H) by the negation rule: 1 − 3/10 = 7/10. And since 90 percent of cases of stomach cancer yield a positive result when the test is applied,

---

*If we wish to distinguish background evidence $b$ from $e$ (the "new" evidence or phenomenon to be explained), Bayes' theorem takes on a slightly more complicated appearance:

$$P[h/(e \cdot b)] = \frac{P(h/b) \times P[e/(h \cdot b)]}{\{P(h/b) \times P[e/(h \cdot b)]\} + \{P(\sim h/b) \times P[e/(\sim h \cdot b)]\}}$$

P(E/H) = 90/100 = 9/10. Furthermore, since we are assuming that the patient has minor stomach troubles if he or she does not have stomach cancer, and since 10 percent of cases of minor stomach troubles yield a positive result when the test is applied, then P(E/~H) = 10/100 = 1/10. Plugging these values into Bayes' theorem, we get:

$$P(H/E) = \frac{3/10 \times 9/10}{[3/10 \times 9/10] + [7/10 \times 1/10]} = \frac{27/100}{27/100 + 7/100} = \frac{27}{34}$$

So, the probability of the hypothesis given the evidence is 27/34, or approximately .79.

You may be wondering whether P(~h/e) = 1 − P(h/e). The answer is yes.[4] In our proof of Bayes' theorem, we saw that P(e) = P(e • h) + P(e • ~h). Now, if we divide both sides of the equation by P(e), we get:

$$\frac{P(e)}{P(e)} = \frac{P(e \cdot h) + P(e \cdot \sim h)}{P(e)}$$

Therefore:

$$1 = \frac{P(e \cdot h)}{P(e)} + \frac{P(e \cdot \sim h)}{P(e)}$$

By the conditional rule, we can replace P(e • h)/P(e) with P(h/e). Similarly, we can replace P(e • ~h)/P(e) with P(~h/e). Making these replacements, we get:

$$1 = P(h/e) + P(\sim h/e)$$

Finally, subtracting P(h/e) from both sides we obtain:

$$P(\sim h/e) = 1 - P(h/e)$$

Thus, if we know P(h/e) = 7/10, we may conclude that P(~h/e) = 1 − 7/10 = 3/10.

In many cases, we do not have adequate grounds for assigning precise numerical values to P(h), P(e/h), and/or P(e/~h). Does it follow that Bayes' theorem is inapplicable in such cases? Not necessarily. Even if we cannot assign precise numerical values, we may be able to assign relative values. For example, in a given case, we may have good reason to suppose that $P(h) \geq P(\sim h)$. And we may be able to settle, by argument, that $P(e/h) > P(e/\sim h)$. In such a case, we can conclude that the evidence under consideration favors $h$ over $\sim h$. This is so because whenever $P(h) \geq P(\sim h)$, evidence $e$ favors $h$ provided that $P(e/h) > P(e/\sim h)$. After all, as we saw in section 11.2, $P(h) + P(\sim h) = 1$. Hence, if $P(h) \geq P(\sim h)$, then $P(h) \geq 1/2$ and $P(\sim h) \leq 1/2$. And in this situation, if $P(e/h) > P(e/\sim h)$, then $P(h/e) > P(\sim h/e)$. To illustrate this concretely, suppose $P(h) = P(\sim h) = 1/2$, $P(e/h) = 3/5$, and $P(e/\sim h) = 2/5$. Then, applying Bayes' theorem, we get:

$$P(h/e) = \frac{1/2 \times 3/5}{[1/2 \times 3/5] + [1/2 \times 2/5]} = \frac{3/10}{3/10 + 2/10} = 3/5$$

$$P(\sim h/e) = 2/5$$

To generalize, if $P(h) \geq P(\sim h)$ and $P(e/h) > P(e/\sim h)$, then $P(h/e) > P(\sim h/e)$. The important point is that we can sometimes apply Bayes' theorem even when we cannot set precise numerical values. Typically, this occurs when we can provide reasonable arguments to the effect that $P(h) \geq P(\sim h)$ and $P(e/h) > P(e/\sim h)$.

Some philosophers have tried to apply Bayes' theorem to major philosophical issues such as the existence of God.[5] While we cannot here enter into a detailed discussion of such matters, it is important to understand how Bayes' theorem can be used to organize a rational dialogue and develop strategies for argument. To this end, let us briefly consider a version of the cosmological argument for God's existence. Let H be "God exists" and E be "There is a physical universe." A theist may argue that $P(E/H) > P(E/\sim H)$ on the following grounds: first, that God would have a good reason to create the physical universe as an appropriate environment for intelligent creatures; and second, that if there is no God, then there is no explanation for the existence of physical reality—it can only be regarded as a coincidence. Using Bayes' theorem to structure the discussion, the nontheist might respond in three ways:

- Refute the theist's arguments for the thesis that $P(E/H) > P(E/\sim H)$.
- Argue that the prior probability of "God exists" is lower than the prior probability of "God does not exist." If a good case can be made that $P(H) < P(\sim H)$, then this could destroy the force of the cosmological argument, *even if* $P(E/H) > P(E/\sim H)$. (To illustrate, some have argued that $P(H) < P(\sim H)$ because the divine attributes lead to conceptual puzzles—for example, if God is all-powerful, can God create a stone too big for God to lift?)

■ Argue that the probability that God exists is low given some evidence *other than* the existence of the physical universe, such as the suffering or evil in the world.

Obviously, these strategies can be combined. The point here is not to recommend either the cosmological argument or any of these strategies for replying to it but merely to illustrate how the Bayesian perspective can help us structure a rational dialogue.

Can a Bayesian approach accommodate a situation in which multiple hypotheses are being compared? Yes. To illustrate, if $h_1$, $h_2$, and $h_3$ are *three mutually exclusive hypotheses that exhaust the possibilities*, then:

$$P(h_1/e) = \frac{P(h_1) \times P(e/h_1)}{[P(h_1) \times P(e/h_1)] + [P(h_2) \times P(e/h_2)] + [P(h_3) \times P(e/h_3)]}$$

In other words, we can accommodate as many hypotheses as we like (provided they are mutually exclusive and exhaust the possibilities), simply by adding relevant clauses to the denominator. To apply Bayes' theorem, we must assign values for $P(e/h_1)$, $P(e/h_2)$, and $P(e/h_3)$, as well as for the prior probabilities of at least two of the three hypotheses. Since we are assuming that the three hypotheses are mutually exclusive and exhaust the possibilities, we can assume that the sum of their prior probabilities is one, just as $P(h) + P(\sim h) = 1$. And given that $P(h_1) + P(h_2) + P(h_3) = 1$, then $P(h_1) = 1 - P(h_2) - P(h_3)$. Similarly, $P(h_2) = 1 - P(h_1) - P(h_3)$, and $P(h_3) = 1 - P(h_1) - P(h_2)$.

The following exercises will increase your understanding of Bayes' theorem and of its application to a wide range of issues.

## ◆ Exercise 11.3

**Part A: Patterns**    Explore Bayes' theorem by answering the following questions.

1. Suppose you are applying Bayes' theorem, and P(H) = P(E/H) = P(E/~H). For example, what is P(H/E) in the following cases?
   * a. P(H) = 1/2; P(E/H) = 1/2; P(E/~H) = 1/2
   b. P(H) = 2/3; P(E/H) = 2/3; P(E/~H) = 2/3
   c. P(H) = 1/4; P(E/H) = 1/4; P(E/~H) = 1/4

2. Suppose you are applying Bayes' theorem and the prior probability of the hypothesis is low, but P(E/H) and P(E/~H) are high and equal. For instance, what is P(H/E) in the following cases?
   * a. P(H) = 1/5; P(E/H) = 9/10; P(E/~H) = 9/10
   b. P(H) = 1/3; P(E/H) = 7/8; P(E/~H) = 7/8
   c. P(H) = 3/8; P(E/H) = 3/4; P(E/~H) = 3/4

3. Suppose you are applying Bayes' theorem and the prior probability of the hypothesis is high, but P(E/H) is low and equal to P(E/~H). For example, what is P(H/E) in the following cases?

* a. P(H) = 9/10; P(E/H) = 2/5; P(E/~H) = 2/5

  b. P(H) = 8/9; P(E/H) = 1/3; P(E/~H) = 1/3

  c. P(H) = 7/10; P(E/H) = 4/9; P(E/~H) = 4/9

4. Suppose you are applying Bayes' theorem and the prior probability of the hypothesis is 1/2, but P(E/H) is greater than P(E/~H). For instance, what is P(H/E) in the following cases? What is P(~H/E) in these cases?

* a. P(H) = 1/2; P(E/H) = 9/10; P(E/~H) = 3/5

  b. P(H) = 1/2; P(E/H) = 7/8; P(E/~H) = 3/4

5. Suppose you are applying Bayes' theorem and one of the probability values is 0. Specifically:

   a. Suppose the prior probability of the hypothesis is 0. Can P(E/H) be determined? [*Hint:* Applying the conditional rule, P(E/H) = P(H • E) divided by P(H).]

* b. Suppose P(H) is high, P(E/H) is 0, and P(E/~H) is not 0. For example, suppose P(H) = 9/10, P(E/H) = 0, and P(E/~H) = 1/10. What is P(H/E)? What is P(~H/E)?

   c. Suppose P(H) and P(E/H) are low, but P(E/~H) is 0. For example, suppose P(H) = 1/10, P(E/H) = 3/10, and P(E/~H) = 0. What is P(H/E)? What is P(~H/E)?

6. Suppose you are applying Bayes' theorem, and suppose P(H) and P(E/H) are both moderately high and P(E/~H) is a bit lower than P(E/H). For example, what is P(H/E) in the following cases? What is P(~H/E)?

   a. P(H) = 7/10; P(E/H) = 7/10; P(E/~H) = 6/10

* b. P(H) = 5/7; P(E/H) = 5/7; P(E/~H) = 4/7

7. Suppose you are applying Bayes' theorem and the prior probability of the hypothesis H is slightly higher than that of its negation, but P(E/H) is slightly lower than P(E/~H). For example, what is P(H/E) in the following cases? What is P(~H/E)?

   a. P(H) = 9/16; P(E/H) = 8/10; P(E/~H) = 9/10

   b. P(H) = 51/100; P(E/H) = 5/10; P(E/~H) = 6/10

**Part B:** Applying Bayes' Theorem    Bayes' theorem has many interesting applications. Some philosophers even think it can be used to set up certain traditional philosophical problems in a revealing fashion. Of course, like other logical principles, the rules of probability seldom solve philosophical problems—that is not their purpose. But the rules of probability, like other principles of logic, can help us formulate questions in interesting ways that help us focus our thinking, ask new questions, and identify difficulties. The following exercises ask you to apply Bayes' theorem to a wide range of questions and issues. In a number of cases, the assignment of numerical values is deliberately contrived, for the sake of making a definite answer possible. But keep in mind that Bayes' theorem can sometimes be applied even when precise numerical values cannot be assigned.

* **1.** Bloggs is an impoverished college student working 40 hours a week. Due to the shortage of time, Bloggs prepares for only 40 percent of his exams. Bloggs passes 70 percent of the exams he prepares for. But he only passes 30 percent of the exams he does not prepare for. Furthermore, Bloggs passed his most recent exam. How probable is it that Bloggs prepared for his most recent exam?

**2.** A veterinarian has diagnosed a dog as having either leukemia or severe anemia (but not both). Given the symptoms, 90 percent of dogs have severe anemia and 10 percent of dogs have leukemia. So, the vet initially surmises that the dog has severe anemia. Later, however, the vet conducts a test on the dog that turns out positive. Seventy percent of cases of leukemia yield a positive result when this test is applied, and 20 percent of cases of anemia yield a positive result. What is the probability that the dog has leukemia given the results of the test?

**3.** Police detectives have determined that Smith and Jones are the only two possible murderers of McCann, and it is known that the murderer acted all by himself. (Thus, Smith and Jones are not both guilty of the murder.) Because Smith has a prior criminal record, Detective Wills initially gives odds of 5 to 3 that Smith is the murderer. However, while at the scene of the crime, Detective Wills finds the murder weapon, which has Jones's fingerprints on it *and not Smith's*. Detective Wills gives 9-to-1 odds that Jones's fingerprints are on the weapon *given that* Jones is the murderer; whereas Wills gives only 3-to-7 odds that Jones's fingerprints are on the weapon *given that* Smith is the murderer. (It is possible, but unlikely, that Smith somehow set Jones up.) Given Detective Wills's assessment of the odds, how likely is it that Jones is the murderer *given that* Jones's fingerprints are on the murder weapon? How likely is it that Smith is the murderer *given that* Jones's fingerprints are on the murder weapon?

* **4.** Valerie is trying to assess the evidence for the existence of a God who is all-powerful and perfectly good. Given her background evidence (e.g., she is aware of the cosmological and design arguments for God's existence), Valerie gives even odds that God exists. However, Valerie has recently heard of the so-called problem of evil. She finds it plausible to suppose that some of the suffering in the world, such as the suffering of animals, is not a necessary means to a greater good. Furthermore, Valerie is convinced that if God were all-powerful and perfectly good, then God would not permit any suffering unless it were a necessary means to a greater good. On reflection, Valerie gives only 1-to-3 odds that some unnecessary suffering occurs *given that* an all-powerful and perfectly good God exists. But she gives 2-to-1 odds that

some unnecessary suffering occurs *given that* an all-powerful and perfectly good God does *not* exist. Given Valerie's assignments of probability, what is the probability that God exists *given that* some unnecessary suffering occurs?

5. Nate is a sprinter at a college that hosts relatively few track meets. In fact, only 30 percent of Nate's races are at his own college. Nate wins 90 percent of the races held at his own college. But he wins only 40 percent of the races at other colleges. Nate won his last race. How likely is it that the race was at Nate's own college?

6. Sally claims to have telekinetic powers. She claims that she can cause a die to turn up any number she chooses. A *fair* die is produced, and Sally predicts that she will role a six three times in a row. She proceeds to do just that. Our evidence and hypothesis are:

   E: Sally rolls a six three times in a row (without cheating).
   H: Sally has telekinetic powers.

   Given that Sally has telekinetic powers, E is just the sort of thing we should expect. So, assume that P(E/H) = 1. But *prior* to considering E, we are understandably skeptical, giving odds of 1 to 9 that Sally has telekinetic powers. Assuming chance is the only alternative to Sally's alleged telekinetic powers, what is P(E/~H)? (*Hint:* You will need to use the restricted conjunction rule.) What is P(H/E)?

7. Zachary is evaluating the evidence for two worldviews, theism and naturalism. Theism is the view that a perfectly loving and all-powerful God exists and that God created the physical universe. Naturalism is the view that only matter exists and that matter is entirely governed by natural laws (such as the law of gravity). In Zachary's estimation, the probability that either theism or naturalism is true is very high. In fact, Zachary regards other worldviews as too implausible to be worth serious consideration. Zachary is aware of the standard arguments for God's existence as well as the problem of evil, which is usually considered the strongest argument against the existence of God. On this basis, Zachary initially gives 1-to-2 odds that God exists and 2-to-1 odds that naturalism is true. However, Zachary goes on to consider his firm belief that people are morally responsible. He takes it as obvious that people cannot be morally responsible unless they have free will. Yet, it appears to Zachary that free will is most unlikely given naturalism. For, given naturalism, every event is the result of past states of the physical world plus the operation of natural laws. And since we have no control over the past and no control over which (or whether) natural laws hold, it seems that we humans lack free will *given* naturalism. Accordingly, Zachary gives only 1-to-5 odds that humans have free will given naturalism, while he gives 5-to-1 odds that humans have free will *given* theism. (Zachary reasons that a God of love would likely provide some of his creatures with free will in order that they might love freely and not of necessity.) Given Zachary's estimates, what is the probability of theism *given that* humans have free will? What is the probability of naturalism *given that* humans have free will?

8. Suppose the police know that either Jones, Smith, or Dobbs stole the jewels. Furthermore, the police know that the thief acted all by himself. $H_1$ is "Jones stole the jewels," $H_2$ is "Smith stole the jewels," and $H_3$ is "Dobbs stole the jewels." The hypotheses are equally likely on the background evidence (e.g., the criminal records of the three suspects). Also, suppose the evidence at the crime scene allows us to assign these probabilities: $P(E/H_1) = 1/4$, $P(E/H_2) = 1/2$, and $P(E/H_3) = 3/4$. What is $P(H_1/E)$? $P(H_2/E)$? $P(H_3/E)$?

9. Chris thinks the prior probability that reincarnation occurs is low for two reasons. First, it is unclear what links any given soul with any given body (e.g., why does Jones's soul wind up in Smith's body?). Second, there seems to be no good answer to the question, "How long has reincarnation been going on?" The usual answer is that the process is beginningless (infinite). However, this seems unlikely since, according to recent work in physics, the physical universe itself has only been in existence for 15–20 billion years—a finite period of time. (And, obviously, there were no physical bodies for souls to transmigrate to prior to the existence of matter.) For these reasons, Chris initially gives odds of only 1 to 3 that reincarnation occurs. But then Chris encounters new evidence in the form of a book about apparent past-life recall. (In the more interesting cases, a young child claims to be someone else, someone who lived and died in the surrounding area in the recent past. And in some of these cases, the child claims to remember the sort of thing that can be checked—for example, the location of some object—and his or her apparent memory turns out to be correct.) Chris becomes convinced that apparent past-life recall sometimes occurs and that in some cases the apparent memories turn out to be correct. Chris realizes that the probability of accurate (apparent) past-life recall *given reincarnation* is very high. In fact, Chris offers 9-to-1 odds that accurate (apparent) past-life recall occurs *given reincarnation*. Chris finds it rather difficult to assess the probability of accurate, apparent past-life recall *given that reincarnation does not occur*. Chris judges that this depends on the probability of obtaining information about someone else's past life through some paranormal experience or through spiritism (mediumship). Chris is rather skeptical of these possibilities and, hence, gives only 2-to-3 odds that accurate (apparent) past-life recall occurs *if reincarnation doesn't occur*. Given Chris's probability estimates, what is the probability that reincarnation occurs given the evidence of accurate (apparent) past-life recall?

10. Suppose there is a fair lottery for which 1000 tickets have been sold. There will be only one winning ticket, and each ticket has a 1-in-1000 chance of being selected. Suppose Smith purchased exactly one ticket. What is the prior probability that Smith will win? Now, let our evidence and hypothesis be:

   E: A reputable local newspaper, which makes a point of reporting lottery winners, carries a story reporting that Smith won the lottery.
   H: Smith won the lottery.

P(E/H) is surely very high. That is, if Smith won, we would expect a reputable local newspaper (that makes a practice of reporting lottery winners) to report that Smith won. Thus, we give 9-to-1 odds that (E/H). However, P(E/~H) is surely quite low. How often does a newspaper report that someone won the lottery if he did not in fact win? Very seldom indeed. Accordingly, we give odds of 1 to 99 that (E/~H). What is P(H/E)?

11. Let H be "God exists" and E be "the universe is orderly and its order can be expressed in terms of scientific laws." Suppose P(H) = P(~H). Now, some theists have argued that P(E/H) is greater than P(E/~H) on the grounds that (a) a good God would have a reason to create intelligent life and there can be no intelligent life without order, and (b) there can be no scientific explanation of the orderliness because the fact that the universe operates in accordance with scientific laws is part of the phenomenon to be explained. Suppose these theists are right. Can we conclude that P(H/E) is greater than P(~H/E)?

12. Suppose that there are just three possible hypotheses that can account for E, the fact that I seem to see physical objects:

> $H_1$: Physical objects exist, and my sensory experiences are produced by them.
>
> $H_2$: There are no physical objects; I am simply experiencing a vivid dream.
>
> $H_3$: There are no physical objects, and I am not dreaming, but a powerful demon is causing me to have hallucinations of physical objects.

Suppose I can somehow prove that P(E/$H_3$) is less than P(E/$H_2$) and that P(E/$H_2$) is less than P(E/$H_1$). Based on this information, can I rightly conclude that P($H_1$/E) is greater than P($H_3$/E)? Why or why not?

## Notes

1. My summary of these three theories of probability borrows heavily from Patrick Hurley, *A Concise Introduction to Logic*, 6th ed. (Belmont, CA: Wadsworth, 1997), pp. 530–533.
2. For more details, see Alban Krailsheimer, *Pascal* (New York: Hill & Wang, 1980), pp. 14–16.
3. My proof of Bayes' theorem follows that of Brian Skyrms, *Choice and Chance* (Belmont, CA: Wadsworth, 1986), p. 153.
4. I am indebted to Stephen Minister (in conversation) for the proof to follow.
5. Perhaps the best-known example is Richard Swinburne, *The Existence of God* (New York: Oxford University Press, 1979).

# Answer Key

◆ **Chapter 1**

## Exercise 1.1

**Part A:** Recognizing Statements

1. Statement
4. Statement
7. Neither
10. Statement

13. Statement
16. Sentence only
19. Statement

**Part B:** True or False?

| | | |
|---|---|---|
| 1. F | 13. T | 25. F |
| 4. T | 16. F | 28. T |
| 7. F | 19. T | |
| 10. F | 22. F | |

**Part C:** Valid or Invalid?

1. Valid
4. Valid
7. Invalid

10. Invalid
13. Invalid

**Part D:** Soundness

1. Sound
4. Unsound. The argument is invalid.
7. Sound
10. Unsound. Valid, but the first premise is false.
13. Unsound. Valid, but the second premise is false.

## Exercise 1.2: Counterexamples

1. *Form:* No A are B. Some C are not B. So, some C are A.
   *Counterexample:* No fish are cats. Some collies are not cats. So, some collies are fish.

4. *Form:* No A are B. Some C are B. So, no C are A.
   *Counterexample:* No collies are cocker spaniels. Some dogs are cocker spaniels. So, no dogs are collies.

7. *Form:* Some A are B. All B are C. So, some C are not A.
   *Counterexample:* Some animals are collies. All collies are dogs. So, some dogs are not animals.

10. *Form:* All A are B. Some A are not C. So, some C are not B.
    *Counterexample:* All dogs are animals. Some dogs are not collies. So, some collies are not animals.

13. *Form:* All A are B. All C are B. So, all A are C.
    *Counterexample:* All dogs are animals. All cats are animals. So, all dogs are cats.

16. *Form:* Every A is B. No C is A. So, no C is B.
    *Counterexample:* Every cat is an animal. No dog is a cat. So, no dog is an animal.

19. *Form:* All A are B. No C is A. So, no C is B.
    *Counterexample:* All fish are animals. No dog is a fish. So, no dog is an animal.

## Exercise 1.3

**Part A:** Arguments to Evaluate

1.          A                               B
   If the solution turns blue litmus paper red, then the solution contains acid.
           A                           B
   The solution turns blue litmus paper red. So, the solution contains acid.

       1. If A, then B.
       2. A.
   So, 3. B.             *modus ponens*, valid

4.          A                       B
   If Susan is a famous author, then she knows how to write.
                      B                    A
   Moreover, Susan knows how to write. So, she is a famous author.

       1. If A, then B.
       2. B.
   So, 3. A.             affirming the consequent, invalid

7.       A                 B                    B
   Rilke is a dreamer if he is a poet. Therefore, Rilke is a poet.

       1. If B, then A.
   So, 2. B.

   *Counterexample:*
       1. If the population of Nevada is more than 5 billion, then it is more than one
           thousand. [true]
   So, 2. The population of Nevada is more than 5 billion. [false]

10.      A                    B
   If you study hard, you refine your communication skills.
             B                             C
   If you refine your communication skills, then your job opportunities increase.
           A                    C
   Hence, if you study hard, your job opportunities increase.

       1. If A, then B.
       2. If B, then C.
   So, 3. If A, then C.     hypothetical syllogism, valid

13.      A              B
   Sam is wealthy if he has more than a billion dollars.
          *not B*                                *not A*
   But Sam does not have more than a billion dollars. Therefore, Sam is not wealthy.

       1. If B, then A.
       2. Not B.
   So, 3. Not A.         denying the antecedent, invalid

## Part B: More Arguments to Evaluate

      A               B         A            B

**1.** The sky is blue. The sky is cobalt blue only if it is blue. Hence, the sky is cobalt bl

    1. A.
    2. If B, then A.
  So, 3. B.                 affirming the consequent, invalid

          A             B

**4.** Eating meat is unhealthy if meat contains a lot of cholesterol.

        B                        A

Meat does contain a lot of cholesterol. Therefore, eating meat is unhealthy.

    1. If B, then A.
    2. B.
  So, 3. A.             *modus ponens*, valid

        A                  B

**7.** If the zygote lacks a brain, then the zygote lacks a soul.

       B            C

If the zygote lacks a soul, then killing the zygote is permissible.

      A                  C

So, if the zygote lacks a brain, then killing the zygote is permissible.

    1. If A, then B.
    2. If B, then C.
  So, 3. If A, then C.    hypothetical syllogism, valid

      A                B

**10.** Lying causes social discord. Hence, lying is wrong.

    1. A.
  So, 2. B.

  *Counterexample:*
    1. Trees exist. [true]
  So, 2. Unicorns exist. [false]

         A                                      B

**13.** Either the animals used in research are a lot like humans, or they are not a lot like humans.

            A                  C

If the animals are a lot like humans, then experimenting on them is morally questionable.

           B                          D

If the animals are not a lot like humans, then experimenting on them is pointless.

           C                         D

So, either experimenting on animals is morally questionable, or it is pointless.

    1. Either A or B.
    2. If A, then C.
    3. If B, then D.
  So, 4. Either C or D.   constructive dilemma, valid

## Part C: Still More Arguments to Evaluate

      A                   B               *not B*

**1.** Overeating is foolish only if it causes disease. Overeating does not cause disease.

   *not A*

So, overeating is not foolish.

    1. If A, then B.
    2. Not B.
  So, 3. Not A.        *modus tollens*, valid

A              B

**4.** You will win the chess tournament if you are very good at chess.

          *not B*                 *not A*

Unfortunately, you are not very good at chess. Hence, you will not win the chess tournament.

  1. If B, then A.

  2. Not B.

So, 3. Not A.    denying the antecedent, invalid

      A               B

**7.** If God can arbitrarily decide what is morally right, then God can make cruelty right.

          C                  D

And if God cannot arbitrarily decide what is morally right, then morality is not entirely in God's control.

          A               C

But either God can arbitrarily decide what is morally right, or God cannot arbitrarily decide what is morally right.

        B              D

Therefore, either God can make cruelty right, or morality is not entirely in God's control.

  1. If A, then B.

  2. If C, then D.

  3. Either A or C.

So, 4. Either B or D.  constructive dilemma, valid

              A

**10.** The death penalty is inequitably applied to the poor and minorities.

      A                          B

And given that the death penalty is inequitably applied to the poor and to minorities, it is unjust.

      B

Therefore, the death penalty is unjust.

  1. A.

  2. If A, then B.

So, 3. B.      *modus ponens*, valid

         A                B

**13.** Mercy killing is morally permissible only if it promotes a greater amount of happiness for everyone affected than the alternatives do.

                            B

And mercy killing does promote a greater amount of happiness for everyone affected than the alternatives do.

        A

Therefore, mercy killing is morally permissible.

  1. If A, then B.

  2. B.

So, 3. A.      affirming the consequent, invalid

## Exercise 1.4

**Part B:** True or False?

| | |
|---|---|
| 1. F | 10. F |
| 4. F | 13. F |
| 7. F | |

## Part C: Valid or Invalid? Strong or Weak?

| | |
|---|---|
| 1. Invalid and weak | 13. Invalid but strong |
| 4. Invalid but strong | 16. Invalid and weak |
| 7. Invalid and weak | 19. Invalid and weak |
| 10. Valid | |

## Part D: Cogency

1. Cogent
4. Uncogent. The premise is false (for example, penguins and ostriches cannot fly).
7. Valid, and hence neither cogent nor uncogent
10. Uncogent. The argument is weak.

## ◆ *Chapter 2*

## Exercise 2.1

## Part A: Arguments and Nonarguments

1. Nonargument (explanation)
4. Argument. *Conclusion:* Waging war is always wrong.
7. Argument. *Conclusion:* Without us, light does not exist.
10. Nonargument (explanation)
13. Nonargument (report)
16. Nonargument (illustration)
19. Nonargument (conditional)
22. Argument. *Conclusion:* The good don't always die young.

## Part B: Constructing Arguments

1. *Premises:* If it is not morally permissible to experiment on nonhuman animals, then all new medical treatments must be tried out initially on human subjects. But surely not all new medical treatments must be tried out initially on human subjects.
*Conclusion:* It is morally permissible to experiment on nonhuman animals.

4. *Premise:* Sending people to prison tends to make them worse, and there are ways of controlling nonviolent criminals without sending them to prison.
*Conclusion:* Only violent criminals should be imprisoned.

7. *Premise:* Most Americans insist on using their own vehicles as opposed to public transportation, and this pattern of behavior causes severe damage to the environment.
*Conclusion:* Americans are too individualistic.

10. *Premise:* People often disagree about whether a given person or work of art is beautiful, whereas they seldom disagree about the shape or weight of an object.
*Conclusion:* Beauty is in the eye of the beholder.

13. *Premise:* Lying is wrong, and misrepresenting one's income on a tax form is lying.
*Conclusion:* It is wrong to misrepresent one's income on a tax form.

## Exercise 2.2

## Part A: Identifying Arguments

1.    1. The defendant is insane.
   So, 2. The defendant is not guilty.

4.    1. The intelligence can only be led by desire.
      2. For there to be desire, there must be pleasure and joy in the work.
   So, 3. Will power has practically no place in study.

7.    1. Affirmative action involves giving a less qualified person the job.
      2. The most qualified person deserves the job.
   So, 3. Affirmative action is unjust.

10. Not an argument

13.    1. The statement "God cannot be proved" may mean that God's existence cannot be proved beyond the shadow of a doubt, but it may also mean, and often does mean, that there is no valid evidence for the existence of God.

2. These two meanings differ.

So, 3. The statement "God cannot be proved" is fundamentally ambiguous.

16.        1. Empirical data are scientific.

2. Only what can in principle be shown false is scientific.

So, 3. Empirical data can in principle be shown false.

19. Not an argument

## Part B: More Identifying Arguments

1. Not an argument

4.        1. A man in a state of profound hypnosis can be made to remember events that have long vanished from his normal mind and that he is quite unable to recover by ordinary voluntary effort.

So, 2. Our minds contain elements that are normally inaccessible to us.

7.        1. If each culture should be judged only by its own moral standards, then no culture's moral standards should be criticized.

2. Some cultures permit slavery, cannibalism, and/or the oppression of women.

So, 3. The moral standards of some cultures should be criticized. [from 2]

So, 4. It is not the case that each culture should be judged only by its own moral standards.

10. Not an argument

13.        1. Deductive reasoning cannot have certainty about its premises.

2. Inductive reasoning cannot have certainty about its conclusions.

So, 3. Absolute proof is something that the human being does not and cannot have.

16.        1. The civil disobedient withholds taxes or violates state laws knowing he is legally wrong but believing he is morally right.

2. M. L. King led his followers in violation of state laws he believed were contrary to the federal Constitution.

3. Supreme Court decisions generally upheld King's many actions.

So, 4. M. L. King should not be considered a true civil disobedient.

19. Not an argument

## Part C: Argument Forms and Well-Crafted Arguments

1.        1. H.

So, 2. If M, then L.

3. M.

So, 4. L.                    2, 3, *modus ponens*

4.        1. If P, then C.

2. If C, then F.

So, 3. If P, then F.          1, 2, hypothetical syllogism

4. Not F.

So, 5. Not P.                3, 4, *modus tollens*

7.        1. Either D or S.

2. Not D.

So, 3. S.                    1, 2, disjunctive syllogism

10.        1. If S, then C.

2. If C, then A.

So, 3. If S, then A.          1, 2, hypothetical syllogism

4. If A, then U.

So, 5. If S, then U.          3, 4, hypothetical syllogism

6. If U, then W.

So, 7. If S, then W.          5, 6, hypothetical syllogism

## Exercise: Appendix to Chapter 2

### Part A: Argument Diagrams

1. ¹[ Photography makes representational art obsolete] because ²[no one, not even the best artist, can be more accurate than a camera.]

4. While ¹[there is much wickedness in the world,] ²[there is also much good.] For ³[if there is evil, then there must be good,] since ⁴[good and evil are relative, like big and small.] And no one will deny that ⁵[evil exists.]

7. ¹[There is no better way to arouse the American citizen than to order him around or to tell him what to think.] Although ²[there are many people in this country who would like to organize us more thoroughly and tidy up the freedom we have by a little more control,] ³[we still reserve the personal right to plunge our own way into our own mistakes and discoveries, in art, philosophy, education, or politics. . . .]

10. Despite the fact that ¹[contraception is regarded as a blessing by most Americans,] ²[using contraceptives is immoral.] For ³[whatever is unnatural is immoral] since ⁴[God created and controls nature.] And ⁵[contraception is unnatural] because ⁶[it interferes with nature.]

13. ¹[There is no life after death.] For ²[what's real is what you can see, hear, or touch.] And ³[you cannot see, hear, or touch life after death.] Furthermore, ⁴[life after death is possible only if humans have souls.] But ⁵[the notion of a soul belongs to a prescientific and outmoded view of the world.] And hence, ⁶[the belief in souls belongs to the realm of superstition.]

16. ¹[For beginners, portrait painting is perhaps the most difficult branch of art to understand and enjoy *as painting*.] ²[If we happen to know, either from personal acquaintance or from photographs, what the subject of a portrait is actually like in physical appearance, we are inclined to think more about whether it is a good likeness than whether it is a good painting.] And ³[if it is a portrait of

someone who lived long ago but is not in the history books, we may think that because the subject is of no interest to us the painting must also be without interest.]

19. ¹[Violence as a way of achieving racial justice is both impractical and immoral.] ²[It is impractical] because ³[it is a descending spiral ending in destruction for all.] ⁴[The old law of an eye for an eye leaves everybody blind.] ⁵[It is immoral] because ⁶[it seeks to humiliate the opponent rather than win his understanding;] ⁷[it seeks to annihilate rather than to convert.] ⁸[Violence is immoral] because ⁹[it thrives on hatred rather than love.] ¹⁰[It destroys community and makes brotherhood impossible.]

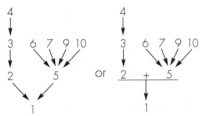

## Part B: More Argument Diagrams

1. ¹[John and Robert Kennedy and Martin Luther King were, like them or not, this country's last true national leaders.] ²[None of John Kennedy's successors in the White House has enjoyed the consensus he built,] and ³[every one of them ran into trouble, of his own making, while in office.] In the same way, ⁴[none of this country's national spokespeople since Robert Kennedy and Dr. King has had the attention and respect they enjoyed.]

4. For a variety of reasons, ¹[private colleges are in trouble.] First, ²[private colleges have repeatedly increased tuition well beyond the rate of inflation.] And ³[any business that increases prices in such a fashion is likely to run into trouble.] Second, ⁴[many people are beginning to question the value of higher education] since ⁵[a college degree no longer guarantees an attractive salary.] Third, rightly or wrongly, ⁶[the American public believes that colleges have not practiced good financial management,] and hence ⁷[the public thinks that tuition dollars often subsidize inefficiency.]

7. ¹[The Peloponnesian War deeply altered the future course of Greek history.] ²[By changing the movement of men, the geographical distribution of genes, values, and ideas, it affected later events in Rome, and through Rome, all Europe.] [...] ³[In turn, in the tightly wired world of today, ... Europeans influence Mexicans and Japanese alike.] ⁴[Whatever trace of impact the Peloponnesian War left on the genetic structure, the ideas, and the values of today's Europeans is now exported by them to all parts of the world.] Thus ⁵[today's Mexicans and Japanese feel the distant, twice-removed impact of that war even though their ancestors, alive during its occur-

rence, did not.] In this way, [6][the events of the past, skipping as it were over generations and centuries, rise up to haunt and change us today.]

10. Not an argument. (*Note:* The passage is an explanation—it explains why the Belgae are the bravest of the Gauls.)

13. While [1][colleges and universities have come under heavy criticism in the last decade,] [2][they will undoubtedly remain a vital force in American social life for generations to come.] For one thing, although [3][both the public and the media seem to have a thirst for stories about people who've gotten rich or famous with only a high-school degree,] the fact remains that [4][a college or university degree is the surest way to increase one's social and occupational status.] For another, [5][college grads as a group indicate higher levels of satisfaction with their lives than do those with lesser educational attainments.] Finally, [6][you show me a nation with a weak system of higher education, and I'll show you a nation with little power.] And [7][Americans will never willingly accept a position of relative powerlessness among the nations of the world.]

16. Not an argument

19. [1][The only proof capable of being given that an object is visible is that people actually see it.] [2][The only proof that a sound is audible is that people hear it;] and [3][so of the other sources of our experience.] In like manner, I apprehend, [4][the sole evidence it is possible to produce that anything is desirable is that people do actually desire it.] Thus, [5][no reason can be given why the general happiness is desirable, except that each person . . . desires his own happiness.]

## ◆ Chapter 3

### Exercise 3.1: Cognitive Meaning and Emotive Force

1.      1. Terrorism in the Middle East is one of the greatest threats to world peace today.
   So, 2. We should kill the leaders of each of the main terrorist groups.

4.      1. Playing the lottery involves paying a sum of money with a very low probability of receiving a larger sum in return.
   So, 2. There is nothing wrong with playing the lottery.

7.      1. The work of a garbage collector is of great importance.
      2. The pay is good and the hours are reasonable.
   So, 3. Your reluctance to take this job is beyond comprehension.

10.      1. If you're against genetic engineering, you're against something recently made possible by science.
   So, 2. You should accept the fact that genetic engineering is here to stay.

13.  1. There is a conflict between criminals and those who keep the law.
     2. Politicians who promote gun control are aiding criminals.
     3. Gun control will not take guns away from criminals.
     So, 4. Gun control is misguided.

16.  1. The world is full of cruelty, poverty, starvation, and debilitating illness.
     2. Some people believe that a loving God controls the world.
     So, 3. People believe what they want to believe regardless of the facts.

19.  1. She is selfish and superficial.
     So, 2. You should not marry her.

## Exercise 3.2

### Part A: Types of Definitions

1. D          10. E or F
4. E          13. F
7. C

### Part B: Lexical Definitions

1. Unnecessarily negative
4. Unsuitable attribute. The conventional meaning is "eight-sided figure."
7. Too narrow: leaves out triangles having sides that are unequal in length.
10. Figurative
13. Too narrow: leaves out lesbians.
16. Unsuitable attribute. The conventional meaning is "having far more material possessions than most people."
19. Figurative

### Part C: More Lexical Definitions

1. Circular
4. Figurative
7. OK
10. Unsuitable attribute. The conventional meaning is "having a round shape."
13. Too narrow: leaves out lizards, turtles, crocodiles, and so on.

### Part D: Precising Definitions

1. Narrow, since so many elderly persons are 92 or younger.
4. Narrow, since many pacifists object not to the use of violence (e.g., think of police restraining an attacker) but specifically to killing (or lethal violence).
7. Narrow, since it rules out teaching a form of evolution that is theologically neutral.
10. Wide, since humans often assert what is false (due to ignorance) without intending to deceive anyone.

## Exercise 3.3

### Part A: Equivocation

1. The equivocation is on "nothing." In the first premise, "nothing" means "no job at all," while in the second premise it means something like "no end humans seek."
4. The equivocation is on "faith." Initially, it means "trust in God," but then later it means something like "a willingness to act on the basis of what is probable but not certain."
7. The equivocation is on "miracles." Initially, it means "wonders of science," and then later it means "divine interventions in the natural order."
10. The equivocation is on "nothing." Boiled down, the argument looks like this: When you choose not to exist, you choose nothing. But it makes no sense to prefer nothing to something. So, it makes no sense to prefer not to exist over being unhappy. In premise (1), "nothing" means an end to existence. In premise (2), "nothing" means nothing *whatsoever*, that is, no entity, state of mind, situation, and so on.

## Part B: Merely Verbal Disputes and Persuasive Definitions

1. Merely verbal dispute. For Mr. X, "homework" means "any assigned work for class." But for Ms. Y, "homework" means something like "assigned work for class that one doesn't enjoy doing."

4. Persuasive definition. Unsuitable attribute: A more neutral (or less biased) description of the goals or values of the Republican party is needed for a rational evaluation of the party as a whole.

7. Persuasive definition. Unsuitable attribute: For the purpose of a rational discussion of the existence of God, the definition of "wrong" is clearly slanted in favor of theists.

10. Merely verbal dispute. The scare quotes are the key. Ms. Y is saying that polygamy is *considered* right (i.e., regarded as morally permissible) by the members of some societies. Mr. X is making the entirely different claim that polygamy is not right, that is, not morally permissible.

13. Merely verbal dispute. For Ms. Y, "artist" means a person who creates objects having beautiful form. For Mr. X, the forms must *depict* something.

## Part C: Equivocation and Persuasive Definition

1. The definition of "self-serving act" is persuasive. A self-serving act is not merely one that accords with one's own motives; a self-serving act aims at selfish ends.

4. The definition of "psychiatrist" is persuasive. Psychiatrists do not merely talk with their patients; psychiatrists treat their patients.

7. Equivocation on "human": In premise (1), "human" means biologically human, that is, an organism with genes of the type associated with *homo sapiens*. But in step (4), "human" means animal with higher faculties. (Fetuses presumably do not have such higher faculties.)

# ◆ Chapter 4

## Exercise 4.1

### Part A: Formal and Informal Fallacies

1. Argument against the person (or *ad hominem* fallacy). "Bonehead" is an abusive term.

4. Appeal to the people (or *ad populum* fallacy, circumstantial). "Hot new thinkers" and "new wave" indicate an appeal to one's desire to be accepted or valued by others.

7. Straw man fallacy. It is a misrepresentation to say that proponents of legalized euthanasia seek the power to kill anyone who has a serious illness. For example, many serious illnesses are not terminal, and some are not especially painful.

10. Appeal to pity (or *ad misericordiam* fallacy). The length of time spent on the paper and the potential probation may arouse pity, but they are not relevant to the conclusion.

13. Appeal to force (or *ad baculum* fallacy). A threat is issued.

16. Argument against the person (or *ad hominem* fallacy, abusive). "Immature" and "cold-hearted" are abusive terms.

19. Argument against the person (or *ad hominem* fallacy, circumstantial). The view is rejected because the person who holds it would benefit if more people held the belief.

22. Appeal to ignorance (or *ad ignorantiam* fallacy). Claim is made simply because there is "nothing in his file to disprove" the conjecture.

25. Appeal to people (or *ad populum* fallacy). "If you want to fit in around here" indicates an appeal to one's desire to be accepted.

28. Appeal to ignorance (or *ad ignorantiam* fallacy). Claim is made simply because "no one has succeeded in proving" the conjecture.

### Part B: Formal and Informal Fallacies

1. Straw man fallacy. No prochoice advocates would accept this description of their views.

4. Argument against the person (or *ad hominem* fallacy, circumstantial). Persons who claim clairvoyant experiences stand to benefit by receiving lots of attention.

7. Appeal to ignorance (or *ad ignorantiam* fallacy). Claim is made simply because "no one has ever shown" otherwise.

10. not a fallacy

13. Two fallacies here. Straw man—hardly a standard formulation of the doctrine of the Trinity, that is, the view that there is one God but three divine persons: Father, Son, and Holy Spirit. Argument against the person (or *ad hominem* fallacy, abusive). "Fools" is an abusive term.

16. Formal fallacy: No A are B. All B are C. So, no A are C. (Counterexample: No dogs are cats. All cats are animals. So, no dogs are animals.)

19. Appeal to the people (or *ad populum* fallacy). "Real men" and "wimps" are key words/phrases in appealing to one's desire to be accepted or valued by others.

22. Straw man fallacy. The views of the evolutionist are being distorted here.

## Exercise 4.2

### Part A: Fallacies Involving Ambiguity

1. Amphiboly. We shall wear no clothes at all, or we shall wear no *distinctive* clothes?

4. Composition

7. Division

10. Equivocation. In premise (2), "reason to believe" means "something to gain by believing"; but in premise (3), "reason to believe" means "evidence in favor of the belief."

13. Not a fallacy

16. Division

19. Amphiboly. "All men are not losers" may mean either "not all men are losers" or "all men are nonlosers."

22. Composition

25. Amphiboly. The sentence structure allows "fish" to be taken as either a verb or a noun.

28. Amphiboly. "That which can not-be at some time is not." Does this mean that those things that can fail to exist will all fail to exist at the same time (call it time "T")? Or does it mean that each thing that can fail to exist will fail to exist at some time or other? The inference drawn assumes the former interpretation, but the latter interpretation makes the first premise much more plausible.

31. Equivocation. In the premise, "your home" means "the home of the driver who has been involved in an accident." In the conclusion, it means "the home of the person being addressed."

34. Amphiboly. The previous employer presumably meant that *the recommendation* did not need to be qualified with statements indicating areas of concern about the applicant. The interviewer takes the previous employer's statement to mean that *the applicant* has no qualifications (experience, skills, etc.) needed to do the job.

## Exercise 4.3

### Part A: Identifying Fallacies

1. Appeal to unreliable authority or *ad verecundiam* fallacy. The president of General Motors is illegitimately assumed to be an authority on the country's religious and ethical moorings.

4. Appeal to unreliable authority or *ad verecundiam* fallacy. The unwarranted assumption is that tobacco companies are reliable authorities on the harmfulness of smoking.

7. False dilemma. The unwarranted assumption is that either men are superior to women or women are superior to men, which ignores the possibility that men and women may be equal in ability, moral standing, and so forth.

10. Begging the question. The premise ("humans have the power to make choices") is merely another way of stating the conclusion ("humans have free will"); thus, the argument assumes the point to be proved.

13. Three fallacies: composition ("each scene was excellent, so the whole play was excellent"); appeal to the people or *ad populum* fallacy ("everybody who is anybody is raving about the play"); begging the question—to say the play is superb is just another way of saying that it is excellent.

16. Complex question. The unwarranted assumption is that Harding was the best president of the first half of the 20th century.

19. Appeal to unreliable authority or *ad verecundiam* fallacy. The unwarranted assumption is that Einstein, who *is* an authority on physics, is *also* an authority on morality.

22. False cause (slippery slope variety). The unwarranted assumption is that the various links in the alleged causal chain are all strong, when in fact they do not appear to be so.
25. False cause. The unwarranted assumption is that if A precedes B, A causes B.
28. Not a fallacy

## Part B: Identifying Fallacies

1. Complex question. The unwarranted assumption is that being a good boy involves eating spinach.
4. Three fallacies: false dilemma (the unwarranted assumption is that one must favor either rehabilitation or deterrence; one might favor retribution or preventive detention instead); argument against the person or *ad hominem* (abusive) ("silly" is an insult); straw man (rehabilitationists do not hold that hardened criminals can be cured so easily).
7. Appeal to unreliable authority or *ad verecundiam* fallacy. The unwarranted assumption is that psychology professors are authorities on the existence of God.
10. Complex question. The unwarranted assumption is that the world contains 10 times as much misery as happiness.
13. Appeal to unreliable authority or *ad verecundiam* fallacy. The unwarranted assumption is that sociology professors are authorities on what's just.
16. False dilemma. The unwarranted assumption is that "either I was hallucinating or he levitated." The possibility that I was tricked has been overlooked.
19. False cause. The unwarranted assumption is that since rock music preceded the military defeat, rock music caused the defeat.
22. Two fallacies: appeal to unreliable authority or *ad verecundiam* fallacy (the unwarranted assumption is that chemistry professors are experts on the relation between language and logic); appeal to the people or *ad populum* fallacy ("any intelligent person will agree that").
25. False dilemma. The unwarranted assumption is that for any doctrine, one must either believe it to be true or believe it to be false. This overlooks the possibility that one might suspend judgment.
28. Three fallacies: argument against the person or *ad hominem* (abusive) ("logic choppers" is a put-down); appeal to ignorance or *ad ignorantiam* fallacy (the philosophical arguments against time travel prove nothing, so time travel is possible); appeal to the people or *ad populum* fallacy ("just about everyone but philosophers thinks…").

## ◇ Chapter 5

## Exercise 5.1

### Part A: Categorical Statements

*Note: The answers are given in the following order: name of form, subject term, predicate term, quantity, quality.*

1. A, hungry cannibals, dangerous people, universal, affirmative
4. E, green vegetables, minerals, universal, negative
7. O, poems, sonnets, particular, negative
10. O, numbers, odd numbers, particular, negative
13. I, celebrities, highly moral people, particular, affirmative
16. E, odd numbers, even numbers, universal, negative
19. I, art critics who like Picasso, snobs, particular, affirmative
22. A, individuals who lie frequently, deeply unhappy people, universal, affirmative
25. E, photons, objects visible to the naked eye, universal, negative
28. O, literature professors who love Tolstoy, good lecturers, particular, negative

### Part B: Standard Forms

1. No human beings are things that can swim across the Atlantic Ocean. **E,** universal, negative
4. Some persons are nerds. **I,** particular, affirmative
7. Some poems are not sonnets. **O,** particular, negative
10. **I,** particular, affirmative

13. Some animals that can fly are not birds. **I,** particular, affirmative
16. All Shawnees are people who were skillful trackers. **A,** universal, affirmative
19. No people who are unlucky are happy people. **E,** universal, negative
22. All lizards are reptiles. **A,** universal, affirmative
25. All birds are feathered things. **A,** universal, affirmative
28. Some paintings are not masterpieces. **O,** particular, negative
31. Some mountains are beautiful things. **I,** particular, affirmative
34. Some trees are ugly things. **I,** particular, affirmative
37. Some animals are vicious things. **I,** particular, affirmative
40. All female siblings are sisters. **A,** universal, affirmative
43. Some living survivors of the Nazi prison camps are people who were tortured. **I,** particular, affirmative
46. Some soldiers are people who will be wounded. **I,** particular, affirmative
49. Some persons who choose not to fight are not cowards. **O,** particular, negative

## Exercise 5.2
### Part A: Logical Relationships
*Note: Superalterns and subalterns are listed in the order in which they appear.*

  1. Contraries
  4. Contradictories
  7. Subaltern/superaltern
 10. None. "Some odd numbers are numbers that can be divided by 2 (without remainder)" is *necessarily* false. If a statement is necessarily false, it cannot be true, but two statements are subcontraries only if they both can be true.
 13. Subcontraries

### Part B: Immediate Inferences

  1. Valid
  4. Valid
  7. Valid
 10. Valid

 13. Not valid
 16. Valid
 19. Not valid

### Part C: Generalizing

  1. If the **A** statement is false: The **O** statement is true (corresponding **A** and **O** statements are contradictories). The truth value of the **E** and **I** statements is not guaranteed.
  4. If the **O** statement is false: The **A** statement is true (corresponding **O** and **A** statements are contradictories). The **E** statement is false (since it implies the **O** statement). The **I** statement is true (since corresponding **I** and **O** statements are subcontraries, and subcontraries cannot both be false).

### Part D: Standard Form

  1.   1. No capitalists are heroes.
      So, 2. Some capitalists are not heroes. *Valid*
  4.   1. All positrons are things smaller than atoms.
      So, 2. Some positrons are not things smaller than atoms. *Not valid*
  7.   1. No acids are bases.
      So, 2. All acids are bases. *Not valid*
 10.   1. All persons who are kept awake for over a week are persons who will go crazy.
      So, 2. All persons who will go crazy are persons who are kept awake for over a week. *Not valid*
 13.   1. No persons who invented the airplane are persons who died flying an airplane.
      So, 2. All persons who invented the airplane are persons who died flying an airplane. *Not valid*

## Exercise 5.3

### Part A: Term-Complements

   1. No things that are not brown bears are nonherbivores.
   4. Some entities that are not unhappy are not nonpeople.
   7. No things that are not great women are nonmen.
  10. Some metals are nonchemicals.

### Part B: Conversion

   1. No maggots are magnates. *Valid*
   4. Some bombs are not explosives. *Not valid*
   7. All copies are forgeries. *Not valid*
  10. Some nontigers are leopards. *Valid*

### Part C: Obversion

   1. No shar-peis are nondogs.
   4. Some heroes are nonmartyrs.
   7. No colonels are objects not weighing at least 100 pounds.
  10. All serigraphs are nonsculptures.

### Part D: Contraposition

   1. All nonpessimists are noncynics. *Valid*
   4. Some dogs are not collies. *Valid*
   7. All noncats are things that cannot run at more than 50 miles an hour. *Valid*
  10. All guppies are things that are not great white sharks. *Valid*

### Part E: Inferences from *A* Statements

   1. Not guaranteed (converse)
   4. T (contrapositive)
   7. Not guaranteed (contrapositive of the obverse)
  10. T (obverse of the subaltern)
  13. T (subaltern of the contrapositive)

### Part F: Inferences from *E* Statements

   1. T (obverse)
   4. Not guaranteed (contrapositive)
   7. F (contraries)
  10. T (contraposition by limitation)
  13. F (No P are O; all P are non-O; so, some non-O are P. Hence, it is false that no non-O are P.)

### Part G: Inferences from *I* Statements

   1. T (converse)
   4. Not guaranteed (contrapositive of the converse)
   7. Not guaranteed (contrapositive)
  10. Not guaranteed
  13. Not guaranteed

## Part H: Inferences from O Statements

1. Not guaranteed (superaltern)
4. Not guaranteed (converse)
7. T (converse of the obverse)
10. Not guaranteed (converse of 5)
13. Not guaranteed (obverse of 6)

## ◆ Chapter 6

## Exercise 6.1

## Part A: Standard Form

1.    1. All novels are books.
     2. Some works of art are books.
   So, 3. Some works of art are novels.

4.    1. Some beautiful things are paintings.
     2. All sculptures are beautiful things.
   So, 3. Some sculptures are not paintings.

7.    1. All sadists are mean people.
     2. All art critics are mean people.
   So, 3. All art critics are sadists.

10. Already in standard form

13.    1. No aspiring actors are saints.
     2. Some aspiring actors are not egoists.
   So, 3. Some egoists are saints.

## Part B: Mood and Figure

1. Second figure: IAI (not valid)
4. Third figure: EOI (not valid)
7. Second figure: AII (not valid)
10. First figure: IAO (not valid)
13. Second figure: AAA (not valid)

## Part C: Putting Syllogisms into Standard Form

1.    1. All cowboys are horse lovers.
     2. Some farmers are not horse lovers.
   So, 3. Some farmers are not cowboys. Second figure: AOO (valid)

4.    1. No cowards are bull riders.
     2. Some bull riders are fools.
   So, 3. Some fools are not cowards. Fourth figure: EIO (valid)

7.    1. No cattle rustlers are good guys.
     2. All cowboys in white outfits are good guys.
   So, 3. No cowboys in white outfits are cattle rustlers. Second figure: EAE (valid)

10.    1. All bulls are things that are hard to ride.
     2. Some broncos are not bulls.
   So, 3. Some broncos are not things that are hard to ride. First figure: AOO (not valid)

13.    1. No trail bosses are hired hands.
     2. Some ranchers are hired hands.
   So, 3. Some ranchers are trail bosses. Second figure: EII (not valid)

## Exercise 6.2

### Part A: Venn Diagrams and Standard Form

1. Some ancient philosophers are people who believed in the unreality of change.

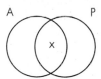

7. No chlorofluorocarbons are things that are good for the ozone layer.

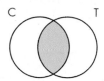

4. All people who deserve harsh treatment from the IRS are tax-dodgers.

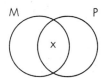

10. No physical entities are spiritual entities.

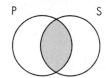

### Part B: Venn Diagrams and Arguments

1. Some chairs are not thrones. So, some thrones are not chairs.

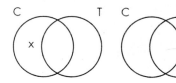

INVALID

4. Some married persons are persons who have attachment disorders. Thus, some persons who have attachment disorders are married persons.

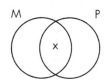

VALID

7. No elephants are beetles. Consequently, no nonbeetles are nonelephants.

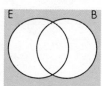

INVALID

*Note regarding the diagram of the conclusion: The area of overlap between nonelephants and non-beetles is the area outside BOTH circles; hence, the area outside both circles should be shaded in.*

**10.** Some wines are not merlots. Therefore, some nonmerlots are not nonwines.

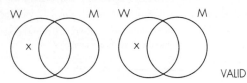

VALID

**13.** Some mammals are edentulous animals. Thus, all mammals are edentulous animals.

INVALID

## Exercise 6.3

### Part A: Argument Forms

**1.**  1. All M are P.
2. Some M are not S.
So, 3. Some S are not P.

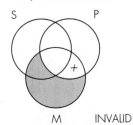

INVALID

**4.**  1. Some P are M.
2. Some S are M.
So, 3. Some S are P.

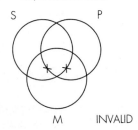

INVALID

**7.**  1. No P are M.
2. Some M are S.
So, 3. Some S are P.

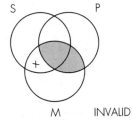

INVALID

**10.**  1. All M are P.
2. No S are M.
So, 3. No S are P.

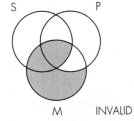

INVALID

## Part B: Categorical Syllogisms

**1.**    1. All Athenians are Greeks.
        2. Some humans are not Athenians.
    So, 3. Some humans are not Greeks.

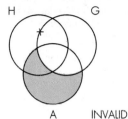

A    INVALID

**4.**    1. All liars are self-deceived persons.
        2. All liars are wicked persons.
    So, 3. All wicked persons are self-deceived
        persons.

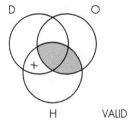

L    INVALID

**7.**    1. No human beings are omniscient beings.
        2. Some divine beings are human beings.
    So, 3. Some divine beings are not omniscient
        beings.

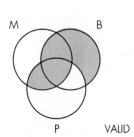

H    VALID

**10.**    1. All brain events are physical events.
        2. No mental events are physical events.
    So, 3. No mental events are brain events.

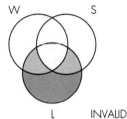

P    VALID

**13.**    1. All similarity statements are
        metaphorical statements.
        2. All statements are similarity
        statements.
    So, 3. All statements are metaphorical
        statements.

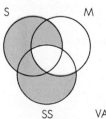

SS    VALID

16.  1. No acts foreknown by God are free acts.
     2. Some acts are acts foreknown by God.
     So, 3. Some acts are not free acts.

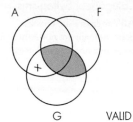

G   VALID

19.  1. All unhappy persons are persons who have inner conflicts.
     2. Some successful comedians are unhappy persons.
     So, 3. Some successful comedians are persons who have inner conflicts.

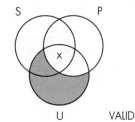

U   VALID

# Exercise 6.4

## Part A: Argument Forms

1.   1. No M are P.
     2. All S are M.
     So, 3. Some S are not P.

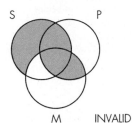

M   INVALID

4.   1. All M are P.
     2. All M are S.
     3. At least one M exists.
     So, 4. Some S are P.

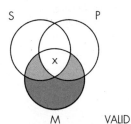

M   VALID

7.   1. No S are P.
     So, 2. Some non-P are not non-S.

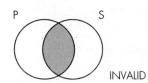

INVALID

**10.**   1. No S are P.
   2. At least one S exists.
   So, 3. Some non-P are not non-S.

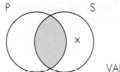

VALID

## Part B: Testing Arguments

**1.**   1. All people who never make mistakes are
      admirable people.
   2. All ideal humans are people who never make
      mistakes.
   So, 3. Some ideal humans are admirable people.

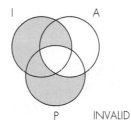

INVALID

**4.**   1. All persons who advocate the use of overwhelming
      nuclear force are persons who lack moral sensibility.
   2. All persons who advocate the use of overwhelming
      nuclear force are persons who should not serve as
      world leaders.
   3. At least one person who advocates the use of
      overwhelming nuclear force exists.
   So, 4. Some persons who should not serve as world
      leaders are persons who lack moral sensibility.

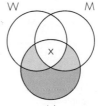

VALID

**7.**   1. All sycophants are flatterers.
   2. All flatterers are disgusting persons.
   3. At least one flatterer exists.
   So, 4. Some disgusting persons are sycophants.

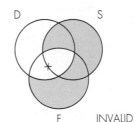

INVALID

**10.**   1. No members of the IRA are members of the IRS.
   So, 2. It is false that all members of the IRA are members
      of the IRS.

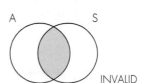

INVALID

**13.**   1. All scarlet things are red things.
   So, 2. It is false that no scarlet things are red things.

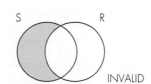

INVALID

16.    1. It is false that some Germans are Zoroastrians.
       So, 2. Some Germans are not Zoroastrians.

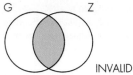

19.    1. No kangaroos are karate experts.
       So, 2. Some kangaroos are not karate experts.

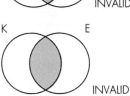

## Exercise 6.5

### Part A: Enthymemes

1.    1. No certainties are propositions that should be
         rejected.
      2. All self-evident propositions are certainties.
      So, 3. No self-evident propositions are propositions that
         should be rejected.

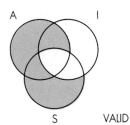

4.    1. All simple substances are indestructible entities.
      2. All atoms are simple substances.
      So, 3. All atoms are indestructible entities.

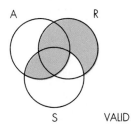

7.    1. All rational statements are scientific statements.
      2. No aesthetic judgments are scientific statements.
      So, 3. No aesthetic judgments are rational statements.

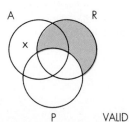

10.   1. All rational beliefs are beliefs that are proportioned
         to the available evidence.
      2. Some beliefs about aliens are not beliefs that are
         proportioned to the available evidence.
      So, 3. Some beliefs about aliens are not rational beliefs.

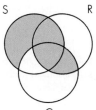

13.    1. All harmful traits are forms of laziness.
       2. All vices are harmful traits.
   So, 3. All vices are forms of laziness.

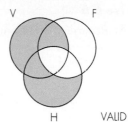

VALID

## Part B: More Enthymemes

1.    1. All events that are foreseen by God are
          predetermined events.
       2. All events are events that are foreseen by God.
   So, 3. All events are predetermined events.

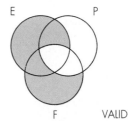

VALID

4.    1. No necessary events are events that can be
          avoided.
       2. All justly punished acts are events that can be
          avoided.
   So, 3. No justly punished acts are necessary events.

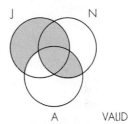

VALID

7.    1. All things that can be annihilated are things that
          can come apart.
       2. No things that have no parts are things that can
          come apart.
   So, 3. No things that have no parts are things that can be
          annihilated.

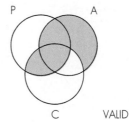

VALID

10.   1. All events are occurrences caused by a deity.
       2. All sins are events.
   So, 3. All sins are occurrences caused by a deity.

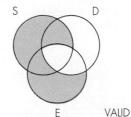

VALID

## Exercise 6.6

### Part A: Removing Term-Complements

1.  1. No M are P.
    2. All S are M.
    So, 3. No S are P.

4.  1. All S are P.
    2. No P are C.
    So, 3. No C are S.

7.  1. All M are P.
    2. All S are M.
    So, 3. All S are P.

10. 1. Some S are M.
    2. All M are E.
    So, 3. Some E are S.

### Part B: Standard Form

1.  1. Some A are B.
    2. All B are C.          Sub 1: Some A are C.
    3. All C are D.
    So, 4. Some D are A.

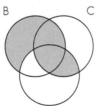

4.  1. No E are C.
    2. All D are E.          Sub 1: No D are C.
    3. All B are D.          Sub 2: No B are C.
    4. Some A are B.
    So, 5. Some A are not C.

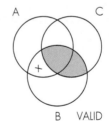

7.  1. All A are B.
    2. No C are B.          Sub 1: No C are A.
    3. Some D are not C.
    So, 4. Some D are not A.

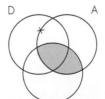

This sorites is not valid.

**10.**   1. Some B are A.
2. All B are C.    Sub 1: Some C are A.
3. All C are D.
So, 4. Some D are A.

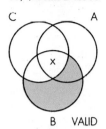

B   VALID        C   VALID

## Part C: Sorites

**1.**   1. All A are T.
2. No T are P.    Sub 1: No P are A.
3. Some D are P.
So, 4. Some D are not A.

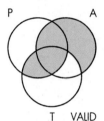

T   VALID        P   VALID

**4.**   1. All Z are D.
2. All D are M.    Sub 1: All Z are M.
3. No E are M.    Sub 2: No E are Z.
4. Some P are E.
So, 5. Some P are not Z.

    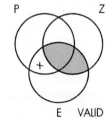

D   VALID        M   VALID        E   VALID

7.    1. All A are P.
      2. All P are R.          Sub 1: All A are R.
      3. Some F are not R.
  So, 4. Some F are not A.

    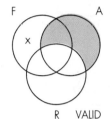

P    VALID              R    VALID

10.   1. All P are R.
      2. No B are R.           Sub 1: No B are P.
      3. All C are B.          Sub 2: No C are P.
      4. Some F are C.
  So, 5. Some F are not P.

        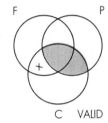

R    VALID              B    VALID              C    VALID

## Exercise 6.7

### Part A: Forms

   1. **EEE**. Fourth figure. Violates Rule 4: invalid.
   4. **AAA**. Second figure. Violates Rule 2: invalid.
   7. **AOO**. Second figure. Satisfies all five rules: valid.
  10. **OOO**. Second figure. Violates Rule 4: invalid.
  13. **OAO**. First figure. Violates Rule 2: invalid.
  16. **AAI**. First figure. Violates Rule 5: invalid.
  19. **III**. Third figure. Violates Rule 2: invalid.

### Part B: Valid or Invalid?

   1. Some M are P. No S are M. So, some S are not P. *Mood:* **IEO**. First figure. The syllogism violates Rule 3: invalid.
   4. All P are M. No S are M. So, no S are P. *Mood:* **AEE**. Second figure. There is an equivocation on the word "animals." In the second premise, "animals" means "nonhuman animals." In the first premise, "animals" means (roughly) "living organisms capable of moving about." The syllogism thus violates Rule 1: invalid.
   7. All M are P. All S are M. So, some S are P. *Mood:* **AAI**. First figure. Violates Rule 5: invalid.
  10. Some M are not P. All S are M. So, some S are not P. *Mood:* **OAO**. First figure. The syllogism violates Rule 2: invalid.

## ◆ *Chapter 7*

## Exercise 7.1

**Part A:** Well-Formed Formulas?

| | |
|---|---|
| 1. Not a WFF | 13. Not a WFF |
| 4. Not a WFF | 16. Not a WFF |
| 7. WFF | 19. WFF |
| 10. WFF | |

**Part B:** Permissible Departures from Strict Grammar

| | |
|---|---|
| 1. Permissible | 7. Permissible |
| 4. Permissible | 10. Permissible |

**Part C:** Symbolizing

| | |
|---|---|
| 1. $C \vee R$ | 13. $\sim S \rightarrow (J \vee T)$ |
| 4. $M \rightarrow N$ | 16. $T \rightarrow K$ |
| 7. $\sim R$ | 19. $(R \bullet \sim S) \bullet (\sim S \rightarrow \sim H)$ |
| 10. $\sim(B \vee S)$ | |

**Part D:** More Symbolizing

| | |
|---|---|
| 1. $S \rightarrow R$ | 7. $B \rightarrow (F \rightarrow \sim P)$ |
| 4. $(W \vee F) \bullet \sim(W \bullet F)$ | 10. $(B \rightarrow F) \rightarrow \sim B$ |

**Part E:** Symbolizing

| | |
|---|---|
| 1. $D \rightarrow A$ | 10. $[(R \bullet A) \rightarrow H] \bullet \sim R$ |
| 4. $(M \rightarrow N) \bullet \sim N$ | 13. $(P \rightarrow S) \bullet \sim(S \rightarrow P)$ |
| 7. $\sim(O \rightarrow E)$ | |

## Exercise 7.2

**Part A:** True or False?

| | |
|---|---|
| 1. F | 16. T |
| 4. F | 19. F |
| 7. T | 22. T |
| 10. T | 25. T |
| 13. T | |

**Part B:** More True or False

| | |
|---|---|
| 1. T | 10. T |
| 4. T | 13. T |
| 7. T | |

**Part C:** Assigning Truth Values

| | |
|---|---|
| 1. P true; Q false | 10. N true; P true |
| 4. A true; B false; C false | 13. H true; J true; K true; L false |
| 7. Y true; Z true | |

## Exercise 7.3
**Part A:** Truth Tables

1.

| A B | A ∨ B, | ~A | ∴ B |     |
|-----|--------|-----|-----|-----|
| T T | T | F | T |     |
| T F | T | F | F |     |
| F T | T | T | T |     |
| F F | F | T | F | valid |

4.

| P R | ~P → ~R | ∴ ~(P → R) |       |
|-----|---------|------------|-------|
| T T | T | F |       |
| T F | T | T |       |
| F T | F | F |       |
| F F | T | F | invalid |

7.

| A B | A · B | ∴ B |       |
|-----|-------|-----|-------|
| T T | T | T |       |
| T F | F | F |       |
| F T | F | T |       |
| F F | F | F | valid |

10.

| F G | ~F · ~G | ∴ ~F ↔ ~G |       |
|-----|---------|-----------|-------|
| T T | F | T |       |
| T F | F | F |       |
| F T | F | F |       |
| F F | T | T | valid |

13.

| D E C | D ↔ (E ∨ C), | ~D | ∴ ~C |       |
|-------|--------------|-----|------|-------|
| T T T | T | F | F |       |
| T T F | T | F | T |       |
| T F T | T | F | F |       |
| T F F | F | F | T |       |
| F T T | F | T | F |       |
| F T F | F | T | T |       |
| F F T | F | T | F |       |
| F F F | T | T | T | valid |

16.

| A B C | A → B, | B → C | ∴ A → C |       |
|-------|--------|-------|---------|-------|
| T T T | T | T | T |       |
| T T F | T | F | F |       |
| T F T | F | T | T |       |
| T F F | F | T | F |       |
| F T T | T | T | T |       |
| F T F | T | F | T |       |
| F F T | T | T | T |       |
| F F F | T | T | T | valid |

**19.**

| A | B | C | A ∨ B, | A → C, | B → C | ∴ C |
|---|---|---|---|---|---|---|
| T | T | T | T | T | T | T |
| T | T | F | T | F | F | F |
| T | F | T | T | T | T | T |
| T | F | F | T | F | T | F |
| F | T | T | T | T | T | T |
| F | T | F | T | T | F | F |
| F | F | T | F | T | T | T |
| F | F | F | F | T | T | F |  valid

## Part B: More Truth Tables

**1.**

| A | B | A • ~B | ∴ ~(A → B) |
|---|---|---|---|
| T | T | F | F |
| T | F | T | T |
| F | T | F | F |
| F | F | F | F |  valid

**4.**

| H | K | ~(H • K) | ∴ ~H • ~K |
|---|---|---|---|
| T | T | F | F |
| T | F | T | F |
| F | T | T | F |
| F | F | T | T |  invalid

**7.**

| A | B | A | ∴ (A ∨ B) • ~(A • B) |
|---|---|---|---|
| T | T | T | F |
| T | F | T | T |
| F | T | F | T |
| F | F | F | F |  invalid

**10.**

| H | J | ~(H ↔ J) | ∴ ~H ↔ ~J |
|---|---|---|---|
| T | T | F | T |
| T | F | T | F |
| F | T | T | F |
| F | F | F | T |  invalid

## Part C: English Arguments

**1.**

| A | E | A → ~E, | E | ∴ ~A |
|---|---|---|---|---|
| T | T | F | T | F |
| T | F | T | F | F |
| F | T | T | T | T |
| F | F | T | F | T |  valid

**4.**

| A | W | ~A ∨ W | ∴ W → A |
|---|---|---|---|
| T | T | T | T |
| T | F | F | T |
| F | T | T | F |
| F | F | T | T |  invalid

7. V L P | V↔L, L→P, P→~V ∴ ~L

| V L P | V↔L | L→P | P→~V | ~L |
|-------|-----|-----|------|----|
| T T T | T | T | F | F |
| T T F | T | F | T | F |
| T F T | F | T | F | T |
| T F F | F | T | T | T |
| F T T | F | T | T | F |
| F T F | F | F | T | F |
| F F T | T | T | T | T |
| F F F | T | T | T | T | valid

## Exercise 7.4

**Part A:** Abbreviated Truth Tables

1. 
| A B C | A→(B→C) | ∴ B→C |
|-------|---------|-------|
| F T F | T | F |

4. 
| J K | J→~K | ∴ ~(J↔K) |
|-----|------|----------|
| F F | T | F |

7. 
| S H U | ~(S•H), | (~S•~H)→~U | ∴ ~U |
|-------|---------|-----------|------|
| F T T | T | T | F |

10. 
| P Q R | (P→~Q)↔~R, | R | ∴ ~P |
|-------|-----------|---|------|
| T T T | T | T | F |

13. 
| Z Y W | (Z•Y)→W | ∴ Z→(Y•W) |
|-------|---------|-----------|
| T F T | T | F |

16. 
| P Q R S | P→Q, | P→R, | Q↔R, | S, | S→R | ∴ P•Q |
|---------|------|------|------|----|----|-------|
| F T T T | T | T | T | T | T | F |

19. 
| Q S T U W | ~(Q∨S), | ~T∨S, | (U•W)→Q | ∴ (~T•~U)•W |
|-----------|---------|-------|---------|-------------|
| F F F F F | T | T | T | F |

**Part B:** More Abbreviated Truth Tables

1. 
| A B C D | ~(A•B), | ~A→C, | ~B→D | ∴ C•D |
|---------|---------|-------|------|-------|
| F T T F | T | T | T | F |

4. 
| V X Y | ~(V•X)→~Y | ∴ ~[(V•X)→Y] |
|-------|-----------|--------------|
| T F F | T | F |

7. Z A B C | ~(Z → A), Z → B, ~A → C ∴ C • ~B

   T F T T | T           T        T         F

10. H S Z P | H ∨ ~S, H → Z, ~S → P ∴ P ↔ Z

    F F F T | T        T        T         F

## Part C: Valid or Invalid?

1. A B | ~A ∨ B ∴ A → B

   T F | T/F        F        valid

4. A B C | A ∨ (B • C) ∴ (A • B) ∨ (A • C)

   F T T | T                  F              invalid

## Part D: English Arguments

1. W B | W → B ∴ ~W → ~B

   F T | T          F         invalid

4. G H I | (G • H) → I, H • ~G ∴ ~I

   F T T |      T        T       F   invalid

7. S P R | S → (P → R), ~(S ∨ P) ∴ ~R

   F F T | T              T           F   invalid

## Exercise 7.5

**Part A:** Tautologies, Contradictions, and Contingent Statements

1. A B | ~A → (A → B)

   T T | T
   T F | T
   F T | T
   F F | T           tautology

4. B A | B → (A → B)

   T T | T
   T F | T
   F T | T
   F F | T           tautology

7.

| P | Q | P → (P → Q) |   |
|---|---|---|---|
| T | T | T |   |
| T | F | F |   |
| F | T | T |   |
| F | F | T | contingent statement |

10.

| R | S | (R • ~R) → S |   |
|---|---|---|---|
| T | T | T |   |
| T | F | T |   |
| F | T | T |   |
| F | F | T | tautology |

## Part B: Logical Equivalence

1.

| A | B | ~(A • B) | ~A ∨ ~B |
|---|---|---|---|
| T | T | F | F |
| T | F | T | T |
| F | T | T | T |
| F | F | T | T |

4.

| S | U | S → U | ~S ∨ U |
|---|---|---|---|
| T | T | T | T |
| T | F | F | F |
| F | T | T | T |
| F | F | T | T |

## Part C: English Arguments

1.

| G | W | G ∴ W → W |   |   |
|---|---|---|---|---|
| T | T | T | T |   |
| T | F | T | T |   |
| F | T | F | T |   |
| F | F | F | T | valid |

4.

| P | E | P ↔ ~P ∴ E |   |   |
|---|---|---|---|---|
| T | T | F | T |   |
| T | F | F | F |   |
| F | T | F | T |   |
| F | F | F | F | valid |

## ◆ *Chapter 8*

## Exercise 8.1
### Part A: Annotating
1. 1. F → G
   2. G → H          ∴ F → H
   3. F → H          1, 2, HS
4. 1. H ∨ ~C
   2. H → ~B
   3. ~C → D
   4. (~B ∨ D) → (K • J)     ∴ J
   5. ~B ∨ D          1, 2, 3, CD
   6. K • J            4, 5, MP
   7. J              6, Simp
7. 1. ~(P • Q) ∨ R
   2. (~E • ~R) → (A • B)
   3. E → (P • Q)
   4. ~R              ∴ B ∨ (F • G)
   5. ~(P • Q)         1, 4, DS
   6. ~E              3, 5, MT
   7. ~E • ~R          4, 6, Conj
   8. A • B            2, 7, MP
   9. B              8, Simp
   10. B ∨ (F • G)      9, Add
10. 1. W → (X ∨ ~Y)
    2. ~~Y • W          ∴ X ∨ ~Z
    3. W              2, Simp
    4. X ∨ ~Y           1, 3, MP
    5. ~~Y             2, Simp
    6. X              4, 5, DS
    7. X ∨ ~Z           6, Add

### Part B: Correct or Incorrect?
1. MT
4. CD
7. DS
10. Incorrect. The main connective of the premise is the arrow rather than the dot, and so simplification cannot be applied.
13. Incorrect. To apply MT, we need both a conditional and the negation of its consequent as premises. And the negation of ~U is ~~U rather than U.
16. Incorrect. This is not CD. To have CD, the disjuncts of the disjunctive premise must be antecedents of the conditional premises.
19. Incorrect. To apply DS, we need a disjunctive premise and the negation of one of its disjuncts, but the first premise here is a conditional rather than a disjunction.

### Part C: Proofs
1. 1. H → ~B
   2. D → B
   3. H              ∴ ~D
   4. ~B              1, 3, MP
   5. ~D              2, 4, MT

**4.** 1. ~A → F
　　2. A → D
　　3. ~D
　　4. F → S　　　∴ S ∨ X
　　5. ~A　　　　2, 3, MT
　　6. F　　　　　1, 5, MP
　　7. S　　　　　4, 6, MP
　　8. S ∨ X　　　7, Add

**7.** 1. ~(S ∨ R)
　　2. B → (S ∨ R)
　　3. B ∨ P
　　4. ~Q ∨ B　　　∴ P • ~Q
　　5. ~B　　　　　1, 2, MT
　　6. P　　　　　　3, 5, DS
　　7. ~Q　　　　　4, 5, DS
　　8. P • ~Q　　　6, 7, Conj

**10.** 1. (B • A) → C
　　2. ~D → (B • A)
　　3. ~C　　　　　∴ ~~D
　　4. ~(B • A)　　1, 3, MT
　　5. ~~D　　　　2, 4, MT

**13.** 1. (T → C) → ~F
　　2. S → C
　　3. T → S
　　4. F ∨ ~P　　　∴ ~P
　　5. T → C　　　　2, 3, HS
　　6. ~F　　　　　1, 5, MP
　　7. ~P　　　　　4, 6, DS

**16.** 1. (E ∨ F) → ~G
　　2. ~H
　　3. H ∨ K
　　4. (K ∨ L) → E　　∴ ~G
　　5. K　　　　　　2, 3, DS
　　6. K ∨ L　　　　5, Add
　　7. E　　　　　　4, 6, MP
　　8. E ∨ F　　　　7, Add
　　9. ~G　　　　　1, 8, MP

**19.** 1. ~~B
　　2. ~C → ~B
　　3. (~~C ∨ T) → P　　∴ P
　　4. ~~C　　　　　1, 2, MT
　　5. ~~C ∨ T　　　4, Add
　　6. P　　　　　　3, 5, MP

## Part D: More Proofs

**1.** 1. P → Q
　　2. R → ~S
　　3. P ∨ R
　　4. (Q ∨ ~S) → (~T ∨ ~W)
　　5. ~~T　　　　　∴ ~W
　　6. Q ∨ ~S　　　1, 2, 3, CD
　　7. ~T ∨ ~W　　4, 6, MP
　　8. ~W　　　　　5, 7, DS

**4.** 1. ~(R ∨ S)
   2. ~(T • V) → (R ∨ S)
   3. ~~(T • V) → W         ∴ W ∨ ~R
   4. ~~(T • V)             1, 2, MT
   5. W                     3, 4, MP
   6. W ∨ ~R              5, Add

**7.** 1. ~F → J
   2. ~F ∨ ~G
   3. ~G → ~H
   4. (J ∨ ~H) → ~K
   5. ~L → K             ∴ ~~L
   6. J ∨ ~H             1, 2, 3, CD
   7. ~K                   4, 6, MP
   8. ~~L                 5, 7, MT

**10.** 1. ~A • ~C
   2. ~C → D
   3. (D • ~A) → (E → ~H)
   4. E • (~F → H)         ∴ ~~F
   5. ~C                   1, Simp
   6. D                     2, 5, MP
   7. ~A                   1, Simp
   8. D • ~A              6, 7, Conj
   9. E → ~H            3, 8, MP
   10. E                   4, Simp
   11. ~H                9, 10, MP
   12. ~F → H           4, Simp
   13. ~~F             11, 12 MT

**13.** 1. (Z • A) ∨ ~Y
   2. (Z • A) → U
   3. W ∨ ~U
   4. ~W                ∴ ~Y
   5. ~U                  3, 4, DS
   6. ~(Z • A)           5, 2, MT
   7. ~Y                 6, 1, DS

**16.** 1. (~M ∨ L) → (~A → B)
   2. ~S → T
   3. R → ~S
   4. ~M • J
   5. R ∨ ~A           ∴ T ∨ B
   6. R → T            3, 2, HS
   7. ~M                4, Simp
   8. ~M ∨ L           7, Add
   9. ~A → B          1, 8, MP
   10. T ∨ B           5, 6, 9, CD

**19.** 1. A ∨ D
   2. ~D
   3. (C ∨ A) → ~E       ∴ ~E
   4. A                   1, 2, DS
   5. C ∨ A            4, Add
   6. ~E                 3, 5, MP

**22.** 1. ~A
2. [~A ∨ (B • C)] → (D → ~E)
3. ~E → ~F
4. (D → ~F) → G      ∴ (G • ~A) ∨ ~H
5. ~A ∨ (B • C)       1, Add
6. D → ~E        2, 5, MP
7. D → ~F        6, 3, HS
8. G          4, 7, MP
9. (G • ~A)        8, 1, Conj
10. (G • ~A) ∨ ~H      9, Add

**25.** 1. (D ∨ C) → (F ∨ H)
2. (H • G) → (F ∨ E)
3. (D ∨ B) → (~F → G)
4. (F ∨ D) • (~F • A)     ∴ E
5. F ∨ D        4, Simp
6. ~F • A        4, Simp
7. ~F         6, Simp
8. D          5, 7, DS
9. D ∨ C        8, Add
10. F ∨ H        1, 9, MP
11. D ∨ B        8, Add
12. ~F → G       3, 11, MP
13. G         12, 7, MP
14. H         10, 7, DS
15. H • G        13, 14, Conj
16. F ∨ E        2, 15, MP
17. E         16, 7, DS

## Part E: English Arguments

**1.** 1. S
2. S → U
3. U → A
4. A → K     ∴ K
5. S → A     2, 3, HS
6. S → K     5, 4, HS
7. K       6, 1, MP

**4.** 1. E
2. E → (D → C)
3. (F ∨ V) → D
4. S → F
5. A • S     ∴ C
6. S       5, Simp
7. F       4, 6, MP
8. F ∨ V     7, Add
9. D       3, 8, MP
10. D → C     2, 1, MP
11. C      10, 9, MP

**7.** 1. P
2. P → A
3. A → (E ∨ F)
4. ~E      ∴ F
5. P → (E ∨ F)   2, 3, HS
6. E ∨ F     5, 1, MP
7. F       6, 4, DS

## Exercise 8.2

**Part A:** Annotating

1. 1. ~~A → B              ∴ A → B
   2. A → B                1, DN

4. 1. ~(E ∨ D)            ∴ ~D
   2. ~E • ~D             1, DeM
   3. ~D                  2, Simp

7. 1. [(P → Q) → R] • (~Q → ~P)       ∴ ~~R
   2. ~Q → ~P            1, Simp
   3. P → Q              2, Cont
   4. (P→ Q) → R         1, Simp
   5. R                  4, 3, MP
   6. ~~R                5, DN

10. 1. [~O → (~M → ~N)] • ~(N → M)       ∴ O
    2. ~O → (~M → ~N)      1, Simp
    3. ~(N → M)            1, Simp
    4. ~(~M → ~N)          3, Cont
    5. ~~O                 2, 4, MT
    6. O                   5, DN

13. 1. ~A                ∴ ~[(B • C) • A]
    2. ~(B • C) ∨ ~A      1, Add
    3. ~[(B • C) • A]     2, DeM

## Part B: Correct or Incorrect?

1. Correct (DeM)
4. Correct (DeM)
7. Incorrect use of DeM. Correct sequence: from ~S ∨ T to ~S ∨ ~~T by DN; from ~S ∨ ~~T to ~(S • ~T) by DeM.
10. Correct (Cont)
13. Correct (Com)
16. Correct (As)
19. Correct (DeM)

## Part C: Proofs

1. 1. ~(C • D)
   2. ~C → S
   3. ~D → T             ∴ S ∨ T
   4. ~C ∨ ~D            1, DeM
   5. S ∨ T              4, 2, 3, CD

4. 1. ~(~A ∨ B)          ∴ A
   2. ~~A • ~B           1, DeM
   3. ~~A                2, Simp
   4. A                  3, DN

7. 1. (A ∨ B) ∨ C
   2. ~A                 ∴ C ∨ B
   3. A ∨ (B ∨ C)        1, As
   4. B ∨ C              2, 3, DS
   5. C ∨ B              4, Com

10. 1. F → (G • H)
    2. (H • G) → J       ∴ F → J
    3. (G • H) → J       2, Com
    4. F → J             1, 3, HS

**13.** 1. $\sim S \rightarrow (T \cdot U)$
    2. $(\sim S \rightarrow X) \rightarrow \sim Z$
    3. $(U \cdot T) \rightarrow X$        $\therefore \sim Z$
    4. $(T \cdot U) \rightarrow X$        3, Com
    5. $\sim S \rightarrow X$           1, 4, HS
    6. $\sim Z$              2, 5, MP

**16.** 1. $(K \vee P) \vee X$
    2. $K \rightarrow \sim O$
    3. $(P \vee X) \rightarrow \sim L$      $\therefore \sim (O \cdot L)$
    4. $K \vee (P \vee X)$        1, As
    5. $\sim O \vee \sim L$         4, 2, 3, CD
    6. $\sim (O \cdot L)$         5, DeM

**19.** 1. $\sim (L \cdot M) \rightarrow \sim (N \vee O)$      $\therefore (O \vee N) \rightarrow (M \cdot L)$
    2. $\sim (M \cdot L) \rightarrow \sim (N \vee O)$      1, Com
    3. $\sim (M \cdot L) \rightarrow \sim (O \vee N)$      2, Com
    4. $(O \vee N) \rightarrow (M \cdot L)$        3, Cont

**22.** 1. $\sim (\sim P \cdot Q)$
    2. $\sim Q \rightarrow R$
    3. $P \rightarrow \sim S$         $\therefore R \vee \sim S$
    4. $\sim (\sim P \cdot \sim \sim Q)$     1, DN
    5. $\sim \sim (P \vee \sim Q)$      4, DeM
    6. $P \vee \sim Q$           5, DN
    7. $\sim S \vee R$           2, 3, 6, CD
    8. $R \vee \sim S$           7, Com

**25.** 1. $\sim B$
    2. $\sim (C \cdot B) \rightarrow C$
    3. $\sim F \rightarrow \sim C$       $\therefore F$
    4. $\sim C \vee \sim B$        1, Add
    5. $\sim (C \cdot B)$         4, DeM
    6. $C$                2, 5, MP
    7. $\sim \sim C$            6, DN
    8. $\sim \sim F$            3, 7, MT
    9. $F$                8, DN

## Part D: Longer Proofs

  **1.** 1. $\sim \sim T \vee \sim R$
      2. $\sim (S \vee \sim R)$
      3. $(T \cdot \sim S) \rightarrow \sim Q$
      4. $W \rightarrow Q$        $\therefore \sim W$
      5. $\sim S \cdot \sim \sim R$      2, DeM
      6. $\sim \sim R$           5, Simp
      7. $\sim \sim T$           1, 6, DS
      8. $T$              7, DN
      9. $\sim S$            5, Simp
     10. $T \cdot \sim S$       8, 9, Conj
     11. $\sim Q$           3, 10, MP
     12. $\sim W$          4, 11, MT

  **4.** 1. $B \rightarrow E$
      2. $\sim F \vee G$
      3. $(B \cdot C) \cdot D$
      4. $(D \cdot C) \rightarrow F$     $\therefore E \cdot G$
      5. $B \cdot (C \cdot D)$      3, As
      6. $B$              5, Simp
      7. $E$              1, 6, MP

    8. C • D          5, Simp
    9. D • C          8, Com
  10. F               4, 9, MP
  11. ~~F          10, DN
  12. G              2, 11, DS
  13. E • G         7, 12 Conj

**7.** 1. ~(B • ~C)
   2. ~B → D
   3. C → ~E        ∴ ~E ∨ D
   4. ~B ∨ ~~C    1, DeM
   5. ~B ∨ C      4, DN
   6. D ∨ ~E     5, 2, 3, CD
   7. ~E ∨ D     6, Com

**10.** 1. ~A → ~B
   2. D → E
   3. (B → A) → (C ∨ D)
   4. C → F         ∴ E ∨ F
   5. B → A         1, Cont
   6. C ∨ D        3, 5, MP
   7. F ∨ E        6, 2, 4, CD
   8. E ∨ F        7, Com

**13.**  1. ~[(M ∨ N) ∨ O]
   2. (P • R) → N
   3. ~P → T
   4. ~R → S       ∴ T ∨ S
   5. ~(M ∨ N) • ~O  1, DeM
   6. ~(M ∨ N)     5, Simp
   7. ~M • ~N      6, DeM
   8. ~N           7, Simp
   9. ~(P • R)      2, 8, MT
  10. ~P ∨ ~R    9, DeM
  11. T ∨ S       10, 3, 4, CD

**16.**  1. ~[(E • F) ∨ G]
   2. (H ∨ ~E) → G  ∴ ~(F ∨ H)
   3. ~(E • F) • ~G  1, DeM
   4. ~G           3, Simp
   5. ~(H ∨ ~E)    2, 4, MT
   6. ~H • ~~E     5, DeM
   7. ~H           6, Simp
   8. ~(E • F)      3, Simp
   9. ~E ∨ ~F     8, DeM
  10. ~~E         6, Simp
  11. ~F          9, 10, DS
  12. ~F • ~H     11, 7, Conj
  13. ~(F ∨ H)    12, DeM

**19.** 1. [(A • B) ∨ ~C] → (~X • ~Y)
   2. ~(Y ∨ X) → Z
   3. ~C ∨ (A • B)    ∴ ~~Z
   4. (A • B) ∨ ~C    3, Com
   5. ~X • ~Y      1, 4, MP
   6. ~(X ∨ Y)     5, DeM
   7. ~(Y ∨ X)     6, Com
   8. Z            2, 7, MP
   9. ~~Z         8, DN

**22.** 1. A ∨ (B ∨ C)
2. ~A • ~C             ∴ [(B ∨ C) • ~(A ∨ C)] • (A ∨ B)
3. ~A        2, Simp
4. B ∨ C        1, 3, DS
5. ~(A ∨ C)        2, DeM
6. (A ∨ B) ∨ C        1, As
7. ~C        2, Simp
8. A ∨ B        6, 7, DS
9. (B ∨ C) • ~(A ∨ C)        4, 5, Conj
10. [(B ∨ C) • ~(A ∨ C)] • (A ∨ B)        8, 9, Conj

**25.** 1. Z • Y
2. T → X
3. ~Y → ~S
4. ~(X ∨ Y) ∨ ~Z        ∴ ~(T ∨ S) • Y
5. Y        1, Simp
6. Z        1, Simp
7. ~~Z        6, DN
8. ~(X ∨ Y)        4, 7, DS
9. ~X • ~Y        8, DeM
10. ~X        9, Simp
11. ~Y        9, Simp
12. ~S        3, 11, MP
13. ~T        2, 10, MT
14. ~T • ~S        12, 13, Conj
15. ~(T ∨ S)        14, DeM
16. ~(T ∨ S) • Y        5, 15, Conj

## Exercise 8.3

### Part A: Annotating

**1.** 1. B ↔ E        ∴ E → B
2. (B → E) • (E → B)        1, ME
3. E → B        2, Simp

**4.** 1. H → (J → ~H)        ∴ H → ~J
2. H → (~~H → ~J)        1, Cont
3. (H • ~~H) → ~J        2, Ex
4. (H • H) → ~J        3, DN
5. H → ~J        4, Re

**7.** 1. M → ~N        ∴ N → ~M
2. ~M ∨ ~N        1, MI
3. ~N ∨ ~M        2, Com
4. N → ~M        3, MI

**10.** 1. (U → U) ∨ (~U → U)        ∴ ~U ∨ U
2. (~U ∨ U) ∨ (~U → U)        1, MI
3. (~U ∨ U) ∨ (~~U ∨ U)        2, MI
4. (~U ∨ U) ∨ (U ∨ U)        3, DN
5. (~U ∨ U) ∨ U        4, Re
6. ~U ∨ (U ∨ U)        5, As
7. ~U ∨ U        6, Re

**13.** 1. ~P → P        ∴ ~P → Q
2. ~~P ∨ P        1, MI
3. ~~P ∨ ~~P        2, DN
4. ~~P        3, Re
5. ~~P ∨ Q        4, Add
6. ~P → Q        5, MI

**Part B:** Correct or Incorrect?

1. Correct (Re)
4. Correct (Dist)
7. Incorrect. From the premise, by Dist, we get $(K \vee X) \bullet (K \vee R)$.
10. Incorrect. DS is an implicational rule and cannot be applied to part of a line.
13. Correct (Dist)
16. Correct (Dist)
19. Incorrect. Simplification is an implicational rule and may not be applied to part of a line.

**Part C:** Short Proofs

1. 1. $\sim M \vee N$      $\therefore \sim N \to \sim M$
   2. $M \to N$      1, MI
   3. $\sim N \to \sim M$      2, Cont

4. 1. $\sim A \vee \sim A$
   2. $A \vee P$      $\therefore P$
   3. $\sim A$      1, Re
   4. $P$      3, 2, DS

7. 1. $(\sim J \bullet K) \to L$
   2. $\sim J$      $\therefore \sim L \to \sim K$
   3. $\sim J \to (K \to L)$      1, Ex
   4. $K \to L$      3, 2, MP
   5. $\sim L \to \sim K$      4, Cont

10. 1. $\sim R$
    2. $(R \to S) \to T$      $\therefore T$
    3. $(\sim R \vee S) \to T$      2, MI
    4. $\sim R \vee S$      1, Add
    5. $T$      3, 4, MP

13. 1. $E \to H$
    2. $(E \vee F) \bullet (E \vee G)$
    3. $(F \bullet G) \to H$      $\therefore H$
    4. $E \vee (F \bullet G)$      2, Dist
    5. $H \vee H$      4, 1, 3, CD
    6. $H$      5, Re

16. 1. $\sim\sim(R \bullet S)$
    2. $T \to (R \to \sim S)$      $\therefore \sim T$
    3. $\sim T \vee (R \to \sim S)$      2, MI
    4. $\sim(\sim R \vee \sim S)$      1, DeM
    5. $\sim(R \to \sim S)$      4, MI
    6. $\sim T$      3, 5, DS

19. 1. $H \vee H$
    2. $H \leftrightarrow \sim J$      $\therefore \sim J$
    3. $(H \to \sim J) \bullet (\sim J \to H)$      2, ME
    4. $H \to \sim J$      3, Simp
    5. $H$      1, Re
    6. $\sim J$      4, 5, MP

22. 1. $P \bullet Q$      $\therefore [(R \vee P) \bullet R] \vee [(R \vee P) \bullet Q]$
    2. $R \vee (P \bullet Q)$      1, Add
    3. $(R \vee P) \bullet (R \vee Q)$      2, Dist
    4. $[(R \vee P) \bullet R] \vee [(R \vee P) \bullet Q]$      3, Dist

25. 1. $(A \rightarrow B) \leftrightarrow C$
    2. $\sim(A \rightarrow B) \vee \sim C$          $\therefore \sim C$
    3. $[(A \rightarrow B) \cdot C] \vee [\sim(A \rightarrow B) \cdot \sim C]$    1, ME
    4. $\sim[(A \rightarrow B) \cdot C]$         2, DeM
    5. $\sim(A \rightarrow B) \cdot \sim C$         3, 4, DS
    6. $\sim C$         5, Simp

## Part D: Longer Proofs

1. 1. $(Z \vee \sim Y) \cdot (Z \vee W)$
   2. $Z \rightarrow \sim\sim U$
   3. $\sim Y \rightarrow (W \rightarrow U)$       $\therefore U$
   4. $Z \vee (\sim Y \cdot W)$       1, Dist
   5. $Z \rightarrow U$       2, DN
   6. $(\sim Y \cdot W) \rightarrow U$       3, Ex
   7. $U \vee U$       4, 5, 6, CD
   8. $U$       7, Re

4. 1. $\sim H \vee (G \vee F)$
   2. $\sim F$
   3. $S \rightarrow \sim(H \rightarrow G)$      $\therefore \sim S$
   4. $(\sim H \vee G) \vee F$      1, As
   5. $\sim H \vee G$      4, 2, DS
   6. $H \rightarrow G$      5, MI
   7. $\sim\sim(H \rightarrow G)$      6, DN
   8. $\sim S$      3, 7, MT

7. 1. $B \vee (C \cdot \sim D)$
   2. $(D \rightarrow B) \leftrightarrow P$        $\therefore P$
   3. $(B \vee C) \cdot (B \vee \sim D)$        1, Dist
   4. $[(D \rightarrow B) \rightarrow P] \cdot [P \rightarrow (D \rightarrow B)]$    2, ME
   5. $(D \rightarrow B) \rightarrow P$        4, Simp
   6. $B \vee \sim D$        3, Simp
   7. $\sim D \vee B$        6, Com
   8. $D \rightarrow B$        7, MI
   9. $P$        5, 8, MP

10. 1. $(B \cdot C) \rightarrow D$
    2. $B$
    3. $Q \rightarrow \sim(\sim C \vee D)$
    4. $\sim Q \leftrightarrow T$        $\therefore T$
    5. $B \rightarrow (C \rightarrow D)$      1, Ex
    6. $C \rightarrow D$      5, 2, MP
    7. $\sim C \vee D$      6, MI
    8. $\sim\sim(\sim C \vee D)$      7, DN
    9. $\sim Q$      3, 8, MT
    10. $(\sim Q \rightarrow T) \cdot (T \rightarrow \sim Q)$      4, ME
    11. $\sim Q \rightarrow T$      10, Simp
    12. $T$      11, 9, MP

## Part E: English Arguments

1. 1. $P \rightarrow (N \vee S)$
   2. $N \rightarrow (M \cdot F)$
   3. $S \rightarrow E$
   4. $P \cdot \sim F$      $\therefore E$
   5. $P$      4, Simp
   6. $N \vee S$      1, 5, MP

| 7. $(M \cdot F) \vee E$ | 6, 2, 3, CD |
|---|---|
| 8. $\sim F$ | 4, Simp |
| 9. $\sim M \vee \sim F$ | 8, Add |
| 10. $\sim(M \cdot F)$ | 9, DeM |
| 11. $E$ | 7, 10, DS |

4. 
| 1. $S \vee (U \cdot P)$ | |
|---|---|
| 2. $(S \vee U) \rightarrow R$ | $\therefore R$ |
| 3. $(S \vee U) \cdot (S \vee P)$ | 1, Dist |
| 4. $S \vee U$ | 3, Simp |
| 5. $R$ | 2, 4, MP |

## Exercise 8.4

**Part A:** Conditional Proofs

1. 
| 1. $Z \rightarrow (\sim Y \rightarrow X)$ | |
|---|---|
| 2. $Z \rightarrow \sim Y$ | $\therefore Z \rightarrow X$ |
| 3. $Z$ | Assume |
| 4. $\sim Y$ | 2, 3, MP |
| 5. $\sim Y \rightarrow X$ | 1, 3, MP |
| 6. $X$ | 5, 4, MP |
| 7. $Z \rightarrow X$ | 3–6, CP |

4. 
| 1. $A \rightarrow B$ | |
|---|---|
| 2. $A \rightarrow C$ | $\therefore A \rightarrow (B \cdot C)$ |
| 3. $A$ | Assume |
| 4. $B$ | 1, 3, MP |
| 5. $C$ | 2, 3, MP |
| 6. $B \cdot C$ | 4, 5, Conj |
| 7. $A \rightarrow (B \cdot C)$ | 3–6, CP |

7. 
| 1. $P$ | $\therefore (P \rightarrow Q) \rightarrow Q$ |
|---|---|
| 2. $P \rightarrow Q$ | Assume |
| 3. $Q$ | 2, 1, MP |
| 4. $(P \rightarrow Q) \rightarrow Q$ | 2–3, CP |

10. 
| 1. $C \rightarrow (\sim D \rightarrow E)$ | |
|---|---|
| 2. $(D \rightarrow \sim D) \rightarrow (E \rightarrow G)$ | $\therefore C \rightarrow (\sim D \rightarrow G)$ |
| 3. $C$ | Assume |
| 4. $\sim D \rightarrow E$ | 1, 3, MP |
| 5. $(\sim D \vee \sim D) \rightarrow (E \rightarrow G)$ | 2, MI |
| 6. $\sim D \rightarrow (E \rightarrow G)$ | 5, Re |
| 7. $\sim D$ | Assume |
| 8. $E \rightarrow G$ | 6, 7, MP |
| 9. $E$ | 4, 7, MP |
| 10. $G$ | 8, 9, MP |
| 11. $\sim D \rightarrow G$ | 7–10, CP |
| 12. $C \rightarrow (\sim D \rightarrow G)$ | 3–11, CP |

13.　1. $(A \lor N) \to \sim S$
　　2. $M \to [N \to (S \cdot T)]$　　　$\therefore \sim(\sim M \lor \sim N) \to (S \cdot \sim A)$
　　3. $\sim(\sim M \lor \sim N)$　　　Assume
　　4. $\sim\sim M \cdot \sim\sim N$　　　3, DeM
　　5. $\sim\sim M$　　　4, Simp
　　6. $M$　　　5, DN
　　7. $N \to (S \cdot T)$　　　2, 6, MP
　　8. $\sim\sim N$　　　4, Simp
　　9. $N$　　　8, DN
　　10. $S \cdot T$　　　7, 9, MP
　　11. $S$　　　10, Simp
　　12. $\sim\sim S$　　　11, DN
　　13. $\sim(A \lor N)$　　　1, 12, MT
　　14. $\sim A \cdot \sim N$　　　13, DeM
　　15. $\sim A$　　　14, Simp
　　16. $S \cdot \sim A$　　　11, 15, Conj
　　17. $\sim(\sim M \lor \sim N) \to (S \cdot \sim A)$　　　3–16, CP

16.　1. $A \to (B \to C)$　　　$\therefore (A \to B) \to (A \to C)$
　　2. $A \to B$　　　Assume
　　3. $(A \cdot B) \to C$　　　1, Ex
　　4. $A$　　　Assume
　　5. $B$　　　2, 4, MP
　　6. $A \cdot B$　　　4, 5, Conj
　　7. $C$　　　3, 6, MP
　　8. $A \to C$　　　4–7, CP
　　9. $(A \to B) \to (A \to C)$　　　2–8, CP

19.　1. $A \to (B \cdot C)$
　　2. $B \to D$
　　3. $C \to \sim D$　　　$\therefore A \to X$
　　4. $A$　　　Assume
　　5. $B \cdot C$　　　1, 4, MP
　　6. $B$　　　5, Simp
　　7. $C$　　　5, Simp
　　8. $D$　　　2, 6, MP
　　9. $\sim D$　　　3, 7, MP
　　10. $D \lor X$　　　8, Add
　　11. $X$　　　10, 9, DS
　　12. $A \to X$　　　4–11, CP

## Part B: English Arguments

1.　1. $\sim V \to (\sim I \lor \sim P)$
　　2. $\sim I \to \sim S$
　　3. $\sim P \to \sim S$　　　$\therefore \sim V \to \sim S$
　　4. $\sim V$　　　Assume
　　5. $\sim I \lor \sim P$　　　1, 4, MP
　　6. $\sim S \lor \sim S$　　　5, 2, 3, CD
　　7. $\sim S$　　　6, Re
　　8. $\sim V \to \sim S$　　　4–7, CP

## Exercise 8.5

### Part A: Proofs

1.  
    1. A → B        ∴ ~(A • ~B)  
    2. A • ~B        Assume  
    3. A        2, Simp  
    4. B        1, 3, MP  
    5. ~B        2, Simp  
    6. B • ~B        4, 5, Conj  
    7. ~(A • ~B)        2–6, RAA

4.  
    1. (H ∨ R) • (H ∨ ~R)        ∴ H  
    2. ~H        Assume  
    3. H ∨ (R • ~R)        1, Dist  
    4. R • ~R        3, 2, DS  
    5. H        2–4, RAA

7.  
    1. Z → (X ∨ Y)  
    2. X → ~W  
    3. Y → ~W  
    4. ~W → ~Z        ∴ ~Z  
    5. Z        Assume  
    6. X ∨ Y        1, 5, MP  
    7. ~W ∨ ~W        6, 2, 3, CD  
    8. ~W        7, Re  
    9. ~Z        4, 8, MP  
    10. Z • ~Z        5, 9, Conj  
    11. ~Z        5–10, RAA

10.  
    1. ~A • ~B        ∴ A ↔ B  
    2. ~(A ↔ B)        Assume  
    3. ~[(A • B) ∨ (~A • ~B)]        2, ME  
    4. ~(A • B) • ~(~A • ~B)        3, DeM  
    5. ~(~A • ~B)        4, Simp  
    6. (~A • ~B) • ~(~A • ~B)        1, 5, Conj  
    7. A ↔ B        2–6, RAA

13.  
    1. D → ~(A ∨ B)  
    2. ~C → D        ∴ A → C  
    3. ~(A → C)        Assume  
    4. ~(~A ∨ C)        3, MI  
    5. ~~A • ~C        4, DeM  
    6. ~C        5, Simp  
    7. D        2, 6, MP  
    8. ~(A ∨ B)        1, 7, MP  
    9. ~A • ~B        8, DeM  
    10. ~A        9, Simp  
    11. ~~A        5, Simp  
    12. ~A • ~~A        10, 11, Conj  
    13. A → C        3–12, RAA

**16.**
1. W → (X ∨ G)
2. G → M
3. ~M                 ∴ ~W ∨ X
4. ~(~W ∨ X)          Assume
5. ~~W • ~X           4, DeM
6. ~G                 2, 3, MT
7. ~~W                5, Simp
8. W                  7, DN
9. X ∨ G              1, 8, MP
10. ~X                5, Simp
11. G                 9, 10, DS
12. G • ~G            11, 6, Conj
13. ~W ∨ X            4–12, RAA

**19.**
1. ~S → (T • U)
2. ~R → ~(T ∨ U)
3. (T ↔ U) → (~~S • R)    ∴ R • S
4. ~(R • S)               Assume
5. (T ↔ U) → (S • R)      3, DN
6. (T ↔ U) → (R • S)      5, Com
7. ~(T ↔ U)               6, 4, MT
8. ~R ∨ ~S                4, DeM
9. ~(T ∨ U) ∨ (T • U)     8, 2, 1, CD
10. (T • U) ∨ ~(T ∨ U)    9, Com
11. (T • U) ∨ (~T • ~U)   10, DeM
12. T ↔ U                 11, ME
13. (T ↔ U) • ~(T ↔ U)    12, 7, Conj
14. R • S                 4–13, RAA

## Part B: Valid or Invalid?

**1.**
1. (F → G) → H          ∴ F → (G → H)
2. F                    Assume
3. G                    Assume
4. ~H                   Assume
5. ~(F → G)             1, 4, MT
6. ~(~F ∨ G)            5, MI
7. ~~F • ~G             6, DeM
8. ~G                   7, Simp
9. G • ~G               3, 8, Conj
10. H                   4–9, RAA
11. G → H               3–10, CP
12. F → (G → H)         2–11, CP

**2.**

| F | G | H | F → (G → H) | ∴ (F → G) → H |
|---|---|---|-------------|---------------|
| F | F | F | T           | F             |

**Part C:** English Arguments

1.　　1. R → (T ∨ P)
　　　2. T → (~L ∨ C)
　　　3. P → (~L ∨ W)
　　　4. R • (~C • ~W)　　　∴ ~L
　　　| 5. L　　　　　　　　Assume
　　　| 6. ~C • ~W　　　　　4, Simp
　　　| 7. ~C　　　　　　　6, Simp
　　　| 8. ~~L　　　　　　　5, DN
　　　| 9. ~~L • ~C　　　　8, 7, Conj
　　　| 10. ~(~L ∨ C)　　　9, DeM
　　　| 11. ~T　　　　　　　2, 10, MT
　　　| 12. ~W　　　　　　　6, Simp
　　　| 13. ~~L • ~W　　　8, 12, Conj
　　　| 14. ~(~L ∨ W)　　　13, DeM
　　　| 15. ~P　　　　　　　3, 14, MT
　　　| 16. ~T • ~P　　　　11, 15, Conj
　　　| 17. ~(T ∨ P)　　　16, DeM
　　　| 18. ~R　　　　　　　1, 17, MT
　　　| 19. R　　　　　　　4, Simp
　　　| 20. R • ~R　　　　19, 18, Conj
　　　21. ~L　　　　　　　5–20, RAA

# Exercise 8.6

**Part A:** Theorems

1.　　　　　　　　　　　　∴ ~(P → Q) → (P • ~Q)
　　　| 1. ~(P → Q)　　　　Assume
　　　| 2. ~(~P ∨ Q)　　　1, MI
　　　| 3. ~~P • ~Q　　　　2, DeM
　　　| 4. P • ~Q　　　　　3, DN
　　　5. ~(P → Q) → (P • ~Q)　1–4, CP

4.　　　　　　　　　　　　∴ (X → Y) → ~(X • ~Y)
　　　| 1. X → Y　　　　　Assume
　　　| 2. ~X ∨ Y　　　　　1, MI
　　　| 3. ~X ∨ ~~Y　　　2, DN
　　　| 4. ~(X • ~Y)　　　3, DeM
　　　5. (X → Y) → ~(X • ~Y)　1–4, CP

7.　　　　　　　　　　　　∴ K → [(K → L) → L]
　　　| 1. K　　　　　　　　Assume
　　　| | 2. K → L　　　　　Assume
　　　| | 3. L　　　　　　　2, 1, MP
　　　| 4. (K → L) → L　　2–3, CP
　　　5. K → [(K → L) → L]　1–4, CP

**10.**

| | |
|---|---|
| 1. P • ~Q | Assume |
| 2. P ↔ Q | Assume |
| 3. (P → Q) • (Q → P) | 2, ME |
| 4. P | 1, Simp |
| 5. P → Q | 3, Simp |
| 6. Q | 5, 4, MP |
| 7. ~Q | 1, Simp |
| 8. Q • ~Q | 6, 7, Conj |
| 9. ~(P ↔ Q) | 2–8, RAA |
| 10. (P • ~Q) → ~(P ↔ Q) | 1–9, CP |

∴ (P • ~Q) → ~(P ↔ Q)

## Part B: Challenging Theorems

**1.**

| | |
|---|---|
| 1. ~[(T → U) ∨ (U → T)] | Assume (RAA) |
| 2. ~(T → U) • ~(U → T) | 1, DeM |
| 3. ~(T → U) | 2, Simp |
| 4. ~(~T ∨ U) | 3, MI |
| 5. ~~T • ~U | 4, DeM |
| 6. T • ~U | 5, DN |
| 7. T | 6, Simp |
| 8. ~(U → T) | 2, Simp |
| 9. ~(~U ∨ T) | 8, MI |
| 10. ~~U • ~T | 9, DeM |
| 11. ~T | 10, Simp |
| 12. T • ~T | 7, 11, Conj |
| 13. (T → U) ∨ (U → T) | 1–12, RAA |

∴ (T → U) ∨ (U → T)

**4.**

| | |
|---|---|
| 1. P ∨ (~P • Q) | Assume (CP) |
| 2. ~P | Assume (CP) |
| 3. ~P • Q | 1, 2, DS |
| 4. Q | 3, Simp |
| 5. ~P → Q | 2–4, CP |
| 6. ~~P ∨ Q | 5, MI |
| 7. P ∨ Q | 6, DN |
| 8. [P ∨ (~P • Q)] → (P ∨ Q) | 1–7, CP |
| 9. P ∨ Q | Assume (CP) |
| 10. ~P | Assume (CP) |
| 11. Q | 9, 10, DS |
| 12. ~P • Q | 11, 10, Conj |
| 13. ~P → (~P • Q) | 10–12, CP |
| 14. ~~P ∨ (~P • Q) | 13, MI |
| 15. P ∨ (~P • Q) | 14, DN |
| 16. (P ∨ Q) → [P ∨ (~P • Q)] | 9–15, CP |
| 17. [(P ∨ (~P • Q)) → (P ∨ Q)] • [(P ∨ Q) → (P ∨ (~P • Q))] | 8, 16, Conj |
| 18. [P ∨ (~P • Q)] ↔ (P ∨ Q) | 17, ME |

∴ [P ∨ (~P • Q)] ↔ (P ∨ Q)

**7.**
$$\therefore [((L \cdot M) \vee (L \cdot N)) \vee ((P \cdot M) \vee (P \cdot N))] \rightarrow [(L \vee P) \cdot (M \vee N)]$$

| | |
|---|---|
| 1. $((L \cdot M) \vee (L \cdot N)) \vee ((P \cdot M) \vee (P \cdot N))$ | Assume (CP) |
| 2. $[L \cdot (M \vee N)] \vee ((P \cdot M) \vee (P \cdot N))$ | 1, Dist |
| 3. $[L \cdot (M \vee N)] \vee [P \cdot (M \vee N)]$ | 2, Dist |
| 4. $\sim[(L \vee P) \cdot (M \vee N)]$ | Assume (RAA) |
| 5. $\sim(L \vee P) \vee \sim(M \vee N)$ | 3, DeM |
| 6. $L \cdot (M \vee N)$ | Assume (RAA) |
| 7. $M \vee N$ | 6, Simp |
| 8. $L$ | 6, Simp |
| 9. $L \vee P$ | 8, Add |
| 10. $\sim\sim(L \vee P)$ | 9, DN |
| 11. $\sim(M \vee N)$ | 5, 10, DS |
| 12. $(M \vee N) \cdot \sim(M \vee N)$ | 7, 11, Conj |
| 13. $\sim[L \cdot (M \vee N)]$ | 6–12, RAA |
| 14. $P \cdot (M \vee N)$ | 3, 13, DS |
| 15. $P$ | 14, Simp |
| 16. $M \vee N$ | 14, Simp |
| 17. $L \vee P$ | 15, Add |
| 18. $\sim\sim(L \vee P)$ | 17, DN |
| 19. $\sim(M \vee N)$ | 5, 18, DS |
| 20. $(M \vee N) \cdot \sim(M \vee N)$ | 16, 19, Conj |
| 21. $(L \vee P) \cdot (M \vee N)$ | 4–20, RAA |
| 22. $[((L \cdot M) \vee (L \cdot N)) \vee ((P \cdot M) \vee (P \cdot N))] \rightarrow [(L \vee P) \cdot (M \vee N)]$ | 1–21, CP |

**10.**
$$\therefore [(A \cdot B) \vee (C \cdot D)] \rightarrow [((A \vee C) \cdot (A \vee D)) \cdot ((B \vee C) \cdot (B \vee D))]$$

| | |
|---|---|
| 1. $(A \cdot B) \vee (C \cdot D)$ | Assume (CP) |
| 2. $\sim[((A \vee C) \cdot (A \vee D)) \cdot ((B \vee C) \cdot (B \vee D))]$ | Assume (RAA) |
| 3. $\sim((A \vee C) \cdot (A \vee D)) \vee \sim((B \vee C) \cdot (B \vee D))$ | 2, DeM |
| 4. $[\sim(A \vee C) \vee \sim(A \vee D)] \vee \sim((B \vee C) \cdot (B \vee D))$ | 3, DeM |
| 5. $[\sim(A \vee C) \vee \sim(A \vee D)] \vee [\sim(B \vee C) \vee \sim(B \vee D)]$ | 4, DeM |
| 6. $[(\sim A \cdot \sim C) \vee \sim(A \vee D)] \vee [\sim(B \vee C) \vee \sim(B \vee D)]$ | 5, DeM |
| 7. $[(\sim A \cdot \sim C) \vee (\sim A \cdot \sim D)] \vee [\sim(B \vee C) \vee \sim(B \vee D)]$ | 6, DeM |
| 8. $[(\sim A \cdot \sim C) \vee (\sim A \cdot \sim D)] \vee [(\sim B \cdot \sim C) \vee \sim(B \vee D)]$ | 7, DeM |
| 9. $[(\sim A \cdot \sim C) \vee (\sim A \cdot \sim D)] \vee [(\sim B \cdot \sim C) \vee (\sim B \cdot \sim D)]$ | 8, DeM |
| 10. $[\sim A \cdot (\sim C \vee \sim D)] \vee [(\sim B \cdot \sim C) \vee (\sim B \cdot \sim D)]$ | 9, Dist |
| 11. $[\sim A \cdot (\sim C \vee \sim D)] \vee [\sim B \cdot (\sim C \vee \sim D)]$ | 10, Dist |
| 12. $[(\sim C \vee \sim D) \cdot \sim A] \vee [\sim B \cdot (\sim C \vee \sim D)]$ | 11, Com |
| 13. $[(\sim C \vee \sim D) \cdot \sim A] \vee [(\sim C \vee \sim D) \cdot \sim B]$ | 12, Com |
| 14. $(\sim C \vee \sim D) \cdot (\sim A \vee \sim B)$ | 13, Dist |
| 15. $\sim(C \cdot D) \cdot (\sim A \vee \sim B)$ | 14, DeM |
| 16. $\sim(C \cdot D) \cdot \sim(A \cdot B)$ | 15, DeM |
| 17. $\sim(C \cdot D)$ | 16, Simp |
| 18. $\sim(A \cdot B)$ | 16, Simp |
| 19. $A \cdot B$ | 1, 17, DS |
| 20. $(A \cdot B) \cdot \sim(A \cdot B)$ | 18, 19, Conj |
| 21. $((A \vee C) \cdot (A \vee D)) \cdot ((B \vee C) \cdot (B \vee D))$ | 2–20 RAA |
| 22. $[(A \cdot B) \vee (C \cdot D)] \rightarrow [((A \vee C) \cdot (A \vee D)) \cdot ((B \vee C) \cdot (B \vee D))]$ | 1–21, CP |

**Part C:** Corresponding Conditionals

1.

∴ [(~A ∨ ~B) • B] → ~A

| | | |
|---|---|---|
| 1. (~A ∨ ~B) • B | Assume |
| 2. ~A ∨ ~B | 1, Simp |
| 3. B | 1, Simp |
| 4. ~~B | 3, DN |
| 5. ~A | 2, 4, DS |
| 6. [(~A ∨ ~B) • B] → ~A | 1–5, CP |

## ◈ Chapter 9

## Exercise 9.1

### Part A: Well-Formed Formulas?

1. WFF
4. Not a WFF. The problem is that *a* is an individual constant rather than a variable. Quantifiers must contain variables. Note that (*a*)Ca is nonsense, like saying, "For all Adam, Adam is cold."
7. WFF
10. WFF
13. WFF
16. Not a WFF. The problem is that *b* is an individual constant rather than a formula. Note that ~*b* is nonsense, like saying, "It is not the case that Bob."
19. WFF
22. WFF
25. WFF

### Part B: Free and Bound Variables

1. The x in Hx is bound by the quantifier; the y in Gy is free.
4. The z in Fz is bound by the (z) quantifier, and so is the z in Gz; the x in Jx is free.
7. The x in (y)Pxy is bound by (x); the y in Pxy is bound by (y). The x in Qx is free.
10. The x in Bx is bound by (x); the y in Dy is bound by (y); the z in Ez is bound by (z).
13. The x in Lx is bound by the quantifier immediately to its left; the x in Nx is bound by the quantifier immediately to its left.

### Part C: Symbolizing

1. (x)(Zx → ~Mx)
4. ~(x)(Mx → Kx)
7. (∃x)Rx
10. (∃x)(Mx • Hx)
13. (∃x)(Px • Gx) • (∃x)(Px • ~Gx)
16. (x)(Sx → Bx)
19. (∃x)(Ax • Sx)
22. (x)(Cx ↔ Px)
25. (x)[Hx → (Fx • Bx)]

### Part D: More Symbolizing

1. (x)(Cx → Ax)
4. (x)(Lx → Wx)
7. (x)Ix
10. (x)(Rx → ~Wx)
13. (x)Mx → (x)~Px
16. (x)[(Px • Sx) → ~Hx]
19. (x)~Gx → (x)(Hx → ~Nx)

22. (x)[Cx → (Lx • Rx)]
25. (x)(Cx → Sx)

## Part F: Challenging Translations

1. *In logicese:* For any x, if x is not equilateral, then it is not the case that x is both a rectangle and a square: (x)[~Ex → ~(Rx • Sx)]. In other words, for all x, if x is both a rectangle and a square, then x is equilateral: (x)[(Rx • Sx) → Ex].
4. (x)(Vx → Cx)
7. [(x)(Hx → Mx) • ~Ms] → ~Hs
10. (x)[(Fx • --(Hx ∨ Mx)) → ~Rx]
13. [Db • (x)(Dx → Ax)] → Ab
16. (x)[(Px • (Hx • Sx)) → Cx]
19. (x)~Gx ∨ (∃x)Ex
22. (x)[Wx → ~(Kx ∨ Fx)]
25. (∃x)(Px • Cx) → Ck  Also correct: (x)[(Px • Cx) → Ck]

## Exercise 9.2

## Part A: Demonstrating Invalidity

1. 

| Aa Ba | Aa → Ba ∴ Aa • Ba |
|---|---|
| F T | T        F |

4.

| Ka Kb La Lb | (Ka ∨ Kb) → (La ∨ Lb)  ∴ (Ka → La) • (Kb → Lb) |
|---|---|
| T F F T | T                    F |

7.

| Ha Hb Ja Jb | (Ha • Hb) → (~Ja • ~Jb) ∴ (Ja → ~Ha) • (Jb → ~Hb) |
|---|---|
| T F T T | T                      F |

10.

| Ra Rb Sa Sb | (Ra → Sa) ∨ (Rb → Sb)  ∴ (Ra ∨ Rb) → (Sa ∨ Sb) |
|---|---|
| F T F F | T                    F |

13.

| Ad Bd | Ad → Bd, Bd ∴ Ad |
|---|---|
| F T | T      T    F |

16.

| Ma Mb Na Nb | (Ma → Na) • (Mb → Nb), Ma ∨ Mb  ∴ Na • Nb |
|---|---|
| F T F T | T                T        F |

19.

| Aa Ab Ba Bb Ca Cb | (Aa • Ba) ∨ (Ab • Bb), (Ca • Ba) ∨ (Cb • Bb) |
|---|---|
| F T T T T F | T                  T |

∴ (Aa • Ca) ∨ (Ab • Cb)
       F

22.

| Aa Ba Bb Ab | ~[(Aa → (Ba ∨ Bb)) • (Ab → (Ba ∨ Bb))]  ∴ (Aa • Ab) → (Ba ∨ Bb) |
|---|---|
| T F F T | T T F  F F F  F T F  F F F        T T T  F  F F F |

25.

| Sa Sb Ra Rb | (Sa • Sb) → (Ra ∨ Rb)  ∴ [Sa → (Ra ∨ Rb)] • [Sb → (Ra ∨ Rb)] |
|---|---|
| T F F F | T F F T  F F F       T F  F F F  F F T  F F F |

28.

| Aa Ba Ab Bb | ~[(Aa → Ba) • (Ab → Bb)]  ∴ (Aa • Ab) → (Ba • Bb) |
|---|---|
| T F T F | T T F F F T F F       T T T  F  F F F |

## Part B: English Arguments

**1.** *Symbolization:* (x)[(Sx • Lx) → Cx] ∴ (∃x)[(Sx • Lx) • Cx]

| Sa La Ca | (Sa • La) → Ca ∴ (Sa • La) • Ca |
|---|---|
| F T T | T                    F |

**4.** *Symbolization:* (x)(Sx → Gx), (∃x)(Bx • Gx) ∴ (∃x)(Bx • Sx)

| Sa Ga Ba | Sa → Ga, Ba • Ga ∴ Ba • Sa |
|---|---|
| F T T | T          T          F |

## Exercise 9.3

### Part A: Annotating

**1.**  1. (x)(Rx → Tx)
  2. ~Tc                ∴ ~Rc
  3. Rc → Tc           1, UI
  4. ~Rc               3, 2, MT

**4.**  1. Hn                 ∴ (∃x)Hx
  2. (∃x)Hx            1, EG

**7.**  1. (y)(Ry → Ny)
  2. ~Ng               ∴ (∃y)~Ry
  3. Rg → Ng           1, UI
  4. ~Rg               3, 2, MT
  5. (∃y)~Ry           4, EG

**10.**  1. (∃y)Py → (z)(~Nz ∨ Oz)
  2. Pn
  3. ~Om               ∴ (∃x)~Nx
  4. (∃y)Py            2, EG
  5. (z)(~Nz ∨ Oz)     1, 4, MP
  6. ~Nm ∨ Om          5, UI
  7. ~Nm               6, 3, DS
  8. (∃x)~Nx           7, EG

**13.**  1. (y)(Dy • Ey)       ∴ (y)Dy • (y)Ey
  2. Dy • Ey           1, UI
  3. Dy                2, Simp
  4. (y)Dy             3, UG
  5. Ey                2, Simp
  6. (y)Ey             5, UG
  7. (y)Dy • (y)Ey     4, 6, Conj

### Part B: Correct or Incorrect?

**1.**  1. (x)Ax → (x)Bx
  2. Ax → (x)Bx        1, UI          Incorrect. UI may *not* be applied to part of a statement.

**4.**  1. (∃z)(Kz • Lz)
  2. (∃z)Kz            1, Simp        Incorrect. Simp may *not* be applied to part of a statement.

**7.**  1. (x)(y)(My ↔ Nx)
  2. (y)(My ↔ Ny)      1, UI          Incorrect. (y)(My ↔ Ny) is not an instance of (x)(y)(My ↔ Nx) because the x in Nx is free in (y)(My ↔ Nx), but the y in Ny is not free in (y)(My ↔ Ny).

**10.** 1. (x)(Bx → (z)Cz)
    2. (x)Bx
    3. (z)Cz            1, 2, MP         Incorrect. To apply MP, we need a conditional on one line and its antecedent on another. Line (1) is not a conditional but a universally quantified statement.

**13.** 1. (x)(Ax ∨ Bx)
    2. Ax ∨ Bx        1, UI           Correct
    3. (y)(Ax ∨ By)    2, UG          Incorrect. The instantial variable (in this case, x) is free in (y)(Ax ∨ By).

## Part C: Proofs

**1.** 1. Ja → Hb
    2. (y)~Hy          ∴ (∃x)~Jx
    3. ~Hb              2, UI
    4. ~Ja               1, 3, MT
    5. (∃x)~Jx        4, EG

**4.** 1. (z)(Nz → ~Ez)
    2. (z)(Sz → Nz)    ∴ (z)(Sz → ~Ez)
    3. Sz → Nz      2, UI
    4. Nz → ~Ez    1, UI
    5. Sz → ~Ez    3, 4, HS
    6. (z)(Sz → ~Ez)  5, UG

**7.** 1. (x)(Dx → Lx)
    2. (∃x)Dx        ∴ (∃x)(Dx • Lx)
    3. Dx              2, EI
    4. Dx → Lx      1, UI
    5. Lx              4, 3, MP
    6. Dx • Lx       5, 3, Conj
    7. (∃x)(Dx • Lx)  6, EG

**10.** 1. (y)(~Py → ~Ly)
    2. Lc ∨ Ld       ∴ Pd ∨ Pc
    3. ~Pc → ~Lc    1, UI
    4. ~Pd → ~Ld    1, UI
    5. Lc → Pc      3, Cont
    6. Ld → Pd      4, Cont
    7. Pc ∨ Pd      2, 5, 6, CD
    8. Pd ∨ Pc      7, Com

**13.** 1. (x)(Ax ↔ ~Ax)           ∴ Bc
    2. Ax ↔ ~Ax              1, UI
    3. (Ax → ~Ax) • (~Ax → Ax)   2, ME
    4. Ax → ~Ax           3, Simp
    5. ~Ax ∨ ~Ax         4, MI
    6. ~Ax                5, Re
    7. ~Ax → Ax           3, Simp
    8. ~~Ax ∨ Ax         7, MI
    9. Ax ∨ Ax           8, DN
    10. Ax                9, Re
    11. Ax ∨ Bc          10, Add
    12. Bc               6, 11, DS

**16.**
1. $(z)\sim[\sim(x)Jx \lor \sim Kz]$     $\therefore Jc \cdot Kc$
2. $\sim[\sim(x)Jx \lor \sim Kc]$     1, UI
3. $\sim\sim(x)Jx \cdot \sim\sim Kc$     2, DeM
4. $\sim\sim(x)Jx$     3, Simp
5. $\sim\sim Kc$     3, Simp
6. $Kc$     5, DN
7. $(x)Jx$     4, DN
8. $Jc$     7, UI
9. $Jc \cdot Kc$     8, 6, Conj

**19.**
1. $(y)\sim(Ly \to My)$
2. $(y)Ly \to (\exists x)Dx$     $\therefore (y)\sim My \cdot (\exists x)Dx$
3. $\sim(Ly \to My)$     1, UI
4. $\sim(\sim Ly \lor My)$     3, MI
5. $\sim\sim Ly \cdot \sim My$     4, DeM
6. $\sim My$     5, Simp
7. $(y)\sim My$     6, UG
8. $\sim\sim Ly$     5, Simp
9. $Ly$     8, DN
10. $(y)Ly$     9, UG
11. $(\exists x)Dx$     2, 10, MP
12. $(y)\sim My \cdot (\exists x)Dx$     7, 11, Conj

## Part D: Proofs

**1.**
1. $(x)[Px \to (\exists y)Oy]$
2. $(\exists z)Pz$     $\therefore (\exists y)Oy$
3. $Pz$     2, EI
4. $Pz \to (\exists y)Oy$     1, UI
5. $(\exists y)Oy$     4, 3, MP

**4.**
1. $(\exists y)Fy \to (y)My$
2. $Fg$     $\therefore Mg$
3. $(\exists y)Fy$     2, EG
4. $(y)My$     1, 3, MP
5. $Mg$     4, UI

**7.**
1. $(x)(Sx \to Tx)$
2. $(\exists y)(Ry \cdot \sim Ty)$     $\therefore (\exists z)(Rz \cdot \sim Sz)$
3. $Ry \cdot \sim Ty$     2, EI
4. $Sy \to Ty$     1, UI
5. $\sim Ty$     3, Simp
6. $\sim Sy$     4, 5, MT
7. $Ry$     3, Simp
8. $Ry \cdot \sim Sy$     7, 6, Conj
9. $(\exists z)(Rz \cdot \sim Sz)$     8, EG

**10.**
1. $(x)[(Bx \lor Ax) \leftrightarrow Cx]$
2. $(x)\sim Cx$     $\therefore (x)(Ax \leftrightarrow Bx)$
3. $(Bx \lor Ax) \leftrightarrow Cx$     1, UI
4. $[(Bx \lor Ax) \to Cx] \cdot [Cx \to (Bx \lor Ax)]$     3, ME
5. $(Bx \lor Ax) \to Cx$     4, Simp
6. $\sim Cx$     2, UI
7. $\sim(Bx \lor Ax)$     5, 6, MT
8. $\sim(Ax \lor Bx)$     7, Com
9. $\sim Ax \cdot \sim Bx$     8, DeM
10. $(Ax \cdot Bx) \lor (\sim Ax \cdot \sim Bx)$     9, Add
11. $Ax \leftrightarrow Bx$     10, ME
12. $(x)(Ax \leftrightarrow Bx)$     11, UG

13.  1. (x)[Bx → (Cx • Dx)]
     2. (∃x)Bx                      ∴ (∃x)~(~Cx ∨ ~Dx)
     3. Bx                          2, EI
     4. Bx → (Cx • Dx)             1, UI
     5. Cx • Dx                     4, 3, MP
     6. ~~Cx • Dx                   5, DN
     7. ~~Cx • ~~Dx                 6, DN
     8. ~(~Cx ∨ ~Dx)                7, DeM
     9. (∃x)~(~Cx ∨ ~Dx)            8, EG

## Part E: English Arguments

1.  1. (x)(Ix → Hx)
    2. (x)(Cx → ~Hx)               ∴ (x)(Cx → ~Ix)
    3. Ix → Hx                     1, UI
    4. Cx → ~Hx                    2, UI
    5. ~Hx → ~Ix                   3, Cont
    6. Cx → ~Ix                    4, 5, HS
    7. (x)(Cx → ~Ix)               6, UG

4.  1. Pg
    2. (x)(Px → ~~Rx)             ∴ Rg
    3. (x)(Px → Rx)                2, DN
    4. Pg → Rg                     3, UI
    5. Rg                          4, 1, MP

7.  1. (x)[Px → (Dx ↔ Sx)]
    2. Sb • ~So
    3. Pb • Po                     ∴ Db • ~Do
    4. Pb → (Db ↔ Sb)             1, UI
    5. Pb                          3, Simp
    6. Db ↔ Sb                     4, 5, MP
    7. (Db → Sb) • (Sb → Db)       6, ME
    8. Sb                          2, Simp
    9. Sb → Db                     7, Simp
    10. Db                         9, 8, MP
    11. Po → (Do ↔ So)            1, UI
    12. Po                         3, Simp
    13. Do ↔ So                    11, 12, MP
    14. (Do → So) • (So → Do)      13, ME
    15. ~So                        2, Simp
    16. Do → So                    14, Simp
    17. ~Do                        16, 15, MT
    18. Db • ~Do                   10, 17, Conj

## Exercise 9.4

## Part A: Proofs

1.  1. (x)Ax → (x)Bx
    2. ~(x)Bx                      ∴ (∃x)~Ax
    3. ~(x)Ax                      1, 2, MT
    4. (∃x)~Ax                     3, QN

4.  1. ~(∃x)~Gx                    ∴ (x)Gx
    2. (x)~~Gx                     1, QN
    3. (x)Gx                       2, DN

**7.**
1. (x)(Nx → Ox)                ∴  ~(x)Ox → ~(x)Nx
2. ~(x)Ox                      Assume
3. (∃x)~Ox                     2, QN
4. ~Ox                         3, EI
5. Nx → Ox                     1, UI
6. ~Nx                         5, 4, MT
7. (∃x)~Nx                     6, EG
8. ~(x)Nx                      7, QN
9. ~(x)Ox → ~(x)Nx             2–8, CP

**10.**
1. (x)(Ax → ~Bx)
2. (y)Ay               ∴ (z)~Bz
3. Ax → ~Bx            1, UI
4. Ax                  2, UI
5. ~Bx                 3, 4, MP
6. (z)~Bz              5, UG

**13.**
1. (∃x)[Bx → (y)~Cy]
2. ~(∃y)Cy → ~(∃z)Dz        ∴  (x)Bx → (z)~Dz
3. (x)Bx                    Assume
4. Bx → (y)~Cy              1, EI
5. Bx                       3, UI
6. (y)~Cy                   4, 5, MP
7. ~(∃y)Cy                  6, QN
8. ~(∃z)Dz                  2, 7, MP
9. (z)~Dz                   8, QN
10. (x)Bx → (z)~Dz          3–9, CP

**16.**
1. ~(x)Mx ∨ (∃x)~Mx
2. (∃x)Sx → (x)Mx
3. Sb ∨ (x)~Px               ∴ ~Pa
4. ~(x)Mx ∨ ~(x)Mx           1, QN
5. ~(x)Mx                    4, Re
6. ~(∃x)Sx                   2, 5, MT
7. (x)~Sx                    6, QN
8. ~Sb                       7, UI
9. (x)~Px                    3, 8, DS
10. ~Pa                      9, UI

**19.**
1. (x)(Lx ↔ (y)My)                 ∴  (x)Lx ∨ (x)~Lx
2. ~[(x)Lx ∨ (x)~Lx]               Assume (RAA)
3. ~(x)Lx • ~(x)~Lx                2, DeM
4. ~(x)Lx                          3, Simp
5. (∃x)~Lx                         4, QN
6. ~(x)~Lx                         3, Simp
7. (∃x)~~Lx                        6, QN
8. (∃x)Lx                          7, DN
9. Lx                              8, EI
10. Lx ↔ (y)My                     1, UI
11. [Lx → (y)My] • [(y)My → Lx]    10, ME
12. Lx → (y)My                     11, Simp
13. (y)My                          9, 12, MP
14. ~Lz                            5, EI
15. Lz ↔ (y)My                     1, UI
16. [Lz → (y)My] • [(y)My → Lz]    15, ME
17. (y)My → Lz                     16, Simp
18. ~(y)My                         17, 14, MT
19. (y)My • ~(y)My                 13, 18, Conj
20. (x)Lx ∨ (x)~Lx                 2–19, RAA

## Part B: Proofs

**1.**
1. $(\exists x)Fx \rightarrow (\exists x)(Gx \cdot Hx)$
2. $(\exists x)Hx \rightarrow (x)Jx$      $\therefore (x)(Fx \rightarrow Jx)$
3. Fx      Assume
4. $(\exists x)Fx$      3, EG
5. $(\exists x)(Gx \cdot Hx)$      1, 4, MP
6. $Gy \cdot Hy$      5, EI
7. Hy      6, Simp
8. $(\exists x)Hx$      7, EG
9. $(x)Jx$      2, 8, MP
10. Jx      9, UI
11. $Fx \rightarrow Jx$      3–10, CP
12. $(x)(Fx \rightarrow Jx)$      11, UG

**4.**
1. $\sim(\exists x)Mx \rightarrow (\exists x)(Nx \cdot Px)$
2. $(x)\sim Px$      $\therefore (\exists x)Mx$
3. $\sim(\exists x)Mx$      Assume
4. $(\exists x)(Nx \cdot Px)$      1, 3, MP
5. $Nx \cdot Px$      4, EI
6. $\sim Px$      2, UI
7. Px      5, Simp
8. $Px \cdot \sim Px$      7, 6, Conj
9. $(\exists x)Mx$      3–8, RAA

**7.**
1. $(x)(Cx \rightarrow Dx)$
2. $\sim(\exists x)Cx \rightarrow (\exists x)Dx$      $\therefore \sim(x)\sim Dx$
3. $(x)\sim Dx$      Assume
4. $\sim(\exists x)Dx$      3, QN
5. $\sim\sim(\exists x)Cx$      2, 4, MT
6. $(\exists x)Cx$      5, DN
7. Cx      6, EI
8. $Cx \rightarrow Dx$      1, UI
9. Dx      8, 7, MP
10. $\sim Dx$      3, UI
11. $Dx \cdot \sim Dx$      9, 10, Conj
12. $\sim(x)\sim Dx$      3–11, RAA

**10.**
1. $(\exists x)\sim Kx \rightarrow \sim(\exists x)Dx$
2. $\sim(x)Kx$
3. $Db \leftrightarrow Qa$      $\therefore \sim Qa$
4. $(\exists x)\sim Kx$      2, QN
5. $\sim(\exists x)Dx$      1, 4, MP
6. $(x)\sim Dx$      5, QN
7. $\sim Db$      6, UI
8. $(Db \rightarrow Qa) \cdot (Qa \rightarrow Db)$      3, ME
9. $Qa \rightarrow Db$      8, Simp
10. $\sim Qa$      9, 7, MT

**13.**
1. $\sim[(x)Ax \rightarrow (\exists x)Bx]$
2. $(\exists x)\sim Cx \rightarrow (\exists x)Bx$
3. $(x)[(Ax \cdot Cx) \rightarrow Da]$      $\therefore Da$
4. $\sim[\sim(x)Ax \vee (\exists x)Bx]$      1, MI
5. $\sim\sim(x)Ax \cdot \sim(\exists x)Bx$      4, DeM
6. $\sim(\exists x)Bx$      5, Simp
7. $\sim(\exists x)\sim Cx$      2, 6, MT
8. $\sim\sim(x)Ax$      5, Simp
9. $\sim\sim(x)Cx$      7, QN

10. (x)Ax            8, DN
11. (x)Cx            9, DN
12. (Ax • Cx) → Da     3, UI
13. Ax             10, UI
14. Cx             11, UI
15. Ax • Cx        13, 14, Conj
16. Da             12, 15, MP

**16.**   1. (x)[(Ax → ~Bx) ∨ Cb]
      2. ~(∃x)Cx
      3. (∃y)By            ∴ ~(y)Ay
      4. (Ax → ~Bx) ∨ Cb     1, UI
      5. (x)~Cx           2, QN
      6. ~Cb            5, UI
      7. (Ax → ~Bx)       4, 6, DS
      8. (x)(Ax → ~Bx)    7, UG
      9. By             3, EI
     10. ~~By          9, DN
     11. Ay → ~By       8, UI
     12. ~Ay           11, 10, MT
     13. (∃y)~Ay        12, EG
     14. ~(y)Ay         13, QN

**19.**     1. [~(x)(R • Px) → (R → ~(x)Px)] → (∃x)[Ax • (y)(~Ay ∨ By)]    ∴ ~(x)Bx
       2. ~(x)(R • Px)               Assume (CP)
       3. R                  Assume (CP)
       4. (x)Px                 Assume (RAA)
       5. Pz                  4, UI
       6. R • Pz              3, 5, Conj
       7. (x)(R • Px)           6, UG
       8. (x)(R • Px) • ~(x)(R • Px)    2, 7, Conj
       9. ~(x)Px            4–8, RAA
     10. R → ~(x)Px         3–9, CP
     11. ~(x)(R • Px) → (R → ~(x)Px)    2–10, CP
     12. (∃x)[Ax • (y)(~Ay ∨ ~By)]    1, 11, MP
     13. Ax • (y)(~Ay ∨ ~By)      12, EI
     14. Ax              13, Simp
     15. (y)(~Ay ∨ ~By)       13, Simp
     16. ~Ax ∨ ~Bx         15, UI
     17. ~~Ax           14, DN
     18. ~Bx            16, 17, DS
     19. (∃x)~Bx         18, EG
     20. ~(x)Bx         19, QN

## Part C: Logical Equivalents

**1.**   1. (x)(Ax • Bx)       ∴ (x)Ax • (x)Bx
      2. Ax • Bx         1, UI
      3. Ax             2, Simp
      4. (x)Ax          3, UG
      5. Bx             2, Simp
      6. (x)Bx          5, UG
      7. (x)Ax • (x)Bx    4, 6, Conj

**4.**

| | | |
|---|---|---|
| 1. | (∃x)Ax ∨ (∃x)Bx | ∴ (∃x)(Ax ∨ Bx) |
| 2. | ~(∃x)(Ax ∨ Bx) | Assume |
| 3. | (x)~(Ax ∨ Bx) | 2, QN |
| 4. | (x)(~Ax • ~Bx) | 3, DeM |
| 5. | (∃x)Ax | Assume |
| 6. | Ax | 5, EI |
| 7. | ~Ax • ~Bx | 4, UI |
| 8. | ~Ax | 7, Simp |
| 9. | Ax • ~Ax | 6, 8, Conj |
| 10. | ~(∃x)Ax | 5–9, RAA |
| 11. | (∃x)Bx | 10, 1, DS |
| 12. | By | 11, EI |
| 13. | ~Ay • ~By | 4, UI |
| 14. | ~By | 13, Simp |
| 15. | By • ~By | 12, 14, Conj |
| 16. | (∃x)(Ax ∨ Bx) | 2–15, RAA |

**7.**

| | | |
|---|---|---|
| 1. | (x)(Ax → P) | ∴ (∃x)Ax → P |
| 2. | (∃x)Ax | Assume |
| 3. | Ax | 2, EI |
| 4. | Ax → P | 1, UI |
| 5. | P | 4, 3, MP |
| 6. | (∃x)Ax → P | 2–5, CP |

## **Part D:** English Arguments

**1.**

| | | |
|---|---|---|
| 1. | (x)(Tx → Dx) | |
| 2. | (∃x)(Tx • (Wx ∨ Cx)) → (∃x)(Tx • ~Dx) | ∴ (x)(Tx → ~Cx) |
| 3. | Tx | Assume |
| 4. | (x)(Tx → ~~Dx) | 1, DN |
| 5. | (x)(~Tx ∨ ~~Dx) | 4, MI |
| 6. | (x)~(Tx • ~Dx) | 5, DeM |
| 7. | ~(∃x)(Tx • ~Dx) | 6, QN |
| 8. | ~(∃x)(Tx • (Wx ∨ Cx)) | 2, 7, MT |
| 9. | (x)~(Tx • (Wx ∨ Cx)) | 8, QN |
| 10. | (x)(~Tx ∨ ~(Wx ∨ Cx)) | 9, DeM |
| 11. | (x)(Tx → ~(Wx ∨ Cx)) | 10, MI |
| 12. | (x)(Tx → (~Wx • ~Cx)) | 11, DeM |
| 13. | Tx → (~Wx • ~Cx) | 12, UI |
| 14. | ~Wx • ~Cx | 3, 13, MP |
| 15. | ~Cx | 14, Simp |
| 16. | Tx → ~Cx | 3–15, CP |
| 17. | (x)(Tx → ~Cx) | 16, UG |

4.  1. $(x)[Kx \rightarrow (Wx \leftrightarrow Ex)]$
    2. $(x)(Px \rightarrow Kx)$
    3. $(x)(Fx \rightarrow Px)$
    4. $(x)(Px \rightarrow Ex)$        $\therefore$ $(x)(Fx \rightarrow Wx)$
    | 5. $Fx$ | Assume |
    | 6. $Fx \rightarrow Px$ | 3, UI |
    | 7. $Px \rightarrow Ex$ | 4, UI |
    | 8. $Px$ | 6, 5, MP |
    | 9. $Ex$ | 7, 8, MP |
    | 10. $Px \rightarrow Kx$ | 2, UI |
    | 11. $Kx$ | 8, 10, MP |
    | 12. $Kx \rightarrow (Wx \leftrightarrow Ex)$ | 1, UI |
    | 13. $Wx \leftrightarrow Ex$ | 11, 12, MP |
    | 14. $(Wx \rightarrow Ex) \cdot (Ex \rightarrow Wx)$ | 13, ME |
    | 15. $Ex \rightarrow Wx$ | 14, Simp |
    | 16. $Wx$ | 9, 15, MP |
    17. $Fx \rightarrow Wx$        5–16, CP
    18. $(x)(Fx \rightarrow Wx)$        17, UG

7.  1. $(\exists x)(Rx \cdot Bx)$
    2. $(\exists x)(Mx \cdot Hx)$
    3. $(\exists x)Rx \rightarrow (x)[Hx \rightarrow (Mx \rightarrow Fx)]$        $\therefore$ $(\exists x)(Mx \cdot Fx)$
    | 4. $Rx \cdot Bx$ | 1, EI |
    | 5. $Rx$ | 4, Simp |
    | 6. $(\exists x)Rx$ | 5, EG |
    | 7. $(x)[Hx \rightarrow (Mx \rightarrow Fx)]$ | 3, 6, MP |
    | 8. $My \cdot Hy$ | 2, EI |
    | 9. $Hy \rightarrow (My \rightarrow Fy)$ | 7, UI |
    | 10. $Hy$ | 8, Simp |
    | 11. $My \rightarrow Fy$ | 9, 10, MP |
    | 12. $My$ | 8, Simp |
    | 13. $Fy$ | 11, 12, MP |
    | 14. $My \cdot Fy$ | 12, 13, Conj |
    | 15. $(\exists x)(Mx \cdot Fx)$ | 14, EG |

## Exercise 9.5

### Part B: Symbolizing

1.  $(x)\sim Lxx$
4.  $(\exists x)[Fx \cdot (y)(Py \rightarrow Rxy)]$
7.  $(x)[Dx \rightarrow \sim(\exists y)(Hy \cdot Wxy)]$
10. $(x)[(Ox \cdot Px) \rightarrow \sim(\exists y)((Oy \cdot Wy) \cdot Rxy)]$
13. $(x)(Mx \rightarrow \sim Mxx)$
16. $(x)(Mx \rightarrow Axb)$
19. $(x)[Sx \rightarrow \sim(y)(Py \rightarrow (z)(Dz \rightarrow Hxyz))]$
22. $(x)(y)(z)[(Fxy \cdot Fyz) \rightarrow \sim Fxz]$
25. $(x)(y)(Nxy \rightarrow Nyx)$

### Part D: More Symbolizing

1.  $(\exists x)[Px \cdot (y)(Py \rightarrow Axy)]$
4.  $(\exists x)(Px \cdot Lxx) \cdot (\exists x)(Px \cdot \sim Lxx)$
7.  $(x)(\exists y)Cxy$
10. $(x)\sim(\exists y)Cxy$

**Part E:** Ready for a Challenge?

1. (∃x)(∃y)[(Px • Cy) • (Hxy • Exy)]
4. (x)[(Mx • ~Ix) → (∃y)(Cy • Pxy)]
7. (x)[(Px • (∃y)(Py • Hxy)) → Hxx]
10. (∃x)(∃y)[(Px • Myx) • (Myj)]
13. (∃x)[Tx • ~(∃y)(Ry • (∃z)(Pz • Lyzx))]
16. (x)[(Sx • Rx) → (y)(My → ~Gxy)]
19. (x)(y)[((Px • Py) • Mxy) → (∃z)(Pz • Wzxy)]

## Exercise 9.6

**Part A:** Correct or Incorrect?

*Note: Inferences are correct unless marked "incorrect."*

1. 1. (x)(y)(Mx • Nxy)
   2. (y)(My • Nyy)                1, UI    incorrect
4. 1. (x)[(∃y)Lxy → Kx]
   2. (∃y)Lby → Kb                 1, UI
7. 1. Eab → Fab
   2. (x)(Exb → Fxb)              1, UG   incorrect
10. 1. (∃x)(y)(Kyx ∨ ~Lxy)
    2. (y)(Kyy ∨ ~Lyy)            1, EI   incorrect
13. 1. (x)[Sxb → (y)Rxy]
    2. Szb → (y)Rzy               1, UI
16. 1. (x)(∃y)Jyx
    2. (∃y)Jyx                    1, UI
    3. Jyx                        2, EI
    4. (x)Jyx                     3, UG   incorrect
19. 1. ~Lnn
    2. (∃x)~Lxx                   1, EG
    3. (∃x)~Lxn                   1, EG
    4. (∃x)~Lnx                   1, EG
22. 1. (∃x)Fxd
    2. Fxd                        1, EI
    3. (x)Fxd                     2, UG   incorrect

**Part B:** Proofs

1. 1. (x)(y)(Rxy → Ryx)
   2. Rab                          ∴ Rba
   3. (y)(Ray → Rya)              1, UI
   4. Rab → Rba                   3, UI
   5. Rba                         4, 2, MP
4. 1. (y)(Bay ∨ Bya)             ∴ Baa
   2. Baa ∨ Baa                   1, UI
   3. Baa                         2, Re
7. 1. (∃x)[Hx • (y)(Hy → Lyx)]       ∴ (∃x)(Hx • Lxx)
   2. Hx • (y)(Hy → Lyx)              1, EI
   3. Hx                              2, Simp
   4. (y)(Hy → Lyx)                   2, Simp
   5. Hx → Lxx                        4, UI
   6. Lxx                             5, 3, MP
   7. Hx • Lxx                        3, 6, Conj
   8. (∃x)(Hx • Lxx)                  7, EG

10. 1. ~(∃x)[Px • (∃y)(Py • Lxy)]      ∴ (x)[Px → (y)(Py → ~Lxy)]
    2. (x)~[Px • (∃y)(Py • Lxy)]      1, QN
    3. ~[Px • (∃y)(Py • Lxy)]      2, UI
    4. ~Px ∨ ~(∃y)(Py • Lxy)      3, DeM
    5. ~Px ∨ (y)~(Py • Lxy)      4, QN
    6. ~Px ∨ (y)(~Py ∨ ~Lxy)      5, DeM
    7. Px → (y)(~Py ∨ ~Lxy)      6, MI
    8. Px → (y)(Py → ~Lxy)      7, MI
    9. (x)[Px → (y)(Py → ~Lxy)]      8, UG

## Part C: English Arguments

1. 1. Soa
    2. (x)(y)(Sxy → ~Syx)      ∴ ~Sao
    3. (y)(Soy → ~Syo)      2, UI
    4. Soa → ~Sao      3, UI
    5. ~Sao      4, 1, MP

4. 1. (x)[(Rx • Ax) → (y)((~Ry • Ay) → Gxy)]
    2. (Rk • Ak) • ~Gkg      ∴ Ag → Rg
    3. (Rk • Ak) → (y)((~Ry • Ay) → Gky)      1, UI
    4. Rk • Ak      2, Simp
    5. (y)((~Ry • Ay) → Gky)      3, 4, MP
    6. (~Rg • Ag) → Gkg      5, UI
    7. ~Gkg      2, Simp
    8. ~(~Rg • Ag)      6, 7, MT
    9. ~~Rg ∨ ~Ag      8, DeM
    10. ~Ag ∨ ~~Rg      9, Com
    11. ~Ag ∨ Rg      10, DN
    12. Ag → Rg      11, MI

7.   1. (x)(Hx → Ax)      ∴ (x)[(∃y)(Hy • Txy) → (∃z)(Az • Txz)]
    2. ~(x)[(∃y)(Hy • Txy) → (∃z)(Az • Txz)]      Assume
    3. (∃x)~[(∃y)(Hy • Txy) → (∃z)(Az • Txz)]      2, QN
    4. ~[(∃y)(Hy • Txy) → (∃z)(Az • Txz)]      3, EI
    5. ~[~(∃y)(Hy • Txy) ∨ (∃z)(Az • Txz)]      4, MI
    6. ~~(∃y)(Hy • Txy) • ~(∃z)(Az • Txz)      5, DeM
    7. ~~(∃y)(Hy • Txy)      6, Simp
    8. ~(∃z)(Az • Txz)      6, Simp
    9. (∃y)(Hy • Txy)      7, DN
    10. Hy • Txy      9, EI
    11. (z) ~(Az • Txz)      8, QN
    12. ~(Ay • Txy)      11, UI
    13. ~Ay ∨ ~Txy      12, DeM
    14. Hy → Ay      1, UI
    15. Hy      10, Simp
    16. Txy      10, Simp
    17. Ay      14, 15, MP
    18. ~~Ay      17, DN
    19. ~Txy      13, 18, DS
    20. Txy • ~Txy      16, 19, Conj
    21. (x)[(∃y)(Hy • Txy) → (∃z)(Az • Txz)]      2–20, RAA

10.    1. (∃x)Sx            ∴ ~(∃x)[Sx • (y)(Sy → (Cxy ↔ ~Cyy))]
       2. (∃x)[Sx • (y)(Sy → (Cxy ↔ ~Cyy))]        Assume
       3. Sx • (y)(Sy → (Cxy ↔ ~Cyy))              2, EI
       4. Sx                                       3, Simp
       5. (y)(Sy → (Cxy ↔ ~Cyy))                   3, Simp
       6. Sx → (Cxx ↔ ~Cxx)                        5, UI
       7. Cxx ↔ ~Cxx                               6, 4, MP
       8. (Cxx → ~Cxx) • (~Cxx → Cxx)              7, ME
       9. Cxx → ~Cxx                               8, Simp
       10. ~Cxx ∨ ~Cxx                             9, MI
       11. ~Cxx                                    10, Re
       12. ~Cxx → Cxx                              8, Simp
       13. Cxx                                     12, 11, MP
       14. Cxx • ~Cxx                              13, 11, Conj
       15. ~(∃x)[Sx • (y)(Sy → (Cxy ↔ ~Cyy))]      2–14, RAA

## Exercise 9.7

### Part A: Symbolizing

   **1.** ~d = f
   **4.** ~(∃x) ~x = x
   **7.** (x)x = x
   **10.** (∃x)(∃y)[(Px • Py • Ax • Ay) • ~x = y]

### Part B: More Symbolizing

   **1.** (∃x)~x = x → (x)~Mx
   **4.** (∃x)(∃y)[~x = y • (z)(z =x ∨ z = y)]
   **7.** (∃x)[(Px • Sxa) • (y)((Py • Sya) → y = x)]
   **10.** (Dk • Gk) • (x)[(Dx • ~x = k) → ~Gx]

## Exercise 9.8

### Part A: Proofs

   1.    1. Na • ~Nb        ∴ ~a = b
         2. a = b           Assume
         3. Na • ~Na        1, 2, LL
         4. ~a = b          2–3, RAA

   **4.** 1. c = d → e = g
          2. d = c
          3. Fg             ∴ Fe
          4. c = d          2, Sm
          5. e = g          1, 4, MP
          6. Fe             3, 5, LL

   **7.** 1. (y)(Ay → By)
          2. Ab
          3. b = c          ∴ Bc
          4. Ab → Bb        1, UI
          5. Bb             4, 2, MP
          6. Bc             3, 5, LL

**10.**  1. (x)(Hx → Jx)
    2. (x)(Kx → Lx)
    3. Hd • Kc
    4. c = d             ∴ Jc • Ld
    5. Hd → Jd        1, UI
    6. Kc → Lc        2, UI
    7. Hd               3, Simp
    8. Jd               5, 7, MP
    9. Jc               8, 4, LL
   10. Kc           3, Simp
   11. Lc            6, 10, MP
   12. Ld            4, 11, LL
   13. Jc • Ld       9, 12, Conj

**13.**  1. (∃x)Hx
    2. (x)(y)[(Hx • Hy) → x = y]       ∴ (∃x)[Hx • (y)(Hy → x = y)]
    3. Hx                                  1, EI
    4. ~(∃x)[Hx • (y)(Hy → x = y)]     Assume
    5. (x)~[Hx • (y)(Hy → x = y)]      4, QN
    6. (x)[~Hx ∨ ~(y)(Hy → x = y)]    5, DeM
    7. ~Hx ∨ ~(y)(Hy → x = y)      6, UI
    8. ~~Hx                      3, DN
    9. ~(y)(Hy → x = y)           7, 8, DS
   10. (∃y)~(Hy → x = y)         9, QN
   11. (∃y)~(~Hy ∨ x = y)        10, MI
   12. (∃y)(~~Hy • ~x = y)       11, DeM
   13. (∃y)(Hy • ~x = y)          12, DN
   14. Hy • ~x = y              13, EI
   15. (y)[(Hx • Hy) → x = y]      2, UI
   16. (Hx • Hy) → x = y         15, UI
   17. Hy                        14, Simp
   18. Hx • Hy               3, 17, Conj
   19. x = y                  16, 18, MP
   20. ~x = y                14, Simp
   21. x = y • ~x = y         19, 20, Conj
   22. (∃x)[Hx • (y)(Hy → x = y)]    4–21, RAA

**16.**  1. (∃x){[(Ax • Bxa) • (y)((Ay • Bya) → y=x)] • Dxb}
    2. Ac • Bca                                   ∴ Dcb
    3. [(Ax • Bxa) • (y)((Ay • Bya) → y=x)] • Dxb     1, EI
    4. (Ax • Bxa) • (y)((Ay • Bya) → y=x)          3, Simp
    5. Ax • Bxa                              4, Simp
    6. (y)((Ay • Bya) → y=x)               4, Simp
    7. (Ac • Bca) → c=x                6, UI
    8. c=x                                7, 2, MP
    9. Dxb                              3, Simp
   10. Dcb                            8, 9, LL

**Part B:** English Arguments

1.  1. (x)(Px → ~Axx)
    2. Aab
    3. Pa • Ph                           ∴ ~a = b
    ⎡ 4. a = b                           Assume
    │ 5. Pa → ~Aaa                       1, UI
    │ 6. Pa                              3, Simp
    │ 7. ~Aaa                            5, 6, MP
    │ 8. ~Aab                            4, 7, LL
    ⎣ 9. Aab • ~Aab                      2, 8, Conj
    10. ~a = b                           4–9, RAA

4.  1. (∃x)(∃y)[(Ox • Oy) • ~x = y] • (x)(y)(z)([Ox • Oy • Oz]
       → [x = y ∨ x = z ∨ y = z])
    2. Oa                                ∴ (∃x)[Ox • ~x = a]
    ⎡ 3. ~(∃x)[Ox • ~x = a]             Assume
    │ 4. (x)~[Ox • ~x = a]              3, QN
    │ 5. (∃x)(∃y)[(Ox • Oy) • ~x = y]  1, Simp
    │ 6. (∃y)[(Ox • Oy) • ~x = y]      5, EI
    │ 7. (Ox • Oy) • ~x = y            6, EI
    │ 8. (x)[~Ox ∨ ~~x = a]            4, DeM
    │ 9. (x)[~Ox ∨ x = a]              8, DN
    │ 10. ~Ox ∨ x = a                  9, UI
    │ 11. Ox • Oy                      7, Simp
    │ 12. Ox                           11, Simp
    │ 13. ~~Ox                         12, DN
    │ 14. x = a                        10, 13, DS
    │ 15. ~x = y                       7, Simp
    │ 16. ~a = y                       14, 15, LL
    │ 17. ~Oy ∨ y = a                  9, UI
    │ 18. Oy                           11, Simp
    │ 19. ~~Oy                         18, DN
    │ 20. y = a                        17, 19, DS
    │ 21. ~x = a                       20, 15, LL
    ⎣ 22. x = a • ~x = a               14, 21, Conj
    23. (∃x)(Ox • ~x = a)               3–22, RAA

⬥ *Chapter 10*

**Exercise 10.1**

**Part A:** True or False?

| | |
|---|---|
| 1. T | 13. T |
| 4. T | 16. F |
| 7. T | 19. F |
| 10. F | |

**Part B:** Identifying and Evaluating Statistical Syllogisms

1. Not a statistical syllogism (In a statistical syllogism, the percentage is greater than 50 and less than 100.)

4. A statistical syllogism. Since Johnark is a U.S. senator and many senators oppose campaign reform, there is a possible fallacy of incomplete evidence here.

7. A statistical syllogism. Since Goggans owns a coffee house, however, it seems likely that he drinks coffee; so there is a possible fallacy of incomplete evidence here.

10. A statistical syllogism
13. Not a statistical syllogism

## Exercise 10.2: Identifying Inductive Arguments

1. Induction by enumeration
4. Induction by enumeration. Sampling error: ±3.
7. Argument from authority
10. *Ad verecundiam* fallacy
13. Induction by enumeration. Sampling error: ±2.
16. Induction by enumeration. The sample is too small.
19. Argument from authority. There is a fallacy of incomplete evidence here, since the authorities (i.e., eyewitnesses) disagree about Black Coyote's role.

## Exercise 10.3

### Part A: Mill's Methods

1. Method of concomitant variation
4. Method of agreement. A better hypothesis: Studying intensely for 3 hours increases the quality of Alonzo's performance on exams.
7. The joint method
10. Method of agreement
13. The joint method
16. The joint method
19. The joint method
22. The method of residues

### Part B: Hypotheses

1. There seems to be no way to test the hypothesis.
4. The hypothesis appears to be low in explanatory power. Bees surely do not generate enough body heat to warm the atmosphere.
7. This hypothesis is inconsistent with well-established theories. Nothing can travel faster than the speed of light.

## Exercise 10.4

### Part A: Analyzing and Evaluating Analogies

1. A is Mars; B is the earth; P is the property of being inhabited by living things. The reply indicates that being a heavenly body that orbits the sun is no guarantee of being inhabited by living things. We might add that Mars and the earth are dissimilar in relevant ways—for example, Mars is much colder than the earth, and its atmosphere contains relatively little oxygen.
4. A is logic; B is whiskey; P is the property of being such that very large quantities should be avoided. The stated reply does not indicate a weakness in the argument, for even if logic does not contain alcohol, one may still be well-advised to avoid taking logic in very large quantities. (The same can be said about aspirin or vitamins.) The vagueness of the phrase "very large quantities" makes it difficult to evaluate the argument. What is a very large quantity of whiskey? Enough to cause drunkenness? Enough to impair one's judgment? Enough so that one is unable to walk? What is a very large quantity of logic? So much that one becomes mentally imbalanced (e.g., unable to appreciate nonlogical aspects of life properly, such as the emotions)? If so, then perhaps the argument is strong. But lovers of logic may rightly observe that very few people take logic in quantities of that magnitude, so the argument is seldom applicable.

### Part B: More Analogies

1. A is dogs; B is mentally deficient people; P is a complicated moral property, being such that one should not be killed merely on the grounds that caring for one is inconvenient. The main point

can be summed up as follows: If it is wrong to kill a human being who is mentally on the level of a dog (simply on the grounds that caring for the human is inconvenient), then it is wrong to kill a dog (simply on the grounds that caring for it is inconvenient). The stated reply is certainly open to question. It seems doubtful that the wrongness of killing is grounded in the shape or looks of the thing killed. To illustrate, if something looked like a dog but had the feelings and mental capacities of a normal human adult, wouldn't such a thing have rights similar to a normal human adult?

4. A is a computer; B is a human brain; P is the property of being aware of one's own thoughts and feelings. The stated reply does not seem to point to an important defect in the analogy. Metal, plastic, and brain tissue are all physical in nature. And metal and plastic can be structured so as to simulate SOME functions of the brain. Of course, it remains an open question whether computers have self-awareness.

# ◆ Chapter 11

## Exercise 11.1

### Part A: Classical Theory

1. 1/52
4. 13/52 = 1/4
7. 1/52

### Part B: Relative Frequency Theory

1. Relative frequency theory: .503. Classical theory: 1/2 or 0.5. (The classical theory has no way of accounting for slight imbalances in the coin.)

### Part C: Subjectivist Theory

1. 4/(4 + 1) = 4/5
4. 17/(17 + 2) = 17/19
7. 2/(2 + 5) = 2/7

### Part D: For Discussion

1. Relative frequency theory. The probability of getting a six on the next roll: 40/100 = 4/10 = 2/5. If we applied the classical theory here, the answer would be 1/6. But the classical theory has no way of accounting for irregularities in the die, and the die appears to be off balance or loaded.

## Exercise 11.2

### Part A: Disjunctions

1. 13/52 + 13/52 = 26/52 = 1/2
4. 1/52 + 13/52 = 14/52 = 7/26
7. 26/52 + 4/52 − 2/52 = 28/52 = 7/13

### Part B: Conjunctions and Conditionals

1. 4/52 × 4/51 = 16/2652 = 4/663
4. 13/52 × 12/51 = 156/2652 = 3/51
7. 1/52 × 0 = 0

### Part C: Various Compound Statements

1. $P(\sim G) = 1 - P(G) = 5/5 - 3/5 = 2/5$
4. $P(M \lor \sim M) = 1$ (tautology)
7. $P(M \cdot G) = P(M) \times P(G/M) = 3/10 \times 9/10 = 27/100$
10. $P[D \rightarrow (G \rightarrow D)] = 1$ (tautology)

**Part D:** The Strength of Arguments

1. $5/(5+1) = 5/6$ and $4/(4+1) = 4/5$. Using the restricted conjunction rule, the probability that Team A will play Team C in the semifinals is $5/6 \times 4/5 = 20/30 = 2/3$.
4. $1/6 \times 1/6 = 1/36$
7. $15/(15+1) = 15/16$. And $20/(20+1) = 20/21$. Using the general conjunction rule, the probability that Ted and Sue were both at the party is $15/16 \times 20/21 = 300/336 = 25/28$.

## Exercise 11.3

**Part A:** Patterns

1. a. $P(H/E) = \dfrac{1/2 \times 1/2}{[1/2 \times 1/2] + [1/2 \times 1/2]} = \dfrac{1/4}{1/4 + 1/4} = \dfrac{1/4}{2/4} = 1/4 \times 4/2 = 4/8 = 1/2$

2. a. $P(H/E) = \dfrac{1/5 \times 9/10}{[1/5 \times 9/10] + [4/5 \times 9/10]} = \dfrac{9/50}{9/50 + 36/50} = 9/45 = 1/5$

3. a. $P(H/E) = \dfrac{9/10 \times 2/5}{[9/10 \times 2/5] + [1/10 \times 2/5]} = \dfrac{18/50}{18/50 + 2/50} = 18/20 = 9/10$

4. a. $P(H/E) = \dfrac{1/2 \times 9/10}{[1/2 \times 9/10] + [1/2 \times 3/5]} = \dfrac{9/20}{9/20 + 3/10} = 9/15 = 3/5$

   $P(\sim H/E) = 2/5$

5. b. $P(H/E) = \dfrac{9/10 \times 0}{[9/10 \times 0] + [1/10 \times 1/10]} = 0$

   $P(\sim H/E) = 1$

6. b. $P(H/E) = \dfrac{5/7 \times 5/7}{[5/7 \times 5/7] + [2/7 \times 4/7]} = \dfrac{25/49}{25/49 + 8/49} = 25/33$

   $P(\sim H/E) = 8/33$

**Part B:** Applying Bayes' Theorem

1. $P(\text{Bloggs prepared}) = .40$, or $4/10$
   $P(\text{Bloggs passed } given \text{ Bloggs prepared}) = .70$, or $7/10$
   $P(\text{Bloggs passed } given \text{ Bloggs did not prepare}) = .30$, or $3/10$
   $\dfrac{4/10 \times 7/10}{[4/10 \times 7/10] + [6/10 \times 3/10]} = \dfrac{28/100}{28/100 + 18/100} = \dfrac{28}{46} = \dfrac{14}{23}$

4. $P(\text{God exists}) = 1/2$
   $P(\text{some unnecessary suffering occurs } given that \text{ an all-powerful and perfectly good God exists}) = 1/(1+3) = 1/4$
   $P(\text{some unnecessary suffering occurs } given that \text{ it is not the case that an all-powerful and perfectly good God exists}) = 2/(2+1) = 2/3$
   $P(\text{God exists } given \text{ some unnecessary suffering}) =$
   $\dfrac{1/2 \times 1/4}{[1/2 \times 1/4] + [1/2 \times 2/3]} = \dfrac{1/8}{1/8 + 2/6} = \dfrac{3/24}{3/24 + 8/24} = 3/11$

# Glossary/Index

*Bold page numbers indicate the page on which the term is defined.*

## LOGICALLY EQUIVALENT STATEMENT FORMS

| *Form* | *Converse* |
|---|---|
| **E:** No S are P. | No P are S. |
| **I:** Some S are P. | Some P are S. |

| *Form* | *Obverse* |
|---|---|
| **A:** All S are P. | No S are non-P. |
| **E:** No S are P. | All S are non-P. |
| **I:** Some S are P. | Some S are not non-P. |
| **O:** Some S are not P. | Some S are non-P. |

| *Form* | *Contrapositive* |
|---|---|
| **A:** All S are P. | All non-P are non-S. |
| **O:** Some S are not P. | Some non-P are not non-S. |

## TRADITIONAL SQUARE OF OPPOSITION

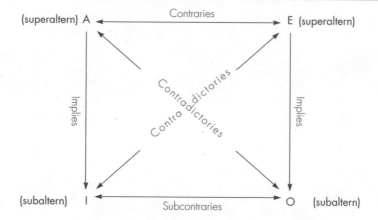

(superaltern) A — Contraries — E (superaltern)

Implies — Contradictories — Implies

(subaltern) I — Subcontraries — O (subaltern)

## VALID SYLLOGISTIC FORMS

**First figure:** AAA, EAE, AII, EIO
**Second figure:** EAE, AEE, EIO, AOO

**Third figure:** IAI, AII, OAO, EIO
**Fourth figure:** AEE, IAI, EIO

## RULES FOR CATEGORICAL SYLLOGISMS

1. A valid standard-form categorical syllogism must contain exactly three terms, and each term must be used with the same meaning throughout the argument.

2. In a valid standard-form categorical syllogism, the middle term must be distributed in at least one premise.

3. In a valid standard-form categorical syllogism, a term must be distributed in the premises *if* it is distributed in the conclusion.

4. In a valid standard-form categorical syllogism, the number of negative premises must be equal to the number of negative conclusions.

5. No valid standard-form categorical syllogism with a particular conclusion can have two universal premises.